After the CRASH

by

Shane Brad Wise

CITI OF
BOOKS

CITIOFBOOKS, INC.
3736 Eubank NE Suite A1
Albuquerque, NM 87111-3579
www.citiofbooks.com
Hotline: 1 (877) 389-2759
Fax: 1 (505) 930-7244
Ordering Information:
Quantity sales. Special discounts are available on quantity purchases by corporations, associations, and others. For details, contact the publisher at the address above.

Printed in the United States of America.
ISBN-13:   Paperback   979-8-89391-611-9
                eBook   979-8-89391-612-6

Library of Congress Control Number: 2025905596

Dedication

To every follower of Jesus Christ who ever thought our Lord had abandoned them.

He is always right, he is always good, and he is always for you.

CHAPTER 1

Blessed

DAY 1

What is this woman doing? Jeremiah thought to himself. She said she'd be out in a moment, but several minutes had passed. It would have been safer not to get his hopes up, but it was way too late for that. So, he whispered a prayer as he paced the hallway. "Father, I love you, and I am trusting you to do this. I need you to do good for me and my wife. You're the God of the impossible and my eyes are on you. You've given us so much and I am thankful. But now, please, Father, give us this too. In Jesus' name, Amen."

He loved Elise with his life and there were times when it seemed like she could do anything. So, why was this so hard? She was taking way too long, and he was growing impatient. She might trip, but he had to intervene.

He spoke as calmly as he could through the closed bathroom door. "Lise, how's it going, babe?"

"Miah, I'm fine" she answered. "Hold on." Elise was the sweetest woman in the world, though not always the most patient.

Jeremiah treaded lightly as he checked on her progress. "You need some help?" he said, laughing at the ridiculousness of his question. If she did say yes, what was he going to do?

"Baby, I can pee, and I can read. No assistance required."

"Oh, okay. Well, then, what does it say?" Jeremiah asked anxiously. "Miah, it don't say nuthin'! I can't go cuz you keep bothering me."

Jeremiah could tell he was getting on her nerves, but he loved to tease her. As important as this was, he couldn't pass on this opportunity.

He spoke as seriously as he could. "Would it help if I went outside and sprayed water on the bathroom window?"

Elise covered her mouth to muffle her laugh as she sat on the toilet. His little comment was funny enough, but she wasn't going to give him the satisfaction of knowing all that. She composed herself quickly and responded, "Miah, stop it now. You play too much."

"Okay, then I'm coming in."

"No, Miah. Please stay out. I'm serious, baby."

"I don't understand why you want to do this by yourself."

"Because if it's not real, I don't want to see that sad look on your face. And if it's real, if this is really happening, then I'm terrified. I don't know if I can do this. I didn't grow up like you, Miah. I don't have any life experience to draw from. So, either way, I need to process...okay?"

"No. It's not okay," Jeremiah said softly but firmly. "Did you just tell me no?" she questioned.

"I did. And I meant it, babe. We're in this together. You're my girl, Lise. I know this is scary but when it's all said and done, and I got my potbelly and my man boobs, and all your stuff starts to sag...."

"Boy, don't be speaking that on me. My stuff ain't go sag! I be working out," she interrupted harshly.

"Sorry. Anyway...," he continued.

"Baby, do you think I'm sagging?" she asked pitifully. "Tell me the truth." "Lise, that's not what I meant...."

"It's yo mama's fault. I don't be wantin' to hurt her feelings and she always cooking somethin' with sugar or carbs," she explained.

"Lise, stop! You're beautiful, babe. Except for the occasional ADD flareup, you're perfect. Now focus. My point is, when whatever happens, it's just going to be us! Miah and Lise against the world. And I wouldn't have it any other way. The best thing you ever gave me was letting me give you my name and you won't ever be able to top that, babe. Anything else is extra. I just want you to know you don't have to give me a kid, you just have to keep on giving me you. Just be you, Lise. You're enough."

"So, what are you saying?" she asked with a sly smile he could see through the closed door.

Jeremiah smiled and cleared his throat as loudly as he could. "What I'm saying is: 'You don't have to be rich to be my girl,'" he sang.

Elise's smile widened as her husband serenaded her in his awful, offkey, tone- deaf falsetto.

"You don't have to be cool to rule my world." "Jesus, help him," she laughed.

"Ain't no particular sign I'm more compatible with. I just want your extra time and your...," Jeremiah waited for her response. That was their song. "Kiss" by Prince. Whenever he needed to make her laugh or feel loved, he would serenade her with it, and everything would be right with the world. He would sing the verse, and Elise would sing the word "kiss" back to him and then give him a real one. But now, she didn't say anything.

"You didn't hear me? I said, 'I just want your extra time and your'"

Elise's silence on the other side of the bathroom door brought a sudden tightness to Jeremiah's chest.

She's not pregnant. The thought invaded his mind, but he quickly dismissed it. He had just prayed and was still holding on to hope as he spoke through the door again.

"Girl, if you make me sang this song one mo time and don't open this door Irepeat, 'I just want your extra time and your '"

Elise slowly opened the door, but she didn't say "kiss" and she didn't kiss him. Her lips said nothing, but her face was wet with tears. Jeremiah's heart sank and he knew his face was showing the disappointment she feared.

He faked an encouraging smile. "Lise, I'm sorry, babe. It's okay. Listen...," but before he could finish, she smiled through her tears and opened her mouth. "Miah, we're pregnant!" she laughed.

Jeremiah picked her up and spun her around. Then he realized she was now in a delicate condition and set her down lightly. He had a blessed life, but having a child with the woman he loved was the one thing that God had never done for him. Elise had never been pregnant, and no clear medical reason had been given. When they were younger the doctors told them to just keep trying. They were happy to comply. It was their inside joke. "Doctor's orders," they would say. But now they were in their forties and Elise would be forty-four by the time this baby came. They didn't really talk about it, but they had both come to accept that a baby was not in God's will for them.

But now the Lord had given them their miracle, and Jeremiah wanted to give thanks. He pulled his wife close to him and began to pray.

"Father, we just want to thank you and love on you right now. You have already done so much. You have always been good. But to give us a child now? All we can say is thank you, Jesus!"

"Thank you, Jesus!" Elise repeated.

"I confess, I stopped expecting this, but now we want to thank you for your overruling grace. And right now, we just want to give this little boy to you."

Little boy? Elise thought to herself. *This man done already decided what we are having.* She laughed to herself even as she agreed with her husband as he kept praying.

"By all the grace you give us and by your Holy Spirit, we will raise him to know you and love you and serve you all his days. I want to thank you for my wife, Father. Thank you for the love and kindness you have shown me through her. I know I don't deserve her, but I am thankful for the blessing that she is. Please protect her. Please protect our son. We bring them under your faithful care and thank you for the years of grace that you have ahead of us. You have always been good, Lord, so now we ask that you keep being good. And Jesus, please let us be a blessing to someone else who may have thought you weren't coming through. Place them in our lives so we can tell them that there is always hope in Christ. Father, this is too big. We don't know how to do this, but we come to you in faith believing that you know what plans you have for this little boy."

There he goes again. Elise smiled as she prayed in her own heart,

Father, please give my man a son.

Unaware of his wife's thoughts, Jeremiah kept pressing in prayer and thanksgiving. "May he know how much you love him and may he give your love to others. Even now, Lord, fill him with your Spirit and make him strong in you and your mighty power. We cannot say thank you enough, Father. In Jesus' name, Amen."

"In Jesus' name, Amen," Elise said. Her tears had stopped and nothing was left but an overwhelming sense of gratitude and love. She stood there in her husband's embrace, the side of her face buried in his chest and joined him in prayer. "Hey, Daddy, it's your baby girl. Me and this wonderful husband you have given me are so thankful. I agree with my husband that you have already given so much. We just want to say that we remember Jesus today and what he did on the cross for us. But God, I have to be honest. Right now, all I can really think about is this perfect little moment you have given us. Me, my man, my baby, and you."

She started to cry again.

"People think that we have it all together but God, you know our sin, our struggles, and all our fears and failures, but your grace keeps coming. Lord, I can honestly say that you don't have to do anything else but if you will keep on blessing, we will do our best to get the blessing to others so they may know you. Thank you for my husband, Lord. Thank you for my baby."

"Our baby boy," Jeremiah corrected.

Elise simply smiled. "Thank you for Jesus. Amen."

"Amen," Jeremiah said, as he wiped the tears from her eyes and kissed her on her forehead. "You good?" he asked her.

"I am better than good. If you look up 'perfect' in the dictionary, you would see this picture right here. Me and you and our little peanut standing here together. Miah, I promise, I could stand here with you forever. I don't want this moment to end."

"Forever?" Jeremiah questioned.

"Why you say it like that?" she responded, her lips contorting. "Jeremiah John Traylor, are you trying to go to the office?" She pulled away from him so she could make eye contact.

"Babe, yes, but only for a few hours, I promise. I just gotta finish something up." "Baby, it's Saturday. You are going to burn yourself out. Besides, we need

to celebrate."

"I know. We are going to celebrate. We'll do it big.   Whatever restaurant you want. Wherever you want to go. Make some reservations for around 7 and we are going to do this right."

"That sounds nice but ummm… I want to celebrate now," she said cooly.

"Now?" Jeremiah was puzzled but the look on her face quickly clarified exactly how she wanted to celebrate.

"Lise. Not now, I gotta go to work. Let me go and I promise when I get back, it's on."

"Fine." She pulled totally away from him and put her hands behind her back. "Go ahead and go." She got up on her tiptoes and kissed him softly on the cheek.

"Lise, don't do that," he protested.

"What I do? I just said 'go' and I kissed you bye. What's wrong with that? See, let me show you. Bye, Miah. I love you. Have a good day." Once again, she raised up and kissed him on the other cheek.

"Elise Janelle Traylor, you know those are not goodbye kisses."

"Why, whatever do you mean?" she said as she tilted her head slightly in feigned ignorance.

Jeremiah gave her the side-eye. "You know what you are trying to do, Elise." "Baby, I am telling my hardworking whole snack…I mean hardworking husband goodbye. I want to send him off with love. That's all I am trying to do. I am just gonna stay here all by myself. I am not sure what else you're thinking but I am not trying to do anything else. So go, baby. See you later." She kissed him again but this time a little longer and on the neck. "I think I'm going to take a bath. I'm feeling a little… dirty. I need to wash off." She slipped her house shoes off.

"Elise, the longer it takes for me to leave, the longer it will take for me to finish and get back. Stop it now."

Elise tried to sound as innocent as she could. "Wow. Just wow. The devil be- est busy. But Lord, I rebuketh this spirit of confusion. Thoust man that thoust hast giveneth to be my husband and I be-est not on the sameth page. He seemeth to think that thoust most favoriteth girlst child is up to something sinistereth. Openeth hist eyes, Lord, so that thou servant may see that thine daughter is of noble character and meanest no harm."

She then unbuttoned the top button of her pajama blouse.

"Okay, now I know you up to something. Up in this joint strippin' and prayin' in King James."

Elise couldn't contain herself. She laughed out loud but quickly got right back into character. "Oh, dear husband, I am sorry if you have misunderstood anything. Go ahead and go but let's talk about this after you get back from, well, you know… grinding."

She opened another button on her blouse.

Jeremiah was quickly forgetting the rather urgent assignment waiting for him at the office. "Okay, okay, okay. Just a few minutes won't hurt but then I gotta go."

"A few minutes for what?" she asked coyly, still unbuttoning her shirt. "For this," Jeremiah said as he pulled her back close and kissed her.

"Sir, I am flummoxed and flabbergasted. Are you trying to seduce me? Where did this come from? Why, I thought you had to go to work?"

Jeremiah didn't have time to play the full spectrum of her little game, so he cut to the chase.

"Yeah. Fine. Blame me. I mean, I'm not the one with they shirt half off but fine. I'm trying to seduce you. But I do have to go to work, ma'am, so it's gonna have to be just a few good minutes, I really gotta go."

"A few minutes? Ummm, is that different than any other time?"

Jeremiah took a step back and shook his head. "Okay. You got me. Full-frontal assault on your man's ego."

"No, baby," she laughed, "I am just playing. Your few minutes are always enough. I know you have to go make it happen for us. I just want to give you a reason to rush back."

"You're always my reason, babe."

Elise's heart melted. Jeremiah always made her feel like the most beautiful woman in the world. And he always made her feel good about herself. Today, that should not even have been possible considering her emotional and spiritual high, but her Miah never disappointed.

"Thank you, baby. Now come on over here and fulfill yo husbandly duties.

Good thing we in the bathroom cuz we both 'bout to need a shower."

CHAPTER 2

Cursed

DAY 1

Joshua returned home from his workout, surprised to see his son's car was there. Robert had graduated college with his Master's degree in education two years ago. He only lived thirty-five minutes away from his parents, but due to a growing estrangement with his dad he didn't come around very often. Joshua couldn't even identify the root of their rift, and every attempt to reconcile only served to widen the chasm between them. Sad as it might be, Joshua had become weary of the rejections and had all but stopped trying.

Their conversations had been reduced to text messages on birthdays and special occasions. It had gotten to the point where his wife, Angela, and daughter, Robin, would have outings with Robert without Joshua. It bothered him but he understood. He didn't want his son to be deprived of his mother and sister because of their issues. But now Robert was here. Joshua hoped they would all be able to go out to dinner or just watch a movie.

He parked his truck in his garage and took a deep breath. He sat in the truck a little longer to gather his thoughts and pray. "Lord, please open this door. Please make my son's and my heart soft and open to you. And please make our hearts soft and open to each other. My eyes are on you, Jesus. Thank you for the victory. Amen."

He entered his home to a sweet greeting from Robin. Like any teenager Robin had her moments, but he was thankful that she was still Daddy's girl.

She rushed into her father's arms and her sweet embrace warmed his heart. "Hey, Daddy! Your son is here," she said, grinning from ear to ear.

"Do I need to get my popcorn ready?"

"Why do you think you need some popcorn, Robby?" he asked, anticipating a humorous and perhaps inappropriate comment.

"Well, if y'all are going to fight, I wanna have a snack. Rob has youth on his side, but the experience and the size factor goes to you. My money is on you in four rounds. I don't think he wants that Daddy smoke."

"Girl, get out!" Angela said as she pointed her finger to the door and laughed out loud.

Joshua shook his head. Robin had no filter. She knew as the baby girl she could get away with certain comments.

"No, baby girl. No popcorn necessary. Unless your brother wants to catch a movie or something. You down, R?"

Robert unseated himself from his position on the couch next to his mom and joined his sister in the embrace. The hug surprised Joshua just a little but he was glad to take one arm from around Robin and put it around his son.

"No, Dad. Not today," Robert responded. "I'm just trying to be a good big brother. I'm taking this thang out on the town," Robert said as he playfully slapped his sister on the back of the head.

"Oh, that's nice. Raincheck, then?" Joshua asked hopefully. "Yeah, Dad. Sure."

"I'm gonna hold you to that, R, okay?"

"Okay, Dad. That's cool. We're headed out now. I will see you when we get back. Come on, girl. You got money, right?" Robert teased.

Robin cocked her head and rolled her eyes at her older brother with all the extraness she could muster. "Of course I do. I have a big brother with a job. I allllwaaaays got money. Move, boy!" Robin said as she shoved her brother away and reclaimed her father's arm. "Bye, Daddy. I love you. See you later," she said, raising up on the top of her toes and kissing her dad on his cheek. "You're still the best daddy in the whole wide world," she whispered.

The extra attention from both kids was pleasantly surprising. *Not a bad way to start the weekend,* he thought.

"Bye, sweetie. Have fun. And don't spend up all your brother's money." "Okay, Daddy. I promise not to spend up all his money. Just most," she said.

Robert grabbed his little sister by the arm. "Whatever, girl! You gettin' McDonald's today…and no fries either. Come on. We'll see y'all later," he waved as they walked out the front door.

Joshua walked over to his wife and kissed her on the forehead. "I guess that wasn't too bad. He looks good. Looks like he's working out. It's nice to see him coming to check on his sister. I like that. At least he likes two of the three people that live here," he quipped. His levity hid the sadness of just how true he thought his statement was.

Angela didn't respond. Her silence was a little awkward. She seemed preoccupied but Joshua figured she was just in one of her moods.

"I'm gonna shower right quick," Joshua said, breaking the silence. "Do you want to get something to eat and catch a movie?"

Angela sighed. "No, Josh. We need to talk." "Oh, okay. But can I shower first?"

"No, Josh. We need to talk now."

"Uh-oh. One of those, huh?" Joshua asked as he prepared himself for battle. "Yeah. It really is one of those," Angela agreed. "Sit down, please."

Joshua couldn't imagine what urgent matter had arisen, but he sat down and tried to be fully present. "Okay, I'm listening. What's up? And do I need to order us something to eat? You look like you got a lot on your mind," he said, attempting to lighten the mood.

"No, we can eat later. We need to do this first." Angela looked him squarely in the eyes. "Joshua, I want a divorce."

Her eyes were devoid of any emotion. Her demeanor was calm. Her tone was cold. Her words were clear. And they seeped into Joshua's soul like poison. They certainly didn't have a perfect marriage, but a divorce? Now? After twenty years, one child out of college, and the other on the way? This wasn't the first time Angela had mentioned what they called the "d word." Previously, it would always come to nothing. But this time it hit different. It hit different because it was different. This was calculated. Angela had a horrible temper, but this wasn't a threat coming off the springboard of an argument about money, sex, or the kids. Despite the obvious issue at hand, Joshua still knew his wife. And he knew she was done.

Still, he struggled to process and to find a response. All he could think to say was "A divorce?"

"Yes, I want a divorce, Josh. This is over. I am not living like this anymore. I deserve better and I want better. And believe it or not, I want better for you too."

Joshua looked around at their five-bedroom house. "Angela, I'm sorry. But live like what?"

Angela remained calm. She knew her words were unexpected. She wanted to help him process but didn't want to give in to any sympathy that might give him false hope. Their marriage was over. She wanted out but she didn't want to destroy him in the process.

"Josh, we've got to face this. What we have is not what God intended," she said as she motioned her hands between the two of them. "I know you might not want to admit it but that doesn't mean I can't. I truly love you, but I am not in love with you. I know this hurts but I am not sure if I ever did. And if I did then at some point it stopped. I don't know when. I just know it's not there anymore and it hasn't been for a very long time. If you would be honest, I think you would say the same thing but even if you don't, I am not doing this anymore. I deserve to be happy." Joshua's head was reeling. This was not what he expected to come home to, but he knew he had to say something. "Angela, I want to make you happy. I want to be happy. But not at the expense of our marriage. Not at the expense of disobeying God."

Angela shook her head. "Wow. Josh, do you see? That part right there! Did you hear what you just said? So let me get this straight. We just have to be miserable because of a mistake we made more than twenty years ago?"

"Hold on, Angela. First of all, I am not miserable. I am sorry that you are. And I never thought our marriage was a mistake. But regardless, no, we don't have to stay miserable. We just need to face it and work it out together."

"I am tired of working it out and talking about it, Joshua. Nothing ever changes. We don't act like or look like other couples who are happy. Who are we... no, I am sorry, I'm going to say it, who are you trying to fool? Joshua, are you even still in love with me? Can you honestly say I am still or ever was the woman of your dreams? It's okay to admit it."

Angela's words pierced him. Was she right? Was their marriage that bad? He couldn't get distracted now. He needed to focus.

"Angela, baby, listen," he said softly. "If you are talking about emotions and feelings and romance, then yes, we're lacking in that department. We've let it get stale and predictable but that's no reason to ditch over twenty years of life together."

"It is when it's like this. We tried. We failed. We need to move on."
"Move on and do what?"

Angela softened. "Josh, sweetie, move on and live! Enjoy life. Be free." "So that's it. You want to be free of me?"

"Yeah, Josh. I am sorry but I do. I want to be free. I don't want to be married anymore. And I am not the only one here who feels like that. I noticed you never answered my question about being in love with me. I think on some level you feel the same. You just don't want the people at church to know that the amazing Brother Dupree doesn't have a perfect home life. But I don't care what they think. I am not living like this anymore."

"Angela, of course I love you. I want to make this work and not just because of what people will say. I'm sorry that I have so obviously let you down to a point where you don't realize this, but our marriage matters. Our family matters. Our kids matter. And yes, what God has to say matters. For all those things we need to communicate and work this out. If we've failed, fine, but God can turn this around. We need to show the kids what happens when we really bring the Lord into this. Not that we just gave up and said the heck with it because it got tough or we weren't happy."

"Josh, Robert is grown, and Robin is strong enough to get through this." "I know that, but we still need to think about how this will affect them." "Well, how did they look to you tonight?" Angela asked.

"They looked fine," Joshua answered, wondering where she was going with this. "I agree. They're good. Josh, they're great. And guess what else? They already know. That's why Robert came by. I spoke to him a couple of weeks ago and asked him to come and get his sister so we could talk. Well, you know that boy loves his mama. He could tell something was up, so I let him know what I needed to talk to you about."

Joshua struggled to process the onslaught of different emotions. There was shock, sadness, and confusion. But Angela taking this to Robert without telling him made him angry.

"Angela, are you saying you already told Robert all this? Before you told me?" Josh said, trying to keep his feelings in check.

"Yes, Josh, I did. And you know what? He wasn't the least bit surprised. He said he never thought we would stay together. Even when he was little, he never thought it. For me, it was just confirmation from someone who had seen our lives up close and personal. And I'm sorry, we may as well just rip the Band-Aid off, Robin knows too."

Joshua stood up instinctively. "Wait a minute. I can't be hearing you right. You told Robin? You told my daughter that you wanted to leave me? Is that why she was so clingy with all the 'you're still the best dad' stuff?"

"Josh, calm down. You know she adores you. Be thankful that she's concerned. Both of them are, actually."

Joshua took a step toward Angela. "And you thought that was a good idea?

You thought that was how to handle this?"

Angela was never one to back down from a confrontation and she stood up boldly to face him. "Well, that's how I handled it, so I guess I did," she said defiantly.

Joshua could feel his heart racing. "And you didn't think I should be a part of that conversation?"

Angela could tell Joshua was becoming angry, but she wasn't about to back down. "In hindsight, yes, I guess I should have told you first

After the Crash

but you're making it sound worse than it is. The part with Robert is on me but he is a full-grown adult. After I spoke to him, he thought we should tell Robin together, to help her through it. I am sorry if that hurts you but at least you don't have to have that conversation."

"Angela, it's beyond hurt. It's intentionally disrespectful. And I can't believe you didn't realize that."

"You're right, Josh," Angela nodded in agreement. "It was disrespectful. But at least I told you. Kind of like when you told me you had been watching porn. It was disrespectful but hey, at least you told me. So, all good, right?"

Her words hit Joshua in the gut. He had confessed to Angela a struggle he had with pornography but at this point it had been years. He thought it was behind them. But now, of all times, it had surfaced again. They hadn't mentioned it in years, but she apparently had it loaded in the chamber for later use.

Joshua sighed. "Angela, that was years ago. I can't believe you're bringing that up."

"You're right. But I forgave you so you will just have to forgive me too. It took me a minute to get past it. I understand it will take you a minute to get past this. It's my first divorce so I may not do it perfectly."

Joshua looked at her face and searched for some softness. Some opening. But he found none. His anger had only served to escalate the volatile situation. He needed to calm down, but this battle was on ten and he still had questions.

"So, this is what you want to do?" he asked. "Abandon our marriage? Our kids? Our home?"

"Joshua, I am not going anywhere, sweetie. We can work out the details, but I intend to stay here. Robin only has one more year of school left but she still needs her stability."

"Ohhh, so you want me to leave?" Joshua asked, already knowing the answer. "Josh, it would make sense. But if you want the house, so be it. It's an acceptable loss for my peace but I am pretty sure you know that Robin will want to come with me. She's old enough to make that decision on her own. But for your sake and hers, don't put her in the position to have to tell you that. It will just make things worse."

Joshua's head was pounding. This wasn't happening. When was he going to wake up? The throbbing in his head only served to make his patience wain.

"Okay, Angela. You got it all worked out, don't you?" he said sarcastically. "I'll just punk out and leave. You get the house. The kids. And I'll just walk away. Is that what you want?"

"Josh, you can do whatever you need to do but this is happening. If you would just stop and think, you would see it's not nearly as bad as you are making it out to be."

"Oh, it's bad, Angela. It's very bad. Just because you're cool with all of this… with this master plan you have, doesn't mean it's right or good or fair. No, I don't think I'm the one who needs to stop and think. You need to stop, think and, oh, here's an idea, actually pray, and see what God has to say instead of leaning to your own understanding."

"Whoomp. There it is!" Angela said as she mockingly clapped and pointed at him. "That's the word right there. Go ahead and preach, Joshua. You know you're the only one in this house that loves Jesus. Go ahead and tell me how I'm going to hell if I divorce you."

"I never said anything like that, and you know it. This whole thing is ridiculous. 'Josh, I want a divorce.' You hit me with this? Now? Like this? 'Hey, Josh, me and the kids were talking, and we don't need you anymore and Imma need you to bounce most expeditiously. I don't love you, so you need to accept that and move on. No big deal.' Well, I'm sorry, Angela, but I am not going quietly. I'm going to fight even if I have to fight by myself. Do I love you? Yes, I do. But right now, I don't like you. Not in the least. I've never been more disappointed with someone in my life. No, I'm not the only one here who loves Jesus, but I do appear to be the only one who cares what he thinks right now. I'm the only one who's thinking at all. So, no. I'm not going anywhere. You wanna fight? Fine, let's fight. Our marriage isn't like others? How about you just come to your husband and actually say that? Just say 'Josh, I'm struggling. Josh, I'm confused. Josh, I'm not happy.'"

"I have. For over twenty years I have. Now I'm tired of talking."

"That's a lie, Angela, and you know it. Have you complained? Yes. Have you walked around like I'm the Boogeyman? Yes. But you haven't ever met me in the middle and said let's work on us."

"I thought you were supposed to be the leader. Isn't that your job?" Angela jabbed.

Joshua had to concede her point. "Yes, it is. And I can admit I've fallen short but don't act like I never tried. When I asked you what was wrong or what I could do, you never had anything to say. You said you were fine or that you wanted to work it out on your own. So no, you didn't talk. You sat there and let it build to this. You saw the building was on fire and never once pulled the fire alarm. You must have wanted it to burn down."

"You're right," Angela agreed.

"Wow. Just wow, Angela. So, you agree?" he asked.

"Josh, what did you think I was going to say? I'm sorry, boo boo, but it's all over but the crying now. And I'm all cried out."

"Hmm. Okay then. But same question…what did you think I was going to say to all of this?" Joshua asked with genuine curiosity.

"Honestly, I hoped you would say, 'You know what? I'm tired too. Let's just work it out and be cool.' There are plenty of couples who split and find themselves in a better relationship with each other afterwards. If you let it happen, we can end up closer because of this."

Angela's ludicrous statement quickly subdued Joshua's calm. "I can't believe you let that come out of your mouth. That's the stupidest thing you could have said, Angela."

"Oh, so now I'm stupid?" she said as she took a step toward him. She turned her head to the side, daring him to repeat the statement.

Joshua knew he should backtrack, but he was tired of taking the high road. "Yeah, Angela, it's pretty stupid to just let a marriage disintegrate and never say a word until you think it's over. And yeah, it's stupid to tell a man's kids you're leaving him without even telling him first."

"I told them for everyone's sake, including yours. They needed to process too, and they can't do it with you. All you were going to do was shove the Bible down their throats. They needed a parent, not some spiritual advisor. They don't relate to you, so they don't talk to you. So now they know. You're welcome."

"Oh, I'm supposed to say thank you? Thank you for not loving me? Thank you for putting up another wall between me and the kids?"

"Don't blame me for that, Josh. Get a mirror. I haven't done anything to get between you and the kids. That's all you, bruh. But you know everything so I'm sure you'll figure it out. You mad that I didn't talk? Why talk with someone who has all the answers anyway? You didn't need me. Except for sex, I guess, and that's not even that good."

"Well, I guess I didn't have much motivation on that front, did I, Angela?" Joshua retorted coldly.

Angela was surprised at Joshua's comeback. And oddly, a little pleased. "Okay, Josh. I see you. Way to stand your ground. Well played. But I am still not staying in all of this. My point is you've been a solo act from the beginning. I'm just making it formal."

"If I'm solo, it's because you never wanted us to be one. You never joined me in trying to make things better. With anything. With the kids or especially with Robert."

"Josh, I really do feel bad about you and Robert. I can't tell if you two are just too different or too alike. Either way, I can't do anything about it."

"You could have stood with me and let him know that despite our differences, he needed to love and respect his dad. Instead, you just coddled him like I was someone he needed protection from."

"Sometimes he did need protection. You rode him way too hard. I don't care what you say. That's why he's distant from you now and why he and I still have a good relationship."

"Y'all have a good relationship because you don't check him on his crap. Oh, you might say something if he makes you mad, but you don't cut it straight with him on stuff that's not directly affecting you. So, I always have to be the bad cop." Angela felt herself getting more and more frustrated. The marriage was over.

Why did they have to keep fighting? "This is ridiculous," she said. "I am not going to keep going round and round with you. Especially about Robert. It's not fair, it's not like you ever really had a chance anyway."

"I never had a chance? What does that mean?" Joshua asked her.

Angela uncharacteristically stumbled for words. She usually had a quick comeback. Especially in a fight.

"Josh," she stammered, "like I said, y'all are just different. Don't worry about it." "No, Angela. That's not what you meant. What do you mean I never had a chance?"

"Josh, let it go. This is about me and you. I'm tired and now is not the time to press me," Angela warned.

"No, dammit! I'm not letting it go!" Joshua shouted. "What are you gonna do? Leave me? No, I want to know. What did you do now? How the hell else have you been undermining me with my son?"

Joshua rarely raised his voice at Angela. And it was even rarer for him to curse at her in any way. His words and accusatory tone caught her off guard and before she could catch herself, she blurted, "Josh, I haven't undermined you! He just isn't your son."

Angela's news about the divorce was like poison. But this was like a shotgun blast to the chest.

Just a few short moments ago she said she wanted a divorce, and he knew she was serious. He knew she was just as serious now. But all he could do was stand there. Frozen. He couldn't speak. He couldn't move. He couldn't think.

Angela's fierce countenance gave way to one of deep regret and sympathy. She hadn't meant for that to come out tonight. She hadn't meant for it to ever come out. Robert was twenty-four years old. There was no need to ever open that particular can of worms.

It was likely only moments, but it felt like hours that they stood there in their living room, face to face, with no words.

Angela broke the silence. "Josh, why don't you sit down?" she spoke gently.

Defeated. Josh complied.

"Joshua, I really am sorry. You know I have a temper. I don't have the ability to just sit back when someone comes for me. I know you won't believe me, but I didn't want to do this. Especially this way."

Joshua should have been in utter disbelief, but he wasn't. Still, estranged or not, Robert was his son. And regardless of their recent disagreements, he still loved his boy. How could this be?

"Josh, I need you to breathe, baby. Do you want some water?" Angela asked him.

Joshua just sat there. All he could do was muster a simple nod. He still had not spoken.

Angela returned with a bottle of water and a cool towel. She gently placed the bottle to his lips and placed the towel on the back of his neck. This was not what she had wanted. You just had to win, didn't you? she asked herself in disgust. She found herself gently stroking the back of his head. This wasn't part of the plan.

But surprisingly, Joshua accepted the comfort. He finally spoke, but "Angela, how?" was all he could muster.

Angela sat back down opposite him. "Josh, I didn't always know. There was a part of me that suspected, but I never knew for sure. I'm not perfect now and I was less perfect when we met. When we first met, there was someone else in my life. Somebody that shouldn't have been. When I realized I was pregnant I knew I wanted it to be you, so I didn't question it. You said you loved me and wanted to marry me, and I just couldn't tell you there was a possibility of the baby not being yours."

Angela paused. Joshua looked at her and ironically, for the first time tonight she seemed sweet and concerned.

She continued her explanation. "As seems to be the theme tonight, yes, I was wrong. But I truly wanted it to be you. You were and are such a good man. I knew the baby could be yours, so I buried my head in the sand and prayed for it to be yours." Joshua grasped for a final straw of hope. "And why do you think he's not?" he asked.

"It haunted me over the years," Angela responded. "It's ironic but only now am I remembering that we did have some good times. I just never knew how to bring it up. How do you tell your husband his son might not be his? But when Robin was born, she looked just like you. I mean people say Robert looks like you, but Robin, though? That girl looks like you had her and that brought up those old fears. So, one day I went and got DNA testing done. That's when I found out you weren't Robert's biological father. But Josh, no matter how he is tripping now, Robert loves you. You're an amazing father and an amazing man. Don't let my issues take that away from you."

"Does Robert know? Does his father know? Oh my God! Angela, does Robin know?"

Angela listened to his questions and knew they were fair. Joshua's anger was gone. He was just a man searching for answers.

"No, Josh. I promise. You're the only one who knows. So, here's your chance. You can cuss me out. Call me out my name. Whatever. I deserve it. I can't change it, though."

"Angela, I don't want to do any of that. Let's just finish this later. I don't think I can even eat. I need to lay down."

"I understand. We can table it for now. But about laying down…I have fresh sheets in the guestroom. Do you want me to sleep in there tonight?" Angela offered.

Her words were a bitter reminder. Their fight had begun because she wanted a divorce. Regardless of this unexpected revelation about Robert, she wasn't going to back off that and Joshua had no fight left in him. He almost had to laugh at his naivete. With all that he had heard that day, it had never entered his mind that he and his wife wouldn't sleep in the same bed that night.

"No. It's fine. I'll take the guestroom," he conceded.

"Josh, you need to eat something. I'll bring you something back. Okay?" Angela offered.

"Okay," Josh agreed.

"Cool. I will be right back," she said.

Joshua waited in their living room until he heard her car leave the garage.

He took a deep breath. He couldn't handle this, but he knew the One who could. He was more than a conqueror and this weapon wasn't going to prosper. But his Savior wasn't there. At least he could not feel him. All he could feel was an overwhelming sense of loneliness and defeat. All he could remember was every point of his life where he had sinned and fallen short. He was supposed to serve a forgiving God of grace who didn't remember sin. But obviously he served a vengeful God with an excellent memory.

The Lord was far away and silent, but the devil was happy to join him and speak clearly.

"You thought you were free? You thought all was forgotten? Dude, God has not forgiven you. He just wanted to let you get comfortable so he could blindside you now. And it's your own fault. Nobody told you to have a kid and not be married. And he's not even yours? Wow, Josh. And she doesn't even love you anymore? Did she ever? You call yourself praying for people but obviously your prayers bounce off the ceiling. Look around, Joshua. Who's here? Nobody. That's who. Get used to it. Because your wife and your kids are gone. And dude, why didn't you ask about Robin? Are you that stupid? You do know she's probably not yours either. But go ahead and get into your prayers, Josh. I mean, you're going to be talking to the same God that didn't bother to warn you about your wife or about your son. But hey, maybe he will listen now. Give it a try."

Joshua knew he was under attack. But there was still power in the name of Jesus. He needed to pray. He needed to cry out to the Lord. God promised not to leave him or forsake him, and he was still for him. But when he opened his mouth to say "Father," all that came out was an indiscernible wail as tears flooded his face. He tried to compose himself. He tried to get down on his knees to humble himself before the Lord, but instead he just fell onto the floor and wept uncontrollably.

CHAPTER 3

Foul

DAY 1

Case McBride didn't like to wait but he was known to do so occasionally if it worked to his benefit. This was one of those times, so he sat calmly as he anticipated his lunch companions' arrival. He had sacrificed on many previous dealings with them. Now he was looking forward to reaping the benefits of his sacrifice.

Case was the owner of Jacebre Construction. Thanks to the work of his son and some up-and-coming senior project manager named Jeremiah, Jacebre had vaulted into position as the fastest-growing construction company in the state. Now Case was primed and ready to take his company to the next level.

The first of his companions arrived. Vance Cobb was the owner of Union Construction, undeniably the largest construction company in the state. Though technically the two men were in competition, they had worked out a mutually beneficial, though illegal, business arrangement that had shown to be quite profitable.

Vance was Case's former boss and mentor. By Case's loose definition, Vance was a friend. They had a bit of a falling-out when Case started his own construction company twenty years ago, but they were happy to sacrifice their rift on the altar of profits.

Case was at least three inches taller than Vance and had more than forty pounds on him. What Vance may have lacked in physical prowess, he more than made up for with his intellect and business acumen. That intimidated Case but he couldn't let him know it. Especially not today.

"Case!" Vance greeted him warmly as he joined him. "How are

you, my friend?"

"I'm good, Vance. How are Karen and the kids?" Case asked. Karen was Vance's trophy wife. He wondered if Vance had ever suspected the affair Case had with her prior to starting his own company.

"They're great," Vance responded. "How is your son? You got him groomed to take over yet?"

"Oh, he's ready to run the company but I keep reminding him not to get too big for his britches," Case said. "If he wants to truly run things, he can do what I did and go out on his own. But if he wants to run my company he can wait until I don't want to do it anymore."

Vance laughed inwardly at Case's false bravado. Case was an exceptional businessman, but he was only able to start his company because of a sizable inheritance left to him by his deceased father.

"Where are Ramsey and Dale?" Case asked.

Ramsey and Dale were owners of their own construction companies and partners in the business arrangement.

"Yeah, about that," Vance answered, "Ramsey feels like he wants to go in a different direction. He no longer feels comfortable with our... arrangement."

"What?!" Case exclaimed. "I should have known he would take all he could and then jump ship. He's benefitted as much as anybody from this...arrangement. So now what? He's got cold feet?"

Vance was well acquainted with Case's temper and remained calm as he spoke. "You could say that. Unlike you, he is ready for his kids to take over the business and he would prefer they not participate in dealings like this."

"What a wimp!" Case spat angrily.

Vance laughed. "Case don't worry about it. We've worked it out. Ramsey won't be a problem."

"And what about Dale?" Case asked.

"Come on, Case," Vance said directly. "You and I both know it's only two alpha personalities in this thing and they aren't named Ramsey and Dale. Dale will do whatever I advise him to do. I hope you will too, but I know you won't."

"What's that supposed to mean?" Case asked suspiciously.

"I mean that we've made some good money on this run. But we're getting a little greedy. Our circle has gotten too wide, and this project is too big."

Vance leaned forward and lowered his voice. "There could be a lot of eyes on this. Federal eyes."

"Come on, Vance. Not you too," Case said louder than he intended.

"Hear me out," Vance pressed his point. "Whenever more than one person knows a thing, you can guarantee it's no longer a secret. True enough, Ramsey didn't have the balls for this type of thing, but in this case, I see his concern. This project is way too high-profile. I think we should just play this one straight."

Case was prepared for this moment. Vance's reference to him being an alpha personality hadn't gone unnoticed and he wanted to show him just how true his statement was.

"Damn it, Vance," he said as he leaned forward not very far from Vance's face. "You all owe me. You especially. You were the one who showed me how to do this, but I was the one who perfected it. And I was the one who sacrificed the most. I always got the last bite of the apple while the rest of you prospered. Hell, I know you didn't need it, but I've seen the yacht so it's obvious you are benefitting. And Dale? Look me in the eye and tell me you think he would be a major player if it wasn't for this."

Vance sat silently as Case continued.

"So, and I know you already know this by the way, I've been waiting. Up to now, I've let you guys take the big ones and I took the little ones. You guys reaped. You profited. And I waited. I waited for this one. And you're gonna come through and do your part like I did for you. It's Jacebre's turn now and I'm not letting you guys back out."

"You finished?" Vance asked calmly. "For now," Case said sternly.

"Case, everything you said is true. I can give you what you want but I don't know that you are going to want what you get. You need to be careful."

"I'm always careful, Vance. We turn in numbers Monday. Can I count on you to do what you said? And what about those other two?"

"Like I said," Vance said, "Dale will do whatever I ask him to do. Remember, he used to work for me too. He will make sure your number looks good. And let's just say Union Construction has way too much on its plate and we don't feel we want to take on a project of this magnitude right now."

"And Ramsey?" Case asked.

"Ramsey is going to go for the job aggressively on his own," Vance replied. "He can't even do the job," Case protested. "He doesn't have the staff or the knowledge. Why, he can't even…." Case cut himself off mid-rant as he noticed the sly expression on Vance's face. He sat back in his chair and calmed himself.

"That's the point, huh?"

"Exactly," Vance confirmed. "Ramsey isn't a factor. He wants to be a big dog, but he can't play in this kind of yard. Not on a project like Vista Ridge. There are only three companies anybody who had any sense would want to do this job. I am bowing out and Dale is willing to play ball because I am telling him to. Ramsey is going to have the low number. But they aren't going to use him. They know he can't deliver the goods. You just have to grow a pair and hold your ground. They will try to use his number as leverage against you. But you already know the score. So be an alpha and you will get what you want. Jacebre's name will be on a bonafide skyscraper, the biggest one in DFW. And of course, this conversation never happened. You go down, you go down like a man. Leave us out of it. Including Ramsey."

"That's fine by me," Case said confidently. "And don't worry. I'm not going down. I have some insurance policies in place."

CHAPTER 4

None the Wiser

DAY 1

Jeremiah struggled to stay on task. He smiled from ear to ear as he thought about the wonderful morning he had just experienced with his wife. As important as this project was, all he wanted right now was to see Elise again. He wanted to hold her like he had that morning and thank God for the miracle she carried inside her.

Work had to be done, though. This project was crucial to the company's success. He was doing a final review of his presentation and pricing. He was very pleased with his presentation. He offered multiple options that demonstrated the attention to detail that he hoped would set their proposal apart. If he could land this project, it would posture the company for a huge leap in the market and likely mean a huge promotion for him.

His company, Jacebre Construction, was on the verge of becoming the leading construction company in the state. Jeremiah started there as an intern while he was still in college and had worked for Jacebre his entire professional life. The projects were diverse and challenging. The staff was intelligent and innovative. And the pay was great. None of his college classmates could boast salaries even close to Jeremiah's. Jacebre was a great place to work. Mostly. The one drawback was that Elise could not stand the owner of the company, Case McBride. She never called him that, though. She called him "S & S," which was short for "Shiesty & Shady." Jeremiah didn't necessarily disagree with her, but Case was the boss and for the most part Jeremiah was empowered to get his job done. But still, working for Jacebre was one of the few points that Elise and he could never get on the same page about. Jeremiah had been courted by several other construction companies and Elise had always encouraged him to consider a change. But Case would always convince him to stay by matching or exceeding any potential offer. Despite her distrust of Case, Elise couldn't deny the rewards so she would always acquiesce.

Jeremiah was completing his review when the phone rang. It was Case. Oddly enough, Case and Jeremiah rarely spoke. When he did talk to Case, however, it was about one thing: profits. Jeremiah could never get him to understand that there had been quite a bit of business lost because of Case insisting on unreasonably high profit margins. It was as if he wanted to lose some of the work. Even more puzzling, Case would never sit down with him to actually crunch the numbers. He would just say, "If you want you and your employees to continue to have a place to work, you need to figure out how to sell at a higher price. We can't make it unless you do." So, Jeremiah would push the envelope as much as he could. And even though it didn't make sense, he couldn't deny the results; it seemed that for every job he felt they lost because of being overpriced another one would come, and they would land it.

Now Case was calling him, on a Saturday. Jeremiah was sure it had to be related to this project. He answered the call in his most welcoming voice. "Hi Case. What can I do for you?"

"Jeremiah?" Case asked, sounding surprised. "Are you working, brother? I didn't expect to get you. I was going to just leave you a message for you to call me Monday before you sent Vista Ridge. What are you doing there? Is everything okay? Any problems?"

"No, Case," Jeremiah answered calmly. "We're in good shape. I figured you were calling about Vista Ridge. I am just triple-checking the numbers and going over our presentation. I want it to be the first thing they see when they get to the office Monday morning."

"Outstanding!" Case exclaimed. "And how are those numbers looking? We have good money in it, I assume."

Jeremiah paused. He didn't want to spar with the owner of the company on a Saturday and potentially ruin this perfect day, but he felt he needed to speak up. "Case, about that," he said. "I know how you feel about profits, but I'm afraid if we keep our margins like we have been applying them recently we won't get this job. We need to be sharper on these numbers. If we aren't, then Liberty or Union construction are going to get it."

Case knew he had to be careful. If it had been anybody else, he would have just told him to shut up and do as he was told. But he was well aware that Jeremiah could work anywhere else, and he needed him there. He also needed him in the dark, so he chose his words wisely. Jeremiah didn't have many weaknesses but the ones he had were glaringly obvious to Case. Jeremiah was a nice guy who was more concerned about people than anything else. Case knew he could use that.

"Jeremiah, I hear you. I really do. And you know what? I trust you. But I've been doing this for about twice as long as you so can you hear me out?" Case asked politely.

"Of course, Case," Jeremiah responded. He could imagine Elise twisting her lips had she heard Case's fake attempt at courtesy.

"You say you're worried about us not getting this job, but I recall us having a similar conversation on the Regal Hotel project a couple of years ago. Refresh my memory on that one, Jeremiah."

Jeremiah hated Case's condescending tone. He knew where he was going. "Case, you know what happened. We didn't get the job but the company that did lost a boatload of money."

"Yeah, that's how I remember it too. In fact, you hired up a couple of their guys because we had plenty of work and were financially strong. Oh, and what happened on that Grand View mall remodel? Oh, I remember. I think that's the only time I saw you mad, Jeremiah," Case prodded him. "You said we were going to miss out on a great opportunity because we weren't competitive. But we got that job and I recall some fat bonus checks getting written. The fattest one went to a guy whose name started with a J. I think he's still with us."

"Ha. Yeah, Case. He's still here," Jeremiah said dryly.

"I know I'm being a bit of an ass, Jeremiah. But this isn't just about bonus checks. You tell me all the time about us being more aggressive and getting more projects. Well, maybe I'm out of touch, but I don't want you guys working for free. If we get the job and it's making money, then great. But the less money we make, the harder it is to keep on the little guys on our crews. I hear you talking about how we can thrive on less and I admit it, you're right, we can. But what about the guys in our company who don't get six figures like you? What about them? That's all I want you to think about, Jeremiah. It's your call, though. I am trusting you to get it right. Let's get the job and let's get it profitably. Fair enough?"

"Well, when you put it like that, yes, that's fair," Jeremiah conceded. "So, you got everything together?" Case asked victoriously.

"Yes, sir. It's ready and I will make sure there is plenty of money in it. If we get it, then the little guys will be well taken care of."

"Great work, Jeremiah. And I am sorry for disturbing you while you are giving your Saturday up for the company. You get that taken care of and go spend some time with that pretty little wife of yours and tell her I said hello."

Jeremiah cringed at the compliment. He could hear Elise now: "You tell that shiesty, shady, steroid-takin' joker I am not the one."

"Will do, Case," Jeremiah responded. "Take care and thanks for the call." Jeremiah thought about the conversation. Case hadn't said anything wrong, but he still felt troubled.

His mind went back to Elise. Not only had she wanted him to look at other offers, but she kept telling him that he should do his own thing. "Miah, start your own business," she would encourage him. "You can do anything you set your mind to. You don't have to work for anybody. Especially Case's shiesty butt."

He was tempted but the timing never seemed to be right. Stepping out on his own in the commercial construction industry would be a major undertaking, particularly for a black man. He enjoyed the life he was able to provide for his wife and wasn't sure he wanted to take the risk. On top of that, although he enjoyed his job, he wasn't sure it was his passion. Sure, the money was great, but a lot of stress came with it, along with a lot of hours away from Elise. The thought of spending his Saturdays at the office, even if it was for his own company, when his son came made him sad. Still, Elise made him feel like Superman. If she thought he could do it, perhaps he should.

He sat there lost in his thoughts for a moment when Elise texted him. "You still at it?"

"Yeah, babe - but almost done," he replied. "Good - we miss you."

Jeremiah almost asked her, *"Who is we?"* Then he remembered. There was an addition to the family on the way.

"I will be home soon. You mind getting me something ready to wear?"

"Already done," she texted back, "you not going out with me looking all discombobulated."

"LOL. Whatever, girl."

"But umm - there is a little problem with the baby," she texted.

Jeremiah's heart sank as he read the text. He instantly called her. She sounded surprised as she said, "Hey, baby."

"Lise, what's wrong with the baby? What happened? Do I need to come home?" he asked anxiously.

Elise felt bad but tried to play it off. "Umm, no, baby, it's just that your son is a little upset with you."

Jeremiah could hear by her tone that everything was cool, and Elise was just being Elise. "Why is my son upset with me?" he said, anticipating some Elise shenanigans.

"Well, your son said he does not appreciate the way you defiled his mama today and he said when he gets big, you and he are going to have words," she said as she laughed.

Jeremiah joined her in her laughter and told her, "You tell that little bun that if it wasn't for me defiling his mama he wouldn't even be in the oven. But if he still feelin' froggy about it when he gets past puberty, you tell him jump. Pop is here for it."

"Miah, don't you hurt my son!" she exclaimed, still laughing. "So, you've accepted that he's a he, huh?"

"Whatever, I'm just trying to let you have your little boy fantasy until your little princess comes and steals your heart from me."

"I cannot with you right now, Lise. Let me finish my work so I can come home."

"Fine, bye," she said as she smacked her lips together, giving him a mock kiss through the phone. "I love you, Miah."

"Hey, Elise, one more thing." "What up?" she asked.

"If it is a little girl, I mean it's not but hypothetically, if it is, don't worry about her stealing my heart from you. You are my heart, babe. Always have been. Always will be."

Elise was silent on the other end of the phone.

"What are you doing? Smiling or crying?" Jeremiah asked confidently. "Both," she said. "I can't stand you, Miah."

"Umm, I think you can."

"Whatever, boy. But hey, I've got one more thing too. What we talked about with Mari. That's still on, right?"

"Of course it is. We prayed and fasted about it and agreed that's what God wanted for us. If God wants to give us a double portion, then that's fine but we aren't changing course," Jeremiah reassured her.

"Good. Miah, I am sooo happy. Hurry home, okay?" "I will, babe. Almost done."

Jeremiah disconnected the call and refocused for a quick final check. Everything was done. He looked at his pricing one last time and thought about his conversation with Case. With a click to his spreadsheet, he added a few more margin points to the job. If that's what Case wanted, then so be it. He hit send on the email and headed for the door to go celebrate with his wife and child.

CHAPTER 5

Perfect Day

DAY 1

"Miah, dinner was so good. That steak melted in my mouth like butter," Elise said. "I'm glad I rocked your world earlier, because I'm going to sleep."

"You can't go to sleep just yet," Jeremiah said. "I need your help on something."

"What do you need help with?" she asked.

"Well, I took a little side project for a friend. I am helping him remodel a house he bought for himself."

Elise turned in the passenger seat and faced Jeremiah. "Jeremiah, that's why you've been so tired lately. You're working weekends and doing side projects. How much are they paying you?"

"I'm not charging. It's for a friend."

"A friend wouldn't let you do that!" she said as she tilted her head and leaned toward him. "Miah, you have a wife and child to think about. You out in these streets working for free and got the baby at home talking 'bout 'I want my daddy.' Then I have to be the one to tell him, 'Don't worry, baby. Mommy will take you to soccer practice.'"

"Whoa!" Jeremiah said as his eyes widened. "Extra much? First of all, the baby you speak of is at best a few weeks in existence and I am pretty sure he can't talk, make up stories like his mama, or go to soccer practice yet. He'll be fine."

"Umm-hm," Elise said as she squared back up in her seat and folded her arms. "She, and I do mean she, how you like them apples, is a genius and knows how to express herself and she doesn't appreciate this one bit."

"So now that you in your feelings, it's a girl?"

"Durn skippy. If you knew how to act right you would have had an ally on this boy journey, but now you on your own. Sucks for you."

"Okay. Both of you just chill," Jeremiah told her. "Just come see it. I want your opinion before I show it to them."

"Miah," she said as she softened her voice, "I don't have to see it. I know if you did it, it will be nice. I just don't want you killing yourself. And definitely not for free."

"Babe, it's about done. It's just a few more things I want your thoughts on." "Fine," she agreed, "but you are for sure not getting any fresh-baked cookies

tonight. Imma let you make it because I don't wanna fight in front of the baby, but I don't like this, Miah."

"I understand," Jeremiah said calmly.

He was actually too calm for Elise's taste. It was unlike him to see that she was bothered and not make more of an effort to smooth things over.

"Where is this house, anyway?" she inquired, still a little annoyed. "It's in Colonial Park."

"Colonial Park?!" Elise exclaimed. "That's snazzy! But I guess they can afford it since you're working for free," she said, getting one more jab in.

Jeremiah's heart often overruled his common sense and people would sometimes take advantage of his generosity. Elise would warn him, but he would just tell her he knew but that he wasn't just doing it for them, he was doing it for the Lord. Outwardly she would complain but inwardly she was thankful to have such a giving and kind man as her husband. The thought of his kindness melted her frustration.

"Oooh, Miah, do you remember that house we saw on the lake a few years ago? Can we go by there? That was my joint! It was so nice."

"Oh, yeah, about that…," Jeremiah said reluctantly.

"Jeremiah, what now?" she asked suspiciously, peeping his tone. "It's just that…," Jeremiah still hesitated.

"What?" she asked. She couldn't imagine what his hesitation was about.

"Well, about that house. That's the one he bought."

"What?! Jeremiah John Traylor, no the H-E-double-hockey-sticks you did not remodel my house for someone else. You know I loved that house, Jeremiah. We even prayed over it and walked around it seven times, like that did any good."

Jeremiah shot her a disapproving glance.

"Fine. I'm sorry, Jesus," Elise said as she looked up. "But this is the husband you gave me's fault. He gave my house away, Lord!"

"Elise, he bought the house and he asked for help. I didn't know he picked your dream house," Jeremiah explained.

"Umm, umm, ummm," Elise said, shaking her head. "Did I say no fresh-baked cookies tonight? Baybay, you 'bout to lose some weight. You about to get lean, cuz you not getting any of this sugar for a minute. You might finally get those abs." Jeremiah reached over to hold her hand. "Don't be mad, babe," he said sweetly.

Elise interlaced her fingers with his. "I can't be mad at you, Miah, but if I let you off the hook, you won't learn nuthin'." She kissed his hand. "You better enjoy that, sir, cuz heh-heh-heh, bruh, that's gon be the most physical affection you get for a minute. I mean it's going to be a while. Giving my house away," she sneered. "The nerve."

They rounded the corner into the gated community and Jeremiah punched in a code to open the gate. Elise had only been there a few times. She could swear when she drove through those gates, she could hear angels singing. Every house was unique and every lawn perfectly manicured and landscaped. She hadn't thought about the house in some time, but she always hoped they could live there one day. But for now, their little three-bedroom was fine. She already had everything she needed. *Maybe one day,* she thought.

They turned down the street where the house was, and Elise's eyes went straight to the end of the cul-de-sac. Her eyes widened as they approached it. It was even more beautiful than she remembered. Jeremiah had added some wonderful touches to it.

Jeremiah drove up into the driveway and couldn't help but notice her staring. "I'm the man, ain't I, babe?" he said conceitedly.

"It's lots of men like you," Elise said as she turned her nose up at him. "Benedict Arnold…for one."

"Elise," he said, amused at her attitude.

"Darth Vader," she continued.

Jeremiah just shook his head and smiled. "Judas!" she spat the word at him.

"Judas?!" Jeremiah exclaimed as he laughed out loud. "Okay, that's harsh, don't you think?"

"I think that's about right, sir," she said as she turned her head away from him. "What you are about to do, sir, do quickly."

Jeremiah got out of the car and walked around to her side to let her out. He gently pulled her out and walked her toward the entrance. "Girl, get out your feelings and tell me what you think," he said.

Elise took a breath and settled back into her role as a supportive wife. "Miah, it's amazing. I love the traditional look. I love the paint. I love the brick and the stone. You changed the window surrounds too, didn't you?"

"I did," he said proudly. "That was actually your idea. I remember you didn't like the old ones."

"Oh, I know whose idea it was. Just like those limestone columns. Those were my ideas too, boy. I would ask for a design fee but you ain't getting paid."

"But you like it, though, right?" he asked.

"It's aight," she said as she shrugged her shoulders.

"Uh-huh," Jeremiah said, seeing through her facade. "Come on. Let me show you the inside."

Elise decided to just go with the flow. She remembered that just this morning she was in perfect bliss. She wasn't going to let this put a hiccup in their perfect day. The house was elegant, but it also looked like a real family could live there.

The color of the walls perfectly blended with the wood and carpet flooring combinations. The carpet was the same style and color she had pointed out to Jeremiah one day when they were shopping. The kitchen was adorned in the most beautiful marble she had ever seen. The countertops sat on top of the most amazing custom cabinet work. Elise struggled not to be envious, but the more she saw the harder that became. When she saw the house years before, it was so full of potential. Now everything that Jeremiah had done for his friend had made that potential a reality.

"Miah, did you do all of this?" she asked.

"I did some of it. But mostly I just managed the process. It was a whole lot of 'Say, bruh, that don't go there' and 'Dude, I told you.' But it was cool."

"When did you have time?"

"There were quite a few quick Zoom calls and there may have been a few Saturdays where I had to swing by here to check on some things."

"Imma fuss at you later. You know that, right?" she said. "I know. But what do you think?"

"Miah...this is so dope. I love it. I don't think I would change a thing. I mean I would change my man remodeling my dream house for somebody else but other than that, I am really proud of you. It was beautiful before, but this is absolutely gorgeous."

"Thank you, babe," he said as he kissed her cheek. "Let's see the rest."

The rest of the house included four bedrooms, an office, a game room, and a theater. But the master bedroom topped them all. Unlike the rest of the house, it was fully furnished. The bed was a full king with an exquisite comforter set, with the most beautiful array of pillows. In the corner was an elegant woodburning fireplace.

"This woman is like me," Elise said.

Jeremiah was used to it now, but it took him a while to get used to Elise and her plethora of pillows on the bed. "Babe," he would complain, "it takes us five minutes just to get in the bed every night.

Do we really need all these pillows?" Elise would quip back, "Jeremiah John Traylor, I don't ask for much, but you are not getting in between me and my pillows!"

The bedroom windows had exquisite curtains that looked like they came straight out of the featured house in some elite interior design magazine. And as seemed to be a recurring theme, it was something that she would have picked herself. As the thought ran through her mind, she got a very nervous and a very good feeling at the same time. *No!* she thought. *You trippin', girl.*

"So do you think my friend will like it?" Jeremiah asked.

Elise's heart sank just a little. She was right. Her passing thought was too good to be true. But still she wondered. The columns…the kitchen…the curtains… these were all things she liked. There were so many aspects of the house that reminded her of conversations she had with Jeremiah.

And now this bedroom with a bed and pillows for days. "Jeremiah," she said, trying not to get her hopes up. "Who did you do all this for? It seems like a lot of work for free. Did your friend tell you he wanted all this?"

"Sort of. I just know what they like. Your man got some skills, right?" he gloated.

"Yes, Mr. Humility. I love it. But what friend? I know all your friends and ain't nobody I know mentioned buying a house like this. Whose house is this?" she pressed.

Jeremiah ignored her and grabbed her hand. "Let's look outside," he said. "Miah, why won't you tell me whose house this is?"

"I told you, it's for my friend," he said casually as he opened a sliding door and walked her out onto the spacious balcony.

The balcony overlooked the spacious backyard and a beautiful lake. The sun was setting and glistened off the clear waters. The sight took her breath away.

"Miah, please tell me whose house this is," she said, trying to sound calm.

Jeremiah stood behind her and wrapped his arms snuggly around her stomach as he kissed her softly on her cheek.

Before he could speak, she said sternly, "And boy, you bet not tell me it's for your friend."

"Well, I can't tell you that. It is for my friend. It's for my best friend. It's my friend who I can tell anything to and not be condemned. It's my friend who believes in me even when I don't believe in myself. It's for my friend who prays for me and with me. It's for my friend who loves me unconditionally. It's for my friend who tells me like it is when I'm wrong but lets me know they will ride or die with me until the end. It's for my friend who dreams with me and then shows me how to make those dreams come true."

"Sounds like a good friend," Elise said as she felt her heart racing in her chest. "Like I said, my best friend."

"Do I know this best friend?"

"Of course you do," he said as he kissed her again. "So, what's this friend's name?"

"I think you know her name, Lise."

"Well, it better not be Shawneequa from the choir or somebody getting cut." "No, it's not Shawneequa from the choir."

"And it better not be Vicki. Talking 'bout being the church secretary and keeping the books. She need to keep her eyes off my man."

"Nope, not Vicki either."

"Well, if it's not Shawneequa, and it's not Vicki, then could it possibly be forrrr...." Elise was afraid to say it out loud even though it was obvious. "Me?" she asked sheepishly.

"Of course it's for you, babe. I've been working on it for a while now. I'm sorry I had to keep it secret, but I wanted to see the look on your face when you saw it for the first time. Do you really like it?"

"Miah...I love it. I'm speechless. This is our house?" "Yeah, babe. It's ours."

"Miah?"

"Yeah, babe?"

"You still not getting no cookie tonight," she laughed.

"Dang, Lise, a brutha done got you your dream house and still can't get no love?" "Don't worry, we can get up early before church and I will send you into the house of the Lord with a smile on that handsome face."

"Welp, time to go get some sleep then," Jeremiah said emphatically.

"Nooo, Miah, not yet. I want to stay here in your arms until the sun goes down." "That's exactly what I wanted to hear, Lise. We can stay as long as you want."

CHAPTER 6

Enlarged Territory

DAY 2

Church service was amazing! As usual, their pastor, Wayne Gregory, had delivered an encouraging word that brought the congregation to their feet in praise. But now it was time to go home. Jeremiah was still basking in the euphoria of being a father and he wanted to get home and relax with Elise.

But today, duty called. Pastor Gregory, or Pastor G., as Elise affectionately called him, had asked him to meet with them both after church. Pastor Gregory was not someone you easily told no. Not because he was overbearing or demanding, it was actually just the opposite. Pastor Gregory had a way of making you want to please him without demanding it of you. So as much as he wanted to just go home, he quickly agreed to stay a little longer to see how he could help. But now he had to wait. Pastor Gregory considered it a mark against his pastoral character if he didn't personally shake every man's hand, hug every sister, and kiss every baby at the end of service. And of course, there were always those who needed impromptu counseling sessions or prayer, making the wait longer. To the casual observer, it may have appeared to be an inconvenience or simply the man doing his job. But Jeremiah knew neither was the Case. For Pastor Gregory, the people of God were his life and he somehow never seemed to run out of energy, patience, or love.

Jeremiah held Elise's hand as they sat in an empty pew waiting for him to finish. Unlike Pastor Gregory, Elise had already run out of patience.

"Miah, what he doin'? I'm 'bout to die. I'm sooo hungry, baby. Tell them folks leave my pastor alone!"

"Babe, he has to do his thing. You wouldn't want him rushing if he was talking to you," Jeremiah told her calmly.

"That's because he wouldn't rush if he were talking to me. It's not my fault I'm his favorite. Besides, I wouldn't be bothering him after he just preached with some of this foolishness!"

Elise changed her voice as she mocked what she imagined some of the conversations Pastor Gregory had to endure were like: "'Pastor, can you pray for my grandbaby? She got the sniffles something fierce. We shole is worried about her. And pray for my one hundred and thirty-five-year-old Aunt Janey Mae. She's in hospice but we speakin' life over that thang. We declarin' and decreein' she gon live and not die!' Fool, let Janey Mae go see Jesus. I assure you she ret to go!"

"Elise, not now, babe. It's too many people here for you to be showing out," Jeremiah said, stifling his laughter.

But Jeremiah trying to calm her only made her want to cut up all the more. "Uh-uh. I'm just getting started. If me and our little bundle of joy gon have to die of starvation in the house of the Lord, then I'm gon speak my truth before I see my redeemer! These folks taking up my Pastor G's precious time cuz Pookie and Ray Ray back in jail on more false charges. 'Pastor, we just praying the truth come out and the lies of the enemy don't prevail.' Baybay, they got Pookie and Ray Ray on high-definition camera with them folks' televisions and couches in they hand. Where's the lie?"

Jeremiah released his laughter as he heard a sweet familiar voice. "Is she on one again, Jeremiah?"

"Yes, Sister Faye. She is. Plus, she's hungry," Jeremiah said.

"And bad as I don't know what," Sister Faye said as she embraced them both. Sister Faye was Pastor Gregory's wife and the consummate First Lady. She loved the Lord and his people. And she most definitely loved Wayne Gregory. Not that they needed it, but Pastor Gregory and First Lady Faye were like a second set of parents to Jeremiah and Elise.

"So, how's my favorite couple doing?" Faye asked.

"We hungry, First Lady!" Elise said much more loudly than necessary, hoping Pastor Gregory would hear her in the distance.

"You two kids waiting on Wayne?" Faye asked.

"Yes, ma'am. You know he has to make his rounds," Jeremiah responded.

Sister Faye gently took both of their hands and looked at them sweetly. "Well, I just want to encourage you two to keep being thankful and to trust the Lord. You children are some of the brightest lights in this church. I appreciate the way you love my husband and support the work of the Lord. And just remember, where much is given, much is required."

"Okay. Thanks for that. What do you know, Sister Faye?" Jeremiah asked, wondering what prompted her statement.

"I don't know what you mean, sweetie," Faye said coyly. "Now do you want me to get my husband so you can get back home with your precious wife?"

"He does, First Lady," Elise said emphatically. "Yes, ma'am. That would be nice," Jeremiah agreed.

Faye subtly waved to her husband and without saying a word let him know it was time to move on to the next task. Pastor Gregory quickly made his exit and joined them. He kissed his wife on the cheek and then enveloped Jeremiah and Elise in his huge arms.

"Hey, you two. Thank you so much for waiting," Pastor Gregory greeted them warmly.

"It's no trouble, Pastor G," Elise said sweetly.

Jeremiah and Faye made eye contact with each other and then both gave Elise the side-eye.

"Why are y'all looking at my baby girl like that?" Pastor Gregory asked. "Because they're haters, Pastor G! Don't worry about them. What do you

need?" Elise said as she snuggled up sweetly to her pastor and stuck her tongue out at Jeremiah and Faye.

Pastor Gregory placed his arms around his daughter in Christ and smiled. "I don't want to hold you long, but I have something important for Jeremiah to pray about. I wanted to pitch it to you both since we really need you both to buy in. The Lord is blessing our little church.

We're growing and we want to make sure we have leadership in place so our next generation will be discipled by loving and mature Christians. A big part of that is also making sure we start now with making sure our Elder Board is strong."

Elise's heart warmed as she anticipated Pastor Gregory's next words.

Jeremiah, however, didn't quite know where he was going with it. "How can I help, Pastor?" he asked.

"You can help, son, by agreeing to start the process of becoming an Elder here in our church."

Jeremiah simply stood there…speechless.

Pastor Gregory whispered into Elise's ear, "Baby girl, is he breathing?" "Give my baby a moment," Elise said. "Him just humble. Others sometimessee how amazing he is before he does."

"You okay, Jeremiah?" Faye asked as she placed her hands on his shoulders. "Huh? Oh, yes, ma'am, I'm fine. But Pastor, you mean me? For the Elder ministry? Don't you have to be… an elder to do that?" Jeremiah asked as he processed his pastor's proposal.

Pastor Gregory laughed. "Well, yes, son, you do have to be an Elder to be an Elder, but I am pretty sure you are asking me if your age makes a difference. If that's the case, then no. You meet all the biblical qualifications. But it is a whole new level of ministry. Up to now, you have been carrying and implementing the vision. Now, if you feel called to do so, and I mean only if you feel called to do so, you will be working with the voting Elders to decide the direction of the church. You will be involved in major decisions regarding finances, discipleship, outreach. You name it. Plus, we think with your mind and heart you will bring a much- needed freshness to the table."

Jeremiah's heart began to slow as he settled into the reality of this awesome request. But one thought came to the forefront of his mind. "Pastor Gregory, is this because of my dad? Did he recommend this?"

"Well, if you mean is it because your dad raised a responsible Christian man who is Spirit filled, gifted, and able to lead, then yes, it is because of your dad. But this isn't a fraternity, son. We don't hand out Eldership because of family connections. All the elders, including your dad, have been praying about this. I actually asked your dad to make the presentation to you, but I guess he knows his son. He wanted me to do it so I could assure you that we are considering you only after carefully seeking the Lord. We have observed your heart, your home life, and your efforts in the church. It's because of those things that the Lord has opened this door for you. So…what do you think?"

"Pastor. I am having trouble taking it all in. It's overwhelming."

"Good! It's supposed to be, Jeremiah. If you didn't think it was a big deal, then I would know I had the wrong man. You don't have to answer now. You take my daughter home and you two pray about it. Let me know how you feel the Lord is leading and if you have any questions. Good enough?"

"Yes, Pastor. That sounds good. I am still at a loss for words, but I'm honored that you would think of me for something like this."

"It's not just me, son. Listen to your wife. We all see God's hand on your life.

You just need to walk in your calling and let him have his way."
"Amen," Elise said, still smiling.

"And do you have any questions, daughter?" Pastor Gregory asked her. "Welp, time to go!" Jeremiah said humorously as he nudged Faye with his elbow.

Elise cut her eyes at her husband and then turned them back to Pastor Gregory. "Yes, sir, I do, actually," she said. "Once Jeremiah accepts, and we all know he's going to accept, does that mean everybody in the church has to call me Elderess?"

Pastor Gregory shook his head. "No, daughter, I am sorry but that's not what that means."

"Oh, well, that's disappointing. But you do know that will be the first motion Elder Traylor makes? In the meantime, I will settle for the honorary title of Pastor G's favorite daughter."

"You are a mess, girl!" First Lady Faye interjected.

"I ain't playing. Oh, and speaking of official church titles, Elder Traylor's second motion when he takes office is to forbid everyone in the church from calling you Pastor G."

Pastor Gregory tried to sound innocent. "Why, daughter, why can't they call me Pastor G?"

Elise's arms were still wrapped around him, and she playfully hit him on his chest. "You know why. That's my name for you and they stole it from me. I know you have to pretend you like them, but you're my Pastor G. Not theirs."

"Somebody's hungry, Jeremiah. Take my daughter home and feed her," Pastor Gregory said.

Jeremiah smiled. "Yeah, she would be like this on a full stomach, but I will take care of it. Come on, Lise, let's go get something to eat, babe."

"Fine," Elise grunted. "But can I at least get one of those big church hats?" "If you want one, then you can have one. Get the biggest one you can find, daughter," Pastor Gregory said.

"Yay, Jeremiah, put that on your church credit card."

"Get her outta here, son!" Pastor Gregory said as he laughed from his belly.

CHAPTER 7

Mari and the Traylors

DAY 2

"Miah, what if she says no?" Elise asked nervously as she checked the smothered chicken. She was excited to tell Jeremiah's parents everything about the baby and the house. But she found herself getting anxious about another matter. "What if who says no?" Jeremiah asked obliviously as he tried to figure out a way to sneak a premeal taste.

"Here, take this so you can concentrate," she said as she cut a piece of chicken and put it in his mouth. "I'm talking about Mari. What if she doesn't want to do it?" "Babe, she ain't gonna say no. Why would she?" Jeremiah smacked as he struggled to enjoy the juicy but piping-hot chicken.

"I feel like we are proposing to her at a football game or something and all the cameras are going to be on her. It's like she's going to feel forced to say yes so she doesn't embarrass us."

"Lise, it's okay to be nervous. This is big. I felt the same way when I proposed to you." Jeremiah took a step back and posed for her. "I was so young and foolish. Like you were ever going to be able to turn down all this unbridled manliness," he said with a sly grin. "But I was still scared, though," he said in a more serious tone, "so I talked to Pop. He prayed with me and told me he felt the same way when he asked Mama. And we know how both of those stories turned out. Mari wants this too. Don't worry about it."

Elise stared her husband down. "You know, bruh, you would be on point with your encouragement game if you had left out that 'unbridled manliness' comment and that ridiculous Arnold Swartzanegro pose."

"Girl, please, you know this manliness is off the charts. If I could figure out how to bottle it, I would get out of the construction game, you could stop selling houses, and we could just go to the beach and chill with Elon Musk."

"Oh, so yo Jeremiah manliness pill gon put us up there with Elon?" she asked skeptically.

"No, not with him. Past him. Elon would be our butler," Jeremiah said, struggling to keep a straight face.

"Wow…that's delusional, sorry…I mean that's delightful, sir."

"I don't know, kid, you didn't seem to think this manliness was delusional this morning. You were for sure delighted," Jeremiah said confidently.

"I can't stand you, Miah," she said as she shook her head and blushed. "Yes, you can."

Before they could continue their banter, they were interrupted by an exuberant voice in the background. "T Lise! Uncle J! We're here."

Hearing that voice calmed all of Elise's concerns. She sang out her response. "Mari, we in the kitchen, baby."

Jeremiah and Elise met Amari by what most would call sheer coincidence. Elise had been volunteering at an afterschool care center that the little girl was attending. Amari was withdrawn and very slow to trust. But Elise was quickly able to form a bond with her. She went on and on about her for several weeks and asked Jeremiah to meet her. When he did, it was love at first sight! Amari had endured some serious abuse with her previous foster family and was staying in a group home at the time. So, her caseworker was happy to transition Amari to them. Now Jeremiah and Elise were hoping things would become more permanent.

Amari ran into the kitchen and hugged her Uncle J around the waist.

"Hey, beautiful!" Jeremiah said warmly. "Did you enjoy Mama Etta and Papa John?"

"Yes…well, sort of. Mama Etta is always trying to get free labor. We spent a lot of time in the garden, but it was fun, though. She let me eat whatever I wanted," Amari said as she turned her head slyly to Elise.

"Whatever, little girl. Don't be throwing shade cuz I want you to be healthy," Elise said as she scrunched up her lips. "You can let your Uncle J go now and come love on me too. Please and thank you."

"Aww, her jealous, Uncle J, let me share the love. I would tell her to come down here and hug me but she's not that much taller than me," Amari quipped, causing Jeremiah to laugh from his soul.

"Oh, you got short jokes, huh? This is what we doin', little girl? Fine, I don't need no hug. Let me find my spoon," Elise said aggressively. She grabbed a large wooden spoon and Amari was off to the races with Elise hot on her heels.

"Papa John! Help! T Lise is tryna get me!" Amari giggled as she ran into the living room and found safe harbor behind Jeremiah's father.

"Hey, Daddy. How are you?" Elise said sweetly.

"Hey, Daddy's Girl. I'm doing fine now. How is my little ray of sunshine doing?" John said, matching Elise's energy.

Elise put her arms around him, then slickly reached around his back and playfully popped Amari with the spoon.

"Amari, you know you can't hide from yo T Lise behind Papa John," Jeremiah's mother said. "You better come over here with Mama Etta for that."

Amari joined Jeremiah's mother on the couch and snuggled up next to her, matching John and Elise's pose.

Etta Ween loved seeing her husband dote on Elise. Jeremiah always referred to his father as "Dad" or "Pop," but one "Daddy" from Elise and that man was no good. "Girl, you are just a whole mess," Etta Ween continued. "Elise, you too old to

be this spoiled. Got my pastor and my husband wrapped around your fingers. Amari is supposed to be the baby."

"Am I too old for you to spoil me, Daddy?" Elise asked innocently.

"No, you are not," John defended.

Jeremiah followed behind and playfully tried to join in John and Elise's embrace. "No! My daddy," Elise objected as she pushed Jeremiah away and squeezed John more tightly.

Jeremiah shook his head and turned to his mom. "Mommy!" he said mockingly as he went to the couch to hug her.

Etta Ween quickly joined in. "Hey, sweetest bestest baby boy who never does anything wrong. Come here and sit on Mommy's lap with the other baby. I don't care that you are a grown man," she laughed.

Elise and John looked at each other. "Haters!" they said in unison.

"Come on, Daddy," Elise said as she squinted her eyes at Jeremiah, Etta Ween, and Amari. "Let me make sure you get the big piece of chicken. If you haters are finished being jealous of me and my daddy's love, I guess y'all can come too. We have some news to share!"

CHAPTER 8

No One Left Behind

DAY 2

"Baby girl, baby girl, baby girl! That's the best...I mean second-best smothered chicken I've ever had," John said as he leaned over and kissed his wife on the cheek. "That's okay, sweetie. I'm happy my daughter has perfected my recipe," Etta Ween said. "She's come a long way, though. I remember the first time she asked me to help her make something for Jeremiah. I said, 'Baby, when you feed my son this, you better be naked and have a bowl of cereal on standby.'" "Mama!" Jeremiah objected as he nodded in Amari's direction. "Oh...sorry, Amari," Etta Ween said.

"It's okay, Mama Etta. I know Uncle J and T.T. have praise and worship grown version," Amari giggled.

Jeremiah turned his head and looked directly at Elise. "Praise and worship grown version, huh? Really, Elise?"

"These kids say the darndest things. I cannot imagine where she heard such a thing," Elise said, trying to sound innocent.

"So, Elise, what's this big news?" John asked, attempting to throw his daughter-in-law a lifeline.

"Good save, Daddy. Miah, you go first."

Jeremiah reached for Elise's hand. "Well, the Lord is doing a lot and we just wanted to share it all with you. But first we want to talk about what you already know. Pastor Gregory approached me today about becoming an Elder."

"Amen," John said proudly. "And?"

"Well, Dad, just be in prayer. Elise says I can do it, but I want to be sure. I also want to say that if our pastor and our church sees anything good in me, then it's because of how you two raised me. Dad, you always have been and always will be my hero. I know what a man of God looks like because of you. You walked so close to God in front of me and gave me a roadmap. Mama, I know what love looks like because of you. When Elise was playing hard to get, I was able to see past it because regardless of what she said, her eyes looked at me the way you look at Dad. She could lie, but her eyes couldn't. We love you both and we thank God for you. I know you already know that, but I just wanted to say it again."

"My baby is so sweet," Elise gushed. "But he didn't tell me we were doing parent appreciation, so I will have to improv my part. Mama Etta. Daddy. Some things can never be said enough. Y'all are my second chance. You know I didn't really have a relationship with my mother and never knew my father. I didn't really know what I was missing until I met you. You welcomed me and loved me unconditionally. You have always treated me like I was your own and I want to thank you for that."

"Ya durn skippy!" John agreed. "I told Jeremiah a long time ago, 'You let that girl go if you want to. We ain't letting her go.'"

"And you been spoilin' that little thang ever since," Etta Ween laughed out loud. "Elise, you are our daughter. We love you and we thank you for loving our son. And Jeremiah, we are so proud of you, baby. It's your time. Let the Lord use you."

"Okay, family," John said. "Now that we got all this mushy stuff out of the way and talked about all the things we already know, can we get to the stuff we don't know? This itis about to hit yo old man with a vengeance."

"Okay, Pop, way to ruin the emotional moment," Jeremiah said. "Well, we have good news, better news, and the best news. The good news is…drumroll, please, babe."

Elise drummed her hands loudly on the dining room table. "We bought a new house. We will be moving soon."

"A new house? When did this happen?" John asked, slightly put off that his son hadn't shared such big news with him.

"Dad, it's a long story. We will give you the details later, but now Elise has the better news. Trust me…you want to hear this."

"Daddy…first of all…I'm just appalled," Elise said. "The first thing I told Jeremiah was that he should be ashamed of himself for not talking to you about this."

Jeremiah and Etta Ween looked at each other and shook their heads.

Elise laughed and continued. "But he's right…you want to hear this. Yesterday morning I woke Jeremiah up and told him I was several days late."

Etta Ween smiled and gasped.

"Late for what? Did you miss an appointment?" Amari asked innocently. "Yes, I did, baby, but not that kind of appointment," Elise answered. "I realized

I was late for something that was supposed to happen every month that hadn't happened yet."

"Come on now!" John exclaimed.

"Y'all have to let me finish!" Elise laughed. "So, Jeremiah jumps up immediately and goes to the pharmacy."

"Were you sick?" Amari asked.

"No, baby. T Lise wasn't sick. Uncle J went and got me a pregnancy test." "Annnnddd?" Etta Ween asked excitedly.

"It was positive!" Elise shouted. "We're going to be parents and you two are going to be grandparents."

"Thank you, Jesus. Thank you, Jesus. Thank you, Jesus!" Etta Ween shouted. "A grandbaby! Praise the Lord."

"Good job, son. I'm proud of you," John said.

"John, baby, hush! Why do men always say such foolish things?" Etta Ween said. "Talkin' 'bout 'Good job,' like he just completed one of his construction projects."

"Mama Etta, I know, right?" Elise laughed.

"So y'all are going to have a real baby? Your own baby?" Amari asked. She sounded more worried than excited.

"Well, yes, we are, baby," Elise said as she noticed the concern in the little girl's eyes. "But you know we said we have good news, better news, and the best news, right?"

"Uh-huh," Amari said quietly.

"Come here, baby girl," Jeremiah said. "It's my turn. I get to tell you the best news."

He picked her up from her chair and placed her in his lap and then took Elise's hand again.

"You see, me and T Lise, we're kind of nervous. We've never had to take care of a little baby before. When you came to live with us, you could already walk and talk and feed yourself. We don't know how to teach a little baby all of that. We think we're going to need some help. We need someone to help us love the baby and take care of the baby. And we were hoping you would be the baby's big sister."

Amari's eyes brightened a little. "I can do that," she said.

"Baby, do you understand what I'm saying? T Lise and I want you to stay with us permanently. We don't want you to just be our foster child anymore. We want to adopt you. Do you know what that means?"

"I guess it means I'm not really yours, not like your real baby, but I'm kinda yours." Jeremiah put both arms around her. "Amari, listen, baby. We love you. No, T Lise didn't have you but if you let us adopt you it will be just like she did. So, no, you wouldn't be kinda like ours. You would for real be ours. Forever. We would change your name and everything. Would you like that?" "You don't like my name?" Amari asked.

"That's not what Uncle J means, baby. He just means your new name will be Amari Traylor. We won't be Uncle J and T Lise anymore. We will be Mommy and Daddy, or whatever you want to call us," Elise explained.

"I don't think I've ever called anyone Mommy or Daddy. I tried one time but the lady I was staying with said don't call her that," Amari said somberly.

Elise leaned in close, as Jeremiah continued to hold her. "We won't ever say anything like that, baby. Now, there's some legal things we have to do. But we need to make sure that this is what you want. You're still a little girl but I think you're old enough to say if you don't want to do this or not. Don't be afraid to hurt our feelings."

"No, I want to. It's just that…it doesn't matter. But yes, I would like that," Amari said.

"But it's something else. Let us help you, baby," Etta Ween said.

"Well, when I first came here, everybody was so nice. But I was afraid you would get tired of me like the other ones did or start being mean. Or that you would make me leave. But you kept being nice even when I would get in trouble. So, I stopped thinking about it. I guess I just thought that I was already yours. And now y'all are going to have your own baby and I don't think you will want me anymore," Amari said as she broke down crying.

Elise rubbed her back as she sobbed in Jeremiah's arms. "Mari, we will always want you. Didn't you hear what Papa John and Mama Etta just said about me? They love me more than they love Uncle J and they had him," Elise said as she tickled her lightly under her chin.

"Totally unnecessary comment, Elise," Jeremiah said.

"Baby, this family takes people in. It doesn't matter about who had who. We love you. We want you to be our daughter. We want to be your mommy and daddy. And our new baby wants you to be his big sister."

"And we want to be your grandparents," John said.

"As soon as you take your nap?" Amari said, returning to her normal self. "That part," Elise laughed. "So, what say you, T.T. baby? Do you want to be

Mama's baby?"

"Yes. Forever," Amari said.

CHAPTER 9

The Glowing Man

DAY 2

"Miah, this was the best weekend ever," Elise said to Jeremiah as she snuggled close to him. "I know I should be tired, but I still have so much energy. I just want to go out and yell in the streets, 'Jesus loves me!' I'm so thankful for you. The baby. The house. Amari. Miah, it's all so perfect. I love you, so much, baby."

Jeremiah raised his eyebrows. "Oh, so you love me?" he asked with a cunning grin. "Yes, Miah. I love you," she said suspiciously.

"And you said you still have so much energy?" "Yes, but…."

"No, hold on," he interrupted. "You said you had so much energy and that you wanted to go out and yell in the streets. I mean it's my responsibility as your husband to keep you safe. So, I can't just let you run willy-nilly in the streets, but I also have to help you with all this pent-up energy."

"And what would you suggest, Miah?" Elise asked, already knowing his answer. "Babe, I mean it's been a while."

"Miah, it hasn't even been a day! You don't remember this morning? And yesterday morning? I'm taking you off those vitamins cuz bruh, you be doin' the most."

"Well, maybe, but it is a special weekend. Don't you think we should end it… with a bang?"

"Miah, I cannot stand you," Elise hollered.

"Yes, you can, but hear me out. I'm just sayin'…."

Before Jeremiah could plead his case any further, there was a knock at the door.

Elise laughed. "Sorry, Daddy. Your future daughter is at the door. Come in, sweetie."

Amari opened the door and stood beside the bed.

"Hey, Mari. What's wrong, baby girl?" Jeremiah asked. "I had a scary dream," Amari responded.

"Do you want to tell us about it?" Elise asked.

"Uh-huh," Amari said as she crawled in between Jeremiah and Elise. "I was playing soccer, and I was holding the baby, and you all were there cheering me on."

"You were holding this baby?" Elise asked as she pointed to her own belly. "Uh-huh," Amari answered, "and then while I was running and holding the baby, I scored a goal."

"That's my girl! Winning in your dreams," Jeremiah encouraged.

"But when I turned around, Mama Etta wasn't there anymore. It was only Papa John and y'all. But I was still holding the baby. And then I got the ball again and you all were cheering again, and I scored again. But when I turned around this time Papa John was far away. I could see him, but it wasn't like he was really there. But you and Uncle J kept cheering and said, 'Keep playing, baby. You can do it.' And I got the ball again and I scored. But this time when I scored, a really ugly man came and said I couldn't hold the baby anymore. But I told him y'all said I could. Then a glowing man said that the baby and the ugly man had to both come with him, but he told me that I should keep playing. I didn't want to let the baby go but the glowing man was nice, so I gave the baby to him. I thought y'all were going to be mad but when I looked for you, I couldn't see you anymore."

"Like Papa John?" Elise asked.

"No, I didn't see you at all, but I kept playing because the glowing man said to. But when I got the ball again, this time nobody was there to cheer me on and everybody else started booing me. I kept trying but no matter how hard I tried, I couldn't score. And nobody on my team would help me. And I called y'all. I remember you said you would be my real mommy and daddy so that's what I said. I said, 'Mommy! Daddy!' But a witch came and said I couldn't call you that. So, I called you and said, 'T Lise! Uncle J!' and she said, 'They aren't coming either. They're gone. You have to come with me now.' And she took me to an ugly place with all sorts of ugly things there."

"Ugly things like what, sweetie?" Elise asked.

"I don't want to talk about it," Amari said. "Just very ugly things."

Elise scooted closer to Amari and sandwiched her tightly between herself and Jeremiah. "Baby girl, that sounds scary, but it was just a bad dream. That won't ever happen. We love you and we are always going to be here for you. And I wish...no, I hope...no, here it is... I pray somebody would boo you. I promise you they would never, ever boo anybody else in life. Trust and believe!"

Jeremiah leaned over and kissed her on the forehead. "Mari, I promise you that was just a bad dream. It's not going to happen. We aren't going anywhere, and nobody is taking you to an ugly place. As far as me and T Lise are concerned, you are already our baby girl. You are as much ours as the little baby growing inside T Lise. And nobody is ever going to change that."

"Or T Lise will cut them or shoot them?" Amari said, smiling.

"We skippin' straight to shootin', baby!" Elise said enthusiastically. "Or...or...maybe we just reasonably and lawfully protect and cover you. No need to cut or shoot anybody," Jeremiah corrected.

"There was one kind of good part to the dream," Amari said. "What was that?" Jeremiah asked.

"Even when I was in the ugly place, the glowing man was there. Really, he was there the whole time. He didn't say much but even when I was sad or afraid, he stayed with me. It made me feel like everything was going to be all right because he was there. He said not to be afraid because he was going to send a prince to take me from the witch and the ugly place and help me find you. I asked him who he was, and he said to come ask you and then I woke up and came in here. So, who was the glowing man, Uncle J?"

"Baby, I've never had a dream like that," Jeremiah answered. "So, I can't say for sure, but a glowing man that stays with you, even when

After the Crash

you're sad or afraid, sounds like Jesus. Or maybe an angel watching over you. Either way, God is always there for us. He lets us know everything will be all right."

"I'm still scared, though. Will you pray for me, Uncle J?"

"Of course, I will," Jeremiah answered. "Lord Jesus, we pray for your precious daughter…and for our precious daughter. We thank you for her. In your name, Jesus, we chase away all her fears, and we place her in your hands and trust you to ease and comfort her and give her peace. We pray your Holy Spirit replaces the bad dreams with sweet dreams so she can rest. In Jesus' name, Amen."

"Amen," Amari and Elise said in unison.

"Thank you, Uncle J," Amari smiled. "I feel better now. I'm so glad you're going to be my daddy."

Elise turned her head hoping Jeremiah couldn't see her giggling. For certain, Amari was sincere, but game recognized game and Elise knew her soon-to-be- daughter had an ulterior motive.

"I'm glad you're going to be my daughter, Mari," Jeremiah gushed.

"But I would feel better if you let me sleep with you guys…since I'm your daughter and all," Amari smiled.

"You little con artist!" Jeremiah accused.

"Pretty please, Uncle J?" Amari said as she clasped her hands together and batted her eyes.

"Aww, her said 'pretty please,' Uncle J. You know you can't resist those pretty brown eyes," Elise supported.

Jeremiah shook his head as he realized he was outnumbered. "You two…," he said as Elise cut him off.

"Are irreplaceable, priceless, and beautiful," she finished his sentence as she chuckled. "Come on, hun. Get under these covers and get some sleep. Tomorrow is a school day."

"Hey, Lise, weren't we having a conversation?" Jeremiah asked.

"I don't know, Daddy. You might have to get used to fewer conversations." "You guys can keep talking," Amari said sweetly. "I won't interrupt." "Yeah, it's not that kinda conversation," Jeremiah grumbled.

"Boy, turn that light off and snuggle up with your little Mari and your wife. I am sure we can talk later."

"Yeah, Uncle J. Y'all can talk later," Amari said victoriously.

Jeremiah squinted at her. "Mari, I will give you $100 to go back to your room." "Miah, leave that girl alone and go to sleep, boy," Elise laughed. "Goodnight, sweet baby."

"Goodnight, T Lise. Goodnight, Uncle J," Amari said, securing her spot in Jeremiah's arms and taking her T Lise's arm and pulling it around her.

Jeremiah was silent.

"Tell him you love him," Elise whispered. "I love you," Amari said.

"Tell him he's the bestest uncle, daddy, husband in the whole big wide world," Elise said.

"You're the…," Amari started.

"You two do know I can hear you both, right?" Jeremiah said.

"Well, then say goodnight to your favorite girls, then," Elise told him. Jeremiah sighed. "Goodnight, my favorite girls."

"Hey, Mari," Jeremiah said, accepting his fate. "So, the baby in your dream.

It was a boy, right?"

"Yeah, Uncle J. It was a little boy. He looked just like you only littler and cuter." "Goodnight, baby girl. I love you."

"Goodnight, Uncle J, I love you, too."

CHAPTER 10

Math Is Not Mathing

DAY 3

Jeremiah settled into his office. He was on a high from the amazing weekend, but it was still a Monday morning. He checked through his calendar and took a sip of coffee as his phone rang. It was Elise.

"Hey, gorgeous!" he said happily.

"Hey, handsome! Sooo, how long before I get cravings?" she laughed. "Babe, I think you have to wait until after the first doctor's appointment before you get to use that excuse."

"Hater!" she laughed. "I'm going Wednesday." "We're going Wednesday," he corrected. "Aww, you want to hold my hand?"

"You know I want to be there when the doctor tells us about our little boy!" "Miah, if I can't have cravings yet, then it's also too soon to tell what the baby is." "Oh, well…whatever, I'm still coming."

"I figured. I scheduled it early in the morning, so you won't be too late for work. Oh, I also heard from Amari's caseworker. Everything is looking good so far for the adoption. They just have to doublecheck some things."

"Doublecheck what?" Jeremiah said, not hiding his annoyance. "She's been with us all this time. What are they worried about now?"

"Calm down, Daddy," Elise soothed. "They just have to confirm that all the boxes are checked with her biological parents."

"You mean the ones she doesn't remember, and we haven't heard from in three years?"

"Yeah, those ones. It's just preliminary."

Jeremiah heard a knock at his door. It was Paul. On paper, Paul was his boss. But Jeremiah and he actually had two distinctive roles. For the most part, Jeremiah had full autonomy over his team and his projects. Paul was a good person, though. Unlike Case, Jeremiah always felt at ease with him. Plus, Elise liked him.

"Let me call you back, babe. Paul is here." "Okay. Tell him I said hi. I love you."

"Love you too, babe," Jeremiah said as he disconnected the call. "Hey, Paul. What can I do for you?"

"Hi Jeremiah. How was your weekend?" Paul asked, shutting Jeremiah's door. "Pretty nice, but that closed door has got me wondering how yours was.

What's up?"

"Jeremiah, listen. I appreciate you keeping me in the loop on things. And I know you know what you're doing…."

"But you saw the Vista Ridge numbers?" Jeremiah asked. He had been anticipating this conversation.

"Well, yeah, I did. Jeremiah, I don't get it. How do you expect us to win a job like this at these prices? I thought we would have been a little…no, quite a bit sharper."

Jeremiah paused and measured his words in his mind before he spoke. "Paul," he began, "I hear you. And I'm not saying you're wrong. I actually agree with you. But I'm under a lot of pressure to increase profits on the projects." "Pressure? From who?"

"Well, who else can pressure me?" "You mean Case?"

"Yes, I've been fighting this battle for a few years now. I've seen us win jobs, and Case will come in here and sit right where you are now and tell me how I'm going to run his company into the ground. He would come in here screaming, 'Jeremiah, you're winning battles but you're losing the war!' Then we lose jobs and I think he's gonna have a fit and he's like 'Don't worry, you'll get the next one.' And you know what? I can't argue with him because we do. It doesn't always make sense to me either, but the numbers don't lie."

"Do you really think we still have a shot at it?"

"No, Paul. I don't. I think Liberty or probably Union will come in with the low number."

"Jeremiah, that's unacceptable. I can't imagine someone of your talent and skill level saying that! You're the gatekeeper, if it doesn't fly in your mind then it doesn't fly period as far as I'm concerned. Why not just ask Case's forgiveness instead of asking his permission and price the job like it needs to be priced for us to win?"

"Paul," Jeremiah said calmly, "that is exactly what I was trying to do. I came in here Saturday, triple-checked all my files, and finalized the presentation and the pricing. I was just going to send it and let Case go off on me after the fact. I figured, 'What's he going to do? Fire me for winning a job?' But that idea got torpedoed when he called me Saturday and asked about the pricing."

"He called you? On a Saturday?" Paul asked, surprised.

"Yes, he did. He gave me the old 'we have to get more so we can take care of our crews' speech."

"And he asked you to put these numbers on it?"

"No, Paul. He doesn't work like that. I've tried to sit him down and show him our pricing models, but he doesn't want to see them. He always says it's up to me…just get more."

"Jeremiah, I have to tell you. I looked at some other jobs. Your jobs. I'm a little confused too. I do see an odd pattern of getting jobs that seemed high. But this one…I don't know."

"Paul, I don't know either. But as Case always reminds me, the money is coming in."

"Listen, I wasn't trying to come down here and ride you or anything," Paul said contritely.

"I didn't take it that way, Paul. I have no problem being held accountable. It's just an unusual circumstance."

"So, this is going to sound strange coming from your boss," Paul said as he held up air quotes. "But what would you do if you had these concerns?"

"I'm not you. But I've already done what I would do. Paul, this isn't new. Over the past three or four years, I've tried several times to really sit down with Case and help him see what I'm talking about. But it's a hard argument when our company keeps growing. If you're concerned, go talk to him yourself. Make your case, no pun intended," he smiled, "and stand your ground. But know he's going to stand his as well."

"You wanna come with me?" Paul asked, hoping Jeremiah would say yes. "No. You should go by yourself. If Case wants to talk to me, he knows where

I am. You can handle it."

CHAPTER 11

Wasted Breath

DAY 3

"Good morning, Case," Paul said.

"What can I do for you?" Case said, not bothering to look up from his desk. "It's about Jeremiah Traylor."

"What about him?" Case said, still focused on his work.

"I just came from his office. I reviewed his numbers for Vista Ridge, and honestly I'm a little nervous. I told him point blank there's no way we're going to get that job at the prices he submitted. I also spot-checked some of his other projects. He seems to have a pattern of overpricing."

"Why are you looking at Jeremiah's numbers?" Case asked. He still hadn't looked up but intentionally put an accusatory tone in his voice.

The question caught Paul off guard. Vista Ridge was a gamechanger, but Case didn't seem concerned at all about potentially not landing the project. "Case, it's my job. Jeremiah reports to me. Aren't you worried about what I just said?"

"No, not at all. And I've explained to you before, too many times in fact, that you and Jeremiah have two completely different roles. I want Jeremiah to stand guard over our major projects. I want you over new business and vendor procurement. I pay you both very nicely and you should be doing your own jobs. Why do I need Jeremiah if you are going to be watching over his shoulder? I don't want you in the projects. Let Jeremiah handle it. He's qualified to make the best business decisions for this company on these matters."

"So, you don't think I'm qualified?" Paul asked, a little hurt at the implication.

"It's not about qualifications or your ego. It's about business," Case said, leaning back in his chair and looking up at Paul for the first time. "But if you want to go down that road…no, you're not qualified. The projects are Jeremiah's wheelhouse. If you're going to be a good leader, you have to let your horses run free."

Paul's ego was bruised, but he wasn't going to roll over so quickly.

"Then let him run! Why are you calling him checking on his numbers if it's his wheelhouse?"

"Yeah, shame on me for keeping tabs on the high-profile projects in my own company. I'm just focusing a little extra attention where it matters. Jeremiah oversees all the big-ticket projects, right?"

"Yes," Paul agreed.

"So, doesn't it make sense to check in with him occasionally? We all know it's the jobs you don't get that save the company. Price the wrong job too low and none of us have jobs. I am just making sure Jeremiah doesn't forget that. But it's still his show to run. We put him there for a reason and we are moving him and you up for a reason. You need to worry about getting us new partnerships and vendors. Let Jeremiah handle the projects. Unless you're telling me Jeremiah can't handle the responsibility, I don't see a problem."

"Case, he can handle it. Honestly, he can do my job and your job. That's why you watchdogging him doesn't make sense."

"Well, if he can't speak up for himself, and you can't focus on what I need you to do, then maybe I have the wrong two people in mind to help get this company to the next level," Case said, scowling.

Paul saw that the conversation was going nowhere. "We're not tracking together, Case, but to be clear, Jeremiah is good to go and so am I."

"I already knew that, Paul."

Paul just shook his head. "Well, I'm glad you know," he responded.

"Paul, remember, I have forgotten more than you will ever know about this business."

"How could I?" Paul asked. "You never let me forget."

"Close the door on your way out, please," Case said, refocusing on his computer screen.

Paul complied and closed the door behind him. Something felt off, but he hoped he was making much ado about nothing.

As was usually the case, he walked out of Case's office feeling defeated. The conversation was fruitless and left him more frustrated than he was when he walked in. *"No, you're not qualified."* Case's words echoed in his head. He had long given up hope of earning Case's respect. But there was still a longing deep inside him that wanted to be loved as his son.

CHAPTER 12

Ascending the Mountain

DAY 30

Jeremiah got to the meeting room first. He always liked to settle in before the rest of the senior staff and VPs came trickling in. This had to be it! One thing Case didn't like was wasting time. Him suddenly calling this "all hands-on deck" meeting had to mean good news. Jeremiah had been finalizing details on the Vista Ridge contract for the last month. The job was theirs verbally, but nothing had been signed yet.

Ironically, with all of Case's prodding about margin, Jeremiah hadn't been very optimistic they would have a chance at the job. But somehow, they had come in with an extremely competitive price. Jeremiah could only assume their competitors were afraid of tying up their resources on such a challenging project and had priced themselves out of it. Case's meddling bothered him, but once again it appeared he was right. Still, the job wasn't secured yet, and nothing was for sure until a contract had been signed.

He tried to calm himself when a text came in from Elise: "Hey, Miah. I love you. Don't be anxious. God's peace is yours…Daddy, I give all my husband's anxiousness to you. We petition you to prosper him and his team with this project he has worked so hard for. We thank you for victory and we thank you for giving him a peace that surpasses understanding. I thank you for giving me him. And we both thank you for Jesus. It's in that perfect name that we pray, Amen."

"Amen. I needed that. Thanks, babe. You're the best!" Jeremiah replied. Jeremiah could feel his spirit calming as the rest of the senior staff joined him.

They immediately began barraging him with questions. "Jeremiah, you think we got it?"

"Jeremiah, what have you heard?" "Jeremiah, what did they say?"

Jeremiah smiled pleasantly and tried to share his recently discovered peace. "Hey, guys, first, I am fine. Thanks for asking," he said sarcastically. "I'm sorry, but I don't know anything for sure. I can tell you that the only thing left to do would be for Vista Ridge ownership and for Case to sign. Everything is in place, and we're gonna have to strap in and hit it hard once it comes through."

"So, you do think we're going to get it? That's what this is about?" one of the project managers asked enthusiastically.

"I never assume, man," Jeremiah responded.

"But fingers crossed...oh, I'm sorry, Jeremiah. You don't cross fingers, do you?" another asked.

"No, I don't, but prayers have gone up," Jeremiah said confidently.

"Well, can you please ask Jesus to hurry up, Jeremiah? And while you're at it, can you ask him to let the Dallas Cowboys go to the Super Bowl this year?"

"Oh, you do want a miracle, don't you?" Jeremiah said as the team laughed with him.

"Glad you all are having so much fun on company time!" Case's booming voice bellowed through the room as he walked in.

Case was a large and some would say intimidating man. He had participated in several bodybuilding competitions and had joked often that he would have won some if it were not for him moonlighting as the CEO of Jacebre.

"Well, let's get to it," Case said. "We're hemorrhaging money with all of you sitting here."

Case sat down at the head of the table. Jeremiah sat on his left and Paul on his right.

"Well, even in my position, I hear all the water cooler talk, and I know you are all on pins and needles. So, I will turn it over to Jeremiah to update you. Go ahead, Jeremiah," Case said.

Jeremiah liked to think he stayed on top of things, but he was in the dark. Had he missed a memo? Was he supposed to run this meeting? He looked over to Paul for some hint, but he simply sat there looking as if he too were waiting for some fresh revelation.

"Case...I'm not sure what you mean. You called the meeting. What do you need me to give an update on?"

"Come on. Don't be shy now, Jeremiah. You know what everyone came here for," Case said.

"Well, everyone is hoping we have some good news about Vista Ridge," Jeremiah said. "But that's in your court."

"What do you mean it's in my court?" Case said, sounding slightly perturbed. "Case, I sent you the latest and hopefully final draft a couple of days ago. The only thing missing is your and the Vista Ridge reps' signatures."

"Oh, you're right. You did send me that. Yeah, I'm pretty sure Vista Ridge already signed. But this place is never going to scale up if you don't stop waiting on me and take some ownership. Why don't you sign it?" Case said, grinning slyly. Jeremiah returned the smile as he caught on to the game that was being played.

Case wasn't necessarily a nice guy, but if what he suspected was happening, then this was a pretty nice gesture.

"Case, I can't sign it. It has to be signed by a vice president," Jeremiah said simply. "Oh, you're not a vice president?" Case asked innocently. "Who knew? Well, if I want to get out of the signing business, I guess I better make Jeremiah a VP." Case turned to another executive. "Can we get that handled?" he asked.

"Already done, Case," the exec confirmed.

"Good. So, Jeremiah, are there any other excuses as to why Vista Ridge isn't signed yet?" Case asked.

"Well, we have to switch the names in the system and on the contract," Jeremiah said, anticipating Case's response.

"Pretty sure that's handled too," Case asserted.

Jeremiah grinned. "Well, I guess I will just run to my office and sign it then." "Already on that too, sir," Case replied. "In fact, we have a special delivery for you."

Case motioned with his hand and a team member opened the conference room door. Elise walked in, looking her absolute best, carrying Jeremiah's laptop. Behind her was his assistant Susan and a team of caterers rolling in food and buckets of champagne.

Jeremiah was stunned. Elise set his laptop in front of him and stood behind him with her hands on his shoulders.

"Elise, how? You knew this already?" Jeremiah asked.

"Not exactly. Susan asked me to be in the neighborhood today so I kinda suspected."

"Yeah, that part was Susan's idea, Jeremiah," Case said. "I didn't think you would want the old ball-and-chain around, but she said you would."

Elise smiled through her annoyance but dug her nails into Jeremiah's shoulder, reminding him how much Case got on her nerves.

"Well, she was right, Case. I'm very glad to have Elise here for this moment. Thank you, Susan."

"You're welcome, Boss," Susan responded.

Jeremiah didn't really like the title "Boss," especially from Susan, who was at least twenty-five years his senior. But he had come to appreciate the title as a term of endearment from someone who respected him.

"So, for those of you who haven't figured it out yet," Case continued, "once Jeremiah, our new Vice President of Construction, signs this contract, Jacebre Construction will be on the hook for the biggest building project the city of Dallas has ever seen. This is a team effort. Every one of you plays a critical role, even if you're not working on this project."

"Although most of you will," Jeremiah interjected.

"Power's gone to his head already!" Case joked. "But as I was saying…it's a team effort. No doubt. But we do have to give credit where credit is due. I've intentionally taken a step back to focus on other aspects of the company. And along with other key team members here, we're trying to pave a path for the future. But Jeremiah has been handling the now. And it's not just this project. Virtually every big project we've gotten over the last few years has had his hand on it. We've entrusted a lot to him, and he hasn't let us down. We're not all here about to sip champagne without Jeremiah Traylor. So, let's get a glass in our hand. We do have some nonalcoholic options for Jeremiah and…well, for Jeremiah."

Everyone laughed as they raised their glasses.

"To Jacebre. The best construction company in the nation. To you, the best team in the nation. And to you, Jeremiah, I toast you. Well done, all of you."

The team clinked their glasses together and drank to their victory. "Mr. Vice President. You ready to pull that trigger, sir?" Case asked.

"Oh, I signed it five minutes ago while you were talking, Case," Jeremiah chuckled as his coworkers joined him in his laughter.

"Big bonuses coming soon!" one of the executives said to everyone's approval.

Paul struggled to be as exuberant as everyone else. He knew as well as anyone that Jeremiah's praise was well deserved. He had worked tirelessly on the project for months. But no one mentioned that though Jeremiah was responsible for the project itself, it had been Paul who wooed and pursued the client to get them in the door. Again, Case's words haunted him. *A few key team members,* he thought to himself. Case hadn't even bothered to mention that along with Jeremiah's promotion, Paul also had been promoted. He looked across the room at Jeremiah as the team surrounded him. He searched himself inwardly and was embarrassed at the jealousy forming in his heart. It only deepened as Case stood at Jeremiah's side. He watched his father as he shook Jeremiah's hand and patted him firmly on the back, giving him the approval he so desperately wanted.

CHAPTER 13

Descent to the Valley

DAY 31

Joshua's soul continued to weaken under the weight of his failing marriage and the revelation that his estranged son was not truly his. Angela's bombshell had robbed him of any joy or peace. After several sleepless nights, sheer emotional and physical exhaustion took over, and he finally slept through the night. He woke up particularly hungry. He looked at his phone and realized why. It was already 9:43 A.M. It was very unusual for him to sleep that late, but his body felt the benefits of the sleep, even if his defeated spirit did not.

He sat at the edge of the bed and contemplated his dreary day. He had come to despise weekends. Work provided a much-needed refuge from his deteriorating home life. His house had become a nightmarish place to be. There were awkward moments of passing conversation as he and Angela tried to be civil. They spoke only when necessary as it pertained to Robin, important financial matters, or during their counseling sessions.

Counseling? What a joke! he thought bitterly to himself. They had indeed gone to counseling, but he quickly realized Angela was only going as a formality. She made it crystal clear to the counselor that she wanted a divorce, and no one was going to change her mind. The counselor had challenged him to persevere, regardless of Angela's attitude. "You have got to go after her the way the Lord came after you, brother," he encouraged. "Be a man and fight for your family." On that point, Joshua knew he was epically failing. He had made a few halfhearted efforts, but Angela didn't acknowledge them and certainly didn't reciprocate. He came to realize that giving love where it was not wanted or appreciated was not something he was built for. So, he just withdrew more and more. He wanted his marriage. He wanted Angela. But he also wanted her to want him.

His early morning hunger mercifully overruled his descent into self-pity. He left his new accommodations in the guestroom and made his way downstairs to look for something to eat. He went to the kitchen and noticed a plate covered in foil. Angela had prepared breakfast and made enough for him. Whether it was a peace offering, simple courtesy, or she simply had made too much, he should at least say thank you. It would take all the Jesus in him to do so. Talking to her had become a chore. Every look on her face was one of disdain. She maintained polite decorum with her words, but her face communicated what her mouth did not: "I'm tolerating you for now, but this is not your home anymore. I can't wait for you to leave."

He crossed the living room to the bedroom he had been ostracized from. The closed door clearly communicated another clear message: "This is not your room, and you need permission to come in." But the laughter on the other side of the door cut even deeper. He heard Angela's voice, but she wasn't alone. Robin and Robert were in there also. There were no hushed tones. No quiet rumblings. Only boisterous laughter. Laughter that communicated another message. Not only was he not missed; his wife and children were enjoying life and were fine without him. Perhaps better off…and totally fine with the current state.

He lifted his hand to knock on the door…but stopped. He wasn't sure why. Perhaps it was the heartbreak of knowing that his family was fine without him. Perhaps it was the small modicum of pride he had left refusing to let him ask for entry to a place he knew he wasn't welcome. Regardless of why, the sound on the other side of the door was enough. He didn't need to see his family enjoying their Saturday morning without him, and he didn't need to see them look disappointed to see him. He took the plate back to the kitchen and scrambled upstairs. He dressed as quickly as he could. Then he made his way downstairs, got into his truck, and sent a simple text to Robin: "Going out. Let me know if you need anything."

CHAPTER 14

Housewarming

DAY 31

"Elise, tell your daddy what you did to my son!" Etta Ween said as she playfully tapped Elise on her backside.

"Mama Etta, I'm sorry," Elise giggled. "I'm eating for two, so now I guess I have the strength of two. I ain't know. I sawwy, Miah," she said in her little baby voice.

"Tell me what happened, Daddy's Girl?" John asked.

"Daddy, Jeremiah's boss is up there with his old steroid-taking self, calling me a 'ball-and-chain.' I was like 'ball-and-chain'? You don't realize that's a trigger word for black folks?" she laughed.

"Pop," Jeremiah interjected, "your precious baby girl dug these nine-inch nails right through my shirt and into my skin. I got lacerations up in this mug. I was like 'what the what'!"

"I said I was sorry, baby," Elise said. "Susan just asked me to come up there. I forgot your ole shiesty shady-tail boss was gon be up there. But y'all would have been so proud. I will give the man credit for this; he really gave Miah his due. Right there in front of everyone. You can tell they really respect him."

"Well, I respect him too," Shania said. Shania was Elise's best friend. They served in the Army together and had been inseparable ever since.

"Jeremiah, this house is so beautiful," Shania continued. "You a real one, big bro. Thank you for taking care of my bestie."

Jeremiah appreciated the compliment but was troubled by it at the same time. "Come on, babe," he said, taking Elise by the hand and escorting her to the center of their new home. "Hello, everyone," Jeremiah said to their guests. "Can

I interrupt you for just a moment? Again, thank you for coming to our little housewarming celebration. The Lord has been good, and we wanted to celebrate his kindness with you all. But I've heard a few comments tonight. Comments about how blessed Elise is, how wonderful it is that I surprised her with this house, and how good a husband I am. But if you don't know, I need you to know that none of this happens without Elise. When I was in college, chasing after her, she made it clear she wanted a man who was serious about his relationship with Jesus Christ. I called Pop that night and asked him, 'What must I do to be saved?'" he said jokingly as their guests laughed.

"Seriously," he continued, "I was already saved, but seeing Lise, I knew I couldn't get her without the Lord's help. And because God does what he does, he used my pursuit of her to bring me closer to him. Elise also told me she wanted a man who knew what he wanted to do in life, and again, I called Pop. I said, 'Pop, I think I need to pick a major.' He said, 'It's about time, son. You been there four years!'"

"Now that part is true!" John shouted.

"It wasn't four years, Daddy," Elise defended.

"And that part right there," Jeremiah said seriously. "I just thought I was in love. I didn't know I had fallen for an angel who would defend me from her heart. Who would stay with me no matter how bad it ever got. Who would pick me up when I was down. And who would not only love me when I wasn't lovable, but who would honor me when I didn't feel worthy of her respect. I didn't know I had fallen for someone who was willing to forego her dreams, so I could achieve mine. A lot of you don't know this but Elise was the one who held it down when we were a young married couple. I was in college and couldn't really make good money and go to school, but Elise made sure we could make it and didn't have to depend on anybody. I didn't know I had fallen for an entrepreneur who could sell sand in the middle of the desert. Some of you know what I'm talking about. I see a lot of faces out there who got into your home because Elise prayed, worked tirelessly, and found a way. Many of you would call her and tell her it wasn't time, and she would tell you not to give up, and the next thing you knew, my Lise had you in a house. And I haven't even mentioned how she leads God's people in praise every week. And how she prays for people when they're down. How she can make you laugh when all you want to do is cry. How she loves our soon-to-be-daughter. And as much as it kills me to admit it, how she's everyone's favorite person…including my own parents. I mean how did that happen? Who steals a man's parents?"

"We love you too, baby," Etta Ween encouraged.

"See!" Jeremiah exclaimed. "Not, 'you're still our favorite' but 'we love you too.' But I can't get mad," he said as he looked at Elise, "because you're my favorite too, babe. You don't just make my dreams come true. You are my dreams…every last one of them. You're my best friend, the mother of my children, my ride-or-die. I loved you the moment I saw you. I love you now. And I'll love you forever."

A chorus of "awws" came from their guests.

"So, anyway…with all due respect, you can miss me with all that how blessed Elise is stuff. I'm the blessed one. And I just wanted you all to know that."

"Mari," Elise said, not missing a beat, "you can't sleep with us tonight, baby."

CHAPTER 15

Bittersweet

DAY 84

"Miah, you wanna sit down, baby? You need me to get you some water?" Elise asked. "No. I'm good," Jeremiah responded.

"It's okay that you want a boy, Miah. Just don't trip if it's a girl."

"I won't. But…I mean we already got Amari. So, you know…come on with the boy, Jesus!" he said as he shook imaginary dice and threw them across the floor.

"Is this what we doin', Miah? Excuse me…Elder Traylor. We throwin' make- believe dice in Jesus' name?"

"Oh, you wanna blow on them?"

"No, I don't. I just want you to chill and enjoy the moment with me," Elise said softly. "We are one step closer to our miracle. We're twelve weeks in and there haven't been any complications. Our baby is healthy. Your wife is healthy. So as long as we have that, we're good, right?"

"Yeah, babe. You're right. We're good."

"But you still want me to blow on your little fake dice, don't you?" Elise said, contorting her lips.

Jeremiah shrugged and smiled. "I mean, if you want to." "Put 'em up here," Elise said, smiling and shaking her head.

Jeremiah held the imaginary dice up to Elise's mouth, and she blew on them like she was blowing out a thousand candles.

"Not like that, babe! Gently."

Elise sighed, then gently took Jeremiah's hand in hers and blew softly. "Now say it," he instructed.

"Come onnnn, boy!" Elise said as enthusiastically as she could.

Jeremiah threw his dice and snapped his fingers. "I think that's it, babe. I can feel it."

"You need help, Miah," Elise said as the doctor joined them.

Dr. Kakarla was a short and cheery Middle Eastern woman. She was fit, especially for her age. Jeremiah teased Elise that the only reason she picked her was because she was shorter than she was.

"So," the doctor said excitedly as she rubbed her hands together, "I hear we need to find out if we need pink or blue paint?"

"Oh, it's blue, Doctor. It's blue for sure!" Jeremiah said confidently.

"Yes, Jeremiah," the doctor continued, "I understand from Elise, you really want a boy, right?"

"Yes, ma'am," Jeremiah confirmed.

"But as long as we have a healthy baby, that will be enough," Elise added. "Well, let's see what we have here," the doctor announced. "Elise, let's lay back and lift up your shirt."

Elise lay down and tried to relax as the doctor squeezed the cold fluid onto her belly that still hadn't started to protrude. She felt Jeremiah's hand grasp hers.

"Baby, I'm sure it's a boy," she reassured him.

The doctor began to roll the instrument over Elise's belly and, in just a few moments, found a strong heartbeat.

"Is it supposed to sound like that?" Elise asked, concerned about what sounded like a rapid pace.

"It's perfectly normal. You and the baby are doing just great, Elise," Dr. Kakarla said. "But is your husband okay?"

Elise turned her head to Jeremiah as he struggled to keep his emotions in check. "You okay, baby?"

Jeremiah leaned over and kissed Elise. "I'm fine. But you're right. It doesn't matter whether it's a boy or a girl. As long as y'all are good."

"So do you still want to know the gender?" the doctor asked.

"It doesn't matter, Doctor. The only thing that matters is this beating heart," Jeremiah said.

"Uh-uh. That's just emotion, Doc. He wants to know. Keep checking," Elise said.

"Well, for the little boy," Dr. Kakarla said in her thick accent, "we are looking for what we call the little turtle shape. Hopefully the baby is positioned right so we can see. They don't always cooperate."

Several moments passed and the doctor maneuvered the device along Elise's belly.

"Everything okay?" Elise asked.

"Yes," the doctor said, "I just have to get it to the right spot. Yes, there it is.

Mr. and Mrs. Traylor, you have a baby boy!"

"Praise the Lord, we have a baby boy, Miah!" Elise exclaimed. "Thank you, Jesus!"

Jeremiah's newfound contentment quickly fell by the wayside, and his response wasn't quite as spiritual as Elise's.

"Uh-huh! Uh-huh! What now? Who's the man?" he bellowed as he beat his chest. "Told you we was having a boy!" He put his face near Elise's belly. "That's right, lil' man. Daddy know how to hit the target!" he yelled triumphantly.

"Oh, he did this?" the doctor asked Elise.

"All by himself," Elise said, shaking her head.

"I can't tell if we are at my office with other patients or a football game," Dr. Kakarla said.

Elise whispered through gritted teeth, "Jeremiah, hush, boy. It's white people in here!"

"Oh, I'm sorry, Doc. Just a little victory cry," Jeremiah said, smiling from ear to ear.

"That's okay," the doctor replied. "You first-time fathers can be very funny.

Let me print you a picture. Elise, I will see you in one month."

They walked into the waiting room and all eyes in the small office turned on them.

"So, we heard a rumor you guys had a boy on the way," another father said. "Oh, yeah, we got a boy, y'all!" Jeremiah said as he beat his chest.

Another father egged him on. "Yeah, we didn't know. I mean we heard some minor commotion but weren't sure. So, you sure it's a boy, right?"

Jeremiah took the newly printed sonogram picture to the stranger. "Oh, yeah, man. We're sure. Check this out. Look at them baby man parts. You'd swear he was already seven or eight years old from that."

"Oh, my goodness. I am so sorry, everybody," Elise said as everyone in the waiting room burst into laughter. "Let's go, Miah!" Elise said as she took his arm. Elise noticed a young man standing alone in the corner as she tried to pry Jeremiah away from his audience. He was well built and handsome. Perhaps of Hawaiian or Samoan heritage. He looked to be in his twenties or maybe his early thirties. He seemed pleasant enough but while the rest of the room enjoyed

Jeremiah's humorous show, his countenance was more focused and serious.

He seemed out of place but before she could process it any further, Jeremiah's audience demanded an encore.

"Sir," a mother asked, "forgive me, but we only have girls and my daughter just asked, and I quote, 'Mommy, can I see the little boy's baby man parts?'"

"Of course, she can," Jeremiah replied.

Jeremiah knelt down next to the little girl, who looked to be the same age as Amari. He tactfully showed her the "turtle" outline the doctor had shown them.

"See, sweetie. Those are my son's…well, you know, baby man parts." "Do you mean a penis?" the little girl asked innocently.

Jeremiah looked at the girl's mother, who was totally unbothered at the exchange.

"Well, yeah. I guess you can call it that too," he said carefully.

We goin' to jail! Elise thought to herself.

"My mommy's having a baby too," the little girl said sweetly. "But we're having another little girl. Mommy does that mean Daddy can't hit the target?" the little girl asked innocently.

"You heard that too?" Jeremiah asked, showing embarrassment for the first time.

"Yes!" they all responded.

"And with that I am taking my children home," Elise said as she pointed to her belly and to Jeremiah.

As they walked to the car, the young man Elise noticed from the corner caught them in the parking lot.

"Hey, you two. May I have a word?" he asked.

Jeremiah positioned himself between the young man and Elise. "What can we help you with?"

"I have a word from the Lord for you if you will receive it," he said.

Jeremiah looked at him cautiously. "Our Lord is Jesus Christ," he said seriously. "Jesus is Lord of all, Jeremiah," the young man replied.

"Okay, and what do you have to say?" Jeremiah asked skeptically. "Jeremiah, when there is only darkness, your Father will be your light. When you lose all hope, he will be your salvation. When all you trusted in is gone, he will be your source. A new thing will spring forth out of your wilderness. For no one who trusts in the Lord will ever be put to shame. What the Lord gives, no man can take away from you.

"Elise, your Daddy sees you and even where sin increases, his grace increases all the more. When you run back to him, he will run to you, cover you, and comfort you as you mourn. Everything that the devil steals will be given back to you, and even that which you give away will be restored.

"The Lord has blessed your life together and his hand is on you, even as a time of great testing approaches. The enemy will appear to have his way for a season, but the Lord will not allow your faith to fail. He is faithful to his promise, and he will be close when your hearts are broken, and he will save you when your spirits are crushed. And after you have suffered a little while, the Lord will restore you and make you strong. The Lord is your healer and a life giver. He will heal your marriage and your life. He will heal you to the uttermost in soul, spirit, and body. And when this time of testing is done, you will see his beauty in the sunset and his faithful promise in the sky and know more than ever that the love of Jesus Christ did not, has not, and will never fail."

Jeremiah and Elise stood there next to their Mercedes SUV, attempting to process what they had just heard as the young man's somber countenance transitioned into a huge friendly smile.

"Goodbye, Jeremiah and Elise," he said as he returned to the doctor's office.

CHAPTER 16

Processing

DAY 84

"Miah, what just happened?" Elise asked, troubled by the young man's haunting words. "If God wants to communicate something to us, then so be it. But that was…ominous. He was odd all over. Did you see how he acted when you were doing your shenanigans? Everybody was laughing but him. He just sat in the corner and watched. It was a little creepy."

"He was in the office?"

"Miah, yeah! You didn't see him?" "No, I didn't."

"Baby, he was standing right there in the corner."

"I'm sorry, Lise. I didn't notice him. I was in full proud daddy mode." "Okay, fine. But what did you think about what he said?"

"I'm not sure. It did have a happy ending. But you're right. Some of it was ominous."

"Do you really think God was speaking to us?"

"I don't know, Lise. I'm very skeptical of the 'God told me to tell you' thing. But a lot of what he said was straight scripture. Which is good. At the same time, he might be just some random dude who thinks he has a word for everyone. Either way, God has us, no matter what he says."

"He wasn't a random dude, baby," Elise said with certainty. "Why are you so sure?"

"Because Miah…he knew our names."

"He probably heard somebody say our names. Or maybe one of the nurses told him."

"Miah, don't grasp at straws. Did you know any of the people in there? No, you didn't. And nurses aren't going to just give our names out all willy-nilly to strangers."

"He probably heard our names when she called us back."

"Strike one, Miah. The nurse doesn't call me Elise. She calls me Mrs. Traylor. She's old-school like that. And she for sure didn't call your name. As far as they are concerned, you are our plus-one. You're just along for the ride. You don't have to push a human out of your hoo-ha. And even if she did call our names, he wasn't even there when we went back. I observe stuff with my keen militarily trained eye. He wasn't there until we came out. So how did he know our names?"

Jeremiah laughed. "Okay, well, he heard it somewhere."

"Somewhere, Miah? Unless you think we have a stalker, then that's strike two." "Lise, that office is small. He was probably in the hallway when we were talking to the doctor and heard our names."

"And then decided to tell us a time of great testing was coming?" she asked skeptically.

"I guess so," Jeremiah shrugged.

"Okay, but like I said. I observe stuff. Forget the names since you are trying to rationalize your way out of this conversation. Riddle me this: When you pray you always say Father or Lord. You get all reverent and stuff. But when I pray, I call God 'Daddy.' When he spoke to you, he referred to God as your Father but when he spoke to me, he said 'your Daddy.' That distinction is too specific to be a coincidence."

"I have to admit, that's a good point," Jeremiah conceded. "But just don't let it stress you out."

"I'm not, but I do need you to tell me something. And I need you to be honest.

Are you not happy with me? Is there something I've done?" "Where is that coming from?"

"Miah, you heard the same thing I did. This dude just walked up on us and told us the sky is falling. If everything he said is right, then our marriage needs to be healed. I know where I am. I love you, more than ever. But if you're not happy with me, I want to know!"

Jeremiah pulled into their driveway and parked the SUV. "Lise, I don't have all the answers. Did God send this dude to speak into our lives as some word of warning or prophetic message? I can't say for sure. But this I do know…you're still enough. And it's still Miah and Lise against the world. Right now, all is good. We aren't going to sit around in fear waiting for something bad to happen because this wanna be prophet thinks he has a word."

"Don't do that, baby. Like you said, he was coming with the word. We shouldn't despise prophecy."

"You're right. But we also test everything."

"That's why I'm asking, Miah, I'm scared. What he said surfaced some other things."

"Okay. What are you afraid of, babe?"

Elise shook her head. "It's just that…Miah…I'm old," Elise confessed, her shoulders slumping and her countenance changing.

Jeremiah turned his head slightly so she couldn't see his expression. "Jeremiah are you laughing at me?" she yelled, slapping him on his shoulder.

"You know how hard that is for me to admit?"

"Babe, I'm sorry. It's not what you said. It's just that look on your face. You look so cute and pitiful. Your little lip poked out and everything. But you are hardly old."

"I'm baby-having old. What if something happens to the baby because my womb is all spider-webby, geriatric, and discombobulated? And you bet not laugh, Miah!"

"Babe, you not exactly helping me be serious. Up in here talkin' 'bout a spider webby womb."

"Miah, I'm serious. I can't lose him now. I don't think I could take it." "You're not going to lose him," Jeremiah consoled. "You and my little man are doing great. And God is going to take care of you. So calm down, breathe, and give me your hands."

Elise placed her hands in his as he prayed. "Father, we don't know what to make of what we have heard today. We confess our fears and trust you for grace to walk in victory and in faith. We will accept whatever you allow, Lord, but we trust that you will protect us by the power of your name. I want to thank you for my wife, Father. There is no greater gift a good Father could give a son, and I pray that your love would reach in right now and ease this burden and give her peace. And Father, thank you for our son. We look forward in faith to a safe and healthy delivery for our baby boy. We thank you for keeping us and comforting us as you always do. To the name of Jesus be the glory. Amen."

"Hey, Daddy," Elise continued, "It's your baby girl. We do want to thank you. I am sorry for being fearful when you have been so good. I will always praise your name for giving us this blessing, and I am going to trust you to finish it. And even though he laughed at me, thank you for my Miah. He think he funny, but he's a good husband. And no matter what comes, I know you are faithful. We trust you and thank you in Jesus' name, Amen."

"Feel better?" Jeremiah asked. "A little."

"I'm sorry I laughed," he said contritely.

"It's okay. It actually got me out of my head. Ole boy just need to work on his delivery…with his cute Bruno Mars-looking self."

"Oh, so he was cute, huh?" Jeremiah asked, purposely showing his jealousy. "Baby, yes!" Elise said, a little more enthusiastically than Jeremiah would have preferred. "He was a cute, ripped Bruno Mars lookalike," Elise added. "Okay, cute and ripped?" Jeremiah asked, getting more annoyed by the moment. "Miah, yaaasss! Muscles just rippling through his shirt. With his little perfect teeth."

"Oh, you saw his teeth too?"

"I did. They looked like pearls standing in formation." "Anything else you notice about prophet Bruno, Ms. Harris?"

"Oh, you mad, bruh?" Elise laughed. "You only call me by my maiden name when you mad. You leaving me?"

"I'm just saying. You out here looking wanna be Bruno up and down.

Anything else?"

"Ooh, Miah," Elise continued, undeterred by her husband's jealous annoyance, "he smelled good too. It wasn't a cologne. It was like a natural, manly musk."

"Elise, you could not smell that man!" Jeremiah insisted.

Elise laughed out loud. "I'm playing, baby! Nobody is cuter than my Miah." "And my teeth?"

"He has nothing on that smile of yours." "And my muscles?"

"Did I mention you have a nice personality?" she laughed.

"Whatever, girl. So, you good?"

"Is it still Miah and Lise against the world?" she asked. "Always." he affirmed.

"Then, I'm good."

CHAPTER 17

Love Is Blind

DAY 99

"Hey, Mom. How are you doing?" Paul asked his mother.

"Well, well, well. To what do I owe this surprise?" she responded.

"Very funny. Honestly, I was just checking on you. Case said he wanted to come by. He said it was something important but didn't want to talk on the phone. I guess I got in my head a little. I thought something had happened to you and that's why he wanted to come by. He's never been here."

"I'm fine, honey. Give him the benefit of the doubt. Maybe he just wants to talk." "You know you don't believe that, Mom. But okay."

"Be nice, Paul. Regardless of how he treated me…or you, he's still your father." "Yeah. Okay. I love you. He's at the door now. I will talk to you soon."

Paul hung up with his mother and took a breath. His heart was racing. He felt like he was about to go through a military-style inspection. What could Case want, he wondered?

"Hey, Case," Paul said as he let his father in. "Hi son. Thanks for having me over."

Son? Paul questioned in his mind. He tried to think if Case had ever referred to him that way. Paul rarely referred to him as Dad. Not out of disrespect, but because Case preferred it.

"Can I get you anything?" Paul asked him, noticing how spent he looked. Maybe he had the wrong parent in mind. Had Case received some disturbing medical report that suddenly had him visiting and calling him son?

"No, son. I really need to just talk. Best we don't do this in the office or over the phone."

"Well…okay…now you're scaring me. What's wrong?"

"Yeah," Case replied. "We have some scary days in front of us. But before I tell you why, I need to do something you know I'm not good at, Paul. I need to apologize. I hitched our wagon to the wrong horse, and it could cost us everything. I just want to say it wasn't intentional. I really thought it was the right business move. I guess I got caught up in appearances and wasn't paying enough attention. Now all our futures are in jeopardy."

"Case, slow down. What are you apologizing for? What horse? Tell me what's going on?"

Case paused and took a breath. "Yeah, I'm sorry, son. I guess you're not used to seeing your old man like this."

"It's okay…Dad. Just start over and tell me what's happened."

"Son, I just spent most of the day on the phone with legal and the Department of Justice."

"The Department of Justice?!" Paul exclaimed. "For what?"

"We and a few other local companies are under investigation for bid rigging. Son, I could just kick myself. I should have been paying more attention. I just always thought Jeremiah was such a standup guy."

"Jeremiah! You think he has something to do with it? That doesn't track," Paul said, shaking his head in disbelief.

"That's what I was thinking. But then I remembered you saying you looked at some of his old projects and thought they were high."

"Okay. Case…Dad. Let's calm down. Jeremiah has been with you longer than I have and he's doing well. You think he would jeopardize it for…well, whatever?"

"Greed doesn't always make sense, son." "Well, what evidence do they have?"

"They aren't going to tell me all of that, son. But I know this for sure. Jeremiah even told you. We've let the buck stop with him on all our major projects. Maybe he figured out a way to get something kicked back to him. Or maybe he wanted to get more money in the door to justify the promotion he was bucking for. He's a smart guy and to my shame doesn't have very much oversight. Everybody on the staff loves him so they probably wouldn't question it if he did something he shouldn't. Either way, I'm sorry, son. We've got a tough road ahead of us."

"Case, I have to say it because it's going to come up."

"I already know, son. Jeremiah's going to say I kept pushing him on the numbers. Well, you can look at all my emails, as the government plans to do, and any records. I have said time and time again to Jeremiah that the final decision is his. If you recall, I told you that when you came in my office just a few months ago." "Yeah, you did. It's just that…Jeremiah? I can't believe it. Maybe it's nothing.

Just them fishing."

"Either way, we have to protect our company. This thing is going public tomorrow, and we need to be ready. The first order of business is to fire Jeremiah. We need to send a clear message that we aren't on board with all of this."

"Dad, that's not going to go over well with the team."

"What team, son? My only team is here in this room. I'm not going to let Jeremiah tear down everything I've spent my life's blood building. I know I should have paid more attention, and I know I should have had you more involved. I can't fix what's done. But we can fix it going forward. Tomorrow morning we're firing Jeremiah Traylor and tomorrow afternoon we're holding a press conference."

"A press conference?" Paul asked.

"Hell yeah, son. We need to get ahead of this. Now, I'm gonna take the hit and look like a fool. The old man who let a fox into the henhouse. I'm gonna keep you clean. When the time comes, all you have to do is tell the truth. We entrusted that responsibility to Jeremiah, and he let us all down."

"Dad, I don't know."

"Okay, well, let's figure out what you do know. Did you price and manage any of those projects?"

"No, I didn't."

"Did you make any recommendations on how they should be priced?" "You know I didn't; I was working on business development."

"As you should have been. So was I. There's no one left, son. Now to be fair, like you said, maybe it's a mistake. But are you willing to leverage the entire company on that? I'm not. Jeremiah has to go. Now are you with me, son?"

"Well, yeah, Dad. I am."

"I knew you would be. Listen, we have a long day tomorrow. Get some rest and get in early. We have to meet with legal and HR. Wear a suit and tie for the press conference. We'll get through this, son. I love you."

Paul couldn't recall the last time those words had come from Case's mouth. Had they ever? Case stood and hugged Paul. Perhaps for the first time in years. But as much as Paul appreciated the words and the embrace, he still felt the same heaviness that he felt every time he and Case interacted.

Jeremiah doing something illegal didn't make sense. But Case was right. Those projects were his responsibility. The Department of Justice was involved now, and for the first time in his life, Paul's father needed him. He didn't want to let him down.

CHAPTER 18

Terminated

DAY 100

"What's up, fellas? All hands on deck today?" Jeremiah greeted Sam and Kyle. They were security guards but normally only one of them patrolled the front lobby.

"Good morning, Jeremiah," Sam said seriously.

"You okay, man?" Jeremiah asked. Sam wasn't his normally jubilant self. He seemed sad.

"Yes, sir. I'm good," he responded simply.

"Okay, I'll see you later," Jeremiah responded, trying not to overthink Sam's mood.

"Hey, Jeremiah," Sam said.

"Yeah, buddy. What's up?" Jeremiah responded. "You…you take care, okay?"

"Okay, Sam," Jeremiah smiled, curious about his demeanor. "I will, you do the same. I'll see you later."

"I'm gonna ride up with you, Jeremiah," Kyle said.

"Your boy LeBron is aging like fine wine, man. You see him the other night?" Jeremiah asked on the elevator.

"Yeah…good game," Kyle said somberly.

"Take care, Kyle," Jeremiah said as they got out of the elevator.

"Jeremiah, would you mind coming with me to the conference room real quick?" "Kyle, I got a full day. What's wrong? Is it Sam? Y'all are acting weird." "Jeremiah, I really am sorry, brother, but I got a job to do," Kyle said. "Okay, well…I'm not stopping you," Jeremiah said, confused. "Go do your job." "I am, Jeremiah. That's why I need you to go with me to the conference room."

Jeremiah didn't like to flaunt his status, but he also wasn't used to being ordered around his own workplace. He turned and faced Kyle. "Kyle, are you asking me to come with you to the conference room or are you telling me to?"

"You and me have always been cool, Jeremiah. Please, just come to the conference room with me."

Jeremiah knew something wasn't right, but he could not for the life of him figure out what Kyle wanted. His feelings escalated as he looked around the office. Jeremiah usually was one of the first ones in the office, but it seemed to be full. And all eyes were turned on him.

"Okay, Kyle, I'm just gonna take my stuff to my office and I will join you," he said calmly.

"I'll come with you," Kyle said firmly.

"So, you have to come with me to my office?" Jeremiah said, unintentionally raising his voice.

"Yes, sir, I do. I'm sorry." "Never mind. Let's go."

Jeremiah followed Kyle to the conference room. Case sat at the head of the table. Paul flanked him on his right. With them were Sidney, an HR executive, and Fred from legal. They were all immaculately dressed. Way too much for a typical workday.

Sidney spoke first. "Good morning, Jeremiah," she said calmly. "Thank you for joining us. Please have a seat."

Jeremiah sat down. "What's going on? Has something happened?" he asked. "Jeremiah," Case said. "Yesterday we were advised by the Department of Justice that Jacebre Construction is under investigation for bid rigging. Virtually every project named in the documents were projects you were directly involved in, including Vista Ridge. We cannot ignore this connection and we have to protect the future and the reputation of this company. We can't appear to condone any illegal activity. In view of these rather serious allegations and your connection to the projects in question, we have no choice but to terminate your employment effective immediately."

"Case, you're firing me? This doesn't make any sense. Bid rigging for what?" Jeremiah asked.

"Jeremiah, in all honesty, Case has already communicated what needed to be said. Kyle is waiting on you. We are going to allow you to gather your personal items so he can escort you out," Sidney said.

Was this a joke? Jeremiah looked at their faces for a sudden smile or burst of laughter. Nothing of the sort came. He then surveyed the room, hoping to find an ally. "Case, you can't possibly believe this. I've been with this company for almost twenty years! Paul, you know me. You know this isn't true. Why would I risk my career and my family?"

"You heard her, Jeremiah. This decision has been made, and we don't have anything else to say on the matter. Let's not make it more difficult. Kyle is waiting," Case said coldly.

"You said the Department of Justice. You mean the FBI? Do I need a lawyer?" Jeremiah asked, calming himself.

Sidney looked over to Fred, who answered, "We can't advise you on that matter. That's a question for you and your family."

"Please, Jeremiah. We know this is a difficult day. We don't want to hold you up," Sidney told him.

Jeremiah looked Paul in the eye. "Do you believe this, Paul?" he asked. "Look me in the eye and tell me you believe this!"

Paul glanced at Case, then barely made eye contact with Jeremiah. "You heard Sidney, Jeremiah," he said, holding back his desire to say, "I'm sorry."

"This is wrong," Jeremiah said firmly as he stood up. He took a deep breath and joined Kyle in the hallway, closing the conference room door behind him.

"Case, I still don't think this was the best way to handle this. There are lots of questions. Are you sure?" Fred asked.

"I'm sure," Case said.

CHAPTER 19

You May Now Begin Your Test

DAY 100

"Hey, Miah. Why are you sitting here in the dark?" Elise said to Jeremiah as he sat alone in their living room.

"Hey, babe. I thought you had appointments all day?" Jeremiah asked. "I did. The day is over."

"Already?"

"What do you mean 'already'?" she asked. "Miah… it's six o'clock. Didn't you go to work today and just leave after 5:30 like you normally do? And speaking of normally, sir, just because I'm busy doesn't mean I can't get a 'Hey, gorgeous' or a 'You good?' text from my husband. I called to see if you could meet for lunch, but you didn't pick up. Did you have a rough day?" she asked, turning on the lamp. He looked as tired and worn as she had ever seen him. "Miah, what's wrong?"

"Babe…I got fired today."

"Fired?!" she exclaimed. "That doesn't make sense. You just landed the biggest job in the history of the company, and you just got promoted," she said as she sat next to him.

"I know, babe. Let me try to explain. Do you remember me talking to you about bid rigging?"

"Yes. You talked about people going to prison behind trying to be shady and how boring the training videos you had to watch were."

"Jacebre is under investigation for bid rigging." "Who investigates that?"

"The Department of Justice." "You mean the FBI?"

"Ha. You sound like me. Yeah, that part. The FBI. They are looking into the Vista Ridge job and apparently some of my other projects as well. In a nutshell, the accusation is that we conspired with other bidding companies to determine who would win certain projects in order to drive up prices."

"They're just looking at your projects?" Elise asked.

"Mostly. It's my responsibility to oversee that process, but Case wouldn't even talk to me. I'm sure it's just a mistake. I know I didn't do anything wrong. If we got the jobs, it was because we made the most sense. The work should speak for itself."

"So why did you get fired?"

"They said they can't appear to condone any illegal activity. I can understand it, but I just thought they would at least stand with me and give me the benefit of the doubt."

"So, your company is under investigation, and they fire you for that? They didn't even ask you any questions?" Elise asked as her phone rang. She didn't recognize the number and let it go to voicemail. "Miah, that doesn't sound right," Elise continued. "Shouldn't they circle the wagons? You're a VP now."

Jeremiah shrugged his shoulders and shook his head. "I guess they don't want to take any chances."

"So, they're saying that you got these jobs by conspiring on the pricing with other companies?"

"Basically."

"And to what end? How were you supposed to benefit from this?"

"Babe, I tried to talk and ask but they shut it down. Lise…they had security escort me out of the building. I hired most of the people there and they walked me out in front of them like I…," he paused as he considered the irony of what he was about to say, "…like I stole something."

Elise took his hand and kissed the back of it. "I'm so sorry, baby. But it will be all right," she comforted.

"Yeah…there's more. An agent called me today. He wants me to come in and talk." "An FBI agent called you?"

"Yeah. He was asking all sorts of questions." "Which, please baby, tell me you didn't answer!"

"Well, I probably would have. I don't have anything to hide. But then he made it clear that the conversation was part of a federal investigation. So, I told him I didn't feel comfortable speaking to him without a lawyer. He said that was my right, but that I needed to be prepared to answer some difficult questions under oath. He said I would be hearing from him again soon. I spent the day looking up similar cases and situations. And researching lawyers. Then I came in here to pray." "So, since Jacebre has cut ties with you, we have to pay for our own lawyer?"

"Yeah, babe."

"Okay, so what did you find out?"

"Mostly what I already knew. Babe, if this doesn't go right, it could mean up to ten years in federal prison."

Elise was unbothered. "It's going to go right, Miah," she said confidently. "I know you're good with the Lord but umm…my Daddy loves me. There's too much he has for us, and this is just the devil tryna cut up. But I do want to know something. Now that you've had time to process and pray, how did we get here?"

"Babe, I just explained."

"No, those are the facts that are on the surface, but what's really happening? Why are we here? Why do you think Jacebre is cutting ties with a newly appointed VP? Their star! Why are all eyes on you?" Elise asked as her phone rang the second time from the same unknown number. She ignored it again.

"Elise, I guess it's just like they said. They are being investigated and my projects are at the heart of the investigation. It sucks, but they have to distance themselves from me until this is cleared up."

"So, this is just a mistake? They are going to investigate and not find anything?

And then Case is going to say, 'Sorry, Jeremiah, come on back'?"

"Babe, I hope so. I know they aren't going to find any evidence of me doing anything illegal, because I didn't."

"Okay, I knew you were going to say that. I'm coming over, sit back," Elise said.

Elise took off her shoes and jacket and sat in Jeremiah's lap.

"Baby, you are so sweet and good. But I'm sorry. You have no game, so you don't recognize game. For years, you have come home talking about how Case rides you about pricing. How he's always pushing you for better numbers. Even though you thought the jobs were already profitable. Didn't you tell me you didn't even think you would get Vista Ridge? You said you hated doing all that work and going in with such a high number. And this isn't the first time you've said that."

"Yeah, you're right," Jeremiah agreed.

Elise rubbed the back of his head and kissed him on the cheek. "Baby, he's playing you. I am not sure why or how, but he is. You may not know anything about this, but I promise you he does. That's why he's cutting ties. He's going to try and put all of this on you. You know how you said you used to try to talk specifics with him and he always just said handle it? That's why, baby. I bet you don't have one thing in writing or a single email that shows how he was pushing you. He was always calling you or coming to your office, right?"

Jeremiah nodded as the weight of her words hit him.

"Baby, I will never doubt your ability to lead this family, but I gotta go hard in the paint on this one. Listen to your wife. God is going to clear this up, and when he does, you gotta give Case the deuce of all deuces. And as far as I'm concerned, you don't have to use the index finger when you do it. Don't you ever go back and work for that man again. I've never trusted Case. I'm not saying I thought it would ever come to this, but honestly, I'm not surprised."

Elise's phone chimed again. This time it was a text from the same unknown number.

"Is that a client?" Jeremiah asked. "You might want to get that. We might need the money."

"No, I don't know who this is. Let me see."

Elise read the text out loud: 'Hello Elise. My name is Candace. I am Susan's daughter. She has been advised not to reach out to Jeremiah, but she wants him to know that she doesn't believe a word of what is being said. She wanted me to send you this. You might want to look at it now. You and your husband are in our prayers.'"

"What did she send?" Jeremiah asked. "It's some link. Let's see."

Elise opened the link. It was a press conference. Case was dressed in a black business suit. Behind him was the same group that fired Jeremiah, along with some key members of Jacebre's executive team. Case was addressing a small band of reporters in the Jacebre building lobby.

"Thank you for meeting with us today. For over two decades, Jacebre Construction has built a reputation for serving our nation's construction needs through innovation and excellence. But innovation and excellence mean nothing without integrity. For the first time, our integrity has been brought under scrutiny. When you found and own a company, it is like having a child. With that in mind, I am sad to report that I did not properly protect my child. I have placed people in power who I thought had the same commitment to honesty and fair play that this company was founded upon. To my shame, I was wrong. We called you all here today because we wanted you to hear it from us first. Jacebre Construction is under investigation by the Department of Justice for bid rigging. We highly suspect this to be the work of just one individual. That individual has been relieved of his responsibilities with this company. We are cooperating fully with the Department of Justice with the goal of determining the truth and restoring trust in our organization. Since this is an active investigation, we will not be taking any questions today."

Case turned around and exited as a barrage of questions echoed in the background.

"Are you acknowledging that you agree criminal activity did occur?" "What projects are under investigation?"

"Who was relieved of their position?" "Were they the only ones terminated?"

Case didn't answer any questions. He simply left.

Jeremiah and Elise tried to process what they had just seen when Jeremiah's phone rang. This also was from an unknown number.

"Baby, I think you need to pick that up," Elise advised.

"Hello," Jeremiah said reluctantly. He had no desire to answer a robo call. "Mr. Traylor," the voice on the other end of the line said. "My name is Shantell

Broussard. I am an investigative reporter with Channel 8 News." "How did you get this number?" Jeremiah asked.

"Mr. Traylor, we will be running our story on the bid rigging incident tonight. We wanted to give you an opportunity to comment. Can you make arrangements for an interview?"

Elise grabbed the phone and muted it.

"We're not talking to the press, baby. We can't control what they edit or how they put your comments out there. Just say 'No comment.' They are going to say whatever they want to say anyway."

"I'm not commenting right now," Jeremiah said.

"Are you sure, Mr. Traylor?" the reporter pressed. "It's already been made clear you were fired today. And that you were the only one. We want to give you an opportunity to get ahead of this and tell your side of the story. I do have to tell you, other parties have agreed to speak with us."

Elise shook her head and reasserted herself. "Don't do it, baby. 'No comment.'"

Jeremiah agreed. "Thank you, ma'am. No comment. Goodbye," he said as he hung up the phone.

"Baby, this is the time of testing the guy at the doctor's office warned us about," Elise said seriously.

Jeremiah just nodded, still trying to process his plight. "The work of just one individual. That individual has been relieved. What does that mean?" Jeremiah asked.

"Baby, it means you're his scapegoat. He's already ahead of us, so we need to catch up. Tomorrow we are going to get us the best lawyer in town and get ready for the FBI. Tonight, we need to make sure Mama

Etta and Daddy know what's up. She just said they are going to air tonight. She called you for comment. That probably means they are going to mention your name tonight and say that they tried to call you, but you had no comment. That's fine, but they need to hear this from you and not the evening news."

"Okay," Jeremiah nodded.

"It's going to be okay, Miah," Elise said sweetly.

"I know…but go ahead and say it," Jeremiah said. He knew what had to be going through her mind. She had to be thinking of all the times she told him she didn't trust Case and that he should make another move.

"Umm, okay. I love you," she said with a kiss on the cheek.

"Ha. Thank you. I love you, too. But no. Not that," Jeremiah smiled weakly. "You're the best husband in the whole wide world," she said with another

kiss.

"I appreciate that, Lise. But not that either."

"Oh, my…you little mind reader," she said slyly. "I mean this is a time of family crisis, but if you're gonna make me say it…fine. Miah, I'm horny. There it is. I was hoping to romance you out those boxers, but who am I to argue if you want to get straight down to business?"

Jeremiah shook his head and for the first time that day, he laughed. "Lise, I appreciate you, babe. But you were right. So go ahead and say it. I should…."

"Keep being the man you are? Yes, I agree. The only thing I can add to that is that it's Miah and Lise against the world. Nothing else I could say right now matters."

CHAPTER 20

Closed Doors

DAY 160

"Zach, I really appreciate you coming by man. Thanks for checking up on me live and in person," Jeremiah said.

"Anything for my college roomdog. Thanks for having me out to your hacienda," Zach replied. He looked around at Jeremiah's home. "J, this is nice, man! And you said you did all this?" he asked.

"Mostly," Jeremiah responded, appreciating the compliment. "But Elise put the finishing touches on it."

"Y'all always have been a great team. How's my petite princess doing?" Zach joked.

"Ha. She's good, man. She's really picked up her clientele since I got let go.

She's hustling and holding it down for us."

"Dude! I was on the interstate the other day and I saw her billboard. 'Come see Elise.' I said, 'That's my little buddy!'" Zach exclaimed. "So, she's moving a lot of houses, huh?"

"Yeah, for sure. She's even looking into commercial properties. I lost my job and she just kicked everything up another gear. It doesn't replace my salary, but we still got lights," Jeremiah said halfheartedly. He was proud of Elise, but not providing for his family was a hard pill for him to swallow.

"Okay. Let's just address the elephant in the room," Zach said seriously. "Is it fair to say that you invited me here because you want to come to work for us?"

Jeremiah's heart lightened. Zach was a good friend, and he knew Jeremiah needed work. It would be just like him not to make him beg.

"Well, Zach. Yeah. If you think you have a spot for me. I would love it. I actually have some ideas for you that can really grow the company."

Zach paused and sighed heavily. "Jeremiah, I know you do. I've always known. But man, I'm just gonna say it. I wish you would have come years ago, when I was begging you to. I know we could have done a lot of damage with someone like you."

"And now?" Jeremiah asked reluctantly, fearful of his answer.

"Jeremiah, I've already run it past my father-in-law. It's still his show. I'm not all talented like you. I just married the boss's daughter."

Jeremiah could tell by the look on Zach's face what had been said, but he had to ask, "Okay, what did your father-in-law say?"

"Jeremiah, we've been talking this over ever since we heard the news. I told him I don't believe for a second you had anything to do with it. He knows Case and let's just say they are more than business rivals. They're darn near arch enemies. He can't prove it, of course, but he thinks Case tried to work something with some of the larger outfits around town and let you take the fall when it went south. I mean, he doesn't even know you, but he said, 'That kid really got screwed over.'"

"Well, since he knows that," Jeremiah said, "is he willing to give me an opportunity? I'm not begging for a handout, Zach. You know what I can do. I just need an opportunity. If you give me one, I promise I can get you guys to the next level."

"Jeremiah, I know that. I've always known that. That's why I've always wanted you on our team. But things are different now. We may be smaller than Jacebre, but we are starting to hit our stride. We've been getting awarded some nice contracts."

"So let me help you get more!" Jeremiah pressed. "I can get you guys up there with the big boys." Jeremiah hated selling himself like this. He wasn't sure if he was coming on too strong or not. Jacebre was the only place he had ever worked and when other opportunities did come up, the companies were trying to woo him. Now he was in the unusual position of trying to convince someone of his worth.

"Man, J, I'm sorry, but some of these are government contracts. We can't do anything that may appear less than above board. And right now, and it kills me to tell my friend this, Jeremiah Traylor is not above board. I mean, dude, if they set you up...." Zach noticed Jeremiah's change in facial expression. "Forgive me. I don't mean if. What I mean is...they set you up good. I can't prove it, but I know it in my heart because I know you. But brother, I can't go to our clients talking about what's in my heart. And I can't go to our other employees and explain we lost work because I wanted to be a good friend. I promise, as soon as this blows over, as soon as you are cleared, we have a place for you. But right now...it can't happen."

Jeremiah's heaviness returned as he processed Zach's words. "Zach, I appreciate you shooting straight. I do have another question for you. Have you spoken to anybody else in the business? I mean, if you are saying this and you know me, what are they saying?"

"Jeremiah, most people feel just like me, especially anyone that knows you, knows of you, or knows Case. It doesn't add up, and they know it. Now, there are others who just read the papers or watch the news and talk about the guy from Jacebre. The guy that got caught with his hand in the cookie jar on the biggest job in the city. They're hypocrites! Every last one of them! Most of them have done exactly what they are trying to judge you for. Either way, though, I think it's gonna be hard for you to find work in this business. You're a smart guy. You might want to consider a career change. If anybody can do it, you could."

"Zach, I wish it was that easy. I've tried that. It's not just the construction industry. This whole deal is an attack on my character. Nobody in any industry wants to touch me. They don't want to chance it. I can tell them all day long about how unfounded the charges are, and how I'm fighting it, but it doesn't matter. There are smaller opportunities out there with companies that could give a care about my reputation, but they say I'm overqualified."

"I get it," Zach said sympathetically.

"Zach, I don't think you do. It's not just about me. You know how few black men get to my position in this business? They took my job, my career, and my reputation. They took my face and my name and put it on the evening news. I know this sounds arrogant, but there were people who looked up to me. And now I'm painted like I'm crooked. It's infuriating, embarrassing, and frustrating all at the same time. Elise has always been a baller, but she used to be able to pick and choose her opportunities. Now, here she is almost six months pregnant, and she's out there working harder than ever because I can't work. I bought this house thinking we would be making more than ever, but the salary I was depending on is gone. And don't get me started on the law firm we retained. They want all this money, but they make no promises on the outcome. And…."

Jeremiah looked at Zach's face and realized he was rambling.

"I'm sorry, man. I didn't mean to dump all that on you. I appreciate you more than you know."

"Jeremiah, you don't have to apologize. This is too much for anyone. Do you mind telling me what your attorneys are saying? How's the case shaking out?"

"Cases like this can take years. In the meantime, it just hangs over my head. They've said that I should consider taking some sort of plea bargain. But that would imply I was guilty…and I'm not. You're right. Case set me up good. He says he empowered me to close those deals, and it's basically my word against his. The FBI dug through my financials. They didn't find anything, mind you. But they are implying I could have done it to curry favor with the company to earn some of the raises and promotions I've gotten over the years. Ironically, me just having bought this house doesn't look good either."

"Man, that sucks. It really does. But I truly believe you are gonna land on your feet," Zach encouraged.

"That's what I'm praying for."

"Hey, court cases and unemployment aside…you got a kid coming! Man, I am so happy for you guys!" Zach said, trying to cheer up his friend.

"Yeah, man. We're also adopting our foster daughter. My mom and dad are healthy. And Elise is breezing through this pregnancy like a champ. And that's it right there! Every time I'm tempted to complain, I remember that regardless of all this nonsense, God has kept our family whole and healthy. It's been rough, but as long as I got them, I know I'll be all right."

CHAPTER 21

Elise's Odd Theory

DAY 160

"Honey, I'm home!" Elise said cheerfully. She normally liked to be home when he arrived. But now he was usually the one at home waiting for her. Still, she did her best to bring a little light and love home with her.

"Hey, gorgeous!" Jeremiah smiled, appreciating her energy. He was down because of his conversation with Zach, but he didn't want to bring her down with him. "How was your day, babe?"

"The closing went great. I put it on the tee, and my Daddy knocked it out of the park! Praise the Lord! How did it go with Zach?" she asked.

"Oh, he's fine. He asked how his petite princess was," Jeremiah replied. "That's nice," she laughed. "But I didn't ask how he was. I asked how it went.

I am assuming he doesn't have a spot for you, or you would have told me already." "Nah," Jeremiah replied dryly.

"What did he say?" she asked.

"What I expected. Even my friends can't hire me," he said dejectedly. "I'm sorry, baby," she said as she kissed him on the cheek.

"You know what really gets me? The FBI hasn't found one credible piece of evidence. They do all this posturing and threatening but nothing."

"We knew they weren't going to find anything, baby. You didn't do anything." "Yeah, but while they're sniffing for stuff they aren't going to find, we haveto pay lawyers and worse yet, with this case hanging over my head, I can't work." "It's going to be all right, Miah. Our savings are a little shot, but so what? We haven't missed any meals or any bills. Your wife is out in these streets selling houses like hotcakes and, dare I say it…looking cute doing it."

"Yeah," Jeremiah nodded.

"Yeah?" Elise questioned. "Sir, certainly you misspoke. You mean 'Amen,' don't you? Especially to the part about your wife looking cute."

Jeremiah smiled. "Amen, babe. God is providing and yes…you look cute. I just don't like not doing anything for us, and I especially don't like you having to hustle like this when you're pregnant."

Elise wrapped her arms around his neck. "I know you don't like having a sugar mama, baby. But we're in this together. You can let me do the heavy lifting until God turns it around for us. Until then, I got you."

"Whoa!" Jeremiah jumped. "You have to warn a brother when that's going to happen."

"When what is going to happen?" she asked.

"When you're going to get more beautiful…you can't just spring it on me like that."

"Thank you, baby," she said, happy his spirits were lifted. "So, you good?" "Yeah. I'm good. I love you, Lise."

"I know, baby," she responded. "I love you, too." "Lise, I know you didn't sign up for all of this." "All of what?" she asked.

"Court cases, potential jailtime, unemployment… what happened last night," he said as he shook his head.

"Oh, you mean, when our friend refused to stand up and salute?"

"Don't joke about it, Elise! Some things are never funny and that's one of them."

"Miah, you have a lot on your mind. It's okay. Besides, I know you're not a machine. It's hard…no pun intended," she grinned, "to keep up…again, no pun intended," she laughed out loud, "with all this pregnant fire."

"Elise, stop!"

"I'm sorry, baby. But it really is okay. We will have a raincheck later. And by the way… you're wrong."

"About what?" he asked.

"I said sickness and health, richer or poorer, until death do us part. So yeah, I did sign up for it. And I'd do it again, and again, and again, just to be right here with you. I wouldn't be anywhere else in the world, baby. We just gotta believe that God is on the way. This movie just started. The hero is coming soon to save the day…and he always comes through. And speaking of him coming through… everything went perfectly with my doctor's visit."

"Thank you, Jesus," Jeremiah said.

"But something interesting did happen. I was in the waiting room yesterday and I saw a few of the same people who were there when you put on that little show when you found out about our son. And I got to thinking about our little Bruno Mars-looking friend. So, I asked some of the other moms if they remembered that day, and Miah, it was so funny, they were like, 'Yes, girl. We remember you and your proud, loud husband.' So, we chitchatted, and they teased me a little. All fun and games, right? So, then I asked them about the other father that was in the corner. I described him, and I'm sorry, baby, but you know I had to say how cute he was."

"Uh-huh, I remember. The teeth, the muscles, let's move on," Jeremiah said dryly.

Elise laughed. "Baby, I had to. I had to make sure they knew which one I was talking about. So, I begin to describe him, and yes, I mentioned the body, the teeth, that cute little Bruno Mars face. And I told them how he was just standing over in the corner and had followed us out and came back in. Now here's where it gets interesting. Miah, do you know not one of them knew who I was talking about? One of them was sitting in the same chair she was in last time. You remember the mom whose little girl wanted to see our son's baby man parts?" she chuckled. "There was no way she could not have seen him. That office isn't that big, but she was like drawing a blank. When he walked out, he would have had to pass all of them, but none of them remembered him."

"Okay," Jeremiah said cooly, "I mean I didn't notice him in there either." "Exactly. So, he's sitting up there in the corner looking all…."

"Elise!" Jeremiah said sharply.

"…not quite as sexy as you, but ain't nobody noticed him?" she continued. "I thought that was strange."

"He probably made more of an impression on us because of what he said to us," Jeremiah reasoned.

"I knew you would say something like that. I already got my Sherlock Holmes on. I spoke to the receptionist. Same thing. I described him to a T. Told her where he was. And before you say she can't give out patient information, I told her I didn't need a name or address or anything. I just wanted to know if there was a young father there that met that description or if she saw him. She was like 'No, girl, but if you see him again tell him I'm single.'"

"Yeah, you described him too good," Jeremiah said.

Elise laughed again. "I know, right, but that's so crazy that nobody noticed him. I asked about other people who were there that day, and they remembered them. But not him."

"Yeah, I guess it is kinda weird," Jeremiah agreed.

"I'm glad you agree. Sooo, I have a theory. It's gonna blow your mind but check this out. Sit down," she said, breaking their embrace.

"Okay," Jeremiah said, taking a seat.

"Miah…," she said, pausing for dramatic effect, "I think ole boy was an angel."

"An angel?" he questioned. "An angel!" she reasserted.

"Okay," he said, turning his head away from Elise so she could not see his expression.

"Jeremiah John Traylor! You gon stop laughing at yo helpmate when I'm droppin' knowledge!"

"No, babe, I'm not laughing," he chuckled. "That's interesting. You know, you might be right. Matter of fact, I have been noticing my mama's biscuits have been particularly moist and fluffy lately. You think they are actually manna from heaven?"

Elise put her hands on her hips. "Oh, so now you got jokey-jokes? Fine. You scoffer! You God mocker! You…you…you blaspheming, uncircumcised Philistine you. Go ahead and laugh. You are from a wicked and adulterous generation, and you refuse to believe," she said, wagging her finger at him.

Jeremiah let his laughter burst forth. Partially at the idea of this angelic visitation, but mostly at his wife's humorous rant.

Elise was annoyed but also very happy. He hadn't laughed like that in some time. It felt good to see him like that even if it was at her expense.

"So, babe, we saw an angel?" he asked, still laughing.

"Yes. We. Did," she said firmly. "And don't you worry about that raincheck. If you can't respect my ideas, you can't enjoy this pregnant deliciousness," she said, turning to the side and showing her baby bump.

"I'm sorry, babe," he said, controlling himself. "Come here." "Ain't!" she said, folding her arms and turning her head.

Jeremiah tugged her by her blazer and sat her in his lap. "I said I'm sorry, babe. You're right…it could have been an angel," he said rather unconvincingly.

"Boy, don't patronize me. I'm serious!"

"I know," he said as he kissed her on the cheek.

"Nope…not gonna work!" she insisted. "No raincheck for you, sir." "I know," he said, kissing her again. "No raincheck."

"Miah, you're not taking me seriously. He was letting us know that we had this little hiccup coming but that God is faithful. This is our time of great testing. The Lord just wanted to prepare us. But he hasn't forgotten us. He's always come through for us, and he's going to do it again. We just have to trust him."

"Babe, you know I always care about what you think. Whether it was an angel or not…it's obvious there was some truth to it. We're being tested. I just pray we pass the test soon. I want this all behind us before the baby comes. Sooo, are you sure no raincheck?" he smiled.

"Positive, besides we have to get to Mama Etta and Daddy's. They're waiting on us for dinner. And don't worry…I'm sure all of this will be over soon."

CHAPTER 22

Ambushed

DAY 160

Jeremiah, Elise, and Amari were greeted by the intoxicating aroma of Etta Ween's home cooking. His dad welcomed them with a warm embrace. Jeremiah noticed that he held on longer and squeezed him tighter than normal.

"You okay, Pop?" Jeremiah asked.

"I'm okay, son," John replied simply, still holding his son tightly.

They joined Etta Ween in the dining room, where she had a royal feast awaiting them. There were ox tails, smoked turkey legs, collard greens, cornbread, candied yams, rice and gravy.

"Mama, why did you do all of this?" Jeremiah asked. "You don't want it?" she asked coyly.

"Oh, no… I want it but dang, Mama!"

"Mama Etta, if this is a challenge, I'm throwing in the towel!" Elise said. "You win."

"It's not a challenge. I just wanted to do something special for my children." Etta Ween put her arms around Elise and pulled her close. "I am so happy for you two. I know these last two months have been rough. But God is going to turn this thing right around. You watch and see. And when he does, you remember what I said."

"Mama Etta," Elise said, "we were just talking about that. But can you let us tell you while we eat? And more importantly, can you release this grip you got on me? You go squeeze the baby out!"

"Oh, I'm sorry, baby. You know Mama Etta don't want to hurt this precious cargo." She kissed Elise on the cheek and gently rubbed her belly. "I love you, sweetheart. I am so glad you are here. Come on, let's eat. Honey, they look hungry. We need a short grace," Etta Ween told her husband jokingly.

John looked lovingly at his wife as he took his seat at the head of the table. "I'm going to pray as long as the Spirit leads, baby," he said seriously.

Etta Ween simply smiled at her husband.

"Father, we want to thank you for this special time. Everything about you is good, Lord. You are a good father, a good shepherd, and a good friend. We need you now, more than ever. And right now, we need you closer than ever before. We need you to stick closer than a brother. We know our red-scarlet sins are white as snow because of what your Son Jesus did for us on the cross, and we give you thanks. He who knew no sin became sin for wretches such as we and we give you thanks. Lord, you are good. We're going through some things, but you are good. They are lying on my son, but you are good. We don't know what tomorrow holds but you are good. You're a protector. You're a provider. You're a peace giver. And precious Jesus…you're a healer. Lord, you're everything we need you to be. And on this day where my wife has prepared this wonderful meal and given her best for this family…." John paused.

Jeremiah looked out of the corner of his eye. Was his dad getting choked up over grace?

John cleared his throat and continued. "…we thank you for giving us your best through Christ. We won't lie and pretend there are not other things we are desperate for you to do, Lord. But you've given us Jesus. You've given us each other. You've given us now. So, we say thank you, Father. Thank you for our children and our grandchildren. Thank you for this food my wife has prepared. Thank you for my wife and the love you have given us through her. Thank you most of all for the bread of life that is your Son Jesus. In that perfect name we pray, Amen."

"Mama Etta, I'm glad you asked him for a short grace," Elise quipped.

John laughed. "Quit meddling, yo daddy girl. Didn't you say you had to tell us something?"

Elise shared her theory about their encounter with the young man as they enjoyed their dinner. Both John and Etta Ween were very open to the possibility. "I don't think it's too farfetched to think that the Lord would have an angel

speak a special word into your lives," Etta Ween said.

"I agree, honey," John confirmed. "We can't possibly understand and fathom all of God's ways. But scripture confirms we may sometimes entertain angels unaware."

Jeremiah cut his eyes at Elise. She was gloating because she knew he wasn't going to cross his mom and dad.

"That's what I said, Daddy! I told Miah that and he just laughed at me," she tattled.

Normally, John would have rushed to Elise's defense and chastised Jeremiah for her benefit. Instead, he just whispered to her, "Daddy, gon get him later, baby girl."

"Kids," he continued, "speaking of angels, there are some things going on that we need to share with you. Things that need heavenly intervention. With everything happening with you, son, we wanted to hold off telling you this. But we think that we've held it too long."

John paused again. The way he did earlier when he was praying. He looked at his wife. His mouth quivered slightly but no words came from his mouth. Etta Ween reached to him and grabbed his hand. Her touch calmed him and gave him strength.

Jeremiah looked at his parents. He didn't know what it was, but something was wrong.

Elise saw Etta Ween reach for John and likewise reached for Jeremiah's hand. "What's wrong, Daddy?" Elise asked.

"Your mom went to the doctor the other day. Truth is, she was getting a second opinion."

"A second opinion on what?" Jeremiah asked, fearing he already knew the answer.

Again, his father struggled to form the words. Etta Ween stepped in and answered.

"I got a second opinion from an oncologist," she said plainly. "My doctor discovered a tumor in my breast. It's cancerous."

"Does that mean you have cancer?" Amari asked fearfully. "Come over here, sweetie," Etta Ween said to Amari.

Amari crawled into her lap.

"Yes, baby. That does mean I have cancer. But we don't want you to be afraid. God takes real good care of your Mama Etta." She kissed her on the cheek and tickled her under her arm, but Amari barely responded.

Jeremiah contemplated telling Amari to leave the room, but his parents had intentionally made this announcement in front of her. Amari was young but she was old enough to understand what cancer meant. Eventually she would have to know. He looked at her in his mother's arms and realized she was in the safest place she could be.

"Mama Etta, what are the doctors saying? What's the plan?" Elise asked.

Etta Ween held on to her husband with one hand and snuggled Amari with her free arm. She gave Jeremiah and Elise her eyes.

"It's too far along and inoperable, baby. They can't do anything."

"What do you mean it's too far along?" Jeremiah asked. "When was your last breast exam?"

"I may have missed a couple of years, baby," Etta Ween confessed. "Mama! A couple of years?" Jeremiah exclaimed in disbelief.

"Miah, let her talk, baby," Elise said, squeezing his hand and communicating that he should tone it down.

John just sat there, obviously trying to hold his emotions in check. Jeremiah's frustration was compounding. He was already dealing with a lot. But this was too much.

"I'm sorry, Mama. So...what else can we do? Can you get another opinion?" Jeremiah asked.

"We've already had two different doctors say the same thing.

Surgery. Chemo.

Radiation. They don't think it will do much good."

"There was one other option," John said firmly, breaking his silence. "What is it?" Jeremiah asked hopefully.

"John, honey, we talked about this," Etta Ween said sweetly.

"I don't think we're finished talking," John said sharply. "We said we wanted to tell them, so we're telling them everything. Kids, there is something experimental going on. I guess there always is. They've had some success. Even in patients your mother's age. Your mom doesn't want to try it, though."

"Mama, we have to try! What's the problem?" Jeremiah asked.

"What your father isn't saying is that this experimental trial is very expensive, and the side-effects are much worse than traditional chemo or radiation. The cure is worse than the disease."

"And what your mother isn't telling you is that in cases where they succeed, the patients recover and live another five to six years!" John snapped.

Elise knew no marriage was perfect. Perhaps Jeremiah had seen glimpses of this, but in her twenty years of being in this family she had never seen these two at odds with each other like this. Still, Etta Ween held John's hand.

"Mama, we have to try. Tell her, Lise," Jeremiah said.

Elise looked into her Mama Etta's eyes. The same love that she always saw was still there. She was concerned but there was no fear. She wasn't concerned for herself. Her concern was for the people in the room right now. For a husband and a son who couldn't imagine life without her. For the precious girl sitting in her lap trying to understand what was happening. Right now, she didn't need to be pressured. She just needed to be supported and to be loved.

"Miah. Daddy. I think we need to take a second and listen to Mama Etta. I think she has more to say."

Etta Ween looked at Elise and said thank you with her eyes. "I just want to say I'm sorry. I so want to be here with you. I want to see this little one grow up and I want to spoil my grandson. I want to live. I really do. But that's the word. Live. The doctor said this medicine they use is very strong. If it works, it really does a number on cancer, but it also does a number on your body. I feel good and I look good. I want y'all to remember me this way. Strong and alive. Not some messed-up, shriveled-up thing clinging to life just so she can breathe and take up space. I want to put this in the Lord's hands. He's a healer and if he wants me healed, then cancer is no hill for him to climb. If he doesn't, then no medicine or experimental treatment can change his mind."

"So, we are just going to give up without a fight?" Jeremiah asked harshly. "No, son. We are just going to give it to the Lord."

"Mama, I'm all for giving it to the Lord. But we have to take advantage of whatever he provides. If it's the money, then me and Elise will cover it."

"It's not just the money. Jeremiah, I don't think you're listening. I know this is hard to hear, but yo mama is at peace. I want you to be too."

"Mama, I can't be at peace knowing you're giving up. Dad said that the procedure can give you another five or six years. If you don't do anything, how much time do you have?"

"Two months. Maybe three," Etta Ween said somberly. Her words struck Jeremiah like a fist.

"Mama, you say I'm not listening but are you listening to yourself? Elise will still be pregnant in three months. If you don't fight, you won't ever meet your grandson."

"Baby, don't you think I know that? That scares me more than anything," Etta Ween said.

"Jeremiah, we're not going to solve all this tonight. Let's take a beat and process this," Elise said, trying to calm the situation.

"Process what, Elise?" Jeremiah asked, raising his voice. "We have to do whatever we can. And since we don't have many options, we have to take whatever is left. We need to do this!"

"Jeremiah, you keep saying 'we.' We don't have to do some experimental procedure. We can't endure this for her any more than you can have this baby for me! We have to process what she is saying, and we have to consider what Mama Etta wants to do."

"This is about all of us, Elise!"

Jeremiah. Elise. Amari rarely heard them call each other by their full names, but it seemed like they were always mad when they did.

"Y'all, please don't fight," Amari pleaded.

"We're sorry, Mari. I know it sounds like it, but we're not fighting… not really.

We just want Mama Etta to be okay," Jeremiah tried to explain.

"I'm sorry. This is too much for her. This is not how I wanted this to go. I didn't want to upset everybody," Etta Ween said.

"Mama, I'm sorry for raising my voice. But we have to deal with this. We can't just let this slide. Dad, what do you say?" Jeremiah asked, searching for an ally. He couldn't believe what he was hearing. Cancer was bad enough. But his mother saying she wasn't going to do anything about it and Elise willing to go along with it made it all the worse.

"Son," John replied. "I want your mother to be happy and to be at peace. But I also…." John's voice broke again as he struggled to complete his thoughts. "I also want her here."

John's words broke the dam of his emotions. He took hold of his wife's free hand with both of his and laid his head on it as he broke down and wept. In over forty years of life, Jeremiah could not recall his father crying. He was sure he must have. John wasn't a hard man, but right now he could not think of a moment where his dad had lost control. But that's exactly what was happening now. His father had laid his head on their dining room table and was weeping uncontrollably in front of everyone who considered him to be a hero.

"Baby, I don't want you to go. I'm sorry!" he wailed.

Elise called Amari back to her. She could comfort her. Right now, Mama Etta needed to be a wife.

Jeremiah tried to be strong, but the sight of his broken father was more than he could bear. Soon they were all crying for the woman who was everything to them. John wept for the love of his life. Jeremiah wept for his best friend. Elise wept for the only mother she had ever known. Amari wept for her precious Mama Etta. They wept for the glue that held their family together.

Etta Ween was the only one who held her tears. She wanted to cry. She needed to cry. But not here and not now. She still had strength and right now her family needed it.

When their tears slowed, Amari asked a rather simple question. "Uncle J, why don't you just pray and ask God to heal Mama Etta?" she asked. Without waiting for a response, Amari got out of Elise's lap. "It's okay, Papa John, get up. Come on, everybody," she said as she formed the family into a circle. "I will go first," Amari said confidently.

She started as only a little girl could.

"Lord Jesus, please help Mama Etta not to be sick anymore. And please help us not to be scared so we won't be sad. We hope that you take this cancer away and make her feel better. Amen… I mean in Jesus' name, Amen." Amari pulled Jeremiah's hand. "Go ahead, Uncle J," she encouraged.

Jeremiah took a deep breath. He was encouraged, and a little embarrassed, by his soon-to-be-daughter's faith. "Father, we thank you for the faith of our little girl, and how she has reminded us to pray. So, Father, we trust you now. We pray for your presence, your wisdom, your guidance, and your healing. We thank you for being for us. And we believe that even this…cannot be against us. We join our faith together and believe you to turn this thing around. We ask for life, and we ask for more time. Please show us what to do. We are caught off guard, but you are not. We trust you and thank you. The weapon is formed but please don't let it prosper, as you protect Mama by the power of your great name. We speak life, health, and recovery in Jesus' name. We declare your faithfulness and trust you for greater grace. We ask that this sickness not end in death. But that you would use it to make another notch in your belt as you show the watching world the love you have for your children who call on your name. You said we have not because we ask not. So, we ask that you heal Mama and that you spare us this sorrow. Our eyes are on you, Jesus. We know you will not fail us. It's in your name that we pray, Amen."

Amari smiled brightly. "It's going to be all right now. God always answers Uncle J's prayers."

CHAPTER 23

Selfless

DAY 160

Etta Ween lay on John's chest. They didn't speak, but after fifty years of marriage words were unnecessary. His breathing pattern told her he was not asleep. His arms wrapped tightly around her told her that even now in the darkest point of her life, she was safe. His occasional whispers told her that he was praying. And she knew exactly what for. She knew everything about him. This was her husband…her life partner…her prayer partner. But right now, they could not pray together because they were not in agreement. For certain, they wanted the same thing. But she knew from her soul it could not be. The Lord had shown her his will. She wanted to tell him it was going to be all right. That her love for him would not die with her and that the Lord would see him through. Maybe she would tell him later. For now, she would let him pray and let him hope. Perhaps the Lord would change his mind because of his faith. She smiled as she recalled the countless times he had prayed for someone else and the Lord had come through. Maybe this was one of those times? So, she let him hold her while he prayed and she herself prayed silently.

"Master, please. I know what you told me. I hear your call so forgive me for asking this. Father, are you sure there is no other way? I don't ask for myself, Lord. You can search my heart for any deception. You know I long to be with you. I'm ready, Lord. But Father, my husband and my children…they aren't ready. If not for me, Father, then please, for them.

"Lord, you are showing me so much. I don't understand it all, but

I will trust you. I pray for my grandson, and I pray for Amari. I don't understand why you are leading me to pray this way. I know Jeremiah and Elise will be wonderful parents.

But Father, I am asking for a covering over their lives and that you please protect them from all the evil influences and all the foolishness around them. Jesus, I don't understand my own words, but please raise up people to love and cover them. Please protect them by the power of your great name and give strength to those who love them and take care of them. Lord, I don't understand but my Jesus, I trust you. I know my path home to you is a rough and bitter one. But even right now I praise you for the day I will see you. I don't want to leave my husband, Lord. But I know what you have shown me. So, in faith and obedience, I will come. Please, Father, won't you do a healing work in my husband and my children? The enemy has plans to steal and to kill and to destroy, but I call on your word that my husband, my children, my grandson, my granddaughter have an abundant life. They will cry but God, you are their comforter, their refuge, and their healer. Don't let them give up, Lord. Don't let them give in. And Jesus, if they fall, I call on your word that you pick them up. You're calling me, Lord… not them. So, please keep them…forgive them…and encourage them. Build them up better than ever before. Let it be known in their spirit that you didn't forget them. You didn't forsake them. You didn't fail them. Lord, let them know that you were there all the time and that even when your ways and thoughts are higher than ours you still love with an everlasting love.

"And Master…Lord…Father…my precious Savior… I will ask this one last time. You've done so much. I give you praise. You've been so good. I give you praise. You've covered my sin and you've healed my sin-sick soul and I give you praise. But Jesus…if there is any way. Please, Father…please, Lord…just once, let me hold my grandson. I dare not instruct you, Lord. But if I must come to you now, could you let me stay long enough to snuggle up with him? I want to kiss his little head and play with his little feet. And maybe I could hold him in my arms, and we take a nap together and then after that… you can call me home.

"Lord, I'm asking that you open up Jeremiah's eyes and let him see your greatest blessings. You've made him so successful, but now I ask that you let him see what success really looks like to you. Let him come through this fire refined like pure gold. Thank you for such a wonderful son, Lord. I couldn't have asked you for more.

"And Jesus, thank you for Elise. Your will didn't allow me to have a baby girl but Father, you always come through. Thank you for my daughter. They gon all lean on her, Lord. When she breaks, please restore her gently, Lord."

Etta Ween's prayer was interrupted by John's voice. "Baby. You 'sleep?"

"No, honey," she replied.

"I was talkin' to the Lord," John said.

"I know you were…did he talk back?" Etta Ween asked. "No," he said honestly. "So I'm just gon tell you what I want." "I'm listening."

"Baby, let's fight it," John pleaded. "So, what if the odds are against us? Wouldn't it be just like God to let you be the one to beat it? I know you are the one that has to go through it, but I promise I will be with you, Weenie. Every step of the way, baby, please…."

"Baby, stop. You don't have to convince me you are with me. I've known that from the moment I met you. I just don't know if we can stand in the way of this," Etta Ween reasoned.

"Weenie, we have to. It's still too much to do. I don't want to play with my grandson without you. Or go to church without you. Or have Sunday dinner with the kids without you. I don't want to do anything without you. I don't want to live…."

"Stop it, honey," Etta Ween interrupted. "Just stop. You gon run yoself crazy. And I don't wanna hear about you not living. Don't you know it breaks my heart to think of you wasting away, not enjoying the life the good Lord gave you because I'm not here?"

"Well, Weenie…that's what's gon happen. So, I guess you need to live."

Etta Ween sighed. She hoped her husband would speak a word of faith. A word he had gotten from the Lord assuring him that this sickness would not end in death. But these were not words of faith.

They were the words of a desperate man who knew his time with the love of his life was short. She had given her whole life to him, and if he needed it, then he would have this too."

"John, baby. If it's what you feel is best, then of course I will try. Now… you rest, my love."

CHAPTER 24

Wrong Enemy

DAY 160

Jeremiah lay still in the bed. He faced away from Elise. She tapped him on the shoulder, but he ignored it and tried to pretend he was asleep. She snuggled as close to him as she could and put her arm around him.

"You know, I just realized something," she said. "I thought your silence was about Mama Etta's bombshell. But it's not, is it? It's about me. You're mad at me, aren't you?"

"Elise, it's late. Not now."

"Yes, now. What did I do that would make you turn away from me? Why are you shutting me out?"

"Why did you entertain that foolishness, Elise?" he said as he sat up in the bed, breaking her embrace.

"What foolishness?"

"With Mama talkin' 'bout she doesn't want to get treatment. I can't believe you would support that!"

"Miah, baby," she said patiently. "I support her. I support her wishes. And I trust her. You've never experienced loss. I have. And I remember that look on her face. It was the same look my grandmother had before she went home. It's a look that says, 'I love you, but I have to leave you and I need you to be okay with that.'"

"Well, I'm not okay with it. We were just talking about God coming through, and now we hear some bad news and all of a sudden he's not able? I understand she's scared but that doesn't mean she gets to quit. And for you of all people to, just go along with it…Elise, she trusts you. You would be able to convince her that she needs to fight."

"Jeremiah, that's not my place. Or yours. Or even Daddy's. I already looked up this trial she's talking about. They are very transparent about the side-effects. And if the doctors are already saying she's terminal, why make her go out in pain?"

"So, you have given up?"

"No. I'm going to believe God for a miracle. But I want us to honor her wishes and her faith. She has given us everything. We can give her this."

"You don't understand, Elise. You weren't close to your mom."

"That was ugly and unnecessary. I may not have been close to my mama, but I am close to yours."

"Well, I'm sorry, but I need you to believe with me. Not just say 'whatever.' This is my mama we're talking about."

"I understand that, and I know you are in your feelings right now, but please don't make me the enemy."

"I'm not trying to but…." "But what, Jeremiah?"

"Elise, I thought you always scheduled her appointments with yours. You didn't know she wasn't going?"

"Oh. Wow. You do think this is my fault. Jeremiah, yes, I schedule them for her. I'm sorry. I did know of at least one she missed, but I didn't know it had been a couple of years. And she didn't tell me one way or another. She looks good and acts like everything is fine. I guess I didn't follow up. I didn't see it coming."

"And now we're here."

"Yeah. I guess we are. Just a few hours ago it was all about how much we loved each other. Now I'm the Grim Reaper. Now I'm the one who singlehandedly made Mama Etta sick. And now I'm just ushering her on to glory because I'm so irresponsible and unconcerned. You know what, bruh? We got four other bedrooms and multiple couches up in this joint. Pick one. Use them all. I don't care. You wanna turn over and face away from me? You wanna be mad because I'm listening to Mama Etta? Fine. Let me turn over too so you can kiss my behind on the way out!"

Jeremiah just sat there.

"Oh, you still here? Fine, I can go. I don't have to be anywhere I am not wanted."

Elise got up out of the bed and headed to the door. Jeremiah caught up to her as she was halfway down the hall.

"Elise, wait," he said as he attempted to put his arms around her.

"Jeremiah, leave me alone. I don't want to wake up Amari. This is hard on her," she said as she pulled away from him.

"Okay, then come back and let's talk."

"I tried to talk but you wanted to lay blame. I'm so done with you right now." "Elise, I'm sorry. I was wrong. I just…I can't explain it. But I was wrong.

And I'm sorry. Please come back to bed."

"How could you just turn on me like that?" she asked. "I didn't mean to."

"But you did. I wanna know why."

"Babe, it's just a bad day. Zach was the last shot I felt like I had. I don't know what I'm going to do for work. I didn't plan on all of this. And hearing Mama today…it was too much to handle. I got to thinking about your angel and…."

"You were like 'Why, Lord?'" Elise finished his sentence.

"Yeah. I guess I've gotten used to being in control and now everything is out of my control. It doesn't feel good. Me and you are usually on the same page, and I guess when I felt like you were siding with Mama it was one more thing out of my control."

"I never thought you wanted to control me, Miah."

"That's not what I mean. But Lise, I can't lose my mom. Especially not right now. If there's a chance for her to live, we have to take it."

"Miah, you always want to solve everything at once. Give it some time. We don't know what God has in mind. Baby, I am always on your side. But it would destroy you if you strongarmed her into something she didn't want to do and it didn't go well."

"Babe, please come back to bed. I handled this bad, but I can't deal with it all right now. I just want to hold you and go to sleep."

"That's what I was tryna do." "I know. Again, I was wrong."

"Miah, I don't do well with mistreatment. You've always been good to me, so I'm not used to you going off like that. You have to treat me right. It should be enough that I'm your wife, but I'm not just your wife anymore. I'm the mother of your child. Your children, actually. I need you to turn to me when it gets rough… not on me."

"I'm sorry," he said, placing his arms slowly around her. "Please come back to bed."

"No. I'm still mad," she said in her baby voice. "I'm sorry, gorgeous. Please forgive me."

"Are you going to be nice to me now?" she asked, easing closer into his embrace.

"Yes. I promise."

"Okay, well, I will see you when you get back." "Back?" Jeremiah asked.

"I want tacos from Jack in the Box and the baby wants an apple pie and fries from Whataburger. I will let you snuggle after you get back. Bye."

CHAPTER 25

Mother and Daughter

DAY 200

"Father," Etta Ween prayed, "I'm here on my knees loving you and trusting you. They say I have to trust you even when I can't trace you. But my God, by your grace that's not my story. I can trace you. I feel like you are closer than ever before. And that's why I am so ashamed, Lord. I feel your presence. I feel your love. Now I ask you to let me feel your forgiveness because I have a complaint. Father, I am hurting in my heart, my soul, my spirit…and especially in my body. This treatment is doing everything but help me. I was hoping you would give me one of those testimonies about not having any bad reactions, but Lord, that's not what's happening. I can't eat because I'm throwing up all the time. I can't sleep. You've taken my health and now, Lord, you've taken my hair. Father, I hate to be prideful, but you know I loved my hair," she laughed. "I'm just so tired. And I know I told you I would obey your call. I know I told you I wasn't afraid. But Father…."

Etta Ween's emotions would not allow her to finish her plea. She knelt on her living room couch and allowed her tears to speak for her. After a few moments of weeping, a new sense of peace and calm came over her. She knelt in silence for a little while longer. Then she simply said, "Yes, Lord."

She got up from her knees and sat down on the couch until she heard Elise's keys rattling at her front door.

"Hey, beautiful!" Elise said sweetly as she joined her.

"Chile, please," Etta Ween objected. "You know I am far from beautiful. But you, you are absolutely glowing. Waddle yo cute self over here and give me a hug and a kiss."

"Okay, I will be over in a minute," Elise joked as she exaggerated her pregnant walk. "Hold on, Mama Etta. Hugs and kisses coming, but umm…I may, I repeat… I may have gained a few pounds, and you may have lost a few. So, when I sit down don't go flyin'."

They both laughed out loud. Elise sat near her on the couch, locked arms with her, and leaned on her shoulder.

"How are you, Mama Etta?"

"I will tell you later, sweetheart. I promise…but you first. How are you? And how's my son?"

"Mama Etta, we're good. We're more concerned about you, sweetheart." "Elise, baby, don't do that. Don't treat me like a China plate. Tell me what's happening," Etta Ween insisted.

"Okay, Mama Etta," Elise sighed. "You want the truth? The real truth?" "That's what I want, baby."

"Well, first, there is some good news. Me and the baby are doing well. The doctor couldn't be more pleased, and we are looking forward to a healthy delivery. And the other good news is that the Lord is really blessing my business. I am closing a lot of deals and it's keeping us afloat."

"And what else?" Etta Ween asked. "You ain't told it all, baby girl."

"Mama Etta, you are going to get me in a lot of trouble. Don't break up my happy home."

"This is a mother-daughter conversation, baby. Just us girls," Etta Ween assured her.

"Well…it's getting a little bleak. Miah is under a lot of stress right now. The whole thing is still far away. They haven't come up with any proof of wrongdoing, but the investigators keep implying he must have been complicit in some way. His lawyers said it may come to a point where they recommend that he pleads guilty. If he does, they can get him probation and no jailtime. But Jeremiah isn't going to say he did something wrong when he knows he didn't. The problem is that it's hard to prove he's innocent. And if he doesn't plead guilty and the case goes to trial, he could face prison time if he's not acquitted. I don't want to believe that could ever happen, but the thought of him not being here for us is horrifying."

"And he still can't find work?" Etta Ween asked.

"No, he can't. Not really. He's driving Lyft and Uber to bring in a little money, though. He hates just sitting around. As far as fulltime work, though, he's overqualified for most positions and others won't touch him because they know about his situation. It's like a dark cloud is following him. I can tell he gets down sometimes, but he's still trusting God and staying positive. I am so thankful for his faith. He keeps telling me that God is going to come through for us and when he does, we don't want to be all surprised by it. He says he wants us to wait in expectation."

"That's my son," Etta Ween said. "But that's not everything, is it?"

"No, it's not. We're hemorrhaging money. Between him not working and attorney fees and…some other stuff, it's hard to keep up with this house note. I mean we had plans to pay it off in ten…maybe fifteen years…but now? I think the writing is on the wall. We may have to sell it. There's not much equity in it right now, but we aren't going to be able to handle that note for much longer."

"By other stuff, you mean y'all paying all the money for this experimental treatment?" Etta Ween asked.

"Mama Etta, you know we would pay a thousand times more to help you." "I do know that. And I know it's what your daddy and he wanted. I know it was out of love, but I just hate that y'all are in this bind now and I am not getting any better.

"This whole thing is like the perfect ugly storm. If Jeremiah was working it wouldn't even be an issue," Elise said.

"I can't stand them lying on my baby like that. They know he didn't have anything to do with this foolishness. I hate y'all have to go through this as hard as you have worked."

Elise laughed. "Mama Etta, I told Miah we should rob a bank. You know, just playing with him, trying to cheer him up. Then we got to thinking about it. That would never work because Miah ain't got no thug in him."

"Haaa!" Etta Ween laughed from her belly. "My baby so sweet. He would be up in there robbing the bank just as polite. I can hear him now. 'Ma'am, you sit down right here, okay? Don't be afraid. This ain't even a real gun.'"

Elise laughed with her and then asked, "Sooo… what do you want to tell me?

I told you mine. Your turn. What's happening with you and what can I do?"

"Baby, it depends on the moment. Sometimes I have faith that can move mountains and other times I feel like the Father must be angry with me. But right here, right now…with my daughter. I'm good."

Elise smiled at her words as Etta Ween continued.

"It's just that." Etta Ween stopped herself. "Never mind. It doesn't matter."

"Yes, it does matter. It's just that what?" Elise asked.

"Baby, it's so many 'just that's.' It's just that I wish I could feel better. It's just that now my family really needs me, but I feel so useless. I'm just sitting around being sick. It's just that I hate being mad. I'm praising the Lord one minute, then I'm mad at him the next because I know he's good. I know he's faithful. I know he's all powerful. And I know he's a healer. But he's not healing me."

"Mama Etta, we don't know that. God is more than able," Elise encouraged. Etta Ween continued as if Elise said nothing. "It's just that sometimes I get so anxious, I literally want to scream. I'm not used to feeling this way. It's just that I don't want to go through this anymore, but I don't want to leave y'all. It's just that I keep telling everyone that God is faithful but some days… baby girl, it's like the devil himself is leaning over my shoulder. He's saying, 'It won't be long now. I'm gon get you out of the way. Then I'm gon get yo whole family.'

"It's just that my husband is broken and trying to be strong, and he can't lean on my son because he is under attack himself. It's just that I wanted to see Amari grow up. She was so broken when you found her. I wanted to see God's grace on her life as he finished his work. And it's just that you have this beautiful life growing inside you and he will never know me. I won't ever hold him or play with him. I won't be able to tell him, 'Little boy, get down from there!' I won't ever be able to fix him his favorite dish. I don't even have my grandparent name yet. But even if I did, I won't ever hear him say it."

"Mama Etta, don't say that. We are still believing God for your healing. We have to trust him."

Etta Ween looked Elise in the eye. "Baby, I need to tell you something," she said as she repositioned herself on the couch so she could face Elise. "And it's going to be hard to hear, but I can't hold it anymore. The Lord has already let me know I am coming home to him. I knew the night we first told you. I knew when Jeremiah and your daddy asked me to take this treatment. And I know it right now. It's funny how God works. Before you got here, I was about to plead with the Lord one more time to give me more time. And…I don't have a fancy way to say it, but I feel like he spoke to me. In all of my hurt and disappointment and confusion… he spoke. He said I have finished my race and it's time to come home."

"How do you feel about that?" Elise asked.

"Baby, all I felt was…this overwhelming sense of his love…his kindness… and his patience. He was close and sweet and gentle with me. I was crying but now those tears have washed away my fear, and all that is left now is my faith. My faith tells me he is good. My faith tells me he will take care of you all when I am gone. My faith tells me that his grace is sufficient, and Jesus is enough. There is still a part of me that wants to stay, but I can't ignore his call or be mad about the way he sends for me. How can I be mad about where I'm going?"

"Mama Etta…I have to tell you something too," Elise said.

"You already know, don't you, baby?" Etta Ween asked, anticipating her thoughts.

"I do. It's like you said that first night. I saw something in your eyes. I could tell you were already at peace. I don't think Miah and Daddy can see it…but I can. It doesn't mean I want you to go. I can't tell you how much I want you to stay. But if you have to go, I want to say as many times as I can that I love you more than words can express. You mean so much to me. So much of the good the Lord has allowed in my life is because of you. I don't know if I will ever make it but when I grow up, I want to be just like you." Elise smiled even as she fought back her tears. "And if you need somebody to say it, then I will. Mama, if you have to go, then go. If the Lord is telling you to come home, then go to Him in peace. Go get your 'well done.' And by all the strength and grace the Lord will provide, I promise you that I will take care of everyone you leave behind. I can't replace you for Daddy, but I will take care of him. I'll make sure he eats, goes to his checkups, and I will make sure he lives and not just survives. I will be there for him when he cries and when his crying stops, I will make sure he laughs. I promise you; Amari will never forget you and we are going to talk about you so much your grandson will feel like you were always there. And you already know I am going to take care of Miah because I love that man. I got you."

"Thank you, sweetheart. I already knew that, but hearing you say it means more than you will ever know. Knowing I can leave my family with you gives me a peace that I can't even explain. And thank you for calling me Mama."

"Huh?" Elise was confused. "I always call you Mama."

"No, baby, you always call me Mama Etta. But a second ago, you just called me Mama. I like that. Just plain ole Mama."

"Oh, well…you are. Or at least I always wanted you to be. It always felt like that."

"It's always been like that," Etta Ween said as she kissed her cheek. "And before we both start crying like babies, I just want to encourage you to be strong. Even if you have to suffer a little while, I want you to have faith that God will restore you."

Elise's eyes widened at her words. "Mama, can I ask you a question?" she asked, almost sounding afraid.

"You know you can," Etta Ween responded gently.

"Do you remember the night you told us about the cancer?" "Of course I do. Why do you ask?"

"Do you remember Jeremiah laughing at me because I said we saw an angel?" Etta Ween laughed gently and nodded her head. "Yes, I do, baby."

"Well, one of the things he said was just like what you just said. He said after we have suffered a little while the Lord would restore us. Mama, I'm a little scared about what's next. Miah didn't just lose his job. They took his ability to make a living away. And they might take him away altogether. And now you? I wonder what's next?"

Etta Ween looked sweetly at Elise. She tried to pour all her love and care into her gaze. There was much to say, but not to Elise.

"Baby, all I can tell you is Jesus will not fail you." "Mama! See! That part! He said the same thing too!"

Etta Ween laughed. "Well, then take it as confirmation. The Lord will restore you and he will not fail you. Nothing else matters. Now I want to have some fun with my baby girl. What we doing?"

"I have something I want to give you."

"Baby, I don't need anything," Etta Ween said.

"Mama, let me do this. But you would have to go someplace with me." "Elise, that's sweet but I thought we would just stay here and laugh and talk."

"That's what we are going to do. We are going to laugh and talk right here. But we're also going someplace. We just have to use our imagination and do a little roleplay."

"Okay, so what do I have to do?" Etta Ween asked curiously.

"Like I said, just go with me. I want you to imagine we are all in the delivery room. I am about to give birth," Elise explained.

"I'm in there with you?" Etta Ween asked.

"Of course you are. Daddy not gon be in there cuz he don't need to be seeing my bizness, but you are for sure going to be in there. So, tell me what happens next. Use your imagination."

"Okay, well, it hurts because you don't have an epidural, but I keep telling you that you're going to be okay."

"Wait. What? No epidural?" Elise asked.

"Girl, hursh now. You said you wanted to play. So, your daddy is outside with Amari. And me and Jeremiah are on both sides of you. We're holding your hands. Jeremiah keeps telling you how beautiful you are and what a good job you're doing. He's feeding you ice chips and kissing you on your forehead. All that good stuff. Then he goes to the business end with the doctor and the doctor says push and I say, 'I've got you, baby girl. You can do it,' and you cry and scream and push and next thing you know the doctors and nurses are just amazed because they have never seen such a beautiful baby boy."

"I'm feeling some kind of way about this tough girl no having an epidural thing but other than that, I'm here for it. What next?" Elise asked eagerly.

"Later, I go to the nursery to see him but he's not there." "Where my baby, Mama?"

"I look around and we find all the nurses have him in a special room and they are fighting over who gets to hold him, but I put the bum rush on 'em and say, 'Give me my grandbaby. His mama misses him.' And I bring him back to you."

Elise nodded her approval. "Okay, Mama. I see you. You got the hang of this." "But I don't know his name yet. What did y'all decide?"

"The only name that fits…Jeremiah John Traylor II. But we are going to call him J.J."

"J.J., I like that!" Etta Ween agreed.

"More importantly," Elise asked, "what is your grandma name going to be? You too fly to be 'Granny.' I know you and I'm vetoing that right here and now."

Etta Ween laughed, then smiled peacefully. "I just decided that I want him to call me what you and Amari call me. Mama Etta is perfect. No need of fixing something that's not broken."

"I agree," Elise said. "So, let's get out of the hospital now. Next scene…I call you on the phone, in the middle of the night, mind you, so you better pick up!"

"You know I'll pick up, baby," Etta Ween said sweetly. "So, what do you say when you call?"

"Mama Etta," Elise said, pretending to be frantic, "J.J. won't go to sleep. He just keeps crying and crying. Should I take him to the doctor?"

"Will he nurse?" Etta Ween asked, playing along.

"No, I pop the boob in, and he pops it right out of his mouth," Elise paused and put a sly grin on her face. "He's not like his daddy."

"Girl, you a mess," Etta Ween laughed. "Get back to the scene. Has he had a bowel movement?"

"Mama, you don't even know. I think Miah done snuck this boy some steak and potatoes."

"Okay, I know what's wrong," Etta Ween concluded. "Have you swaddled him?"

"Have I what?" Elise played dumb even though she knew what she meant.

Etta Ween also knew that Elise was well aware, but they both just played each other's game. "Baby, you just need to get his blanket and make a little burrito out of him. J.J. is just missing the womb. He felt safe there and all of this is still new to him."

"Mama, you are doin' this!" Elise beamed. "Okay, I got another one. It's cute but it's kinda corny...and boring."

"Baby, when you get to be my age, boring ain't always bad. What is it?" Etta Ween asked curiously.

"Mama, I see you sitting in a rocking chair with J.J. in your arms. You're smelling his little head, soaking in all the baby smells...the nice baby smells," she emphasized. "You're playing with his curly hair and kissing his little feet. I try to get him and both of you look at me like 'Are we bothering you?'" Elise laughed. "Eventually you both fall asleep, but J.J. has this sweet smile on his face because everything is right in his world when his Mama Etta has him. And I see y'all are worn out and I get him, and I kiss you on your head and let you rest. Is that corny? That's corny, isn't it?"

"No, sweetheart. That's not corny at all. It's perfect," Etta Ween said. "Can you picture it?" Elise asked.

Etta Ween remembered her prayer. The image of her unborn grandson in her arms appeared clearly in her mind and tears of joy escaped her face. "Yes, baby. I can picture it."

"Mama, I'm sorry. You didn't like that one?"

Etta Ween struggled to speak. When she did, she said, "Thank you, Jesus." "Do you want to stop?" Elise asked her.

"No, baby. I don't want to stop. That was the best one of all. But we can keep going. I like this."

"How far do you want to take him?"

"Oh, that's easy, baby girl. I want to take him all the way until he marries someone just like you."

CHAPTER 26

New Light Shines

DAY 230

"Father," Jeremiah prayed, "I come to you remembering the cross… remembering the shed blood of your son…and I come trusting that you will remember me with grace. I come not based on anything I could ever say or do. I come based on my faith in the finished work of Christ on the cross. I come to you now with all that makes me weary and heavy laden, and I trust you for the rest that only you can provide. Jesus, I need you. Please don't let me be put to shame. I am putting my faith in you, so please be the author and the finisher of that faith. I am putting all my hope in you. You promised me that my hope would not disappoint me. Father, I believe that all these weapons that have been formed will not prosper. Let every lie be drug in to the light and exposed. I have hope in you, Lord, that you are working all of this for my good. I don't understand, but I trust you. It doesn't feel good, but I trust you. I don't see any answers or a way through, but I trust you. And if you have brought me to this place, so I could truly understand what it means to totally depend on you, then I am here for it, because I believe your promise not to leave me and not to forsake me. Lord, didn't you promise to be for me? Didn't you say it would not matter who would be against me? And didn't you say that along with Christ Jesus, you would graciously give me all things? So, Father, if you will give me grace, then I will consider it pure joy as I face this trial. It is a long trial, and it is a difficult trial, but I am going to trust you. As for me, I will always have hope. Lord, I have hope for Mama. I petition you in Jesus' name to take up the infirmity and carry the disease. I have hope for my reputation that you are my strong tower. I run to you, Jesus, and declare safety in your name. I have hope that the enemies who seek to devour me will stumble and fall, and even as war has broken out against me, I don't have to fear. Father, I have hope for my finances. You're my provider and you meet all my needs according to your glorious riches. I have hope in you for my family's peace. Please grant grace that we have peace that surpasses understanding. And with it, Lord, please give us your joy. You promised to be our very present help in our times of trouble, and Father, I need you to manifest that promise and be close to us now. I want to thank you for all you have done, and I want to thank you for my wife, for Amari, for J.J., my mom and dad. Father, your word says you do more than we can ask, imagine, or think, so I just use my imagination right now and in Jesus' name I imagine and think about my family being whole, restored, healed, and provided for. I imagine your mercy and grace providing blessings, victory, joy, and kindness in such a glorious way that we would forget the troubles we are enduring right now. Jesus, you are the faithful one. The healer. The author of life. You hold all power in your hands, and I believe that you always come through. You always rescue your people. So please show us your glory as you keep your word that my fervent prayers avail much. I believe you, Jesus. In faith, I choose not to believe the voice of the stranger in my ear. You will heal. You will set free. You will deliver. You are faithful. You are mighty to save. Lord, if you give me grace, I will not listen to the voice of the stranger. But Father, he is screaming! I try to ignore him, but he screams every day. He screams that Mama won't live. He screams that I won't ever find a job. He screams that I am going to jail. He screams you have forgotten me. He screams that you don't care. I confess sometimes I feel like you are just watching. You won't speak and you won't help. I confess that sometimes I feel like you don't see me. But I repent from those thoughts in Jesus' name, and I declare you are my refuge and my rock, and I humble myself under your mighty hand, believing in faith that in due season you will exalt me. And I believe that though you have made me see many bitter troubles that you will restore me to life again. So, I cast my cares on you knowing you care for me. You gave Jesus up for me so how will you not, along with him, graciously give me all things? Father, please grow me in your grace and accomplish your work in this trial. Please help me so that my faith doesn't fail. I want to be found trusting you. I want to be found expecting you. Please grant me the courage you granted to David, and as I face my Goliath, let me speak faith and victory as I fight in Jesus' name for your glory.

I plead with you not for what I deserve, but for what your grace has already provided for. I am in the fire, Lord…me and my whole family. But I believe you, Jesus, that you are in the fire with us, and when you bring us out, we won't be burnt up or destroyed, because you were there with us, and you covered us. I love you, Jesus. I confess there is still fear but I love you, with all my heart, mind, soul, and strength. And because I know that I'm dust, and that I am only flesh and blood, if the day comes where I can't take another step, then I still trust you because you are my shepherd who carries me forever. Lord, please grant your strength to your servant and let me have enough strength and love for Elise and my family. Please don't let me fail now, Lord. Please don't let me fail you or my family. You said you were able to keep me from stumbling, so please keep me now. Won't you please, Lord Jesus, according to your word, hold me up in your righteous right hand and give me victory? I trust you for all these things and more. In Jesus' name, Amen."

Jeremiah completed his prayer as he sat parked near the Dallas Fort Worth Airport. He checked his phone and saw a notification for a rider. Driving for Lyft and Uber wasn't exactly his dream job, but it was better than letting Elise support the family on her own. Thankfully, this would be a lucrative ride. He would have to take the rider from the airport all the way to the distant suburbs. He found the rider and helped him to get his bags into the trunk. The rider was a slim but athletic- looking white guy. He was perhaps ten years Jeremiah's junior, but he had the demeanor of a polished businessman.

"Have you lived in the Dallas area long?" his passenger asked in a friendly tone.

"Yeah, man, all my life, actually," Jeremiah responded, trying to match his energy.

"So, is it safe to say you like it?"

"Well…it's home so I may be biased, but I think it's great. In my former job, I had to travel all over the country. But I always loved coming back here."

"Man, I hope I do. But I don't think I will. I'm a California boy through and through. Texas? Yeah, great cost of living but forget all that. I love LA."

"So, you're moving here?" Jeremiah inquired. "It's looking like that," the man said rather flatly. "Don't worry, man, you'll like it."

"I hope so, man. You said you used to travel a lot. What did you do?"

Jeremiah wondered how transparent he should be but decided he might as well use this talkative stranger he would never see again for free therapy.

"Well, you might not believe it, but I was a project manager and for a short time, the vice president for a commercial construction company called Jacebre. I started out with them as a project engineer and eventually was vice president of construction."

"I've heard of Jacebre. That's a pretty big company. Feel free to tell me to mind my own business, but if you don't mind my asking…."

"Why am I driving you around?" Jeremiah finished his question. "Well, yeah. Do you just like getting out of the house or what?"

"Ha. It's definitely 'or what,'" Jeremiah said. "A few months ago, we were awarded one of the biggest jobs in the state, and by far the biggest in company history. I was promoted to vice president on the same day. Well, a little time goes by, and I come into the office one day and they fired me on the spot. They said the FBI had accused us of bid rigging, and my projects, especially the big one I mentioned, were at the center of it all. They wouldn't even let me explain. Then they had security walk me out. They had a press conference and everything. My name got put out on the news and more importantly to every other firm in the city. Makes it kind of hard to find work. So now, I'm driving you."

"Wow, man. That sounds like it was brutal," the rider said sympathetically. "Was?" Jeremiah said. "It still is. The FBI is still investigating. It takes time

for them to review everything and decide what to do. My lawyer says if I am telling the truth, which I am by the way, that it might not even go to trial. If it does, he's optimistic that I would be acquitted. But there's always the possibility that it won't go my way. For now, I am essentially blackballed in the construction industry. No one wants to hire me with this hanging over my head. And we recently got a new house and I no longer have the salary to support it. Oh, by the way, my wife is pregnant with our first child and my mom has cancer…so there's that. But don't worry, man. I am sure Texas is going to be much kinder to you," Jeremiah said, trying to lighten the mood.

His passenger just sat in silence, and Jeremiah realized he had probably given out too much unwanted information.

"Hey, sir, I'm sorry," Jeremiah said humbly. "I didn't mean to dump all of that on you."

"No, dude, I asked. Really, it's okay. If you don't mind, can you tell me a little more?" the rider asked, leaning toward the front seat.

Jeremiah was surprised by the question…and a little annoyed. What else did he want to know? And why? "That's really the heart of it," he responded.

"Well, let me be clearer. In a nutshell, you're telling me you didn't do anything wrong?"

"No, sir," Jeremiah said, trying to be patient. After all, he was the one who opened his mouth and told all his business. "Except for maybe being a little naïve," he added.

"Like I said," his passenger continued, "I've heard of Jacebre. I know they're a pretty big company. It's sad that they didn't stand with you on this, but that's not where I am going. Let me just get to it. It's obvious you know commercial construction. And it's obvious you need work. Have you ever considered residential construction? There may not be as much scrutiny with the right company."

"It's funny you say that. That house I was telling you about. I essentially remodeled it for my wife. It was a lot of work, but I really enjoyed it. I hadn't thought about residential, but you might be right. I don't have any connections in that arena, though."

"Well, you do now. What's your name, man?" "Jeremiah."

"Jeremiah, my name is Chad Wood. I own Trinity Homes with my older brother and my dad. We're developing several neighborhoods in the area, and we have really struggled to find the talent and experience needed to get the job done. That's why I'm having to move here. My brother made the last move. And understandably, he says it's my turn. I've tried for over a year now to find someone to drive this forward, but until now I have failed. I don't believe in coincidences. I'm looking for a construction manager, you're out of work, and I happen to get you to drive me to the development? Things like that only happen in the movies. But this is real. What do you think?"

Jeremiah wanted to slam on the breaks, jump out of the car, and shout. But disappointment after disappointment had left him a little jaded about how real this too good-to-be-true opportunity was.

"Mr. Wood, I'm flattered, and I appreciate the opportunity, but it's a different direction for me. I would like to try but I don't want to let you down," Jeremiah said.

"Jeremiah, hear me on this. I've only known you for a few minutes, but I make quick decisions. I believe your story and I believe in you. So, if you're telling me I'm making a mistake, well, I guess I have to believe that too. So, is that what you're saying? Would I be making a mistake to bring you on?" Chad asked bluntly.

Jeremiah smiled, said a quick "Thank you, Jesus" to himself, then said out loud, "No, Mr. Wood. You would not be making a mistake to bring me on."

"That's what I thought. And it's Chad. But listen, I do have to run this by my brother and my dad. They're gonna grill you a little harder than I did. My brother is going to want to know more about your abilities. And my dad is going to want to get some assurances about this bid rigging accusation. But you have me in your corner. What are you doing the rest of the day?"

"Well, I am supposed to spend some time later with my mom to see how she is doing."

"That's totally understandable, but can you spare a couple of hours?" "Yeah, I can do that," Jeremiah said eagerly.

"Good," Chad nodded. "The place you're taking me is the development site. I just want you to listen in on the team meeting so you can get a feel for some of our goals. Then, I want to get you on a call with my dad and my brother. You make a good first impression, brother, and believe me, you're going to need to. This thing isn't in the bag yet."

"So, Chad…question?" "Go ahead, buddy."

"Is all this just so you don't have to move to Texas?"

Chad laughed. "Dude, I despise Texas and I've only been here for twenty minutes. But I despise failing even more. I think you can help us succeed, and I think you need a second chance with someone who isn't worried about all the political bull. Now I can tell you already, you aren't gonna make what you were making with an outfit like Jacebre, but we will take care of you."

"Sounds like a plan," Jeremiah said as he smiled from ear to ear. In his mind, he added to his previous prayer. *"Father, that part about not hearing from you and you not seeing me…my bad. Good looking out."*

CHAPTER 27

New Victory

DAY 230

Elise sat at her computer preparing her appointments for tomorrow. She had several opportunities to close on some very lucrative properties before her son was born. They would need every dime from the commission checks. She was hoping to take at least a full year off after J.J. was born, but that wouldn't be feasible without Jeremiah working. Etta Ween's medical bills, attorney costs, and their new mortgage had put them in unfamiliar financial distress. Still, she was at peace.

"Daddy," she prayed. "Thank you for everything you have done for me and my family. I love you, and I know you love me. When you let me have this blessing, I told you it was a perfect moment. And Daddy, it still is. But we need you. We need you to come through for us. And I need you to come through for my husband. You made him to be a protector and provider and he feels like you have taken that away from him. Daddy, I know you give, and you take away, but I am asking as your daughter that you please give it back. Please restore him and grant back to him everything the enemy has stolen. I trust you so much. Please get us through this season and show us your glory. In Jesus' name, Amen."

"Amen," Jeremiah agreed.

"Boy, what you doin' home and listenin' in on my prayers? Is nothing sacred?" "I'm sorry, gorgeous. But thank you for praying for me."

"Excuse me. I didn't hear you. Say that again," Elise said. "Umm… thank you for praying for me," Jeremiah teased. "Before that, sir."

"Oh, Amen," Jeremiah said. "Wonderful prayer, babe." "Strike two, Elder-in-Waiting Traylor."

"Oh, you mean the part where I called you 'gorgeous'?" "That part!" Elise confirmed. "You know, you could...."

Before she could finish her thought, Jeremiah turned her office chair around, knelt down in front of her, and kissed her.

"How rude," she stammered, a little taken aback by his passionate kiss. "First you listen in on my prayers and now you won't let me talk."

"Yeah, let's continue that...hush and listen." "I know you didn't just tell...," Elise started.

"Did," Jeremiah cut her off again. "I told you to hush and listen," he said, sealing his words with another sweet kiss. "Babe...thank you. Thank you, for loving me. Thank you, for sticking with me. Thank you, for believing in me. Thank you, for holding this family down. Thank you, for never saying 'I told you so.' Thank you, for carrying my child. Thank you, for bringing Amari into our lives. Thank you, for being my wife. After almost twenty years, you keep topping yourself. Everything you say, everything you do, shows me God's grace because I know I could never deserve you. I appreciate every joke. Every prayer. Every conversation. It's hard to describe, but through all these last few months, my life with you...it's like I'm climbing Mount Everest and I think I'm at the top. I'm just about to plant the flag but then you come in and say, 'Oh, we can go higher. There's more to me and it's even better. Let's go.' I am still in awe of you, babe. You're my everything and I love you with everything in me."

"Hush and listen?" Elise asked.

Jeremiah's eyes widened. "Is that all you heard?" he asked, shaking his head. "Oh, for sure, I heard that," Elise said, pretending to be angry.

"Okay, my bad, babe. Let me have it."

"Oh, I am going to let you have it all right, mister," she said, articulating every syllable. "First of all, Mr. Traylor, let me tell you something," she said as she pulled his face back to hers and returned his kiss. "Secondly," she continued, "hello, handsome. How are you?"

"I was good, but I'm better now," he responded.

"Just coming off in here kissing folks. Boy, I'm eight months pregnant, you know I be snackin'! I could have had food in my mouth," she laughed.

"So, am I forgiven for daring to tell you to hush?" Jeremiah asked.

"Well…I guess. But I also want to say thank you. God, for whatever reason, has allowed us to be tested. I don't think either of us were ready for all of this, but I just want you to know that I am here for it! I'm here for you, baby. I would go through all of this with you a thousand times over as long as you are here. You have been, you are now, and you will always be my history-making, lifechanging love of my life. Forever my boyfriend, my man, my husband, my Miah. You have my heart, and I don't want it back because I know it will always be safe with you. Sooo…now that we've said all that…what's up? You tryna get some of this scrumptu-licious loving before you go see Mama Etta? Cuz it ain't take all that. I'm jus' sayin'."

"Huh?" Jeremiah asked innocently.

"Negro, don't huh me. Don't get me wrong. You sweet and all that but you ain't came up in here with all this unbridled affection and gushy, mushy words for nuthin'. Talkin' 'bout Mount Everest knowin' you don't like the cold. You either tryna sneak me to the bedroom before Amari come knockin' or something else has happened. What's up?"

"Welll…I meant all that stuff…so there's that," Jeremiah said.
"But?" Elise asked.

"But…something did happen. Babe…I got a job. A real job. A pretty good job, actually," he announced proudly.

"Yesssss! Thank you, Jesus," Elise screamed with joy. "Ooh, Miah, please tell me it's a direct competitor of Jacebre? I want you to stick it to them. Tell me everything!"

"Babe, it literally was nobody but God. I was driving and I was just praying for the Lord to help us. So, I pick up this rider and he and I just get to talking. I don't know why but I told him everything that I went through with Jacebre. It turns out he's a homebuilder and he didn't care about all that nonsense. Long story short…he said he wanted me. We went to his development site, I met his team, and God just started moving. He gave me all the right questions to ask and all the right things to say. We were really vibing."

"Baby, do you know anything about residential construction?" Elise asked. "Not a darned thing, ma'am, but we're back to hush and listen," Jeremiah said.

"Oh, sorry, sir! Please continue," Elise said, smiling from ear to ear. She was so happy to see him like this. He looked like the whole world had been lifted from his shoulders.

"Thank you, ma'am. I will. So, after the meeting he wants me to have a conference with his dad and older brother. They all own the company together. The brother…he wanted to try me."

"I know he did not try to try my baby," Elise said jokingly.

"Oh, yes, he did," Jeremiah confirmed. "He got to asking all sorts of questions, scheduling, dealing with subcontractors, how I deal with delays and problems. Just goin' in on yo man."

"And my baby answered them all cuz he is…wait for it…the man!" Elise encouraged.

"Well, I was gonna say God just gave me the right answers…but your answer works."

"Uh-huh. I notice you didn't tell me to hush and listen that time but proceed."

Jeremiah laughed and continued. "Then he says to his younger brother, the one who wants to bring me on, his name is Chad. He says, 'Chad, I see where you are going with this. I agree with it as long as you're going to ride shotgun with him for the first few months. I think it will work. At the end of the day, construction is construction, right?'"

"That sounds good, Miah."

"It is, but now I get nervous because the whole point for Chad wanting me is so he won't have to move here. He might not want to do that. But then Chad goes, 'Yeah, I figured you'd say that. That's what I had in mind. I can spend one or two days a week with him here and come down if there are emergencies.'"

"You got that favor, baby!" Elise shouted.

"But I still have to get past the dad. He asks me about Jacebre. He starts talking about character, reliability, loyalty, and trust. I assure him I believe in those same things and how important it is for me to show that, considering the allegations. Then he asks me point blank were any of the accusations true. I looked into the screen and told him, 'No, sir, not at all.' He said he believed me but that he wanted something in writing saying that my employment would be probational, contingent upon currently known facts. Then he tells Chad, right there in front of me, that it's on him if it doesn't work out. And babe, Chad doesn't bat an eye. He says, 'Dad, it will work out. This is gonna be good for the business.' So, his dad says, 'Okay, let's do it,' and welcomes me aboard."

"Miah, I am so proud of you," Elise said, still smiling from ear to ear. "Sooo… not that it's important, but how much money you gon be making? Asking for a friend. It's me. I'm the friend."

"Babe, it's a smaller company. I'm only going to be making half of what I was making at Jacebre."

"Baby, half is great. We would have consistent money coming in to stay solid on the house note, pay our lawyer, and the medical bills. And don't you worry yo little handsome self about the rest. Yo sugar mama will handle it. I am sure we can figure out other ways for you to contribute," Elise said slyly.

"Oh, really? Well, you know I want to contribute but I don't know what to do. What could I give you?" Jeremiah asked.

"You know, you two should really take a tour of this house and start using all these bedrooms. You can't be exposing my baby brother to these grown people shenanigans when he comes," Amari interrupted.

"Amari! I'm gon put a bell on you. What you need, baby?" Jeremiah asked as he wondered how long she had been there.

"Well, little kids need love too, Uncle J. Just sayin'."

"Mari, T.T. is going to take Uncle J upstairs for some… praise and worship grown folks version and then we can get some snacks together for our night with Papa John and send your Uncle J to his date night with Mama Etta."

"Lise, we reaaally gotta talk about our parenting approach, babe," Jeremiah said, shaking his head.

"Boy, she don't know all the ins and outs…even though I know you do," she whispered. "She just knows that's our private time together. And she also knows it's because we love each other and are married. Stop being so stiff…well, not all of you but you know what I mean."

"I can hear you, T Lise!" Amari said loudly.

"Did you hear the part where I said mind ya bizness?" Elise laughed.

CHAPTER 28

Mother and Son

DAY 230

"Hey, Mama!" Jeremiah greeted Etta Ween enthusiastically. "Guess what?" "You found a job! Baby, I'm so proud of you. My baby gon be building houses," Etta Ween said happily.

"Elise told you?" Jeremiah said as he imagined Elise picking up the phone the second he left the house.

"Oh, you wanted to tell me?" Etta Ween asked.

"It would have been nice…but yeah, Mama. I got a job."

"This Chad sounds like a nice fella. His brother and daddy like you too. That's God's favor right there, baby."

Jeremiah laughed. "Oh, so you know my boss's name and everything, huh?" Etta Ween laughed with her son. "Baby, it 'bout would have killed Elise to hold that in. Let her brag on her man. I am so glad to see you. Come sit with me for a minute."

Jeremiah sat next to her. The thin, frail, balding woman beside him was almost unrecognizable as his mother. Her body was worn but there was still that familiar spark of love in her eye. A spark that let him know everything was going to be all right. Now he needed to let her know everything was going to be all right as well. "Mama…Elise and I have been talking. Well, Elise has been talking. I've just been trying to listen."

"What have y'all been talking about?" Etta Ween asked.

Jeremiah sat for a moment. He had to pause. If he spoke now, he would only cry.

"Take your time, baby. What you got to tell Mama that got you like this? I already know you got that fast thang pregnant. Y'all married, though. It's okay," Etta Ween teased him.

Jeremiah smiled as his mother's humor helped chase his fears away. "Mama…Elise told me that I should tell you some things. I think you already know but I want to say it again. I want to tell you that you're more than my mother. You're my best friend. Pop taught me the power of God. But you taught me his grace and his love. I always wanted to make Pop proud. But you were the one I always wanted to make happy. I hope all that makes sense."

"It does, baby," Etta Ween confirmed. "And I am happy."

"I also wanted to say that I'm sorry. I made you feel bad because you didn't want to take this treatment. I should have listened to you and thought about you more."

"Baby, that was you and yo daddy. And you know what? It's okay. At least we know we did all we could. Mama not mad. At you. Your daddy. Or at the Lord. I'm mostly at peace."

"Mostly?" Jeremiah questioned.

"Yes, mostly. I think I can only be at real peace once I know you and your daddy are. So, are you at peace, baby? Tell me the truth."

Jeremiah felt his emotions taking over again. "Mama," he said, struggling to speak, "I'm trying to be at peace with all of this. I'm trying to be thankful. I'm trying to trust. But I want you here. It's still hard to accept that it's your time. I keep trying to figure out what God is doing and nothing tracks. I'm trying to remember he's good, but this doesn't seem good."

"Oh, this is definitely not good," Etta Ween said, rubbing her hand across her nearly bald head. "But will we take good things from our Father and not bad? Are we so quick to forget his kindness to us? Are we the ones who forget the cross when life is not easy? Are we the ones who forget he works all things together for our good? And are we so quick to forget we are not home? And that where we are going is so much better than where we are leaving? Don't get me wrong, baby. I want to stay here with you. I want to see all the amazing things God is going to do. But baby…he's shown me plenty. Plenty of love and plenty of mercy and plenty of grace. I'm not saying I understand it all, but I do understand it's time."

"Mama, I know you're right…I just honestly thought that if we prayed hard enough…fasted long enough…that God would come through and heal you. I thought we were acting in faith and that God would respond."

"Baby, we did…and God did. Or at least he will." "Say more," Jeremiah said.

"What I mean is, we did act in faith, and He will heal me. And not like you mean. And not just a little bit. Not just so I can die in a few years anyway. His healing will be perfect. He will heal me so I can know him and love him forever. Baby, I'm sorry that you are going to have to cry. I would do anything to spare you from it…I would. But you need to know that before too long yo mama won't ever cry again. Try to take comfort in that. And remember the good times. We had a good run, didn't we?" she said as she patted him on his thigh.

Jeremiah leaned over and kissed her on the cheek. "We did, Mama," he smiled even as he allowed his tears to flow. "But this is hard. I guess it's a good thing you built my self-esteem…and taught me to pray… and taught me how to declare God's promises for my life…and taught me to not give up…and taught me to trust God when I couldn't trace him. If you hadn't, I don't know if I could make it through all of this. But you did. And Mama…I can make it. I just want you to know that." "Come here, Mama Baby," Etta Ween said as she struggled to put her arms around him. "I know you can. But thank you for saying that. I know it's hard and what I have to say now will be hard too. But I need you to listen."

"Okay," Jeremiah said reluctantly, wondering what she could possibly have to say.

"Baby, you need to steady your heart. This little job thing…this little legal stuff…baby, that's nothing. Your faith is going to be tested like it has never been tested before. The Lord will allow your heart to be broken but even in the brokenness he will be close. You won't see him or feel him, but he will be near. Your spirit will be crushed but he will save you. I don't know why the Lord has chosen you for this, but he has and you have to trust him. It's going to look like he has forgotten you because he will allow the unimaginable and the unthinkable to overwhelm you. You will run to shelter, but your hiding places will hide from you. You will want to give up, curse God and die. Everywhere you look there will be destruction and despair as the enemy crashes everything around you. But hear me, baby…after the crash, when all is lost and you are in your lowest valley, I want you to open your mouth and praise the name of Jesus. And soon after…he will turn it around. The trial won't last forever."

Jeremiah shook his head. "Mama, I don't know what to do with all of this." "I know, baby. But God knows exactly what to do. Keep your eyes on him. I wish I could stay here and fight with you, but Mama can't stay here. Not like this. God allowed this. He is preparing my spirit for him by allowing my body to break. But he's not angry and he is not weak. He loves us and he won't stop. And I won't stop loving you."

"I love you too, Mama."

"But I do have one more thing I feel the Lord would have me tell you." "What is it, Mama?"

"You need to forgive Elise. This is hard for a mother to say, but I'm glad it's true. That girl loves you even more than I do. So don't you let her go. I don't care what happens."

Her statement confused Jeremiah. "Mama, me and Elise are good. I promise.

There's nothing to forgive."

Etta Ween looked deeply into her son's eyes. "Did you hear me?" "Yes, I did."

"That's all that matters. It doesn't make sense now but when the time comes, it will. She is your wife. God gave her to you. You make sure you protect her and cherish her and keep her. What is that she says all the time? She will drive and kill for you?"

"No, Mama," he laughed. "That's ride or die. Although with Elise, the first statement probably isn't too far off either."

"Whatever," she giggled. "You just hear me. You stick with your wife no matter what. If she rob a bank, you drive the getaway car. And if she falls in a pigpen, you better be the first one there with a bucket of water and soap. I know you don't understand. Just put this in your pocket and save it for later. Now come on. Help me up."

"Where we going?" Jeremiah asked.

"We goin' to the kitchen. You gon help me fix dinner like when you were little."

"Mama, no. You don't have to do that."

"Little boy, this is my date night. I can get what I want. And this is what I want. Don't worry. It ain't big. Elise marinated the chicken for me. You and I just have to drop it in some grease. She also made the greens for me…and the rice and gravy…and the cake… and the tea," she laughed.

"Dang Mama…did you make anything?" Jeremiah meddled.

"I made you, boy!" she quipped as she jabbed her finger in his chest. "Now turn that burner on and let's fry this chicken."

Jeremiah reached for the pan full of the chicken that was ready to be cooked. On it was a note from Elise: "Hey, baby. I love you. Enjoy this time. I will wait up for you so you can tell me how everything went. Remember what I told you to tell her. We will make it through this. Forever your girl - Lise."

Jeremiah smiled. He remembered his mother's words from just a few moments ago as he helped her with the chicken. He trusted his mother's discernment, but he couldn't imagine Elise doing anything that would warrant him having to be told to forgive her. He would have to mull that over later. This was his mom's time. And it was a good one.

Dinner was simple but delicious. In this space there was no sickness, no questions, and no insurmountable problems. There was just a mother and son enjoying each other.

"Mama," Jeremiah said, "I just want you to know I remember everything." "Like what, baby?" Etta Ween asked.

"Like when I got that bad grade, and I was talking about being stupid. I didn't think I would ever be able to figure out math and you just kept encouraging me. And like when I snuck out, stole Daddy's car, and put that ding in it. You knew he was going to kill me, but you covered for me even though you knew I was lying."

"Boy, I ain't covered for you. I thought you was telling the truth!" "Oh...my bad. But yeah, I was lying...water under the bridge," Jeremiah said

casually.

"I'm gon water yo bridge. Bad tail little boy!" Etta Ween teased.

"Anyway," Jeremiah said, continuing their walk down memory lane, "remember when me and Elise were first married? We had a big ole fight and she stormed out the house."

"And came here!" Etta Ween burst forth laughing.

"I was like… 'how she gon leave me and go to my mama and daddy house?'"

"But you know what? That's when I knew that was my baby girl. Baby… mama sorry, but we talked about you like a dog that night."

"Mama!"

"Well, you be lying about stealing folks' cars, I had to make Elise feel like she had somebody to vent to. At least I sent her home after we talked about you."

They continued to share stories like that, and Etta Ween thought it would be nice to have the entire family there.

"Baby, call your daddy and tell him to come home." "Mama, you tired of me? I thought we were having fun?"

"We are. Let's do this right. Tell your daddy to come home. And tell him to bring Elise and Amari."

CHAPTER 29

I Don't Need Anything Else

DAY 230

John, Elise, and Amari had joined Etta Ween and Jeremiah. Etta Ween was snuggled next to her husband with Amari close to her side. Jeremiah and Elise sat opposite of them.

"Haaaa!" Elise laughed. "Mama, why you tell Jeremiah my bizness? He don't need to know everything.

"Baby, we just been telling all the family secrets tonight. Everybody can get it," Etta Ween said.

"Weenie, speaking of getting it. We need to get on our son over there," John said.

"What did I do?" Jeremiah asked.

"It don't matter," Etta Ween said mischievously. "You gon get it. What we gettin' him for, baby?" she chuckled. She was exhausted but absolutely did not want this night to end.

"Oh, I'm gon tell you, baby. Jeremiah, I been meaning to ask you, why didn't you tell me and your mama you was working on that house? I could have helped. I could have made some runs for you. Checked on things for you. You 'bout drove yoself crazy sneaking about and trying not to let Elise find out. You should have let me help you."

"Oh, my bad, Pop. I'm sorry. It was just a surprise for Elise," Jeremiah said. "That's fine, son. But why didn't you let me and your mama help you?" John asked. "That bothered us, right, Weenie? Every time I bring it up, yo mama get all quiet. And I just let it go cuz I don't want to upset her." "Uh-huh," Etta Ween said sheepishly.

Elise turned her face into Jeremiah's shoulder to hide her expression.

"Y'all shole is quiet. I thought everybody could get it. So, let's get him. And Elise, are you laughin' at over there? I'm serious, baby."

"I know, Daddy," Elise said, trying to contain herself. "It's just that…Daddy, they hate us because they ain't us. They don't understand what me and you got. But it's okay."

"Elise, what you talkin' about?" John asked, confused.

"Baby, just go ahead and tell him. We done held this too long," Etta Ween said.

"Well…," Elise started.

"Nope," Etta Ween stopped her. "Make Jeremiah tell him. We women can't do everything. Man up, boy! Talk to yo daddy. Tell him what you did."

"Woowww, Mama. It's real uncomfortable under this bus you just threw me under."

"Mama Etta is right, baby. Go ahead and tell Daddy what you did," Elise said. "Et tu, Lise? What happened to Miah and Lise against the world?"

"Oh, that's still in effect…but this is Daddy we talking about. Handle yo bizness.

Jeremiah took a deep breath. "Okay, Daddy. What had happened was…." "Oh, Jesus, this 'bout to be some mess!" John said. "Jeremiah, I thought you

was the one with some sense. What did you do and what does it have to do with me helping you with your house and not telling me and your mama?"

"Daddy… you see…like I said. It was a surprise. I repeat, a surprise for Elise. And…well, you know how you are with Elise. She has you wrapped around her finger, and you would have broken down and told her."

"So, you thought if we knew, we would tell Elise?" John asked.

"Yeah, about that, Pop. You see, I had to get some input. I needed some female guidance on some things. So…."

"Weenie, he told you!" John exclaimed.

"He did, baby. We have a good son but he shole did you wrong on that one," Etta Ween said, her eyes half closed.

"Well, why didn't you tell me, baby?" John asked. "He swore me to secrecy, baby. It was awful."

Jeremiah looked at his mother in disbelief. "Nope. Uh-uh. I'm not letting you get away with that, Mama. Daddy, Mama said you can't keep nuthin' from Elise and I bet not tell you or you was gon mess up the whole thang. So Mama did you just as wrong as I did."

Etta Ween snuggled just a little closer to her husband. "Well, you can tell on yo mama all you want to. My husband ain't gon get mad at me. Are you, baby?" Etta Ween said confidently.

"No, I'm not, baby. Jeremiah, I can't believe you. Telling everybody but me. And then don't know what you talkin' 'bout. Elise don't run me. If you needed me to keep a secret from her, I would have."

Everyone paused and looked at John before letting their laughter explode. "Daddy, it's okay," Elise comforted. "Miah just knows how you are about me.

And I'm here for it. But umm…you know you would have let the cat out of the bag. I wouldn't even know and you'd be all smiling. I'd have known something was up and after that, I'd just bat these eyelashes, give you one of them 'Hey, Daddy, what's up's', and all the little beans just be spilt."

"No, they would not have," John objected.

"Daddy, come on now," Elise said, smiling sweetly. "Look me in the eye and say that one more time."

John stared at the wall. "I wouldn't have told you anything." "She said look at her, Papa John," Amari added.

"Okay, then maybe I would have," John conceded. "I just wouldn't have wanted you to wait all that time. That's all,"

"It's okay, Daddy. So, you forgive my Miah?" Elise asked him.

"Yeah, I guess so. But not 'til tomorrow. Yo mama is tired. Y'all go on home and me and my son can make up proper then."

"Nooo," Etta Ween objected. "This is so nice. Let's just stay out here and talk."

"Slumber party!" Amari exclaimed. "Yay. Slumber party," Elise agreed.

They stayed up laughing, talking, teasing each other, and remembering their life together. They ate leftover chicken and splurged on Elise's cake. They made popcorn and enjoyed each other. In some ways, it was like it always was. They were just a small family who loved each other. Still, something was different about this moment. Something very precious. The evening gave way to morning and exhausted as she was, Etta Ween wanted more.

"Amari, can you do Mama Etta a favor?" "Yes, ma'am."

"I want you and T Lise to sing that song you have been working on." "Mama Etta, that song is so hard. It's not ready yet. Can you wait until we sing it at church?"

Elise looked at Etta Ween. They shared no words, but they communicated. "It's ready, Mari. Come sit with me. I will sing it with you," Elise said.

Amari got up and stood near Elise.

"It's okay, baby, just relax and remember what we talked about," Elise encouraged her.

"I would only do this for you, Mama Etta," Amari said nervously as she took a deep breath and started to sing.

Bless the Lord Oh my soul, Oh my soul
Worship his holy name
Sing like never before, Oh my soul
Worship his holy name, I worship your holy name

The sun comes up, it's a new day dawning
It's time to sing your song again
Whatever may pass and whatever lies before me

Let me be singing when the evening comes

Elise stood next to her and began to sing with her.
You're rich in love and you're slow to anger
Your name is great and your heart is kind
For all your goodness I will keep on singing
10,000 reasons for my heart to find

Elise carefully lowered her pregnant frame to the floor and knelt in front of her mother. She gently grasped her hands and sang the last verse by herself.

And on that day, when my strength is failing
The end draws near and my time has come
Still my soul will sing your praise unending
10,000 years and then forever more

Bless the Lord Oh my soul, Oh my soul
Worship his holy name
Sing like never before, Oh my soul
Worship his holy name,
I worship your holy name (Matt Redman, "10,000 Reasons")

Elise finished her song but she and Etta Ween did not let go of one another's hands. No one spoke for fear of ruining the moment.

Etta Ween eventually broke the silence. "I love you, daughter," she whispered. "I love you, Mama," Elise responded.

"Come here, Amari," Etta Ween said. "I want to hug both my girls. Thank you, Baby Girl. That was beautiful. Mama Etta is so proud of you. I want you to make me a promise. I want you to promise me you will never forget how beautiful you are, how much I love you, and how much God loves you. Can you promise me that?"

"Yes, ma'am. I promise," Amari said. "I love you too."

"Now, you two let me sit with my husband," Etta Ween told them.

Elise released her and turned off the lights before she sat back down with Jeremiah and Amari. The only light remaining was from the nearby kitchen. No one questioned why she did that. They were all still afraid to speak.

Eventually, John broke the silence again. "Amari, did I ever tell you how I met your Mama Etta?" he asked softly as he pulled his wife back into his embrace.

"Yes, sir. But I love that story. You can tell it again."

"Yes, baby. Tell it again," Etta Ween whispered as she closed her eyes. "It's simple, really," John started. "I went to go see Wayne preach." "You mean Pastor G.?" Amari asked.

"Ha, yes, baby. Pastor G. Well, he was nervous and he wanted a friendly face in the crowd that he could see. So, he asked me to sit on the front row of the church.

It didn't really bother me, so I found a spot in the front so I could support my friend. And the next thing I know, your Mama Etta came bouncin' in talkin' 'bout 'Good morning.' Now mind you, baby, this was a night service, but she said 'Good morning' like it was seven A.M. And I saw her and was just awestruck. I had never seen someone so beautiful. It was like the sun had come out in the middle of the sanctuary. She lit up the room."

"But you were afraid to talk to her, huh?" Amari asked.

"Baby, let me tell my story," John laughed. "But yeah, your Papa John was afraid. She was clearly out of my league. I did want to talk to her, but I had no idea what to say. But God made a way. Pastor G. preached a good word, and he made a few funny comments, and that allowed us to talk and laugh with each other. I thought she had the sweetest voice. And I guess she thought I was funny."

"So y'all two just on the front row talking in church?" Elise asked. "The whole time. Just up in there cuttin' up in the house of the Lord."

"And when service was over?" Jeremiah asked, already knowing the answer. "Hush, boy, we still not friends yet," John jokingly snapped.

"No, I don't need anything else," Etta Ween said.

They all looked curiously at each other in the dimly lit room. No one had asked Etta Ween a question that would prompt that response.

"Yes, I am," she continued. "I know you will."

"Baby, are you okay? What are you talking about?" John asked as he kissed her sweetly on the forehead.

"I'm fine, baby. Keep talking. I love this story. I'm listening. Tell them what happened next."

"Well, as your son has already implied, church was over but I was afraid to ask you your name or where you were going or if I could see you home. You told me to have a good night and you walked away. I felt like you had taken my heart with you. But what I didn't know was that you did. You had been praying all night that I would ask you your name and ask you out. And you prayed that the Lord would give you my heart. And the Lord answered your prayer because even though I was afraid, the Lord had already given you my heart."

"Tell us about the next time you saw her," Elise asked.

"The next time I saw her, I was helping greet people at some church function.

And she showed up."

"She was fine, wasn't she, Daddy?" Elise teased.

"Daddy's Girl, I gotta tell the truth and shame the devil! Yes, yo Mama Etta was fine," John confirmed. "And still is."

"And you was still scared?" Jeremiah teased.

"You 'bout to get writ out the will, son. Go on now. And yes, I was still scared but I knew I had to say something, so I remembered how she walked in at night the last time talking about 'Good morning' and how we sat together on the front row. So, I said, 'Good morning, front row!' She laughed and we got to talking and ever since that day, it's been a good morning for me because of my Weenie. Ain't that right, baby?" John said as he shook her gently. "Ain't that right, baby?" he said again. "Baby? Baby?" John repeated, shaking her gently.

"Weenie?"

CHAPTER 30

Angel Takes Flight

DAY 231

"Shh, shh, it's going to be okay, Mari," Elise comforted. "She's in heaven now."

"I don't want her to go. I thought God was going to heal her. We prayed!" Amari protested.

"He did, baby… maybe not like we wanted or asked…but your Mama Etta is healed. It's okay to cry, though."

Jeremiah knelt next to his father, who was still holding tightly to his wife. He searched for the words, but they wouldn't come. All he knew to do was put his hand on his shoulder.

"I thought we had a little more time, son," John told him. "But I bless God. I think she knew. That's why she had you ask me to come home. That's why she wanted the girls here. This is how she wanted to leave. I thank God she died in my arms. Thank you, Jesus."

His father's faith encouraged Jeremiah and gave him the words he was looking for. "This was a good night, Pop," he said. "This is how Mama wanted to leave." "How much time do we have before the funeral home gets here, son?" John asked.

"I don't know, Pop. You want me to call them again?" Jeremiah asked.

"No, not really, son. The truth is…," his father's voice cracked, "the truth is," he repeated as he struggled to control himself against the weight of his emotions, "I know I'm not holding her anymore, but I still don't want her to go."

Elise continued to rock Amari, who was slowly crying herself to sleep when the doorbell rang.

"Miah, that's them," Elise said. She looked at John as he held on to Etta Ween's shell. "Tell them we need a minute."

"Okay," Jeremiah agreed.

Jeremiah went to the front door to let the young man from the funeral home in.

"Hello, sir. My name is Glen Johnson. I am sorry for your loss. I am here to pick up your loved one."

"Hi Glen," Jeremiah responded. "We need a few minutes, please." "Yes, sir, I understand."

Jeremiah returned and found his dad still cradling his mother in his arms. Elise laid Amari down and stood next to Jeremiah, who instinctively grabbed her hand. Her touch strengthened him.

"Pop," he said gently, "it's time. Do you want to be by yourself with her for a moment?"

"I don't know what to say, son. I guess I have to, don't I?" he asked, almost as if asking his approval.

"Well, eventually, yes, Pop. But if you need a little bit, it's okay."

"My Weenie is gone, isn't she?" he asked. His voice was calm even as the tears streamed down his face.

Jeremiah and Elise allowed their tears to flow as well.

"She's gone in the way that we are used to, but she will always be with us, Pop."

"Son, I don't know what to do," he said, still cradling his wife.

"You don't have to know, Pop. You taught me everything. I'm here. Elise is here. God is with us." Keeping hold of Elise's hand, he knelt next to his father and placed his hand on his even as he held on to his wife. "Father," he prayed, "we just want thank you for the wonderful gift you have given us through my dad's wife and our mother. You have loved us through her for so many years. And now that you have brought her home, we want to give you praise even as we weep before you. We pray your strength in the days to come. And we pray your strength right now. Please keep us and help us to find our way together by the power and presence of your Holy Spirit. We know she is with you already but in faith we release her and trust you for victory and joy. Thank you, Jesus, Amen."

"Amen," they all repeated.

"Help me lay her down gently," John requested. "Come on, young man," he said to Glen.

"I am going to take good care of her, sir. I promise," Glen said kindly.

He began making his preparation with calm and careful movements. With John's assistance, he gently wrapped Etta Ween's body until she was fully covered.

"Do you want to help me move her to the gurney?" Glen asked. "Yes, young man."

John went to her head and gently placed his hands underneath her shoulders while Glen grabbed her by the feet. They gently lifted her from the couch to the gurney and readjusted her wrappings. As they moved her, Elise noticed her feet had become uncovered.

"Miah, cover her feet," she pleaded. Perhaps it was an odd request. But she simply wanted her feet to be covered.

They followed him out of the house as he rolled Etta Ween to the van. Their hearts breaking a little more with each step. Glen opened the back of the van and rolled her inside.

"Thank you, Glen. You've been great brother," Jeremiah said.

"It is my pleasure, sir. And once again, I am sorry for your loss," Glen said as he got into the hearse.

Elise turned her attention to John as Glen drove Etta Ween's body away. "Daddy, do you want to spend the night at our house?"

"No, Daddy's girl," John said, "I think I want to stay here."

"Oh, I'm so sorry, Daddy. I said that completely wrong. What I meant was, Daddy, get a bag. You are staying with us. Miah, go pack a bag for Daddy. Please and thank you."

John looked at Jeremiah, who just shrugged his shoulders. "Is this how it's gon be?" John asked.

"Yes, Daddy. This is how it's gon be. Your grandson will be here soon, and you can take care of me then. But until then, I run this. Miah, baby, you still standing here?" she chuckled.

Jeremiah kissed her on the cheek and whispered in her ear, "I love you, babe."

CHAPTER 31

Ride-or-Die

DAY 231

"Baby, what are you doing?" Elise asked Jeremiah. "You disappeared on me." "Oh, I'm sorry. You need anything?" he responded.

"Yes. You to come to bed. It's four in the morning. Mari is settled in. She's snuggled up next to Daddy. I told her he might want to be alone, but he insisted she could sleep with him. So, you're the last child I need to put to sleep."

"Go ahead, babe. I will be up later. I need to finish this." "Miah, finish what?"

"I need to do a little research on this company. I didn't exactly vet them. Beggars can't be choosers. And I'm also doing some research so we can make some funeral arrangements."

"Miah, you got the job. It's going to be fine. You can be Mr. Alpha Male later.

And I've already made the funeral arrangements." "What are you talking about?" Jeremiah asked.

"Baby, Mama Etta and I talked about everything she wanted weeks ago. It's already set. Pastor G. knows what to do. The menu and the programs are ready. You and Daddy can look at everything tomorrow for final approval, but I promise you'll like what we did."

"Can I see the program?"

"I will share the link with you tomorrow, but I promise you it's beautiful. Pastor G. is going to speak from 2 Timothy 4:7-8. You know, 'I fought the good fight, I finished the course, I kept the faith.' Sister

Vicki is catering everything for the repast. We just have to dot some I's and cross some T's. It's handled, baby. I got you."

"Okay, thank you, baby. I appreciate it. But go to bed. I'm just gonna do a little research. I wanna be prepared for this job. I can't mess this up."

"Baby," Elise said as she put her hand gently on his shoulder, "I know what you're trying to do, but you can't avoid this. It's going to happen and it's probably going to happen more than once. Let this first time be with me. Remember what you told me when we first thought I was pregnant? You said, 'We're in this together,' so you don't get to have this moment without me."

"Babe, I really don't know what you're talking about."

"It's okay...I do. Come upstairs...now, Miah," Elise said as she gently shut his laptop, grabbed his hand, and led him upstairs.

Jeremiah sighed heavily to indicate his annoyance. Elise was used to getting her way with him, and her pregnancy really made it harder for him to tell her no. "I don't care about you breathing all heavy. This has to happen, baby," she said softly.

They got upstairs and got into bed.

"Give me," Elise said, indicating she wanted his arm.

Jeremiah complied as she eased her back against his chest and stomach. She took his other arm and placed it on her pregnant belly.

"I love you, Miah. It's okay. Just hold on to me. I'm here, baby."

"I know. I love you too, Lise. I mean I'm not sure why you made me come to bed like I'm a little kid, but I love you," he said sarcastically.

Uncharacteristically, Elise said nothing. They lay there for a short time. Elise kissed his hand a few times and returned it back to her belly when she felt his body jerk slightly against hers. She heard an indistinct yelp come from his throat as if he started to scream and someone had covered his mouth.

"It's okay, baby. Let it go. I'm here. Don't be afraid," she said gently.

Jeremiah pulled her as closely as he could without hurting her. "Lise, my mama is gone," he said, releasing his tears. "My mama is gone! Jesus, please help me, my mama is gone!"

Her touch. Her presence. That was all the comfort he needed, but she still spoke to him as he began to sob for his lost mother.

"He hears you, baby. Let it out. We'll get through this. I promise."

CHAPTER 32

If It Ain't One Thing…

DAY 246

"Monique, I am sorry, but this doesn't make any sense," Jeremiah said, trying to hide his frustration. "She's been with us for three years now. I'm not even sure we knew she had an aunt. Elise may have known but if she did, she didn't think it was relevant."

Monique was Amari's caseworker. She loved working with the Traylors because they made her job so easy. Today was not easy, though.

"Jeremiah, I understand your frustration. This surprises us as well. But it does all check out. I have tried to explain to the judge that there are extreme circumstances. The child has been in your care for an extended period of time, and you want to adopt her. But generally, the Court is going to favor keeping families together."

"But that's what I'm saying," Jeremiah said. "We are her family. She is a part of our lives, and we are a part of hers. This isn't right. After the first few months… maybe. Even a year ago I might be able to see it, but to try and come to claim her after three years just isn't right. We're going to fight this!"

"Jeremiah, I'm not sure what you can do. The judge's orders are clear. We need to prepare Amari for the transition. It will be a lot easier for her if you cooperate."

"Monique, we are absolutely not cooperating. I don't know if you can understand this, but she's not just our foster child. I don't know if she ever was. Amari is our little girl. If we have to, we'll get a lawyer."

Jeremiah's words scared him. He truly wanted to fight for Amari, but an additional set of attorney fees wasn't exactly appealing. His new job was going well but they still weren't on stable financial grounds. Still, Amari would have to come first. There was no way he was going to stand by and let them take their daughter.

"I am sorry you feel that way, Jeremiah. In the end, you will likely only make things harder on Amari."

"I'm not making things harder on Amari. I'm protecting her. She belongs with us. She has a good life with us. It's this ridiculous system that's making things hard on her. Monique, please don't do this. I am not asking for me. I am asking for Amari. You know us. You've met us. You've seen how she is with us. You know we love her, and you know the life we can give her. Can you say the same about this aunt who has all of a sudden come on the scene? Can you honestly say that you think Amari is better off with her?"

Monique was silent for a moment, then responded with the most professional answer she could. "Jeremiah, the judge wants Amari with her biological family. I am sorry but that is not you and Elise. Please have her ready by the end of the week. I will give you and your family time to adjust and speak to her and prepare her. I will also make an appointment with you so I can meet with her and explain everything that is happening. It will be hard on her at first, but children are very resilient. She'll be okay. I'm sorry, Jeremiah. I know she's not going to want to hear it but give my best to Elise. Goodbye."

"Monique, if we let this happen, the only one who's going to be sorry is Amari. You and that judge and whoever else will listen will be hearing from our lawyers. Goodbye."

Jeremiah disconnected the call, dropped to his knees, and made another call. "Father…okay…I recognize my place in all of this. You are God and I am not.

I've heard the warning about what's coming. But Lord, please… not this. This is too much. You always do what is right and this is not right. You took Mama and we were comforted because she had a good, long life. But God…not Amari. Not now. Whatever tests you have, then your will be done, but please leave our daughter out of this. Put it on me. She doesn't deserve this. If I can't take the thought of her being away from us, then I don't think she can either. I know Elise can't. We need you, Lord. We are powerless against that which is coming against us, but I place my eyes on you. I thank you for Jesus. The son you gave up for us all. I hold you to your promise to be for us. You have given us this precious child to love. I can't believe you brought her into our lives just to take her. Please cover us. I plead with you in Jesus' name that you would keep her with us, Lord. I know what the courts say. I know what the system says. But Lord, doesn't heaven rule? Don't you have the final say? So, Lord, I ask that you intervene and give us favor that overrules man's decisions. Give us the answer, Lord. Send us to the right people. Soften the judge's heart and let him see past what he can see on some piece of paper and let him see in his spirit what is really best for her. Father, please protect our baby girl, heart, soul, mind, and spirit. Let her know in the depths of her little soul how much you love her and let her never be able to forget that we love her. Jesus, you have allowed some hard things for us lately. But I am not going to stop praising you. You are God and you are good. I trust you to do what is right. I am caught off guard, but you know the end from the beginning, and I know you have an answer. I give this to you in faith and I thankfully expect victory. I remain your servant and your son, Lord. I trust you and I love you. In Jesus' name, Amen."

CHAPTER 33

Road Blocks

DAY 248

With all they had been through, somehow Elise had maintained her glow. Jeremiah was never sure if it was just his love for her or if it was something everyone saw. Regardless, right now the glow wasn't there. She looked burdened. Even defeated. She didn't say a word, but it was clear she hadn't had a good day. "Hey, gorgeous," he said as he kissed her on the cheek and sat beside her.

"How did it go?"

"Miah, are we going to lose her?" she asked somberly. "Babe, I don't know. Tell me what happened."

"I've been on the phone all day and went to three different attorneys," she said.

"You found appointments that fast?" Jeremiah asked.

Elise turned her head at glared at him. "Miah, this is me, baby. I just walked in and charmed them."

"Charmed?" Jeremiah questioned.

"Well, okay. I acted a fool in one office. I may have implied I was going to burn the building down if no one saw me. I pretended I was going into labor in another. But in the last one I really was sweet, and someone came out to talk to me. "Will anyone take our case?" Jeremiah asked, resisting the urge to ask how much it would cost.

"A few were interested. But they all said it's tough to keep a child away from family. And Miah, it's a lot. A whole lot. You don't wanna know even though I know you want to ask lot. But it's not even that to me. I just don't have confidence that they see us as anything more than a paycheck. They just want their money. They don't care about Amari."

"We'll figure it out, babe."

"Miah, what did we do? The Lord need to tell us so we can repent!" "We didn't do anything, babe. And it's going to be all right."

"It's not going to be all right. I got a call from Mari's school today. One of the kids in her class, her father is a policeman. He came to her class to see his daughter. Mari thought he was there for her. She had a fit and ran down the hallway screaming for us not to let them take her. Maybe we shouldn't have told her?"

"Babe, we had to."

"Miah, can we just run away?"

"Ha. No, babe. We can't run away," he said as he slipped his arm around her. "You not taking me serious, Miah. Let's just start over. They can have this house, the cars, all of it. Let's just go get Daddy and find a cheap flight to Cuba or

Puerto Rico or some other non-extradition country. As long as we're together." "Babe, Puerto Rico is part of the United States."

"Jeremiah, now is not the time!" she snapped.

"I'm sorry," he smiled. "We'll figure something out."

"Monique is coming tomorrow. She's coming to take our child. How are we going to figure this out?"

"She's not coming to take her. She just wants to talk."

"Miah, I don't buy this. I mean why now? I know I talk a lot of junk, but this doesn't make sense. Why does it take three years to come and get someone you love? Because she's family? Uh-uh. I am sorry but from the beginning, family would have said 'No, she's not going to foster care. She can come with us.' I talked to Monique. She's trying to be politically correct, but she doesn't like it either. I can tell. I think this aunt wants a little extra cash and she realizes the Court will pay her to take care of Amari. She's not thinking about her. She hasn't been for three years. And I'm sorry. Biology doesn't mean anything if there is no love. Trust me, biological family can hurt you just as bad as a stranger can. Sometimes it's worse."

"I hear you, babe. We just have to pray that doesn't happen to her."
"So, we're giving up already?"

"No. But we have to be prepared for the worst," Jeremiah explained.

"No, Miah! We need to fight for her. Please tell me we will fight for her," Elise insisted.

"Babe, I promise we will, but I'm not seeing a whole lot of options here. You searched all day and didn't find anything."

"Then we try again tomorrow. And the next day. And the next day until we find an option! But we won't just abandon her because it's no longer convenient. She can't fight for herself. We have to! You don't know what this can do to her. I do."

"Lise, I know you're worried about Mari but is there something else?" "There is. I never told you about the family I lived with after my grandmother died."

"Yeah, you did. The little old lady with the two-legged dog? Y'all had fish sticks every Friday. I thought she was cool?"

"She was actually my second home," Elise revealed.

"You never told me that. Where did you go first?" he asked, surprised about this new information about her.

"I went to stay with my aunt and her husband." "Aunt? I didn't really know you had any relatives."

"Miah, everybody has relatives. They just don't all relate, if you catch my meaning."

"Why didn't you ever mention them?"

"It hurts. I mean it was over thirty years ago. But it hurt."

"What happened? Did her husband do something to you?" Miah bristled. "Calm down, my brown knight. Yeah, I guess he did but not like what you're thinking. They agreed to take me after my grandmother died. I think they were actually the ones who were supposed to take me in after my mother passed. But I ended up with my grandmother. They had a good life. Really, they had it going on. He was some kind of engineer or something and she was a surgical nurse. Miah, don't get me wrong. I love this house but it's really because I love you, and I know you did it for me. But baby, these folks were living like the Beverly Hillbillies after they came up."

"They had a cement pond?" he joked. "Yes…inside and outside the house." "Oh…like that, huh?"

"Yeah, like that. Anyway, it was okay living there. I mean I know you think I'm street, but I had good old-fashioned home training from my grandmother. I pulled my weight, did well in school, behaved…I tried to show I was thankful. I don't think it's anything they ever did, but somewhere along the line I started to believe they loved me. I remember they got a dog, and I loved that dog so much. He was so cute. He was my best friend. I thought I was going to have a good life. Then my aunt got pregnant. She was going to have twins. I mean the dog was cool, but two little babies running around the house? Please, just like Mari, I was so excited. But unlike Mari, they never actually told me they wanted me to be a part of the family. I never will forget it. I came home from school one day. My aunt was about five or six months along. She and her husband sat me down in the kitchen and explained, very bluntly I might add, that they were going to have their own children. It wouldn't be fair to me to make me stay there because they weren't going to treat me the same way they did their own. They wanted their kids to have the best education and life and me being there would make that hard to do. So, I was going to have to leave."

"Babe, are you serious?" he asked, angered at the thought of her rejection. "Oh, it gets better. I'm about ten, I think. I'm processing this but next thing I know the doorbell is ringing. Miah, they didn't even let me spend the night. A caseworker was there ready to take me. And here's the tearjerker. I'm holding the dog. My little buddy. And I'm trying to explain that I'll be good. 'I'll do better. I'll help more. I don't need anything. Just please don't make me leave. I thought you loved me.' I mean, I know you think I'm cute as an adult, but if I say so myself, I was a pretty cute little kid too. They aren't even moved, though. I'm crying and everything and the husband tells me it's going to be all right. Then he pats his leg and whistles, and the dog jumps out of my lap. I was like 'I know this bleeping fleabag ain't Judas'd me.' And I didn't say bleeping either."

Jeremiah struggled to contain himself. Elise was naturally hilarious, but she likely didn't mean to be in this moment.

"It's okay," she said, seeing his struggle. "You can laugh. It was a long time ago."

"I'm sorry, babe. It's not funny, but it's the look on your face and the way you tell it. But that's awful. So, you think that's what we're doing to Mari?"

"I do think that's how she's going to feel. We've done an awful job, Miah."

"Wait! What? Lise, come on now. We've done right by Mari."

"We've done right by her for our lifestyle. But she's not ready to go back into the system. She's the center of everything here, like a child should be. She's not ready for that to change, and I feel it in my spirit that this chick ain't no good for her, Miah. If she leaves it will break her or it will change her. I don't want either of those things to happen. So, pinky promise me we will fight."

"I pinky promise," Jeremiah agreed as he extended his right pinky finger to hers.

"I mean it, Miah. If they come, you got to fight like…like they was taking me. I mean furniture moving, they got to call the SWAT team, they need hostage negotiators. But we are going to fight for her. Or we just go to Puerto Rico. Whatever you prefer. You can't break the pinky promise."

"I won't break the pinky promise," he smiled.

CHAPTER 34

Negotiations

DAY 252

Monique dreaded this visit. She placed Amari with Jeremiah and Elise three years ago and there had been absolutely no issues. Amari was a success story. A much-needed win in a profession where she often wondered if she was truly helping the children she served. The Traylors were excellent foster parents, to say the least, but when she found out they wanted to adopt Amari it nearly brought tears to her eyes. The young girl had been through more than her share of trauma, but the Traylors had turned it around. They wore their love for her on their sleeves. Amari's aunt was a different story altogether. Monique didn't exactly get warm and fuzzy feelings as she communicated with her. Cherese said most of the right things. She mentioned she was concerned about her niece's upbringing and being connected to her real family. But Cherese became very defensive when asked why, after more than three years, she was only just now inquiring about Amari's wellbeing or whereabouts. She simply said that was her niece and that blood was thicker than water.

Nevertheless, everything checked out and keeping a child from her biological family wasn't something the Court was in the practice of doing. There was no evidence that would lead the Court to think Cherese would not be an appropriate guardian. Unknown to the Traylors, Monique had advocated for them to keep Amari. She knew it was a longshot but she felt in this case an exception should be made to the status quo. Considering that Amari had been with the Traylors for three years and that they had now started the process for formal adoption, she had hoped the judge would be less rigid. But he simply brushed her off and sternly warned her she was barking up the wrong tree.

So now she was forced to do the worst part of her job. She drove into the driveway of the Traylor's' beautiful home. The yard was immaculate and was topped off by a beautiful flower garden near the entryway.

She knocked on the door and was greeted with a very warm welcome by Jeremiah.

"Hello, Monique. Welcome. Come on in."

Given the circumstances, Monique appreciated the courtesy. "Hi Jeremiah, it's good to see you again. Although I wish it were under different circumstances." "Yes, ma'am, so do we," Jeremiah replied. "But hopefully we can work something out. Can I offer you anything?"

Monique wanted to get to the point of her visit. There was no need to prolong it. "Oh, no, thank you. I just wanted to speak with Amari and answer any additional questions you all may have."

As she came further into their spacious living area she saw John, Elise, and Amari. Amari leaned snuggly against Elise with her hand on her very pregnant belly. Elise smiled at her, but Monique could sense she was on the defensive. If there was going to be drama, Elise would likely be the spark.

Still, everyone greeted her warmly. Everyone except Amari. Amari would not even make eye contact with her.

Jeremiah invited her to sit down, and Monique sat in a comfortable chair near where Amari was sitting with Elise.

"Hello, Amari. How are you?" Monique asked.

"Fine," Amari said quietly, still not making eye contact.

The last time she saw her, Amari was a confident, energetic, and friendly little girl. But the little girl she was seeing now was more reminiscent of the young girl she had first met. The young girl who had come out of one abusive foster family after another. She was already snuggled closely to Elise but somehow, she leaned in even further. She held on to her like a life preserver.

"Amari, do you know why I am here?" Monique asked.

Amari turned to her and this time made full eye contact. "You want to take me away from my family," she said with an accusatory tone.

"Well, sweetheart. It's not what I want to do. But it does appear that you have an aunt who loves you. She wants to take care of you," Monique explained.

"Everyone here already takes care of me," Amari objected. "I have my own room in two different houses. I can go see Papa John and he really needs me because Mama Etta is in heaven now. I have friends. I make all A's in school. I sing at my church and T Lise is teaching me to play the piano too. Uncle J coaches my teams and I do good. I don't want to go and live with my aunt. I don't even know her. Uncle J and T Lise are going to adopt me and we have a baby coming. I want to stay here."

Although she couldn't fully express it, Monique's heart was broken for the child. There had been times in her career where, for the child's wellbeing, she had to take children away from parents that they loved. This situation was different. There was nothing leading her to believe that removing Amari would be for her good. It only checked a box for people who really had no connection or, worse yet, interest in the good of the child.

But her hands were tied and all she could do now was try to soften the blow. "Yes, sweetie, I know that. I know you have people here that love you. But you are soooo blessed that other people want to love you too. You will have to get used your new home, but you will adjust."

"Monique," Elise said, "did you speak to her aunt about what we spoke about?"

Monique nodded her head. "Yes, Elise, I did. She's not interested in meeting with you to discuss a compromise. She says her mind is made up."

"Well, our mind is made up too, Ms. Lacroix," Elise countered rather aggressively. "This is not going to stand."

Jeremiah sensed his wife's emotions escalating at the negative news and wanted to defuse the situation. There could be no good in making Monique an enemy.

"Monique, can you join my father and me in the dining room?"

Jeremiah asked her.

"Where are y'all going?" Elise asked, clearly agitated.

"Babe, let me and Pop handle this. Cooler heads, okay?" Jeremiah said as he leaned over and kissed her forehead. "Stay here with Mari."

Elise relented and Monique joined Jeremiah and John in the dining room. "Monique," Jeremiah said, "you've known us for three years now, and I know you know that Amari is loved and well taken care of. Can't something be done?"

"Jeremiah," Monique answered, "first, thank you for calling me Monique. I see Elise has promoted me to 'Ms. Lacroix.'"

Jeremiah and his dad made eye contact and laughed.

"Don't take it personally, Monique. My baby girl is in full mama bear mode," said John.

"And that's totally understandable, sir," Monique answered. "And yes, of course I know she is loved, but imagine if it were your niece. How would you feel if you were deprived of her?"

"I don't think I could look myself in the mirror and say I was deprived of someone who I had not tried to make contact with in three years," Jeremiah answered. "And let's not forget, she was with several families before she came to us, Monique. So, we have to ask, where was she during all that time? This is fishy and I think you know it. Like Amari said, she doesn't even know her."

Monique kept her poker face, hoping Jeremiah could not see just how much she agreed with his assessment.

Jeremiah continued his plea. "I know I am biased," he added, "but what about the adoption? And isn't there some sort of child abandonment rule we can cite?"

Monique sighed. "Gentlemen, I can't really advise you on that front. I know it's hard to process, but the aunt says she just needed time to get things together. There is no evidence that she can't provide a safe environment for Amari."

"Okay, fine," Jeremiah pressed. "Can you give us more time? Can you give us until next week? Just a full week to either find another solution or at least prepare her? Nobody's thinking about Amari. This is already very traumatic for her."

"Jeremiah, many times we just have to rip the Band-Aid off. I know it sounds cruel, but there is no way to do things like this without tears or pain. And I can tell you that would likely be the longest week of her life. Delaying this would only make it harder."

"How about this, ma'am? Give us three days, then," John countered. "Friday. Give us until Friday, and if we can't get it figured out by then you can come and take her. That's only two more days than what you wanted."

Jeremiah looked at his dad with pride. He would be well within his rights to be grieving his wife, but he wanted to be in the thick of things with his family during this time.

"Well, it's what the judge wanted," Monique said defensively. She hated being in this position. "But okay, Mr. Traylor. I can give you until Friday. But on Friday I will be here to get her. I need you to have her here and ready. We can work out a time. But when I come, I need you to be cooperative and help me, so it is not overly traumatizing for Amari."

"If you have to come, Monique, we will comply, but we are going to do everything we can to make sure you don't have to," Jeremiah said.

"And Elise?" Monique asked with concern.

Again, Jeremiah and his dad made eye contact and laughed.

"Well, no promises but we will do the best we can, Monique," said Jeremiah. "Then all I can do is pray with you that God works this out for Amari's good.

I hope we can agree on that," Monique said. "We can," Jeremiah confirmed.

"Well, then, thank you both. And by the way, I do want to extend my condolences about your wife and your mother. She was a joy to be around."

Jeremiah smiled. "We can agree on that too, Monique. See, we are all sitting around here just agreeing. Before you know it, you are going to be agreeing with us on some other things as well."

Monique wanted to tell them that she already advocated for Amari to stay with them, but she thought better of it. She simply said, "We'll see, Jeremiah."

Monique got up from the dining room table and rejoined Amari and Elise in the living room. Amari's face was pressed against Elise's protruding belly, speaking to the little baby inside. Monique's heart melted at her words.

"Hey, J.J.," she said. "This is your big sister. I can't wait to meet you. I will see you soon."

This was going to be tough. She had seen a lot over the years. Foster parents who didn't care properly for children. Biological families who wanted to take care of a child but simply could not. But this was the first time in her career a foster family had wanted to fight to keep a child. The notion of it was sweet as she considered that Jeremiah and Elise had their own baby on the way soon. In all her years, she could not recall hoping a family's situation would work out more than this. But for now, she still had a job to do. Still, she could not ignore the nagging feeling she felt in her belly. It may cost her a reprimand, but there was one more card she could play for the Traylors.

"Amari, I'm leaving now. Your Uncle Jeremiah and I spoke. I will be back to get you in three days, sweetie. Don't worry. It will be all right," Monique said.

Amari said nothing but Elise responded in her place with a surprisingly gentle tone.

"Thank you, Ms. Lacroix. You're correct. Everything is going to be all right.

Right, baby?" she said as she kissed the child on the top of the head.

Amari looked up at Elise, smiled, and nodded her head. "Let me show you out," Jeremiah offered.

"Oh, thank you, Jeremiah," Monique said. "Ummm, actually I could use a hand. I have some huge files in my trunk that I need to transfer to my back seat. Would you mind helping me real quick?"

Jeremiah was puzzled. Monique's request seemed out of character, but he wanted to get whatever brownie points he could.

As they walked outside, Monique turned and faced him. "Jeremiah,

I don't need any help, but take this card and call it immediately. And you didn't get this from me. Goodbye."

"Goodbye," Jeremiah said, still confused.

He then looked at the card. It wasn't Monique's card. The card read: "Norman Valero – Family Law."

CHAPTER 35

Light at the End of the Tunnel

DAY 253

Jeremiah wanted to get as much work in as he could before the baby came, so they decided it would be best for Elise to visit the lawyer on her own. He tried to concentrate on his workload but was anxious about her report. He was happy to see her face come across his phone.

"Hello, gorgeous!" Jeremiah answered Elise's call, hoping for good news. Her joyful scream let him know it was forthcoming.

"Ayeeee. Yesssssss, baby. When I tell you God gonna work it out, Imma need you to believe me," she said excitedly.

"Okay, so what happened? What did he say?" Jeremiah asked.

"Miah, this lawyer is legit. He specializes in cases like this. He says he fights for the underdogs in family cases. Fathers who have been deprived of their children. Underprivileged families. Cases like that. He wants to help us."

Jeremiah sat silently on the other end of the phone. "What's wrong?" Elise asked.

"Babe, I am just wondering if he would consider us to be the underdogs. Some people might consider us to be the bad guy taking a child away from her family. What does he say about that?" Jeremiah asked.

"Miah, I went over all of that. He agrees with us. Homechick ain't been on the scene in three years. Now she wanna play auntie? He also agrees that Amari has emotional ties to us and breaking them now could damage her. He says we just need someone who knows the system to fight for us. He says our case is unusual but not unheard of. He is prepared to draw up papers preventing them from taking Amari until further investigation. But we have to move now. And, yeah, we gon be paying on your student loans for a little bit longer, but we can deal with that later. Now he isn't making any promises, but he has a good relationship with the judge and feels like he can get us another few weeks. Miah, he picked up the phone while I was there in the office and called the judge! We already have an appointment to meet with the judge Friday morning. That's the day Monique is supposed to come get her, but if that meeting goes well then we can keep her for a few more weeks while he does a private investigation. We have to be there, though. He stressed that. Me, you, and Amari. Daddy should come too. He said that it's vital that we show the judge just how serious we are about this and how we are prepared to give Amari a permanent home. So, I need you to put that Jeremiah Traylor charm on your new boss and tell him you need the morning off. Maybe the day. We need to be ready."

Jeremiah was hoping for good news but was concerned that Elise may be getting her hopes up. Still, it sounded promising, and he didn't want to discourage or distress her. "Okay, babe," he agreed. "I will talk to him. I am sure it will be fine," he assured her.

"Miah, God is doing it. I mean everything the devil tried to do and is trying to do is failing. You're working. They still haven't found any evidence against you. Me and yo 'can't sit down and be still' son are doing fine. And baby, I feel it in my spirit. Mari is not leaving us. Thank you, Jesus," Elise said victoriously.

Again, Jeremiah was silent.

"Miah, I can hear your wheels turning over the phone," Elise said calmly. "Yes, baby. It's going to cost a lot. A whole lot. We made a commitment to her. We have to protect her. That's our baby, right?"

"Of course she is," Jeremiah reassured. "It's just we have been taking a lot of hits in the pocketbook. With me being unemployed right after we got the house and the new job not even replacing half of my old salary and paying the lawyers for my case, it's not much left. And now we are getting more lawyers."

"Miah, I know it's a lot of pressure. You have always provided for us. I know things haven't been what you're used to, but baby, I need you to believe me when I tell you that you are enough and if we have to go to the projects, then I will go as long as it keeps our family together. Let's do this."

Jeremiah paused and said mischievously, "Well, Lise, it's easy for you to say that. You still got a lot of the projects in you. For you, that would be like going home."

"Oh. No. He. Did. Not," Elise said, trying to hold back her laughter. "Miah, are you throwing shade? Are you coming for me with absolutely no invitation? Are you sure you want this heat?"

Jeremiah laughed out loud. "I'm playing, babe. No. I don't want that heat. And you're right, let's do it. Pay him and let's get the ball rolling. Operation Keep Mari is in full effect. I'm on board. Go ahead and check the accounts, but I'm pretty sure we are going to have to tap into a credit card."

"Soooo, about that," Elise said with feigned sheepishness.

"What did you do, Elise?" Jeremiah asked, already anticipating the answer. "Baby, what had happened was, he said we needed to move fast. I knew you would want us to get this taken care of and I knew you would want what is best for Amari and I knew you would want me to be happy, so I just did what you would have done anyway. Oh, and don't use the Capital One card. I mean like never again in life, don't use it. I mean like erase that mug from your memory. No. Better yet, erase it from your soul."

"Okay, babe," Jeremiah agreed as he shook his head.

"Oh, and you might wanna lay off the Mastercard too. Let's just let that one rest just a little too," Elise said mischievously.

Jeremiah just took a breath and agreed again. "Okay, babe."

"Oh, and someone may be calling you about a loan application. Just say yes." "Elise!" Jeremiah exclaimed.

Elise laughed out loud. "I'm messing with you, baby. Gotta keep it light. But ummm, yeah, keeping it 100, let's let Capital One and that Mastercard gather some dust for a second. Mastercard say they 'bout to be our master for real."

"Girl, let me go back to work before you say something else crazy."

"Miah, wait."

"What, babe?"

"You said I still have the projects in me. Do you think your wife is ghetto?

Do you think I'm hood? Can you not take me anywhere? I wanna know." "No, Lise. I think my wife is perfect," Jeremiah said simply.

Elise gushed at her husband's words. "Awe, Miah. You are so sweet. Thank you, baby."

"You're welcome. I gotta go. I love you. Bye." "Miah, wait."

"Elise, what? I have to get back to work." "Umm, did you just curse at me, sir?" Elise said.

"I apologize," Jeremiah relented. "Lise, what is it, babe?"

"Baby, I was just thinking. If I wasn't pregnant, I could wear that cute little red dress you like and bat my eyes at that judge. He might just go ahead and award us full custody right there on the spot. I wonder if I can find a sexy maternity dress?" Elise pondered.

"That's gonna be a hard no. The only thing you puttin' on to go see this judge is the full armor of God, young lady. If there is such a thing as sexy maternity dresses, you can buy it for me. My eyes only," Jeremiah said firmly.

"Ooo, Miah. I love it when you get all jealous on me. Just a little friendly flirt for the family wouldn't hurt, would it?" she laughed.

"Lise, I can't with you right now, babe," Jeremiah laughed.

"Okay, I will quit. Miah, it's going to work out, right?" she asked seriously. "Yes, babe," Jeremiah said. "Everything is going to be good. I will see you later. Bye."

As they disconnected, Jeremiah thought about his words. More importantly, he thought about his mother's words to him. He couldn't help but to wonder if his words of comfort to his wife were true or not.

CHAPTER 36

Where's Daddy?

DAY 255

Amari was overjoyed and found herself grinning from ear to ear as she awoke from her peaceful sleep. It had been a while since she had spent the night at Papa John and Mama Etta's house. Papa John and she had just had a nice movie night. They made up a little mini fort in the living room floor and had pizza and snacks the night before. She wanted to make sure that her Papa John was taken care of. Whenever people would ask him how he was doing he would say he was doing fine, but Amari knew he missed Mama Etta because of how much she missed her. But it wasn't just the festivities of the previous evening that had the little girl brimming with joy. Today they would go to the courthouse and meet the judge to explain why she should be allowed to stay with Uncle J and T Lise. She prayed that God would help her. The idea of leaving her family terrified her, but she truly believed that God was on their side.

It took her a moment to realize that Papa John was not lying in his spot next to her. But she wasn't surprised. Most of the time, he would not stay on the floor with her all night. He would often wait for her to drift off, then he would go get in his own bed. When she was smaller he would carry her to her bed, but as she got a little bigger, he would complain. "Sweet baby," he would say, "Papa John gotta save his strength to run off the Boogeyman if he try to come get my baby girl. I can't be using my good strength toting yo sweet 'two good legs having' self 'round this house."

Even as the thought of his warm smile comforted her, she could not help but notice the house seemed to be unusually silent. Papa John always woke up before everyone, but where was he now? She didn't smell anything coming from the kitchen or hear any of his normal rattling of pots and pans. Mama Etta and she used to laugh at how much noise he made when he cooked. She laughed as she remembered Mama Etta's teasing. "Mari," she would meddle, "Papa John in there making you some good food, ain't he, baby? I would tell you to call your Uncle J and T Lise, but they can probably hear him from their house." But there was no clanging or banging of pots, so he was probably not in the kitchen.

She went to his bedroom. The door was closed. She knocked but there was no answer. After a moment, she went in, but he wasn't there.

Before she could continue her search, she heard T Lise's voice. "Mari. Daddy.

Why y'all can't answer a phone? Where y'all at?"

Amari's heart sank. *Oh, no. What time is it?* she thought to herself. *Did Papa John forget to wake me up?*

"I'm coming, T.T.," Amari replied as she hurried back down the hallway. "Mari, where's Daddy?" Elise asked, noticing she was still in her sleep clothes.

"We have been calling y'all for forty-five minutes. It's time to go, baby!" she said. "I'm sorry, T.T. I just woke up. I will go brush my teeth," Amari answered, picking up on Elise's frustration.

Elise saw that she had projected her exasperation onto the little girl and tried to calm her. "It's okay, baby," she said gently, "but we need to do this super-fast. Miah, please go get Daddy."

"Okay," Jeremiah responded. "Hey, Mari. How is Uncle's Baby doing? Let me get my hug."

"Nope,," Elise protested. "Miah. You can hug and kiss your Mari all you want after we are finished. Heck, I will drive and y'all can snuggle in the back seat. But right now, I need to get her ready and you need to go get Daddy."

Jeremiah knew now was not the time to push Elise's buttons and complied. "Pop," he called, "where you at? Elise say you gon get it if you ain't ready in five minutes!" he meddled.

"Shole did," Elise agreed as she took Amari to the bathroom for a quick makeover.

But John didn't answer.

"Pop!" Jeremiah called again, but still there was no answer.

He checked the kitchen but there was no sign of him. He went into the laundry room and noticed the door to the garage was slightly ajar.

"Pop, really? So today of all days we have to tinker in the garage?" Jeremiah asked as he opened the door to the horrifying sight of his father laid out face first in the middle of the garage.

Jesus, please. Not this! he thought, momentarily frozen in fear.

Elise's voice jarred him back to himself as he heard it faintly from the back. "Miah, did you find him?" she yelled.

"Elise. Come quick!" he bellowed as he joined his father on the floor. "Dad. Are you okay? Can you hear me?" he asked as he placed his hand underneath his father's face.

He heard Elise gasp in the background as she joined them. "Baby, what happened?" she asked. "Did he fall?"

"Lise, I don't know. He was like this when I opened the door."

"I'm calling 911," Elise said as she fumbled for her phone and clumsily tried to maneuver her nearly full-term pregnant frame on the floor with her husband and father-in-law.

"Babe, I don't think he's breathing," Jeremiah said, trying to hold his emotions in check. The family was still stinging from losing his mother, but there had at least been time to prepare. But this? He couldn't lose his father. He felt selfish as the thought of his son never knowing any of his grandparents invaded his mind.

"Yes, ma'am. Please," Elise said to the operator. "Send someone quick. We found our father on the floor. We're not sure how long he's been here. He's seventy-three."

Amari joined them as Elise tried to listen to the 911 operator. "What's wrong with Papa John?" she asked.

"Shhh, baby. We don't know. Hold on, I have to listen," Elise told her as she stroked the back of her head.

Jeremiah gently rolled his dad from his belly to his back. Elise noticed his face was drooping and contorted on one side and told the operator.

"He has likely had a stroke," the operator informed her. "We have someone on the way. If he is not breathing, then you need to perform CPR."

Jeremiah heard the instructions and proceeded. He never imagined his father's life would literally be in his hands.

"Amari, go finish getting dressed, baby. We're gonna have to go," Elise instructed.

"Is Papa John going to be okay?" Amari asked.

"He's going to be fine. It's okay, baby. Now go," Elise comforted.

Amari obeyed. But even to her young eyes, nothing looked like Papa John was going to be fine and nothing seemed like it was going to be okay.

Jeremiah continued his chest compressions until the EMTs arrived. He relinquished his position and helped Elise to her feet as they prepared his father and loaded him into the ambulance.

CHAPTER 37

Taken

DAY 255

Jeremiah anxiously waited in the emergency room with Elise and Amari. He put on a brave face as he tried not to dwell on the inescapable flood of negative thoughts in his mind.

Lord, please. Not something else, he prayed silently. *Jesus, I can't do this. Not Pop too. Lord, please. Stand up for us. Not Dad. Not now. Please, God.*

He took a deep breath and tried to focus on Elise and Amari.

"Welp. At least we look good," Elise said, trying to lighten the mood. Jeremiah and Elise had wanted to look their best for the judge and had on their

Sunday best when they arrived at John's house. So, when Elise told Amari to get dressed, she naturally put on the new dress that they bought her to wear for court. Jeremiah appreciated the gesture and chuckled, but Amari didn't respond.

"Mari," Elise said sweetly, "don't be afraid. Your Papa John is going to be just fine."

"Do you think it's cancer too? Like Mama Etta had?" Amari asked innocently. "No, it's not cancer!" Jeremiah answered, sounding sterner than he intended. Elise shot him a "get it together" look and he quickly corrected himself. "I'm sorry. Come here, Mari."

Jeremiah placed her in his lap and kissed her forehead.

"Baby, T Lise is right. Papa John is going to be fine. We can't be afraid. We are going to pray and believe and trust God that everything is going to be all right." "But Uncle J, we prayed really hard for Mama Etta and God didn't heal her.

What if God doesn't make Papa John better?" Amari asked.

Jeremiah glanced at Elise, who simply smiled at him with a "You're up, Daddy" expression.

"Mari," he started, "I have to be honest, baby, I am wondering the same thing. I've asked God a few times why he didn't heal Mama, and I am really wondering why this had to happen to Dad. Especially today. But you know what Papa John always told me when I was little and bad things would happen and I didn't understand why?"

"No, what?" Amari asked.

"He would tell me, 'Son, no matter how bad things are, I want you to remember something,' then he would put me on his lap like you're on my lap now and tell me this. He would say, 'God is always right. God is always good. And God is always for you.' He looked me in my eyes the way I am looking in your pretty brown eyes right now, and he said, 'It doesn't matter what happens; those three things are always true.' Then he made me say it after him like I am going to do with you right now. You ready?"

"Uh-huh," Amari nodded.

"Say 'God, I thank you for always being right. For always being good. And for always being for me,'" Jeremiah instructed her as he pulled her close.

Amari repeated his words. "God, I thank you for always being right. For always being good. And for always being for me."

"That's good, sweetie, and don't you let what you see or how you feel make you forget that. Does that make sense?" he asked, hoping he had just slam-dunked his point home.

"Sort of," Amari responded in a not-so-confident voice. "What doesn't make sense?" Jeremiah asked hesitantly.

"Well, God knows everything, so I understand that he is always right. But...," Amari paused. "Never mind."

"It's okay," Jeremiah comforted. "But what?"

"If God is so good, then why do the bad things happen?" Amari asked. "That's a good question," Jeremiah agreed. "Sometimes God lets bad things happen so he can show us how he can help us when things are bad. He wants to show us that no matter how bad things are that we can trust him to keep loving us and help us. Like how he helped me. I lost my job, but he gave me another one. And even though he took Mama Etta to heaven, we all still have each other."

"But wouldn't it be easier if he just let you keep your old job and let Mama Etta stay here?" Amari asked.

Elise stroked the back of Jeremiah's head as he tried to avoid the landmines in Amari's field of questions.

"Baby," Elise interjected, trying to save her husband, "we aren't always going to have the answers. What your Uncle J is trying to say is that we are going to keep trusting God even when we don't understand."

Jeremiah looked at his wife. "Thanks for the assist," he said.

"It's okay, baby. I just think more like a little girl than you do," Elise said as she grimaced a little.

Her expression didn't escape Jeremiah's notice. "You okay, babe?" he asked. "I'm fine, Miah," Elise replied. "I am just worried about Daddy and your son can't seem to get comfortable."

Before Jeremiah could inquire further, Amari continued her full-court press. "T Lise, are you saying you guys don't understand why bad stuff is happening to us either?" she asked.

"I will let your Uncle J handle that one. Go ahead, baby. Do we understand?" Elise asked as she maneuvered in her chair, trying to find a comfortable position. "No," Jeremiah said reluctantly as he kept a concerned eye on his wife. "We don't understand. But we trust God anyway. And that's okay. It's okay to tell God that you don't understand something. God knows that we don't have all the information like he does. He doesn't expect us to know or understand everything."

"Or like everything?" Amari asked.

"No," Jeremiah chuckled. "He doesn't expect us to like everything either. But he does want us to trust him no matter what."

"Good. Because I don't like this," Amari said. "Why are the doctors taking so long?"

"You're right, sweetie," Elise agreed, still grimacing. "Imma need an update."

As she spoke the words, her phone rang. It was Mr. Valero. The lawyer they retained to advocate for Amari.

Elise answered the phone praying the judge would understand their absence.

But Mr. Valero didn't have very good news. "Mrs. Traylor, I am sorry to call you like this," he said. "I know you guys are having an awful morning. But as I mentioned before, it was very crucial that we do this today. Considering your absence, the judge is insisting that the child be turned over immediately."

Elise started to object when she felt a sharp pain in her abdomen. "Mr. Valero, please just talk to my husband." She handed the phone to Jeremiah and told him, "Miah, the judge is upset because we missed the meeting. They want us to turn her over. Handle this. Please."

Jeremiah grabbed the phone and prayed some supernatural wisdom would come to him as he spoke. "Mr. Valero, we're sorry we didn't show up. We are at the hospital right now. Can you get the judge to postpone this?"

Mr. Valero continued. "Mr. Traylor, your wife can tell you, I called in a lot a favors with the Court but this particular judge can be very, let's say, inconsistent and moody. He seemed very sympathetic in our previous conversations, but he is known to be very harsh at even the slightest hint of disrespect. And in his mind not showing up for something like this, when he is making a very out-of-the- ordinary exception, is considered disrespectful."

"Disrespectful?!" Jeremiah exclaimed. "Mr. Valero, we are not being disrespectful. Did you explain that we found our father collapsed on the floor? We are at the hospital. Certainly, the judge understands there are extenuating circumstances."

"I'm sorry about your father, Mr. Traylor, but that really doesn't matter to the judge at this point," Mr. Valero answered.

"What do you mean that doesn't matter to him?" Jeremiah asked as he struggled to keep his composure. "So, you're telling me it doesn't matter that someone can't meet with a Family Court judge because they actually have a family emergency? No. That's not right. What can we do? There has to be something."

"Mr. Traylor, right now I would suggest cooperation. If you butt heads with the Court, you will lose and likely destroy any chances of ever getting Amari."

"We aren't giving up that easy, Mr. Valero," Jeremiah said defiantly. "This would have been worked out had my father not had this episode. I can't believe the judge can't work with us. Amari is staying with us."

Mr. Valero continued. "Mr. Traylor, I am sorry, but you aren't hearing me. The judge agreeing to allow you to keep Amari after today was never a guarantee, and it was definitely contingent on his meeting with you as well as her aunt. Her aunt is here, and she has all the cards in her favor. Monique is on her way right now.

She stuck her neck out on this as well. The agreement was that you have Amari prepared today. I am sorry. I am not saying the war is over, but this battle is."

"Okay, so what are our chances of getting her back if she leaves?" Jeremiah asked.

"Mr. Traylor, you have a pregnant wife and a sick father. You have to live to fight another day."

"Mr. Valero," Jeremiah said, calming himself, "please just answer the question."

Mr. Valero sighed and spoke. "Mr. Traylor, today was our Hail Mary and our best chance. I wanted the judge to meet you and your wife. I wanted him to see you three together. I wanted him to experience Elise's heart and passion for Amari. I wanted him to see the love you all have for each other. And I wanted him to see all those things in comparison to this aunt. Now? I am sorry but I don't know. You already had a lot against you with her aunt being a blood relative. This would be hard to overcome. For now, you need to comply with the judge's order. Am I clear?"

Jeremiah felt defeated. "Yeah. You're clear. So, Monique is coming now? To the hospital?"

"Yes, sir. Monique is a professional. It's going to be hard but let her handle it. You take care of your wife and your father. We can circle back once things have settled and discuss your options. Is that fair enough?" Mr. Valero asked.

"It doesn't seem fair at all, Mr. Valero, but I do understand," Jeremiah answered.

"I get it, sir," Mr. Valero said. "I'm sorry, but one more thing. Your wife didn't sound well. Is she okay?"

"Thanks for asking, Mr. Valero. I'm watching her. I think she's just stressed.

Thank you, sir. Goodbye."

Jeremiah turned around as he hung up the phone and looked at Elise and Amari. If the measure of a man was how well he protected his family, then he was about to score low today.

He walked back to where they were seated. As he knelt before them, he noticed small beads of sweat had formed on Elise's forehead.

"Babe. You okay?" he asked.

"Miah, I'm not sure but I think it's time," Elise responded.

"For the baby?" Jeremiah asked excitedly.

"Yes, but it's okay. What did you work out with Mr. Valero? What do we need to do?" Elise asked.

Jeremiah felt horrible. Elise's tone was one of pure confidence. He looked in her eyes and saw no sign that she even suspected he was not able to fix the situation. But as she looked back at him, the expression on his face instantly took that confidence away.

Jeremiah looked kindly at Amari. "Mari. Uncle J tried. I don't know what else to do. Baby, you're going to have to go live with your aunt for a little while."

"No, please, Uncle J! Please let me stay!" Amari protested.

Jeremiah tried to comfort her. "Baby, we want you to stay. But for now, you can't. But we aren't giving up on you. We just have to pray it's for just a little while."

"I guess I won't be able to be J.J.'s big sister, then," Amari said as she broke down and cried.

"Don't be afraid, baby," Elise said. "It won't always be this way. We're going to fix this."

"Please don't make me go. I promise I won't be in the way. And I will help with J.J. like we talked about and everything. I don't want to go!" Amari said emphatically.

"We know, baby girl. And we don't want you to go. We just can't stop this right now," Jeremiah explained.

"But you said you wanted me. You said you wanted me to stay and be your little girl for real. Forever!" Amari sobbed.

Jeremiah and Elise's heart broke at the child's words. They both searched for the right thing to say, but Amari wasn't finished.

"You lied. God isn't right. And he isn't good. And God doesn't care about me. And you lied when you said you wanted me. I knew you didn't love me. You just love J.J. You don't want me anymore because of him!"

Amari's words stabbed at them both. Elise knew she was only expressing a fear that she had been suppressing. Now it was coming out. She didn't want her to leave with that lie in her mind.

Elise stood Amari up and made her face her. She looked deep into her eyes. "Amari Dawn Echols," Elise said softly but firmly, "these lies stop here and now.

You hear me? You know we love you. We know it hurts. We know you don't understand. We don't understand. But we love you and we want you. And God loves you too."

"Then why won't he do anything?" Amari asked, still sobbing.

Elise tried to be strong and hide the fact that she wasn't feeling very well at all. "He is, baby. We just can't see it right now. Uncle J and T Lise will always be on your side. We aren't going to give up on you, but you have to be strong. No matter what. You know your T.T. had to go through what you are going through too, right?"

"But nobody ever came to get you, though," Amari said as her sobbing amplified. "If they take me, you won't come to get me either."

Elise immediately regretted using her childhood as an example. "No, they didn't, baby, but I realize now that God was with me the entire time. He is going to be with you too."

"But you won't!" Amari said with sadness and a touch of anger as well.

Elise wiped the tears from Amari's face. "Baby, all we can say right now is that God wants you to be strong and brave. Don't you stop praying and don't you stop believing. Don't you ever believe that you aren't loved. We love you and God loves you. We are going to figure this out. And if there is any way, then we will get you back."

"Do you promise?" Amari asked.

"We promise we will try," Jeremiah said, trying to be as careful with his words as he could.

"Hey, kids!" Pastor Gregory's familiar voice chimed in behind them. "We got here as soon as we could. What's happening?"

"Pastor, it's all bad," Jeremiah said as he rose to greet Pastor Gregory and First Lady Faye. "We still haven't heard back about Dad, and now everything is falling apart in our plans for Amari. We missed our court appearance with the judge this morning, and the caseworker is on her way right now to come and get her. Oh, and we think Elise may be in labor."

"Labor!?" First Lady Faye exclaimed as she rushed to Elise's side. "Children, we are so sorry. That's so much for you to have to deal with at once."

As the words came from Faye's mouth, Jeremiah saw Monique enter the emergency room.

Amari saw her as well and her sobbing graduated to hysteria. "Nooo!" she screamed. "Uncle J, please! Please don't let her take me. I don't want to go. I don't want to go. You said we were going to be a family. I promise to be good. Please!" Amari jumped into the seat and threw her arms around Elise's neck and squeezed as tightly as she could, praying her T Lise wouldn't let her go.

Monique steeled her heart at the scene. She had done all she could and now, unpleasant as it might be, she had to do her job.

"Amari, sweetheart. We have to go now," she said.

"No!" Amari refused as she tightened her grip around Elise.

Elise knew in her mind that there was nothing more to be done, but the combination of labor and emotional pain had stolen her logic. She returned Amari's tight embrace and pleaded with her husband. "Jeremiah, we can't let her take her. This is our child. We have to do something."

"Elise, we've done everything. We have to let this happen," Jeremiah said, holding back his tears.

Monique spoke again but this time with more authority in her voice. "It's time to go, Amari."

But Amari wasn't ready to go. Worse yet, Elise was not ready to let her go. "Dammit, you wait!" Elise snapped harshly.

Jeremiah patted Monique on the shoulder, hoping she would not respond to Elise's outburst. Then he knelt back down in front of his wife as she held on to Amari. "It's not her fault, babe," Jeremiah soothed her. "She has a job to do. We have to let her go."

"Miah, you said we would fight," Elise said. Her tone was almost accusatory. "We will, babe. But it's too many battles right now. Dad. You're in labor. The Court. We have to fall back and regroup," Jeremiah responded. "We can't win this

battle like this."

Jeremiah's voice calmed Elise some. She knew he was right, but she also knew in that moment that it had not occurred to her that they really might lose Amari. She hadn't prepared herself emotionally for the possibility that Amari would actually have to leave. Still, she needed to be strong for her.

"Listen, baby," Elise said softly, "I need you to be my big girl and go with Ms. Monique. Okay? Don't you be afraid. You be T.T.'s strong, brave girl."

"I'm trying not to be afraid, T.T.," Amari cried as she hugged Elise's neck even more tightly.

"Jeremiah," Monique said, "a word, please." Jeremiah joined Monique just a few feet away.

Monique whispered to him, "Jeremiah, I know this is hard for everyone. But Amari can't let go because Elise won't let her go."

"Monique, you just heard her tell her she has to go," Jeremiah defended. "Yes, sir, I heard her. But I also see the death grip they have on each other,"

Monique countered. "Now, I don't want anything even close to a physical confrontation. I don't want to reach in there and just grab Amari and make Elise even more upset. I need your help."

"Okay. I will handle it," Jeremiah said. Jeremiah leaned over and whispered in Elise's ear, "Lise, let me hold her, babe."

"Miah, please, just wait. She just needs a moment," Elise pleaded.

Jeremiah kneeled again at Elise's feet and gently caressed one of her hands that were wrapped around Amari. He brought her hand slowly to his mouth and kissed the back of it.

"Come here, baby. It's going to be okay," he said softly to Amari.

Elise said nothing but shook her head as one last plea. But there was nothing else that could be done.

Amari exchanged Elise's neck for Jeremiah's and held on just as tightly as before.

"Sister Faye, can you help Elise up, please?" Jeremiah asked her.

Faye helped Elise to her feet and Elise wrapped her arms around Amari and Jeremiah. "Father," Jeremiah prayed, "please cover our little girl. Please protect her by your name. Please fill her and let her know your love. And even now where it's dark, we ask that you please be her light. We trust you still, Jesus. Amen."

Elise pulled Amari's face close to hers. She kissed her and placed her cheek on hers as their tears mixed.

"We love you, baby girl," Jeremiah said. "You will always be our Mari. Don't you ever forget that." Then Jeremiah, holding on to Amari with one arm and releasing Elise with the other, turned his body away from Elise, shielding them from each other.

But Amari wasn't ready to go and let everyone know it. "Please, T.T., no!

Please don't make me go. Please, Uncle J!"

"We have to, baby girl. Uncle J is sorry. I love you, with all my heart, but we have to let you go," Jeremiah said.

"Miah. No. Please!" Elise begged, but before she could utter another word a contraction hit that almost doubled her over.

Sister Faye held her up, and all she could do was watch as Jeremiah walked Amari over and placed her in Monique's arms as Amari released a bloodcurdling scream.

Monique took her and whispered in Amari's ear, "Baby, I know this is hard and I know you are afraid, but we have to go. It's going to be okay."

"T.T., please!" Amari begged. "I'll be good!"

Elise tried to block out the sound of her voice as Monique carried her away. The memory of her similar experience as a child echoed in her mind. She didn't hate her aunt and husband. But she had never forgotten how they made her feel that day. Was Amari going to think the same of her?

Monique tried to sooth her, but Amari was inconsolable. She just kept screaming.

The last thing they heard as Monique took her out of the emergency room doors was "Uncle J, please don't forget your promise!"

Her words echoed in Jeremiah's ears and tore at his soul, but he held his tears. They would do Amari and Elise no good. Amari was gone. All he could do now was return to his wife and hold her as she cried.

CHAPTER 38

Exiled

DAY 255

Monique was sick to her stomach over the episode. Never in her career had she felt less at ease about her job as she felt right now. Amari cried hysterically in her passenger seat, pleading with her to take her back. All Monique could do was pray silently for her. She prayed the Lord would protect this little girl. She prayed the Lord would comfort the Traylors. And she prayed the Lord would give Cherese the patience and love needed for this transition. But her conversations with her weren't exactly encouraging. Cherese didn't seem to be a bad person, and she said all the right things. She stated in her interviews that she wanted to take care of her niece. That she wanted her to be with family. She said she wanted Amari to know she had not been forgotten. But the conversation always ended with her getting confirmation of how much she would be compensated for by taking Amari in as a foster child. Monique had been rooting for the Traylors to get the delay approved and was hopeful the judge would side with them. Though their absence was understandable and unavoidable, he had lost all patience when they could not make the scheduled appearance. Now it might be too late. There were too many factors against keeping Amari with the Traylors. Amari was going to be with blood relatives, and likely the Traylors would soon forget her once their newborn child was with them. That left Amari, once more, in the care of a system that had failed her before.

They arrived at Cherese's apartment. Monique wanted to do the best she could to cheer Amari up. Her frantic crying had subsided to a more controlled weeping, but she was still obviously in emotional distress. The poor child looked exactly like she felt. Monique did her best to clean up her face and calm her.

"We're here, sweetie," she said as kindly as she could. "It's going to be okay, Amari. Your aunt is very nice."

She almost choked on the words as they came out. She wasn't at all sure if what she had just stated was true or not. Still, she had to complete this task. "Come on, honey. Let's go."

Amari simply sat in her seat, hoping that if she didn't move, Monique would change her mind and take her back. But her hopes were dashed as Monique reached over and unbuckled her seatbelt. Monique got out of the car, walked around to Amari's side, and opened the door.

"I'm sorry, baby, but we have to do this," she said softly but firmly.

Amari had one more plea for mercy left in her tired body. "Please, Ms. Monique. Please don't make me go in there. Please, I want to go home."

Monique's response was to pick Amari up. She was obviously old enough to walk, but Monique couldn't help but think this might be her last real hug for a while. She held Amari close as she carried her to Cherese's apartment. She then put her down and told her, "It's going to be all right, Amari," as she knocked on the apartment door.

Cherese quickly answered. "Well, well, well, what do we have here? Who's this pretty little princess?" Cherese asked enthusiastically.

Monique couldn't help but think to herself, *Woman, don't show out for me.*

"Is this my beautiful little niece?" Cherese asked.

Regardless of her uncertainty, Monique wanted to encourage Amari. "Well, yes, it is," she responded with a smile. "But I am afraid she's not exactly having a great day."

"Well, I'm sorry to hear that, because I've been looking forward to this for a while now. You guys, come on in," said Cherese.

For Amari, there was no Uncle J. No T Lise. No Papa John. Monique was the last familiar person she knew. She squeezed her hand tightly as they crossed the threshold of Cherise's apartment.

Cherese had everything in its place. The home smelled like it had just been cleaned.

Monique continued her efforts to comfort Amari. "Amari, this is your Aunt Cherese. She has been looking forward to meeting you."

Amari responded by turning and wrapping her arms around Monique's legs. "Hi Amari. I wish I could see your pretty face," Cherese encouraged. "Do you want to see your room?"

Amari didn't turn around. She simply shook her head and said, "No, I want to go home."

"Well, you are home now," Cherese said rather coldly.

Monique gently removed Amari's arms from around her legs and did her best to push this awful event forward. "It's okay, Amari," she encouraged, "Go see your room."

"Come on, let's go see," said Cherese.

Amari's head pounded from her crying. Her strength was gone. Mama Etta was in heaven. Papa John was sick. Uncle J and T Lise prayed for her, but still they had let her go even as she begged to stay. No one was coming. Mama Etta used to tell her that God would answer her prayers, but maybe she had done something wrong. Maybe God was mad. She couldn't think of anything she had done wrong. She had tried hard in school and tried to be obedient. So why was God mad at her? Did Uncle J and T Lise mean it when they said they wanted her? Her questions only compounded her headache. She almost didn't hear Monique telling her goodbye.

Amari turned to see Monique heading for the door. Monique turned one more time and waved to her as she closed the door. The click of the door closing brought a harsh finality to the horrific day for her. This was her life now. All she could do was hope this aunt she had just met wouldn't be like the foster parents she had before the Traylors.

Cherese led her to her room. "Well, little girl," she said, "I guess it's just you and me now. Did you eat yet? Are you hungry?"

Amari was starving but couldn't imagine eating anything right now. She simply shook her head.

"Well, you are going to have to get used to being here, little girl. I don't know what you think all this crying is going to do. I'm sorry but those tears don't really move me. You actin' like they brought you to prison or somewhere. You should have seen where I grew up. Trust me. It's worse places for you to be."

Before Cherese could continue, there was a knock at the door. Amari's heart revived. *God, please let it be my Uncle J and T Lise!* she pleaded silently. *Please let them come and get me.*

"Stay here, little girl. I'll be right back," Cherese said.

Amari obeyed. Sort of. She peeked her head out of the door of her new room and prayed to hear those familiar voices. For a moment, her imagination ran wild. T Lise would storm in and say, "Woman, I don't know who told you what, but they told you wrong. Now give me my child back. You don't want this heat." Then Uncle J would explain, "Ma'am, we're sorry but there's been a mistake. We're going to take Amari home now. Thank you for understanding." Then T Lise would call her name. "Mari! Come here, baby. T.T. sorry. Let's go home." The very thought of the scenario brought a huge smile to her face. But the voice she heard from around the corner was an unfamiliar one. It wasn't Uncle J or T Lise. It wasn't even Monique.

"Hey, you," she heard. It was a man's voice, but it certainly wasn't Uncle J's. "What you doin' creeping around my door?" Cherese said coyly.

"My bad. I didn't think I had to creep," the voice responded confidently. "Oh, you thought you could just come around whenever you wanted?"

Cherese asked.

The voice responded again, "Yeah, I kinda thought I did. But let me know if I'm wrong. I can go. I mean… if you got plans."

"Boy, hush and come on in here," Cherese said joyfully.

For a moment Amari didn't hear anything else, but after a few moments she heard Cherese's voice again.

"Uh-uh. Stop now. I told you I got my niece now." "Oh, damn. My bad," the voice said.

"It's okay," Cherese responded. "Umm, come on to the back."

Amari ran back to her bed and pretended to be there the whole time.

Cherese and the young man were soon standing at her door. He was tall and dark. He had a friendly smile.

"Amari, this is… my friend Eric," Cherese said.

"Hey there, lil' bit. How you doing?" Eric greeted her with a smile.

Amari wasn't sure how she felt about Cherese, but this young man seemed nice. She gave a half smile and waved at him.

"Has she been crying?" Eric asked sincerely.

"She will be fine," Cherese responded. "Little girl, me and Eric need to talk about some things, so you just chill out here in your room."

Amari's head continued to throb as she realized her hunger was now overwhelming her hurt feelings.

"Can I have something to eat, please?" she asked.

"I just asked you and you said you didn't want anything. You can wait. I'll be back in a little bit," Cherese said, annoyed. She grabbed Eric by the hand and led him to her room.

"You not gon get her somethin' to eat?" Eric whispered with genuine concern. "She just got here. You know they didn't bring that girl over here hungry. She need to learn that I'm not gon jump every time she say so. Besides. I think you a

little bit hungry yourself, sir. Let me take care of you."

Eric was tempted at the offer, but his heart went out to the little girl he had just barely met.

"Come on, Cherese. Let's get her something to eat and then…," he paused and looked at Amari, "well, you know."

"Fine," Cherese said reluctantly. "Come on, little girl." "What you want, little bit?" Eric asked in a friendly voice.

"Grits, egg whites, and grilled chicken," Amari said rather simply. But the looks on both Eric's and Cherese's faces let her know she had likely overstepped.

Eric smiled at her. "Umm, yeah, little bit. I don't get all of that and I…well, I don't get all of that."

Cherese was not so gentle. "Who this little thang think she is?" she said rather harshly. "Egg whites? Grilled chicken? So, I guess you think this is a five-star hotel?"

"No, ma'am," Amari said respectfully. "That's just what T Lise usually makes for me. She doesn't let me eat that much pork."

"Are you allergic to pork?" Eric asked.

"I don't think so," Amari said. "My T Lise just says it's not good for me." "Well, you gon have to get used to pork over here, boo boo," Cherese scolded.

"And I got regular eggs. Talkin' about some damn egg whites. Da hell she think this is?" she said as she looked at Eric.

Eric just put his head down and patted Amari on her shoulder.

Amari felt the tension and hoped to make it better. "But pancakes are okay too. They are my favorite. Uncle J makes them for me for dinner when T Lise is at choir rehearsal. Hers are better, though, but I don't tell him," she said, trying to smile.

Cherese threw her hands up in frustration. "Imma tell you what, little girl. I got cereal and sausage. Pork sausage."

Cherese placed a box of cereal and some milk in front of Amari, along with a package of sausage.

"Here, little girl," Cherese said. "You can make you some cereal. Go to town. And you can put a couple of these sausages in the microwave. That will hold you for a little bit. And let me help you out," Cherese said, bending over and making full eye contact with Amari. "My name ain't T Lise or Aunt Jemima. And ain't no Uncle J around here either. I don't want to hear jack else about them, you hear me?"

Eric didn't like Cherese's response but it was her business how she handled her niece. Besides, he had other things on his mind.

Amari simply nodded as she wondered what she had done wrong. "Come on, Eric," Cherese said. "We need to talk."

"I'll see you later, little bit," Eric said sweetly.

Amari heard Cherese's door close as she was left alone in the kitchen. She made her breakfast as Cherese instructed and went back to her room. There were no posters. No neon signs with her name on it. No pictures of family. No stuffed animals. The bed was comfortable enough, so she lay down. Perhaps she would have been able to fall asleep, but her stomach was now bothering her. She probably should not have eaten the sausage. Even in her feelings of abandonment, a smile made its way to her face. She recalled a time where Uncle J and Papa John had forgotten to bring her special order from their favorite Chinese restaurant.

"What in the world?" T Lise exclaimed. "How y'all gon forget my baby's order?"

"That's a pity and a shame," Mama Etta joined in. "They know that baby hungry."

"Don't worry, Mari," T Lise continued her rant. "We got you. But first, it's gon be some furniture moving."

"Lise. Stop it, babe. We're sorry," Uncle J pleaded.

"Uh-uh. Nope. Stop. Flag on the play. Technical foul. Players are ejected!" T Lise said as only she could.

"Babe, what are you doing?" Uncle J asked her.

"I told you it's gon be some furniture moving and I meant it," T Lise said.

Then she moved the furniture in the living room and challenged Uncle J to a wrestling match.

"Elise, I weigh almost a hundred pounds more than you. Stop now. Let's move the furniture back. I'm not fighting you, babe. Mari, I'm sorry, baby," Uncle J pleaded as Amari smiled from ear to ear.

"Oh. You thought this was a choice?" T Lise replied. "This is happening, Jeremiah John Traylor. I gots to defend my baby's honor. Now lay down and take this butt whoopin' like a man."

"I have to lay down on the floor?" Jeremiah asked.

"You heard me. You too, Daddy. You just as wrong as your son," Elise commanded.

"Daddy's girl, come on now, we just forgot," Papa John protested.

"Well, I bet after this y'all won't forget again," Mama Etta said.

"Now you heard her, John. Jeremiah, help yo daddy get down on the floor. We don't want him to get hurt before we whoop him," she said as she laughed.

Reluctantly Jeremiah and John lay down on the floor as Elise climbed onto the couch.

"Don't worry, Mari. They will rue the day they forgot my baby's order," Elise said.

Amari didn't know what "rue" meant, but she was pretty sure it was a good thing for her.

Elise jumped off the couch like a professional wrestler and dropped the atomic elbow on her husband and father. She lay down on top of them while Mama Etta counted them out. Then they both stood over them with their hands raised in victory.

"Now will we be forgetting the baby's food in the future, gentlemen?" Elise asked sweetly.

The men looked at each other as they agreed to never make such a mistake again.

"That's your wife," Papa John whispered to Uncle J.

"Your wife was her partner in crime, Pop," Uncle J countered. "Y'all talking down there?" Mama Etta said.

"No," both defeated men said in unison.

"That's what I thought," T Lise said. "Now Mari, come give your Uncle and Papa a hug and let them know you forgive them."

Amari quickly ran to the floor still giggling and smiling. "I forgive you," she said as she lay on top of them, hugging and kissing them both.

The pleasant memory warmed her heart. She thought she was loved. She thought she was important. Now she didn't know what to think. Uncle J and T Lise always talked to her about God. Maybe all the nice things they said about him weren't true. It hadn't even been an hour since she had been taken away, but it seemed like such a long time ago. Now, no one cared about what she was eating. No one cared that she was scared and alone. No one seemed to care about her at all. The smile brought on by the pleasant memory quickly dissipated and gave way to a quivering lip as the tears returned to her little eyes.

CHAPTER 39

J.J.'s Birthday

DAY 255

Elise's contractions were getting closer and stronger. It was becoming clear that little J.J. had decided to come early. After consulting with Elise's doctor, they both felt that she would be fine to go to her hospital. Jeremiah and Elise had just enough time to run back to the house to get her hospital bag. Thankfully, Pastor Gregory and First Lady Faye were happy to stay at the hospital with John and wait for the doctor's report. They promised to give him an update as soon as they heard anything and insisted he get Elise to the hospital.

Jeremiah's heart became heavy as he ran into the house to retrieve the bag. This was supposed to be Amari's job. She would be responsible for grabbing the bag and putting it in the car when it was time to go. She was so excited about her little assignment. Jeremiah recalled teasing her. *"Baby girl, if you forget that bag, you know you gon have to drive back to the house by yourself to get it, don't you?"* But Amari always had something to say and quickly responded, *"You just don't forget T Lise. Then we will really have a problem."* Amari was likely at her aunt's house by now. Jeremiah prayed she had calmed herself. As much as he hoped they could find a way to get her back, he also hoped she would be well taken care of.

This was supposed to be a great day. Their son was being born. It should have been a day of rejoicing and praise. But even the joy of having a new baby couldn't get his mind off his ailing father and Amari.

He joined Elise in the car still not knowing what to say. He prayed she understood, but he could not help but wonder if he somehow looked weak in her eyes. Was she wondering how he could let this happen? Or perhaps even blaming him?

"How are you feeling, babe?" he asked her as he pulled out of their driveway. "I'm okay," she responded, still sniffling from her tears. "Miah, is she going

to be all right? Why is all of this happening? It doesn't make any sense."

"Lise, we can't think about that right now. We have to get you to the hospital.

We will check on Amari after you have the baby. It will be all right."

"Miah, it's not going to be all right! Did you hear what she said? She thinks we don't want her. She thinks she is being replaced. We said we were going to take care of her like she was ours. We promised each other. We promised her. We promised God. And now she is in a stranger's house thinking we don't care! That's not okay, Miah! That's not all right!"

Another contraction hit her as she spoke. Jeremiah reached over and held her hand as he pressed down on the accelerator.

Jeremiah gave her a moment to breathe through the contraction. "Lise, all I mean is that we have to address you and the baby first," he explained. "Amari is going to be fine. She's safe. And we're not giving up. Okay? We're going to keep our promises to each other, to Amari, and to God. We just have to get through this detour. So, I need my baby, you I mean, not J.J., to breathe and chill," he smiled. "God has us. He always has and he always will. We are going to come out on the other side of this thing, and it's gonna be good, gooder, and gooderer."

Her husband's smile reassured Elise and she returned it. "Okay, baby. I will breathe and chill. But as soon as I push out Jeremiah John Traylor II, Imma need you to go get his big sister and make sure his granddaddy is all right," Elise said emphatically.

"Elise, I am not leaving y'all at the hospital," Jeremiah argued.

"Miah, you're going to have to!" Elise countered. "I know you can't be in two places at one time. This is just going to be a routine delivery. Me and our little man are going to be just fine. Shania will come up there if I need anything. Daddy is going to need you and Pastor G. can't do everything. We gotta think this through, baby. I need you to be the brains of the operation while I'm recuperating. You make sure Daddy is good and you get 'Operation Rescue Amari' underway. Like I told you before, if we need to kidnap her and move to Mexico, Puerto Rico, Hawaii, or some other non-extradition country, I'm down."

"So, now Puerto Rico and Hawaii are included in your list of non-extradition countries?"

"Are!" she said as she turned up the corners of her lips, daring him to contradict her.

"Okay, babe," Jeremiah smiled. "I mean, I already thought I was the brains of the operation but okay."

"Jeremiah, I know I did not just hear you say you thought you were the brains of this operation," Elise said, smiling.

"Oh, I said it. I mean, leave it up to you and we gon be kidnapping kids and moving to Hawaii so the law can't track us down. So yeah, I think the important decisions need to be left up to me, sweetie."

"Don't you 'sweetie' me, Jeremiah," Elise said as she squeezed his hand as hard as she could.

"What's wrong with me calling you sweetie, sweetie?" Jeremiah asked innocently, barely noticing the tightening of her grip.

"Cuz you know you have all sorts of sweeties, Jeremiah. Only one time out of ten do you really mean it. The other times, sweetie, is your polite way of saying 'Chile, please go sat down somewhere.'"

"Lise, have I ever told you to go sat down somewhere?"

"No, cuz you know what would happen if you did. That's why you just say okay, sweetie," Elise laughed.

Jeremiah laughed with her, then smiled back at her. "Well, maybe, but the truth is you always get the good sweetie," he said as he brought her hand close to his face and kissed the back of her hand.

"Oooh, J.J., yo mannish daddy tryna start something on the way to the delivery room. Get him, baby," Elise said as she giggled.

"Don't listen to your mama, J.J. Daddy is just tryna get you to the hospital so he can meet you."

"No, he ain't, J.J.," Elise argued. "He tryna...ooo...." Before Elise could continue her argument, another contraction hit.

"Breathe, babe," Jeremiah comforted. "We're almost there. I got you." Elise breathed and squeezed Jeremiah's hand until the contraction subsided.

"They're getting closer and stronger, baby. This is happening. We're having a baby," she said.

"Yes, we are, babe," Jeremiah said. He was happy to see she was starting to enjoy the moment in spite of all that seemed to be against them.

"Miah?"

"Yeah, babe? What's up?"

"We're going to be okay, right?" Elise asked.

"Yes, babe," Jeremiah answered confidently. "We're going to be just fine." "You promise?"

"Yes, Lise. I promise we are going to be okay. It's going to be better than okay. I told you, God has us. Our son is about to be born, Pop is going to pull through, and we are going to get Amari back. We're going to look back on November 13, 2022, as the best day of our lives."

"Miah?"

"Yes, Elise."

"You know what I said about taking Amari and running away to a non- extradition country?"

Jeremiah smiled. "Yes, babe. What about it?" "You know I'm serious, right?"

"Oh, yeah. I know," Jeremiah agreed.

"That applies to you too. If you go to jail, I already have a plan to break you out. You know that, right?" Elise said seriously.

"I didn't do anything, Elise. God is going to let the truth come out."

"Miah. Baby. Sugar Plumb. We ain't talking about the truth and all that right now. I said if you go to jail, I already have a plan to break you out. Don't have me at the fence talkin' 'bout 'Lise, we just need to wait on God.' Imma need you to come on when I hatch my escape plan. Am I clear?"

Jeremiah gave in. "Okay, babe. It's not going to be necessary. But if it is, I will follow your lead."

"That's all I needed to hear. Miah and Lise against the world. Right?" Elise asked.

"Miah and Lise against the world, babe," Jeremiah agreed. "But how we gon escape the long arm of the law with Mari and a baby?"

"Oest, thou most highest God," Elise prayed in King James. "Thoust hast favored thine most precious of daughters witheth such an amazaneth man. But now in this mostest desperateth of hours, makest him humble beforest hist help- mateth, that he wilst knoweth, I goteth this. In the nameth of Jesus, thoust only begotten son, I prayeth to thee, Amen."

"So, we prayin' in King James again?" Jeremiah asked.

"Yeseth! Thou most highest God inclineth hist ear morest closely when we imploreth him in King James," Elise laughed.

Her laughter gave Jeremiah peace. He stopped the car at the red light and enjoyed the moment. Regardless of everything against them, he still believed God was for them. He pulled her hand back to his lips and kissed the back of it again.

"Thank you, Jesus," he said as she smiled at him.

He took his foot off the brake and gently accelerated. He returned her smile but was confused as her peaceful expression morphed into one of horror. He wondered if she had another contraction. But it wasn't a contraction. Jeremiah couldn't see what she saw. A car was speeding toward them on Jeremiah's side. The driver was going too fast for this area. Before Elise could say his name and before Jeremiah could ask what was wrong, the car collided with them.

CHAPTER 40

Trapped

DAY 255

Elise was disoriented. She felt pressure on the side of her face, shoulder, and neck area but she couldn't imagine where it was coming from. Somehow her body was contorted and seemed to be folded in on itself. It took her a moment to realize that she was upside down and pinned against something. Her vision cleared and she saw the cracked glass of their SUV as she realized she was still in the car. Her senses began to return to her, and she remembered seeing another car speeding to Jeremiah's side.

"Miah!" she screamed. "Miah, are you okay?" Jeremiah didn't answer.

She tried to push up against the roof of their flipped-over SUV so she could turn her body when she realized she was still holding Jeremiah's hand. But he wasn't holding hers. She squeezed it but he didn't respond.

"Miah, baby, please answer me. Can you hear me? Are you okay?"

But he still didn't answer. Her seatbelt painfully cut against her body. She released herself and instantly regretted it as her body crumpled to the roof. But at least she was free. Before she could maneuver to check on Jeremiah, another excruciating contraction hit her. She tried to breathe through the contraction that seemed to last for an eternity. She had never had a baby before, so she had never been in labor. But this contraction seemed different. Something was wrong.

As her pain subsided, her mind shifted from Jeremiah to her child.

She had to get help. She tried to open the door, but it wouldn't budge. She managed to turn her body so she could see Jeremiah. What she saw horrified her. His body was twisted similar to hers and he was still in his seatbelt. He was bleeding from his head, his nose, and his mouth. His eyes were closed, and he was totally motionless. "Daddy, please don't let this happen. Please, Jesus," she prayed out loud, as other drivers on the busy street stopped to assist.

She heard a man's voice come from the outside of the vehicle. "Are you okay in there?" the man said.

"No, please!" Elise exclaimed. "We need help. I'm in labor and my husband is bleeding. Please help us!"

"Did you say you're in labor?" the man asked. "You're having a baby?" "Yes. I'm having a baby!" Elise said.

"You mean now? You're having a baby right now?!" the man asked.

Had the situation not been so dire, Elise would have had some choice words for him, but this was no time for her to show off her smart mouth.

"Yes!" Elise said, trying to press her point. "I am having a baby right now.

This minute! We need help right now. Please."

"Okay," the man said as he struggled to open her door. "Stay calm. I can't get the door open, but help is on the way."

"Please hurry!" Elise pleaded.

She turned her attention back to Jeremiah, noticing the color seemed to have drained from his face. She prayed silently as she took hold of his wrist to find a pulse. His pulse was faint, but it was there. He was still alive.

Elise heard another man's voice on the outside. "Sir, you have to move! You're in danger there. We will handle this. Ma'am, are you okay? How are you doing?"

Elise looked out of the window and saw a fireman. He was on his knees and bent over as low as he could go.

"Please hurry. I think my baby is coming and my husband isn't saying anything. He isn't moving. He isn't...." Suddenly she felt a warm rush of water streaming from her body. It seemed to not want to stop. "I think my water just broke," she said. "I can feel it."

"Let's move!" the fireman shouted with urgency. "Get that equipment over here now so we can get the vehicle stabilized. Ma'am, we're coming but you have to be still. We have to get your vehicle stabilized before we cut you out. Try not to move."

"Let me get in there, Chief," a young lady said.

"You make it quick. And I mean real quick," the Chief responded as he exchanged places with a young woman.

"Hi ma'am, can you tell me your name?" the young lady asked. "Elise!" she cried.

"Hi Elise. I'm Jada. I'm an EMT," the young lady said. "How are those contractions coming? How far apart are you?"

"I'm not sure," Elise said, "but my water just broke and I think another one might be coming soon. The last one was really bad. I can't stay in here."

"I need you to lie still, Elise," Jada instructed her.

"Okay, but I've been moving. I think I'm okay. Please just get us out of here," Elise pleaded with her.

"We're trying, Elise. Your car is a little twisted up, okay? We're going to have to do some cutting to get you out. Beside the contractions, is anything hurting you?" Jada asked her.

"No, I mean…wait, I feel another contraction coming." "That's okay, I'm with you. I'm not going to leave you."

Although it was unadvisable, Jada reached through a small opening of the totaled vehicle and laid her hand on Elise's shoulder as she endured another contraction.

This contraction was more agonizing than the last. She couldn't help but wonder what would happen if they couldn't get her out before the baby came. She abandoned her breathing and screamed instead. Jada rubbed her shoulder until it ended.

"Elise," Jada asked calmly. "I know it's hard but try to think. How long ago was the last contraction?"

"I don't know. Five minutes. Maybe less. But they are getting stronger every time," Elise answered.

"Okay. We're going to get you out of here. Chief, we have to get her out now," Jada insisted.

"We have to stabilize the car first," the Chief replied.

"I don't think we have time. This baby is coming. We need to get her to the hospital," Jada responded.

"We don't have a choice!" the Chief snapped. "We have to stabilize the car, so it doesn't roll again. You need to get out of there. Now!"

"I can't leave her," Jada argued.

"That's an order! You're hurting her more than helping right now."

Jada relented. "Elise, I have to go so they can stabilize the car. I promise I will be right back."

Elise heard clanking and banging on the outside of the vehicle as the rescue workers attached their equipment to stabilize it. She wasn't sure what all of that meant. She just knew she wanted them to get her and Jeremiah out.

"Miah, can you hear me, baby?" Elise asked as she did her best to clean him up. "We are going to be okay. Like you said, God has us. You stay with me, baby. You stay with us. Your son is gonna be mad if you're not here to greet him. Come on, baby. I can't do this without you." Elise paused and grasped her husband's limp hand. "Please, Jesus, help us." But Jeremiah was still unresponsive.

"Ma'am," the Chief's voice returned, "we are almost there. Hang on!" "They're going to get us out, baby. Hold on," Elise said.

Elise lay there and tried not to cry. But she knew another contraction would be coming soon, and she was in no position to deliver a baby.

"Elise, we have the car stabilized." It was Jada's voice. She had returned as promised. "We're going to have to cut you out. Keep facing away from the door and cover your face. We're coming. You hold on. Okay?"

"Okay," Elise responded. "But my baby isn't being so patient." She didn't want to let go of her husband's hand. She was afraid this may be her last time holding it. But she had to get help for her and the baby.

She pulled her hand from his and extended it to cover his face as she covered her own with the other. She had never been so uncomfortable in her life. She felt like a pretzel. Twisted and turned in on itself.

Elise heard the saw cutting through her passenger-side door. She couldn't quite perceive everything that was happening. She didn't realize that not only had the car flipped over but that it had flipped over into a ditch and was in danger of turning over again into a steeper embankment. The firemen and EMTs were working feverishly to get Jeremiah and her out but it was no easy task to extract them.

But moments after the cutting had started, the firemen pulled the mangled door away from the car. In a moment Jada was lying next to her.

"Well, hello, my friend," Jada said encouragingly. "It's nice to see you up close and personal. We don't have much time. I am going to brace your neck and pull you out of here."

"What about my husband?" Elise protested.

"We're going to get him too. We're going to take care of you both," Jada assured her.

Jada carefully lifted Elise's head to place the neck brace on her. Elise didn't think it was necessary, but she held her protest. Soon enough, Jada was able to pull her from the mangled SUV and placed her gently on a nearby gurney. Elise caught a glimpse of where they were and realized why it had taken them so long to get to her.

Elise started to ask about Jeremiah again, but her labor would not let her mind focus on her husband. Another contraction came. They were getting closer, stronger, and lasting longer.

"Come on, Elise," Jada encouraged. "We're with you. Breathe, sweetie." After the contraction subsided, they moved her quickly to a nearby ambulance. "You have to take care of my husband!" Elise cried out.

"We are already seeing to him," Jada responded.

Once she was loaded into the ambulance, Jada asked her if she could check her. "Elise, we need to see if you're dilated."

"Now?" Elise asked.

"Yes, sweetie. Right now," Jada said firmly. "I think you're really close. Trust us, okay? We're trained for this."

Jada checked and as she suspected, Elise was close to being fully dilated. The baby was coming soon.

"Okay, she's set. Let's roll!" Jada ordered.

Elise heard the door of the ambulance slam shut and the sound of the engine roaring and sirens blaring. She remembered her words to the Lord when they first found out about her pregnancy. *"Right now, all I can really think about is this perfect little moment you have given us. Me, my man, my baby, and you."* But now none of that was certain. Her life was unraveling. Nothing was as it should be. Mama Etta was gone. Amari had been snatched away from them. And there was no way to know what would happen with Daddy and Jeremiah.

She didn't care who heard as she cried out to the Lord. "Jesus, please take care of my baby. And take care of Jeremiah. Jesus, please. We need you."

CHAPTER 41

Emergency

DAY 255

Elise was met at the hospital by a team of nurses who quickly transported her to a room. They worked feverishly attaching monitors to her and her belly as Dr. Kakarla joined them.

"Hello, Elise," she said. "I hear you had a hard ride here, but we are going to take care of you."

The doctor checked her heartrate and blood pressure and didn't try to hide her concern.

"This is not looking good, Elise," she said. "Your blood pressure is very low and seems to be dropping."

"How is my baby?" Elise asked.

"We're checking him now, dear," she responded.

The doctor applied the familiar cool gel to Elise's belly and began moving the device around in search of J.J.'s heartbeat. Elise tried to relax as she awaited the sound of her child's heartbeat. But her waiting was met with a deafening silence. "Elise!" the doctor exclaimed suddenly. "We are going to have to put you

under. We need to do a C-section."

"Why?? What's wrong?" Elise screamed. "What's wrong with my baby?" "Elise, we don't have time. We have to get the baby out now," the doctor told her.

Before she could protest or ask another question, the anesthesiologist had covered her face and Elise was out.

CHAPTER 42

Unimaginable

DAY 255

Elise came out of the anesthesia confused by her surroundings. After a few moments her confusion waned, and she realized she was in a different room. She took a breath and gathered her thoughts. Where was her baby? She looked around to see any signs. There was no baby carriage near her bed, which made sense. She was obviously in no shape to take care of her little man. Still, a sweet anticipation came over her. She reached for the device to call for help, but before she could, a nurse was in the room.

"Mrs. Traylor, good, you're back with us," the nurse said. "How are you feeling?" "I'm just a little bit groggy," Elise responded. "Can I see my baby now, and

is there any news about my husband?"

"Let me check you out first," the nurse said. "How is your pain level?"

"I'm probably going to need the good stuff later on, but I'm okay for now. How is my son? I mean I know I probably can't keep him right now, but can you bring him here? And can you check on my husband? Have you heard about him?" "Let me check your vitals, Mrs. Traylor, and I will let your doctor know you're up." Elise was never patient. In that regard, she was the polar opposite of Jeremiah.

But she knew that in her condition it would be a while before she would be able to take care of J.J. and she didn't want him to be known as the angry black woman's baby, so she held her peace for the time being.

The nurse finished checking her vitals. "You're in great shape, Mrs. Traylor.

Your doctor will be here in just a moment."

"That's fine," Elise said. "While she's coming, can you or someone else bring my baby?"

"Let me check on that, Mrs. Traylor," the nurse responded as she left.

Several moments went by as Elise waited. Too many moments. Under any other circumstances, Elise would have marveled at her care. In addition, to the first nurse, other nurses were in and out of her room every few minutes or so. They were attentive and caring. Physically she felt fine. She was in pain, but it was tolerable as long as she lay still. But this wasn't a normal circumstance. She hadn't had her appendix removed. She had a baby that she hadn't seen yet. None of the nurses had any information on her husband and when she asked about J.J., they simply told her the doctor would be there soon.

She did her best to process the harrowing day. Her unanswered questions tormented her. How was Daddy? How was Jeremiah? Was Amari okay? And when were they going to bring J.J.? She remembered her husband's words just a short time ago. *We're going to be just fine. God has us.*

"Daddy, you be doin' the most sometimes," she prayed. "But we are still here praising you and trusting you. My eyes are on you, Daddy, in Jesus' name, Amen." She took a breath and visualized her pending blessing. The nurse would soon come in with J.J. "You have a visitor," she would say. And she would place little

J.J. in her arms. She visualized his little nose, his eyes, and his curly hair. Then Jeremiah would come in. Perhaps a little banged up. The horrible gash he had in his head would be stitched up but other than that, he would be just fine. She imagined his sweet, strong voice speaking to her. "I'm sorry, babe," he would say. "They kept on poking and prodding me. But I'm good. Just a little headache. So, I see our little man is tougher than all of us. Not a scratch, huh, J.J.? I see you, boy! Little old car wreck can't hurt Daddy's man. Don't worry, babe.

Pastor G. just saw Dad. He's good. It was just a minor stroke. They just want to watch him close. He said he wants to see you and the baby as soon as he can. And I promise, we are going to handle this thing with Mari. It's not over. God has us, baby."

Her thoughts overjoyed her, but the anticipation they brought also robbed her of her last bit of patience. She reached her hand out to one of the nurses. "Ma'am," she said, not trying to hide her anxiety. "You guys have had me here for a while now but I'm fine. I need you to bring me my baby. And for the umpteenth time, is there any news on my husband?"

"Ma'am, I know it's a lot, but we honestly don't know," the nurse told her. "I'm probably saying too much but I don't think your husband is at this hospital. But someone is checking, and we will let you know as soon as possible. And I promise, your doctor is on the way."

"Uh-uh! No! That's not good enough!" Elise exclaimed, intentionally raising her voice. "Being patient and nice obviously is not y'all's language, so let me speak clearly. Let me get ethnic. I want my baby here right now! I don't want to hear your damn excuses and the 'I don't know's and the 'please be patient's and 'the doctor is on the way's anymore. You can't tell me that nobody knows where my husband is. There were ambulances and firetrucks and police cars everywhere. I don't want to be like this but I'm about to lose it and if it were your family, you would too!"

"Elise, it's okay. I am sorry but I am here now, and I brought a friend." It was Dr. Kakarla.

Elise's soul leaped as she anticipated J.J. being brought in, but instead First Lady Faye followed in behind Dr. Kakarla.

"Oh, Hey, Doctor Kakarla. Hey, First Lady. Uhh, did y'all hear me?" she giggled. "I'm sorry, but I can't always keep hood Elise in check. It's probably the anesthesia."

"It's fine, Elise. I can answer your questions. Nurse, you can go," Dr. Kakarla said. "I will let you know if I need you."

The nurse looked at Elise. "I will be back soon," she said sweetly.

Elise appreciated the look of concern on her face. "Thank you. And I'm sorry," she said, trying to calm herself.

"It's okay. I will be right outside," the nurse responded as she left.

Dr. Kakarla came and stood next to Elise's bed while Faye stood on the other side. "Elise," she started, then paused and breathed heavily. "I am sorry. We did all we could, but the trauma of the accident was too much for the baby. Your child died an hour ago."

Elise couldn't quite process the words. They simply did not make sense. "What?" she asked, hoping against all hope that she had heard incorrectly. "I am sorry, Elise, but your baby did not survive," Dr. Kakarla reasserted the nightmare.

Elise looked at First Lady Faye and prayed she would overrule what her doctor was saying. But Faye simply placed one hand on Elise's head and held her hand with the other.

"That's not true, Doctor. I'm fine. How could I survive and my baby not?

There has to be some kind of mix-up."

That was it. That must be it. There had to be another accident with another mother and child. Her Daddy would not do this to her. Hospitals make mistakes and this was one. Her child would soon be in her arms. But the tears that streamed down her face let her know that her heart had already accepted what her mind could not. She would never hold J.J. He would never see his room. He would never climb into the bed with Jeremiah and her when he got afraid at night. He would never grow up. And even if they got her back, Amari would never get to be his big sister.

"It's okay, Elise. I want you to try to breathe," Dr. Karkarla said.

Faye could feel Elise's body tensing as her whole body began to shake. "No! No! No!" she repeated as she frantically shook her head in a last attempt to deny the horrible truth she had just heard.

"I'm here, sweetheart," Faye said as she tried to comfort her, but Elise's grief only escalated.

Her mouth gaped wide open as she screamed in horror. At first, the sound born from her pain didn't escape. But when her breath returned, her voice produced a scream that echoed throughout the entire floor.

Dr. Kakarla and Faye continued to try to comfort her, but Elise was inconsolable. She began kicking and screaming, and before they could subdue her she leaped out of the bed, ripping the I.V. tubes from her arm. But her legs were still weak and she fell hard to the floor.

"Bring me my baby!" she cried. "You are all liars. What did you do to my child?"

The nurses came in to assist. Elise saw the needle they were preparing but she had no intention of letting them sedate her. The last time she woke up they told her that her child was dead. She wasn't going to give them another chance. She mustered all her strength and somehow scrambled to her feet. She made her way to the hallway, still screaming, "Bring me my baby!"

Ignoring protocol, Faye rushed past the converging nurses. "Elise, let First Lady help you, baby."

Elise was still screaming but somehow heard Faye's voice. She spoke with compassion, but she also spoke with authority. Faye's voice calmed her momentarily and the nurses saw their opportunity. They rushed to Elise, but Faye blocked their path to her. She raised her hand, commanding them to halt. She had no such authority, yet they all obeyed her.

"Elise, it's me, baby. It's First Lady. I know it hurts. I know you're scared. But I'm here. I am going to walk you back to your room so you can rest, baby. It's going to be okay."

"Don't let them get me, First Lady," Elise pleaded.

"They aren't going to get you. They don't want to hurt you," Faye said sweetly. She turned to the nurse and to the security staff that had just arrived. "Y'all back up, please. She'll be okay. Let me handle this. Elise, you're safe, baby. I see you. The Lord sees you."

"He doesn't see me, First Lady."

"Yes, he does. That's why he sent me. So, you could have someone to tell you that he loves you. Come on now. It's okay. Let's get you back to your room." Faye put her arms around her and started the walk back to her room. "Y'all give us some space," she chastised the nurses. "She's okay now."

The nurses continued to comply with Faye's instructions. In any other situation, Elise would have already been forcibly sedated for her outburst. But Faye had managed to calm the situation.

"Let's get you in this bed," Faye said gently.

The nurses assisted Elise back into her bed when another nurse, who obviously didn't know how to read the room, tried to approach her with a sedative.

Faye shot her a disapproving look. "Sir, I don't think she needs that. Elise, baby, do you want to go to sleep?"

"No," Elise said. "I want to see my baby."

Faye looked at Dr. Kakarla, who was still trying to process what just happened. "Can you make that happen, Doctor?"

"Yes, we can."

"I think we can all see Elise is fine now. May I speak with her for a moment while you bring her child?"

Elise looked at the nurses as they exited. One of them looked familiar. He looked like the young man that spoke to Jeremiah and her at Dr. Kakarla's office. The one she said was an angel. He smiled at her as he walked out of the room. But she couldn't process one more piece of information.

"It's going to be okay, baby," Faye said as she gave her a sip of water.

"First Lady, it can only be okay if my baby is okay. I know what the doctor said, but I need you to believe with me. I need you to pray that the Lord give me my baby back. I know I sound crazy, but I waited forty-four years for this. I don't believe my Daddy would let me get pregnant only to take my son away from me now."

Faye's heart raced. Elise was quite literally asking her to pray for the impossible. She had heard of testimonies where God had done things like what Elise desired. But she never thought she would be asked to pray for a literal resurrection. Still, if Elise believed, she was going to believe with her.

"Precious Jesus, we pray you ease Elise in her heart, mind, soul, and spirit. We trust you, Lord. This weapon is formed but it won't prosper. Jesus, please don't let the devil win. And no matter how bad it looks, please show this precious child who is like a daughter to me that she can never fall beyond your grace, mercy, love, and forgiveness. We pray for her family, Lord. Won't you have mercy, Jesus? Won't you please show compassion? We ask in faith that you please make Elise and her family an object of your amazing grace right now. Please spare her sorrow upon sorrow. Please command your mighty angels concerning them to guard them in all their ways so their feet are not stricken against the stone."

As Spirit-filled as Faye's prayer was, it was also a safe prayer. And Elise didn't want a safe prayer. She wanted her baby back.

"First Lady please pray the Lord bring my baby back," she pleaded.

Faye had to decide what to do. She could stay in the shallow water and talk about the will of God, or she could launch out into the deep and believe that God would show unusual mercy to this mother. She chose to believe.

"Father," she continued, "to you who take up the infirmity and carry the disease. To you who said all things are possible for us as we believe. To you who said there was nothing too hard or impossible for you. To you who raised Lazarus from the grave and who raised his own son from the grave. To you, Lord, we lift up little Jeremiah John Traylor II, and we ask with all the faith you give us in Christ that you bring him back to his mother alive and whole and that this mother be allowed to raise her son."

"Yes, Daddy, please," Elise agreed.

"Father, we pray and believe you for a miracle and trust you for victory. We believe you for the impossible and we thank you in advance. And when you do it, we promise to give you all the glory. In Jesus' name, Amen."

Dr. Kakarla came in the room with a nurse as Faye concluded her prayer. They rolled J.J. in a small cart. He was wrapped from head to toe.

"Can I hold him?" Elise asked Dr. Kakarla.

"Of course," she answered as she gently placed the lifeless baby in Elise's arms.

"Thank you, First Lady. Thank you, Dr. Kakarla. I would like to be alone with my baby, please," Elise said calmly.

CHAPTER 43

Wasted Efforts

DAY 255

"Hey, Ang. How are you doing?" Joshua asked his wife. "Hey, Josh. I'm okay," she replied.

"Thanks for letting me come over," he said as he cautiously leaned forward to hug her.

Angela returned the embrace. "It's fine. I needed to know why you haven't signed the divorce papers anyway. Is there a problem?"

"Ha," he laughed nervously. "Wanna jump right in, huh?" "Yes, I do," she asserted. "What's the holdup, Josh?"

Joshua took a deep breath. "Angela, I've got a lot of mixed feelings. In spite of everything with Robert and all the stuff we've been through, I still think we need to fight for our life together."

"Ooh, Josh," she said as she shook her head, "you always have been a glutton for punishment. But believe it or not, I don't wanna punish you. I just want us to be free."

"I know, Angela. But just hear me out. It's still not too late. Honestly, I don't know what to say, but I'm hoping me coming here would show you and the Lord that I haven't given up."

"Josh, I can't speak for the Lord. But me? I'm done. Don't do this to yourself.

Please."

"It's not just about me, Angela. It's about us."

"Well, us is not blackmailing me. You are!" she said aggressively.

"Blackmail?" he asked.

"You're holding up this divorce and you know I'm ready to move on. Then you say you won't sign the papers unless we talk. That's blackmail. And it's a waste of my time."

Joshua tried to process the flood of emotions that accompanied her dark energy. *Was she always like this?* he asked himself. *Is this the same person I fell in love with and would have done anything for? Was my love blind, crippled, deaf, dumb, and crazy?*

He fought back his emotions. He didn't want this to turn into a knockdown drag-out.

"So, what do you want to talk about that we haven't already talked about?" she asked.

"Angela, that's just it. We never really talked about it." "That's because I am tired of talking," she interrupted.

Josh breathed. "Like I said, we never really talked about it. You came to me one day and said you weren't in love anymore and that you couldn't remember the last time you were. I know I was supposed to fight harder for you. But I just couldn't do it. I don't know why."

"Josh, you couldn't fight because you didn't want to. And that's okay. I wish you would just listen to your heart. In your heart, you know you don't want this. You know this doesn't work. But you rationalize everything. All this stuff you doin' now is just making things worse. I told you I love you, and I meant it. But I do not love you like a wife is supposed to love a husband. You don't have to keep putting yourself through this. It's over and I have gone as far as I plan to go. I'm not going any farther. Not with you. Not like this."

"Angela," he said, staying composed. "Would you please just try to listen? The same way you don't remember when you stopped being in love with me, I don't remember when I stopped truly functioning in my role as your husband. But I did and I want to fix it. I want to make it right."

He took a breath and reached for her hand, but she quickly folded her arms. "Listen," he continued, "we have to know there is another side to all of this.

You're right, there is a big part of me that wants to give up. But I still think we should try."

Angela realized how she must have sounded to him and tried to soften a little. "But Josh, what would be the point? We aren't happy. I don't know if we ever were."

Joshua felt her guard might be coming down, and he wanted to be as honest as possible. "I'm not sure either," he responded. "But we're here now. Can't we try? Angela, I will do most of the work. I know it's my responsibility. You don't even need to meet me halfway. I just need you to meet a quarter of the way. An eighth of the way?" He tried to smile through all his mixed emotions. Was he getting through to her? Did he even want to?

"Josh, you need to leave. This is pointless. Sign the papers. Don't sign them. Either way, I'm done. And I am not going to sit up here anymore and pretend to be your wife. Not for you, not for the kids, not for anybody. You sad, Josh? You mad, Josh? You lonely, Josh? Well, welcome to my world. Sucks, doesn't it? Like I said, you don't know what it's like to dread coming home to somebody. To breathe but only getting foul air. To have them touch you and to feel totally and completely repulsed when you feel their hands on your body."

"So, you feel repulsed when I touch you?" Joshua asked.

"I'm sorry. That was ugly. Like I said. This is only making things worse. You really need to go."

"You heard her, homie," a deep voice said from the top of the stairs. "Jemarcus. No," Angela said.

Joshua looked her squarely in the eye to see what she would do. True to form, Angela looked straight back at him.

"I tried to tell you you should leave," she said unapologetically.

"Yeah, homie. Stop embarrassing yourself. Time to bounce," Jemarcus said.

Joshua stood up and faced the stranger in his house. "Why don't you show me to the door?" he said defiantly.

"Jemarcus, I told you to stay out of this. Go back upstairs. Josh, you need to leave," Angela said.

"I'm leaving, wifey. As soon as your friend Jemarcus shows me out."

Joshua was by no means a small man, but Jemarcus was considerably broader and a little taller. He came down the stairs and stood just a few inches from Joshua's face.

"Time. For you. To go. Homie," he said, poking at Joshua's chest with each word.

Angela knew that was a mistake but before she could intervene Joshua took Jemarcus's arm and flipped him over his shoulder, destroying the coffee table in the process. Joshua scrambled to the floor and placed his knee in Jemarcus's spine as he twisted his arm painfully behind his back.

"Hey, wifey," Joshua said calmly. "Do you mind handing me those divorce papers you were so concerned about?"

"Josh, please. Let him up!" Angela pleaded.

"Jemarcus, you'd better tell my wifey, who I can only assume you are here to pray with and encourage, that she need to get yo homie those papers so you can escort me out. Oh, and a pen too, please… wifey."

"Baby, get him the papers!" Jemarcus pleaded.

"Baby?" Joshua said as he wrenched Jemarcus's arm just a little tighter. "Yeah…baby. Get me those papers," Joshua goaded.

Angela complied and brought Joshua the divorce papers and a pen.

"This might be a little sloppy, wifey. Just tell the judge I had to use my left hand because my right hand was, you know…full. I mean, you obviously understand having your hands full, don't you, wifey?" he asked sarcastically.

Joshua signed the papers on Jemarcus's back and threw them casually at Angela's feet. He leaned forward and whispered in Jemarcus's ear as he noticed a tear coming from the larger man's eye, "Hey, Jemarcus. Just FYI, my wifey over there, well, I guess ex-wife now, you know, the one you just called 'baby,' she knows full well what I'm capable of. If she really cared about you, she wouldn't have had you here when I was. Just think about it. Now, just so you know, if I wanted to, I could take your little arm with me. But I'm gonna let you keep it. Then I'm going to walk out of the house that I paid for, and you can do you. Ha.", he looked up at Angela with disgust, "Or my ex-wife. Or whatever. All that's hurt now is your pride. Ice up and you will be okay. Now I know the pain is excruciating. But my brother, please listen. This is important. When I let you go... don't you say a word. Just let me go. And don't you get up until you hear my truck drive away...homie."

Joshua gave Jemarcus's arm one more twist and slowly got up. He released him and walked away intentionally not looking at Angela.

CHAPTER 44

Helpmate

DAY 256

Jeremiah sat in the corner of Elise's hospital room holding J.J. They were both fast asleep.

"Daddy, thank you for my little miracle," Elise said.

"Elise, you have had a day, sis! I can't believe you guys went through all of that. But God!" Shania said.

"But God is right," First Lady agreed. "But Shania, you should have seen yo sister running up that hallway. Babay, every patient on this floor got up out the bed to see what the goins-on was."

"Elise, sis, did you clown?"

"I may have had a moment," Elise said sheepishly, recalling her outburst before J.J.'s miraculous resurrection.

"But Jeremiah, though?" Shania continued. "Got everybody scared and he just needed ten stitches and some dangum Tylenol."

"Well, I was the first one to get it," one of the nurses said. "I was like, 'this little thang here is about to deal with me!'"

"I'm so sorry," Elise said humbly. She didn't mind any of the good-humored teasing. All that mattered was that the Miracle Worker had returned her husband and child back to her safe and sound. Jeremiah was okay and J.J. was alive and well. Just like First Lady prayed.

"It's okay," the nurse comforted. "That was way too much for anyone.

Besides, anyone can see that this is from God. We're all so happy for you." "Thank you," Elise said.

"And I know you are rejoicing in your miracle," the nurse said in a more serious tone, "but legally, your husband can't sleep and hold the baby. We could get in a lot of trouble."

"Aww, him so tired," Elise said as she looked at her husband and her child. "But we don't want to be any more trouble. We want y'all to remember us for our miracle and not for us breaking hospital rules."

"Or acting a plumb nut and running all over the hospital," Shania teased. "Leave me alone, girl, and bring J.J. to me. I'll take him, nurse. I will be up for a little while. I'm too thankful to sleep," Elise laughed.

"No, ma'am," the nurse contradicted. "I don't think you understand. We take the rules here very seriously. Your husband has to leave and we're taking the baby." "Ma'am, I said I'm sorry. He'll wake up. Please. We've had a very hard day.

We just want to be together. Miah, wake up, baby."

"He's not waking up, ma'am, and the baby is coming with me," the nurse said coldly.

Elise tried to protest but an invisible hand pressed against her chest and would not allow her to move. She tried to scream but nothing would come out.

The nurse violently ripped J.J. from Jeremiah's arms and started out of the room carrying his little body by the feet. Jeremiah didn't move.

"Ma'am," First Lady said sweetly. "Can't you give them another chance?" "What difference does it make?" the nurse said. "This baby is dead anyway." "You're always running around here thinking you're so special, Elise," Shania said harshly. "Now look at you. You won't ever see your baby again."

Elise continued to struggle but the unseen hand wouldn't let her move. She looked at Shania and First Lady hoping they would help, but they just looked at her. They shook their heads like they were blaming her. She gave up her struggle to move and tried to scream until her words finally escaped her lips.

"Daddy, please help me. Please don't let her take my baby."

A harsh and angry voice answered her, "No, you shouldn't have done this." "But what did I do? Please, Daddy. What did I do? What did I do? Please tell

me and I will fix it. I promise. Please, Jesus, I prayed for this. Please don't take my baby. What did I do?"

"Elise, baby, wake up. It's okay. We're here. It's just a bad dream. Wake up."

Elise woke up to First Lady's face as she gently stroked her cheek.

"Hey, sis. It's okay. We're here," Shania said as she gently held her hand. "Is this real?" Elise asked.

"Yes, this is real, baby. But we're here," Faye answered gently. "Did they tell you?" she asked Shania.

"Yeah, sis, First Lady told me. I came as soon as I could. And I am so sorry, but God is going to bring you through this."

Elise didn't want to hear about God right now. She just needed to know where her husband was. "Jeremiah?" she whispered.

"Baby, Jeremiah was hurt pretty badly in the accident. They have him stabilized. He's at Memorial Hospital downtown. They have the best trauma unit in town," Faye explained.

"How is he?"

"Baby, Wayne is with him. I've already texted him. He's going to call and let you speak to Jeremiah's doctor."

"Is it that bad that you can't tell me?"

"Elise, I'm not going to lie to you. It sounds serious but I'm not a doctor and I won't be able to…." Faye's phone rang as she was trying to explain the situation to Elise. "Hey, Wayne. Yes, she's up. I have you on speaker. She can hear you."

"Hey, daughter. It's Pastor G. How are you?"

"Pastor G., please tell me Jeremiah is okay," Elise pleaded.

"Daughter, I am here with the doctor now. He wants to talk to you. Doctor, this is his wife. She can hear you."

"Hello, Mrs. Traylor. This is Dr. Allen. We are seeing after your husband." "Is he okay?" Elise asked.

"Ma'am, his injuries are very severe. He took the brunt of the collision. He has a tough night ahead of him. He has an array of internal injuries. We had to remove his spleen and he has some extensive kidney damage, along with a collapsed lung. His leg is broken in two places, his arm is broken, and he has several broken or cracked ribs. But none of those injuries are life threatening. We are most concerned with his head injury. His brain is swelling against his skull, and we need to perform surgery to relieve that pressure. Afterward, we will have to induce a coma while he heals. I know this is a lot to process, but do you have any questions?"

"Is my husband going to live?" Elise asked very simply.

"We will do everything we can to pull him through, but right now I can't make any promises. We'll know more in the next forty-eight to seventy-two hours. Right now, I need to get back to your husband. He's stable for now, but he has a long night and perhaps a long few days in front of him."

"I will be there right away, Doctor. Please do everything you can to save my husband's life."

"We will, ma'am, thank you. Goodbye."

"Baby girl, did I hear you right? Did you say you would be here right away?

Listen to Pastor G. now. You need to rest."

"Pastor, I will see you in a little bit. I love you. Bye."

"Now Elise...," Pastor Gregory started to protest before his wife intervened. "Wayne, I will handle this end. I will call you back," Faye said as she disconnected the call. "Elise, it's 3 A.M., sweetie. You've just had a...surgery. Why don't you try to rest? Wayne will tell us if there are any changes with Jeremiah."

"Three A.M.!" Elise hollered. "I can't believe I fell asleep. The last thing I remember was you leaving when they brought me the baby... and... and... I don't want to talk about it, but then they came and took him, and I just sat here. I must have fallen asleep. I need to go be with Jeremiah."

"You can't go anywhere right now, sweetie. They need to observe you." Elise looked Faye squarely in her eyes. "First Lady. You know I love you.

Thank you for being here. But you are either going to get me out of here or you are going to get out of my way. Either way I am going to be with my husband."

Shania reached across from the other side of the bed and gently touched Faye's arm. "We're not going to be able to stop her, First Lady. Not when she's like this. We just need to try to help her."

"So, we're doing this?" Faye asked.

"We're doing this," Elise confirmed. "You tell them to bring me whatever forms I need to sign, but I need to go be with my husband."

CHAPTER 45

Why Did I Wake Up?

DAY 266

Jeremiah opened his eyes to sheer agony. Even the slightest twitch was excruciating. His vision was blurred and he was totally confused. *Where am I?* he thought. He tried to sit up, but his body punished him for the effort. He slowly turned his head and saw a heart monitor and several I.V. tubes in his right arm. *Am I in the hospital?* he asked himself. *Why am I here?* He tried to think. *If I'm in the hospital, where's Elise? Where's my mom and dad?* What could possibly have happened to put him in the hospital?

He tried to process his situation as his head throbbed. If they had given him anything for the pain, it must have worn off. *I should have a buzzer for the nurse if I'm in the hospital,* he thought.

Before he could look for it, his nurse came in. He was a pudgy, short, older gentleman whose voice was totally different than his appearance.

"Mr. Traylor, you're back with us, I see," he said with a powerful bass voice. "The doctor will be in soon. Let me check your vitals."

Jeremiah tried to speak. "What's happening? Why am I here?" He tried to articulate his words but for some reason he couldn't open his mouth.

"Mr. Traylor, you have several injuries, including a broken jaw. We had to wire your jaw shut. That's why it's difficult for you to speak. They had to perform surgery on your head to relieve some pressure. You have broken bones along the left side of your body, including two breaks in your leg, a broken arm, and several broken ribs. There are some other things going on that your doctor will explain. For now, just know that you're safe."

"How long have I been here?" he asked as best he could, considering his jaw was broken.

"Mr. Traylor, you were in an accident. You've been here for ten days, sir." "Ten days?!" he exclaimed as his body jolted instinctively. An action he quickly regretted, as it only served to send an excruciating burst of pain through his whole body.

"Please stay calm, Mr. Traylor. We had to put you in a coma while the swelling in your brain went down. The doctor will explain everything. I will let him know you are awake."

"Where is my wife?"

"This is actually one of the few moments she hasn't been by your side. She won't even let us touch you without explaining what we're doing and why. We tease her that she can go ahead and apply for her nurse's license after you're discharged. But she can't be in two places at once. I am sure she will be back soon. Now tell me, on a scale of one to ten, how is your pain level?"

"I'm not sure," Jeremiah responded weakly. "Maybe an eight if I just lay here.

Nine if I talk. Ten if I move."

"Let me adjust your I.V. drip and see if we can bring it down some, but it's best not to talk or move right now."

"Is my wife okay? Was she in the accident too?"

"Mr. Traylor…she's fine. She's just worried about you more than anything.

Like I said, I am sure she will be back soon."

Jeremiah started to ask more questions when he suddenly felt like he couldn't keep his eyes open. The nurse's adjustment to his I.V. was doing its job on his pain and his restlessness. Soon he was asleep.

When he woke again, his mind was less foggy, and his pain had decreased some. He examined himself and realized his entire left leg was in a cast and suspended in the air. His left arm was also in a cast up to his elbow. His whole left side felt discombobulated.

His thoughts quickly returned to Elise. He didn't have to search for her, though.

"Hey, handsome, how are you?" she said as she got up from a nearby couch. Her voice was comforting, but it didn't have the same ring he fell in love with.

He remembered the nurse telling him he had been there for ten days, but from her appearance he would not have been surprised if she would have told him it had been ten years. She looked exhausted. The nurse told him she had constantly been by his side, but it wasn't just fatigue. Something was different…and something was wrong.

"Lise, what's going on?"

"Miah, baby, I am so sorry. I promise you I've been here, but I've been going back and forth checking on Daddy too. Pastor G. and First Lady have been helping me out, but when you woke up yesterday you caught us in transition while nobody was here."

"That was yesterday?"

"Yes, baby. But I'm here now. The doctors say you're a miracle, but I already knew that."

Her words lifted his spirits, but he could still tell something was wrong. "Why did you have to check on Pop?"

"Miah," she said as she gently stroked his good arm, "tell me what you remember."

"What do you mean?"

"The doctor said you might have some memory loss and might need help remembering what happened. I need to know what's the last thing you remember." "I remember waking up yesterday and wondering what was going on," he mumbled.

"Do you remember the accident? Or what happened with Mari and Daddy?" Elise asked him.

"Babe, it's really hard to think. Can you just tell me what's going on? Are Mari and Daddy okay? And what about Mama?"

Elise closed her eyes and searched for the right words. She hadn't expected to have to remind him his mother was gone. "Baby…Mama Etta is gone. I know it's hard, but you have to try to remember. We buried her a few months ago. Don't you remember?"

"I think so," he said as the sad memory regenerated itself in his mind. I remember her being sick. You and Mari sang to her, we were all talking…and then she was gone."

"I'm sorry, baby. But that's good. It's not a good memory, I know, but it's good that you can remember. Now do you remember what happened with Daddy and with Mari? Elise asked, hoping he would spare her having to tell it all over again.

"I'm not sure," he said. "I think Daddy fell and I remember Mari crying but I don't remember why.

"Miah, Daddy didn't just fall. He had a massive stroke. It's bad but he's holding on.

"Is he going to be all right?" Jeremiah asked, fearing her answer.

"He's still with us. That's all we can ask for now." "Is Mari okay? Was she in the accident?" he asked.

"Mari is safe," Elise said. She was too emotionally and physically exhausted to recount losing their daughter. She would have to explain that later. "But Miah," she continued, "what about me? Do I look different to you?

"Babe, you look a little tired," he said, trying not to hurt her feelings.

"I know I look a mess, babe. But that's not what I mean," she said as she took a step back, turned to the side, and pulled her top tightly to her belly.

For the first time, Jeremiah's eye's brightened and a hint of a smile danced across his damaged face. He didn't remember much but he remembered that his wife was pregnant, and he was about to have a son.

"Lise! You had the baby!" he exclaimed, ignoring his pain. Elise nodded and held back her tears.

"Where is he?" he asked as he tried to figure out the best way to hold his son with only one arm. Maybe Elise could just lay him on his chest? But Elise didn't seem very excited.

"Miah, if I could fix this for you, I would. I wish I could lay him in your arms.

And I wish he was here instead of me."

"What do you need to fix?" he asked. "Lise...where's our son?" "I'm so sorry, Miah."

"Lise...babe. Where's J.J.?" he pleaded.

Elise knew he had to hear the words. She could only hope his injuries and his faith would keep him from reacting the way she did when she was told the terrible truth she was about to tell him. "Miah, we got hit by a drunk driver. I don't think you ever saw him. J.J. didn't make it. It was too much for him." son.

Jeremiah shook his bandaged head in disbelief. Not his son. Anything but his

"Lise...are you telling me our son is...dead?" he asked. "I'm sorry, Miah," she tried to comfort.

Questions flooded his mind. *How did he die? What happened? Did he suffer?*

But he didn't get any answers to his unspoken questions as his grief overwhelmed him.

"J.J.!" he called out, not expecting an answer. "Lord, please. Not my son, Jesus," he said weakly as he began to weep.

Elise lowered the guardrail on his bed and lay her head next to him. She didn't have much strength left but whatever she did have, she would give to him.

CHAPTER 46

Unreachable

DAY 280

"Don't worry about that, sweetheart. I will handle it," Elise told John's nurse. "It's no trouble," the nurse reassured her.

"I know it's not. And we appreciate you. I just feel so helpless. I want to do something for him. Besides, I have his favorite scents and lotions. I'm going to give him a little makeover before I go back to check on my husband."

"And how's he doing?"

Elise didn't want to lie and didn't have energy to explain. She simply shrugged her shoulders.

"Okay," the nurse said, "I will leave you to it as long as you promise not to try to turn him over!"

"I won't," Elise promised as she started her pampering session on John. "Hey, Daddy. It's me. Daddy's Girl. We gon get you spruced up, okay? But when you wake up, we are going to have words, young man. If you wanted a break, you just had to say so."

Elise poured some warm water in the bowl and mixed it with John's favorite scent for his sponge bath.

"Now I sensed the last time that you were a little embarrassed. I'm going to need you to just let your daughter take care of you. Don't be all sensitive about me seeing your…well…you know. We won't ever speak of it. And if you don't like it, here's a thought…just wake up and wash your own little sweet tail."

Elise wiped him gently but thoroughly from head to toe and patted him dry before applying his favorite lotion.

"I'm actually becoming a pro at this. At least your son will move a little bit. You just lying there like a bump on a log getting all this attention. You Traylor men," she continued. "You love to smell good but if all these women who be sweatin' y'all only knew…y'all cute but just as ashy as you want to be. Can't have my daddy sittin' up here dry as the dangum Sahara Desert. There you go. Now let's get this scruff handled," she said as she ran her fingers on the side of his face. "Now Daddy, when, and I did say when, you come out of this, you can fuss

but I don't know if I'm gon be able to shape up your goatee like you like it. I'll try, though. I'm gon get the sides all baby face like you like it, and I will do my best with these clippers. Don't be mad if it's not perfectly symmetrical, okay? Can't have my daddy looking like Grizzly Adams up in this joint. Mama Etta would kill me. I could hear her now, 'Elise, you had one job, baby.'"

Elise heated up the water and lathered John's face.

"I know, I know…shave with the hair so you don't bump up. I got you, Daddy. Ooh, wee, Daddy," she said as she finished his shave. "Lookin' good. Okay. Here we go with the clippers. I'm just gon take my little time and edge you up. Daddy, I'm just gon say it. Ya baby girl got skillz. I don't believe you been paying folks to do this all these years. You coulda let me do it. It would have given us more time to kick it together. But we're going to have plenty of time. Right? Plenty of time," she said, more to herself than to John.

Elise finished her makeover and continued her one-sided conversation. "Daddy, if I took a picture of you and sold it, would you let me keep all the money? I think I could get a nice little piece of change with you looking like this. But anyhoo…I digress. I know you have a lot of questions. Jeremiah…is doing okay. He's not talking too much. And it has nothing to do with his jaw. He just kinda lays there. He misses you. Like me, I think he just wants you to come back and tell him everything is going to be all right. I have to be hypocritical, Daddy. When Mama Etta was ready to leave, I told Jeremiah he had to let her go. I hope you're not ready to go, because I'm not letting you. You have to stay, Daddy. On life, you have to stay. I'm sorry, but you've spoiled me. Now you have to do what I say. But back to your son…he's had three more surgeries. One on his arm and two on his leg. He had an infection, but they caught it early and he's doing better. He's going to have a nice scar on his head. He hasn't mentioned it, but I know he's thinking about it. Lowkey, you know yo son is a pretty boy, right? I guess it will be my job to let him know he's still the most handsome man in the world. Daddy, I know he doesn't feel good. But why won't he talk to me? I really need him to talk. I really need him to tell me it's okay. What's that? You're telling me it's going to be okay? Daddy, I knew you would say that. You're so sweet! I remember when I sold my first house. Jeremiah threw a little party for me to celebrate. Yes, Daddy. I know it was actually your idea. He wasn't quite super husband yet. But you were such a great coach. Thank you. But anyway, I remember you gave such a simple toast. You said, 'Elise, I love you and I'm proud of you. You will always be Daddy's Girl.' Daddy, you don't know how that gassed me up. That was the first time you ever called me 'Daddy's Girl'. I mean I ran off of that for years. Doggone John Traylor is proud of me? Shoot! It don't get no better than that. So, I have to tell you something. I've never lied to you. Never had to. And I've told you more than what most daughters-in-law would share, but I've done something. Something I'm ashamed of…or at least I should be. I know you wouldn't be proud. I need this confession to be enough because I know you wouldn't understand if I gave you the details. Just please know that I hate myself more than you ever could. So, I need you to let me keep being Daddy's Girl. And I really need you to come back. I need you to wake up. I need you to hold me while I cry and tell me, 'Daddy is here.' God took him, Daddy. He took my baby, and I don't know what I'm going to do. He took Amari too. Even when Jeremiah gets better, I don't know how I'm going to make it past this. But you know what keeps me going? Your wife. I promised Mama Etta I would take care of you, and that's what I'm going to do. So, I just need a little bit of you back. I will love you and take care of you, but I need that smile. I need my hugs. They say you won't ever be able to walk or talk again. So be it. But I need you to come up with a little hand signal or an eye twinkle that says, 'Leave my baby alone.' Okay? I need you. You don't get to love me for the last twenty-three years and ditch now. No, sir. What's that? You miss your wife. I hear you. I do too. But I promised to take care of you, so this is happening. Daddy, if there is any way, I need to you to come back before this funeral. Pardon my language but this has been absolute hell on earth. Jeremiah can't leave the hospital and we won't have the funeral without him there. But I can't even get closure. They are going to put my baby in the ground and we need you there. Please, Daddy. You have to hear me. You know you can't tell me no, so stop trippin' and wake up. I meant now, sir. No? Okay, worth a try. Just be back before the funeral and I will let it slide. I have to go see about Jeremiah now. I'll be back soon. I love you, Daddy."

CHAPTER 47

Defeated

DAY 285

"Hey, girl," Elise greeted Monique as she remembered how she treated her during their last couple of meetings. She tried to channel her inner Jeremiah. If there was going to be any hope of getting Amari back, then they needed an ally.

"Hi Elise," Monique greeted her. "How are you doing? How's everyone?" "We are all doing as well as could be expected. We're hanging in there." "Praise the Lord for that," Monique said.

"I guess you know I'm calling about my little girl." Elise knew that was a strong term to use, but at this point it didn't matter.

"Elise, I figured that but I'm not sure what you want me to say. You've been through so much. I don't want to make things harder on you."

"I know you don't and Monique…I'm sorry. I know I was awful to you. I called myself being protective of my child. But I just want to let you know that I know none of this is your fault and I am sorry for how I acted."

"Apology totally accepted and appreciated, Elise…really… thank you for saying that. Oh, and thank you for calling me Monique again. You only called me Ms. Lacroix when you were considering violence."

"Ha. I know, girl. I'm sorry, though. My bark is generally worse than my bite.

Short girl syndrome and all that."

"It's totally understandable, Elise. Sooo...is there anything else I can do for you?"

"Monique...I don't ask favors easily. The first half of my life nothing was given to me and the last half...well, I thought I had everything but for the most part I never had to ask. But now I'm asking...there has to be a way. Amari doesn't belong with her. What's our move? I know this doesn't sound good, but you know what all has happened. Please, there has to be a way."

"Elise, there is nothing I can do but tell you the hard truth. The same truth I told your lawyer the other day that I'm pretty sure he relayed to you. I'm sorry, but there are no other moves to be made. Officially, all I can say is that Amari has been placed with a blood relative and she's safe. This is the judge's decision, and at this point he is not inclined to consider the last three years. And Elise, I want to stay Monique, but this part might put me back in Ms. Lacroix territory, even if Amari's aunt were not in the picture, it would be hard to get you reinstated as her guardian right now. I can't pretend I don't know what your family is going through. Your mother-in-law's passing. Your father-in-law is seriously ill. Your husband is critically injured...and you've endured other traumas. You need to heal, Elise. Amari's safe."

"Monique, I don't just want her safe. I want her home. I know you can understand that."

"I do. I really do but it's out of my hands. Elise, I'm so sorry. But I know you are a family of faith. I know the Lord will see you through this."

"Is she okay? Have you seen her?"

"I have dozens and dozens of other kids on my caseload, but I have made a couple of extra visits to her. She's making it. That's all I can say."

"Does she ask about us?" "Elise...she's fine." "Monique, please."

"Yes. And I tell her what I just told you. I tell her you are all fine." "Do you think her aunt would let me see her?"

"No," Monique said bluntly. "I don't think she would allow that at all. I'm sorry."

Elise didn't respond. "Elise...are you still there?"

"I'm here," Elise said in defeat. "Listen, I need to get back to my husband and daddy. Thank you, Monique."

"I'll be praying for you, Elise. Take care."

"Okay. Goodbye," Elise said as she disconnected the call.

Elise sat alone in her beautiful new home. Some of the rooms still smelled of fresh paint. Less than a year ago, it was a sign of God's blessing on her life. Now it just seemed like an empty shell. There was no love, laughter, or life in it, which was fitting because that's exactly how she felt.

CHAPTER 48

Pastor G. and First Lady

DAY 300

"Master," Pastor Gregory prayed, "I've been preaching your word most of my life. I've never preached for money or notoriety but in your kindness, you have provided and given me favor. You've given me a good wife, a good life, and a good church. You've blessed me to carry them in my heart and my spirit as your under shepherd. I've tried to love your people, Father. I've tried to be faithful. And with every trial and tragedy, I have pointed your people back to the cross. Back to you. But this, Lord? What I have to do today. I don't know that I can do it. I'm struggling, Lord. Even though I know you will work out everything for good, I have to ask how. And Father... I have to ask why. Why these kids? Why so much pain at once? Lord, please have mercy. I plead with you for them, and I plead with you for me. We just buried my sweet little sister Etta Ween. My best friend is hanging on to life. And now you want me to preach a funeral for a baby who barely even got a chance to breathe? And you want me to tell a young man who is broken physically and spiritually to take joy in you? How could this be your plan, Lord? Father, I never ran from the call you had on my life. You said 'go tell them about my son' and I went. No matter what it cost me, I went. But I am ashamed to say that right now in this moment, I don't want to be a pastor. I don't even want to be a pew member. I don't know how to encourage this family. What am I supposed to say? 'Hey, son, your mama is gone, your daddy is suffering, your baby never got to see a sunrise, the devil has unleashed every lie under the sun against you, and your body is broken. But hey, Jeremiah, God is a good God. Oh, yes, he is. And Elise, don't you worry, just try to have another baby, that's assuming your husband doesn't go to jail. Don't worry about it. This setback is just a setup for a comeback.' Father, right now I don't know if I believe all of that, so how can I tell them? I know now how Jonah felt, Lord. I know I have to obey you, but I want to run in the other direction. If I didn't think there was a storm and a huge fish waiting for me, I would run out of this church."

"Well, you do know, don't you, Pastor?"

Pastor Gregory was startled to hear the voice of his wife. He had been so deep in prayer; he hadn't noticed her come into his office.

"Honey, what are you doing?" Faye asked. "It's time."

"Baby, this whole church has been looking forward to this birth. I don't know what I am going to say. And I don't know how to comfort those kids. I don't know how to explain all of this to them, so it makes sense!" he explained.

"You doin' too much, honey," Faye said plainly.

He looked at his wife with a puzzled expression. "What do you mean?" "You're putting on yourself what only Jesus can bear. Only God knows why

he allowed all of this, and he doesn't report to you. Quit worrying about what you don't know and what you don't understand, and then you tell them what you do know. You know Jesus is on the throne. You know he died on the cross for their sins and was raised from the dead. You know his grace is sufficient even when he doesn't take the thorns away. Just tell them that he sees their broken hearts and he is close and tell those kids that we are all hurting with them. And don't let your pride get in the way."

"Pride?" he asked, taken aback by her words.

"Yes, honey…pride. You know how you preachers can get. You get so concerned with folks telling you how you preached that thang and getting all those amens and telling everybody in town how you tore up the church. Right now, I think a few 'I don't knows' are appropriate because I promise you Jeremiah and Elise don't know. And you pretending like you have all the answers won't help them or God's people. But telling them you still trust God in the dark will. Telling them that their pastor loves them will. And you telling them that Jesus is closer now than he's ever been, that will help them. And even if they can't receive it right now, God will be glorified. And that's your job, Pastor."

"Baby, I am not trying to be prideful," Pastor Gregory argued. "I just don't want to do this. I wish I could take their pain away."

"Amen, Pastor," she said enthusiastically. "Say that!"

He smiled at his wife. "I know what you're trying to do, baby, but I just wish somebody else could do this."

"I don't. You have been my husband for forty years. But right now, it's not my man that they need. They need God's man. And you are that man. So, this is what we are going to do. Your wife is going to pray for you. Then you are going to get up and go be God's man for those kids. And I believe that when your feet hit the water, when you go in that room, when you lead them down that aisle, and when you open your mouth to preach, God is going to stand up in you and you will know exactly what to say."

She turned his chair around and gently hugged him close to her bosom. "Precious Lord, your servant is broken. Put him back together so you can use him. Help him and help us in our unbelief. Help us in our hurt. Right now, we need you to give him what Elise and Jeremiah need. Stand up in him and speak through him Jesus. The devil is on a rampage but God, we trust you now. We don't see you. We don't feel you. We don't understand you. And Lord, we're sorry but we don't like this. But we love you and we trust you. So, we ask in the name of Christ Jesus the risen savior that you don't just go with my husband, but God, go in him. Grant him your strength and we promise to give the glory back to you. And Father, please manifest your power and presence today, Lord, because Jeremiah and Elise and this entire church are slipping. We can't hold on, so we ask that you hold on to us. In Jesus' name, Amen. Come on, baby, they're waiting."

Pastor Gregory got up and his wife helped him put his jacket on.

"You know what, baby?" he said as he smiled warmly at her. "I think I'm gon keep you."

"Well, I think I might just stay," she smiled back. "Let's go."

CHAPTER 49

Dearly Beloved, We Are Gathered Here Today…

DAY 300

Pastor Gregory and his wife joined Elise and Jeremiah in the family waiting area. The room was full but quiet as everyone spoke in hushed tones. *Nobody knows what to say,* he thought to himself. Besides Jeremiah and Elise, he did not recognize many of the other family members. Jeremiah had a small family and Elise had no significant connection to her blood relatives. Along with John and Etta Ween, he and his wife Faye were her parents and the closest thing she had to family were the members of their small church. He and John used to argue over which one of them was her favorite. "I'm the pastor!" he would assert. But John would always trump him with "I'm the daddy." Elise loved it. He always thought it was an amazing demonstration of God's love that this young lady who had no parents as a child now had two sets as an adult.

His eyes found Elise's as she sat next to Jeremiah in his wheelchair. She returned a faint smile as she sat as close to her husband as she could. There seemed to be a distance between them, though. The grief and pain that separated them was almost visible. Jeremiah looked as if he was a million miles away. He must have lost at least twenty pounds over the last six weeks. And with it, all his hope.

Pastor Gregory felt his wife squeeze his hand. "Time to go to work, Pastor," she whispered.

Faye sat next to Jeremiah. It was fitting since he could not feel the comforting touch of his mother. Pastor Gregory sat next to Elise.

"We're here, kids," Faye said gently.

"Hey, First Lady," Elise responded. "Hey, Pastor G."

"It's time. Are you ready to go in?" Pastor Gregory asked.

Elise looked to her husband, who hadn't acknowledged them yet. "Baby," she said gently, as if she didn't want to startle him from a peaceful sleep. "You okay?" She gently shook his hand.

"Oh, yeah, babe, I'm fine," Jeremiah responded halfheartedly.

"I just want to echo what my wife just said. We're here. Please know we're taking these steps with you," Pastor Gregory said as he called everyone to gather closely for prayer.

Jeremiah remained in his wheelchair and a chair was placed next to him for Elise. Pastor Gregory and First Lady Faye stood behind them. Pastor Gregory prayed as the remaining family and friends circled around them and extended their hands towards Jeremiah and Elise.

"Father," he began, "we give you praise in Jesus' name. Our hearts are broken…but we give you praise. We don't understand…but we give you praise. Lord…we confess we're angry…but we give you praise. And Lord, out of the depths of our pain, despair, and confusion, we want to declare our trust in you. We stand on behalf of your son and your daughter and believe together that this weapon you have allowed to be formed against them won't prosper. We give praise to the God who works all things, and Jesus, we believe you meant all things, together for their good. As my friend, their father, would say, we still believe you are God. You are always right, always good, and always for us. So, we seek you for Jeremiah and Elise. You have allowed much to be taken from them, but we know you have not removed your love or your grace. Grant your strength to them, we pray, Father. You have let the devil sift them as wheat, so now we need you to pray for them, Jesus, so their faith does not fail. Lord, won't you renew their strength? Won't you revive them again? Won't you show them your brand-new mercies? Oh, God, we believe together right now, hoping against all hope, that you will do all of that and that along with Christ you will graciously give them all things. And Lord, as John, my friend, my brother, their father, clings to life, we drop him at the feet of Jesus. We ask that you spare this son and daughter sorrow upon sorrow and return their father to them. Return our brother to us. Lord, I acknowledge my selfishness, but please return my friend to me as well. Jesus, we need you. And

Father, even in our broken heartedness, we want to thank you that this little precious boy is safe with you. And in this space, we trust your sovereignty, along with your love, and believe that even as these precious parents feel like they can't go on that you are the good shepherd who will carry them forever. And Jesus, we don't want to forget little Amari. You have allowed her to get a special place in our hearts. Would you take care of her, Lord? Would you protect her, Lord? Would you let her know that she is not forgotten? Lord, we give praise to the God who won't leave and won't forsake, and we know you will watch over this precious child. And now, Lord, we have to do something that we don't want to do. We have to say goodbye to Little J.J., who we never got a chance to know. All we can say is have mercy on us, Lord, and help us. We trust that you will. In Jesus' name, Amen."

Pastor Gregory leaned over and whispered in Jeremiah and Elise's ear, "Let's go, kids."

Now Elise seemed to have joined her husband in some faraway place. There were no tears. No sadness. She was just simply there. He felt nothing but emptiness from her and it concerned him. He called Faye close to him, but she spoke before he could.

"I have her," she reassured him, "Don't worry."

They lined up in the church foyer and started the long walk down the center aisle. At the end of the aisle, directly in front of the pulpit, was a small casket holding the body of their infant son, who only lived a few minutes. Pastor Gregory fought against his unbelief and his own tears as he began reciting Psalm 23. He had done so perhaps a hundred times in his ministry but didn't recall a moment where it had been so hard not only to say, but to believe what he was saying. But now was not the time for his doubts. He pressed through as he asked the Lord for strength. He moved behind the pulpit and continued his scripture reading as the family procession finished being seated.

As painful as the occasion was, he took joy at the overwhelming show of love and support. The church overflowed with their regular congregation, along with a multitude of others he assumed were from other parts of Jeremiah and Elise's life. The program was a traditional one for the most part. It included Old and New Testament scripture readings and selections from the choir. But after careful thought, it was decided there would be no words of encouragement. "Pastor G.," Elise told him, "the only one I can take right now is you. If somebody get up there and say the wrong thing at my baby's funeral, they gon see a side of me they not ready for. We just want you talking. You do whatever you feel led to do. We trust you."

Jeremiah's request was simple. "Pastor, just be led by the Holy Spirit but if there is any way to bring God glory and to make our child's life matter in this space, we want that to happen."

The choir finished their selection and Pastor Gregory took his place once again behind the pulpit. He locked eyes with Faye in the front row as she held Elise's hand. Faye returned an encouraging smile.

"Praise the Lord," he began. "Thank you, choir. And thank you, saints, for coming here today to mourn with our dear brother and sister in their time of bereavement. Some of you may have noticed, and may even be feeling some kind of way, that there will be no words of encouragement for the family. You might be thinking, 'I want to express my love for them too.' I assure you there will be plenty of opportunities to do that in the days and weeks to come. This is gon be a marathon...not a sprint. So, today, by the grace of our savior Jesus Christ and by the preference of our beloved Jeremiah and Elise, the only words of encouragement will come from me. Can I get an 'Amen' on that?" Pastor Gregory asked.

"Amen," the congregation said in unison.

"Besides," he continued, "y'all know black folks don't know how to stick to the two-minute rule anyway."

The congregation laughed to themselves.

"Oh, you can laugh out loud. Y'all know nobody ever just talks for two minutes and sits down. But seriously, today is a challenge for our dear brother and sister. It's a challenge for our church. And it's a challenge for your pastor. I have to be honest with you family. Can you allow your pastor to get real with you? Can I keep it 100? Can I keep it a buck, as the young folks say?"

"Amen. Keep it real, Pastor," his congregation agreed.

"Family, I didn't want to be here today," he said as he looked at Jeremiah and Elise as they sat in the front row. He wanted to remind them that they were not only special to the Lord but special to him as well. "Elder in waiting Jeremiah," he said. "I didn't know what I could say to you, son."

"Amen," the church agreed.

"My sweet daughter Elise, Pastor G. doesn't know how to make this better.

But baby, you need to know I would if I could." "I know, Pastor," Elise whispered to him.

"But thank God, we are not a people depending on the wisdom or the oratory skills of Wayne Gregory. Amen? We are a people depending on the finished work of Jesus Christ, and we believe that he who knows the end from the beginning knows exactly what needs to be done today!"

"Amen," the church agreed as they applauded his words.

"But as I was saying, family," he continued, "I didn't want to be here. And one of the reasons I didn't want to be here is because I didn't know what to say. I didn't want this precious couple or this great church the Lord has allowed me to serve to think their pastor had no answer… no comfort…no word. And I absolutely did not want to get up here and give you my thoughts or my opinion. But how many of y'all know you have a praying First Lady?"

"Oh, we know that!" someone shouted.

"Your First Lady and my sweet wife came and picked me up both physically and spiritually. And I don't know how else to say this, but she gave me permission to just be human. And she told me that when my feet hit the water, that the Lord would give me strength and that I would know what to say." He looked lovingly at his wife as she continued to hold Elise's hand. "Baby, I just wanted to say, in front of God and everybody, you were right again. The Lord does indeed have a word."

"Amen!" the congregation shouted.

"You see family, you see Jeremiah, you see Elise. There has to be a space in our Christian experience for the 'I don't know.' A space that acknowledges that Jesus is Lord, we are not, and he is not ever obligated to explain himself. There has to be space left in our lives that only the Lord can occupy, where all he leaves us is his all-sufficient grace. Like Paul, we may plead with him to change a thing, to reverse a thing, to heal a thing, to block a thing, but he does sometimes say, 'No, right here, right now, I have to be enough for you and I am going to exercise my sovereignty and my lordship. I will not explain why you have to go through this but if you trust me, I will see you through it.' So, if God won't explain it, I can't explain it, but I don't want to leave you without hope. Because sometimes even in the darkest places, we as God's people can still dare to hope that what is, will not always be. It was like that for our brother Job."

"All right now, Pastor. We see where you going!" someone shouted from the congregation.

"I thought you might," he agreed. "You see, Job was a man who had everything. He honored the Lord, he had a high standing in the community, he had great land and resources…and he had a family. But the Bible says that when the devil came before the Lord, and how many of us know that the devil still has to come before the Lord? That the Lord offered up Job for the devil's consideration. The devil didn't even ask about Job. Yet the Lord basically said, 'Shoot your nastiest shot at my servant Job and I bet he won't leave me.' And the devil's response was 'You ain't said nothing but a word.' And in one day, Job lost all his oxen, his donkeys, his sheep, his camels, and all his sons and daughters."

He looked Jeremiah squarely in the eye, hoping his gaze could somehow impart life and courage to him. "And the Bible says that 'In all this, Job did not sin by charging God with wrongdoing.'

"But you know it didn't stop there. Because Satan had to come back before the Lord. And y'all know the Lord suggests the devil make a sequel? For the second time, the devil ain't thankin' 'bout Job, but God. See, normally when we say 'but God,' something good is about to happen. I was sick…but God healed me. I was broke…but God provided for me. I was lost…but God found me. 'But God' usually means God is going to turn something around and make the bitter, sweet. He steps in and snatches victory from the jaws of defeat and turns it around for our good. But this 'but God' isn't what I would call good, because the Lord once again offers up our brother Job. And Satan says, 'Oh, I get a part two? I get to make another movie? Lord, I know you think you got it all under control, but I bet I get yo man this time because now I'm about to get really nasty. Before I just got his stuff and his loved ones. This time, I'm getting him.' And even though I think at the time Job would have disagreed, the Lord steps in with mercy and grace and says, 'Hold up now. Do your worst but you must spare his life.' How glad are we that the devil is not an independent agent? How glad are we that he can't call his own shots? How glad are we that when our Lord Jesus sets a boundary that even Satan can't cross it?

"So now Job's finances are depleted, his loved ones are gone, and his body is broken. And in all this, Job still does not turn his back on the Lord nor bring an accusation against him. And it occurs to me that Job is totally unaware of this cosmic showdown as the Lord flexes and shows the devil that for someone like Job, his grace is enough. And whether we want to say the devil took it or the Lord allowed it, Job lost everything except his faith because he says in Job 13:15 that 'Though he slay me, yet will I trust him.'

"Precious family of God, we are all wondering where God is right now. Did he who never sleeps nor slumbers need a nap? Did he change channels and just miss this particular set of events? Does God owe this sweet daughter and faithful son a 'my bad'? Is the Lord of All the Heavens preparing his 'what had happened was' speech for this grieving mother and father? Are God the Father and God the Son looking with the side-eye at God the Holy Spirit and saying, 'Bruh, we left you in charge. What happened?' No, family of God. I say not at all. I still have enough faith in this broken old heart to lift my weary, crying eyes to heaven and say, 'Lord, you're still good and I still trust you.' But there is still enough flesh in me to say, 'I don't like this.' But now is not about this old pastor. It's about these two beautiful sheep the Lord has given me to cover. And Jeremiah. Elise. Your pastor wants you to know that the same Lord you have served since I have known you is still on his throne pouring out grace and mercy. And if you can't receive that right now, it's okay because your church family is going to stand with you and cry with you until you can.

"Still, some of us are wondering, as I alluded to before, where is

God in all of this? All I can say is that he is in the same place he was when Jesus cried out, 'My God, My God, why have you forsaken me?' It didn't look good for Jesus in the moment, but how many of us know what happened three days later?"

"Come on, Pastor G.!" someone shouted.

"So, in that same vein, I want to tell you, your family, our family, that I am believing God for a resurrection for you. I don't mean a literal resurrection of your precious son, mind you. But I mean a resurrection of your faith, your joy, and your peace. I know it looks like the devil is having his way, but we still serve a God who desires an abundant life for us even where the enemy has stolen, killed, and destroyed. Children, I believe that Jesus is not going to let your faith fail. And when this is done, he is going to hold you both up in his righteous right hand and give you victory."

Jeremiah heard the words…but victory? It was hard to remember what it even looked like. Still, in that moment he felt like he might just be able to go on. Crippled? Broke? With a criminal record? Childless? Perhaps all the above, but God certainly would not leave him now and with his help maybe he and Elise could somehow, someway make it back. He wanted to stand but knew he simply couldn't. He wanted to take his good arm and raise it, but right now it needed to stay wrapped around his weeping wife. Instead, he just shouted, "Amen, Pastor!" But the voice that came out was not his normally clear tenor. It was a weak shrill that showed he was still broken not only in body but in soul and in spirit. Regardless, he made up his mind in that moment that he was going to keep trusting the Lord.

"Yes, Pastor," the rest of the church agreed as Pastor Gregory continued. "So, I want to encourage you with the words of David as you think on your son. He's not coming back to you but one day, you will go to him. And when you see him both he and you will be whole and complete, and the Lord will wipe every tear from your eye."

Elise's silent weeping began to graduate to loud wails, but Pastor Gregory didn't feel bad. He knew that was a good thing. She needed to cry. Perhaps even scream.

"And for us, family," he said as he stepped out from behind his pulpit, "do we know we will see our loved ones again? I mean do we know that we know? If we have learned anything as a church, we should know now more than ever that tomorrow is not promised. Life can turn very quickly. When it turns, we need to be ready. And if you're not ready, I have good news for you. But the good news isn't going to be as good if you don't know the bad news. You see, the bad news, my brothers and sisters, is that none of us have a chance with the Lord. None of us are righteous. Not even one! We are all wretched, nasty, sinful people who deserve nothing and can't earn anything. And even if we wanted to do right. Even if we wanted to straighten up and fly right, we are so messed up in the eyes of a holy God we can't even approach Him to have the conversation. We'd be dead before we got close enough to say we're sorry. And I hope you're not banking on any good thing you've done, because the Bible says the best we could do for the Lord would be like filthy rags to him. The Word of God says we have all sinned and fallen short of the glory of God. The Lord doesn't care if you stole a stick of gum or stole someone's reputation or stole someone's life, whatever you and I have done, no matter how small we think it was, that was against God's law deserves death. But praise the name of Jesus for the good news. The good news is that he who knew no sin became sin for us. The good news is that even though the wages of sin is death, the gift of God is eternal life in Christ Jesus our Lord. The good news is that because of what Jesus Christ did for you and me on the cross, our wretchedness and wickedness and sin are no longer counted against us because all of God's wrath was poured on him. The good news is that even though Jesus died on the cross, three days later he rose to life again. Death could not hold him down. And even as you sit there with sins as red as scarlet, the good news is that there is a savior willing to heal you and make your sins white as snow. The Good News is that my Jesus took the wrath that we wretched, wicked, and rebellious people deserve. And if we believe on him, God who punished Jesus for our sins, no longer has to punish us. We who believe in the finished work on the cross have been justified. In Christ, we're no longer guilty. The Holy, Righteous God now becomes a Father who is free to respond to us with his amazing grace. So, my brother, do you believe? So, my sister, do you believe? Do you believe in your heart that he died on the cross and was raised from the dead? If so, while there's still time, will you come? Will you call on the name of the Lord so you can be saved? Will you trust him as your sin bearer? If so, will you just come up here with me? Let me show you my Jesus. He loves you. He forgives you. He wants to turn it around for you. Won't you come?"

Pastor Gregory stood silently and braced for the normal awkward stillness that followed every invitation. "Lord," he prayed silently, "let there be one." But before he could even finish the thought, he saw a young man coming down the aisle with tears streaming down his face. Soon the altar was flooded with people. The church applauded and praised the Lord as people continued to leave their seats.

But Elise found no solace as she continued to scream. Most of her words could not be understood, but a few were clear as she cried, "Why, Lord! My baby! Please!" Those words were clear, and they tore at everyone's soul.

Still, the people continued to come forward even as her wailing intensified. Pastor Gregory wanted to attend to her but knew she was safe with Faye. Right now, the Lord was moving, and he needed to be God's man. He asked those who had come to close in tightly so he could pray for them.

"Father," he prayed, "we thank you for these whom you have drawn to yourself. May they know forever that they are saved by faith alone in Christ alone. May they know forever, Father, that it is by grace they have been saved, through faith. And this is not from themselves or their own efforts. It is your gift given to those who believe in your precious son. We place them in your hands by faith. And we thank you that you have given them faith to believe you for salvation and eternal life in Christ Jesus our Lord. We pray their lives never be the same. Jesus, as your grace has given them faith to believe, we thank you for choosing them even where they would not have chosen you. And even as little Jeremiah John Traylor II is safe with you now, we know in our hearts that you are still the God who works all things together for good for those who love you and are called to your purpose. And for that, God, we give you praise. It is fitting that in this place of death and loss you have chosen to give life, eternal life. And for that, God, we give you praise. So, take these, your new babies, and please grow them in your grace and fill them with your Spirit so they may glorify your kingdom and your name. We thank you for your word that promises that no one can ever snatch them from your hand. And for that, God, we give you praise. In Jesus' name. Amen."

Pastor Gregory allowed those who had flooded the altar to return to their seats before placing the proceeding into the hands of the funeral directors. The ushers began directing the full house, starting from the back of the church, so they could say their final goodbyes to this infant soul they never got a chance to know. Pastor Gregory's heart tightened as Jeremiah and Elise came forward to say their goodbyes. Faye helped Elise to her feet and a deacon rolled Jeremiah forward. Elise's eyes locked in on her lifeless child and another heart-wrenching wail escaped her mouth. She reached for her child, but Faye was ready. She restrained her with enough force to hold her in place but with enough gentleness to let her know she was loved and safe.

Elise collapsed to the floor and continued screaming, but this time her words were very clear. "Please, Jesus, I'm sorry!" she cried. "Please don't take my baby. I'm sorry, Lord. Please don't take my baby!"

But the only response Elise heard was her own wailing. She couldn't hear Faye whispering in her ear that she was still loved. That God was going to turn it around. That she wasn't forgotten. That somehow, someway, someday it was going to be okay. But even as she screamed, Faye continued to speak life to her. She knew Elise could not trust right now. So, she was going to trust for her. Elise stopped struggling and lay in the middle of the floor as Faye held her. Shania also came and knelt next to her sister.

Jeremiah was helpless. His injuries would not allow him to get out of his wheelchair and drop to the floor with his wife. The resolve he felt just moments ago was already starting to wane. Chad wanted to help, but he knew his new job would not be waiting for him once he was able to return to work. Whenever that was. The charges against him still loomed large. Everything he had was gone. His wife was overwhelmed with sorrow. His finances were depleted. His mother was gone. His father was just barely clinging to life. His career was in shambles. His body was broken and perhaps would never be the same. And he was about to bury his infant son. He remembered his mother's warning. But he never imagined his test would be losing his son.

He looked helplessly at Elise as she cried on the floor. His only solace came from the thought that there was absolutely nothing else the Lord could allow to come against him. There was nothing else the devil could take. What else could the enemy steal, kill, or destroy? He had already stolen, killed, and destroyed everything. At least things couldn't get any worse.

CHAPTER 50

Salted Wounds

DAY 340

Jeremiah felt helpless. A feeling he was sadly becoming very accustomed to. The bones in his arm and leg were healing, but there was still much rehab to do before he would be his old self. Certainly, he would not be able to help with any of the heavy lifting required for this arduous and depressing task. He had tried to do the little things, packaging and maybe taking care of the trash, but he quickly realized the ladies made him look like he was moving in slow motion with the packaging and the little kids had the trash detail on lock. So, he simply tried to keep out of everyone's way.

Amid the controlled chaos was Elise. Unlike her broken, crippled husband, Elise was doing everything. She looked like a blur as she orchestrated the workers as well as participated in the different tasks needing to be done. And somehow, she did it with a smile on her face. She teased the men as they moved the refrigerator onto a waiting truck. "Brothers, y'all looking a little tired up there. Pastor G.! I think we need a fitness ministry."

She loved on a young five-year-old boy as he tried to haul some discarded objects to the throwaway pile. "Look at that handsome, strong little man. You so sweet. I'm gon steal you."

The boy's mother, oblivious to how much pain Elise's own humorous statement brought her, joined in the fun. "Sweetie, you can have him. I ain't worried. You will bring him back."

They both shared a laugh as Elise continued being Elise.

A young teenage girl remarked about how beautiful a certain dress of Elise's was.

"Oh, sweetie. You can have that, baby," Elise told her.

"Oh, no, ma'am," the young lady replied. "I didn't mean that. I just think it's pretty."

"Well, you better take it. You just better not look better in it than me or it's gon be on." Elise then turned her attention to Jeremiah. "Hey, handsome. You okay over there?"

"Yeah, Elise, I'm good," Jeremiah responded. Even though he wasn't.

"Ole one-armed, one-legged sexy thang. Babay, when I get that cast off of you!" she joked.

"Stop it, daughter!" Pastor Gregory laughed.

"But Pastor, we's married now," Elise said innocently.

Jeremiah faked a smile. He knew it was all a show. Elise just wanted to encourage him. And she wanted everyone to think that she was okay. But she wasn't. Today was another notch in the devil's belt. Today was the day they were moving out of their house. The house she saw years ago but never imagined would be hers. The house he had gotten for her to raise the children that were now gone. The house that in many ways symbolized to them God's blessing on their lives. Jeremiah wasn't working and their depleted finances had finally broken under an avalanche of financial obligations. He and Elise both had massive medical bills and the payment for his mother's failed experimental treatment was overwhelming. They had to pay Mr. Valero's fee for the failed attempt to save Amari and they still had to keep Jeremiah's lawyers on retainer. Thankfully, his father was still with them, but he needed around the clock care. Elise insisted he get only the best care available, but it also translated to the most expensive.

So, Elise suggested that they take their losses on the house and move into John and Etta Ween's home. "When Daddy recovers," Elise had said, "we can figure out the next step then. But this makes sense, Miah. We are stressing out over this house. We just have to accept that it was not meant to be. It's not like it's the worst thing we've lost lately. Let's just get it over with."

Jeremiah had not wanted to agree to it, but he felt powerless in his current situation to do anything about it.

But to add insult to injury, Elise also said they should sell most of their items. "Miah, baby, listen to me," she reasoned. "Mama Etta and Daddy's house is already full and we have money problems. Why pay to put the stuff in storage? Let's just get all we can from it to get us some breathing room."

So now all Jeremiah could do was stand and watch as everything he had gotten for his wife was sold because he could no longer provide for her. But Elise kept a brave face and continued to smile through the pain. The day went on and soon all the major items had been sold and the necessities that needed to go to their new, and hopefully temporary, home were packaged.

Elise walked over and stood at Jeremiah's side. "Baby, I think you should say something."

"Lise, I don't know what to say," Jeremiah said dejectedly.

"Just try, baby," she encouraged. "I know this sucks. This is not what we planned but these people came out here to help us. They are paying full price for our used stuff. We need to say something."

"Just ask Pastor to say something on our behalf," he countered. "Or you can. You've been working it all day. No need to stop now. You got this," he said as he gave a fake smile.

"Miah," Elise said, "you, not Pastor G. and certainly not me, are the man of this house."

"You mean the house that I lost?" Jeremiah said.

"But baby, I'm still here!" Elise insisted. "Remember, Miah and Lise against…."

"Elise, I can't right now!" Jeremiah pleaded as he interrupted her and turned his head so she couldn't see the tears forming in his eyes.

Elise wanted to comfort him, but she had no strength left. She had to put on a performance for their friends and needed all her remaining energy for the show.

"Hey, errbody!" she said in a loud, joyous voice. "Okay. We know y'all are getting hungry and, ummm, you know we ain't got no money.

And since Jesus ain't here to multiply the bread and fish, we are going to send you on your way. But in all seriousness, Jeremiah and I want to say thank you from the bottom of our hearts. Thank you for all the heavy lifting and helping us pack and move. And thank you for your generosity. I know some of y'all bought stuff you didn't even need.

"Pastor G.," she continued, "you and First Lady keep outdoing yourselves. Thank you for loving on us and seeing us through. And thank you all. Most of you were here for our housewarming and…."

Elise's voice broke. She coughed and tried to compose herself. Jeremiah took her hand. She hoped he would take over but he did not. Sister Faye joined her at her side and held her other hand, and Elise quickly pulled herself together and continued.

"And we appreciate you as our church family coming out to help and to love on us. So again, Pastor G, First Lady, all of you…oh, you too Shania,", she said sarcastically, "we love you. Thank you for being here for us."

Pastor Gregory came and stood behind the three of them. "Church family, we know it's been a long day, but let's all just come in close and cover our brother and our sister in prayer. Lord," he began, "we won't pretend that today is a good day. But with all the faith you will give us, we declare you are still a good God. As these children of yours make this transition that they would not have preferred, won't you strengthen them and manifest within their hearts that you never leave and you never forsake. We give praise to the God of restoration who makes the dry bones live again. And even where there is weeping in the night, we, your people, believe together that morning is coming soon for our beloved Jeremiah and Elise. Please remember them, Lord, and help us to love them and encourage them with the love of your Son Jesus Christ. In that name, the name of Jesus, we pray, Amen."

Everyone in the small circle echoed Pastor Gregory's "Amen," but as Sister Faye looked out of the corner of her eye, she noticed Elise said nothing.

After the Crash

CHAPTER 51

Fallen Angel

DAY 390

Elise had been working feverishly and it was paying off. Her real estate business was flourishing, and her name was quickly spreading around town as someone who could help with residential as well as commercial properties. With Jeremiah unable to work, they needed the money, but the deeper truth was that her work was a much-needed distraction. The death of her son, nursing Jeremiah and John back to health, along with their plethora of financial challenges had all taken their toll on her. On top of all that, she still thought about Amari and Mama Etta every day. Oddly, to say she was in pain might not be the best way to describe her emotional state. Hers was one of numbness. She wasn't sure whether she was numb because of the passing of time or the fact that she was indulging in more than just an occasional glass of wine. In the past, she would process her deepest feelings through her prayers and her conversations with Jeremiah. Now, neither the Lord nor Jeremiah were viable options. Facing her pain was too much to deal with, so going numb was her last line of defense.

She felt good physically but unfortunately, her doctor had discovered a few complications and suggested she not get pregnant again. Not that she could even consider that at this point. The thought of getting pregnant again and going through nine months of wondering how it was going to turn out terrified her. Of course, it wasn't really a possibility anyway considering her and Jeremiah's love life was all but nonexistent.

She had also faded out of all her ministry work at the church.

Everyone understood and told her to take her time, but only she knew that her absence had more to do with her feeling some kind of way toward the Lord than it did with just having too much on her plate. Her many fervent attempts to get Amari back had all failed and had only resulted in more financial hardships. It was one more crushing defeat in a series of losses they had taken recently. All she had now was her real estate business, her occasional glass or perhaps bottle of wine and, of course, her obligations to Jeremiah and Daddy.

But she still looked forward to her meetings with First Lady Faye. They met often as they could. Faye had a way of letting the game come to her, as Jeremiah said. For the most part, she didn't push buttons or try to pry. She was content to let Elise talk or laugh or joke. Elise enjoyed her company and was happy to just meet and relax as long as First Lady didn't try to get too deep. Elise loved and respected her First Lady. She was afraid that if Faye were to find out how she really felt that she would be disappointed in her. She hoped today would be another nice distraction as she met with her once again. She had no idea that Faye had other plans and was about to change the game.

"So how are we doing today, baby girl?" Faye asked as she sat down at the table Elise had reserved.

"I'm good, First Lady," Elise responded. "Not as good as you, though. You so cute. I don't believe Pastor G. let you out the house looking all sexy."

Faye wasn't going to take the bait. Elise had been using her charm and sense of humor to avoid addressing real issues. Today, Faye was determined to get to the root of her pain so the Lord could begin to plant the seeds of his healing in her life.

"Yes, baby girl, I'm sexy. This I know. But I want to know how you are doing," Faye asked seriously.

Elise smiled and feigned confusion. "I said I'm good, First Lady." She silently hoped Faye would change the subject. She really didn't think she was prepared to know how she was doing.

But Faye pressed her point. "Well, I want to know what good is. We've been doing this for a few months now, and I don't really know how you are doing. We're going to change that...today. So, sip your little wine and get ready to talk," Faye insisted.

"First Lady, you trippin'. You already know everything that has happened," Elise said as she reached across the table and gently grasped Faye's hand. "You've been there for us the whole time, you were with me on that day, and I really appreciate it. I don't know what I would have done without you."

"Baby girl," Faye said as she leaned forward in her chair, "I didn't ask what was going on. I know what all has happened. But you said you're good, so I want to know what that means. Tell me."

Elise looked for a way of escape. No quip or joke came to her mind, and she was honestly annoyed that First Lady seemed to want to ruin a potentially carefree morning with a deep conversation. But if she wanted it, she was about to get it. She took a breath and nodded her head.

"You say you want to know what good is, First Lady?" Elise said as she intentionally changed her tone.

"Yes, baby. I do," Faye said.

Elise sighed. "Honestly, First Lady, I don't think I know what good is anymore. But I heard somewhere that God is good all the time and all the time God is good. Is that true? I used to think it was. Now, I don't know."

"Yes, he is, baby. He is good. And he only does good."

Faye braced herself for the ramifications of her reply. As much as Elise tried to keep their conversations on a surface level, it was clear that her recent trauma had caused her to wrestle with the goodness of God.

"Well, then there you have it. God is good. You want the spinach dip? I love their spinach dip," Elise said simply.

Faye saw through Elise's attempt to shorten the conversation and considered for a moment that she should let her. *You can't answer her questions,* Faye thought to herself. *Let it go and let God handle his daughter.* But waiting for Elise to open up hadn't borne any fruit, so Faye decided to press through and trust God to guide their conversation.

"Baby, the spinach dip is fine. But you still haven't told me how you are doing. You still haven't told me what good is," Faye said. "And I want to hear from you." "About what?" Elise asked, trying to sound brand new. "What else is there to talk about? You just said God is good. You answered my question. What else matters?"

"What matters is how you feel, baby. How you are doing is what matters. That's why we're here. Not to eat spinach dip and laugh. But to find out how you're doing with all of this. Stevie Wonder can see you're overwhelmed, and you and I both know that you're asking, 'If God is so good, then why did he dump all this... sugar honey ice tea on me?' I think that's what we need to talk about. Let's get real and stop pretending you're okay, because we both know you're not."

"Okay, First Lady," Elise said as she nodded her head and pulled her chair closer to the table. "Game on. You wanna get real? You want to get authentic? You want me to be transparent and express my feelings? As you wish, ma'am. I will play. But remember I tried to keep this surface. Rated GC for General Christian audiences," Elise said as she made air quotes with her fingers. "I don't think you really want this smoke, but here it comes."

She breathed hard and Faye prepared herself for whatever was about to come out of Elise's mouth.

"First Lady, since we're talking about... what do you call it? Sugar honey ice tea? I love that, by the way, I would have just used the real word, but I digress. Since we're talking about all this sugar honey ice tea getting dumped on me, if your God is so good, why did he take my baby from me? I'll wait. I'm all ears," Elise said as she took her hand from Faye's, leaned back in her chair, and folded her arms.

Faye smiled gently. "Elise, I'm sorry. I simply don't have that answer."

"It's okay, First Lady," Elise said, leaning forward again and clasping her hands together. "But I will tell you who does have the answer... my husband. That doggone Jeremiah is an O.G. saint. He tells me all the time, 'Elise, we have to remember, God is always good, God is always right, and God is always for us. He is going to bring us through this. We have to trust him now more than ever.' Now coincidently that's exactly what he told Amari right before they came and took her, so do with that what you will. But oh...I don't have to tell you. You were there too."

"Yes, I was." Faye nodded.

"And I will tell you who else has some good answers…our beloved church family. They keep reminding me, 'Look how many people got saved at your baby's funeral. That was God!' Hell, I'm sorry, heck, First Lady, you think I care about that? Those people got saved and went home from my baby's funeral to be with their families. But my baby is in the ground! And before you tell me my baby is in heaven, I know that. I know that's supposed to bring me comfort, but guess what? It doesn't. Me seeing my baby in heaven one day doesn't let me play with him now. It doesn't let me hold him now. It doesn't let me kiss him now. So where is this goodness of God you speak of, First Lady? Where was your good God when that bastard ran me, and my husband, and my baby over? Ah, ah, ah, don't you say it, cuz I know how y'all think. I took your grief-counseling course, First Lady, so I already know what you are going to say." Elise raised her hands, along with her voice, and gestured. "It's Christianese 101; God was in the same place when my son died that he was when his son died. What a copout! He got his son back three days later. But I guess I just have to wait for a lifetime or until he mercifully kills me. Which I have to say, some days, I would be fine with, if only he would just stop killing and taking everything I love."

Faye took a mental note of Elise's comment but let her continue to vent. "Oh, and speaking of that class, I feel like such a hypocrite. I went to grieving people's homes to comfort them and encourage them and let them know they would see their loved one again. 'It's okay,' I would say. 'We're crying with you and Jesus is still on the throne.' First Lady, if I wasn't so prone to fight and didn't have such a bad temper, I would go to every last one of their houses right now and give them permission to slap the ever-loving…." Elise caught herself as she remembered who she was talking to. "Like you say, First Lady, I would give them permission to slap the ever-loving sugar honey ice tea out of my hypocritical self- righteous behind."

Faye attempted to speak but Elise was no ways tired in her rant.

"And you know what the worst part is?" Elise asked as her voice increasingly raised.

"What, baby?" Faye asked sympathetically.

"Me and Miah weren't even trying to have a baby anymore. Truth be told, we had given up. We used to pray and fast about it. And in our prayers, we would tell the Lord how if he would just bless us, we would honor him by raising our baby to love him and honor him. But after I hit forty, we just sort of stopped asking. The disappointment of God saying no became too painful. But then Amari came into our lives, and we were like 'Well, maybe God isn't saying no. Maybe this is just a different kind of yes.' So, we said 'Thank you, Lord. We give you praise, Jesus. We accept this wonderful little gift, and we are going to love her for you just like she came from our own bodies.' Oh, and you said what do I think good is, right?" Elise asked.

"Yes, I want to know what you think good is," Faye answered.

Elise smiled and her voice softened. "First Lady, good is when I got pregnant. That was so good. God was sooo good. That was so sweet. Me and Jeremiah were just living life and making plans and a baby wasn't in them." Elise shook her head. "I can't describe how good that felt. It was like Jesus was showing off just for us. He gave us Amari and we were happy. But a baby too? I was like 'I see you, Jesus.' "And now? Well, now we can't have either of them. He showed them both to us. He let us get attached to Amari and let us get our hopes up about J.J. Then he took them both away from us. On the same day, mind you. And yeah, I said it. Your good God. Took. My. Kids," Elise said as she slapped the table with each syllable. "Oh, and back to church folks. You haven't said it, but I know you've noticed my absences. But it's because I am soooo damn tired, First Lady, of all these hyper-religious, super-spiritual people telling me about the devil being busy. So, you telling me the devil beat God? No, I ain't that far gone to know that's a lie. Last time I checked, God was the sovereign one. God was the all-powerful one. The devil can't beat God so this must be what he wanted to happen!

"Christians are always talking about 'But God.'" Elise let out an eerie laugh as she shook her head. "Isn't that what Pastor said at the funeral? 'But God' is what we're supposed to say when he steps in and overrules and protects and turns things around. But my 'but God' doesn't work like that, First Lady. My 'but God' is him laying everything I ever wanted or prayed for at my feet, only to find out he was just pretending to be good so he could take it all away. He showed me the one thing that he knew I wanted more than anything in the world, and he played with me and toyed with me and let me believe it was mine, and then on a whim he took it away. And now I'm supposed to sit up here and talk about a good God? Now I'm supposed to act like all that didn't happen?

"No, First Lady. That doesn't sound like a good God to me. That sounds like a cruel God. If I did someone like that. Played with someone like that. Showed someone their heart's desire and then yanked it away from them for no earthly reason, you would say I was wrong. But God just gets a pass? Why? Because his ways are higher than our ways? Fine, but I still thought he was a good Father who gave good gifts and a good shepherd who watched over his sheep. First Lady, do you know how precisely this stuff had to line up for all this to happen? We weren't supposed to be on that street at that time on that day. My baby wasn't even due.

You know my husband drive like somebody granddaddy. Stop, look left, look right, look left again. Then go. That man was going so fast that he wasn't even in view before we pulled out. Jeremiah never even saw him. But right on that day, at that precise moment, he was there. God, who knows the end from the beginning, sat on his holy throne and did…wait for it… absolutely, positively nothing. And now, after he's taken my daughter, after he's killed my baby, and after he's damn near crippled my husband, he wants me to trust him? He wouldn't, not that he couldn't, he wouldn't block a simple car crash and now he wants my praise? Really? I'm supposed to get my praise on because I lived and my baby died? I would have gladly died in his place if I could, First Lady. And I would gladly join him now if I could."

"Elise, I am sorry. But I have to say, you are scaring me. That's the second time you have mentioned going to be with your baby. Are you…."

"No, no, no, First Lady," Elise cut her off mid-sentence, "I am not going to do anything to myself. Jeremiah is just now getting back on his feet, and I know he needs me. And I want to be here for Daddy too. Besides, I got too many bills to pay. I ain't going nowhere," Elise said, laughing off the seriousness of the question. "I wish I could tell you why all of this happened, but I have no idea what God is up to. I just know he loves you," Faye said.

"Well, I don't know about the love part," Elise said simply. "But I do know your good God took my child that I waited on for twenty years. But it's not just that he took him. It's how he took him. He didn't let me miscarry. That was my fear. 'What if I can't carry my baby?' But a simple miscarriage would have been too easy for the God of the impossible. No, your good God gave my forty-four- year-old egg drying up behind one good checkup after another. My doctor was amazed. 'No issues, Elise. You and the baby are fine. You aren't going to have any complications.' Of course, she didn't know the God who never sleeps nor slumbers, would need a nap right when I was going to the hospital to make good on his blessing. I guess God said 'Nahhhh, Elise, you'll be aight. You don't need a baby. You got me. Am I not enough for you, Elise?'" she said as sarcastically as she could. "'Oh, and now that I've opened the door for your husband to work again and it looks like he might be restored, I think I will take that from him too. I will take his children, his health, his esteem, and his hope. And even though John Traylor has done nothing but serve me and be faithful to me even after I took his wife, I'm gon let him get jacked up too! Here's a nice little stroke for you, John. But you had better not question me, because I'm God.' You want to talk about your good God? He let an unrighteous man destroy his career, and we still don't know what's going to happen with that. Your good God took the only mother I've ever known and cut her off. We should have had years with her, but he just had to have her."

Faye just nodded. Partially because she didn't know what to say and partially because she knew this was necessary.

"Oh, and hold my mule, First Lady, I haven't even gotten rolling good yet.

We goin' deep, right? We askin' questions, right?" "Yes, we are, baby," Faye said calmly and gently.

"Well, if your good God is sooooo good, why did he let that woman come out of nowhere and take Amari? We were more than fine with her. She was ours! At least he could have let us keep her. If not for our sakes then for hers. I know she's not telling my child anything about Jesus, but that's where he wants her? Really, God? I mean at least if I had her to focus on, it might make things a little easier. But he couldn't even let me have her."

Elise leaned forward over the table just a few inches from Faye's face, totally unphased that their conversation was beginning to draw the attention of those around them.

"Look at my face, First Lady. Look at my eyes. You don't see any tears, do you? That's because I can't even cry anymore. That's because all your good God has left me with is pain and anger.

"And just in case you're thinking, 'You still have Jeremiah.' Do I? I mean do I really? I snuggle up to him in the bed and I may as well snuggle up to my pillow. I should really just get a dog because at least Fido would be happy to see me and would kiss my face, not that I like dogs kissing my face, but it's the thought that counts. At least a dog would want to go on walks with me, but the Jeremiah I knew is gone. He may as well have died that day with our baby because I haven't seen him since. But who could blame him? I think I died that day too, so I'm not mad at him. I love him. I love him more than anything. But maybe I am reaping what I sowed. I don't think Jesus is enough so now my husband doesn't think I'm enough. He doesn't smile at me like he used to. He tells me to keep the faith, but I don't know if he really believes it either. But I understand. He's been through so much. It's too much and your good God has absolutely nothing to say. And that's what really makes me mad. All Jeremiah has ever done is love God and love his people. When did Pastor G. ever call, and he didn't stop everything to see what was needed for the church? And your good God let this happen to him. Okay, Elise still got her flesh…obviously. I ain't good and saved yet, but my husband is. And my husband was faithful to God, to me, to the church, and to everybody. And Jeremiah John Traylor I should have been allowed to raise and love Jeremiah John Traylor II and God wasn't on his job. If he had to kill somebody, why didn't he just kill me? Jeremiah could get through this without me if he knew he had to stay strong for his son. But this? Nobody wins this way. Jeremiah is faithful but God isn't. How did everything, and I do mean everything, get so bad for us? What did I do that was so bad that God wouldn't only stop protecting me, but he would just be totally against me? Nothing is the same. Nothing is good. Jeremiah prays and I listen, but I don't know if he believes what he's praying anymore, and I don't want to ask him because I sure don't want him asking me if I believe. I know he's recovering, but Jeremiah doesn't even look at me like he used to. I can barely get a peck on the cheek. He doesn't even call me 'babe' or 'Lise' anymore. He doesn't sing our song to me. We don't make love. We have sex and it's like 'Let's get this done because we're supposed to.' But I miss him so much. I miss how we used to be. He is hurting so much but I can't reach him to bring him back. But I wonder. Reach him and bring him back to what. To this? To me? To this messed-up version of me? I wouldn't want me either. I hate me! I hate who I have become. I hate how I feel about God and life and everything. But if he would just hold me and tell me that he still loves me and that he wants me and that we are going to get through this, maybe I could make it. And if he would just tell me that I'm enough for him, that would be enough for me. Maybe I could shine again. Maybe I could have hope. Maybe I could believe God is still good, even though I can't see it or feel it. But I don't know if God loves me. And I don't know if my husband loves me. And I don't know if he misses me like I miss him and still wants me back like I want him. We've lost so much, and some things just can't be fixed. You want to repair and rebuild but it's beyond all that. I'm afraid that's where we are. It's like God did an experiment on us to see how much we could take. I'm like, you didn't know I couldn't take this? Really? Cuz I thought you knew everything."

Before she could continue her rant, Elise's phone rang. She saw the name and recognized it as a new client.

"This is perfect," she said, "I forgot an appointment. Hold on, First Lady." She took a deep breath and collected herself before she answered.

"Hello, yes sir, I am so sorry. Are you waiting? I can be there in twenty minutes. I am coming there right now. Please forgive me. Okay, you're so sweet. Thank you for understanding. Okay, I will see you in just a bit. I am really excited for you. Goodbye.

"First Lady, I'm sorry, but I have to go. I completely forgot this appointment and ya girl gotta get the bag," Elise announced.

"Elise, just wait, baby," Faye objected. "I think there's still a lot we have to do. I know your work is important, but can you cancel? I really feel like we need to finish this. There's a lot on your heart and I want to hear it. I think you should stay."

"First Lady, I am sorry, but I have to work. We've already lost our house. We don't want to lose anything else. Oh, yeah, did I complain about that part? Our house? I mean, you were there too. You're always there, First Lady, Elise said sincerely. "You helped us pack our stuff and move out of the house Jeremiah built for me because we couldn't afford it anymore. I thought that was such a blessing, but that was just one more thing for your good God to take away."

"Elise, sweetie, I know it's hard but don't let yourself become bitter," Faye warned. "Especially against the Lord. You're only going to hurt yourself."

"I'm not bitter!" Elise snapped, surprising them both with her harshness and her volume. Elise recognized her disrespectful tone, and she took a pause before she continued. "I'm sorry, First Lady. I'm not trying to be rude, but we do need the money. I'm just saying we couldn't afford our house anymore. Even if he could get hired, Jeremiah can't work yet so I am our only source of income. If I don't close deals, we don't eat. We got medical bills for Mama Etta, Jeremiah, Daddy, and me. We owe Jeremiah's lawyers and the lawyer we got for Amari. So, it's not that I'm bitter. These are just facts."

Elise didn't know how to interpret Faye's expression. Was it pity or disappointment? Or perhaps it was frustration that one of her mentees, someone she had personally discipled, seemed to be so off course. Whatever the look was,

Elise felt ashamed of her behavior. She knew she was lashing out at someone who only wanted to help. But she still had to go.

"I love you, First Lady, and I'm sorry," Elise said contritely. "Please don't worry about me. I will get over myself eventually. Tell Pastor G. I love him and I said hello."

Faye stood up, pulled Elise close and wrapped both arms snuggly around her. She just wanted to protect her and cover her. She prayed silently that the Lord would communicate his love and healing through her touch. But Elise wasn't ready for that kind of love, and she quickly broke Faye's warm embrace. Faye grabbed her hand before she could totally pull away.

"I love you, baby girl. I know you can't receive this now, but so does the Lord. He hasn't abandoned you and he hasn't forgotten you. I am always here if you need me," Faye said sweetly.

"I know, First Lady. I love you, too," Elise responded.

Faye kept her gentle grip on Elise's hand and attempted to dissuade her from leaving one last time. "I still don't think you should go. I feel the Lord would have you stay. You won't get all your answers today, but you need to be with someone who loves you. Please, Elise. We can talk. We can pray. We can cry. I might even sneak a glass of wine with you. We can do whatever you want. Just stay here with me, baby. Please don't go," Faye pleaded.

Elise heard the urgency and concern in Faye's tone. She also knew in the deepest part of herself that she should trust it and stay. But the conversation had already gone much deeper than she had planned, and Elise quickly shut out the voice inside her telling her she should listen to Faye.

"First Lady," Elise smiled, "you act like I am going to war. I'm just going to show a house. Nothing bad is going to happen just because I keep an appointment with a new client. But we'll talk soon. Goodbye," Elise said as she pulled her hand from Faye's and walked away.

CHAPTER 52

At First Sight

DAY 390

Joshua had been impatiently waiting at his appointment for thirty minutes. He was annoyed but it wasn't like he had anything else to do. Robin was in college now and he often found the walls of his apartment closing in on him. He wasn't even sure that now was a good time to purchase a home, but he at least wanted to see what his options were. Elise Traylor's name kept coming up as someone who could help him find the perfect spot, but so far, she had not lived up to her reputation.

Who has to call and remind a professional about an appointment? he thought. Even though he was annoyed, he decided to wait because he honestly didn't have anything better to do. At worst, he would see a few nice houses and kill a few hours. He prayed Elise would be able to find him something in his price range. He was looking for a more welcoming environment that would make it more appealing for his children to come by and hang out. He wanted a place that they might consider to be their home as well.

He sat in his car in front of the house she planned to show him. He was about to check his watch again when a white Lexus arrived on the other side of the street.

Elise waved at him through the windshield, and he politely waved back as she stepped out of the car. He wasn't prepared for what he was about to see.

Wow. You were worth the wait, Ms. Traylor.

He got out of the car to greet her. She wore a simple white blouse, slacks, and a blazer. She looked like a runway model as she glided effortlessly across the street in her heels. The closer she got, the more beautiful she became.

"Mr. Dupreeeee!" she said with a glowing smile. "Hi, I'm Elise. I apologize, sir. I feel so bad." she said, extending her right hand.

Joshua shook it gently as he very intentionally focused on her eyes. He was sure she was used to men gawking at her. He didn't want to make the same mistake but his strategy backfired as he realized she had the most beautiful brown eyes he had ever seen.

"Don't worry about it. Stuff happens," he said in his most understanding tone. "But this won't ever happen again, sir. I promise you that," Elise said. "I treat my clients better than this. So, we've got a full afternoon, right? Let's get this started."

Elise escorted him to the front door and let him in. The house was gorgeous.

Elise immediately noticed the pleased expression on his face.

"Ohhh, him like it," Elise teased him. "Sir, I am going to need you to play a little harder to get. I work for my money, okay? At least let me get you out of the entryway before you make an offer."

Joshua was happy to play along. "So, be cool?" he asked.

Elise giggled. "Yes, sir, please be cool. Eyes just wide open and grinning." "So, you sayin' I look house thirsty?" Joshua asked.

"You look a little parched, sir, yes," she said, causing them both to laugh. "But that's okay," Elise said seriously. "It's good to want something nice. We should all have that sometimes. Let me show you around so I can get a feel for what you like."

I'm pretty sure I see what I like, Joshua thought. But he wasn't able to enjoy his sudden infatuation very long. Elise pointed him to the kitchen with her left hand, and his heart sank as he noticed a beautiful wedding ring he knew he could never afford on his vice principal's salary.

Of course she's married, stupid. Why wouldn't she be? he thought. "You okay?" Elise asked him.

Joshua was zoned out in his disappointment and didn't respond.

"Mr. Dupree. Come back to the light, sir," Elise said, wondering how she had lost his attention so suddenly.

Joshua snapped back to reality and replied. "Oh, I'm sorry," he said, trying to recover. "I just got distracted. But I'm good." *Oh, well, Mrs. Dupree. It was nice while it lasted*, he thought to himself.

Elise continued with her house showing as she carefully asked him all his thoughts and concerns about the home. She truly seemed interested in helping him make the right decision. Joshua couldn't remember the last time anyone had asked him what was important to him, and it was especially nice coming from this beautiful woman.

After they concluded the showing, Elise suggested they visit a few other properties. Joshua gladly accepted her invitation and they went back to their cars so they could go to their next destination.

"Be thinking about what you liked about this one, okay? There will be a quiz later," Elise joked. "I want to make sure you get what you want."

Joshua knew that was going to be a problem. Because he couldn't remember one detail of the house he hadn't even driven away from yet. All he could think about was her.

CHAPTER 53

Existing

DAY 390

Elise parked her car in John and Etta Ween's driveway. She had done it a hundred times before for various visits and family occasions. But now things were different. Mama Etta was gone, and it wasn't clear if John would ever return. Now, she was home. Or at least what she was calling home since they lost theirs.

The house was eerily haunted with memories that should have produced smiles and pleasant feelings. This was where John and Etta Ween so effortlessly lived life out loud in front of them. There were so many memories of love, laughter, and life lessons. She recalled joyful memories of Amari when they would come to pick her up after her weekend visits. Amari would run and hide but was always so incredibly easy to find because she couldn't control her giggling. She thought of Etta Ween's cooking lessons and her playful teasing. "Don't worry, baby," she would say, "just make sure you wear something cute when you feed him, and he will be fine."

Now all the people that used to make this house a place she wanted to be were gone. Their absence made her sad and she did not want to go in. Yes, Jeremiah was inside. At one time, that alone would have levitated her from her car to his waiting arms. But that was another time, and this was another man. The man inside wasn't the Jeremiah she had married. He was still kind and somewhat sweet. But that was just his nature. Now, he wasn't attentive. He wasn't joyful. He wasn't her Miah. But she was afraid to say anything for fear he might tell her that she was no longer his Lise either.

She sat in the car and mentally prepared herself to go inside. She struggled to think of occasions where she wasn't happy to see her husband. Likewise, Jeremiah always made her feel like he was happy to see her. If he had a tough day at the office, he would let her know that being with her brightened it up. And even in happy times, he would tell her she was still the best part of his day. She missed what they had and wondered if it was gone forever. Being Jeremiah's wife used to be as natural to her as breathing. Now it was a grueling day-to-day effort, and she was getting tired of the seemingly fruitless work.

Her personal life may have been a mess, but she was still managing to soar professionally. In that regard, today was another good day. She didn't know his full story, but she could tell Joshua Dupree was a good guy. She really enjoyed their interaction and was hoping she could help him find a place to call his own. But she would have to focus on that later. *Let's go in here and exist,* she thought to herself.

"Hey, Miah. I'm home," Elise said, trying her best to shine for him. She hoped he could not see just how much effort she was having to put into a simple greeting.

"Hey, Elise," he responded kindly but unenthusiastically.

Elise's heart went out to him. They had both lost so much but at least she still had her career. Jeremiah was right back in the same old rut. He would be medically cleared to work again soon. He reached out to Chad hoping for another opportunity. Chad was sympathetic but told him he had to fill the position. Other doors of opportunity kept being slammed in his face. He was either overqualified or the word had gone before him spreading the news of his pending court case and the charges against him. No matter how much he tried to tell potential employees that the accusations against him were baseless, no one wanted to touch him. He had become a pariah in the industry, and it seemed to be no escape from it. But this was still her husband and she wanted to be there for him.

Jeremiah was in the kitchen making dinner. She walked up behind him and wrapped her arms around his waist.

"Hey, handsome. How are you doing?" she said sweetly. She stood on her tiptoes and kissed him sweetly, and perhaps a little erotically, on the back of his neck. Normally, he would have taken the hint and immediately turned the stove off and turned around to return the affection. Or at minimum, he would have joked with her. She could hear him now: "Woman, I have told you I need fuel to put out your fire. Let me eat. Then I will tend to yo fast tail." But now he just stood there stirring the vegetables as if it was his mother or sister or, worse, an unwanted stranger with their arms around him.

"You hungry? You ready to eat?" he asked simply.

"Sure," she said, frowning just a bit and removing her arms from around him. "Thank you, baby. It smells good."

"Oh, no, thank you, girl. You're the one holding everything down for us. I can at least cook dinner," Jeremiah said.

"Miah, we're a team. 'Miah and Lise against the world.' Remember?" Elise encouraged. "We're both holding this thing down."

"I don't know, Elise," he said. "If we were on a seesaw, I'd be the one all up in the air and you would be the one firmly on the ground. You're holding everything down by yourself."

Elise put her hands on her hips and cocked her head to the side. "What you sayin', Miah? I'm holding the seesaw down? So now I'm fat, huh?" she said playfully.

"No, Elise," Jeremiah said seriously. "You're not fat. You're just making it happen for us. And I appreciate it."

Elise knew he was trying. It bothered her that he didn't want to join in with her shenanigans, but it was nice to hear that she was appreciated. His words were nice even though she would have preferred he just take her in his arms and kiss her on the forehead. But she would settle for a quiet dinner at home with her husband.

"You're welcome, Miah. Thank you for saying that. I appreciate you too, baby," she said as she put her arms back around him, holding out hope he would pull her close. She just wanted to be near him. "You want me to set the table?"

"No, that's okay. Actually, I think I'm gonna take a walk. I need to pray and think a little bit. I'll be back later," he said.

"Jeremiah, you're not gonna eat with me?" she asked, disappointed.

"No, not tonight. I've got a lot on my mind," Jeremiah said.

Elise was disappointed but she didn't want to fight. She wasn't in a praying mood, but he didn't know that. He could have at least invited her to come. He probably knew deep down she wouldn't be a vital contributor on his spiritual hike. Or worse, maybe he just didn't want to be around her.

"Okay," Elise acquiesced. "Enjoy your prayer walk."

"You want me to make your plate?" Jeremiah offered.

Elise nodded her head. "Yeah, that's fine. I'm just gonna take a quick shower, check some emails and send some texts. I will see you when you get back."

"I will be a while. Don't wait up."

"That's fine," Elise said, now pretending it didn't matter. "Hey Elise."

"Yeah?"

"I love you. You know that, right?" Jeremiah asked.

"I know, Jeremiah. I love you, too. I will see you later…tomorrow…whenever."

Jeremiah watched her walk out of the kitchen and thought to himself. *Dude, what is wrong with you? Snap out of it. Stop feeling sorry for yourself.* But he still didn't have any fight. Right now, he was doing good to just survive. Elise was strong and he knew she understood. One day he was going to show her that he was still the man of her dreams. Somehow he was going to get everything back that they had lost. Or at least the things he could get back.

Elise finished her shower and went to the kitchen to get her plate. She was famished but still didn't feel like eating. She sat down in the living room and turned on the television. *Wish I had someone to Netflix and chill with,* she thought. *Wait. Aren't I supposed to? Whatever.*

She sat there looking at her plate and the blank TV screen when her phone chimed with an incoming text. It was from her new client. It read: "Hi Mrs. Traylor. Or is it, Elise? House lady? Realtor? Thanks for the special attention today. They said you were the best. I appreciate it. Not sure if any of them are a good fit, but thanks for your time."

Elise responded quickly. "Well, hello, Mr. Dupree. Or is it, Joshua? House dude? AKA thirsty-for-a-house dude? Client? LOL. You're so welcome! You're not giving up on me, are you? Let's chat soon. I know I can help you. I have a great feel for what you are looking for now. Are you available next Saturday?"

Joshua responded quickly as well. "LOL - well first. I think I kinda like the sound of 'client.' And sure. If you think it makes sense, let's meet again soon. Saturday is perfect."

"Perfect!" Elise texted back. "I will see you then. But feel free to reach out if you have questions. Take care… CLIENT. Signed, REALTOR. LOL."

"LOL - I may have a lot of questions," Joshua responded. "Let me know if I get on your nerves."

Elise smiled as she responded. "No worries. I have had clients who didn't understand any real estate concepts. Loans. Money down. Closing costs. I will guide you as we go."

Joshua didn't want the conversation to end. "Wayment! Am I going to have to pay for this? I don't think you mentioned that part, ma'am."

Elise literally laughed out loud, then replied, "HA! LOL!!! - SIR - DO NOT PLAY. Yes, at some point you will have to come off some money. Don't worry. I got you."

Joshua looked at her reply. He wanted so much to reply back "YES, YOU DO." Instead, he simply texted, "Cool. Talk soon. Thanks, Realtor."

"Thanks, Client," Elise replied.

Elise felt a nagging in her belly. She recalled how Faye didn't want her to go to this meeting but tried not to think about it. She checked her calendar and refused to acknowledge her disappointment that it would be a whole week before she would see Joshua again. She put her phone down and paid no attention to the inappropriateness of her desire for the conversation to continue. She looked at her reflection in the glass coffee table and tried not to dwell on how she was no longer sad but now grinning from ear to ear. She picked up her plate and tried to ignore the fact that somehow, suddenly her appetite had returned.

CHAPTER 54

Walk of Faith

DAY 390

Jeremiah walked through the neighborhood he grew up in. He started taking prayer walks after seeing his father practice them for years. "I love walking with Jesus, son," he would say. "It's something about getting your blood flowing and just walking outside and talking with the Lord. I think that's what Adam did. When I go on my prayer walks, it's like every step is bringing me that much closer to the Lord and to victory."

And Jeremiah desperately needed a victory. He had taken one "L" after the other and even though the same father who taught him this discipline could no longer walk or talk, he still believed his comeback could be just one more step and one more prayer away.

But his father had also taught him to be authentic with the Lord. "Son, the Lord already knows what you are thinking," he would say. "You need to be real with him. He can handle it." Jeremiah felt he might test his father's theory today. "Father, I'm sorry, but I'm not really feeling the 'I come to your throne of grace with confidence' stuff tonight. You know my innermost being, and you know I don't have much confidence left. But with all the faith I do have left, I want to let you know that I still believe you are there. So, I ask for grace because all that you have allowed is much more than what I can bear. I can recite scripture and say all sorts of sweet-sounding things to you, but you would know what remains in my soul. So tonight, I'm not holding back. Tonight, I need to get real with you. It's been over a year now since you let the bottom fall out of my life. And yes, I know that sounds dangerously close to an accusation, but Father, aren't you the one in control? I know you saw these things coming. You even told me they would.

But hearing it and living it are two different things and I don't understand, Lord. How could I interpret any of this as your love? How can I declare your praise when it's like this? Is this how you get glory? I thought you protected. I thought you covered. I thought you kept. But nothing has been protected. Nothing has been covered. And nothing has been kept. Not my career. Not my reputation. Not my finances. And for sure not my family. Why didn't you stand up for us, Lord? You didn't protect Mama. You didn't protect Amari. You didn't protect Pop. You didn't protect me and Elise. And you didn't even…I can't get into that right now. I can't even say it. But I don't understand, Lord? Why did you have to take my mama? All she did was praise you and serve you. Why did you let this happen to Pop? And why after we prayed and fasted about Amari, why after we asked you if it was your will, why after three years would you come and take her from us? I don't understand why you wouldn't protect a little girl.

"And I don't understand why you don't have anything to say. I know you're not cruel but God, your silence…to me… it seems cruel. I thought you would protect me by the power of your name. I thought you wouldn't let the weapons formed against me prosper. I thought if my ways pleased you that you would make even my enemies be at peace with me? Lord, I am not seeing you watch over your word to perform it. I have so many questions, but it seems to be a waste of time because you have nothing to say. Why, Lord? Please just tell me why. You know I tried to honor you with my life. Why is it right for Case to lie on me and flourish while I can't find a job? Why would you let my character and reputation and name get destroyed? I thought you said that if I trusted you that you wouldn't let me be put to shame, but I'm feeling pretty ashamed. You say that you are with me, but you don't stand up for me. If I did that you wouldn't let me rest. If I saw someone being attacked and abused and didn't rise to help, you would charge me with sin. So why didn't you rise up to defend me? Why didn't you step in?"

Even in his frustration, Jeremiah remembered Pastor Gregory's charge to him. *In all this Job did not sin by charging God with wrongdoing."* He paused and tried his best to change his tone.

"Lord, I'm sorry, but you have to know I can't see what you see, and I can't know what you know. If you would only tell me what you are up to. But you still don't say anything? You don't want me to complain. You want my praise and my trust, but you are the sovereign God who took my mother, but how dare I complain about that? Why was there no miracle healing for my mother? She served you. Why did you let her die like that? Certainly, we are not more faithful than you? So why didn't you show up? And why is my dad still suffering and clinging to life? If you want him, then please just take him but don't leave him like this…a shell of himself.

"And Lord Jesus, how am I going to fix it with Elise? Why can't we connect? I used to be able to tell her anything, good or bad, but I can't tell the woman I love that I'm lost and don't have any answers. How can I be the priest of my home and you don't tell me anything? I know this is a sin, Jesus, but I am afraid. I am terrified. I can't tell her that I don't think our lives will ever be the same. I can't tell her I am afraid that the last twenty years were a fantasy and now real life has begun. Now we're going to live in lack and misery and defeat for the rest of our days. And I sure can't tell her that I don't try to make love to her because I'm so stressed out, I don't think I can perform like she needs me to. I can't tell her I don't feel like a man anymore because she is doing everything while I just cook and clean. How can I tell her I am ashamed that I have to depend on her? Lord, what did I do to get here? Please tell me. I promise I will do my best to make it right. Would you please stop standing on the sidelines? I need you to get in this game because I am getting blown out.

"Father, I can't do this anymore," he said, allowing his tears to flow. "Please don't leave me here. Please don't leave Elise where she is. Please pick us up and bring us back to yourself. Please take all this pain and fear away. I'm so tired of hurting, Lord. I'm tired of being afraid. And since you already know, I have to say this. For the first time in my life, I'm afraid of you God. And I don't mean the good kind of fear you are worthy of. I mean the run to the corner and hide kind of fear. But I can't hide from you and I'm afraid of the next thing you might allow. And Lord, I'm afraid to even talk to you about my son. You're God and

I am not. You know my faith is failing and when I think about him it's hard to believe you care. If I talk too much about him, I'm afraid I will say the wrong thing and if I do there's no telling how you might respond.

"But Jesus, even as I cry, I know he is with you. I'm ashamed for saying this, but right now I find no comfort in that. Please forgive me but I want him back. I know he's gone but I still want him back. I'm sorry, Lord. I know this might not make sense, but will you please tell him that his daddy and his mommy love him and that we miss him? Please tell him that Daddy is sorry I didn't protect him. I don't know much these days, Lord, but I know one day I will meet him, and you will make it all right. I know you will wipe these tears."

Jeremiah measured his words. He had already said more than he intended. "Jesus, you know my thoughts and you know my heart. I'm sorry, but I feel like you let me down. I want to please you, but I feel like you don't care how I feel. I need you and I feel like you're in some ivory tower someplace and I am out of sight and out of mind. Jesus, why did you have to take my son? Why did you let that man hit us? You didn't even let me hold him. What am I supposed to do with that? What is it that you want? What sin did I commit that deserves this level of wrath from a God of love and grace? But you promised not to leave me. You promised not to forsake me. And I remember your words on the cross, you said 'Father, forgive them because they don't know what they're doing.' So, I ask that you remember that prayer for me and for Elise because right now we don't know what we're doing. And if this is a test we're failing, so please forgive us.

"Please help us, Lord. I want to keep my eyes on you. I want to point my wife to you but I don't know where you are. Why are you hiding? Won't you please show up?! I know I haven't said it, but I love you, and I'm trying to trust you. I'm trying to hold on. I'm trying to keep the faith. But Jesus, please don't leave us here. Not like this. Not defeated and broken and ashamed. Please come and get us. And please, Father…no more. We can't handle one more thing. No more deaths. No more trials. No more tests. No more sickness. No more defeats. I pray you forgive us of our sins. I still know that you only do good. I pray you forgive me of every error of my foolish, finite heart.

"I pray for your healing, your help, and your restoration. I know I can't have my son back but God…I pray for Amari, I pray for my dad, I pray for my wife, and I pray for my life. The enemy has stolen. Please show me where he took everything and give me your favor and power to fight and get it back. Please show me the land where you want me to set my foot and I will walk it. And Jesus, if you don't do anything else, please show me and Elise the way back to you…and back to each other. All the faith, all the hope, and all the trust I have left…I put in you, and I praise you. I'm broken and defeated, but by your grace I declare my faith. You are still God. You are still good. You are still right. And you are still for me. In Jesus' name, Amen."

CHAPTER 55

Falling

DAY 420

"Client!" Elise exclaimed, sounding far more enthusiastic than she had intended.

Joshua laughed out loud. "Realtor!" he responded with equal enthusiasm. He resisted the urge to embrace her as her intoxicating perfume dared him to throw caution to the wind. He played with the thought that she might have put it on just for him. He tried to stay focused as he questioned how she had become more beautiful since they had last seen each other. This was their fourth meeting in as many weeks. But they had exchanged dozens of phone calls. He would call under the guise of gathering information on his potential purchase, but his true motive was simply to hear her voice. He couldn't help but wonder if his very beautiful but very married crush was playing along for similar reasons considering the absurdity of some of his questions. "Hey, Realtor, are solar panels extra?" he would say. "Boy, what am I gon do with you? You know solar panels are extra!" she would laugh. "Don't worry, I will get you a hookup if that's what you want," she would say to spare his dignity.

"How are you?" Joshua asked.

"I am well. How are you?" Elise replied.

"I'm good and at your disposal. Do your thing, ma'am," Joshua said.

Elise smiled brightly. "Well, I intend to. Thanks for meeting me so early in the morning. I wanted to make sure I showed you everything.

Now Client, full disclosure, this first one is just slightly above your price range, but I couldn't live with myself if I didn't show it to you. You're going to love it."

They walked in and Joshua immediately knew what she meant. It was as if she picked the house just for him.

"Umm, is this the part where I'm supposed to play it cool, so you don't know how much I like it?" he said playfully.

"Yes, sir," she nodded. "That look right there says 'Take all my money. It's okay.' I am so glad you're with me cuz bruh, that poker face of yours ain't working for you at all."

"Yeah, my ex used to tell me I was pretty see-through," Joshua said as his pleasant tone changed.

"That's not a bad thing, Client," Elise encouraged. "You're easy to read because you have a good heart. That's a good thing."

It had been a while since a woman, a woman he was attracted to, had said something nice to him, and he enjoyed it. *Lord,* he thought to himself. *Why do you have to be married?*

"Thanks, Realtor. I appreciate that," Joshua said.

"How long have you been divorced?" Elise asked him. *Why did you ask him that, Elise?* she thought to herself. *It's not going to help you sell him a house, and it's none of your business.*

But Joshua was happy to answer. He wanted her to know everything about him. "Well," he started, "we've only been divorced for a few months, but the marriage kinda took an official nosedive around fourteen months ago."

"Official nosedive? What does that mean?" Elise asked.

Joshua chuckled. "It means that it was probably falling apart a long time ago. My dumb behind just couldn't see it. Long story short, I came home one day, and she told me she didn't love me and didn't think she ever did. We got into this big fight. About the marriage, our life together, the kids…and especially our son."

Mentioning Robert hit different in Elise's presence. Joshua and Robert still rarely communicated. He tried not to let it consume him, but for some reason, mentioning his estranged son in front of his crush released a flood of emotions he couldn't hide.

"Hey…you okay, Client?" Elise asked, noticing the change in his countenance. "It's hard to talk about," he confessed.

Elise's heart went out to him and she instinctively, if rather inappropriately, put a comforting hand on his shoulder. You don't have to talk about it if you don't want to, but did you guys lose a son?" She wondered if he was perhaps going through the same thing she was.

"No, it wasn't that bad," Joshua told her as he composed himself. "It's just that…she told me that night he wasn't mine."

"What?" Elise asked as her voice changed octaves. She knew they had strayed far from the path of a professional sales conversation, but she was in too deep to back out now.

"You heard me right," Joshua said, gathering himself even more. "She had known for years but never told me."

"Client, I can't even imagine. How did your son react?" Elise asked him, not believing the change of course their conversation had taken.

"We haven't told him. It just seems to be so much. Right now, my son and I aren't in a good place. I don't want to put this on him." Joshua thought about his statement. "Well, that's not entirely true. The real truth is that I don't know if I can take one more thing. When your marriage falls apart after twenty years and everything you thought was real turns out to be a lie, you don't go around trying to poke the bear. I seem to be the only person in the world who thought the divorce was a bad idea. I couldn't handle it if I told my son I wasn't actually his biological father, and he just shrugged his shoulders like it was no big deal."

"I am so sorry, Client. But I can see why you were done, and you guys couldn't work it out."

"I wasn't done. My dumb butt actually kept trying!" Joshua said emphatically.

Elise couldn't help herself. She kept digging. "So, even after all that, you still wanted to stay married to her?"

"I did. At least I think I did. I tried to talk to her, I was gonna… nah…I can't have you thinking I'm a simp."

"I won't think that at all. What were you going to do? Enquiring minds want to know."

"Okay, this has to stay between us, though," Joshua said, unable to resist her. She could have asked him his deepest darkest secret and he would have told her. "Cool. Pinky promise," Elise said as she smiled and extended her right pinky finger to him.

"Huh?" Joshua said.

"Boy, don't ack all brand new. You know what a pinky promise is. Here," she insisted.

"Okay," he said as he shook her pinky with his and released it. "I was going to beg her. I mean literally…on my knees, I was going to beg her to work it out." he confessed.

"Oh. Okay. Keith Sweat style, huh?" she said.

"Worse than that…full-blown Jodeci. 'Baby, I'm begging, baby, I'm begging, baby, baby,'" he sang.

"But?" she asked as they both laughed.

"But before I could get to that point, another guy came walking down the stairs of our house."

"Client, noooo! Shut the front door. What did you do?"

"I flipped his a…I mean I flipped his behind over my shoulder, put my knee in his back while I twisted his arm, and told her to bring me the divorce papers." "Please tell me you broke that joker's arm off. No, wait. Don't tell me. I don't want to be a witness. But next time I see a one-armed man, though…I'm gon be like that's what you get for messing with my client."

"Nah. I didn't break his arm off. But between that and her telling me she was repulsed by my touch…."

"She said that?" Elise asked, shocked. "She said you repulsed her?" "Yeah," Joshua acknowledged, thinking he had revealed too much.

"Client," Elise said sympathetically. First of all, I know there are two sides to every story, but I assure you there's nothing repulsive about you. It's a little sad that you would have to do that, but I think it's very sweet…and very romantic that you were willing to lay it all on the line for the woman you love. And secondly, Elise Traylor Properties is a full-service organization. These earrings and heels can be off in a moment. I keep tennis shoes in the car. And a .45 in my purse. Just give me an address and go someplace where there are plenty of witnesses, so you have an alibi. Your Realtor will handle the rest.

Joshua smiled. It was nice to have someone take up for him. But it was particularly special coming from her. "It's okay, Thug Life," he teased.

"Thug Life?" she laughed. She found his playfulness endearing. It reminded her of how Jeremiah used to play with her.

Joshua continued his explanation.

"Hearing that comment and seeing another man in my house helped me realize that regardless of whose fault it was, my marriage was over. Her heart was already too hard to be reached and that moment hardened mine. But don't worry. I am sure that won't happen to you. I peeped that chandelier on your finger. How long have you been married?" Joshua asked.

Joshua's question was intentional. He wanted to remind himself that he was speaking to a married woman. As beautiful as she was, and as much as they seemed to be connecting, he wasn't going to cross that line. A divorce was bad enough, but he wasn't going to add adultery to his growing list of defeats. Besides, she was probably just trying to be nice.

"It's funny, Client. We've been married twenty years as well," Elise responded.

"Nice," Joshua nodded. "Kids?" he asked.

Elise's expression changed. "No. No kids," she said, hoping he would not push the issue.

Joshua could tell he had touched a nerve. He had just been extremely transparent with her, but he didn't want to force anything out of her. So, he pivoted the conversation back to the home they were supposed to be viewing.

"So, what's in this one, Realtor?" he asked.

"Client! This one is everything!" Elise was thankful for the escape hatch and refocused on showing him the house.

With every word, every smile, every move, Joshua became more enamored with her. Normally, he was a very private person. But he was an open book with Elise. Every word she spoke stirred something deep inside him. She made him laugh. She made him think. She made him want to protect her. She made him feel safe enough to be himself. He remembered crying when Angela said she wanted a divorce. But he didn't do that in front of her. And of course, he couldn't deny that she was the most beautiful woman he had ever seen. *Don't do this to yourself, J. She's married,* he said to himself.

Elise knew this was the perfect house for him. It had everything he needed, and she was confident the owner would negotiate the price. Normally, she would close the deal right then and there. Instead, she said, "Client, I know this might work for you, but there are a couple of more properties I want you to see. Do you think you might want to check them out? They are a little pricier, but it won't hurt to make sure."

Elise wasn't quite sure what she was doing. But she knew she wasn't ready for their day to be over. There would be no harm in working a little longer just to make sure her client was well taken care of.

Joshua loved the house he was standing in, but there was no way he was turning down an opportunity to spend more time with her. *Just a few more hours with her won't hurt,* he thought. But a few more hours turned into them spending the rest of the day together. Two more houses morphed into several and Joshua ended up ordering lunch for them. They barely looked at the homes they visited. They mostly talked and laughed.

The day zoomed by as they arrived at the last house. This one was the most luxurious of them all. It was obviously more than what Joshua could afford.

"So, Client," Elise started, "I will tell you now, you can fall in love with this house all you want but there is no way I would sell it to you. I don't want you going bankrupt on this note, but it is very nice. I mean we can dream, right?"

"Okay, Realtor, let me see it. No harm dreaming," Joshua agreed.

They went inside the breathtaking house, which was even more extravagant than what Joshua had expected.

"This is nice, Realtor!" he exclaimed. "Let's do it! I could swing it if I didn't have electricity and ate TV dinners every night," he said jokingly.

"But how are you going to heat up the frozen dinners if you don't have electricity? Asking for a friend," she joked.

Joshua cut his eyes at her and pretended to be annoyed. "Okay, smart butt.

You know what I mean," he said as they laughed together.

"Seriously, Client. I just wanted you to see it because I knew you would like it."

"I do like it, Realtor But this actually isn't the nicest one I've seen," Joshua told her.

Elise put her hands on her hips and cocked her head to the side. "Well, sir, it's by far the nicest one I've shown you so, do tell, where did you see something nicer, and double do tell… who showed it to you? Huh, Client? You stepping out on me?" Elise said as she playfully pointed her finger. "Hell hath no fury like a realtor scorned."

"No, Realtor, I promise," Joshua laughed as he raised his right hand. "I'm a faithful client. But I did go on the internet and look at a few listings to get some ideas."

Elise gasped dramatically. "Clutch the pearls. Client, you went to the internet… instead of me?"

"It was just a few pictures," Joshua defended himself, trying to control his laughter.

"Just pictures, huh? And you think that makes it okay? I feel so betrayed. Got me out in these streets trying to find you the perfect domicile and you out here gawking at other realtors'… well, you know what you did, sir. I can't even look at you right now," Elise said as she playfully turned her head.

Joshua burst into laughter. Her playfulness made her all the more attractive.

Elise continued her humorous rant. She folded her arms and pretended to sniffle. "Okay, tell me what you saw. Don't leave anything out because I will know. A realtor knows these things."

Joshua played along. In his most remorseful tone, he told her, "Well, Realtor, what had happened was...you see, it was late... and I figured I didn't want to disturb you."

"Oh, don't you dare make this about me, sir!" she snapped playfully. "I told you I was going to take care of you. But okay, I get it. You're a client and you have your… your needs. So continue, what did you do?"

"I just saw a few houses, Realtor. And it didn't mean anything."

"Oh, it meant something, sir! Or you wouldn't have been gawking at those other realtors'… I can't say it… listings," Elise snapped as she playfully jabbed her finger in his chest. "And what did they have that I haven't shown you?"

"Really, it was nothing. I promise."

"Tell me the truth, Client. What was this amazing house that was the nicest thing you have ever seen?"

"Well, there was one house that was mind-blowing. It was in Colonial Park. But it listed for a cool one million dollars. Realtor, it was sooo dope. I mean I'm sorry, but a client got needs."

Joshua thought they were both enjoying the playful exchange and was surprised that she did not quip back. Instead, Elise's expression became very somber and he realized that once again he said something that hit a sore spot. But this time he didn't feel like he should change the subject. If she was hurting, he wanted to help.

"Whoa. What's that look? What did I say? Because your whole vibe just changed," Joshua asked.

"Yeah, it's a lot, Client." Elise admitted reluctantly.

"Well, I don't want to pry. But you did just make me cry, so you can share if you want," Joshua said, hoping she would let her guard down. He enjoyed their jesting but wanted to know her on another level.

"Boy, you did not cry!" she exclaimed.

"I wanted to though," he retorted. "And I told you all my bizness. So, what's up?"

"Fine," Elise said. "That house in Colonial Park was actually mine. I mean me and my husband's. He bought it and remodeled it for me. It was my dream house."

"What happened?" Joshua asked. "Why aren't you guys there anymore?" "Client…life be lifin'," Elise said as she shrugged her shoulders. She didn't

even try to mask her sadness. "I mean it's a whole thing." "I got time, Elise."

"Oh, we're using real names now? You think you're out of the doghouse?" Joshua just smiled. He didn't want her to deflect out of this moment. "No, seriously, Elise. I'm interested. If you want to share."

Elise did want to share. She felt very safe. "Well, probably about the same time you were going through your divorce, my husband got falsely accused of what they call in the construction industry, bid rigging."

"Elise, this is crazy but yeah, I know what you're talking about. I remember seeing something on it in the news. Jacebre Construction? Is that who he worked for?"

"Yes, that's it. But again. It's false. My husband is an honorable man."

Joshua didn't know how he felt about hearing her defend her husband. It was just one more reminder that she was off limits. Still, he wanted to know her.

"No judgment," Joshua reassured her. "I'm just telling you I know what you're talking about. So how did that come out?"

"Well, it hasn't. It takes a while for these things to go through the court system. I believe the owner of the company, who I never liked by the way, who I tried to told my husband was shady…."

"You tried to told, Elise?" Joshua interrupted with a smile.

"Okay, Mr. Internet Searcher, so we're correcting grammar from the doghouse? You sure that's what you want to be doing?"

"Oh, my bad. Please continue, ma'am. You tried to told your husband the boss was shady. And?"

"And that part. I tried to told my husband that man was shady. He made him the scapegoat and tried to pretend like he knew nothing. But my husband only did what he was asked to do. He didn't have any knowledge of any under-the-table deals."

"Well, your husband is a blessed man to have you in his corner," Joshua said reluctantly. "So is that why you guys aren't in the house? He lost his job?"

"Mostly. They fired him but they also have done everything they could to destroy his name. He was a star in the construction industry. Before he could have worked anywhere, but now no one will hire him. Every place he would go to find work said that they couldn't take a chance on bringing him on with such a public scandal hanging over his head. We thought we had our stuff together financially, but it has been so overwhelming. We are trying to fight the allegations and we have to prepare to defend my husband if it goes to court. Then there are medical bills out the wazoo. Fulltime care for my father-in-law. Funeral expenses. We couldn't hold all that down without his salary."

"Wait. What? I get attorney fees. But what medical bills? What funeral? Who died?" Joshua asked.

"Oooh, Client, you don't even know."

"Elise," he said seriously, "I think this is a 'Josh' conversation." "Okay, Josh. But you sure you're ready for all this?"

Joshua measured his words. He wanted her to know he was there for her. For whatever she needed. But he wanted to do it without making a fool of himself. "Oh, I'm here for it. Step into my office."

Joshua pulled out a stool for her and they sat at the bar of the luxurious home. "Well, CliffsNotes version," Elise said. "Around the same time my husband lost his job, our mother, and I say 'our' because she was so much more than a mother-in-law to me. She was really my mama. The only mother I ever really knew. Well, she got cancer and lost that battle. That was one funeral. And here is where it gets interesting. Jeremiah, that's my husband, found a nice little job. It didn't pay as well as his previous one, but he was enjoying it and was feeling like himself again. We were like 'Okay, God, not what we had in mind, but we see you working it out. We're gonna make it.'

"While all of this is going on, we're in the process of adopting our foster child. Her name is Amari. Josh, you would love her. She's such an amazing little girl! But even that got all messed up. Her biological aunt said she wanted her, but we were trying to fight it. I know that makes us sound like monsters, but bear in mind that she lived with us for three years and there was no peep from this aunt that entire time. So, we're going to meet the judge to see what we can work out but the day this was supposed to happen our father, same thing, he's Jeremiah's dad but that's my daddy too, he has a stroke so we miss the court appearance and they took her away from us."

Elise thought about telling him about the baby she had lost on that day. But it seemed too much. Too intimate.

"Oh, wow, Elise. That's rough."

"Hold your horses, Mr. 'I'm Here for It.' I haven't even gotten to the good part yet," Elise exclaimed. "So, on the same day our father has this stroke, me and Jeremiah get into this awful wreck. My husband had multiple breaks in his leg and his arm. He had a traumatic brain injury and memory loss. They had to cut open his skull and had to put him into a coma while the swelling in his brain went down. And of course, that meant he lost the new job he got. Like I said, my daddy, Jeremiah's dad, he needs round-the-clock care now and we are still not sure he's out of the woods. He's alive but he's not really living.

"So this last year has been the worst. I mean emotionally, mentally, and financially. So don't let the billboards and the website with pictures of me closing deals and getting people into houses fool you because this, sir," Elise pointed both thumbs at herself, "is a literal hot mess. Look up 'hot mess' in the dictionary. You will see my profile pic. Just a grinnin'."

Joshua shook his head at her story. His heart broke for her. "You're not a mess, Elise. I don't believe that at all. But you're right. It's a lot. And I'm sorry you're going through all of that."

"Thank you, Client," Elise said, appreciating his compassion. Joshua shot her a disapproving glance.

"I'm sorry. Thank you, Josh. Sometimes I wonder if whoever said 'When life gives you lemons, just make lemonade' got this damn many lemons. Oops. I'm sorry, Josh."

"It's okay, Elise. And I wish I had an answer but I gotta tell you, you don't look like what you have been through. I mean, no one would be able to tell with the way you carry yourself. You just seem to have it all together. And that has to be God working in your life. Really, I am humbled that you can have gone through all of that and still be hanging in there."

"You still here for it?" Elise asked him seriously. "Of course," he responded.

"Josh, me and God ain't too good right now. You might want to step back. I don't want you to get struck with my lightning bolt."

"No, I get it, Elise. Really, I do. Sometimes the creation looks up at the creator and asks, 'What's up?' But he still knows what's best. He's still in control. I know that sounds like church talk, but it's still true. I'm not one of those 'God said' types, but I do feel God would say 'I need you to keep believing no matter how it all looks.'"

"Josh, that's it, though. It's not that I don't believe. It's the exact opposite. I believe everything. I believe God opened the Red Sea for his children to walk through on dry ground. I believe Jesus gave sight to the blind. I believe God gave a dead son back to his mother." Elise's voice trembled at her own words. She hadn't meant to stir up those emotions. But Joshua was extremely easy to talk to. She wanted him to know about J.J. But she didn't know how she would act or how he would respond if she broke down in front of him. She paused as she composed herself. "But he just won't do those things for me. And I'm mad at him. I know I'm not supposed to be, but I am."

"You're just in the storm now, Elise. It won't always be like this," Joshua encouraged.

"Well, my Bible says he can speak to the storm! So why won't he say, 'Peace be still'?"

"I can't say for sure, but my guess is it's probably because he's not finished doing what he wants to do. I'm not trying to make this about me because I can't even imagine what you're going through. But on a smaller level, I can remember when I was going through my divorce, I would come home, sit in the car and pray for strength. Elise, I did not want to go in that house. It was like I wanted to be anyplace else in the world. I mean my ex was there. My kids were there. But I was all alone. Being lonely when you're around the people who are supposed to love you the most is the saddest, emptiest feeling in the world. I wouldn't wish that on anybody." Joshua said as the painful memory overwhelmed him.

"I'm sorry, Joshy," Elise said as she wiped away the unexpected tear that had rolled down his cheek with her thumb.

Bruh, I know you did not just cry a real tear in front of this woman! he thought to himself as he realized his emotions had gotten away from him. He wasn't sure if he was crying because of the sad memory he had just shared or because of his concern for the woman in front of him.

"Dang allergies!" he said, attempting to recover his dignity.

"You don't have allergies, Joshy. You just have a soft heart. I love that about you, actually," she said sweetly, ignoring her inappropriate choice of words.

"I'm not soft!" he insisted as her words warmed his soul.

"I didn't say you were soft," Elise clarified. "I said you had a soft heart. There's a difference. But to be clear, I don't think having a soft heart makes you weak. And I get what you're saying about being lonely. Josh, I mean, I'm not gonna lie. My prayer life is nonexistent right now. So, I don't pray, but I do sit in the car some days just not wanting to go inside."

"I get it," Joshua confirmed.

Elise lifted her hand and extended her pinky to him. "Pinky promise?" Joshua shook his head. "We doin' this again?"

"New subject...new pinky swear! That means you can't tell anybody," she insisted.

"Alrighty then. I will go back to kindergarten with you," Joshua chuckled as he took his pinky and wrapped it around hers. But this time he didn't release it. And Elise didn't try to take hers back. "Pinky swear. This is the circle of trust. What's up?"

"Please don't take this too literally, okay? I mean, I'm fine…but Josh, there are days I don't even want to be here anymore. I just want to…."

Elise paused as she struggled to keep from crying. She thought the tears were gone but her thoughts returned to her son. To Amari. And to the husband she had lost connection with. But Joshua's warm smile and her pinky embrace with him calmed her. Even though she knew she should feel uncomfortable. This wasn't right. This wasn't who she was supposed to be sharing this with. Even Jeremiah didn't realize how her prayer life had fallen off the rails, but she had just shared it so easily with Joshua.

"You're safe, Elise. Tell me." he said, gently interrupting her private thoughts. "I'm not going to harm myself, Josh. Okay?" she continued.

"Elise, I believe you. But?"

"But just everything. Everything is so messed up. Nothing I see is lining up with what I thought God was going to do. And I'm not a complete heathen. I still believe in the deepest part of myself that the Lord loves me. I just can't do this anymore. He keeps taking everything. And I don't know what to believe. I'm like 'Okay, Jesus. I flunked my test. Fine. Bring me home. I don't need a mansion. I grew up in the projects on earth, just put me in the projects in heaven and I'll be good.'"

Joshua turned his head away as he tried to hide his amusement at her comment. "Joshua Dupree! Are you laughing at me while I'm pouring out my heart?" "Elise, I'm sorry, but come on now… projects in heaven?" he asked as he shook his head, still trying to contain his laughter.

"Oh, they got projects in heaven," Elise insisted. "I'm sure of it. When Jesus was talking about his many rooms, that's what he was referring to. They for us saved but not sanctified folks. Laughing at me. I ain't laugh at you when you was having your moment."

"No, you didn't," Joshua agreed. "But I didn't start talking about projects in heaven either."

Elise glared back at him. They both paused until neither of them could contain their laughter.

"Well, I guess we both just some soft punks," Elise said, still laughing. And still holding on to Joshua's pinky.

"Yeah, soft like baby boo boo," Joshua agreed.

"But you were the only one who cried though," she teased. "I ain't cry!" Joshua denied.

"Joshy, yes you did!" Elise said, refusing to let him off the hook. "I got your DNA on my thumb. It's okay though. I appreciate you trusting me like that. And just know that your man card is safe. This is our circle of trust. No one will ever know," she assured him.

They smiled at each other as they remained connected by their pinky fingers. "So, seriously, Elise. You're good, right?"

"Yes, Josh, I'm good," she said. Her heartrate increased as she realized, in this moment, with this man, this man who was not Jeremiah, she truly felt good. But she was getting used to not facing her thoughts and now, when everything seemed okay, was not the time to challenge this likely momentary sense of joy, peace…and love.

"Listen," he said as he leaned closer to her. "I don't think God is defining you by one season of doubt in your life. I bet there's a mansion for you, and I bet there's still some great stuff for you here."

"I don't know, Josh. I just feel…worthless."

"You're not worthless to me! I can't tell you how great you have been. This has been more than just house hunting. I really needed this. Anybody else, I would just be sitting at home…well, you know… looking at pictures of houses on the internet," Joshua said, trying to make her smile.

"Little ole bad tail," Elise laughed. "But keep going. You might get forgiven." Joshua laughed and continued. "My point is, you have helped me so much.

You're special, Elise. Anybody can see that. And no matter how sideways you are with God, he loves you. He is going to work it out."

"Aww, Joshy, that's sweet. And you're pretty special too."

Joshua's heart melted at the comment as he continued to enjoy the embrace of their pinky fingers. He wanted to tell her, "Okay, Elise. You got me. I am figuratively and literally wrapped around your finger. Oh, and by the way, 'Joshy'? Yeah, nobody has ever called me that. But I'm here for it."

But, of course, he couldn't tell her that. Instead, he just said, "This is true. I am sweet. And I tell you what. We will just call it even. No charge for my counseling session. And umm, no charge for this house. We good or nah?"

"Boy, bye!" Elise laughed out loud. "You betta leave me alone. I'm tryna cut you a deal. Don't make me have you paying double."

"I'd pay double if you asked me. I think I'd do anything for you, Elise," Joshua said seriously, not believing he just let those words come from his mouth.

Elise felt her face flush and hoped her blushing wasn't noticed. She pressed her lips together to keep herself from smiling.

Too far, J, Joshua thought to himself. *Now you've gone and made it awkward.*

Elise tried to recover. She glanced at their pinkies that had been embraced way too long. *Elise, you doin' waaayyy too much, girl,* she thought to herself.

She gently shook Joshua's pinky and took hers back. She could tell he was embarrassed, and she didn't want to make it worse.

"Joshy, that's okay," she said as she looked into his eyes. "I may be low key... or even high key backslidden but I'm still a woman of integrity. I wouldn't do you like that...I would never want to do anything that would hurt you...or anybody else for that matter."

Joshua clasped his hands together. Her message was clear enough to make the point but subtle enough to spare his ego. "I know you are, Elise," he agreed.

"So, Client, since you're such a sweet guy. I am going to recommend we put in a bid on that first house. That's your spot. It checks every Joshua Dupree box. Let's do it."

Joshua sighed. He was "Client" again. But what else did he expect? Not too much had gone his way lately, so of course he would fall for a married woman. Elise was somebody else's. And apparently somebody else's who was going through a terrible time. As bad as things were for him, whoever this Jeremiah guy was, obviously had it a lot worse. He needed Elise far more than he did. And she was his wife. Not his. Being the nice guy sucked. They always finish last. But he still had a conscience. He hadn't heard from God in a while, but he was pretty sure he wasn't going to send him a married woman. Still, there was so much he wanted to say. But instead, he just agreed with her.

"Okay, Realtor," he said as he faked a smile. "Let's do it."

Joshua wanted to embrace her, but they only stood and shook hands as they went to their cars and their separate ways. If Joshua and Elise could have read each other's minds, they would have known that each of them felt very empty. They both would have known that the other didn't want this day to be over and that one more suggestion, one more inappropriate comment and they would be willing to throw it all away. But the house would soon be Joshua's and their relationship would be over. There would be no reason to call or text. There would be no reason to meet.

Joshua cursed himself. How could he have fallen so far so fast? He didn't even know this woman. Not really. He thought about the night Angela said that she wanted a divorce. He remembered how he could almost literally feel his heart break when she told him Robert was not his son. He remembered his humiliation when she told him she was repulsed at his touch. And now he was in his feelings about a married woman he had only known for a few weeks. Not being with Elise could not possibly be worse than all of that, but somehow it was. He started his car and began the journey back to where he was staying. But he wasn't going home. Today...being with Elise... that felt like home. He felt like he was going back to an even lower place of emptiness and loneliness. Elise was his only salvation, and she couldn't help because they could never be.

Elise drove away in the opposite direction and did her best to rationalize her conflicted feelings. She had enjoyed herself more than she should have. Joshua didn't know it, but she had blown off three other lucrative opportunities that day showing him houses she knew weren't a good fit for him. He listened to her. He cried in front of her. He encouraged her. He told her she was special. Jeremiah used to do all those things and more. And now, here she was, once again feeling some kind of way as she made her way home to be with her husband. Her body would be with Jeremiah but her mind, and perhaps her heart, would be with Joshua.

CHAPTER 56

Confrontation

DAY 425

Shania and Elise sat down at the corner table of their favorite restaurant. It had been a while since they had just hung out, and Shania was overjoyed that Elise finally agreed to another girl's night out.

"Ooh, I'm so excited to be in these streets with my girl. Elise, it's so good to see you. I missed you, sis," Shania beamed.

"Aww, I missed you too," Elise said. "I decided I would come up for air and check on my girl. How are you doing?"

"I'm doing good, but you had me worried. You don't return my phone calls or texts. You don't come around."

"Well, I'm here now. So, no fussing," Elise told her.

"What is there to fuss about? You look amazing. The Lord has really been keeping you, hasn't he?"

Shania's comment was intentional. Elise was MIA from most of her usual church activities. First Lady Faye had mentioned her concern for her, but Shania wanted to see for herself where Elise was emotionally and spiritually.

Elise simply responded with a halfhearted "Yep."

Shania ignored her lack of enthusiasm and kept pressing. "Girl, everyone from the choir has been asking about you, but I told them to stop blowing up your phone."

"Aww…they're sweet, honey," Elise said as she smiled. "Send them my love." "Our small group has been asking about you too. They wanted to see if you would be open to them just coming over for a special time of prayer."

"No. Not right now," Elise said abruptly. "I know they're praying, and I appreciate it. But I have to get some stuff together and now isn't a good time."

"Elise, when is there a bad time for prayer? It doesn't have to be everyone. We could get First Lady Faye and maybe just a few others to come by. Or we could just have a special time of prayer to cover you after church. Assuming we could get you to come to church."

"Is that shade?" Elise asked.

"Hee-hee…maybe just a little teensy-weensy shade. But Elise, if someone else was going through like you, your little intrusive tail wouldn't even ask. I could see you now if it was me. You'd be like 'I'm on the way, don't make me break the door down.'"

Elise smiled at her friend. She knew Shania was telling the truth. It was true that not too incredibly long ago, she was the one who believed God for the impossible. But that was a different person. The person she was now, wasn't a prayer warrior nor did she particularly want prayer.

"Shania, I know you love me. I love you too, but I talk to First Lady all the time and right now I just can't do the church thing. I am trying to piece my life back together, and I need to do it without all the prying eyes and unsolicited advice from the saints."

"I can understand that. But can we at least talk about it? Just me and you?" Shania asked.

Elise squared herself in her seat and looked directly at her friend. "There's nothing to talk about. I just need you to be my sister. Don't try to check the church box with me. I just want to chill with you and enjoy the evening."

"I want that too, but it's hard to enjoy you when I know you're hurting. Why won't you talk to me?" Shania implored.

"Because you can't help. I will figure it out," Elise countered.

"Elise, I don't know what to do with this. I've tried to give you your space, but I can't say you're my sister and just let you drift like this. I need my friend back. The one who taught me that God is faithful and who used to talk to me about everything.

"Shania, sweetie, I am sorry but she's not available right now, and I don't think she's coming back. And I'm telling you as my friend…you don't want this smoke. I already had to apologize to First Lady but you ain't First Lady. Let's not do this."

"Do what?" Shania continued her press. "Talk? Be real with each other? Pray?

Why would those things bring the smoke?"

"I'm gonna go," Elise said as she grabbed her purse and began to get up. "Elise, please. Let's talk," Shania pleaded.

"No, this is not why I called you. I just wanted to escape for a second but you out here doing way too much. All this is not desired, required or even helpful."

"Well, then tell me how I can help." "You can't!" Elise snapped.

Elise saw the hurt in Shania's expression. It was the same disappointed look she had seen on First Lady's face. She stayed in her seat and tried to calm herself. "Shania, you are my best friend and my sister, but I am just not in a place to be ministered to right now. I know this is hard to hear, but to me, all the church talk just sounds like the teacher on Charlie Brown. Yes, I am avoiding people, but I am not doing it to be hateful. I just don't want to mess up someone else's faith just because I've lost mine. People are expecting me to say, 'God is Good. God is faithful. God is holding on to me.' But the truth is that this Elise doesn't believe those things anymore. And I don't believe prayer is going to make one bit of difference, at least not for me. God is going to do whatever he wants to do, so I'm going to let him do it. He doesn't need my input. But I know most people can't take hearing something like that and I don't want them to be where I am. I want them to believe. I want for them to have faith. So, it really is best I keep a safe distance. Misery loves company, but I wouldn't wish how I feel on anybody. I would rather stay in it by myself than to destroy somebody else."

Shania hung her head.

"And see, look at you now. Looking like I shot your dog," Elise continued. "I don't want to make people feel bad. If God is out to get me for whatever I've done, then so be it, but I'm not giving him any more sticks to beat me with. I don't know if you realize this but he's a savage when he comes for you."

"Elise, don't say that," Shania said, shocked at her friend's words.

"I said what I said," Elise said defiantly. "He knows it's in me anyway. I just feel bad because now I got you looking at me like I'm the devil's evil twin sister. I can perform for so long, but sooner or later, this person talking to you now escapes, and I don't want her to hurt anybody. I have to perform for Jeremiah because he's hurt. I have to perform for my clients because I gotta get the bag. I tried to perform for First Lady, epic fail by the by, that's why I don't really talk to her that much anymore. The only one I don't have to perform for is... well, forget it," Elise said, deciding it would be best not to mention Joshua. "But Shania, I can't perform for you. You either got to deal with full-frontal jacked-up Elise or nothing because I don't have any more performances left."

Shania reached across the table and gently took Elise's purse from her. "Sis, I don't want you to have to perform for me. I don't think First Lady does either. Just know that I love you, and I'm here for you. Please don't leave. I'll back off. Let's just order and chill," she said as their waiter approached them. "Hi, we'll start with two white wines, please."

"Change mine to a Hennessy and Coke, please," Elise asked. "Whoa! Got a lot on your mind, don't ya, sis," Shania said.

"Grown woman problems...grown woman drink. Do I need to get my purse back?" Elise threatened.

"Nope...backing all the way off and changing the subject. How's my brother?"

"Jeremiah's a lot better. He's close to one hundred percent recovered. He's just down because he can't find work and he's stressed about the investigation."

"And Mr. Traylor?" Shania asked.

"He's still not walking or talking, but he's able to feed himself if he's patient. I look into his eyes and it's like he's trying to tell me, 'Hold on, Daddy's Girl. I'll be back soon.' Girl, he held my hand the other day. He just kept squeezing it. It was so sweet. Every time I said I had to go;

he would squeeze it more. I had to cancel an appointment. My Daddy wasn't having it," Elise smiled.

"I love y'all's relationship," Shania affirmed.

"I do too. I miss him so much. I think if he was okay things would be better. We would have his quiet wisdom to guide us. But now with Mama Etta gone, it's just me and Jeremiah. I used to think that was enough. That we could face anything and do anything together. But things are so different now and I don't know if we are going to make it through this. A lot of couples don't recover after they lose a child, and we lost two."

Elise felt herself about to tear up and caught herself. She cocked her head and squinted hard at Shania.

"Heffa, you think you slick," she said as she sipped her Hennessy and Coke. "How you gon try and backdoor me into a deep and meaningful conversation? Girl, bye. I ain't getting deep with you. What you been watching on Netflix?"

"I ain't even do nuthin,'" Shania laughed as she tried to hide her concern with Elise's newfound fondness for stronger drink. "I know there's more and I'm here for you. But I'll take that moment of transparency as a win. You just let me know when you want to say more."

"Now all the ooey-gooey stuff aside," Shania said, lightening her tone, "girl, check out that whole snack that just came in the door. I don't care what you say... my God is awesome. Babay, I am sorry, but he is fine. Looking like an extra-large version of Jeremiah Traylor. Check your left shoulder...don't be obvious, though. And try not to be so cute. I always look like the ugly friend when I'm with you."

Elise laughed. "Girl, stop. You know you cute. Let me check this brutha out for you."

Elise turned to her left and saw who Shania had spotted. It was Joshua. She had mentioned they would be there and was pleasantly surprised he had come by. She smiled as Joshua waved to her and made his way to the table.

"Girl, is he waving at you? Is he coming over here?" Shania asked. "I told you not to let him see you. I can't stand yo pretty tail! Already got a man and messing it up for everybody else."

"Girl, calm down. That's just my client," Elise explained. "Hey, Realtor," Joshua smiled. "You doin' okay?"

Elise returned his smile. "Hello, Client." Shania softly kicked Elise under the table.

Elise took the hint but kicked her back to show her annoyance. "Joshua, this is my best friend, Shania. Shania, this is Joshua."

Joshua politely extended his hand to Shania. "Hi Shania. It's nice to meet you."

"You too, Joshua. Is my girl taking care of you?" Shania asked as she shook his hand and smiled from ear to ear. She hoped the instant attraction was mutual. "Oh, yeah, most definitely," Joshua answered. "She's a real one. I just hope I don't have to get a second job to afford whatever she finds me."

"Client! Stop it," Elise said, playfully hitting him on his arm. "I told you I got you. Stop worrying."

"Elise and I come here all of the time," Shania cut in but took note of the playful hit. "Have you been here before?"

"No, I haven't. Realtor here let me know about it. I just wanted to get out of the apartment for a second. It seems nice…good vibe…good music. I hope the food is good."

"It is," Shania continued. "If you're not meeting anyone, you're welcome to join us." Shania had no intention of letting this tall, handsome gentleman get away. "I don't want to intrude," Joshua replied. "Realtor here might be getting tired of me."

Elise saw what Shania was doing. She wasn't sure how she felt about it, but she decided to let her have her fun. Besides, she was very happy to see him. "No, Client. Please join us."

Shania, rather obviously, moved over so Joshua could take the seat next to her. "What do you do, Joshua?" she inquired.

"I'm the vice principal at Conrad Hutchinson High School." "Do you enjoy it?"

"I do. I love the kids. For years, I felt like God was calling me to step out of the classroom. Then one day I saw an opportunity to take some graduate-level courses to get my Master's and Doctorate. I took it and my life hasn't been the same since. My position now lets me support parents, students, and teachers. I'm thankful for where God has placed me."

"Client. I am so sorry," Elise said.

"About what?" Joshua asked with a puzzled expression.

"I should have been calling you Dr. Client all this time. My bad." Joshua laughed. "Your friend is special," he said to Shania.

Shania shot a quick disapproving glance at Elise. She needed her to be seen and not heard at this particular point and time.

Shania gently touched his arm. "Joshua, that's refreshing to hear. It's good to see someone who follows the Lord and is willing to step out and go get what he wants when he sees it."

Elise took another sip of her drink and shook her head at her friend's rather unsubtle hint.

"Yeah, like Realtor says…it's okay to want nice things," Joshua said, looking directly at Elise.

Shania didn't really want to talk about Elise, but she had to know. "What in the heck is this 'client and realtor' stuff?"

Joshua and Elise both laughed out loud.

"That's this one right here," Elise pointed to Joshua. "I would have to show you the text but long story short, he said he wanted me to call him 'Client,' so I said he has to call me 'Realtor.'"

"Alrighty then," Shania said, wondering why the two of them thought that was so funny.

"It's okay, Shania. It was funny in the moment," Joshua said.

"Yeah, I guess you had to be there," Elise said, calling the waiter back over. "Can we get a Diet Coke and ice water for our friend, please?"

Interesting, Shania thought to herself. *So you two have pet names and you know what he wants to drink.* "So, what kind of house are you looking for, Joshua?" she asked, hoping to get a little of his attention.

"Your girl found me a nice spot near Pearson Lake. It's nice. I think we're just finalizing some things with the owner. It has everything I want…," Joshua paused and fixed a smiling gaze on Elise. "It's my…."

"Deluxe apartment in the sky," Joshua and Elise sang in unison as they laughed and high-fived each other.

Hmm…so you also have pet names, you know what he wants to drink, and private jokes, Shania thought.

As the evening progressed, it became unmistakably clear to Shania that Joshua was far more interested in conversing with Elise than her. *Men are so dumb,* she thought. *Always trying to obtain the unobtainable.* She was actually used to it. Elise often garnered a lot of attention from men when they were out. What she was not used to was Elise's response. Elise was an expert at keeping men at a safe distance, but she wasn't exercising that skill with Joshua.

She also noticed Elise had abandoned her second job: being Shania's personal matchmaker. It was a job she wasn't particularly good at, but it wasn't for lack of effort. Elise made no effort to deflect Joshua's attention away from herself and back to her single friend. Normally, a nice single brother would have to hear about how amazing Shania was. It was annoyingly sweet. But not this time. Now they were sitting with this handsome, single, well-employed Christian brother, and Elise made no attempt to be a good wingman. Joshua and Elise bantered back and forth, and it became clear to Shania that she was the third wheel. It was also clear that this wasn't the first time these two had engaged socially with each other.

They enjoyed their dinner and Joshua graciously picked up the check. "Elise, I need to get something from your car before you leave." That was their bff code for "Don't leave. I need to talk to you."

"Okay, girl. Come on," Elise said. "Bye, Client. I will give you an update soon."

"Bye, Realtor. Bye, Shania. Nice to meet you," Joshua said.

"Thank you for dinner…Client. Or can I call you that?" Shania asked. "No, you may not," Elise objected. "Only I can call him Client." "Yeah, gotta keep it in the family," Joshua agreed. "Goodnight, ladies."

Oh, yeah, Shania thought. *I don't care if she gets mad. We're talking about this.*

Shania joined Elise in the passenger seat of her car. "So how long has this been going on?" she asked directly.

"How long has what been going on?" Elise responded.

"Uh-uh. We're not doing this. You don't want church folks in your business?

Fine. Let's take it to the street. Have you slept with him?"

"Girl, are you crazy?" Elise asked, her voice going up two octaves. "Did you take a sip from my glass? No, I haven't slept with him!"

"But you want to…don't you?" Shania asked bluntly.

"Shania, I am sorry that me opening up to you made you think I'm a complete heathen, but I assure you I am not. I'm married."

"Elise, I know you aren't used to this. I'm usually the one who's needing guidance. But that doesn't mean I'm dumb, it doesn't mean I don't know you, and it doesn't mean I don't know men. That man likes you. And he wants you. And you want him too. Now we both know what you should do, but I'm not going to shove something down your throat that you can't receive right now. But please let me be your friend. I've confessed a many failures right here in this Lexus because you always made me feel safe to do so. You're safe too. What's happening?"

"What do you want to know?" "I want to know about Joshua."

"Shania, seriously… we're just friends. He's one of those challenging clients who's looking for a very particular kind of house in a very particular price range. So, I have to spend a little extra time with him."

"Say more…please," Shania insisted, knowing Elise hadn't told the full story.

Elise sighed. "…Okay…I may have started to enjoy our conversations a little too much…and there may have been a few times where I called him when a text would have sufficed or where I met up with him when a phone call would have sufficed. He's a good listener and I like talking to him. But that's it."

"And he just happened to show up here tonight?" Shania asked skeptically. "Well…I may have told him I would be meeting a friend and to say hi if he decided to come through." "Okay, so you invited him?"

After the Crash

"Not exactly. I figured he would just say hi and go sit down someplace else.

You were the one that asked him to join us."

"Elise…hear me…you are not built for this," Shania warned. "Built for what?" Elise asked.

"An affair, that's what!" Shania exclaimed, growing weary of Elise's denial. "An affair? I told you I'm not sleeping with him! Nothing even close to that is happening…nor will it."

"It's already happening, you either don't realize it or don't want to admit it. You have pet names for each other, you know his drink… Elise, you finish each other's sentences. You have inside jokes. So, you two may not be sleeping together, but it's just a matter of time."

"We're just friends, Shania."

"But Elise, you are attracted to each other…thus the extra phone calls and meetings. I'm not going to get all super spiritual with it, but I will kick it to you real. You don't want to perform? Fine. You can't talk to First Lady? Fine. And since you obviously can't talk to Jeremiah about this, talk to me."

"So, be completely real?" Elise asked.

"Yes, and I don't want the *Lifetime* movie version. I want the late-night when you don't think anybody else is watching and you have to pay extra version."

"Shania, he is so sweet. When I'm with Josh, it's whatever. I can either forget my problems or I can talk about them. It doesn't matter to him. I can clown or I can cry. He gets me and he makes me feel good about myself. I can't show him a dishwasher without him making it sound like I'm the most amazing person in the world. We laugh with each other. We laugh at each other. And…he lets me in. He confides in me about his deepest darkest and I love that. When I talk, he listens and hangs on every word. I admit, it's inappropriate. But I say again… nothing is happening. I know where to draw the line. So, there it is…I know you're coming for me, so let's get it over with."

"Sis, I'm not coming for you but…that's a whole lot! If I didn't know better, I would think that you were talking about Jeremiah. But you're not. You're talking about another man. Speaking of Jeremiah…you know…your husband…that Jeremiah…what's happening with you and him that I would even have to have this conversation with you?"

"Me and Jeremiah are just existing. None of the things that used to make us us are there anymore."

"You mean all the things you just said are happening with you and Joshua?" "Shania, don't punish me for being honest."

"I'm not punishing you. But I won't lie to you either. I'm going to say this one time and I will leave it alone. Elise, you need to run as far as you can, as fast as you can from that man. Let someone else sell him a house. That man is the spark, you're the forest, and you two are about to burn everything up…including your marriage. Ole hot selves."

"Girl, I am not hot! Did I say one thing sexually related?"

"No, you didn't and that actually makes it worse…Elise, it's emotional. You're laughing with him…you're crying with him…you're confiding with him…he has your heart. Girl, that serious. And I'll say it again. You are not built for this."

"Well, it doesn't really matter. I've already got a property for him. The owner is just moving slow, but I'll have him closed soon and then neither of us will have an excuse to see each other."

"Oh, you mean like tonight?"

"Oh…well, I explained that," Elise said, hoping Shania would accept her explanation.

"Elise don't make me look at you with the side-eye. You told him you were going to be someplace, and he showed up. That's just one step closer to where you don't want to be! What are you going to do when I'm not around to block?"

"I'm not going to have to do anything. I've been alone with him plenty of times and nothing has happened. Maybe he does like me but he's not like that. He knows I'm married."

"He's a man, Elise. An attractive man. An attractive man that obviously reminds you of Jeremiah. You keep on dangling yourself in front of him if you want to, and one of you is going to break. Get away from him."

"Shania, I hear you. But it's not as evil as you're making it out to be and it's not as simple either. Joshua and I enjoy each other's company. We've both been through a lot. But we're not sleeping with each other. Maybe I should run but you're asking me to run from the little peace and joy that I have left. Like I said, it's not as simple as you make it sound."

"Thank you for being honest with me. But you still need to cut it off. Yes, it will hurt…that's what happens when you have a soul tie. Kick him to the curb and let me know when you do so I can show up at his school and comfort him. 'Oh, Josh. I'm so sorry that mean ole Elise doesn't want you. How can I make you feel better?'"

"Stop it!" Elise exclaimed.

"Ha. You know I'm playing…mostly. But you also know I'm right." "I do," Elise agreed.

"Amen. And I'm right about this too. You need to talk to Jeremiah." "And tell him what?"

"Elise, just tell him you're not happy. At least give him a chance to try. Now I'm not saying you should tell him about Joshua setting your forest on fire," she laughed. "But just tell him all the things that you don't do anymore that you want to get back. Tell him you miss laughing with him. Tell him you miss talking to him. Tell him you need to cry, and you want to cry with him."

"He's got so much on his plate right now. I don't want to be a burden."

"He signed up for you to be a burden. That's in his job description. He doesn't have a job, make him do that."

Elise slapped Shania's wrist. "Girl, don't talk about him! That's not his fault." "Yasss. That's what I'm talking about. Take up for your husband. That's my sister right there."

"Girl, shut up," Elise laughed.

"And one more thing…," Shania said as she leaned in closer over the center glove compartment, "…you listening?"

"Yes, Shania…what?" "Tell Jeremiah you horny!"

"Haaa. I can't stand you," Elise bellowed.

"I'm serious. I know you say you don't want to talk about the Lord, but my Bible teaches me that the Lord smiles on married folks when they do the nasty. He comes into the bedroom with them and cheers them on. Tell Jeremiah that the big cheerleader up in the sky is sitting on the bench bored, because he hasn't been scoring."

"Get out, girl!" Elise hollered. "I absolutely cannot and will not with you." "Girl, I'm serious. The Lord is up in the heavenlies cheering, 'Jeremiah, he's our man, if he can't do it no one can.' Oh…and I do mean no one."

"Girl, you know I stay strapped. I'm about to reach in this purse," Elise laughed.

"Okay, but one more, one more thing…while you're smiling." "Go ahead," Elise said, bracing for more foolishness.

"No judgment…just a question. Hennessy and Coke? I've never known you to drink like that. Ever."

Elise shrugged her shoulders. "What can I say? It takes that edge off." "Elise, seriously…you can search all over…the job, Jack Daniels, Joshua, even Jeremiah…ooh, come on with the J's Holy Spirit. Anyway…you're only going to find your peace in one place. And you know that. The 'J' you need right now is Jesus. Mmmm…that will preach! Look at God."

"I'm sorry…Shania," Elise said seriously. "But you said I didn't have to perform. I don't know that anymore. I don't know where my peace is. There's so much I don't understand, and at this point I don't think I care to learn. I know that's disappointing. Trust me, I'm disappointed in myself."

"I won't argue. But if you'll let me, I want to pray for you." "If you want to, that's fine."

Shania gently took Elise's right hand. "Our Lord Jesus, you know I am not the one who comes with eloquence or the one who comes with the plethora of scriptures. But I'm the one who you found when I was lost. And you used your precious daughter here…my friend…my sister, to do it. So now that's she's hurting and feeling abandoned and alone I ask that somehow, some way you come and find her. We pray for comfort, encouragement, and forgiveness. We pray you heal her broken heart, and you restore her. We pray you keep her, and we pray you bless her. Lord Jesus, I remember that when Peter was about to sink all he had to do was say 'Lord, help me' and you reached out your hand and pulled him out of the water. So, Lord, in Jesus' name, please help Elise. She needs you and I need you because I want my friend back and I want her to be healed. In Jesus' name, Amen."

"Aww…Amen. Thank you, girl. I love you." "One more, one more thing?" Shania asked. "Of course," Elise replied.

"Elise, that is a good-looking man. I don't blame you, girl. I don't see how you held out this long. I'm serious…when, and I do mean when, you kick him to the curb. You tell him I got the good to go with his googa-mooga. Whew…and he smelled so good! Smelled like heaven and lust."

"Shania!"

"Okay, I'm sorry, I don't mean to disrespect your side piece. Just one more, one more thing…go home and tell Jeremiah you need some wood for the fire. Get it? Wood? You see, wood is a euphemism for…."

"Shania, get out! I know what wood is a euphemism for."

"I love you, sis," Shania said. "Let's do this again real soon…just me and you…okay?"

"Okay," Elise agreed.

Elise's phone chimed with a text message just as Shania closed her passenger- side door. It was Joshua. His text message read: "Hey Realtor – Just making sure you made it home. Let me know our next appointment. Thanks for the evening." Elise considered her conversation with Shania. But now she wondered if openly discussing her feelings had made the situation worse. She smiled as she typed her reply. "Hey, Client. No…still here. Shania had some catching up to do." "You're still here?" Joshua replied quickly. "I actually went back inside to listen to the band. I got a seat for you if you want."

Elise thought about all the possibilities of his offer. Then she thought about Shania's warning.

She typed: "I'd better not. Driving home now. My husband is

waiting.

Goodnight," and hit send.

She looked at her screen to see if Joshua would reply. He didn't. Part of her was relieved but another part, the part Shania was concerned about, was disappointed that he didn't.

CHAPTER 57

Warning Before Destruction

DAY 430

"Come on, son. Let it out," Pastor Gregory said patiently, realizing Jeremiah was struggling in their latest counseling session.

"Pastor…listen. I appreciate you but this isn't getting us anywhere. Can we call it a day?"

"Jeremiah let's take a step back. Can I offer you some coffee? You know me, you, and yo daddy all like our coffee the same way we like our women," Pastor Gregory kidded him.

"Yes, sir…sweet with extra cream," Jeremiah agreed. He appreciated his pastor's attempt to lighten the mood. It was a running joke Elise had started with his dad, Pastor Gregory, and himself concerning the similar appearances and personalities of their wives. "I knew I had that man the second I saw how he liked his coffee," Elise would joke.

"Here you go. Just the way you like it," Pastor Gregory chuckled as he served him. "Now take a sip of that brew and tell me what's going on. Shoot it to me straight."

"Pastor…oh, that is good…thank you," he said as he took a sip. "Anyway… I guess it's that I used to have such a blessed life. I know it wasn't perfect, but I knew the Lord was with me. I was the one with the great wife, the great career, and the great life. People came to me for prayer and encouragement, and I always pointed them to Jesus. Now, I don't know where he is. And… we're shooting straight, right?"

"Keep it a buck, son," Pastor Gregory said.

Jeremiah laughed. He found it amusing when Pastor Gregory and his dad used the younger generation's vernacular.

"I used to look at people who were constantly down and defeated like, I don't know…."

"Like what's wrong with them that they can't seem to get right?" Pastor Gregory said.

"Well…yes, sir. It doesn't sound good but part of me looked down on them. 'Just pray and believe,' I thought. 'It will be fine.' But that was then, and this is now."

"And what's happening now?" Pastor Gregory asked.

"What's happening now?" Jeremiah repeated as he pondered the question. "What's happening now is that I'm the one everyone feels they need to be praying for. Now I'm the one who's fallen and can't get up. I'm the one whose wife is slipping away but can't bring her back. I'm the one with all the questions but none of the answers. And keeping it a buck…even though I know it all comes from a good place and even though I appreciate you, I'm the one who's tired of hearing 'Trust in the Lord,' 'He'll make a way,' and 'Joy comes in the morning.' Those words used to strengthen me. Now they just sound like cute clichés."

"That's an interesting choice of words," Pastor Gregory said. "May I ask you a challenging question?"

"I haven't exactly been meeting challenges well lately but go ahead."

Pastor Gregory took another sip of his coffee and leaned in closer to Jeremiah. "When did the word of God become just a cliché to you, son?"

"When I woke up from my coma and heard that my son was dead," Jeremiah responded bluntly, not missing a beat.

Pastor Gregory paused a moment to take in the weight of Jeremiah's words. "I appreciate your honesty. And all that is real and understandable. Your emotions are a result of your very real experience. And I know you don't want to hear the clichés, but God is up to something. When this much happens at once, I can guaran- doggone-tee you he has an end in mind for your good and his glory."

"But Pastor, what's the point? I hate to look at this from a child's perspective, but that's what Amari asked me right before they took her. She asked me why God was letting all the bad things happen and I told her, 'God lets bad things happen so he can show us how he can help us when things are bad.' And she was like

'Wouldn't it have been easier to just not let the bad things happen?' So now I'm like…she has a point."

"I can't argue with you, but we both know there are times when we have to say, 'Thy will be done' and let God be God. We won't always understand God's ways. But you can't give up."

Jeremiah said nothing as he took another sip of his coffee and nodded.

"I know what that silence and that nod means," Pastor Gregory said. "That means, 'You don't get it old man.' And you know what? You're right. This is your own unique trial, and I won't claim to know or understand how you feel. But I know this. Since it's unique to you, how you respond to it will have a lot to do with how it comes out."

"And I need to tell you something else," Pastor Gregory continued. "Jeremiah, I'm concerned about you and I'm really concerned about Elise. Something is very off with her. I'm saying that not only as her pastor but also as her second daddy. My wife is concerned too. I know you're wounded. You both are. But we men don't get time off even when we're hurting. I know it's tough, son, but you owe it to Elise and to yourself to dig in and ask the tough questions and do the work of covering your wife. Are you communicating? Are you praying together? Are you moving forward in life? Are you asking her how she is dealing with this trial you are going through? Are you asking her how she is dealing with the pressure of carrying your family financially? Are you asking her how she is dealing with the trauma of losing Amari and your son? Have you done any of these things or asked any of these questions?"

"Not like I should," Jeremiah admitted.

"Okay, I appreciate your honesty, but tell me, what do you two talk about?" "Well, you know, the usual. I mean, I can't really contribute much to any conversation. I don't have the most exciting life right now. I still drive Uber, I volunteer here at the church, and I go home and make sure the house is clean and dinner is cooked."

"Well, first, let me say the Lord and everybody, including Elise, knows that you're doing everything you can. But let's stay on point. Does Elise try to talk to you?"

"No, she doesn't say very much. She might occasionally talk about work. But for the most part she's pretty quiet. And we don't pray together anymore either.

We used to do this thing where I would start, and she would finish. But we don't do that anymore. To be honest, I'm not really sure when I last heard Elise pray."

"So, in other words, you two aren't communicating and you're not praying together," Pastor Gregory said bluntly.

"No, sir, not really," Jeremiah admitted. "That's concerning. Why do you think that is?"

Jeremiah took a deep breath and thought about the question. "Pastor…you know how they tell lawyers in a courtroom to never ask a question they don't already know the answer to?"

"I'm familiar with the concept," Pastor Gregory responded. "But how does that apply to you and Elise?"

"I'm afraid of what some of those answers would be. It's almost like being sick and afraid of what the doctor might find…so you don't go. But it's more than not knowing…it's my total inability to give any answers or meet any of her needs. It took me a while to remember everything, but I have all my memories back of everything leading up to our crash. Right before we got hit, she asked me if we were going to be okay and I promised her that we would. And Pastor, I truly believed it. Then we got hit and our son died. Before that, there was some confusion and some doubt, but I knew God would come through. And I knew me and Elise would make it. Whether it was losing the job, the case hanging over my head, or the finances. I knew we would make it. Mama died and we mourned but we kept trusting. We found Pop on the floor and that scared me, but I still believed that God wouldn't add sorrow upon sorrow. They took Amari and I truly believed we would find a way to get her back. We just kept telling each other, 'Miah and Lise against the world.' But after that day, after our son died, after the crash, everything was different. The Jeremiah and Elise that got hit aren't the same two people that came out of that crash. We're different now. And I'm afraid to dig in and ask questions because I don't want to know just how different the two people who came out of that crash are. So, I don't tell her how I feel. I don't ask her deep questions because I'm afraid of what she will say. Part of me knows that she still thinks the world of me but in a way that makes it worse."

"How does that make it worse?" Pastor Gregory asked him.

"Because it still leaves me in a place of being so useless. I can't provide for her like I used to. I can't make her happy. And I can't take her pain away. I used to feel like we were king and queen. Now we got this princess-and-frog thing going on and I don't know what to do in this space. She deserves more and I can't give it to her."

"Son…you're offtrack," Pastor Gregory said seriously. "I can't help how I feel, Pastor!" Jeremiah insisted.

"I'm not talking about how you feel," Pastor Gregory said calmly. "I'm talking about what you're doing. I remember I was discussing you with another brother one day. This is what he told me. He said, 'Jeremiah is messing it up for us all. He gon have all the wives expecting their husbands to treat him like he treats Elise. We all gon have to step up our games because of him.'"

"Who said that?" Jeremiah asked.

"Yo daddy," Pastor Gregory said as he smiled. "Pop said that? About me?"

"Yes, he did. And do you want to know when he said it?" "When?" Jeremiah asked curiously.

"This was about two years after you and Elise got married." "When I was still in college?"

"That's right. She was still in the military, you were trying to graduate, and y'all lived in that little one-bedroom apartment. She was making most of the money, but you were working and going to school. And somehow, some way you found a way…with yo broke, struggling tail to make sure that girl knew she was loved. And you didn't need money or position or ease and comfort to do it. I don't think you need it now. That's what you gotta get back, son. The other stuff…well, we just keep praying and believing…but loving your wife? Uh-uh, that's in your hands. You can do something about her right now."

Pastor Gregory put his hands on Jeremiah's shoulder. "Son, I know it's not easy. Most brothers would be plum crazy having gone through what you've endured. But you're still here and I don't care if you lying on the mat. You still gotta fight! You bite the devil on his ankles if you got to. But you fight in Jesus' name!"

"I want to, Pastor, but I feel like my front teeth have been knocked out." "Well, then you gum that dirty son of a gun then."

Jeremiah had to laugh. "That's funny, Pastor, but…it's just so much failure. It's so embarrassing, no, it's utterly humiliating, for your wife to have to do everything for you. It's not just the job situation or the money. There was a time where I couldn't even wipe my own behind good. But then here comes Elise with the rubber gloves and washcloths."

"Yeah, brother. I feel you on that one. It's pretty embarrassing to have a wife who will stick with you through better or worse," Pastor Gregory said sarcastically.

"Pastor, that's not what I meant."

"I know, son. But I'm trying to make you see there is still good in all this. You think you lost everything, but you haven't. Keep your eyes on Jesus and pay attention to your wife. You know what to do, you just need to do it. Find a way to reconnect with your wife. Find a way to let her know she's loved and that she still matters. Jeremiah, Elise has gotten very used to your love and affections. Now I know you have been too, but she's been through tremendous trauma. You have to show up for her."

"Pastor, I don't know that I have anything to give."

"Now we're going in circles. That's not true, son. I've already explained that. You still have your love to give. Yes, it may be a wounded love or a confused love, but it's your love and it's the love you promised the Lord to give her. She's struggling now but I know that girl well enough to know that's all she wants."

"But I don't know how to love her like she needs to be loved…not like this." "That's your pride talking. And it's the voice of the stranger.

You want to be the man and that's fine. But you want to be the man under your own terms. You want to be the man with the great job. The man with the answers. But the Lord can use you even when you're down and still searching for answers. You can do all things through Christ, son. And you can do this. You can love your wife. You can allow Christ to do it through you. He took five raggedy barley loaves and two small fish and fed the five thousand people, and he can take whatever you have left emotionally, physically, spiritually, and financially and love your wife back to healing if you just give it to him. God can use you in your weakness, son. In fact, my Bible says his power is perfected in weakness."

"Now, we still have to acknowledge and deal with your pain. But things like this will sometimes take time. There's a journey to your healing, but while you're on that journey you still have to keep fighting. Trust me, the devil ain't gon ease up just because you're down and depressed. He's gotten in some mighty blows but don't think he's finished. He's looking for the killing blow. But God has something else in mind. You're in the fire, son. Now it's up to you. You can invite him in, and he can use the flames to perfect you, or you can do it on your own and the same flames can burn you up."

"But Pastor, perfect us for what?" Jeremiah asked, frustrated. He's not perfecting us to be good parents because he took our children away from us. There's not much money left so he's not perfecting us to be good stewards. And I'm sorry, but our marriage was pretty close to perfect before, so please tell me, what's the point of the fire?"

"Jeremiah, all I know is that he still loves you and has not forgotten about you. I know you have questions, but you have to accept that you may never truly understand why he allowed all of this. And God is under no obligation to explain himself. He may or he may not. Either way, you have to trust and obey."

"But Pastor, I do trust God and for the life of me I can't imagine where I have been so disobedient that all of this would happen to me. Maybe I did do something wrong, but was it so bad that I deserve all of this?"

"You know how I am about the word 'deserve,' son. We deserve hell and judgment. Every last stankin', nasty, wretched one of us. We're only here by His grace. But no, I don't think you've done anything wrong. And I'm not here to accuse you. I'm here to love you and support you. You may not know everything you need to do, but the one area where I want you to exercise faith and obedience is in dealing with your wife. You are still her husband. You are still the man. You're still her man. And most importantly, you're still God's man. It matters not about the money or the job. This is your gig. Love, honor, and protect her. You promised the Lord you would do that. I was there, if you remember," he winked at him.

"Any ideas?" Jeremiah asked.

"How about a simple date?" Pastor Gregory suggested. "I get the feeling you two aren't really spending much time with each other."

"You're right," Jeremiah agreed.

"Just figure out something nice for you two to do together. Nothing too elaborate. You still know your wife. Ask yourself, what might make her smile? Annnddd, if you don't mind me asking, how's the bedroom life?"

"Whoa there, Pastor. Too far," Jeremiah objected. He wasn't sure he wanted to go down that road.

"I don't think we've gone far enough," Pastor Gregory disagreed. "What's happening in your bedroom is a strong indicator of what's happening in your hearts. So, what's up? I know your dad is down so I'm here. You ain't got to give me details. Just tell me… are you making love to your wife?"

"Uggghh…don't you have other appointments, Pastor?" Jeremiah asked, hoping for an escape.

"Son, I schedule your appointments, then I block out the hour before and after so you will have my undivided attention. So, tell me… you and your wife gettin' it on to the break a dawn or what?"

"Please, Lord, just rapture me right now," Jeremiah pleaded.

"Ha, ha, ha, I'm sorry, son. Just keeping it light…but seriously… how are you guys doing in that area?"

"Okay, listen. We've always connected pretty well in that way," Jeremiah started reluctantly.

"But?" Pastor Gregory asked him.

"Well, I've been a little stressed, so it doesn't always happen like I want it to happen. It started even before the crash, when I was stressing over the court case, when, you know…umm…well…."

"What? You couldn't straighten up and fly right?" Pastor Gregory asked him, grinning from ear to ear.

Jeremiah cringed at his pastor's meddling over this uncomfortable and embarrassing subject.

"Yeah, let's just say that. But now, it's worse. She says it doesn't matter but it matters to me. And so, a lot of times I don't try because I'm thinking about it and I don't want her to have one more thing to think less of me of. Plus, we don't play like we used to. It was always fun and games before and sex came very naturally for us. Now it's forced."

"Okay, you said a lot there and thank you for trusting me with all of that. Jeremiah, I would start there, with the fun and games, get the relationship going on an emotional level and get yourselves back to a place of comfort with each other. Then you can get jiggy with it," Pastor Gregory said, slapping him on his shoulder.

"Not helping, Pastor," Jeremiah said, shaking his head.

"I'm serious, son. And…well, I'm a little older than you, so I know about these challenges. I got a nice stash of those little blue pills. They will give you some confidence until you get over the hump and, you know…start humping on your own. Sister Faye highly recommends them."

"Definitely never wanted to think of my sweet First Lady like that, Pastor," Jeremiah said.

"Well, if that bothers you, you'd really have a fit if you knew yo mama was the one who told Faye about them," Pastor Gregory said unmercifully.

"Wow, Pastor!" Jeremiah said as he stood on his feet. "Where did the time go? So, quick recap… trust God, bite the devil on his ankles. love my wife, and… "

"Let's get it on!" Pastor Gregory sang as he sounded way too much like Marvin Gaye.

"Bye, Pastor," Jeremiah said as they both laughed and embraced.

"Bye, son. You know I'm always here for you and for Elise. See you next week?"

"Yes, Pastor, see you next week."

CHAPTER 58

Almost There

DAY 436

"Hey, gorgeous. How are you?" Jeremiah greeted Elise.

His talk with Pastor G. helped him realize he had been failing his wife. He hoped a simple lunch meeting would provide a pleasant break in her day and help them reconnect. Their interactions used to be so natural. But lately everything was forced.

"Gorgeous? Jeremiah, what did you do?", Elise asked with only the slightest touch of humor in her voice.

"I didn't do anything. Just saying hello to my beautiful wife. How was your morning?"

"It wasn't bad," she said as she softened a little bit. "I've already had three showings. I have one house I am trying to close for a recent divorcee. The owner has been stalling on me for some reason. Jeremiah, I really want to help this guy. He's such a sweetheart."

"Babe, you know you got this," he encouraged.

"Hmmm…babe? Gorgeous? Lunch? And now you gassin' me up. Jeremiah, did you erase my TV shows on the DVR?" she said with more of her normal wit.

Jeremiah laughed and reached for her hand. "No, I did not. But I'm sorry that me being sweet to you is such a surprise."

"Oh…I'm sorry, Miah. It's not a surprise. Well, not too much. I appreciate you. How was your morning, handsome?" she said, attempting to match his energy.

"Same old, babe…prayed, met with physical therapist, checked for any job offers…nothing on that front." he said dryly. "Then I ran by the church and picked up a care package for one of the members. And now I am sitting here with the most beautiful girl in the world."

Elise pressed her lips together and turned her head slightly away from him. "Wait…what's that funny thing you're doing with your mouth? Are you…smiling?" he asked.

"No," she said, turning her head completely away from him. "Are you blushing?" he teased.

"No. It's a rash," she quipped.

Elise was pleased. Perhaps this little outing might represent some light at the end of the long, dark tunnel they had been in. It had been a while since he had been so intentional about spending time with her but if he was willing to try, so was she.

"Miah, are you feeding me?" she asked sweetly. "Your Lise is hungry. And if you don't feed me, I will get angry. And then we know that becomes…"

"Hangry!" they both said in unison.

They smiled at each other for the first time in a while. Jeremiah wanted to lean in and kiss her. It shouldn't have felt awkward, but it did. Instead, he just answered her question.

"Well, madame, we are keeping it simple," he said as he did a very bad impression of a French waiter. "Your meal will be light enough so you don't need a nap after and heavy enough to get you through your grueling day. The chef, that's me, I'm the chef, has specially grilled you some chicken and made you a salad."

"Miah, you made my grilled chicken salad? That's so sweet." "Wow," he said as he stared and leaned back.

"Miah, what? Is something on me?" she asked nervously as she examined herself and prepared to run from the evil lizard or insect that was plotting to take her life.

"No," he said, shaking his head. "I just can't figure out how you got more beautiful in the last two minutes."

"Miah, stop. You play too much!"

"Wait…yep, no doubt, folks. This woman is smiling and blushing," he teased. "Miah, leave me alone. I can't stand you," she giggled.

"I don't know, Lise. I think you can," he said as he felt some of their old energy returning.

I am such an idiot, he thought to himself. *This is all it took? Lunch and a few compliments?*

They sat down on a nearby bench to enjoy their midday getaway. The conversation was light and humorous, and the food was good. Jeremiah couldn't recall the last time he felt nervous around her, but he was. He wanted to let her know how important she was. It used to be as easy for him as breathing, but now it seemed like something he had to work at. Still, he wanted to try.

"Hey, Lise, I know we don't have much time…."

But before he could finish his thought, her phone rang.

"Hold that thought, baby. This is that homeowner I was telling you about. Hello, Mr. Jackson. How are you? I was going to call you this afternoon. Mr. Dupree has everything together and is ready to close."

Elise paused and her countenance changed. Whatever she was hearing on the other end of the line wasn't good.

"Well, yes, sir, you certainly have that right," she said rather dejectedly. "No, sir," she said very authoritatively. "That is not what we had agreed on, and my client won't be able to do that. No, sir, I know what he requires and that won't work for him. I won't try to talk him into that. What has changed? I do need to remind you that you gave your word. Yes, sir, again, that's your right, of course. It's your home but I prefer not to be involved if that is the case. We spoke at length and you and your wife were extremely pleased at the time. No, I prefer not to be involved under these circumstances. This isn't professional. I am sorry. I wish you well. I do hope you find what you are looking for. Thank you. Goodbye.

"That dirty bleepity bleeper!" Elise said angrily but still censoring herself. "What happened?" Jeremiah asked.

"What happened is that I found the perfect house for this divorced guy I was telling you about. We settled on a good price. The homeowner was going to make great money on it and my client was going to really be able to start over. Now, the homeowner is looking at the market value and feels like he should be able to get more for the house. He no longer wants to sell it for what we agreed to. But my client was already at his limit. I won't try and push him up. He needs some breathing room. He's trying to put his daughter through college. He's just trying to make a new life for himself, you know?" Elise explained.

"I do know. I'm glad he has you," Jeremiah encouraged.

"Miah, I need to get on this. Okay? But this was sweet. I wish we could do more of this," she said transparently.

"We can, babe. Things are going to be different. I'm gonna need your help though."

"Different would be nice, Miah. And yes…I want to help. I always have." "Sooo…see you when you get home?" he said, hoping she would take the hint.

"You mean see me? Or you mean…see me see me?" she responded, making it clear she got the hint.

"I mean see you see you," he emphasized, confident he wasn't going to need Pastor Gregory's little blue pills.

Elise leaned her face toward his and stopped her lips just short of his. "Umm… no," she teased. "I want you to think about it. You can see me later. Oh, and you will see everything. They might not let you be Elder after I'm done with you. Married or not, pretty sure you're about to sin, sir.

Jeremiah lowered his head and chuckled. "Hmmm…now who's blushing?" she asked softly. "Just come home as soon as you can, babe." "Roger that, sir," she smiled.

Elise returned to her car. She was happy about the time she had just spent with Jeremiah, but she had to admit she was also happy that the deal for Joshua's house had fallen through. She missed meeting with him, and was excited about the prospect of spending more time with him. She wasn't worried about Joshua being disappointed. She was about to give him some very bad news. But she knew he wouldn't be upset. Butterflies floated in her belly as she dialed his number. She considered just sending him a text, but she owed it to him to speak to him and let him know what was going on. Hearing his voice had nothing to do with anything. Better yet, she should likely just meet him.

"Realtor!!!" Joshua said enthusiastically as he answered the phone. "It's good to hear from you. What's good?"

"Client! I am well. But we need to meet. When are you free?"

CHAPTER 59

Together Again

DAY 436

Joshua rushed from school as quickly as he could. His duties as a vice principal rarely allowed him to leave the school early, but he had a great relationship with his principal, and she knew he was trying to find a house. Truth be told, he wasn't anxious about the house. If it happened, it happened. But he was excited about seeing Elise again. With them landing on a house, she had been appropriately quiet recently. He foolishly hoped she was feeling his absence like he was feeling hers. He knew it was a fantasy. Worse yet, he knew it was a sin, but he couldn't help but wonder if somehow, some way something special could happen between them. Regardless, he was going to get to see her now, and for that he was grateful.

He walked into the coffee shop and saw her wave from the corner. He was disappointed as she extended her hand to shake his, but he knew he could not expect anything more. Her greeting was even more disappointing.

"Mr. Dupree, how are you? Thanks for coming."

He decided not to let the cool greeting go. "Oh, Mr. Dupree, huh? No 'Client'?

No 'Joshy'?"

Elise smiled. "Bruh, I'm trying not to block. I know you see all these women checking you out. Coming in here with your suit on looking like a GQ cover model."

"There she is," Joshua said. "Now that's my Realtor. And no, I didn't notice anyone checking me out, but I can guarantee you they're not what I'm looking for. And as far as looking like a GQ cover model… those are your words…not mine."

"Uh-huh. I'm gon check out your school's performance record, sir. I bet them poor kids ain't learning a thing," she said humorously.

"Hold up now," Joshua objected. "I take our students' education seriously.

Why would you say that?"

"Because all your female teachers probably running around all day thinking about Principal Dupree and what they need to do to be the next Mrs. Dupree. They not concentrating on those kids. Imma need you to dial it back for the sake of America's youth, sir."

It hadn't been very long, but Joshua missed talking with her like this. He missed her smile. He missed her humor. And he missed her. "I'll try," he said humbly.

"Soooo…Client. There's a problem with the house." "Okay, what's wrong?" he asked calmly.

"The owner wants more for it. A lot more. He feels the market will bear it and that if he holds out, he can get more."

"Well, how much more does he want? Maybe…."

"Josh, no," Elise cut him off. "It's not a good deal for you. I told you I wasn't going to let you get into a bad deal. This is bad for you. I will just have to find you something else."

"Oh, no. This is terrible." he said jokingly. "This means I have to have more appointments with you, and listen to your corny jokes."

"You are the one with the corny jokes, sir. I'm hilarious." She appreciated his humorous way of making it clear he enjoyed their time together.

"Okay, Realtor. I'm gonna need you to come through. A client has needs. You don't want me going back to internet listings, do you?"

Elise played right along. "Boy, you bet not. I told you; I will destroy the whole innanet, sir."

"Innanet?" Joshua asked.

"You heard me. Inn. A. Net. I will destroy the whole darned thing, sir. You know how they put www for world wide web in front of everything? When I'm done, it's gon be jafp for just a few places in front of everything. Don't play with me."

"Okay. Super realtor and a cybercriminal. Got it. Okay then, for the sake of modern civilization I will exercise some self-control. I guess I'm back in your hands. What's next?" he asked.

"I will have to regroup because I didn't expect this, but I will be in touch soon.

Trust me. I got you."

Yes, you do, Joshua thought to himself.

"Listen, I have to go to another appointment, but I will be in touch soon." "You have to go?" Joshua said, not trying to conceal his disappointment. "Can

I get you a coffee or something?"

"Nooo, I'm sorry, Joshy. I do have to go. But I did get you a coffee. Sweet with extra cream...right?"

Joshua was pleasantly surprised she knew how he took his coffee. "That's right. How did you know?"

"I just had a feeling."

CHAPTER 60

He Ain't Listenin'

DAY 436

Girl, you need to slow down, Elise thought to herself. As had become a pattern, the conversation she just had could have easily, and more considerately, taken place on a phone call. But Joshua, as always, was overjoyed to hear from her and was happy to meet. She thought about her little comment regarding his coffee order. To him it was innocent, but he didn't know the history behind it. She felt guilty about being so excited about another man.

She was navigating unfamiliar territory. With the loss of her child, she had also lost connection with the Lord, her husband, and herself. She was thinking things and doing things that were out of character. Just a few hours ago she was planning a rendezvous with her husband. A rendezvous she delayed so she could see Joshua.

The issue was easy enough to resolve. Shania had already told her. All she had to do was disconnect from Joshua. She told herself that would be unprofessional, but the uncomfortable truth was, she simply didn't want to. For now, she tried to compartmentalize her emotions. For the first time in a while, Jeremiah had made an effort that she could relate to. Perhaps an evening with him would help her remember that he loved her and valued her.

Despite her conflicted feelings about Joshua, she looked forward to connecting with her husband physically. There was no way she could tell him everything that was happening in her heart but maybe if she just lay in his arms, she could open up just a little. She rehearsed her lines in her mind. *Baby, I've been very confused lately. I feel lost and I don't know how to explain it. Can you just pray for me?* Her prayer life may have been nonexistent, but Jeremiah was still faithful in his.

She walked into the house and Jeremiah greeted her. His intentions were clear. He had showered and put on the pair of silk boxers she bought him for their planned interludes. For the top, he wore a plain muscle shirt. His outfit revealed some of the scars from his various surgeries, but it also revealed he was making a comeback. She loved his new look. He had grown his hair out to hide the scar in his head from the surgery and most of his atrophied muscle tone had returned. He looked good and smelled better. *Joshua who?* she said jokingly to herself.

He walked toward her, pulled her close to himself and kissed her passionately...like he used to. "Babe, I thought you would never get here," he said softly.

"I'm sorry, Miah," she said, regretting making him wait. "I had to take care of my client. But I'm here now. You have me all to yourself."

"Well, before that I have some good news to tell you," he said enthusiastically. "Baby, I got something good for you," she said with a seductive smile. "I promise. But you smell great, and I smell like outside and coffee so I'm gonna shower...wanna help?"

"Babe, you always smell like heaven and springtime. But yeah...I can help.

One hundred percent, I can help. But first, listen. This is good."

She sighed. "Okay, Mr. Self-control. What's the good news?" she asked. "Babe, Chad just called me. He has a job for me," he said excitedly.

"Miah are you serious? Baby, I am so happy for you. No matter how hard they try to keep my man down, you keep bouncing back. Is it the same development or another one?" she asked, trying to match his energy.

"...It's another one," he said with some hesitation.

"Oh, okay," she said, sensing he wasn't telling her everything. "So, when do you start and what part of town is it in?"

"Well, he needs me to start as soon as possible...in the next two to three days, actually. And babe, hear me out, but the job is in Denver."

"Denver!" she exclaimed. "How is that going to work?"

"He said we could work out the details but it's a four-to-six-month schedule. I would just have to look for opportunities to come back whenever possible. And here's the best part, he knows that's a big ask so he's paying me twenty percent more than what he was paying me before, and they are going to cover me a place to stay while I'm there."

"So, you want to go to Denver for six months?" she asked skeptically. "Four to six months," Jeremiah said optimistically. "You know your man always performs above and beyond. Now let's go get that shower going." Elise released herself from his arms.

"Jeremiah, Denver is too far. I would never see you. Before, you worked almost every Saturday for them. When would you come back?"

"Babe, I would come back as much as I could. I know it's not ideal, but we need this."

"Jeremiah…no. We will never see each other. Just tell him you can't take it," she said firmly.

"Babe, why would I tell him no? We need to get some more money coming in."

"No, sir, actually we don't. I respect what you're trying to do, and I love you for it. But we're okay. We're not where we were, but I have closed more deals this year than the last two or three combined. The lights are on and we're getting Daddy the best care. I have been quiet because I know you're going through a lot. But this doesn't work for me and it's not necessary. Jeremiah, we don't even have a house note. I know I haven't been all that lately and I'm sorry. But I've tried my best to keep my promise to stand by you. Now I need you to stand by me. You don't talk to me. You don't confide in me. You don't let me in. You don't make love to me. You don't tease me. You don't hold me. But dammit, at least you are physically present to not do all those things. So no, you don't need to go to Denver. I know it's not fun. I know it's beneath you but go and drive Uber during the day and come back home to your wife. That's fine. We will get through this. When you were in college and I was working and making most of the money, you had no shame because we were a team. There's no shame now.

Jeremiah, I am very lonely and very afraid right now. I don't even know who I am anymore. I can be those things and make it if you're at least physically here. But I can't be lonely and afraid and confused, and you not even be around. I need you here when I'm here. If you don't want me, then stay on your side of the bed like you've been doing but you are going to get in the bed with me. If you don't wanna chill with me, then fine but we aren't going to live separate lives. I can't take any more, Jeremiah! I am at my limit on this. You're just taking something to take it to satisfy your manly pride. We eat. We're warm. We're covered. I'm a good wife. I support you. I listen to you. I encourage you. I have sex with you whenever you want it. And on everything else, I submit to you. But on this, I say no." Elise was surprised at her rant, but she was even more surprised at Jeremiah's response.

"Elise, you don't get to tell me what I can and cannot do for the family like I'm some child that needs your permission. You think I don't know I suck as a husband lately? You think I don't know none, yeah, I know, none of your needs are getting met? And now I have a little bit of a chance to get just a smidge, just a touch, just a sprinkle of my manhood back and you mad because I might not be around as much? You say we're okay. Fine. Now we can make it even better if you just let me be a man. So, stop being selfish and stop trying to rule. Oh, and by the way, I am totally aware of how well you are doing. I see your little billboards all over town. 'Just see Elise.' That's nice. I mean I don't see Elise because you're always in the streets, but you're supporting the family so what can I say?"

"Wow. You had all those bullets loaded up, didn't you? I'm selfish but I work seven days a week and, on top of that, go see Daddy every day. Let you be a man? When have I stopped you from being a man? I bring my commission checks home and just step back while you make all the decisions. Little billboards? When have I ever minimized your successes? When have I ever done anything but support you? And when was the last time I asked you for anything? You can't answer that, because I don't."

"You never had to ask!" Jeremiah exclaimed, raising his voice. "We always had everything but now we don't. I know you feel good because you're still doing what you do best. But I'm not doing anything. Why can't you understand that?"

Elise tried to soften. "Baby, I do understand. But you're not listening. Miah, I can't explain it, but I am in a very bad place right now. I don't even recognize myself when I look in the mirror. I used to look at myself and see Jeremiah's wife and I was special. I used to look at myself and see God's child and I was special. Now I don't know the person looking back at me and I don't know what she's capable of. I just need you to be my husband. I know you wanna work. I know you want to provide. But please, Miah, just provide what I really need. I know it's a sacrifice but give yourself up for me! I need to know that I am enough for you. And I need to know that you feel like as long as I love you and am here for you, everything can be taken away and you can still be good because I'm your wife. It won't be good for us if you take this job. You're doing the same thing you did before Mama died. You're trying to fix everything according to what you want, but you're not thinking about what the people you love really need. You just promised me that things would be different. This is not the different I wanted. Go find a retail job. Go do customer service. Heck, go into business with me. Go get your realtor's license. Nobody can block that. We can be a team and wreck this town together. I will show you everything you need to know. But don't leave me, Jeremiah. You really don't understand, and I can't explain it to you, but don't do this. I promise you it won't be good."

"You're right. I don't understand," he said plainly. "Men have to make sacrifices for their families. Soldiers have to go to war and have to leave for months at a time. So, this is no big deal. We can get through this. We can adjust. It's only a few months."

Elise's anger returned with a vengeance. "Boy, you ain't no damn Navy Seal defending your country against all enemies foreign and domestic. You aren't listening to me!"

"Elise, I need to be productive. When a man is working and his wife isn't, that's okay. But it's not okay when it's the other way around. So, I'm sorry we aren't in agreement on this but either way, I need to do this. I'm making this decision as your husband, and I need you to trust me."

"I do trust you, but what the hell happened to Miah and Lise against the world? I guess the same thing that happened to we're gonna fight for Amari," Elise said, now intentionally trying to wound.

"That's not fair and you know it!" Jeremiah defended.

"All I know is I hope nobody comes and gets me because I know who won't climb any mountains to come rescue me."

"I can't believe you just said that! I've been trying to fight. I loved her every bit as much as you did. And if you wanna talk about Miah and Lise against the world, let's talk about how I can barely get you to say a word with me in prayer."

"You don't know what you're talking about, Jeremiah!" "I know prayer still works!"

"Yeah, name one prayer God has answered in the last year and a half," Elise challenged.

"Elise, you're not a babe in Christ. Grow up!" Jeremiah said, not believing this was his wife talking.

"Dude, trust me, I'm good and grown. I'm writing grown folks' checks, selling grown folks' houses, and doing grown folks' business. I'm fully grown."

"And there it is. And that's why I'm going to Denver. I won't just sit up here weak and helpless playing Mr. Mom. There ain't even any kids to take care of."

"Well, next time look both ways before you cross the street, Jeremiah, and maybe J.J. would be here!"

Elise's words shocked her. Not one time had she blamed Jeremiah for the accident. No matter how dark her emotions, she knew there was nothing he could have done. But her anger and her hurt had come together and forced something from her lips that she couldn't take back. She knew she should apologize but they were too far gone for that.

"Ha. You know I could never win a fight with you, Elise. Well done. You won another one. Say what you want. Blame me for everything. Either way, I'm going to Denver. You need to deal with it."

"Jeremiah, I thought things couldn't get any worse. But this? This is worse. Your wife is pleading with you to stay with her, but you are bound and determined to do whatever you want to do. I may as well be talking to a brick wall. You say I never had to ask you for anything but now that I am, now that I am standing in front of you with tears in my eyes, begging you to not do this one thing, you dismiss me. So, no, Jeremiah. I don't win. You win. Congratulations. Go do you. Peace out!"

"Elise don't be like that. It's not that serious."

"No, Jeremiah, it's not that serious to you. To me, it's crucial. But that's not important to you anymore. I guess I'm not either. Do what you gotta do. I will be fine. But I don't need to be around you right now. I've already said too much."

"Elise, don't you leave this house," Jeremiah warned.

"Didn't I just tell you I was fully grown? Boy, I wouldn't know my real daddy if he came through that door right now, but I for sure the hell know he ain't you," she said as she headed to the door.

Jeremiah knew he should stop her. *Just go put your arms around her,* he thought to himself. *Tell her you love her. Tell her you're going with her. Tell her whatever she needs to hear, but don't let her leave.* But instead he just stood there. *She'll be fine after she calms down,* he thought. *She'll understand later.*

CHAPTER 61

Opportune Time

DAY 436

Elise sped down the road ranting out loud to herself. She recalled Jeremiah's words. "'Trust me, Elise.' Ha! Look where that got me. Trust yo butt for what? You don't talk, so what exactly am I trusting you for? 'Lise, go see about Mom. Lise, go see about Dad. Lise, hold everything down while I figure everything out. Lise, I love you, even though I barely say it and never show it. Lise, I've been through a lot. I mean I know you have too, but it's harder on me. Lise, we won't let them take Mari. God has us.'"

Her phone rang in the middle of her lone rant. It was Jeremiah. She quickly dismissed the call.

"I don't want to talk to you, boy. We already talked. You have nothing to say that I want to hear," she said as she continued releasing her anger. "What are you calling for? To say you're sorry? To try and get me to say I'm sorry? Good luck! You want me to come home? What for? 'Lise, I'm gon do whatever I want to do anyway but we can just look at each other.' Not tonight. I don't want to just look at you and exist. I am tired of holding everybody up and nobody holding me up." Before she could get the next word out, First Lady called. She didn't want to disrespect her, so she let it ring until it went to voicemail. They had only had a few short conversations recently, but they hadn't met in a few weeks. Jeremiah had probably called her to tell her to check on her.

"I don't feel like going back home, First Lady," she continued to talk out loud. "I might go get a hotel room or drive all night to make that fool worry. I can show him selfish," she laughed wickedly. "Then again, Jeremiah will probably just go to sleep. That boy ain't worried about me. If he was, I wouldn't be out here. If he was so worried about me, why did he let me leave? He was 'bout happy to see me go so he didn't have to deal with me. Fine, I don't want to deal with you either. I can do bad by myself."

Elise continued to drive and slowly began to calm herself. But as her anger waned, it gave way to the same emptiness and loneliness that seemed to consume her life now. She felt the tears roll down her cheek as her thoughts were again interrupted. This time by a text from Shania.

"Hey, sis, either come over here or go home. Jeremiah and First Lady are worried about you. It's not that bad. TTYL - love you."

Shania always came through, but she didn't even want to talk to her now. She knew she was right and she should go home. But not yet. Jeremiah wasn't getting that satisfaction. She just kept driving until she reached a movie theatre almost an hour from their house. She stopped in hopes of seeing something that would help her to escape. She walked up to the window to see what was showing next and heard a familiar voice speaking to her.

"So, Realtor, are you stalking me?" It was Joshua. He was no longer in his suit, but he looked very nice in his casual attire.

"Client!" she exclaimed as she reached her arms around him for a full-frontal embrace. She had never done that before. Joshua was pleasantly surprised at the greeting but was happy to return the gesture.

"Ma'am, last I checked you were on the case tryna find yo boy a domicile. So, unless you're planning on converting this theater, Lucy, you got some s'plaining to do," he said jokingly.

"I'm sorry, Joshy. I'll be on the case again tomorrow. It's a long story but today was the worst. I just wanted to get out, have some me time, and try and unplug."

"Are you okay? I'm not trying to pry…but you look like you've been crying." "I'm okay," she said, embarrassed at how she must have looked.

"So, what's good? Is anything funny out?" she asked, trying to change the subject.

"There's a decent buddy cop movie out. I was gonna see that," he advised. "Oooh, Joshy, I know what you're talking about. Let's go see that," she said exuberantly.

Joshua felt awkward. Here she was. His dream girl. Yes, his very married dream girl. She had obviously been crying. Had her husband done something to her? He felt bad but there was a dark and pathetic part of him that hoped he had. He didn't want her to hurt, but he was also looking for whatever justification he could find for his feelings. Regardless, he wanted to make sure she was all right. Besides, she had just called him Joshy again. He was no longer responsible for his actions. He wondered if she knew just how much control she had over him.

"Where do you like to sit?" she asked him.

"Oh, I don't know," he said casually. "Not too close to the screen and kinda in the middle, usually."

"Well, here," she said. "Just pick. My mind is cluttered with thoughts of getting your picky behind in a house. I don't have any brain energy left for this kind of stuff."

Joshua laughed and stepped forward. "J9 looks good," he said.

"Got it," she said as she pulled out her credit card and inserted it in the kiosk. "Elise, wait, you don't have to buy my ticket," he objected.

"Hush, Client. I let you down today. Let me make it up to you. Let Mama handle this. Shhhh!" Elise knew she was totally out of line but right now, she didn't care. Joshua made her feel loved and wanted and she needed that. Besides, it was just a movie. It wasn't as if anything was going to happen. Still, she was careful to use her business credit card. It was less likely to come across Jeremiah's radar. "Well, I don't like this, but you got to at least let me get the snacks. Whatever you want," Joshua insisted.

"Aww, him so sweet and innocent!" she teased. "You ain't realized that was part of my evil plot? Joshy, the snacks always cost more than the movie."

Girl, you got one more time to call me Joshy before I throw it all away, he thought to himself.

Elise ignored her racing heartbeat. *It's just a movie,* she kept telling herself.

Likewise, Joshua ignored the nagging voice telling him he should get out of there. But leaving her didn't seem to be an option. He had to make sure she was okay, and he simply wanted to be with her.

They really weren't doing anything. There was no harm in catching a movie with her.

"Sooo…Joshy. Can I have a hotdog and a pretzel?" she said, pretending there was a possibility he would say no.

"A hotdog and a pretzel? Girl, I'm a vice principal, not the Secretary of Education," he laughed.

"So, no pwetzel?" she asked as she shamelessly poked out her bottom lip.

Well, that answers my question, Joshua thought. *You know full well just how wrapped around your fingers I am. And I'm here for it.*

"I'm just kidding," he told her. "What else? Candy? Popcorn? Let's do it. Let's drown this sucky day away with some junk food."

"Now that's what I'm talking about!" she exclaimed. "Finally, someone that gets it. Whoever felt better after eating a salad?"

"That would be nobody," he agreed. "But a good ole movie pretzel? That will turn your life around."

"You betta preach, sir!" she exclaimed.

"Let me get a small popcorn and a medium Diet Coke," Joshua ordered. "Rulebreaker! Hypocrite! Deserter!" Elise accused.

"Whoa! That escalated quickly. What I do?"

"First, we on a bad day destroying mission and you ordering Diet Coke? Second, a small popcorn? You may as well just say, 'Elise, you can't have no popcorn.'"

"My bad. Got it. Yeah, man," he said to the cashier. "Let's make that a medium…."

Elise squinted her eyes at him, expressing her disapproval. "Just kidding, a large popcorn…"

"Layered butter," she advised. "With layered butter and a…Coke."

"Okay, he's getting it," Elise acknowledged. "Oh, and a…Cherry Icee for my friend." "All is forgiven, Joshy. Well done, sir."

They gathered their food and found their seats just in time to catch the previews.

"I love the previews," Elise said.

"Me too. I feel a little funny coming to the movies and not seeing the previews."

"I know, right? Who does that?"

"Communists, Nazis, and unbelievers," Joshua retorted.

Elise laughed out loud. "Boy, you gon get me in trouble."

"With who? It's like twenty people in here. They'll be aight."

"You so wrong. Be good before I find you a house in the hood. You know you ain't gangsta."

"I will just tell them I know you and they'll back off. The boyz in the hood be like 'Hey, bruh, we can't touch the principal. Big Baller Elise said hands off her client.'"

"Oh, I already told them," she laughed.

They bantered back and forth through the previews until the movie started. Both desperately trying to live in the moment as they ignored the voice in both their heads saying that they were in the wrong place. Their uneasiness subsided as the evening progressed. They barely watched the movie. They ate, laughed, teased, and talked. In this little unexpected hideaway, there were no problems. Elise tried to forget why she was there in the first place. Joshua tried to enjoy this moment that he never could have asked for. And even if they couldn't admit it, they both tried to forget she was married.

Joshua walked her to her car after the movie.

"Thank you for the snacks, Joshy," Elise said as she leaned back on her car. There had been so many times where, even though she didn't want to, she had to leave him. She would leave so she could go back home to Jeremiah. But Jeremiah was leaving her soon anyway. So tonight, he was going to have to wait.

"Thank you for the movie, Elise. Thanks for everything." "Everything?" she questioned.

"Yeah…everything. My day kinda sucked too. So, all this tonight? It was nice," he said gratefully.

"I know, Joshy…I'm sorry about the house. I really do feel bad," she said sympathetically.

"No, I'm not talking about the house," Joshua clarified. "I got a superhero for a realtor. I will get a house when it's time. It's just, you know…like you said…life be lifin'. You ever just wake up and realize you are nowhere close to where you thought you would be? Wondering who you are? Wondering where God is? It's scary."

"I know exactly how you feel," Elise confirmed. "I think I told you before. Me and God, we not good right now. I told you about that lightning bolt that had my name on it, and I am quite sure, when it comes, it will shame all past, present, and future lightning bolts heretofore ever seen by man."

"Heretofore? Dramatic much?" he laughed.

Elise laughed with him as they both began to let their uneasiness wane. "Besides, I don't believe that, Elise," Joshua encouraged. "And I don't want you to either. We can't escape God's love."

"Yeah, but we can make him mad. Or, in my case, can get mad at him," Elise said honestly.

"Why are you mad at God? If you don't mind me asking."

"Joshy, life is just not good lately. I'm sorry but God has let so many bad things happen to my family and me at once and like you said, it's made me wonder where he was when my life was falling apart," Elise explained.

"Speaking of bad things," Joshua said, "there's something that has been eating at me, but I never got a chance to ask you. It's personal, though. I'm a pretty good listener, but sometimes I might read into stuff more than I should. So can I ask you a question?"

"Ummm, okay," she said hesitantly. "You can ask. Not sure if I can tell. You got me nervous."

"No, don't be nervous. And I'm not tryna pry. And you don't have to answer. But I was thinking about that conversation we had at the house. You know, the nice one you knew I couldn't afford but you showed me anyway?"

"Really, Mr. Dupree? That's what we're doing? You trying to get intimate information outta me but wanna come for me first? Did you think this through, sir?"

"Maybe not," he smiled. "But seriously, you spoke about the car crash.

Remember?"

"Oh. For sure. I won't ever forget that," Elise said. "What are you wondering?" she asked, curious as to what he was fishing for.

"I remember you said your mom passed and that was one funeral. But the way you spoke, it sounded like there may have been another one. Did somebody else pass?" he asked her.

Even in the night, Joshua could see the sadness overtaking her face. He realized he should have left well enough alone.

"I'm sorry, Elise. I didn't mean to bring up a bad memory. You don't have to talk about it if you don't want to."

"Josh, it's okay," she said, controlling herself. "I'm touched that you listened so closely and picked up all that. It feels good to be heard. And it's not your fault. You can't bring up a memory that never leaves my mind. I'm still surprised I told you, though. I know you're a good person but that's uber personal. I guess I just feel like I can trust you," she revealed.

Her words took hold of his soul. "I'm glad you feel that way. I want you to. I want you to be safe when you're with me." Joshua was surprised at his candor, but he meant every word.

"You're right," she continued. "It was more than what I let on that day. I couldn't talk about it then but someone else did pass. The second funeral was for my baby."

"Your baby?" he asked. "You mean Amari?"

"Thank you for remembering her name, but no, Joshy. Not Amari. I was pregnant with a little boy. We were going to name him Jeremiah

John and call him

J.J. I was in labor when we had the accident...he didn't make it," she said as she allowed a tear to roll down her face.

"Oh, Elise. I'm sorry." he said as he reached over and gently wiped the tear from her cheek.

"Your hands smell like popcorn," Elise said, laughing through her tears. "Sorry, didn't expect to be on tear duty tonight. I should have washed my hands."

"It's okay. You're very sweet. I appreciate you. It sounds crazy, but I feel better when I cry... but it's like I am losing my ability to cry. But I get mad...and I don't like that person."

"Well, I haven't met that person but I'm pretty sure she's amazing too. She's just hurt," Joshua encouraged.

Perhaps it had stopped speaking, or perhaps she was just ignoring it, but the voice telling her to run wasn't there anymore. All she knew was that she felt safe. Joshua got her. He cared. Somehow, he knew her. And she wanted him to really know her.

"Well, I don't know about all that but if you really want to hear the full story, and let me warn you, it's not for the faint of heart, I will tell you."

"I wanna know, Elise. Tell me."

"My husband and I could never conceive. We tried everything. Fertility drugs. Invitro fertilization. We spent a lot of money going to different doctors and specialists, but nothing ever helped. They couldn't necessarily find anything wrong. We just couldn't conceive. So, one day, about a year and a half ago, I told my husband I was several days late. So, he gets excited and goes to the store. He came back with a pregnancy test. I didn't even want to take it. It seemed too good to be true. But he insisted and it turns out that I was pregnant. Not only was I pregnant, I had a dream pregnancy. I mean I gained a little weight and had the cravings, but my doctor was like 'Elise, you are coming through this like a 23- year-old.' She was amazed. And all this happened right before my husband got fired."

"So, this is happening during your mom dying and all of that?"

Elise was touched. He remembered every detail of what she had shared with him. "Yes, everything I told you before. I was pregnant during all of that with my son." Elise's tears started flowing again.

"Take your time," Joshua said as he gently rubbed her arm.

"Do you remember me telling you about my daddy having a stroke and us losing our foster child?"

"Yeah, I remember."

"What I didn't tell you was that I also went into labor on that day. We are at the hospital with her waiting for the doctor. That's when the caseworker came and took her because we missed the court appearance. But we couldn't do anything about it because I was in labor. And here is where I get like 'God, what the….' Well, you know."

"I get you. Keep going," he reassured.

"On the way to the hospital, me and my husband are talking, we are planning, we are hoping. Josh, we are even laughing. We're trusting. The last thing I remember my husband saying before the car hit us was 'Thank you, Jesus.' He never saw the car coming. It was a drunk driver who was speeding through the intersection. He came out of nowhere."

"It sounds like a miracle you survived."

"Well, if God wanted to do all that, he should have let my baby live. If this is his version of a miracle, I'm not the least bit impressed," Elise said rather bitterly. "I'm fine with the car wreck. We all know God has a flair for the dramatic but if he wanted to get some glory, then why not let my baby live? If he wanted to show out, don't get my hopes up about having children and then take them both away. If he's so faithful, then leave my daddy alone and let him live his days out in peace. He wants everybody to think he's so good, but he wants us to overlook all the bad he does. I'm sorry, I'm not an ostrich and I'm not putting my head in the sand and singing 'Lord, you are good and your mercy endureth forever' when he has no mercy for me. He has no sympathy, no compassion, and no kindness, but he judges us when we do the same thing. He's supposed to number the very hairs on our head, but he can't protect one baby in a car wreck? And then he wants us to believe he is working it together for our good? Now that would be a miracle. If he could show me how all this crap can be for my good, then I would be impressed. But until then I will always know he is a God who gets ghost just when you need him the most."

Elise saw the helpless look on Joshua's face, and realized how her tirade must have sounded to him.

"I'm sorry, Josh. I know that sounds horrible. That's why I don't like talking about it. My Christian filter is broken. I just say what I feel, but I don't want to mess up someone else's faith just because I've lost mine."

"It's real," Joshua said sympathetically. "God knows how we feel, though. He can take it. He understands."

"But Josh, I don't understand. Up until all of this, my eyes were on God. Sometimes I ask, 'What did I do to deserve this level of wrath and desertion from a God of mercy and grace?' But the sad part is, I already know."

"What do you mean?" he asked.

"Josh, I don't pray anymore," she confided.

"That's understandable, your faith is shaken. But you'll learn how to pray again."

"No. That's not what I mean. It's not that I don't know how to pray anymore. I just refuse to, she said very matter-of-factly. "Pinky swear again?" she asked.

"Sure," Joshua smiled, excited at the prospect of touching her again.

"I've never told anybody this, Joshy," she said as she wrapped her pinky around his. "You can never tell."

"I promise, Elise."

"After the crash, I woke up by myself in the hospital. That's when they told me my baby was dead. I've heard so many similar stories of how the baby is safe in the womb. But not mine. God wouldn't protect my baby. His little body just couldn't take it. And neither could I. Josh, I straight flipped. I mean it was awful but after I calmed down, I asked them to bring my baby to me. And I truly believed in that space that God had a real miracle for me. They brought my baby to me. He was cold. He was gone. But I began to pray for the Lord to bring my baby back. I said, 'Daddy, even now when it looks like it's all over, I believe you. I don't believe you brought me this far to leave me now. I thank you for this opportunity to see a miracle. I promise you, Daddy, that I will tell the whole world about what you do for me here today.' That's what I told God. I told him that nothing was too hard for him and that I believed him and that I trusted him. I told him I loved him and that if I had done anything good in his eyes before he hadn't seen anything yet, because I was going to tell the whole world about the God who saw me at the worst point of my life and visited me when I was alone and in deep despair and came through with a resurrection. And Josh, mind you, I am not grasping at spiritual straws now. No, I believed it. I imagined myself trying to comfort the doctors and nurses as they came back and saw my baby alive and well and me smiling at him. I would be like 'No, you guys didn't make a mistake. My baby was dead, but he is alive again by the grace, mercy, power, love, and faithfulness of Jesus Christ. I just happen to serve a God who occasionally likes to make it look like all is lost so he can really get glory when he comes through.' I even changed my baby's name. His name was going to be Lazarus Jeremiah John Traylor. That's ugly, I know, but me and little Laz, we were going to do the most. So, I'm sitting there. I'm praying. I'm believing. Five minutes go by. Ten minutes go by. The nurse comes in to check on me and I ask for more time. But believe it or not, I know the Bible, and I know that when Jesus healed it didn't take that long. But I was like 'Bump that!' Jesus is just testing my faith. You know what I'm saying? I mean, I was gonna name him Lazarus and that took four days, right? So, I'm gonna give Jesus just a little more time. I rebuked my doubt and my fears. I kept telling the Lord how much I loved him. I kept telling him how much I trusted him. But my baby wouldn't move. He wouldn't breathe. But I still believed! I'm not letting you go until you bless me and bring my baby back, Jesus. I lifted him up above my head and went Hannah on the Lord. I said, 'Daddy, please do this for me. I promise if you will give my baby back to me, I will give him to you. I will teach him to love you and serve you and honor you every day of his life.' It's not like that wasn't already the intention but you know, even an all-knowing God may need a little reminder every now and then. But still nothing. And I am so ashamed of this Josh, but it's true. I've never had a vision before, but I think I had one. Right there in that hospital bed with my dead baby in my arms, I saw two paths. On one path, there was light and love and mercy in front of me and on the other path, there was darkness and pain and defeat. I felt the Holy Spirit telling me, 'Your baby is with me now and he's safe. Now I want you to come to me, baby girl. Come to the light and I will bring you through this. You are not alone, and my grace is sufficient. Let me love you through this. You're still my daughter and I am still your Daddy.' And I just remember saying…Josh, I can't repeat it. I'm not that far gone but it was like a cold darkness overcame me. On that day, I stopped calling him Daddy and I started referring to him as God. And I said, 'If I can't have my baby, then you can't have me either.' And other than crying out to him at my baby's funeral, that was the last time I actually talked to the Lord. When the nurse came back to check again, I told them they could take him. I didn't even tell my baby goodbye. I didn't kiss him. I didn't even tell him his mommy loves him. I didn't even tell him I would see him again one day, because I don't know that I will. Josh, I can't remember his little face. I have pictures of him in his coffin, but I have to look at them every day to keep his face in my mind! That's why God did all of this. To show me what kind of person I really am!"

Elise began weeping uncontrollably as Joshua wrapped her in his arms and held her as tightly as he could. She did not resist. Instead, she buried the side of her face deep in his chest, the way she used to with Jeremiah. And like Jeremiah Joshua prayed for her.

"Father God, your daughter needs you. You are always quick to forgive, so please show Elise your forgiveness right now. Please give her strength for this trial, and please give her grace to feel your love once again. We ask that you manifest your promise to her to never leave her and to never forsake her. And we ask for your healing touch on her broken heart. Let her see herself through your loving eyes and even where she has gotten off track, we ask you to be her good shepherd and leave the ninety-nine and come and get her. We ask together for healing and restoration, and we receive it by faith in Jesus' mighty name, Amen."

"Amen," Elise said as she rested peacefully in his arms and ignored the inappropriateness of their embrace. Elise had never been held and prayed for like that by anyone else but Jeremiah. She knew she should feel uncomfortable. She knew she should break the embrace, but it felt right. It felt good. It felt safe.

"You okay?" he asked.

"Uh-huh. Thank you, Joshy. And don't worry, I'm very fast. If I hear thunder, I will run as far as I can, so you don't get hit by my lightning bolt."

"It's okay, Elise. If you get hit, then I'll get hit too," he said as he kissed her on her forehead.

"It's not okay," she said as she squeezed him tightly. "I know what I did that day. I denied the Lord's invitation to healing and he has been denying me ever since. I think that's why nothing has gone right for us since then. I chose the dark path and now Daddy won't recover. I chose the dark path and Amari got taken away from us. I chose the dark path and now Jeremiah can't find work. I chose the dark path and now my husband doesn't talk to me. I chose the dark path and now he's leaving me."

Shame and excitement mixed for Joshua. Shame that there was a part of him, a big part, that was happy to hear that her husband was leaving her. And excitement about the same.

"What do you mean your husband is leaving you?" he asked.

"Well, I might be overexaggerating. He's going to Denver to work. That's what we fought about tonight. But it's not just that. I'm not so self-absorbed to think that I'm the only mother who ever lost a child, but other women, other marriages, other families recover. But nothing works for me anymore. Not even God. And it's all my fault. That's probably why he wants to leave. I appreciate when you said I don't look like what I've been through, but I know on the inside I'm ugly and my husband sees that. I don't love this person I've become, so why should he?"

"Elise, you can't blame yourself. What you're talking about is a lot, but that stuff was in motion long before you…well…."

"You can say it. Became an uncircumcised Philistine."

Joshua chuckled as he continued to hold her.

"No, I don't mean that. I mean before everything fell apart. You're broken, Elise. You're hurt. But there's grace for that," he said as he kissed her forehead again.

"Is there grace for me sitting my unhappily married behind out here in a dark parking lot being inappropriately held and kissed by another man?" she asked bluntly.

"Do you want me to let go?" he asked as he kissed her again, in case she said yes.

"No, Joshy. I don't want you to let go." "Good, because I don't want to."

CHAPTER 62

Scorned

DAY 439

"Yeah, Zach. I appreciate it. Five minutes? Bet!" Jeremiah was hoping Elise would take him to the airport, but she didn't seem to want to be around him. They hadn't had a real conversation since she stormed out of the house three days earlier. "Hey, Elise, Zach is only five minutes away. But I can tell him to turn around if you want. We can spend a little time together before I go."

"No, that's okay," she said coldly, not even making eye contact with him as she typed on her laptop. "I have some things I have to do. So that works out great with Zach picking you up."

"Elise...I don't know what else to do. Please don't make me leave like this," Jeremiah pleaded humbly.

"Make you leave?" she asked calmly, still focusing on her laptop. "Jeremiah, I very distinctly, very specifically begged you not to leave. So please don't come in here talking about me making you leave. You're choosing to leave."

"Yes, to support our family," he explained.

"No, to support your pride," she countered dryly. "I don't want to fight, Elise."

"Then I suggest you let it go, Jeremiah."

Jeremiah covered his face with his hands and breathed heavily. "Elise, how did we get here?"

"I don't know. But we're here. This is it. This is us." "Can we at least pray together before I go?"

"I'm not going to tell you not to pray, Jeremiah." "Do you want to start?"

"Probably not the best idea. But you can pray."

Jeremiah gently took her hands. He could feel the tension in them. He could also tell she did not want to be touched. He searched for the right words. Words that would reach the Lord's ears but also touch her heart. But nothing poignant or eloquent came to him.

"Father…we need you. I need you. Please comfort and strengthen Elise. Please give her her joy back. Please save our marriage. In Jesus' name, Amen."

"Amen," Elise said dryly. "I love you, Elise."

"Uh huh…smooches," she said as she refocused her attention on her laptop. Before he could say anything else, the doorbell rang.

"That's Zach. I'll be back in two weeks. I promise," Jeremiah said as kindly as he could.

"Do what you need to do," she said. "But you're doing this because you say we need the money. No need to spend it all up on flights."

"You act like you don't want me to come back," he said, hoping she would disagree.

"Jeremiah, I am as concerned about you coming back as you are about leaving. So do with that what you will," she said as her fingers continued to dance across her keyboard.

Jeremiah couldn't think of anything to say that would make the situation better. This battle wasn't going to be won. Not here. Not today. So, he collected his luggage and left without another word.

Elise sat on the bed in what used to be John and Etta Ween's room and waited until she heard Zach's car pull off with Jeremiah. She picked up her phone and dialed a now very familiar number.

"Hi Joshy, do you have time to meet?" she said softly. "Huh? No, nothing's wrong. I guess I'm just a little tired. I will send you the address. Is thirty minutes enough time? Perfect. See you soon."

CHAPTER 63

The Right Thing to Do

DAY 439

"So, he's gone?" Joshua asked Elise. "You guys didn't make up? You didn't talk?"

"He tried to, but somebody was being a 'B' on wheels, if you know what I'm saying."

"Somebody?" he said, giving her the side-eye.

"Okay. Fine. It's me. I'm somebody," Elise confessed.

"I'm sorry, Elise. But I'm sure it will work out," he said, knowing that was not truly what he wanted.

"Josh, I all but begged him not to go. I mean, not today, today I all but pushed him out the door, but the night we had the fight…."

"You mean the night we saw each other at the movie theater?"

"Yes. I got as emotionally naked as I could, but his mind was made up. Josh, I asked him to give himself up for me. I told him that I needed to know I was enough for him. I may as well have been talking to this granite countertop."

"Elise, why am I here?" he asked seriously.

"Huh?" Elise fumbled for words. "Well, you need a house. I'm your realtor.

Remember our little Client/Realtor schtick? So do you like the house?"

"Ha. Elise, you know I don't like this house," he said plainly. "You know what I like, so again, why am I here?"

"You're not gonna just flow with me? You know how we do. We banter back and forth and talk the day away."

"I love talking to you. You know that too. But I'd appreciate an answer. Why am I here?" he asked again.

"I guess I just needed a friend. I didn't want to be by myself, so I called you.

I'm sorry if I'm bothering you," she said.

"Uh-uh, Elise. Don't do that. Look at my face. Do I look bothered? Do I look like I'd rather be any place else in the world but here with you right now?"

Elise felt her face flush. She wasn't sure where Joshua was going, and she wasn't sure if she would stop him if it went too far.

"And that's why I appreciate your friendship so much," she said, trying to keep the situation in control.

"So, you're just going to keep calling me your friend, huh?" "Josh, I don't know what you mean."

"Elise, you are literally one of the smartest people I know. I think you know exactly what I mean. Now besides asking you to help me find a house, I don't think I've ever asked you for anything. But now I'm asking. I won't hold it against you. And I won't take advantage. You're safe. But I would appreciate the truth. Is that all you think we are? Friends?"

Elise took a deep breath. As dangerous as it was, she wanted to give him an honest answer.

"Josh, you make me feel like I'm loved and wanted. My husband doesn't make me feel like that anymore. I needed to feel that today. I didn't expect you to make me admit it though."

"I'm glad I make you feel that way. I really am. But one more question," he pressed.

"OMG. You are on one, aren't you, sir? What now?" she asked. "Do you love your husband?" he asked her bluntly.

"Why would you ask me something like that?"

"Please just answer the question, Elise. Do you love your husband?" "Josh...of course I do."

"Do you want to stay married?" he asked. "Josh, I don't want to talk about this anymore."

"Okay, then please just listen, because I don't think I will ever have the strength to say this again. I remember the third, maybe the fourth time we met, you took me to a house, and I remember you showing me the backyard. There was this gorgeous fountain and gazebo but all I wanted to do was put my arms around you and hold you. I just wanted you to be mine. And that night at the movie theater...when you let me hold you...when you let me kiss you on your forehead and tell you everything was going to be all right...Elise, I don't care what it would cost me, I would do it all over again for that one moment. I didn't know how broken I was until I met you and started to heal. But I can't do this. You can talk all the junk you want and you can talk about all the lightning bolts, but I see through it. I see the sweet, kind woman of God that you are. You can't stand where this is going, and I can't stand to be the one to take you there. If I break, then so be it. My wife is gone. My son may as well be. All I have left is a daughter in college who has better things to worry about than a dad who couldn't keep his family together. So, if I have to add you to my list of 'L's,' then so be it, but I won't hurt you. And if we keep going...if we keep doing this, you will get hurt, and it will be my fault. I won't do that to you, Elise. You mean too much to me."

"What are you saying?" she asked.

"I'm saying I'm in love with you, Elise. But I'm also saying for your sake, I have to let you go. It's not because I want to. It's because I have to. We can't just sit around pretending you're trying to find me a house. Before, we had the buffer of your husband. Now, there's no safety net and we need to get away from each other."

"Josh, I don't know what you want me to do."

"Just say goodbye. And please don't say goodbye Joshy, because if you do, I won't leave."

"What if I told you that this was crazy?" she argued desperately. "What if I told you that this was all in your mind? What if I told you this was just a harmless crush? Josh, please don't be hurt. But what if I told you I'm not even attracted to you and that I don't find myself thinking about you? What if I told you that if you just give it time you will see we can be really good friends? And what if I said it's fine if you leave because I'm not going to miss you and I certainly won't break down and cry when you go? If I said all that, would you chill and stop trying to be so noble and just keep being my friend? Because I really need you to be my friend. And I really need you to stay."

"I want to, Elise. But I'd better go while I can," he said softly.

"So, that's it? You're leaving me too? No hug? No kiss on the forehead?" "Elise, I'm sorry, but if I ever get you in my arms again…I'm not letting you go."

"Joshy, please don't do this. What about your house?" she asked, grasping at the last straw she could think of. "I thought you wanted a house?"

"I do but it doesn't matter anymore. Guys like me don't get what they want.

Goodbye, Elise."

CHAPTER 64

Crumbling

DAY 460

"Hey…can I talk to you for a minute?" Jeremiah asked Elise.

"Sure, but let's not be late for your flight. I can take you if you want," Elise said to offer some form of an olive branch.

This had been Jeremiah's first trip home in three weeks. It hadn't been exactly memorable. He came in late Friday night and was completely exhausted. They spent most of their Saturday with his dad and had barely communicated with each other. Jeremiah insisted on going to church Sunday morning, and now it was Sunday afternoon and time for him to leave again.

"Elise, I was taking out the trash and noticed there are a lot of empty wine bottles. Did you drink all of that yourself? In just three weeks?"

"Jeremiah, of course not. Look at this house…it's spic and span. If I kept all the wine bottles I drank over three weeks, you wouldn't be able to get in this house. That's more like three or four days' worth," she said flippantly.

"And you drank that all by yourself?" he questioned.

"All by my lonesome, sir. And?" she asked, daring him to continue his line of questioning.

"And?" Jeremiah bristled at her attitude. "And there's a half-empty bottle of Hennessy in the back of the pantry. Is there something I need to know about?"

"Well...since you asked," she said, pretending to hold back her tears. "Yes... there is something you need to know. Hi...my name is Elise...and I'm an alcoholic."

Jeremiah couldn't read her anymore. Was she trying to be funny or dismissive?

"Elise, I need you to be serious. I know you've always enjoyed an occasional glass of wine, but this isn't you."

"Jeremiah, we've barely spoken all weekend. Why do you want to talk about this now?"

"Because it seems serious. Why are you drinking so much?" he probed. "I told you. I'm an alcoholic," she said casually.

"I can't tell if you're being serious or not."

"I know you can't, Jeremiah. It's because you don't know me. But that's not a jab. It truly isn't your fault. I don't know me anymore so I shouldn't expect you to. But I see you're concerned so I'll be nice. I know I'm acting like a 'B word' but no...I'm not an alcoholic. I just... you know...partake a little more than I used to. It helps me forget. It helps me relax."

"Why the step up to Hennessy?" he asked.

"I don't know...it was my drink of choice BC and BJ...you know... before Christ and before Jeremiah. I guess I remembered and wanted to indulge. Technically, it might be better. You see allll the bottles of wine. But that Henn don't take all that. Now if you come back and see a whole bunch of empty Henn Henns...that's when you can worry."

"I'm already worried." "Well, don't be. I'm fine."

"Elise, I call you every day. You sometimes don't even answer and if you do, you rush me off the phone or, worse, act like I'm the last person in the world you want to talk to. I know you aren't on board with this job, but I'm trying to stay connected."

"Jeremiah, whatever we do or don't have, we have a semblance of peace. Why do you want to disrupt it when you have to get on a plane soon?"

"Because I'm trying to figure out what's wrong with you, Elise!" he said, immediately regretting his choice of words.

"You're trying to figure out what's wrong with me? she asked, her patience quickly waning. "Jeremiah, it's figured! This is us. We're not happy. But I don't want to mistreat you. I can be civil as long as you don't push me."

"So, my choice is to ignore what I think is a problem or face the wrath of 'crouching tiger, hidden negro'?"

"That's funny," she laughed. "And accurate. Just let it go."

"Well, I'm not letting it go," he said firmly.

"I wish you would reconsider. The last time we got into it I said some very ugly and untakebackable things. I don't want to do that again."

"Then just talk to me. You've never been one to hold grudges. I know you're mad about Denver, but to ignore me when I call is ridiculous. And now you're drinking like it's going out of style, and when you do go, you sit in church like you'd rather be any place else in the world. What's happening with you? You used to tell me everything... now you don't tell me anything."

"Oh, you really want to do this, don't you? You just let that come out of your mouth. Wow. When was the last time you told me anything, Jeremiah? When was the last time you let me in and really talked to me? You're getting ready to go back to this bullcrap job in Denver that you took with no input from me, but I'm the one who doesn't communicate? Boy, bye. Call an Uber. I will not be interrogated. I'm not staggering or stammering. My eyes aren't bloodshot and I'm handling my business. Go talk to the staff at Daddy's rehab. They see me eh-va-ree day. You may not be impressed with me, but they are! And I'm still out in these streets six and even seven days a week, closing deals and looking cute. All I do is what everybody else wants me to do, but nobody cares what I want. So, if I need a little drinky poo to rest at night, then I'm going to have one. And if folk get on my nerves... like now... and I need a drink, so I don't go all the way off, then I'm going to have one."

"Where are you going?" Jeremiah asked as she turned her back on him.

"I just told you. I'm going to the back of the cabinet and start on the second half of that Hennessy."

"Elise…stop. This isn't you."

Elise ignored him as she poured a rather generous portion of Hennessy into a glass. She waited until he got into the kitchen.

"Cheers!" she said as she gulped it straight. She normally mixed it with something else. The liquor burned as it went down, but she kept a poker face so he wouldn't know just how uncomfortable she was.

"Elise, I don't know what to do with this. What can I do? What do you want?" Elise thought about the day he told her he had taken the job. She thought about how she had pleaded with him not to go and what his response was. To her, the answer was clear. All he had to do was stay. But she wasn't going to ask him again. He should know.

She took another sip from the glass. "I have what I need right here, Jeremiah." "Fine…I'll be back next week. We'll finish this then."

"The last time you left you promised me you would be back in two weeks, and it took three. So just say, 'I'll see you when I see you.'"

"Well…whatever…I'll be back soon. I'm not going to bother praying for the Holy Spirit to do something while you got that other spirit in your hand. I'll call you later. Answer if you want to. I'll get an Uber."

CHAPTER 65

Breaking Point

DAY 460

Elise sat alone on her couch as the afternoon turned into evening. The half- empty bottle of Hennessy was down to a quarter full, but it didn't dull her pain. Instead of just being hurt, sad, and alone, she was now hurt, sad, alone…and drunk. Jeremiah's plane should have landed over an hour ago, but he hadn't bothered to text or call. *Can you blame him?* she thought.

She thought about her deteriorating marriage. She had been wondering if Jeremiah's love for her had grown cold. Now, she was no longer wondering. He looked truly disgusted at her when he left. He didn't want to talk. He didn't try to pray. And he didn't tell her he loved her. Now he was in Denver…alone…angry… disillusioned with his wife…and to the eye of any random woman…available. She checked her phone again. He still hadn't bothered to call. She thought about the dark path that she had confided in Joshua about. Only he knew that full story. Perhaps a different decision on that day would have spared her the pain she was in now, but she couldn't go back in time. She hadn't eaten much, and her head pounded from the combination of too much alcohol and the overwhelming thoughts that were becoming too much to bear.

She grabbed her glass and made her way to the bathroom to find some relief for her head. She found some of Jeremiah's pain medication prescribed to him after their accident. Jeremiah, of course, only took a few. "I'm not putting that crazy stuff in my body," he would say. She was able to convince him to take them only when his pain levels were at

After the Crash

their highest. And when he did, it was a wrap. In a matter of minutes, he would be out like a light. When he would awake, the pain would be gone. That's what she needed. She needed to sleep, and she needed the pain to go away.

She looked at the directions on the label. "'Take no more than two tablets per every 24 hours. Do not take with alcohol.' Oh, well," she said. "Too late for that part." If one pill did the trick for Jeremiah, then it would likely suffice for her. *Let's not play with it,* she thought. *Take two and I'll be out all night.*

She wasn't sure if it was in her head, but she could have sworn she heard a strange voice with another suggestion.

"Or you can take the whole bottle and never feel anything again. If Jeremiah really cared about you, he would have never left in the first place. What do you think he's in Denver doing now that he can't bother to call or text? He hasn't been having sex with you but that doesn't mean he hasn't been having sex. That man is sick of you. You're sick of you. Jeremiah left because he doesn't love you anymore. Why do you want to keep living like this? This isn't even living. Everyone is gone. Mama Etta…Daddy… Amari…J.J.…Jeremiah is next. He will be okay without you. He might be better off. You never got to hold your baby. You know you want to go be with him. There's only one way to do that. Besides…you know what you did. You turned your back on God. That's Judas level right there, and you know what happened to him. You already said nothing works for you, not even God. You may as well do what Judas did. Forgiveness is cool for everybody else but not for you." Elise saw a teardrop splash off the bottle of pills she was holding. Her hands were shaking as she emptied three of them into her hand. *Three might not be enough,* she thought. *I don't want to be a vegetable.*

She put the three pills back into the bottle and brought the full bottle close to her lips. Then she picked up the glass of Hennessy she had brought into the bathroom with her. Her hands shook so strongly, some of the liquor spilled as she struggled to hold the glass steady.

"I'm so sorry," she said, not quite sure who she was apologizing to.

She took the bottle of pills and placed it to her mouth when she received a text. The unexpected chime startled her and she dropped the pills and the glass. The pills emptied onto the hard bathroom floor and the glass shattered. She looked at the newly formed mess of pills, liquor, and broken glass on the floor beneath her. *I can't even do this right,* she thought.

As sad as she was, it made her happy that Jeremiah had bothered to text. She should at least respond. Maybe she should call him and say she was sorry? She reached for her phone as she maneuvered around the broken glass. But to her surprise, the text wasn't from Jeremiah.

It started with a very familiar and warm greeting: "Hello, Realtor."

CHAPTER 66

Life Preserver

DAY 460

Joshua had resisted reaching out to Elise since their last meeting. The signs of a potentially disastrous relationship were all around them and as much as it broke his heart, he didn't want to hurt her. But instead of getting easier, it had become harder and harder to keep his distance as the days turned into weeks. As was his pattern previously, he searched for a legitimate reason to reach out to her. He finally came up with something that seemed reasonable. His text to her read: "Hi Realtor, sorry to bother you. The house search is likely a no-go. Do you happen to know a good website to research apartments?"

It took a few minutes, but Elise responded. "Hi Joshy…umm… apartments?

Don't you already live in an apartment? LOL."

"I want a better apartment," he replied. "Why can't you just let me be great?" "You need to get great at yo lil' lame reasons to text me… that's what you need to get great at. LOL."

"Wow. Just gon call me out like that, huh?"

"I'm sorry…I'll play along. Sure, Client. There are several reputable places I can refer you to for a nice apartment upgrade. I do have to say I can no longer work for you for free. Sooo…you can meet me in one hour at the movie theater and we can discuss your different options. Yes, the tickets AND the snacks are on you. See you in an hour?"

Joshua hadn't expected such a response, but he couldn't pretend like he wasn't happy about it. Still, even though he had missed her, he had also experienced a certain peace in the last few weeks. Now here he was waiting in the movie theater parking lot for her and as much as he wanted to see her, that peace was now gone and was replaced by that same familiar and uncomfortable knot in his soul. But he was there now. He may as well see how she was doing.

Whatever apprehension he had subsided as her Uber arrived.

She got out of the back of the car and approached him. She wore simple blue jeans, a matching jacket, and red Chucks. And still looked like she was red carpet ready.

"Joshy!" she said as she embraced him warmly. She pulled him close, making no attempt to keep an appropriate distance between her breasts and his chest. He was pleased to have her in his arms again, but something seemed off with her.

"Hey, Elise. It's good to see you. How have you been?" he asked.

"I'm okay. Come on. You pick. I don't care what we see. I will meet you at the snack bar. I am going to the bar for a little adult refreshment. Do you want anything?"

"I'm good," Joshua replied, starting to realize what was off with her. Joshua got the tickets and snacks, and they made their way to their seats. "What did you pick?" Elise asked as she took a sip of her drink.

"Same thing we saw last time," Joshua replied simply.

"Oh...okay...I guess it's worth seeing twice. Thank you for coming out on a school night."

"It's the summertime, Elise. No school."

"Haaa. Boy, you know I ain't got no kids. I don't be knowing."
"Well, I know a few things...you wanna hear?"

"I'm intrigued, sir. What you know?" she said as she leaned closely to him. "I know I've thought about you every day for the last three weeks." "Aww...Joshy...stop it. You're gonna make me cry," she gushed.

"I also know hardly anybody's going to be in this theater because the movie's old. We should mostly have it to ourselves."

"So, you're trying to be alone with me? A married woman?" she asked, easing slightly closer to him.

"Yes, I am trying to be alone with you but not for that. The other thing I know is that you're drunk, and you probably need someone to talk to. I figured we'd be safe in here. So, what's up?"

"Aww! Joshy, you really do care!" she said sincerely. "Here I am thinking you brought me up here to take advantage of me, but you really are just trying to be my friend. But I'm still a little offended. Talkin' bout I'm drunk. I'm not so think as you drunk I am, sir," she said, intentionally mixing up the words.

"What's wrong, Elise?" Joshua asked seriously.

"You first. I thought you just had to get away from me. So, why did you text me?"

Joshua thought about her question. "I tried not to, Elise, he answered honestly. "Every day I had to force myself not to reach out. But tonight…," he shook his head, "I don't know…something was different, and I just felt like I needed to reach out to you.

"And what makes you think I'm drunk?" she asked as she took another sip of her drink. "But before you answer, I gotta tell you Joshy, you're way over your rudeness quota. The last time I saw you, you told me you loved me…then you abandoned me! And now you accuse me of being three sheets to the moon. Explain yourself, sir."

"I think it's three sheets to the wind, Elise." he corrected.

Elise playfully hit him on his arm. "Everybody don't have a Ph.D., Josh!" she laughed.

"Just sayin'. But anyway, you didn't drive yourself. That was a clue. But the way you move…your speech…everything…it's not you," he said plainly.

"And you think you know me well enough to make a statement like that?" she challenged.

"Yes…I do. I'm not saying I know everything. Or even that I know you on some deep level. But I know this isn't you. And I know something's wrong."

Elise put her drink down. "Thank you, Joshy," she said sincerely. "For?" he asked.

"For texting me. I really needed a friend tonight. But also for recognizing this isn't me. I don't want it to be. But I also don't want to be the married chick who bamboozles a very sweet guy into a potentially compromising situation. For that… I'm sorry. What can I say? Drowning people grab a hold of whoever is there. You were there…so now we're here…sorry."

"Okay…you're welcome. So, what happened? You and Jeremiah have a fight?"

"I don't know if you could call it a fight. A real fight has to have some emotional spark. I don't know that Jeremiah cares enough to fight with me anymore. I think he's done. I think we're done. But enough about me. Tell me again why you texted me."

"I already did." "Say more, please."

"I guess I had a weak moment," he admitted.

"What does your having a weak moment have to do with you texting me? You made it sound like we couldn't be friends anymore."

"Yeah, I also said I'm in love with you," he reminded her.

"Ooh, Joshy…you can't be sayin' stuff like that. Ole mannish self, got me up in here half…okay, three-quarters lit… picking seats in the back. And you were right. No one else is in here," Elise said as she leaned closer to him once again, her face only inches from his. "You could do whatever you want. I would be helpless to stop you."

"Elise, what are you doing?" he asked. "Why are you acting like this?" "Oh…I'm sorry. I didn't mean to offend you," she said, embarrassed.

"I'm not offended. I'm just concerned," he clarified. "Like I said… this isn't you. So, why are you acting like this?"

"I'm lonely and I'm afraid," she said honestly. "I'm scared to be by myself. Everybody is leaving and I don't want you to leave again. So… you know…I guess it's your lucky night."

"You don't have to do anything to get me to stay, Elise. You never have. I just want to be here for you."

"Ugh. Josh! Dang, I didn't know I was supposed to get you drunk to do this." "Sorry, I don't drink," he laughed as he took her hand.

"Fine. But there are no guarantees that this love train is going to stop again once I'm sober" she warned.

"Oh, I'm sure I'll regret not climbing aboard," he admitted. "But that's not what you need."

"What do I need?" she asked.

"You need to know that I'm here for you…no matter what…and I love you," he said as he slipped his arm around her. Elise snuggled up close to him and laid her head in his chest.

"Joshy?" she said as she closed her eyes. "Yeah, what's up?"

"Check every now and then and make sure I'm still breathing. I might have alcohol poisoning."

"Elise!" he exclaimed.

"I'm kidding!" she laughed. "But it might not be a bad idea to feed me some pretzel."

Joshua pulled her close and kissed her on the forehead. The knot in his belly was still there but the smell of her hair and the warmth of her body made it easy to ignore. Elise reached her arm around his torso as he placed the pretzel in her mouth.

"I'm glad you're here, Joshy," she said as she took a bite. "You really saved my life."

CHAPTER 67

New Opportunities

DAY 462

"Jeremiah Traylor! Also known as…The Man. How are you doing, brother?" Chad's greeting was warm, but Jeremiah wasn't exactly in a friendly mood.

Still, he appreciated the effort and Chad was still the boss.

"Hey, Chad. What's up?" Jeremiah responded, although he hardly matched his energy.

"Just checking up on you, brother. Even though there's not much I think we need to talk about. You really hit the ground running. Everything looks to be on or ahead of schedule. Great job, man. Seriously."

"Yeah, we don't always get second chances in life. I appreciate this one, Chad," Jeremiah said sincerely.

"It's my pleasure. I felt really bad about before…not being able to keep you on. I honestly didn't think you would take it, but when this opportunity came up I at least wanted to ask."

"Well, I'm glad you did."

"Yeah? Well, let's see if you're glad after this conversation," Chad said plainly. "What's wrong?" Jeremiah asked, preparing himself for the other shoe to drop. "It's nothing wrong…but we do need to talk. We have big plans and I need to know what role you want to play in them."

"Oh…okay. I'm listening," Jeremiah said, slightly relieved.

"Well, first of all," Chad continued, "you've always been transparent about the controversy at your old company. What's happening with that?"

"Actually, I'm glad you asked," Jeremiah smiled. "My lawyer has submitted a motion that all charges be dropped. The FBI has been investigating for over a year now and hasn't come up with any convictable proof against me yet."

"If that happens, you know you could sue Jacebre for damages, right?" Chad asked.

"Ha. Yeah. That's what my lawyers are telling me," Jeremiah confirmed. "Traylor Construction...gotta nice ring to me, brother," Chad laughed.

"One step at a time. If I can get this behind me and get my name back, that will be all right...at least for starters. But back to your original question, I take it you're asking because you want to make sure that I will actually be available for anything in the future?"

"Yeah...I mean as opposed to being in federal prison," Chad laughed, hoping Jeremiah would appreciate the levity.

Jeremiah laughed with him. "No, I get it. Until it's all on paper I can't promise anything, but it's looking more and more like a non-issue."

"That's good. And I'm happy for you. But now it gets to be a little more tricky. This gig is temporary. We thought it would take four to six months. You might have it knocked out in half the time. What do you think of something more permanent?"

Jeremiah's eyes lit up. Chad was the polar opposite of Case. He had high expectations, but he also cared about his team. Elise would love him if she ever met him.

"What did you have in mind?" Jeremiah asked.

"Jeremiah, we need someone coordinating our developments on a national level. We basically need another me. I think that me, is you. And we'll make sure it's worth it to you."

This new opportunity excited Jeremiah. He enjoyed his role, but it was nowhere near his previous salary. What Chad was proposing could be just what he needed to get back on his feet.

"Chad, it really sounds like a nice opportunity," Jeremiah replied. We would need to iron out the details and I need some time to think about it. But I'm interested."

"We can table it for now. But there's something else I'd like to run past you. It's business and personal. It would give you something to do for a month or two while you decide what to do. But you'd be working for me personally…not for the company."

"What did you have in mind?" Jeremiah asked.

"I have an aunt who wants to move into your city. We've located a nice property for her but it really needs to be refurbished. I remember you said you did that for your home, and I see what kind of work you do around here. And you and I both know I got better things to do than to hang out in the metroplex. I was hoping you could manage the work for me. I'll make sure you are well taken care of. You can start on that as soon as you finish here. And you'll be home. What do you think?"

"Chad, that sounds good. Thanks for thinking of me." "Sound like a plan?" Chad asked.

"Yeah…I think I can help you," Jeremiah agreed.

"I'm glad," Chad replied. "But about the first gig… I know you can do it. But you've always kept it straight with me, so I need to keep it straight with you. Jeremiah, I'm only home half the time. I'm not just offering this to you because it's good for the business, I'm offering it to you because I've met someone, and I don't want to only see her three or four days a week. If you sign up for this, that's what you're going to be looking at. And it won't just be for a few months. It will be like that all the time. I'm not trying to meddle and I for sure don't want to discourage you, but that kind of distance can be hard on a relationship. How is your wife dealing with you being gone now?"

CHAPTER 68

The Spark

DAY 462

Elise sat in the corner of the coffee shop, waiting for Joshua to arrive. Their affair wasn't sexual. But it was an affair, nonetheless. She thought about their time together just a couple of days ago. Considering her state of mind and her alcohol- compromised inhibitions, had Joshua been any other man, their relationship would have already crossed the line. But Joshua wasn't any other man and he refused to take advantage of her vulnerable condition. He was totally content just to hold her and comfort her. A fact that only served to make him all the more desirable to her.

Her emotions conflicted as they both disgusted and excited her. The place she most wanted to be in the world right now was the exact same place she knew she shouldn't be in. Shania's warning echoed in her mind. *Elise, you need to run as far as you can, as fast as you can from that man.* Jeremiah had made some mistakes, but he didn't deserve this. Neither did Joshua, for that matter. She closed her laptop but before she could make her escape, Joshua came through the front door. His tall frame caught the attention of the server behind the bar. He politely returned the young lady's greeting, then turned all the warmth of his sweet smile on Elise, who instantly abandoned her escape attempt.

"Hey, Elise," he said simply as he sat opposite of her. "Sooo… we not doing the Client/Realtor thing?" Elise asked.

"We can…but I just wanted to say your name," he whispered before jumping into character. "So, what new home opportunities do you have for me?" he asked, overacting.

Elise shook her head. "You are awful at this," she laughed.

"I don't know what you're talking about," he said, continuing his performance. "What wonderful home options do you have for me, your prospective client?"

"Joshy, sit down and hush," she whispered through gritted teeth before joining in their role play. "It's so good to see you, Mr. Dupree," she said professionally. "Why don't you come over here and let me pull some things up for you?"

Joshua sat next to her. Close enough to feel the warmth of her body and smell her perfume but far enough to make it look like they were just reviewing information on the same screen together.

"Oh. Yeah. That seems like a nice one," he said before whispering, "You smell amazing."

"Poor thing," she replied under her breath. "Just imagine the possibilities if you weren't so gosh darned honorable. But I do appreciate you not taking advantage of the opportunity. I won't blame it completely on the Hennessey, but I for sure wasn't at my best."

"And now?" he asked.

"Now?" she asked, stalling as she searched for the proper response. "Sorry, but now you may have missed your shot. Let's just say that Hennessey gave me some liquid courage. And without that? Bruh…jus sayin'…ole girl behind the bar is cute. I would understand."

"Elise, please stop underestimating me. I'm just asking how you're doing now?" he said, slightly offended.

"Josh…I really need you to stop being so nice to me. If you didn't pick up on it, I pretty much just told you I'm not giving it up. This is the part where you fake getting a phone call and go home. Orrr…wait 'til I leave and circle back around to ole…."

"…Ole girl behind the bar," Joshua interrupted. "Yeah, I get it. I missed my once-in-a-lifetime shot. Whatever…now can you tell me how you're doing?"

"I'm well. How are you?" she said all too politely.

"I'm real. That's how I am. You're the opposite," he said directly.

"You're saying I'm fake? Are you coming for me cuz we're in a public place and you think I won't turn it out?" she said in a half humorous and half threatening tone.

"Nah…I don't like that one," he said, getting back into character.

"Okay, how about this one?" she said, playing her part. "Now answer the question," she whispered as she kicked his foot.

Joshua looked at the computer screen as he spoke to her. "Elise, you're obviously going through. Now you can play games talking about 'I'm well,' or you can open up. At least with me, you know you can tell me anything."

"Anything?" she asked seriously. "Yes…anything," he confirmed.

Elise turned her body toward him, momentarily disregarding how anything might look to a casual observer. "Joshua, before you texted me the other night, I had a bottle of high-dosage prescription pain pills in my hand. I was going to take them and kill myself. Is that real enough for you?"

Joshua could tell from her tone that she was serious, but he looked deep into her eyes for confirmation. There was no smirk. No sudden burst of laughter. Nor was there any fear. Her countenance was eerily peaceful considering what she just said.

"Elise, come to my place."

"Josh, I'm sorry. We're not doing that, she said firmly."

"For the second time…please stop underestimating me. I just want to talk to you in peace and not have to worry about when the homeowners are coming back."

"Just talk?" she asked.

"Just talk. Pinky promise," he said, extending his small finger to her.

"Boy, put yo hand down. We can't be pinky promising in public. People shole would be talking," she laughed. "Okay…go ahead and go. I will leave in five minutes…and we can talk."

CHAPTER 69

Dangerous Game

DAY 462

"Don't worry…I got it, ma'am," Joshua reassured the older woman. He had come home to a new neighbor in the middle of her move. She was struggling with a few larger items, and Joshua was trying to help her as much as he could before Elise arrived.

"Ma'am…I'm sorry, but I actually have an important meeting, so I won't be able to get everything," Joshua explained.

"Baby, don't you worry. This is so sweet. I can manage," his new neighbor said. They made their way back to her car as Elise drove up.

"Ma'am, that's my realtor. I really am sorry, but I have to go."

"Baby, I told you, it's okay. Go handle your little business. Oh… she's cute. You might want to get double for your trouble. Get a new house and a new wife. Hee, hee, hee. Don't mind me. I'm just meddling. Hey there, sweetheart," the older lady said as she waved to Elise. "I know y'all have a meeting. I'm not gon hold him."

"Hi," Elise responded simply. "Josh, we can do this later. She needs help." "Well…those opportunities you mentioned sounded like they needed attention now," Joshua replied.

Elise knew she had scared him and that he wanted to talk. "Okay… but let's help her get all this stuff inside and we can look at your options," Elise agreed.

They helped Joshua's new neighbor with her remaining items before adjourning to Joshua's apartment.

"Thanks, you two. I'm Christine Anderson," she said as they made their exit. "Young lady, would you mind helping me in the bathroom for just a quick second?"

"Oh…sure. Yes, ma'am," Elise said as she followed her.

"Baby, I don't need nothin'," Christine said under her breath in the bathroom. "I just wanted to say you got a good one right there. I can read people and that man loves you. Don't let him go, nah."

"Oh…no, ma'am. It's not like that. He's just a client."

"Oh…if you say so. I guess my matchmaking skills ain't what they used to be," she laughed. "Well, enjoy your meeting."

"I will. It's nice to meet you, Christine. I'm Elise."

"She was sweet," Elise said nervously as they entered Joshua's apartment.

She cringed at the thought of what Shania would say if she saw her now. "Yeah, she was sweet," Joshua agreed as he rushed in to straighten up.

Elise's apprehension waned as she tried not to laugh. "Sooo… Joshy," she teased as she observed the surroundings, "Nice place. I love the crown molding and the wood floors. And such a bold choice on the décor. I've said it a thousand times, moving boxes are slept on as a decorative feature."

"You done?" he laughed, amused and embarrassed at the same time.

Elise quickly scanned the disorganized apartment. "Oh, no sir, I think I'm just getting started."

Joshua shook his head and smiled. "Elise, go get something to drink while I get this place halfway presentable."

Elise walked a few steps into the kitchen. With the exception of both sinks being full of soaking dishes, his kitchen was mostly acceptable. Then she opened the refrigerator.

"Umm…Josh…Joshua…Joshy…drink what sir?" she asked, her amusement growing.

"There's nothing in there?" Joshua asked, surprised.

"No, it ain't nothin' in here!" Elise screamed as she examined the sparsely supplied refrigerator. "Boy, you are a grown man. Go to the grocery store!" she chastised.

"I do go to the store," he defended. "I…just…haven't been recently. I'll Door Dash us something. Come on and sit down."

"Boy, I ain't sittin' down unless you can provide a notarized document specifying that them drawls is clean," she said observing the laundry on his couch. "Hold up now. I don't put dirty clothes on my couch. That's where I draw the line," Joshua insisted.

"There's a line?" she erupted in laughter and fell to the floor.

"Yes, there is!" Joshua laughed, still trying to defend himself. "I just haven't straightened up in a minute. But it's normally a lot better than this," he said as he knelt next to her.

"Joshy," she said, controlling herself so she could get her words out. "What do your other female visitors say when they see this? Are they like, 'Oh well, he cute and got a job. I can clean up for him.'"

"You're the only woman who's ever come in here, Elise," he shrugged. "What?" she said, taken aback by his words.

"You heard me. I've had one or two friends over. My daughter's been here.

My son hasn't," he said sadly. "But you're the first woman." "Well… thank you. I'm honored. Except for the mess," she teased. "Is it that bad?"

"No, Joshy. It's not that bad," Elise said, letting up on him. "Honestly, it's just that you're so put together. You always have on perfectly adorned suits or like now…all fly with your matching sneakers and shirt. It's actually refreshing to know you're not perfect."

"Yeah, well I'm hardly perfect," he said. "Plenty of people will attest to that." "No?" she asked, leaving her knees, and sitting down on the floor. "Let's take

the roll, Principal Dupree. You always put others first. Even if it's to your own detriment. When people call…you answer. Even when it's inconvenient. You deny what you want in favor of what other people need."

"I wish my son felt that way," Joshua said sadly.

"I don't have any children…at least not anymore. But if I did, and they treated Jeremiah like your son is treating you? Joshy…hood rat, project raised, system reared Elise is coming out of retirement. Trust and believe that."

"It's not his fault," Joshua defended his son. "I should have done things so much differently with him, Elise."

"And there it is. Another point in your favor. You take the blame even when it's not your fault."

"No. But it is my fault. I should have made sure nothing ever came between us." "No, Josh," Elise insisted. "It wasn't your fault. It was your responsibility. There's a difference. It was your responsibility to love him and raise him and provide for him. And as hypocritical as it is coming from me, to tell him about the love of

Jesus Christ. And to be there for him. Now, you look me in the eye and tell me you didn't do those things and I will be happy to take my little encouragement back."

"No. I did," Joshua smiled. "I still miss him, though."

"He'll open his eyes one day. When I start praying again that will be at the top of my list. Robert will come around. Just watch," she encouraged.

"You remember his name?" Joshua asked, his heart warmed at the thought. "Of course. Robert, Robin, and the 'B' on wheels in the red corner…Angela." "Girl, stop!" Joshua laughed.

"Hey, I'm not one hundred percent backslidden. At least I used the initial. I know I shouldn't call her out her name but hear me on this. I like you. I. Don't. Like. Her. And when I see her…it's on sight."

Joshua laughed again. "Elise, it's not that serious."

"Oh, it is to me," Elise contradicted. "I don't claim to know everything, but I know what you've shown me. You didn't deserve that. I'm not gon hurt her. I'm just gon drag her enough to make her think she gon get hurt. But if she test me… all bets are off. Best she take this kindergarten behind whooping before I take her to grad school."

"Well, let's just keep y'all away from each other. How 'bout that?" "Ooh Joshy…," Elise said rather fiendishly.

"Elise, what is going on in that head?"

"Hypothetically…what if I went to your old house…in my sexiest black dress and heels mind you. I would just knock on the door and let her answer. I would be like, in my innocent white girl voice, 'Hi, is Joshua here?' And she would be like, 'He doesn't live here anymore.' Then I'd pick up the phone and call you…right in front of her, and say, 'Joshy, you won't believe what I just did. I came to the wrong house. Oh well, we'll just have to be late. Do you forgive me? You know you do. You never stay mad at me. Huh? No, I'm just here talking to your ex mother in law. She is so pretty for an older woman.' Then I slip back into ghetto Elise, pull off my heels, and back up slowly, saying with my eyes, Girl, I wish you would come at me. Then I jump into my Lexus and peel off."

Joshua's eyes widened. "Umm, did you just think of that, or have you been saving that?"

"Joshy, I'm a woman. We only need seconds to think up our diabolical plots." "I'll keep that in mind. So, can we get to why we're actually here?" he asked.

"Joshy, I know I look cute on your floor, but I told you the bakery is closed.

No fresh baked cookies for you."

"Elise," Joshua said, slightly frustrated.

"I'm sorry, Joshy. I'm deflecting. I do that. I know I scared you. What do you want to talk about?"

"I want you to tell me about the pills. Before, you said you never thought about hurting yourself."

"I didn't think about it then either." Elise inched away from him slightly. "Are you sure you're not gonna try and open this cookie jar? If you're trying to get deep and personal, I need to turn off the part of my brain that resists you, so I can fully engage my transparent and vulnerable mode. You're not trying to do an end around to get the drawls, are you?"

"You're safe, Elise. I promise. I just want to be here for you. Tell me what happened. What do you mean you didn't think about it?"

"Exactly that. I didn't think. I was just sad, mad, and drunk. And just all of a sudden, I felt the weight of the world on my shoulders, and it wasn't like before where I said I didn't want to be here anymore. It was like, I needed to do something about it. I felt like I was…," Elise stumbled for her words.

"Under attack?" he asked.

"Yeah," she agreed, appreciating his discernment. "I felt like I was under attack. But I didn't wanna fight. I wanted to lose. I wanted to be finished. So, I picked up the pills and my glass of Hennesy. I remember my hands were shaking so bad. But I was going to take them. There's no doubt in my mind that I would have swallowed those pills if you hadn't texted me. So, when I said you saved my life, I really meant it."

"And what if I didn't text you that night?" Joshua asked seriously.

Elise shrugged her shoulders. "Josh, I already told you…I was going to swallow those pills. Whatever happened after that…so be it."

"What did your husband say when you told him?" Joshua asked.

"You're the only one that knows, Joshy. Just like you're the only one who knows what I did in that hospital bed." she confided.

Joshua moved closer to her. "Elise, you have to promise me you'll call if you ever feel like that again."

"Joshy, you are so sweet. But we both know I can't promise you anything. You can't try to take responsibility for something that's not yours. And I'm sorry but I'm not yours. I'm married. If I weren't, things would be different. But nothing can happen here…nothing good at least. And I don't want to hurt you."

"Then why are you here?" Joshua asked her plainly.

"I told you. I'm drowning," she answered honestly. "I'll grab hold of whatever I can. Why did you ask me to come? Are you hoping I would give in?"

"No, it's not that. You're here because what happens to you is important to me. I really need to know that you're all right. And I honestly like the idea of you grabbing hold of me when you aren't. Now as far as you giving in? Don't test me," he warned.

"We're playing a dangerous game, Joshy," she said, easing closer to him.

"I know. I wouldn't have ever planned to play it. But we're here. So, what do we do now?"

"You could put me out and put me in your rearview mirror. I mean…I'm just saying that to be polite. We both know you're not going to do that", she said confidently. "You should, though."

"You're right," Joshua agreed.

Elise punched him softly in his chest. "You're agreeing with me that you should put me out?"

Joshua laughed. "No. Actually, I'm agreeing that I'm not going to do that." "Oh. I sawee, Joshy," she said in her baby voice. "I take my hit back."

"So, since you're staying and there are no cookies, what do we do now?" Joshua asked.

"Well, I would cook you something if you had some dangum groceries. But I can order a pizza and we can do a G-rated Netflix and chill," Elise said, inching herself closer to him and laying her body across his. "And since it makes you so happy, I guess I'll grab a hold of you and let you be here for me."

Joshua kissed her on the forehead. "Oh, this is for me, huh?" he laughed. "Oh…for sure," she said confidently. "One hundred percent. I'm being selfless."

"Oh, well thank you very much," he said sarcastically. "Yeah, yeah, yeah…more forehead kisses, sir."

CHAPTER 70

Never Alone

DAY 520

Amari used to love the summertime. Uncle J and T Lise would take her on the funnest trips to different places with Mama Etta and Papa John. Uncle J and she would ride every ride in the amusement park, and T Lise would let her eat whatever she wanted. Sometimes Uncle J and T Lise would go places by themselves, and she would get to stay with Mama Etta and Papa John. "Me and Uncle J are going away for a little bit, Mari," T Lise would say. "When we get back ask him for whatever you want. T Lise will make sure he's in a good mood." And she was right! Uncle J would be so happy when they came back from their trips and would say yes to everything. She asked T Lise what she did that made him so happy, but she would just tell her to wait until she was older, and she would explain.

But now Amari was glad the summer was over. Cherese never took her anywhere and it was sooo boring. But she still had to get past the weekends. During the week, at least she could go to school. That wasn't exactly fun, but at least she wasn't all by herself. Now, she was by herself all the time. She missed her family, but she prayed for them every day. She prayed Uncle J would find a job and not be in trouble anymore. She prayed Papa John wasn't still sick and wasn't lonely without Mama Etta. She prayed that J.J. was okay without her there to help take care of him. And most of all, she prayed that they would come and get her. But she had been gone a very long time now. They promised that they loved her but maybe they had forgotten her. She was praying for them. She wondered if they were praying for her.

"Amari!" her aunt's shout interrupted her thoughts. "Come here now!"

Amari knew from her aunt's tone that she was in trouble, but she couldn't imagine what she had done this time. She ran to her aunt's voice and found her in the kitchen holding a pizza box she had thrown away.

"Why did you eat all of the pizza?" Cherese asked.

Amari knew she should just tell her she was sorry but instead, she said, "It wasn't that much, it was only a little bit left."

Cherese's response was a slap on the cheek. "Little girl, I told you that you don't live with them rich people anymore. You can't come in here being all selfish."

Amari didn't make a sound, but that didn't stop the tears from coming from her eyes.

"You don't appreciate nuthin'. Yo mama didn't want you and yo daddy don't even know who you are. I give you a place to stay and all you ever want to talk about is your precious family. I'm your family! I'm gon say this one more time. Them folks ain't thinkin' 'bout you. I'm all you have. You need to quit acting like you're the only person in the world. And I don't care about your little tears either. I'll give you something to cry about if you keep foolin' with me. This world gon slap you a lot harder than I just did. You better be ready. Now dry those damn tears," Cherese said as she threw a towel at Amari's face. "I have to go to work. I guess I have to pick up something to eat on the way since you ate all the pizza."

Amari had eaten the pizza Cherese was so upset about four hours ago. She was hungry again, but she dared not tell her that now.

"Lock the door behind me and don't let nobody in here but Eric," Cherese said as she slammed the door.

Cherese always seemed to be mad. The only time she wasn't was when Eric was here. But he didn't come around as much as he used to and that made Amari sad. He was the only good thing about living with Cherese. But it had been three weeks since he had come by. Eric was nice to her, and she missed him. *He's probably not going to come back either,* she thought to herself as she dried her tears.

Uncle J and T Lise used to pray for her when she was sad or afraid. She remembered how Uncle J would sometimes sit with her in bed and read the Bible to her until she went to sleep. She used to like to hear him read Psalm 23. She also remembered Mama Etta and what she told her. *"Baby girl, learn your Bible. Jesus will speak to you if you learn your Bible."* But Cherese didn't even have a Bible, so she would just have to try to remember the best she could. She really liked Psalm 23. She tried to remember the words of Psalm 23 as she imagined how Uncle J used to hug her close and pray for her. She knelt at the side of her bed and tried to do it herself.

"Lord, you are my shepherd that does not want," she prayed. That always made her feel good. God didn't want anything. He just wanted to take care of her and love her.

"You make me lie down with my green pastor in the steel water," she continued, even though she wasn't sure if she was saying that part right or what it meant. She couldn't remember why the pastor was green, and how did the water become steel? And why did they have to lie down? And did the pastor have a bedtime? Was that why he had to lie down too?

"You lead me in paths of richesness for your name saying." This was hard to understand also. She knew God was supposed to take care of her, but did that mean she was supposed to be rich? She wished she was rich. She would buy a big house, and everyone could come and live with her. Well…everybody but Cherese. But one part made sense. She knew about the name! "Ask everything in Jesus' name," T Lise would tell her.

"Even when I walk in shadow death valley, I will fear no evil because of you." This was a little scary, but it also made her feel better to know she didn't have to be afraid.

"Your rod and your staff comfort me." She didn't know how a rod and a staff was going to make her feel better, but she was pretty sure that's what it said.

"You prepare my table, so my cup won't overflow." Maybe this meant God would fix things because he didn't want you to make a mess.

"And goodness and love will be in your house forever." This part made her sad, really. Cherese never took her to church so if that's where God's love was, maybe he couldn't love her anymore.

The more she thought about it, the more she realized she probably wasn't saying it right. But Papa John used to tell her, "Just pray in your own way, sweet baby. God will hear you. He knows exactly what we mean even when we don't." "Lord Jesus, please help me," she prayed. "I am so sad, and I miss my family.

Please don't let them be mad at me, and please ask them to come and get me. I am so sorry for whatever I did wrong. I love them so much, Jesus, and I love you, too. Mama Etta said that you talk to your children, so please tell Uncle J and T Lise for me that I am sorry and that I love them and that I miss them and that I want to come home."

Amari began to cry again. "And even if they don't want me anymore, please take care of them. And please take care of J.J. I am not mad at him even if he took my place. Jesus, please help me. Nobody loves me here and nobody talks to me. I hate my school. All the kids and all the teachers are mean. And I hate my aunt. The only time she talks to me is when she yells. Her boyfriend Eric is nice, though. He's my only friend here. He sometimes brings me stuff and watches movies with me and lets me share his food. I hope I can see him again. Please take care of him and please let him come see me. I love you, Jesus. Please don't make me stay here anymore. If you let my family come and get me, I promise I will be good. In the name of Jesus, I pray, Amen."

Amari was still sad, but she felt a little better after she prayed. She felt a lot better when she heard a tap on her window.

"Lil' Homey...you in there? Open the door."

It was Eric! She got up and ran to the front door. *That worked fast!* she thought. She remembered Uncle J always telling her to be thankful, so she turned around and went back to her bed. "Thank you, Jesus, for letting my friend come see me," she said before she quickly ran back to the front door.

She opened the door and Eric was standing there with his hands behind his back.

"Amari, did you even check the peephole?" he asked.

"It was you. Why do I have to check the peephole?" she asked innocently. "Because it might have been somebody running game. You need to be careful.

This ain't Bel Air and you ain't the Fresh Prince."

"Okay, I will check the peephole next time you come over and tell me to open the door," she said sarcastically. "What did you bring me? I'm starving. I mean little kid in Africa starving."

Eric laughed out loud. He was as happy to see her as she was to see him. "What make you think I brought you something?"

"Eric…don't play with my emotions and don't insult my intelligence. I was born but it wasn't yesterday."

"Lil' Homey, I swear you been here before," he said as he handed her a bag from her favorite burger joint.

"Thank you, Eric," she said as they went to the kitchen to enjoy their feast. "Eric, where have you been?" she asked. "I was afraid you weren't coming back after you and Cherese had that fight." "You heard that, huh?" he asked.

"Eric, the whole building heard it! So, are y'all cool again?"

"I don't know, lil' bit…maybe. But since you all up in my bizness… you two gettin' along?"

"You're not going to tell her what I say are you?" Amari asked.

"Lil' Homey. Snitches get stitches where I come from. Don't worry…I got you."

"Pinky promise?" Amari said as she extended her pinky to him. "Huh?" Eric asked.

"Eric, you have to pinky promise you won't tell," Amari said seriously. "My T Lise used to say that the worst part of the devil's dungeon was reserved for people who break the pinky promise. So, if you pinky promise, I know you won't tell."

"Okay, Amari…pinky promise…I won't tell. So, what's up?"

"I just try to stay out of her way. I used to think that maybe she liked me, but I don't think she does. I don't know why she said she wanted me, because she doesn't. And she doesn't let me do anything.

I asked her if I could try out for the cheerleading team, and she said she didn't have time. And before school was out last year, she wouldn't even let me play soccer. I told her how good I was, but she didn't care."

"I'm sorry, Amari," he said sympathetically.

"Well, if you're really sorry you can come see me more! It was better when you used to come more, but she's always on one when you're not here."

"Yeah…I know…but you know how she is. I just can't handle all her drama." "Eric…why do you even like her? Because I can't stand her."

"I know. But it will get better. Y'all just gotta get used to each other," Eric said optimistically.

"But you didn't answer my question. Why do you like her?" Amari asked again.

"It's hard to explain." Eric said, struggling to find an age-appropriate explanation. She's pretty and I thought she was cool. But it didn't take too long to realize she wasn't pretty on the inside…you know?"

"No, I don't know. I can't see why you ever liked her."

Eric knew exactly what appealed to him about Cherese, but he wasn't going to share that with this little girl. "I guess me neither," he said.

"Well, I'm glad you did, but if you don't like her, why did you come back?" Eric smiled brightly at his little friend. "You, girl! I had to make sure my Lil' Homey was doing all right. I know you tired of cereal, hotdogs, and stuff. I figured I'd hang with you for a little bit. By the time she gets home, she'll be too tired to fight…hopefully."

"Thank you for being so nice to me, Eric. I prayed to Jesus for you to come back and see me and he said yes. He hasn't said yes to anything I asked him for a long time but when I asked him for you, he did. Thank you for being my friend. I don't really have any friends anymore. You're really my only friend."

Her words touched his heart and broke it at the same time. Nobody had ever told him he was an answer to their prayers. But he thought it was sad that this little girl felt like he was her only friend.

"Well, you got a friend in me, Lil' Homey."

"Ooh, Eric, I love that movie! Can we watch it?" she asked excitedly. "Huh?" Eric asked, having absolutely no idea what she was talking about. "*Toy Story*…that's where you got that from…right?"

"I don't play with toys, lil' bit."

"OMG! Eric, you haven't seen *Toy Story*?"

"I have no idea what you're talking about, Amari."

"Woody? Buzz Lightyear? Andy? It's the best! Buzz and Woody are toys but they're very different. Woody's a cowboy and Buzz is an astronaut. But they become best friends. You know…like us. And Buzz promises Woody that no matter how mean his girlfriend is he won't ever stop coming to see him and being his friend."

"Amari… are you tryna play me?"

"Who, me? Your Lil' Homey? Why would I do that?" she smiled innocently.

"Yeah…you definitely running game," Eric laughed. "But respect. Go ahead and finish up, and we'll watch something before your best friend gets back from work."

"Speaking of work…what do you do for a living?" "Huh?"

"You heard me…what do you do for a living?"

"You know…this and that. I don't really have a permanent job." Eric wasn't exactly proud of how he was making ends meet. Amari thought he was an answer to prayer, and he didn't want her to know any different. "I just kind of help friends out doing different things. Deliveries and stuff like that."

"Eric, I told you I wasn't born yesterday, but you don't have to tell me if you don't want to. I'll just use my imagination. I think you're…a spy. That's it. Like Jason Bourne. And that's why you hang out with Cherese. Your enemies dare not attack you here."

Eric busted out laughing. "Lil' Homey, you got jokes."

"I get it from my T Lise. She made everybody happy. Everybody loved her.

She wanted to be my mommy. Well, that's what she said, anyway."

"I'll bet she did, Lil' Homey. Sometimes things change. But she would have been the luckiest mom in the whole world to have a little girl like you."

"Why are you so nice to me, Eric?"

"Whatchu mean? I'm nice to everybody," he said with feigned smugness. "You weren't nice to witchee-poo when y'all had that fight. Eric, you called

her the b word and everything. But you lost that round cuz she called you...."

"I know what she called me, Amari!" he said, cutting her off. "But I'm sorry you had to hear all that."

"My T Lise and Uncle J never talked to each other like that. When they got mad, they just called each other Jeremiah and Elise. But the next day they would always be right back to Miah and Lise. They called me Mari. If T Lise liked you, she wouldn't ever call you what everyone else called you. She would always change it up. She said that's how she let the people she loved know they were special."

"They sound like they were really nice. I know you don't like it here, but it will be okay."

"You still didn't answer my question...for the second time. Why are you so nice to me?"

"I had a little sister. It was my job to take care of her. She got sick when she was little, and we couldn't afford the medicine she needed. She died. That's it. I guess you remind me of her."

"I'm sorry, Big Homey. I didn't mean to make you sad."

"Big Homey, huh? I like that. It's okay, Lil' Homey. I don't think you could ever make me sad. And I can't promise...but I'll try to be like, what's their names? Buzzy and Woodrow and check on you more."

"Eric!" Amari laughed out loud. "It's Buzz and Woody and, uhhh...I may have added a little bit to that story for dramatic effect."

"Yeah, I figured. Come on...let's check it out."

Eric and Amari watched movies until Amari fell asleep on his shoulder. He was tempted to leave before Cherese came home. But his little friend seemed so peaceful on his shoulder. Besides, there would only be one thing to do once Cherese got home.

CHAPTER 71

Impure Motives

DAY 521

"You leaving already?" Cherese asked Eric.

"Nah. I heard lil' bit stirring. I was just gon pick her up some breakfast. What do you want?" Eric asked even though he didn't particularly care what Cherese wanted. He thought about his conversation with Amari the night before. At first, he really did like Cherese, but it quickly waned as he got to know her. But there was something about Amari, and the thought of her left alone with Cherese bothered him.

"Anything from Chick-Fil-A is fine," Cherese said as she rolled over in the bed.

"I was gonna go to McDonald's. Lil' bit likes their pancakes."

"I don't care what she wants!" Cherese objected. "She gets everything she wants anyway."

"I'm sure she don't get everything, Cherese."

"Chile, please. Amari up in here eating me out of house and home. Running up my light bill. Getting in trouble at school. If I would have known she was gon be this much trouble, I woulda let her stay where she was."

"Cherese…just asking…but if she's so much trouble, why did you get her in the first place?"

"I don't know. My mama had been asking about her ever since my sister disappeared. She said we should at least find out where she was. I did some checking around and found out they would basically pay me to keep her. It's not like she's a baby. I figured it wouldn't be that hard. I'll take care of my sister's baby and get a little extra to make ends meet. It's not like I got a man to help me with these bills."

"Oh, so we throwin' shade, huh?" Eric asked, bracing for another fight. "I'm just sayin'," Cherese said simply. "You wanted to know. So now you know."

"Do you like her being here?"

"Eric, I don't know. What difference does it make? Why you so worried about that little girl anyway?"

"Cherese, I know it's none of my business, but she's always talking about her family and stuff. It seems like she had a really good life. If you don't want her…."

"You right!" Cherese interrupted him. "It ain't yo damn business."

Eric could tell by her tone that Cherese's other side was about to break out, and he at least wanted to make sure Amari had a decent breakfast before he made his escape.

"Hey…my bad. I was just asking. Let me get you some Chick-Fil-A."

CHAPTER 72

Date Night

DAY 531

"Elise, where did you find this place? 'Thug getaways-dot-com'?" Joshua teased Elise.

"I know, right?" Elise agreed. "I thought they were gentrifying the neighborhood."

"Well, they got a little ways to go. You got gangbangers coming up in this joint with they head on a swivel."

"Josh, it's not that bad."

"Oh, it's that bad. For real, why'd you pick this place?"

"You know why, Josh. Better not to be around where we might get spotted." "Elise, if we get in a shootout, I'm pretty sure it's gonna draw attention. Why

can't we just go back to my place?"

"Josh, I told you I'm not going back there. Ms. Christine already looking at me with the side-eye. She's seen me twice now. Plus… somebody got a little frisky last time we were alone."

"Yeah…you did get off the chain," Joshua agreed.

"Boy, I know you didn't," Elise shook her head. "I got off the chain? I let you snuggle a little bit, and next thing I know our Disney movie got moved to HBO."

"I thought you liked me kissing you," he said innocently.

"On the forehead, Josh! Ain't nobody told you to go off script. I see now I need the protection of other eyes when I'm around you. You be tryna seduce folks. I thought you was gon be good. I don't mind you sniffing and snuggling with me but if they ever come out with an up-to-date Bible, I don't want to be known as Elise the Harlot."

"They wouldn't say that. I wouldn't let them," Joshua defended. "That's sweet, but you got love goggles on."

Joshua said nothing. He just stared at her and smiled. "What are you smiling about?" she asked.

"I just like hearing you acknowledge that you know I love you." "Joshy...." she started.

"I know, Elise. Run. Put you in my rearview. I get it. And I know in my head that you're right. But I'm not ready to do that. I know it's wrong, but I've felt better sneaking around with you these last few months than I felt in twenty years. I know I'm gonna have to pay the toll. You're gonna wake up one day and say it's over. Or your husband is going to come to his senses and realize he's about to lose the best thing that's ever happened to any man on the face of the earth. Or something that I can't even think of. I've thought about it. It's gonna hurt. But I'm in it until I know you're not going to drown. Maybe when I know you're okay I can walk away. But for now, I'm here. But by here, I mean with you. I don't mean here in this literal hole-in-the-wall. Let's go... now," he said firmly.

Before Elise could respond, a distressed young woman's voice interrupted them.

"Rayquawn, stop!" the young woman said.

"Go wait in the car!" he ordered her as he called the young woman by what certainly could not have been the name her mother had given her.

The embarrassed young woman complied and exited the establishment. "I think you're right, sir," Elise agreed.

"Where'd you park?" Joshua asked her. "I'm in the back."

"Of course you are," Joshua said, shaking his head. "Where there are absolutely no witnesses."

"I'm sorry," Elise giggled. "I grew up around stuff like this, so it doesn't always scare me like it should."

"Well, I'm scared," Joshua laughed. "Let me walk you to your car and we can come up with a Plan B."

Joshua walked her back to the car only to find the couple from inside had continued their altercation in the parking lot.

Their one-sided argument continued as the young man shouted expletives at the young woman. Elise's car was right next to theirs. Joshua placed himself between Elise and the arguing couple. The young man violently pushed the woman by her face to the hard concrete, where she fell at their feet. Joshua gently pushed Elise away to help her up, but the young man was already there and snatched her up by her now bleeding arm. The young woman made eye contact with Joshua, and he could see that her makeup was concealing a black eye. She looked like she may have been his daughter's age.

"Get yo ass in the car and don't say nothing else," the young man ordered. Joshua kept his position between the couple and Elise. "Are you okay, sweetheart?" Joshua asked her while keeping his eyes on her aggressor. "She good, bruh. Mind your own," he said to Joshua.

Joshua ignored him and asked her again. "Are you okay, sweetheart?"

Elise reached inside her purse, gripped her .45, and peeped around Joshua. "Baby, you don't have to take that," she said. "Do you need help?"

"Elise, get in the car," Joshua said firmly. He wanted to help the young lady, but he needed to make sure Elise was safe first.

The young man walked to within inches of Joshua's face and sized him up. He took note of his athletic physique but could clearly see he was younger and considerably larger than Joshua. "Yeah, little man, why don't both of you get in the car. I said mind your own," he said as he turned his gaze to Elise. "Unless you think I can do something for you that he can't."

"You can't do anything for her, man. Let's all calm down," Joshua said trying to deescalate the situation. "Young brutha, we don't want no problems. Let's just take a beat. I'll take the young lady home and she can reach out to you when she's ready. No smoke. No problems. Everybody wins. Everybody goes home."

"Come here, baby," Elise said, gently calling the young lady to her.

The young woman moved hesitantly toward her but was met with a violent backhand fist to her face. The violent blow caused her head to snap around, and she was unconscious before she hit the pavement.

CHAPTER 73

The Flame

DAY 531

"Aaahhhgggg!" the young man screamed as they rolled him into the ambulance. "He broke my arm!" he shouted as he continued to curse.

"Good for his tail!" Elise said as she sat near the young woman as the paramedics attended her.

To her surprise, Joshua had easily subdued the larger man. But the situation demanded they call the police. She was nervous as to how much she would have to testify to in a future investigation. And how she would explain the situation to Jeremiah.

"Ma'am, we have your statement. You're free to go," an officer told her. "What about my client?" she asked nervously.

"Oh, he'll be fine. He says he doesn't need to go to the hospital or anything.

It looks like that guy fooled around and found out," the officer laughed. "Are you going to need me for anything else?" Elise asked nervously.

"Someone will get in contact with you if they need you, but we already checked the security footage. It checks out with what you and your boyfriend both said."

"He's not my boyfriend," Elise corrected defensively. "He's my client." "Oh. I'm sorry. But you are free to go," the officer said.

Elise looked down at the bruised face of the young girl and her heart went out to her. She pulled out one of her cards and jotted a note on it. It simply said: "Call me anytime."

"I'm not your mother, sweetie," Elise told her. "But you need to know, real men don't treat you like this. Let me know if you ever need to talk," she said as she handed the young woman her card.

Elise joined Joshua as he was completing his statement to the police. "Mr. Dupree, I'm going to go. I'm sorry our meeting didn't go better. But what you did was very brave. Are you going to be okay?"

"Thank you, Elise. Yeah, I'm fine. We can meet again soon and talk about some other properties."

Joshua finished his conversation with the officer and limped to the other parking lot where his truck was parked. He had decimated his opponent for certain but had banged his knee on the concrete in the process. That was the least of his concerns though. He was disappointed that his fleeting time with Elise was now over because of this foolishness. He approached his truck and his eyes lit up as he saw the familiar white Lexus parked near it. He walked to Elise's window as she rolled the window down. She shook her head at him disapprovingly.

"What did I do?" he asked, curious about what she might be displeased about. "Why are you limping?" she asked.

"I just banged my knee," he said. "Why are you still here?" he said, hoping he already knew the answer.

"I just wanted to make sure you were okay," she said.

"I can barely move," he moaned, exaggerating his condition.

Elise shook her head and smiled, seeing through his charade. "Boy, you will do anything to get me to your house, won't you? Come on. I'll follow you."

CHAPTER 74

The Fire

DAY 531

"Come on. Take your time," Elise said as she put her arms around Joshua to assist him into his apartment.

Joshua was totally capable of walking. Other than some swollen hands and a bruised knee, he showed no signs of the violent altercation. Still, he would never turn down an opportunity to be close to her. He put his arm around her shoulder and leaned on her, with far more weight than necessary.

"I can't make it, Elise," he joked. "Go on without me."

"Boy, my name ain't Helga and I ain't on the Russian weightlifting team," she laughed.

"Baby, are you all right?" Joshua's neighbor, Ms. Christine said.

Elise's first instinct was to remove her arms from around Joshua, but that would only make their compromised position look worse. *Does this woman ever just stay inside her apartment?* she asked herself.

"Oh…he's fine, Ms. Christine. We were looking at some properties and he had a little accident. I'm just making sure he's okay."

"Well, baby, you need to be careful. Can I do anything?" Christine asked in a concerned voice.

"No, ma'am. My realtor here is gonna get me inside. I'll be fine. Thank you," Joshua answered as they went into his apartment unit across from hers.

Joshua showered and returned a few moments later.

"Josh, you big baby. Hold still," Elise ordered as she applied an icepack. "I'm trying but that's not how you do it," Joshua said, trying to hide his discomfort.

"Are you sure you don't need to go to the hospital? I think your hand is broken," Elise said as she tried to lighten her touch.

"It's not broken, Elise," he said, trying to maintain his bravado. "How do you know?" she questioned.

"Because I've broken my hand before and it didn't feel like this," he said as he flexed his hand.

"Well, excuse me, Chuck Norris black version, but I do feel like I need to ask if I'm in any danger. Are you like a hitman and now I'm a loose end?"

Joshua chuckled. "No, Elise, you're not in any danger. I promise. I only use my powers for good. Besides, you know I'd never hurt you."

"Where did you learn to fight like that?" Elise asked, hoping he didn't notice her blushing.

"I did some boxing coming up. Golden gloves. I almost made it to the Junior Olympics," Joshua revealed.

"But Josh, that was more than boxing. You did some other stuff too. Pardon my French, but you beat the hell out that boy. What stuff you on?"

"Yeah," Joshua agreed, impressed that she recognized that he was more than a brawler. "I'm a blackbelt in Brazilian Jiu Jitsu and Krav Maga. But I promise you. That is the first time in my adult life I have used those skills outside a controlled environment. I don't like violence but when he hit that little girl…," Joshua paused.

"You thought about your daughter, didn't you?" Elise said, anticipating his thoughts.

"Yeah. If my little girl were out there like that, I would want someone to defend her."

"Ooh, Joshy, I thought he killed her! I'm glad you protected her… and me. I saw the way you kept yourself between me and him," Elise said as she kissed him on his swollen hand.

"Well, I wasn't really protecting y'all from him. I was protecting him from you. I peeped you with that hand in your purse."

"Haaaaa! Babay, if he would have got past you, I promise he would not have gotten to me. Trust and believe. I would have shot his big tail right through this Louis Vuitton."

"Not through the Louis," Joshua teased.

"Oh, yeah. No fumbling. I had the safety off and errthang. Then I would have gone straight Hollywood. I would have given a Meryl Streep and Viola Davis level performance. "Oh, no!" she said, changing her tone for dramatic effect. "Someone please come help me. It was awful. I was afraid for my life. Look what he did to this beautiful young girl. Look what he did to my boyfr…."

"Boyfr?", Joshua teased, taking pleasure in her near slip.

Elise ignored his meddling and quickly recovered. "Anyway… chocolate Bruce Lee, what do you mean I'm not doing this right? How am I supposed to do it?"

"I usually just submerge the hands in ice-cold water," Joshua explained. "Well, why you ain't just say that?" she said as she removed the icepack. "You want me to get a bowl or something?"

"No, I like this better," he said as he stared into her eyes. "You just said the other way is better," Elise argued.

"It's better for my hand…but I like you doing it this way. Any excuse to hold your hand."

"Holding hands is all we were supposed to be doing last time, sir!"

"I know…but you were the one that started the kissing this time… jus sayin'." "Boy, I was just kissing your little ouchy away," she laughed.

"This hand hurts too," Joshua said slyly.

"Here," she said as she kissed his hand with an obnoxiously loud and totally unromantic smack. "Is that better?"

"The first one was better," Joshua laughed. "The sonic boom isn't required." "Anyway," Elise laughed. "I want to tell you something… before I go. Even though it's not exactly appropriate."

"We left appropriate a long ways back," he said. "Tell me."

"Umm…I felt some kinda way watching you defend my honor tonight," she said.

"Yeah? What 'some kinda way' are you talking about?" he asked.

"Don't worry about all that," she said, avoiding his eyes. "Do you need anything before I go?"

"I have everything I need right here, Elise," he said as he gently stroked her hand. "But speaking of tonight…we did have a little Bonnie and Clyde thing going, didn't we?"

"We did," she agreed nervously, noticing how attractive he was in the simple T-shirt and shorts he had changed into. And the scent of his freshly showered body wasn't helping matters. She knew she needed to leave.

"I have to go, Joshy. Do you need anything else?"

"I told you I have everything I need right here," he said, as he continued stroking her hand.

"Sir! My hand is fine. I'm not the one who's been out brawling, young man." "You don't like that?" Joshua asked.

"Josh…I'd better go," she said nervously.

Joshua laced his fingers with hers. "Okay," he agreed. "You'd better go." "I am. I'm leaving," she said, rather unconvincingly.

Joshua brought her hand to his lips and kissed it. "Bye, Elise."

"See, this is why I didn't want to be here. You aren't trustworthy," Elise argued weakly.

Joshua leaned over to her and kissed her on the cheek. "I know… you were right. You should escape."

"Joshua Dupree! What happened to the nice guy who didn't want to take advantage of me?"

Joshua pulled her closely to him and kissed her softly on the lips. "He had to go. This is the guy who said if he ever got his arms around you again, he wouldn't let you go. This is the guy who said he was in love with you."

"Well, you tell him if he tries to kiss me again, I'm leaving," she said as Joshua pulled her even closer and kissed her again, far more passionately than he had before.

Elise enjoyed it for a moment before pulling away from him. "Josh…we should stop…this is going too far," she protested, placing her finger over his lips. They sat in one another's arms looking at each other, perhaps for just a moment until Elise moved her finger off Joshua's lips and gave herself over to him.

CHAPTER 75

It Just Got Real

DAY 532

Elise lay in Joshua's arms wondering if he was asleep. Wondering if he was at peace. Wondering if the burden of their sin weighed on his heart as heavy as it did hers. All the warnings she had received about this moment came rushing back to her mind. She remembered the young man at the doctor's office. She remembered First Lady pleading with her to skip her first meeting with Joshua. She remembered Shania's warning. She remembered her promise to Mama Etta to take care of her family and to take care of Jeremiah…her husband. She remembered how she had walked away from the Lord and how she had ignored his voice during every interaction with Joshua. Now it was too late. Now, she was an adulteress. She could no longer justify her actions by telling herself that her relationship with Joshua wasn't sexual. She didn't know what she was going to do but she knew she had to leave.

"Josh…are you asleep?" she asked.

Joshua tightened his arms around her waist and kissed her. "No. Are you okay?" he asked.

"No. I'm not," she replied. "I have to go. We shouldn't have done this." "Elise, don't go," he pleaded. "I know it's complicated but we can figure it out."

"Josh…there is no we. I'm married. I can't even describe how I feel right now, but I have to get out of here. I'm sorry for doing this to you, but you know this isn't right. That's why you tried to walk away from me before."

"And I also came back into your life," he reminded her. "I know it's messy. I know what you're feeling. But I don't want to live without you. There's got to be a way for us to make it work."

"Josh, this can't work. You can't introduce me to your mother or to your children. It's all fun and games now, but it won't be when you have to lie to your kids about how we met."

Joshua was silent. Robin was constantly asking him if he was dating. As much as he wanted to tell her about Elise, he couldn't.

"You see?" Elise said, observing his silence. "There's no scenario where Josh and Elise work. I'm not blaming you, but you were right before. I can't stand this. I can't live like this."

"What do you want to do?" Joshua asked her.

"Right now, I'm going to get dressed. Then I have to go."

They put on their clothes and met each other in Joshua's living room.

"Josh, this is going to sound cruel, but I need to say something before I go. This has to be the last time we see each other. For any reason. You are such an amazing man, and you deserve so much better than this. I know I may have just destroyed my marriage, but I love my husband. What we just did is so much bigger than us. There's a lot of collateral damage and I'm sorry you got caught up in my mess. You're an honorable man but this is dishonorable. This is not you. And I don't want it to be me either. Not anymore. We have to let each other go. I mean for real this time. You have to lose my number. We have to pretend this didn't happen."

Joshua knew she was right, but as always, when it came to his soul tie, his emotions overruled his common sense. "But Elise, it did happen. I know you're right, but I don't know if I can just let you go. I know it doesn't make sense and I know we can never be, but I still love you. Can't we just…."

"Joshua, stop it! I'm sorry, but I don't love you. Not like you should be loved. You deserve someone who will love you like you deserve to be loved. Someone you can love freely. That's not me."

"What are you going to do?" he asked.

"I don't know," she shook her head. But you can't be concerned with that anymore. Please don't call, because I won't answer. And I won't respond to your texts. I don't want you to hate me, but I would be hurting you more if I continued these games."

"Well, I need to say something too, Elise. I've always known this was wrong and I am ashamed. I understand we have to end this. It shouldn't have ever started. You say you don't love me. That's fine but I don't care. I still love you and think you are the most amazing woman I've ever met. All I ever wanted to do was be there for you and make you smile. And no matter what happens, I want you to remember that someone out there thinks the world of you and would do anything for you. I want to ask you not to go but I know you have to. I wish I would have been stronger. I'm sorry for putting you in this position."

"Josh, there's plenty of blame to go around. I appreciate you saying that, though. I have to go."

"Can you stay until morning?" he asked her softly.

"Josh, I can't stay. I have clarity now and if I stay it will leave. You will have clarity soon too. And when you get it, please don't think too badly of me," she said as she headed for the door.

Joshua gently put both arms around her as she reached for the doorknob. "Elise, please…I'll never ask you anything again, just stay until morning."

"Josh," she said softly, "do you remember the night you prayed for me in the parking lot?"

"Of course I do," he answered.

"I do too. I remember every word. You told the Lord how I needed him. You asked him to show me his forgiveness. You asked him to give me strength and to heal me. And you asked him to give me grace so I could feel his love again. And you asked the Lord to show me that he hasn't left me. Well, now he is answering that prayer. This is the worst thing I have ever done, but he's here and he's with me now. And he's telling me it's time to stop ignoring him and to get out of here. If you are the man I know you to be and if you truly love me, you will let me go."

Joshua relaxed his arms and, for what he knew would be the last time, kissed her sweetly on the forehead. "I do love you, Elise."

"I know, Josh, and I'm sorry for hurting you. Goodbye."

CHAPTER 76

Come to Jesus

DAY 533

The weight of Elise's failure crushed her spirit as she drove home. The brief peace she had experienced when she left Joshua's apartment had now been replaced by an unbearable conviction. She had tried to leave God behind, but the burden of her heart let her know that he hadn't left her. Now she had to face her failure. Had it really happened? Had she really just had sex with Josh? She had experienced a moment of clarity before she left Joshua. A clarity she wished she would have experienced before she violated her marriage vows. She had no idea what to do next. She had intentionally rebelled against the Lord. It was her payback for him taking her child. *You really showed him,* she thought to herself sarcastically. She tried to think of a way out, but no solution came to mind. She was on the verge of taking her own life before, but Joshua interrupted her. Maybe that was the right idea, after all. She could find some abandoned stretch of road, find out just how fast her Lexus was, close her eyes, and see what would happen. But no, death was much too sweet a reward for her. Her punishment would be living. She would have to look Jeremiah in the eye, tell him what she had done, and face the consequences.

She pulled into her garage as the burdens of her heart and mind multiplied. She placed the key in the lock but couldn't turn it. There was nothing wrong with the key or the door. Her guilt simply wouldn't allow her to go in. She didn't deserve to. This was Jeremiah's parents' home. This was the first place where she was truly loved and accepted. This is where Daddy doted on her and where Mama Etta told her she wanted her son to have a daughter that was just like her. What would they think of her now? The guilt and shame of her sin overwhelmed her as her fingers held the key that had been placed in the door. The door she was no longer worthy to open. She recalled her encounter with the Lord when her son died. He had invited her to a path of grace and healing but in her hurt, she had chosen her own path. That path was longer and darker than she could have ever imagined, and her failure brought tears to her eyes.

Her tears turned to sobs. Her sobs turned to weeping. Her weeping turned to wailing.

She fell to her knees and released her pain to the only one she knew could help her now.

"Jesus, I'm so sorry. What did I do, Lord? I'm so sorry, Jesus. Please forgive me. Please don't leave me, Jesus! I know I have sinned against you, Lord. My God, what did I do? Jesus, please! I know I left you, Lord. Please don't leave me. I don't have anybody else. Please let me come back."

She stayed on her knees, weeping and wailing in remorse until she couldn't feel her legs anymore. Even in the dark of night, the Texas heat buffeted her body until she was drenched in sweat, but she continued her plea. She pleaded with tears to the God she had abandoned. She prayed he would hear and forgive. When her knees could no longer take the stress of the hard concrete, she sat on her backside and pressed on with her cries to the Lord she had turned away from. Her heart and her head pounded from her wailing.

She sat there with her back to the door, covered with sweat and tears. Burdened by sin and shame. Only now, after she had thrown everything away, did she begin to understand just how far she had fallen. But also, more than ever, she realized that she had not been, nor was she ever, alone. She kept repeating her remorseful plea and slowly, her screams returned to sobs. Her tears still streamed down her face, but she no longer wailed. She simply spoke softly.

"Lord Jesus, I have sinned against you, the husband you gave me, and so many others. I am wrong and I am sorry. Please forgive me, Lord, and please help me." Her soft words gave way to a whisper until finally, exhausted, she fell asleep.

She woke a few hours later. She was no less broken and no less ashamed. But her Comforter was there, and she knew she was forgiven. She returned to her knees and clasped her hands together.

"My Precious Lord, I come to you in Jesus' name covered in the blood that purifies me from my wretched sin. I left you and I'm sorry. I still don't understand all the things you have allowed, but you told me not to lean to my own understanding. So, I acknowledge you as my master and I humbly return to you as your servant. I acknowledge you as my king and I bow before you as your subject, giving up my right to rule my own life. I acknowledge you as my creator, the one who has fearfully and wonderfully made me. I acknowledge you as my Good Shepherd and I thank you that it's not really me returning to you, Lord, it is you who left the ninety-nine and came and found me."

Elise's tears began to flow once more. "And Father, I declare by faith the finished work of Jesus Christ on the cross. I appeal to your mercy and ask that when you look at me you remember what Jesus had to go through for me, and I ask that you not treat me like my sins deserve. I am a sinful, angry, selfish, foolish, and adulterous woman. But God, isn't that why you sent Jesus? For a wretched woman like me? So, because of what Jesus did, I unashamedly acknowledge you not just as my Father but as my Daddy, and I ask that even as I smell like the pigs of my hog pen that you let me return to you as your baby girl. I make no excuse for my sin. You did everything you could to keep me from this place but now I am here, and I plead with you in Jesus' name not to make me stay. I want to come back, Daddy. I want to be clean, and I want to be yours again. I know I don't deserve to ask you for anything. I turned away from you because. " Elise paused as she pondered what she was about to say, but she knew the Lord already knew what was in her heart and she needed to get it out.

"Daddy, I'm sorry but I hated you so much when you took my baby from me. All I wanted to do was to love him and to raise him for you. I couldn't understand why you would be so cruel, and I wanted to hurt you like you hurt me. But Daddy, now that I'm here, below rock bottom, I can't bear it. It's too much. I can't live like this, and I can't die. As messed up as I am, I know you still have plans for me even though I don't know what they are. All I can say is that I'm wrong. I have sinned and I am sorry. I know my life may never be the same again. I turned my back on you, but you said that you would be faithful to me even when I was not faithful to you. So please remember your word and let me be an object of your grace. I know what I have to do, Lord, but Jeremiah won't understand. I will take whatever cup you have for me to drink. No matter how bitter. But please, Daddy, he doesn't deserve this. He is your son, and he is your servant. This is on me. Not him. Please, Daddy, after he finishes being mad…after he finishes being hurt… would you heal him, Lord? Won't you please bring him all the way back? I want my husband back. I want what we had before. But I won't ask you that. He deserves better than this. He deserves better than me. So please give your goodness and your grace to him and let the pain stay with me. And Daddy, even if everything falls apart, I ask that you stay with me too. If you will just stay with me, Lord, by your grace and by the filling of your Holy Spirit, I promise I will do my best to stay with you and never leave you again. Daddy, I have sinned against you and there will be so many people who will be hurt by this. Please help them, Lord. Daddy. Pastor G. and First Lady. Shania. My church family. And Daddy, please help Josh. He knows he is wrong just as I do. But he loves you. Have mercy on him and heal him. Please take him to a place of restoration and show him that you have not left nor forsaken him. Daddy, I promised him that when I started praying again, I would pray for his relationship with his son. There's so much to overcome. But Jesus, you said I could speak to the mountain. So, with all the faith you will give me, I say to the mountain of confusion, unforgiveness, and pride, that has estranged Josh from his son, to move in Jesus' name. And Daddy, in Jesus' name, please cover my baby Amari. Lord, if there is any way for me to love her, not for me, but for you and for her, I'll do it. But not my will, your will be done. You can stop me from being her mommy, but I don't think you will stop me from loving her and praying for her. So please take care of her and allow her to grow in your grace. When the people who were supposed to love me were taken away from me, you came and found me and gave me a good life until I turned away from you. So, I trust you to cover this precious baby and protect her by the power of your great name. Daddy, please let me feel your presence again. Please stay with me, Jesus, because I have missed you. I have sinned. I am wrong and I am sorry. But Daddy, I want to come back. I know I smell like the pigs of my hog pen, but I want to come back. If no one else is happy to see me, then I plead with you by the blood of your son that purifies me from my hideous and rebellious sin that you take me back. I pray that you be happy to see me and that you would hug me and hold me and be glad. I know I deserve nothing, but I expect everything I have asked because you are always right, you are always good, and you are always for me. I declare your all-sufficient grace over my life, and I declare that you are still enough for me, Jesus. I love you, Daddy. From my sin-sick soul, I love you. And in faith I thank you for your forgiveness and your goodness. I can't take back what I've done. But please help me and show me what to do from here. What I need can't be done if you won't help. But I put my eyes on you in faith and I trust you. In the name of my risen savior Jesus, I pray, Amen."

Elise stood slowly and reached again for the key that had been in the door all night. Still, she couldn't go in. She knew she was forgiven but she still wasn't ready. She picked up the phone and called the number she should have called long ago.

"Elise?" Shania asked wearily. "What's wrong?" "I messed up, sis… bad," Elise confessed.

"You don't sound good. Where are you?" "I'm home."

"I'm on the way," Shania said emphatically. "No…don't come here! Can I come there?" "You already know…the light will be on."

CHAPTER 77

That's What Friends Are For

DAY 533

Shania brushed her teeth and splashed cold water on her face as she waited for Elise's arrival. They hadn't had a conversation of any substance in months. Something was wrong. Elise's distance made it clear she was hiding something, and her lack of responses to phone calls and texts further clarified that she didn't want any help. Still, Shania held on to hope that her friend would make it to the other side of her storm.

Elise's headlights flashed across Shania's front windows, and she opened the front door to greet her.

"Elise, what did you do?" Shania asked jokingly. "It's four o'clock in the morning!"

Elise said nothing as she walked to her front door. Shania looked at her closely. If her appearance was a sign of what she had been through, then Elise had been through hell. Shania reached out to her for an embrace, but Elise stopped her.

"Uh-uh, girl," she said softly. "I can only imagine how I smell."

Shania wasn't worried about her friend's odor, though. "It's okay, sis. It's good to see you. I've missed you. What happened?"

Elise shook her head and tried to control her emotions. It was one thing for her to come clean to the Lord. But people, though? That was different. And this particular person had warned her very specifically about the destructive road she just got off of.

"Is it Jeremiah?" Shania asked. Elise shook her head.

Even with all she had been through, Elise was still the strongest person Shania knew. What would have her on her doorstep in the wee hours of the morning afraid to even talk? Then she remembered their last significant conversation. She prayed silently, then asked what she already knew.

"Is it Joshua?" she asked.

Elise nodded as a tear escaped her eye.

"You wanna tell me what happened?" Shania asked her.

"What you told me would happen if I didn't get away from him," she confessed.

Shania pulled Elise close and hugged her warmly. "It's going to be all right, sis," she encouraged. "Now let's get you cleaned up. I love you...but you are musty."

Elise laughed in Shania's arms and her laughter surprised her. She didn't think she could laugh, but Shania knew she needed it, and she knew exactly what to say. Shania walked Elise further into the house. "Come on. Let me get you something to change into and get these clothes washed for you. You know where everything is. Go shower... use all the soap you feel like using. Let the Spirit lead you, girl! Oh... and it's a spare toothbrush in there too. Feel free to partake." "Stop it," Elise laughed as she wiped her tears.

"I'm going to splash a little water myself...so if we have to hug again we can both be fresh... and then we can talk. I mean really talk. Cool?"

"Cool," Elise agreed.

Elise returned to the delightful smell of fresh coffee, pancakes, bacon, and eggs.

"Sis, you didn't have to do all of this," Elise said, touched by the gesture. "It's okay. I'm just happy to see you. I haven't been able to love on my bestie

in a while," Shania beamed.

The two sisters enjoyed their early morning breakfast. Elise described the consequences of her rebellion as honestly and transparently as she could. Shania knew of the anguish her friend endured when her son died, but she didn't know of the conscious decision Elise had made to turn away from the Lord. She knew she and Jeremiah were struggling, but she didn't know about Elise's thoughts of suicide. She knew of Joshua and Elise's mutual attraction, but she didn't know she had continued to play with that temptation. Elise told her everything about Joshua and all the steps she took toward the sin she fell into several hours ago. And she also told her how the Lord met her in that hot garage not only with his conviction but also with his mercy.

Elise braced herself for the pending judgment and the well-deserved "I told you so." But it didn't come. Shania simply raised her hands in praise.

"Yes! Praise the Lord! Won't he do it?" she said happily.

"I don't think you heard me right, sis," Elise questioned. "Did you hear the part about me cheating on my husband?"

"I did…and we'll deal with that together. But the most important thing I heard was that you have come back to the Lord. And that deserves a 'Thank you, Jesus!' Woop-woop!"

"Jeremiah isn't going to feel the same way," Elise said sadly. "Sooo… are you going to tell him?"

"Shania…I have to tell him…don't I?"

"Knowing you…probably. It would kill you to hold it. But we need a plan. This is above my paygrade. First Lady Faye is about to call. We need to bring her in on this."

"Why is First Lady calling?" Elise asked.

"Sweetie…First Lady and I pray for you every morning. We pray that the Lord would heal you and give you strength. We pray for you and Jeremiah. We pray for Amari. We pray that you be restored. And we pray that you would come back to the Lord and to us. He's answered that prayer but now we need some wise counsel."

The phone rang as Shania spoke. "That's her calling now. Let me bring her in on this."

"Okay," Elise consented.

"Hey, Sister Faye," Shania answered. "You're not going to believe this, but our lost sheep has returned home. We need to meet up."

CHAPTER 78

Prodigal Daughter

DAY 535

"Baby, why won't you tell me what this is all about?" Pastor Gregory asked Faye. "First you run out the house like it's on fire, saying Elise needs you, and then you got me up here waiting and won't tell me what's going on. I don't like all this cloak-and-dagger James Bond stuff. Since when do we keep secrets?"

"Wayne, all I can tell you is that your daughter needs her pastor. She has some things she needs to tell you, and you should hear those things from her and not from me," Faye explained.

"But you know already?" Pastor Gregory pressed.

"Oh, yeah…I know," Faye nodded knowingly. "That's why we cleared your calendar."

"Is she okay?" Pastor Gregory asked.

"Let her explain when she gets here," Faye answered calmly. "Well, do I need to call Jeremiah?"

"Wayne, no!" Faye exclaimed. "Whatever you do. Don't do that! You need to talk to Elise first."

Elise poked her head around the corner and smiled. "I won't get a better introduction than that," she said.

"Hey, baby girl. It's been too long."

Elise embraced him nervously. Her conversations with Shania and First Lady had gone well. They were appropriately honest with her but also let her know she was still loved. But a conversation with Pastor G.

was next-level and she wasn't sure how he would respond.

"Hey, Pastor G. I've missed you," Elise said as she enjoyed his embrace.

"I've missed you too, daughter." "I'm here too," Shania chimed in.

Pastor Gregory laughed. "Girl, I see yo little jealous self all the time but come on and get in on this."

Shania joined their hug before they all sat down in Pastor Gregory's office. "So, baby girl, First Lady tells me you have some things on your mind you want to share."

Elise took a deep breath. She didn't want to cry as she made her confession. Tears were appropriate for her actions, but she didn't want Pastor G. to think she was trying to illicit sympathy.

"Thank you for meeting me, Pastor. I know you're busy," Elise said.

"No, baby, actually I'm not. My wife cleared my schedule so I could talk to you. But I'm curious as to why someone who has my phone number, a key to my house, and can talk to me anytime she wants to needs to have an appointment… and an entourage just to talk with me."

"Pastor…Shania and First Lady are here for moral support. They know this is very hard and embarrassing for me. You'll understand why in just a little bit. A few months ago…the last time First Lady and I really connected, I wasn't in a good place emotionally and spiritually. Before I left her, she gave me what I now know was a prophetic warning. We were in the middle of our conversation, and I got a phone call from a client I had forgotten about. I told her I had to leave. She asked me… she almost begged me to stay. She said she felt the Lord wanted me to stay but I didn't see the harm of going to an appointment. So, I left. Now I wish I didn't. I wish I would have listened. I wish I would have stayed with First Lady. I wish I hadn't been so caught up in myself that I couldn't hear her or the Holy Spirit."

"And what happened at this meeting that has you here visibly shaking in front of your pastor?"

Elise looked at her hands and indeed she was noticeably shaking.

"Do you need some water, daughter?" Pastor G. asked her softly.

He already knew whatever was coming was going to be a bombshell, but he also knew she needed to go through this process.

Having him call her daughter normally eased her, but now it made her a little afraid. She wondered if he would still feel that way after she disclosed her sin.

"No, sir…," she continued. "I just want to get this out. After I left, I met a client named Joshua. He was such a sweet Christian guy. He was strong, intelligent, funny…and very handsome."

"Sounds like someone else I know," Pastor Gregory added.

"Well…yes, sir," Elise agreed. "And like me, Joshua was going through a tough season of his own. At first, we were just friends. At least that's what I tried to tell myself."

Pastor Gregory's years of experience allowed him to keep a poker face, but his insides trembled as he anticipated what Elise was about to reveal.

"Shania warned me it was more than that, though," Elise continued. "We started hanging out more and more and to make a long story short…I let things go too far."

"Daughter, we're all grown here but I need you to be clear. Please describe what you mean by 'too far.'"

"I slept with him," Elise said plainly, the words sickening her as they came from her mouth.

"And how long has this been going on?" he asked. It may have just been her imagination or her guilt, but Elise couldn't recall him ever sounding so stern with her.

"May I have that water now?" Elise asked as she continued to tremble.

"Of course," Pastor Gregory said gently. He got up and retrieved a cold bottle of water from his refrigerator and poured it into a glass for her.

Elise sipped the water and calmed herself. "Is that better?" Pastor Gregory asked her. "Yes, sir. Thank you."

"So, you were about to tell me how long this has been going on,"

Pastor Gregory continued.

"A few months...I mean us just seeing each other and talking to each other. But I promise I only slept with him once. Afterward...I felt as bad as I've ever felt in my life. I knew I had to end it and I did."

"And so, you've ended the relationship?" "Yes, sir. I did."

"When did this...incident happen?"

"Two nights ago. That's when it happened."

"Elise, I appreciate you being honest. I know that this is difficult, but I'd like to know what you need from me now."

"What I need the most right now is for you to know that I know that I have sinned and I'm sorry. I don't even want to imagine what you think of me right now, but I do want you to know that what you think of me matters. I'm sorry for letting you down. I know God has forgiven me, but I need you to forgive me also. I wish I would have realized it sooner, but it's hard when you're listening to the wrong voice and out there trying to do everything on your own. After it happened, I tried to go home and forget it, but I was just so heavy with guilt and shame that when I tried to open the door, I couldn't. I couldn't go into Daddy and Mama's house like that. I just fell to my knees and began to pray and ask God to forgive me. I know he has but there is still so much anger and hurt and confusion. Pastor, I want to repent, and I want to be restored. I just need to know what you want me to do. And honestly, I need you to help me find another church. Jeremiah isn't going to be able to accept this and once word gets out, I won't be able to stand everyone looking at me. But I'm tired of doing things on my own. I'm tired period. Rebellion is exhausting. So, I will do whatever you say and take whatever discipline you deem appropriate."

"Scooch over, little girl," Pastor Gregory said as he sat beside her on the couch. He placed his arm around her and pulled her close. "Elise... you are my daughter and I love you. I couldn't have loved you more if I had you myself. That won't ever change. Now that being said, you do need yo little but whooped but I can see the Holy Spirit has done that so I won't add to it. You have confessed and you have repented, so there is no further need for discipline. Don't think this old pastor don't know there are far more scandalous things than this going on in God's house that I never hear about. Then they come up in here all willy-nilly like ain't nothing been done. So as hurt as I am to find you in this position, I honor you for your integrity and bringing this out into the light. As far as restoration goes, you are going to need to reengage with my beautiful wife. The hard truth is, the Lord wanted to use her to keep you from this hour, but you did things on your own and the devil took advantage."

"What about Jeremiah? When should I tell him? Should I tell him?" Elise asked, hoping her pastor had another suggestion.

"What do you think?" Pastor Gregory asked.

"I think I lose either way. If I don't tell him, I will lose my mind with guilt. If I do tell him, I lose him."

"What do you think the best thing you can do from here is?"

"I think I have to tell him and face the consequences," she answered simply. "I agree. It's going to be ugly, but Jeremiah is a good man."

"I don't suppose you can just tell him for me and call me when it's over?" Elise asked only half-jokingly.

"Ha. No…I won't do that," Pastor Gregory said. "He should hear it from you, but I will be with you if you want. This isn't the first time we've had to deal with something like this. We'll sit down with you and give you some steps to assist you in your confession. But it needs to be done sooner rather than later. The longer you wait, the harder it will be. And no matter what, it's not going to be easy, daughter. I think you know that. The devil came into your house, but you and Jeremiah both left some doors open. Our appeal to the Lord should be for wisdom, mercy, and reconciliation. I am assuming you want reconciliation. Is that true?"

"I do,". Elise answered. "But I don't know if I have it in me to ask Jeremiah for that. I never thought I'd be in a situation like this. I think a part of me always thought I was in control and nothing was going to happen."

"That's how sin gets us, daughter. It baby-steps us into catastrophe as we ignore the warnings and convictions of the Holy Spirit. And it always takes us further than we ever planned to go and makes us stay longer than we ever wanted to stay. But you serve a Good Shepherd and now when it's darkest, you have to trust him. And as his under shepherd, as your pastor, and one of your daddies, I need you to know you already have a church home. Now if the Holy Spirit leads you someplace else then his will be done, but don't let the devil have more victory by making decisions based on guilt and shame."

Elise lay her head on Pastor G's shoulder as First Lady and Shania looked at her. She searched their eyes for anger and judgment and found none. She felt foolish for choosing not to see any of the wisdom they had tried to impart. She felt sad for pushing her friends away when they most wanted to be there for her. But she also felt joy. She had fallen as far as she could, and they were still there with her.

"Pastor, I still don't believe this is me," Elise said sadly. "I can't believe I let it get to this. I don't even recognize myself. I don't know if I'm going to make it back from this.

"You will, daughter," Pastor Gregory said as he pulled her a little closer. "Master, we just want to praise you for your Son Jesus. And we want to praise you for your daughter Elise. Her sin has left her so bruised and bloodied that she can barely recognize herself. But we thank you, Jesus. You were bruised and bloodied so bad you could barely be recognized. You did it for her, Lord. She's wounded, Jesus, but you were wounded for her iniquity. Her heart is pierced by her failure, but you were pierced for her transgressions. Lord Jesus, we give thanks for your stripes that heal the breach between Elise and a holy God. Master, she is sorry for her sin, so please restore her and please heal her. Bring fresh springs to the dry ground and restore her once again. We pray for wisdom to know the next step and that those steps would lead to your glory. And we pray for Jeremiah, who's about to get more bad news. We pray you sustain him with the good news of what Jesus Christ did for him on the cross and that you remind him that he is still in your hands. And Father, where it looks the worst, we hold you to your promise to make all things work together for good for Elise and Jeremiah. They still love you and they are still called to your purpose. In your sovereignty, Master, you've let the devil have his day. This is Elise's Friday. The enemy has had his apparent victory, and it looks like he's won another one. But in Jesus' name, I am believing you for a Sunday resurrection that will defeat the devil and put him back in his place once again. And that place is under Elise and Jeremiah's feet. You said nothing was too hard for you, Master. Show us that word now, because if you don't show up and show out…it can't happen…and it won't happen…but our eyes are on you. So, we give our daughter back to you, Lord, covered in the blood of Jesus that purifies her from her sin. She's come running back to you. So, as your servant, I run to her, eager to represent you. Lord, you know she's like a daughter to me, but she was your daughter first and always."

Pastor Gregory leaned over and kissed Elise on the top of her forehead as he continued to pray. "So let this earthly kiss be received as from a forgiving Heavenly Father who is happy to have his child back."

He took his other arm and wrapped it snugly around her. "May these arms be received as yours, representing your warmth and your covering."

He took her hand in his and gently stroked her finger. "I don't have a ring for her, Lord, but as I hold her hand, let it represent a ring on her finger so that she knows in her spirit she is a beloved daughter of the King. And Father, we are going to celebrate. I don't have a fattened calf but it's a dead cow somewhere around here, and we are going to make sure he did not die in vain as we celebrate your daughter's return. In Jesus' mighty name we pray, Amen."

Elise felt at peace, but she still had to talk to Jeremiah. The people who mattered the most had forgiven and received her back. She wasn't sure he would be able to do so.

CHAPTER 79

Homecoming

DAY 537

Elise cleaned every inch of the house and made sure everything was in its place. Jeremiah was on his way, and she was going to have to tell him about her infidelity. His life was about to be turned upside down…again. The least she could do was make sure the man came home to a clean house.

Now that the house was immaculate, she wanted to look good for him as well. She wore her hair in natural curls the way he liked it best. Her outfit was casual. She didn't want to overdo it. She simply wanted to be pretty for him. She wore well-fitting ripped skinny jeans and a casual blouse she knew he liked to see her in. She had bathed and sprayed herself with his favorite fragrance. If he was going to leave her, at least part of him was going to regret it.

She looked fine on the outside, but her external appearance wasn't going to help when she let her husband know what she had done. She freshened up her lipstick as the weight of her sin bore down on her again. The last time she had gotten cute for a man wasn't for Jeremiah. It was for Joshua. As immoral as their relationship was, Joshua cared for her. She recalled their last conversation and prayed it was enough closure for him. So far, he had respected her requests and hadn't reached out. She wondered how he was but resisted every urge to call. That door was closed and needed to stay that way.

Now all she could do was wait for Jeremiah. She had rehearsed dozens of scenarios in her mind. None of them seemed likely paths to reconciliation. She knew eventually Jeremiah would forgive her. But staying with her was another story. She had broken his trust and her covenant with him. He would be justified in leaving. As much as she wanted them to reconcile, she wasn't sure if she could ask him for it. That would be up to him.

She prepared her heart for the worst. Or at least the worst she could imagine. Shania's imagination was far more extreme. "Girl, I love Jeremiah too," she had said. "But there's no telling what that man will do when you tell him. I'm going to hide up in the guest bedroom closet and if I hear some mess…it's on. You messed up but that doesn't mean he gets to act crazy!"

But Elise insisted that Jeremiah would never hurt her. It simply wasn't in his nature. He might yell. He might cry. He might leave. But he wouldn't hurt her. She would be the one doing all the hurting today. She started to rehearse her confession again, but time ran out as she heard Jeremiah's keys at the front door.

She rushed to the front door and fell into his arms. It had been a while since she made him feel welcome. That gesture alone might cause him to suspect something was wrong, but it didn't matter. This could be the last time she felt his embrace.

"Hey, handsome, how are you?" she asked as sweetly as she could.

As she thought, he wasn't expecting that kind of welcome. "Hey, Elise. I'm good…wow…you smell nice. Did I forget something? Are we supposed to go somewhere? I'm sorry if I forgot. There's been a lot happening."

"No, you didn't forget anything. I just missed you and wanted you to come home to something nice. I was gonna cook but there are some things I need to tell you first. Miah, I'm sorry. You can't imagine how sorry I am and how I wish I could get these last few months back. If I could, I promise you I would do everything differently. You are an amazing husband and I let everything we've gone through make me lose sight of that. I need you to know how much I love you. I know I've messed up and I've been awful, but I do, Miah. I've been away from you. I've been away from church. I've been away from God. I've been away from me, and you deserve so much more and…."

"Lise…please," Jeremiah stopped her. "I don't think you're the one that needs to be apologizing. But you're right. We really do need to talk."

Jeremiah led her to the couch and sat down next to her.

"Miah, this is going to be hard…," Elise started, but Jeremiah cut her off again. "Babe, please. I know you have a lot on your mind, and I want to hear you.

But you communicate better than I do, and I need to get this stuff off my chest while I have it fresh in my mind. So, me first…okay?"

"Okay," Elise agreed, not particularly minding her brief reprieve.

"Babe, I'm sorry too. I always felt like we were a team. But when I lost my job and got hurt, you stepped up and started to shine like I never could have imagined. And I didn't handle it well. I should have been thankful that God blessed me with someone like you who could hold things down when I couldn't. It's hard to explain but I really felt weak and helpless. I stopped feeling like a man and I stopped acting like your man. And it wasn't your fault. You tried to be encouraging and supportive. You tried to make me feel good about myself even though you were hurting as well. Lise, I should have told you how much I appreciated you but I'm telling you now. Babe, you're amazing and I want you to know that I see you. And even though I didn't say it or express it as much, I never stopped. We would be here all day if I told you how much I appreciate you. The way you watched out for Mama. The way you still watch out for Pop. The way you hold it down here at the house and in your business. I promised you it would be Miah and Lise against the world, and I let you feel like you were by yourself and for that, I'm sorry. I didn't consider you like I should. I should have told you the truth…but I was being prideful."

"The truth about what?" Elise asked. Part of her almost hoped that he had a confession that would rival hers. Perhaps if he did, they could just call it even and move forward.

Jeremiah's emotions overtook him. He tried to control himself but he started to cry. "It's still hard to talk about," he said.

Elise let her guilt and shame go. Her husband needed his wife and regardless of her failure, she was going to be there for him.

"Can I sit in your lap, baby?" she requested meekly, For the first time in their life together, she wasn't sure what he would say.

Jeremiah nodded as he continued weeping. Elise shifted positions, sat in his lap, and pulled his head close to hers.

"What is it, baby? Whatever it is, it's okay," she assured him.

"Babe," he said, calming himself. "I think I could have handled a lot of things. The job. Them threatening to take my freedom. Mama dying. Pop being sick. Even when I had to take Amari out of your arms and listen to her scream, I knew God was going to show up. But when I woke up and you told me J.J. was gone? Babe, that took my soul. Then I had to watch you scream on that church floor and I couldn't even get down there and hold you. I knew you were trying to get Amari back and all I could do was lay up in the hospital. You were seeing about Pop and me. And my faith was shaken like you wouldn't believe. I felt like God did this to us and I was mad. But I couldn't say it like I wanted to. I'm not saying this to judge you because I understand, but I know you were struggling in your faith also. I didn't know how to say I was too. I should have grabbed your hand and said let's do this together. Let's trust God and fight our way back. But I didn't. All those things just made me feel so weak and so useless."

Elise gently wiped the tears from his face. "Miah, I never thought you were weak. I never thought you were useless. There's a lot I haven't shared with you. Your faith may have been shaken when we lost J.J., but mine was destroyed. You were hurt, angry, and confused but you kept praying and you kept calling on the Lord. I don't blame you for this, but you were so broken, and when I turned to you…you weren't there. I know it wasn't because you didn't want to be. You just couldn't be. Daddy got sick and he couldn't be there. And instead of turning to the Lord, I turned…to other things."

"You mean like the drinking?" Jeremiah asked.

"Well, yes, that…and maybe some other things too. And now I have so many regrets but you're not one of them. You're still the greatest man I know. And no matter what happens, I want you to know that."

Jeremiah pulled her as close as he could. "Thank you for saying that, baby.

But I know I messed up. And I know what you want to talk to me about." Elise's heart skipped a beat. "You do?" she asked.

"I do," he said plainly. "You want to tell me that you're tired and that our marriage is falling apart. Every day I feel you getting further and further away from me. We've stopped communicating. We've stopped laughing. We've stopped praying. We've stopped making love. We've stopped being Miah and Lise. And I have to take responsibility for all that. I want you back. I want this back. Like now, you in my arms, us being us. Like we used to be."

Elise breathed a sigh of relief. She wanted to enjoy this moment for just a little while longer. "Miah, I want us back too but to be honest, it seems like it was such a long time ago. So much has changed, and we've lost so much. And there's so much you don't know."

"I know this," Jeremiah said firmly. "I love you, and I will not lose you. Until lately we never fought, but you need to know that I will fight anybody that tries to take Elise Janelle Traylor away from me. Even Elise Janelle Traylor. So, you can leave me if you want. But I'm coming with you so you may as well stay here."

Elise laughed. "So, you just gon follow me?"

"Ya durn skippy!" he said with an exaggerated nod. "You gon feel foolish tryna sell all them houses and properties with me following you around singing 'Baby Come Back.'"

"Miah, I'm happy but I didn't expect this. Where is all this coming from?" "It took a second, but I finally realized I needed to tell you all those things I just told you. You don't do well in the dark…not knowing what's happening in my head. I prayed about it and realized if I just communicated with you that you would do exactly what you just did. What you've always done…listen, love me, and support me."

"Yeah…Miah, I wish you would have done this sooner," she said sadly. "I'm sorry, Babe. But I'm doing it now while it can make a difference. Plus," he smiled brightly, "there's a lot you don't know either." "Like what?" she asked.

"Like, it's over. We've received notice from the Justice Department that I am no longer a person of interest in their investigation. They have dropped all charges against me. And I have a meeting with Jacebre tomorrow. They know I'm in a position to sue them. My lawyers think they want to settle before that happens."

"What do you want the outcome to be?" Elise asked him.

"You know lawyers…they want to go for the kill, but I don't want to destroy the company. There's a lot of innocent people who work there. I just want to get my name back and just what's due me."

"I'm sure you'll do what's right. You always do," she encouraged.

"No, I don't. It wasn't right of me to leave you like I did. I should have listened. I should have stayed. God was already working things out. You were right. We didn't even need the money. It would have been better all around if I would have just stayed with you like you asked."

"That's all I really wanted. I wanted you to stay. If you had…things would have been different," Elise said as she thought about how this beautiful moment was about to be destroyed.

"Well, things are going to be different," he said confidently. "Chad offered me another job, but I turned it down."

"Why?" she asked.

"It would be a lot more travel and I would be gone half the time. Now that this job is over, I don't ever want to be away from you like that again. We can decide later what our next move is…together."

"Wait…what? The job's over? I thought you had at least two more months?" "What can I say?" he smiled brightly. "I was highly motivated to get back to you, so I thought outside the box, sweet talked our crews, burned the midnight oil, and knocked that mug out. I had to get back to my wife and my best friend." His words brought a smile to her face.

"Yeah, that too. I had to get back to that smile. I missed it. And since you're smiling, I want you to pray about something with me."

"Of course," she agreed. "Whatever you want."

"Lise, I know what the doctor said but what we have is special. We should share it. I know we can't replace Amari or J.J., but I want us to adopt."

Jeremiah's words warmed Elise's soul. This was more than she could have dreamt. "Miah, I can't tell you how happy that would make me," she said. "I would love to share our life with a baby. That is if you could ever forgive me and we could start over."

"Babe, quit saying that. It's on me. I'm your husband. I should have covered you and loved you. I know you're not perfect, but you don't have to be. You're perfect for me. I know there are a lot of questions, but you don't have to have all the answers. We'll find them together. Miah and Lise against the world will always be enough. I guess what I'm really saying is… '*You don't have to be rich to be my girl*'…there's my smile. '*You don't have to be cool to rule my world*'…uh-oh, I'm gettin' a blush. '*Ain't no particular sign I'm more compatible with, I just want your extra time and your*'…Come on, babe, don't leave me hangin'."

"Kiss!" she said as she leaned in and pressed her lips to his. "I love you, Miah.

I missed you so much, baby."

"I love you too, Lise. But I know you have some things on your mind too. So go ahead. I'm listening."

He looked so happy and at peace. He was holding the woman he loved and didn't have a care in the world. She told herself it would be cruel to do this to him now.

"Miah, I do have some things to talk about," she said. "But you kinda got me speechless. We can talk later. For now, can we just sit here and hold each other? Is that okay?"

"Whatever you want, babe."

CHAPTER 80

Recompense

DAY 537

"You sure you don't want me there, Paul?" Fred asked. "I don't like you doing this without legal in the room. It could get ugly."

"Oh…it's going to be ugly," Paul confirmed. "But this is going to be more of a father-son conversation. Once he sees the facts, it'll be okay. I know it sounds funny, but he'll do what's best for the business. Besides, it's really not up to him, is it?"

"No, it's not," Fred agreed. "I just hoped I could spare you this duty."

"It's necessary, Fred. I'll be okay. I'm going in now. I'll call you when it's over. And no matter what you hear…don't come in that room."

Paul was partially joking, but he was fully aware his pending conversation with Case could escalate quickly.

"Case, we need to talk," he told him seriously as he entered his office.

True to form, Case didn't bother to look up from his desk. "I'm busy right now, Paul. Talk to me later. I have a lot of fires to put out."

"I do too, Case. The biggest fire is blazing in this room."

Paul reached over the desk and closed Case's laptop with a defiant authority Case wasn't used to.

"What in the hell do you think you're doing?" Case asked.

Paul sat down. Another bold move, considering he wasn't invited to do so.

But he wasn't in the mood to wait to be invited to do anything.

"Case, I've been wracking my brain trying to figure out so many things. And all my questions start with why."

"Like why did I lose my mind and get thrown out of my father's office? Because that's a why you're going to be asking yourself real soon, son," Case threatened.

"No," Paul responded firmly. "It's more like 'Why couldn't you just do things on the up-and-up? Why was winning so important that you were willing to lose everything? Why do you have no integrity and no conscience? And why, if you had to do all of this dirt, couldn't you just take it on your own head? Why would you try to destroy an innocent man? And why did I believe you?"

"Paul…you got about five seconds before I forget you're my son and throw you out of here on your little ass."

"Five-four-three-two-one," Paul said defiantly. "Now if you're finished posturing, I'll let you know what's going on. Kinda like when you came to my house over a year ago to explain the charges against us…or the way you spun it… against Jeremiah. But the difference is, what I'm about to tell you is the truth. That's more than what you did for me, Case."

"Okay, that's enough. Get out!" Case yelled.

"No, I will not," Paul said firmly. "You're going to listen to me first and when I'm finished, you're going to be the one who has to get out. Three weeks ago, the FBI contacted me. They gave me a full update on the investigation."

"They contacted you? Why?" Case asked. "And why are you just now telling me?"

"Because after what they told me, I had to do what was best for the company. I came in here to tell you they don't believe a word about what you said about Jeremiah. They couldn't find anything to support that he was the mastermind behind anything illegal concerning Vista Ridge or any other past projects. But you know what they did find, Case? And you should listen, because this affects you. They found that all roads of anything illegal or unethical led back to Case McBride. It even seems some of your friends have confirmed what you've been doing. The FBI went after them too, but you were the big fish, and they all sold you out for leniency. I've sat down with legal and to make a long story short…you're out, Case."

"Are you serious?" Case asked. "Do you think I'm going to let you or anybody else take my company…the company I built on my blood, sweat, and tears?"

"Case, you built it on your inheritance and lies. And that's the sad part. You didn't have to. We have a great team here, and you chose to sell out one of your most vital people as an insurance policy instead of just turning him loose so we could all succeed. Now I know it's in your nature to fight. That's fine, but you need to know the battle for control is over. You need to worry about the battle for your freedom. I've agreed to pay the maximum fines and penalties in hopes that they won't come after you for a maximum jail sentence. But Case, there will be some jailtime."

Paul paused and looked at his father. "Wow…do you hear that, Case?"

"I don't hear anything," Case responded solemnly as he processed what he had just heard.

"That's right. Sounds like after all these years I have finally gotten your attention. This is not the way I saw it happening, but whatever."

"So, what are you going to do?" Case asked far more calmly than Paul expected.

"Eventually I'm gonna change the name and try to start fresh. You've never given me much credit but I'm good at this, and believe it or not, I don't want what you've built to be destroyed. But I'm gonna do it right. We may not be the biggest or the best, but we'll have ethics. For now, I'm going to have to lay off more employees because we've done nothing but lose business since all this happened. I don't think it's a coincidence either. Nothing has gone right for this company since Jeremiah left. And I'm going to talk to him too. I'm going to try to convince him not to sue us for everything we're worth."

"Sounds like you have all the answers, Paul."

"No, I don't," Paul disagreed. "I have one more question and I'd like an answer. I think I know why you did it. I don't agree with you…

but I understand. My question is, why didn't you ever tell me what you were doing?"

"I knew something like this could happen," Case said. "I didn't think it would, so I rolled the dice. I didn't want you involved, though. I wanted you clean. That's why the FBI came and talked to you about fines and not jailtime. There was never any suspicion about you because I kept you out of it. I created a whole new business strategy to keep you out of it. It was a smart business move to keep the company in the family and whether you want to acknowledge it or not, it was a way for me to protect my son."

"And Jeremiah?" Paul asked.

"Jeremiah wasn't ever going to go to jail. And I wouldn't either if my so- called friends had just kept their mouths shut," Case said, shaking his head as he thought about the weakness of his co-conspirators.

"Case, the man lost his job and his reputation. With the way things are now, if he comes in here guns blazing, we could still lose this company."

"Well…no plan is perfect," Case shrugged.

"You don't even care, do you?" Paul asked, amazed at his father's lack of concern for his wrongdoing.

"Paul, I'm not a good man. You haven't figured that out yet? You've spent your whole life trying to get my approval but me sitting here, talking to you now, letting you chastise me, that's as good as it will ever get. So, take the win and let me know what I need to do. I don't lose often but I have a feeling this is what it's like. So, what now?"

Paul shook his head in disbelief. This man was about to lose everything and there was still not a bit of remorse.

"By the time you open that laptop up again, you'll be locked out of all company systems. As of this morning, you are no longer the CEO of Jacebre Construction. A letter of termination has been sent to your home address and personal email. I'll help you as much as I can with the legal side. I suggest you cooperate with the authorities. It should help get any prison time reduced. And…Dad, if it means anything, I'm going to do everything I can to stick with you through all of this."

"Well…son…if it's all the same to you, I'd rather you focus on making sure this company doesn't go under. Is security coming?"

"No, they're not. I'll get all your personal items and bring them to you later.

That's more than what Jeremiah got."

"Yeah, when you talk to Jeremiah, tell him no hard feelings," Case said rather nonchalantly.

"Case, when I talk to Jeremiah, I am going to mention you as little as possible."

CHAPTER 81

Vindication

DAY 538

"Jeremiah, I still don't like this. You could get a lot more," Jeremiah's lawyer complained. He wasn't at all pleased with the deal Jeremiah was about to settle for. "They have no sympathy for you, sir, I don't see why you're letting them off the hook."

"Mr. Jackson, I'm not," Jeremiah explained. "But there are decades' worth of friendships out there and I'm not going to sink the company. They have families and it's not their fault. Bring them back in and just get what I asked for. This foolishness cost me and my wife our home. I'm not going to be the reason these other people lose their homes as well. But you make sure they have to honor our stipulations for being so generous."

Mr. Jackson looked at Elise for support. They had been hammering out the details of a settlement with Jacebre's legal team all morning. But Jeremiah was leaving a small fortune on the table.

"Mrs. Traylor, are you okay with all of this?"

Elise put her hands on Jeremiah's shoulder. Neither of them knew it, but she was just happy to be invited. She didn't want Jeremiah to be taken advantage of, but she didn't want to undermine him either.

"Mr. Jackson," she said, "my husband is loyal. Sometimes to a fault. But he's reasonable. Miah, is it okay for me to drive? I know what you want but I also know what you need. When they come back in, let me talk to them."

Jeremiah gently clasped Elise's hand. "You heard her, Mr. Jackson.

Call them in and let Elise get us across the finish line."

Paul and Fred rejoined them in the conference room.

"Gentlemen," Elise started, "we've reviewed your offer, and it's not going to work for us."

"Mrs. Traylor," Fred interjected, "I don't think you understand, it's not just a matter of what we want to do. It's a matter of what we're able to do. To be blunt, you can't get blood from a turnip. This company is literally hanging on by a thread and simply can't offer anything more lucrative."

Elise leaned forward and retained her smile. "No, Fred, I think it's you and Jacebre that doesn't understand. You don't understand how many nights my husband worked late into the night to make sure your projects were handled correctly. I would have to bring him his dinner to make sure he didn't starve. You don't understand that when matters were entrusted to him, there was plenty of blood flowing. The Jacebre he left was growing and flourishing." Elise cocked her head to the side. "Hmm, I wonder what happened?"

"Listen, Jeremiah…," Fred said, ignoring Elise's words. Jeremiah leaned forward in his chair, indignant at his rudeness.

"Oh, no. No, no, no. Don't do that, Fred," Elise whispered as she calmed Jeremiah with a simple touch. "To be clear, sir, you're talking to me now. Let's keep it professional. You see how my husband's whole countenance just changed? That's because he knows I can't stand to be interrupted or ignored. And if I get my little feelings hurt, he's going to feel like he has to go all hero mode and it's going to be a whole Will Smith and Chris Rock thing. Besides, that question was rhetorical. We all know what happened. Now as I was saying, you don't understand what you did to our family and to his reputation. You don't understand how many opportunities he turned down out of loyalty to this company. Now, we know that the primary culprit in all of this has been dethroned, but the damage to our family has been done. Jacebre needs to step up and make it right. Your current offer doesn't do that. But fortunately for you, my husband is not a vengeful man, and he's loyal to the remaining staff you have left. Your offer is not acceptable, but we can accept one hundred percent of every dime he would have made in the time period where you illegally and illegitimately terminated him. That also includes the bonuses he would have received as a vice president."

"But he was only a vp for a few months!" Fred objected.

"Chris…I mean…Fred, sir. I'm about to let my husband's hand go," Elise warned with a slightly devilish grin. "And we also want that same pay for the next twelve months. And this gentleman over here, Mr. Jackson. He costs us a lot of money. We want one-hundred-percent reimbursement for our legal fees."

"Agreed," Paul said.

"Paul, hold on," Fred objected. "Fred…agreed," Paul said sternly.

"Aww, thank you, Paul," Elise said sweetly before changing her tone. But I'm not quite finished. When all this started, you did press conferences and interviews, putting dirt on my husband's name. Now, you can't really fix that. But you need to try. We want that same energy. We want press conferences and interviews and every form of social media brought to bear as Jacebre Construction makes it clear that Jeremiah Traylor is innocent and has been lied on, slandered, and libeled. Fred, I know that sounds like a lot. Your instinct is going to be to fight it out in court. But Fred…that's lowdown dirty and if you'd be honest, that's why you're here now. You know this is right and fair. Plus, if you lose, you're really going to be in trouble. Word on the street is that Jacebre is losing contracts left and right, and the jobs you do have are all over budget and behind schedule. So do what is right and maybe things will turn around for you. But remember why my husband is being so generous…no more of these layoffs. You need to protect the people you have left and this very generous settlement will give you a little breathing room and hopefully…prayerfully you can restore this company."

"Elise," Paul chimed in, "we can make that happen. You're right. It's more than fair. Thank you for getting us to this point. But Jeremiah, I do have some things I want to say. First, I apologize. It should have been plain as day what was going on but we didn't see it. We didn't want to. And I want to let you know that if you could ever get over all of this, there's a place here for you. I appreciate what your wife said. My goal is to restore this company with excellence and integrity. You're what we need to do it. I'll get totally out of your way and let you do your job. And you can write your own ticket."

"Paul, what ticket?" Elise asked. "Sweetie, y'all ain't got no money!"

Paul laughed out loud. "Well, that's why we need your husband, Elise. Please, Jeremiah, give it some thought. Let's build it back right."

CHAPTER 82

A Future and a Hope

DAY 538

"What are you over there smiling about?" Elise asked Jeremiah as they drove home.

"You, babe. Asking for the extra year was on point. But the press conference, social media, and the bonus? I never would have thought of that. It's a good thing for them we weren't going for the kill cuz you woulda showed no mercy," Jeremiah said.

"Nope…no mercy when it comes to you, baby," she said sweetly. "Besides, it was getting late, and I have an appointment this afternoon. I had to move things along."

"Babe, for real though, why'd you call Paul out talking about they ain't got no money? You was all professional and then went straight street on him," Jeremiah laughed.

"I was street?" she asked. "I thought you were going across that table at Fred!" "Babe, I was on the way. I mean…I wasn't gon actually hurt the man but don't

look past my wife when she's obviously trying to help the situation."

"Well, strange as it sounds, I hope it works out for them. I like Paul. He's sweet," Elise said.

"I do too. And thank you, babe. It's no guarantee what would have happened if we went to court, and I really wanted to get this behind us."

"Thank you for trusting me. I know Mr. Jackson was pressing you to fight for more money, but I know why you didn't want to. I just wanted you to be treated right. We should go celebrate when I get back from my meeting."

"That's cool but speaking of celebrating…are we good?" he asked seriously.

Elise wondered what he was fishing for. "Yeah, Miah. We're good. Why do you ask?"

"I'm asking because last night, I felt like we really connected for the first time in a while. It was like we had a fight and made up. But we didn't make up like we usually do. I was just wondering if you were still feeling some kind of way about things. About me?"

Elise scrambled for a response. Jeremiah was definitely in the mood last night. She had made up an excuse, but the reality was she didn't feel comfortable making love to Jeremiah so soon after being with Joshua. She wanted every part of their intimacy back. But Jeremiah wouldn't feel the same once he knew what she had done. Making love to him without him knowing the truth would only add to her betrayal and his humiliation.

"Miah, baby. I need you to be patient with me," she explained. "You know I have to process things sometimes, and the reality is we've been apart for a while. I just need some time."

"Does this have anything to do with what you said you needed to talk to me about?"

"Yes, it does. But right now, isn't the time. Okay?"

"Okay," he agreed. "I said things were going to be different so if you need time, you can have it."

"Speaking of time," Elise said, seeking to change the subject, "what are you going to do with all your free time? Are you going to take Paul's offer and go back to Jacebre?"

"Lise, I think Jacebre's in my rearview mirror. I meant what I said. I don't want to be away from you anymore. You said it in the meeting. A lot of times you had to come up to the office just to see me. I wanna work and be productive and provide, but God is calling me to do it in a different way. I didn't tell you this part, but Chad actually offered me two jobs."

"What?! Praise the Lord. So, technically you have three different offers.

What's the other job from Chad about?"

"He wants me to refurbish a house for him,". Jeremiah explained. "I think I want to do it. Before, it was just going to be an opportunity to get some extra cash while I…sorry…while we, figured things out. Now, thanks to your fierce negotiation skills, I don't need the money, but I still want to do it. When I was working on our house and everything was coming together, it was work but it was fun too. I enjoyed myself. And I find myself really looking forward to this project. So now I think I want to get into the house-flipping business. What do you think?" Elise's face beamed with excitement. "Miah, that's a wonderful idea and you would absolutely kill it! I've told you for years you don't need to work for anybody, so if you want to do your own thing you have my full support." "Your full support?" Jeremiah asked her.

"No, Miah. Just my partial support," she answered sarcastically. "Yes. My full support. What's that look for?"

"Well, I was thinking. I got all the technical things locked down. I can organize all the work that needs to be done and coordinate with all the trades. And I can make the properties ready to sell."

"But?" Elise grinned.

"Get that look off your face," he smiled.

"No, I'm just wondering," she said. "You're going to have all these properties you're flipping, and we both know they're going to be beautiful. What else could you possibly need?" Elise asked with feigned innocence.

Jeremiah shook his head. He loved that she could still see through him. "I need someone who really has an eye for viable properties to make sure I don't buy something that's a loser investment. Then I need someone who can sell snow to a polar bear so I don't get stuck with the properties. Do you know anybody who can help me with that?"

"Oh, I may know someone like that," she smiled. "But with global warming and the ice caps melting, selling snow to a polar bear really isn't that hard. Ooh, Miah, you remember that documentary you made me watch? That poor mommy polar bear was out there swimming the far reaches of the ocean looking for an iceberg for her and her little bitty baby bears. It was so sad."

Jeremiah shook his head and smiled. "Yeah, I remember, babe. Umm, you wanna come back now?"

"Oh, yeah. Sorry, Baby. Yes, I'm back," she said. "So, you're in?" Jeremiah asked.

"All the way in, baby. Always and forever. Miah and Lise against the world.

You fix 'em up and I'll sell 'em."

"Let's run it!" Jeremiah said as he fist-bumped her. "I was hoping you would say that. I have a few notes on a business plan. Can we talk about it tonight?"

"Yes, we can talk as soon as I get back from my meeting."

Elise was elated but her chest was tight. Jeremiah was making plans for the future and wanted her involved in every way. But he still didn't know what she had done. Days had gone by, and she still had not revealed the truth. She wondered if she should just let it be. Telling him would ease her guilty conscience but it would also break his heart… and destroy their marriage. Perhaps she should just live with her failure and move on.

CHAPTER 83

Duty Calls

DAY 538

"Hey, Sister Vickie! How are you?" Jeremiah answered cheerfully.

"I'm fine, Brother Jeremiah. Are you busy? I heard you were back in circulation."

"Yes, ma'am. I'm back in town. I was working on a business plan but it's not urgent. Between us, Elise is going to do most of the work anyway," he laughed. "She's the brains of the operation, but don't tell her I said that."

"Haaaa. I won't say a word, Brother. But you have to pay me back with a favor."

"Sure. What do you need?" Jeremiah asked, eager to help.

"We have a new member who's only recently moved into town, and no one has gone by to visit with her yet. Do you have time to go by and welcome her to the church?"

"Of course, I can do that. Do you think she's available now? I can do it before Elise gets back home."

"That's wonderful. Her name is Christine Anderson. I will send you her address and phone number."

"That's perfect," Jeremiah said. "I will reach out to her and try to meet with her today."

CHAPTER 84

Say What?

DAY 538

"This church is something else! I have never experienced anything like it before," Christine said. "You all have made me feel so at home."

"Well, it is your house," Jeremiah joked.

Christine tapped him gently on his knee and laughed. "You know that's not what I mean. I'm talking about the homey feel of the church and how everyone makes you feel so loved and welcome. And it's so sweet of you to come to my little ole place to check on me."

"Yes, ma'am. I love to do it, but Pastor Gregory also insists on it," Jeremiah explained. "He likes to make new members feel wanted from the beginning, so we always try to start them with a home visit to make sure they know they're loved."

"Well, I'm feeling the love. I appreciate you coming to see an old lady. But I don't think I've seen you at church before."

"You probably haven't, ma'am. I've been working out of town for the past few months so I haven't been consistent with coming to church. But I'm finished with that job now so you will start seeing me soon."

"Well, don't be a stranger. I'm still getting to know people. At first, I was scared about moving here. But everywhere I turn around it seem like the Lord is providing nice young folks to take care of me. Like my neighbor across from me. His name is Joshua. Just a sweet young man. He checks on me all the time. He reminds me of you. He and his little girlfriend helped me move some stuff in on my first day here. She was sweet too. I told them I didn't need no help but she insisted they help me finish. They such a cute little couple. One night, he had an accident and she helped walk him in the house. He's a big fella and she's a little ole thang, but he was leaning on her and she was walking him in."

Christine looked around her apartment as if someone might be listening in. "Now they claim she's just his realtor," she whispered, "but I ain't never met

a realtor that has to make as many house calls as she does. But that little thang know she is pretty. Come rolling up here in that sharp white Lexus. What they say? Oh, yeah…looking like a boss!" she laughed.

A sharp white Lexus? Jeremiah questioned silently. His heart was suddenly racing but he tried to calm himself. After all, there were probably plenty of cute realtors who drove white Lexus's. Still, the coincidence was hard to ignore.

"Sooo," he said as casually as he could, "you think your neighbor and his realtor are more than friends?"

"Ooh, chile, yes!" Christine insisted. "As much as they try to put on that it's just business, that boy love her. He checks on me from time to time and I ask about her. I can see it in his face every time I say her name. I say, 'How's that pretty Elise?' and his whole face lights up. I hope it works out for them. Like I say, they so cute together."

Jeremiah didn't feel or see the punch to his mid-section. But he figured that must have been what happened. Because he couldn't breathe.

"Are you okay, young man?" Christine asked, noticing the color leaving his face. "Elise?" he whispered. "You said his girlfriend's name is Elise?"

"Yes, Elise," Christine confirmed. "She's a sweetheart but she got that boy wrapped all around her little finger," she chuckled.

"Hey…," Jeremiah stammered. "I think I know someone like that. She's a member of our church."

Jeremiah pulled up Elise's website on his phone and showed her picture to Christine.

"Is this her? Your neighbor's girlfriend? The realtor?" he asked, praying that somehow it wasn't.

"Yes!" Christine exclaimed. "That's Elise. I told you she was pretty. She goes to the church too? I haven't seen her."

"Yeah, Elise has been going through some things, so I think she hasn't been able to come. So, she's over here a lot? Working?" he asked.

"Ha. Well, that's what they call it. But I'm gon stay out they business. I was young once too and the Lord is not hardly finished with me yet. I just pray God bless them. She's sweet but she always seems like…I don't know…a little nervous. Like I caught her doin' something."

"Maybe you did."

CHAPTER 85

Cold Busted

DAY 538

Elise sat up with excitement as Jeremiah entered the house. "Hey, baby, I've been calling. Are you okay?" she asked.

"Yeah, I'm good," he answered dryly. "I just had to take care of some things for the church."

Elise was so overjoyed about their plans, she didn't notice Jeremiah wasn't matching her energy.

"Oh, no worries. I just rushed through my meeting because I thought you would be home. I was hoping we'd get a start on that business plan. Miah…baby… this is going to be straight fire! I can feel it in my spirit. And I'm not just talking about us making money. I'm talking about us doing some real ministry. We have to be strategic about it, but we could do jobs for lower margins for young couples or people who might need a second chance. You remember how good it felt when we got our first house? Baby, you know that's the best part of my job and I want to experience it with you. We should also look at some rental properties. That will give us a nice income stream so we can do some jobs for less. But we can't have no Pookies and Ray Rays who don't know how to pay rent. Only solid renters allowed. Oh, and I've got some names. What do you think about these?" Elise put her hands up like a billboard. "Jerelise Properties…get it?" she beamed. "First part of your name, last part of mine? Of course, you get it. You're the president of a multi-million-dollar real estate firm. Or we could keep it simple…Traylor Real Estate Investments. Orrrr….now hear me out on this last one. It's kind of a tearjerker…J.J. Mari Real Estate. I know that we can't get Mari back but she's old enough that she will always remember us, and maybe when she turns eighteen we can reconnect. It would be so dope if we were running this big real estate company and we told her our business was named after her and the little brother she never got to meet. We'd be like 'Mari, don't worry about college, sweetie, we've had that saved up for you since you were twelve. And here's a little Range Rover for you to get around in.'"

Jeremiah looked off into nowhere as Elise realized he didn't seem very enthusiastic about her ideas.

"Oh…am I rambling? You know how I get when I get excited. You're hungry, aren't you? Well, I didn't cook…you may be the president but I'm the vice president of sales and marketing, so we might need to get a chef," she laughed. "Can we order something so we can start working on the plan?"

Jeremiah just stood there.

"Miah, what's wrong?" she asked.

Jeremiah sighed and finally made eye contact with her. He looked tired and worn. His countenance wasn't that of a man who had just won a victory that would make him financially secure for the near future. "Lise, it's been a long afternoon. I got some bad news that I still can't believe. But the more I think about it, the more I think there's some truth to it."

Elise set her laptop aside. "I'm sorry, baby. I was so excited about our business, I didn't read the room. Come sit down and tell me about it." Elise patted the spot on the couch next to her.

Jeremiah sat on the couch but kept a noticeable distance between them. "It took me a while to get home because I've just been driving around thinking and praying. And the more I drove, and thought, and prayed, the more things just started to add up…and I just started to cry."

Elise reached over to him and touched his arm. "Miah, you're scaring me.

What are you crying about, baby? Is Daddy okay?"

"I keep wanting to believe it's not true. That it's just a

misunderstanding. I'm hoping that this nosey old lady just has her facts wrong." Jeremiah touched the palm of his hand to his chest. "But deep down where the truth lives, I know something is off. I know the last few days have been better for us but the last few months…not so much. And then I remembered what you said before, I don't know you anymore. So, if I'm wrong then I'm going to apologize in advance, but I have to ask…Lise, who is Joshua?"

Jeremiah scanned her face hoping for a curious expression or at least a smart- mouthed comment like "Ain't that the dude that hung around Moses?" or a simple "I don't know anybody named Joshua." But the look on her face made it clear that she knew exactly who Joshua was.

Elise cussed silently at herself. There was never going to be a good time for her to admit she had broken her marriage vows, but this wasn't how it was supposed to happen. She should have been the one telling Jeremiah about Joshua, not him telling her. Being confronted by her husband wasn't in any of her scenarios and she wasn't ready to have this conversation.

"Where did you hear that name?" she asked, stalling for time.

"I did a home visit to welcome a new member today. She was a sweet older lady who had just moved to town. She lives in the Oaks Apartment complex across town. But you already know who I'm talking about, don't you, Lise?" he asked her point blank.

Elise lowered her head. "You're talking about Ms. Christine."

"Yeah," Jeremiah nodded, "Ms. Christine. Well, Ms. Christine just talked and talked and talked. She told me all her little business. Nothing bad, though. She was just sharing. Then she told me about her sweet neighbor and how I reminded her of him. You know, Joshua? That's the guy I asked you about. But we'll come back to him."

Jeremiah leaned forward. Elise felt his gaze piercing through her soul like daggers as he continued.

"Then she told me about his pretty little girlfriend and how she drove a white Lexus and how she was a realtor. I won't lie. It scared me when I first heard that but then I was like, 'No, Jeremiah. It's just a coincidence.' Then she started talking about how much this

Joshua guy loves her. 'She got that boy wrapped all around her little finger,' she tells me. Then, without me saying anything. She says your name. Now at that point, even my naïve, gullible behind had to pay attention. But I had to make sure. So, I showed her your picture, and she recognized you immediately. 'That's Elise' she said. So, I leave, and I start putting things together. Ms. Christine knows your face, your name, your occupation, and your car. And she says you make house calls. Then I start thinking about how you have your phone off so much lately. At first, I thought you were just trying to punish me by not communicating. But you didn't want me to know where you were, did you?

Then I remembered how totally unbothered you were when I would tell you I couldn't come home some weekends. Again, I figured you were just mad, but now I'm thinking…me being home would have been an inconvenience. And you said so much when we had that fight before I left, but a few things started to stand out. You told me you didn't know what you were capable of, and it wouldn't be good for this family if I left. So now my mind is wondering about just what you meant when you said that. So, I'm asking again, Lise. Who is Joshua? Why are you at his apartment so much? And why does this old lady think you're his girlfriend?"

Elise clasped her hands together to keep them from trembling. She felt like she had been stripped naked in the middle of the town square. "Miah…I wanted to tell you. I really was going to. But yesterday and today were so nice for us. We were Miah and Lise again. So, I just kept putting it off."

"You wanted to tell me what?" Jeremiah asked. Elise looked into his eyes. After all they had been through and all she had done, she still saw hope in them. Hope that what this looked like wasn't what it actually was. Some would call it foolishness. But Elise knew Jeremiah was anything but foolish. He simply loved and trusted her. And she was about to destroy that.

"Baby, I promise, it only happened one time."

"What only happened one time? You mean you only went to his apartment one time?"

Elise wanted to take the opening, but she had no game left in her.

She had returned to the Lord and the Lord had returned to her, but with his presence she had lost her ability and desire to deceive. All she could do now was tell him the truth.

"Miah, I am so sorry, baby. But it was more than just me going to his apartment."

"What are you sorry about?" he pressed.

"I'm sorry for what I did and I'm sorry you found out this way. I was going to tell you myself, but I kept putting it off."

"Lise, what did you do?" he asked, still hoping he didn't know. "Miah…baby…you already know. I had an affair."

Jeremiah knew what she was saying but now that the words were coming from her mouth, he couldn't accept them. As much as he wanted to, he couldn't hold back his tears. "So, by affair, you mean you got involved with this dude emotionally? You started spending time with him and you began to catch feelings for him? Is that what you mean?" *That has to be what she means*, he thought hopefully. *My Lise would never do this.*

Elise lowered her head again, avoiding his eyes. Jeremiah slid off the couch and got on both knees in front of her. He took her hands in his and gently squeezed them.

"Tell me that's what you mean, Lise, and I'll believe you." He gently placed his thumb and index finger under her chin and lifted her head until her tear-filled eyes met his. "Babe, tell me that's all it is," he pleaded.

Elise shook her head. Jeremiah was begging her to lie, and that's exactly what she wanted to do. She wanted to tell him it was innocent or that she had been tempted but didn't give in. She wanted to tell him whatever he needed to hear. But there was no going back now.

"Baby, at first, yes, that's all it was. We would just talk and laugh. Miah, I never meant for it to get that far."

Jeremiah's expression changed as anger mixed in with his hurt. "Elise, are you telling me you had sex with this man?"

"Yes, I did. But it was only once," she confessed.

"Are you in love with him?" he asked, his voice trembling. "No!"

she said, shaking her head frantically. "I love you, Miah."

"No…don't call me that!" he said as he released her hands and stood up. "I'm sorry," she cried.

"So, if you're not in love with him, why did you sleep with him?" he asked angrily. "Jeremiah, I was in a bad place, and he was there. It's no excuse but that's why I begged you not to go."

"So, this is my fault? You went out and screwed another man because your husband had to work and that's on me?"

"That's not what I meant. I know it's on me."

"Was it worth it, Elise? Was it worth our marriage?" "No, it wasn't," she answered remorsefully.

Jeremiah paused as he tried to process what he was hearing. "Did you enjoy it?"

"What?" Elise asked. It never occurred to her that he would ask that question. "You heard me, Elise. Did you enjoy having sex with another man?"

"Jeremiah, I'm sorry, but I am not answering that."

"Oh, yes the hell you are!" he snapped. "You say it wasn't worth it. Why not?

Was the sex not good?"

"Jeremiah, I said I'm sorry. Please don't try to humiliate me." "That's not your line, Elise. Tell me!"

Elise sighed and tried to put her words together. "It wasn't really about sex. I know this is hard for you to hear, but it's about how he made me feel."

"And how did he make you feel, Elise?"

Elise thought for a moment about the question and answered as honestly as she could. "He made me feel like you used to. Back when things were good. He made me feel important. And special. He made me feel loved. He made me feel wanted."

"So, this guy made you feel so loved that you took your clothes off and let him enter your body?" he asked with as much disdain as he could muster.

"Jeremiah, when you left, I was already in a bad place. I was going to talk to you about it and then you told me you were leaving. I begged you to stay and quite honestly, I thought you would. I thought all I would have to do was tell you I needed you and you would stay, and we would eventually be okay. But you didn't. You left anyway. And things got worse for me when you did."

"I'm so sick of you putting this back on me," he said with disgust.

"I'm not trying to put it on you. I'm just trying to explain that it's complicated."

"It seems pretty simple to me, Elise. You went out and had sex with another man." "Jeremiah, please forgive me! You don't know how sorry I am."

"Did you bring him here? Jeremiah asked aggressively, ignoring her plea. "To my parents' house?"

Elise stood up. "Jeremiah, no! I promise you I would never do that. We only had sex one time and it was at his apartment. Yes, I went there more than once but we only had sex the one time."

"And what did you do the other times?" he asked.

"We would just hang out. We mostly just talked and laughed. Sometimes we would cry. We were both going through a lot, and we let things get out of hand."

"How did you meet?" he asked.

"He's my client. I was just trying to find him a house," she explained.

"So, is that why business is so good, Elise? You hook up with your clients? How long have you been doing this?" Hurt and confused as he was, Jeremiah knew there was no truth to his accusation, but it didn't matter. Right now, all he wanted to do was hurt her.

Elise saw through his words. "I know you don't mean that, but I guess I've given up the right to be insulted so I will answer. No, that's not what's happening. I'm successful because I'm uber focused on the business. And I'm focused on the business because I wanted to help our family. I wanted to help you. You know I'm not capable of what you just said. But I know why you said it and I deserve it."

"I don't know what I know, Elise. But you were right about what you said before, I don't know you anymore."

"Jeremiah, I am sorry for everything. I am sorry for betraying you and I am sorry that you found out this way. I have no right to ask you this. I didn't think I would. But I'm asking. Please forgive me, baby. I still want to be your wife. You are still my heart. I have never begged anyone for anything, but I am begging you now, please, let me make this right."

Elise took a step toward him, but Jeremiah put his hand up and backed away. "Unless you can go back in time and un-sleep with him, you can't make it right. I still can't believe you would do this." "I can't either," she agreed.

Jeremiah continued his inquisition. "Does he know you're married?"

"Yes, but it's not his fault. He didn't break trust with you...I did. I know you don't want to hear this, but he's not an evil guy."

Jeremiah bristled at the thought of his wife defending her lover. "So, this is what you're doing? Defending the not-evil guy who you're cheating on me with?" "Jeremiah, I promise you it's over. But it's not so black-and-white. And no,

I'm not defending him. I'm just trying to make you understand. I got to a place where I didn't even want to live anymore. And when I was in that dark place, Joshua reached out and I responded. If he hadn't, I don't think I would be here."

"Ya think?" he snapped. "Yeah, for sure we wouldn't be here if you hadn't responded."

"That's not what I mean. I mean I gave up. The day you left I finished off that bottle of Hennessy you found, and I had the pain pills they gave you from the accident in my hand. I was about to swallow them when Joshua texted me. I didn't want to be here anymore. I felt like everyone would be better off without me. I know I was on one that day, but usually you would at least say you loved me before you left. That day you just walked away, and you looked like you had given up on me. You didn't even text or call when you landed. My relationship with God was already in shambles and I felt like I didn't have anyone left. And right before I was about to put those pills in my mouth, Joshua texted me. I was drowning and, in that moment, he was my life preserver."

Part of him wanted to hold her and let her know he was still there for her. But his hurt and anger wouldn't allow it.

"So instead of killing yourself, you slept with him?" he asked coldly.

"Is that what you would have preferred? A dead wife over a cheating one?" she asked, subtly defending herself.

Jeremiah ignored the insensitivity of his words as well as her question and continued digging. "I still want to know how you ended up sleeping with him."

"It's not as simple as me just sleeping with him," Elise responded. "I know it was wrong and I know it's not your fault, but you and I weren't connecting. Joshua wanted to be there for me, and he wanted me there for him. We comforted each other and laughed and listened to each other. We did all the things that you and I used to do."

"So, you do love him?" he accused.

"Jeremiah, it's complicated but I don't want to be with him. I want you." "So, you want me, but you slept with him?" he asked.

"Yes. One time. And then I ended it." "Okay, when?"

"Jeremiah, please. Does it matter?"

"Yes, it does. When did you sleep with him, Elise?" Elised sighed heavily and confessed. "Five days ago."

"Five days ago?" he shouted. "And I'm supposed to believe it's over? It's not over, Elise. You just got caught."

"That's not true. I instantly regretted it, and I told him it was over. You can ask Pastor G. and First Lady. I told them everything."

"Pastor and First Lady know?" Jeremiah asked.

"Jeremiah, I had to tell somebody. I was lost and I needed help. I reached out to Shania, and she said I should bring them in."

"So, everybody knows my wife is sleeping around but me. Were you ever really going to tell me?"

"I honestly don't know. At first…yes, I was. But you came home, and you wanted us to be us again. Then you started talking about us adopting a baby and starting a business together. I thought we had a second chance. I know it's a copout, but part of me started to wonder if I should just keep it to myself. I would just carry the burden alone and make it up to you by being the best wife I could be."

"You can't make this up to me, Elise. I've never been more disgusted and disappointed with anyone as I am with you right now. As bad as things were, I always thought we would get to the other side. I thought sooner or later God was going to turn this thing around for us. But I never in a million years would have thought that you would do the one thing that there was no coming back from."

"Jeremiah, please don't say that!" she pleaded desperately. "I know this won't make sense, but this is me…the real me."

"Oh, so the fake you screwed Joshua? Is that it, Elise?"

"Jeremiah, please just calm down. I know this is unforgivable, but I am asking you to forgive me. I promise you this won't ever happen again. And I don't care if you get mad but Miah, I love you. We can make it back from this!"

"How can we make it back from this when I can't even stand the sight of you," he said, still trying to wound her.

"Do you want me to leave?" she asked, defeated.

"I wouldn't do you like that, and you know it. I'll find someplace to go." "Jeremiah, this is your mom and dad's house. I should be the one to leave." "I'm not holding you hostage, Elise. But I'm not asking you to go either. I

just know I need to leave. I'm not myself right now."

"Miah, please don't go. There's still a lot I want to explain."

"I'm through talking, Elise. I'm through period. For the first time since I met you, I don't care about how you feel and that scares me. If I keep talking it would only be to hurt you. I don't want to do that, so we shouldn't be around each other right now."

"Jeremiah, I'm sorry, but what about Daddy? He's expecting us tomorrow." "No!" he shouted. "You will not do that! You will not use my father to get to me or to justify your…your…."

"My what, Jeremiah? Go ahead and say it. We're both thinking it.

My whoreishness? Is that what you want to say?"

"Elise, I'm not doing this with you. That's my father. I'll take care of him. Pop isn't your concern anymore," he said coldly, getting one more blow as he stormed out the house.

CHAPTER 86

The Reckoning

DAY 538

Joshua sat alone in his living room taking a hard look at the trajectory of his life. He was fifty years old and thought that by now he would have gotten a better handle on this life thing. He should have an adoring wife and children, a house, a dog, and maybe a goldfish. More importantly, by now he should be a man of faith and integrity. Presently, he was 0 for 7. There was no adoring wife. He was still estranged from his son. He had gone from a five-bedroom house to a one-bedroom apartment. His faith and integrity were hardly pleasing to God. And he didn't even have a dog or goldfish.

His divorce had left him with a crushing emptiness. For a short time, his soul tie with Elise had filled that void. Now she was gone, and the emptiness had returned and taken her shape. She was the only one who could fill it, but the relationship was over. As much as he wanted to, he knew he couldn't ask the Lord to restore their adulterous relationship, but he could still ask the Lord for help.

"Lord," he prayed. "It wasn't supposed to be like this. I'm not supposed to be like this. I know this was not your plan for me, but I also know I have sinned. I ignored your warning and disobeyed your command. I have nothing to offer you now but this confession and this desire to repent and get back in alignment with you. I pray for your mercy and your help. I pray for those I have wronged. I have sinned against Elise and her husband. I have sinned against my own body. And I have sinned against you. Please don't let it end this way for me, Lord. Please be the God of a second chance. I bring myself under your hand

and pray you have mercy on me according to your unfailing love and great compassion. Please don't—"

A knock at his door interrupted Joshua's prayer. He went to the door and checked the peephole. He had never even seen a picture of Jeremiah, but he knew it was him standing on the other side. He silently asked the Lord to give him some word…some scripture for this moment. But the only scripture that came to his remembrance was a Proverb. "But a man who commits adultery has no sense; whoever does so destroys himself. Blows and disgrace are his lot, and his shame will never be wiped away. For jealousy arouses a husband's fury, and he will show no mercy when he takes revenge." He had told Elise that he would have to pay a price one day. That day had come.

Regardless of the consequences, he knew he had to open the door to face the one he had wronged. He whispered one last prayer before he did so. "Lord, please protect this man."

"Hello, Jeremiah," he said calmly as he opened the door.

Hearing his name come from this stranger that was all too familiar with his wife angered Jeremiah. He wasn't at all sure what the point of this confrontation was, but a dark part of him wanted it to be violent. It didn't matter that the man standing before him was appreciably larger. Jeremiah wasn't particularly concerned with the outcome. Whether he hurt Joshua or Joshua hurt him didn't matter. He just wanted to feel something other than what he was feeling right now, and anger seemed a more pleasing emotion than the pure anguish he was currently experiencing.

Jeremiah was a planner by nature, but there was no plan in place for facing the man his wife had committed adultery with. This man had been with Elise more recently than he had, and that specific thought infuriated him even more.

"You Joshua?" he asked.

The question was ridiculous. Who else would he be? But Jeremiah hadn't really thought the conversation through. He left Elise with no destination in mind, and before he knew it, he was at Joshua's door.

"Yes, I am," Joshua responded calmly.

Jeremiah took a slight step forward and looked Joshua in his eyes.

Joshua could see the anger and the pain on Jeremiah's face and prepared himself for what would come next.

"Joshua, I came here to tell you to stay away from my wife," he said plainly. He prepared…even wished for some nonchalant or disrespectful response, but Joshua didn't oblige him.

"I plan to, Jeremiah. I'm sorry about what happened. I was wrong and I promise you it's over."

"Oh, I know you were wrong," Jeremiah said, inching forward. "I don't need you to tell me that!"

Joshua took a step back as he searched his mind for the right words to deescalate this tense situation.

"I know you don't, but I wanted you to hear me say it," Joshua explained. "Hear what?" Jeremiah asked aggressively. Why was this guy so calm? He was hoping he would say something more along the line of "Yeah, I smashed your wife. And?"

"Jeremiah…," Joshua said.

"Quit saying my name like we friends!" Jeremiah snapped. "You don't know me."

"I'm sorry…sir, I wanted you to hear me say that I know I was wrong and I'm sorry for what I did. I can't take it back and I can't ask you to forgive me, but I can tell you I regret it. And I can tell you that what I did does not represent the kind of man that I want to be."

Jeremiah's frustration increased. The man before him didn't seem like the demon he had imagined, but it didn't matter. If Joshua wasn't going to choose violence today, then he was.

Jeremiah bumped the larger man with his body, stepped across the threshold of Joshua's apartment, and stood within an inch of his face. "So, what kind of man do you want to be?" Jeremiah asked angrily, hoping in his heart Joshua would give him an excuse to escalate the situation.

Joshua was well within his legal rights to respond aggressively, but instead he took another step back. After all, the disrespect Jeremiah was demonstrating was nothing compared to the disrespect Joshua had shown him. Joshua instinctively evaluated the man he would normally consider an opponent. Jeremiah wanted vengeance but unlike Joshua, he was obviously untrained. His fists were clinched but remained harmlessly at his side. He stood fully upright before him, and his stance exposed him to whatever attack Joshua's years of combat training wanted to utilize. He was full of rage and prayed Joshua would give him an outlet for that rage. Joshua prepared himself to be the object of Jeremiah's wrath, but he would not retaliate. Whatever happened next would be in Jeremiah's hands…and God's.

"I want to be the kind of man who acknowledges his own sin and takes responsibility for his actions. I know why you came here, Jeremiah. And I understand. Do what you have to do."

"So, you just gon stand there?" Jeremiah asked.

Joshua shook his head. "Yeah, I'm just gon stand here. I won't give you what you came here for, but I have this coming."

Joshua allowed his body to go limp and commanded himself not to respond no matter what his aggressor did. Jeremiah responded with a violent shove. Joshua could have easily countered the unskilled move, but he allowed himself to fall to his backside.

"Man…get up and fight me!" Jeremiah yelled as he stood over him.

"No, I'm sorry," Joshua said. "That I won't do. Go ahead and finish. I won't stop you."

Jeremiah stood there trembling with anger. He looked down at Joshua as he sat there waiting for his attack. Jeremiah had pushed him literally and figuratively and still had not gotten the altercation he wanted. He searched Joshua's eyes for fear or aggression but only found regret. This man had done him great harm. But he wasn't trying to harm him now, and Jeremiah released his desire to leap on top of this seemingly defenseless man. He unclenched his fists as he realized he no longer had the desire to fight.

"Stay away from my wife," he said as he turned his back and walked away.

Joshua got to his feet and said nothing as Jeremiah returned to his car and drove off.

He closed his door, picked up his phone, and dialed as Jeremiah's car left his line of sight.

A frantic voice answered the phone after the first ring. "Hello, Josh! Is everything okay? What happened?"

"Calm down, Elise. Nothing happened. At least nothing important. It was just like you said. He was just mad. He tried to press me but when I didn't respond, he walked away."

"So, he's okay?" Elise asked. "Yes, he's fine," Joshua confirmed.

"And you? Are you okay?" she asked.

"I'm good," he said, grateful for her concern.

"Joshua, thank you for not hurting him. We both know you could have." "I already did hurt him. I just didn't want to add to it."

"I'm sorry for putting you through all this, Josh."

"You were going through a lot, Elise. It's on me. But I appreciate the heads- up. If he would have shown up without me being prepared, things may have been different."

Elise wanted to say more. There was still a part of her that wanted to talk to him. But she had played with this fire before and the burns were still fresh. She wasn't going back down that road again.

"Josh, thank you again. I'd better hang up. Please take care of yourself." "Are you gonna be okay?" Joshua asked, resisting the desire to tell her how much he still loved her.

"I will be, Josh…eventually. I may lose my husband, but the Lord will take care of me."

"I'm never going to talk to you again, am I?" Joshua asked sadly. "No, Josh. You won't."

"You'll always be in my prayers, Elise." "And you in mine. Goodbye, Joshua." "Goodbye, Elise."

CHAPTER 87

Crushed

DAY 538

Jeremiah sat in silence as he looked at the headstones of his mother and son. Had they lived, he always imagined they would be close. So, it always brought him comfort knowing that their final resting place was together. He desperately needed that comfort now but found nothing but anger and pain.

He regretted letting Joshua off the hook so easily, but Elise was right. He wasn't the one who broke their covenant. She had. He tried to envision a scenario where he would have broken his marital vows, and he could not. How could she do this? Why would she do this? And why now, when things were turning around for them? He looked around the cemetery at all the different headstones. His marriage was now dead, so it was fitting he now sat in an environment of death. His anger forced his sadness to the background as he fumed over his situation. But it wasn't Joshua or Elise that was the object of his rage. Elise wasn't the only one breaking promises. There was someone else who had truly let him down, and it was time He got told about himself.

"You know," he said out loud. "I'm beginning to realize something; you don't really do any of the things you say you do, do you? You say you answer prayer, but nothing ever really changes. You say you heal, but people stay sick and die. You say you're a rescuer, but you don't ever show up. No, you don't do any of those things. You know what I just realized? You just have a really great marketing team. We all talk about your goodness and your grace and make excuses for you when you don't show up. But not me. Not anymore. I. Am. Done.

"No more. I told the daughter I thought you gave me that you were always good, always right, and always for her. But you just sat on the sidelines while the man who taught me that got attacked and you took my daughter away while she screamed for me to help her. Your grace. Ha. Your mercy. Ha. Your love put an innocent child in the arms of a stranger.

"I am soo done," he continued, summoning all the vitriol he could. "You took my mama, and I praised you for a life well lived and for the time you gave me with her. You tried to take Pop and I prayed in Jesus' mighty name that you would heal him. You straight killed my son when you know I would have gladly died in his place, but I kept calling on your name. You took my career and my reputation, and I kept trusting you. And now I see you're still not finished…ha…being faithful," he said with all the sarcasm he could muster.

"Once again, you let it look like you were going to turn it around for me. But now you let another man have my wife? And I'm supposed to trust you? No. I'm good. You know everything so you must know that I don't care anymore. Mama said when this moment came that I should praise you. Well, I don't have any praise left. I don't have anything left. So do what you have to do and take whatever else you want to take. You say it's the devil killing, stealing, and destroying, but I think it's you. So, here I am. You can destroy me, or you can do what you do best… ignore me. Either way, I'm done. I'm not wasting breath or emotional capital on praise and prayer. And I'm not going to run around lying for you anymore, telling people that you're a God of love. This is not love. I don't know what I'm going to do but don't worry…I won't bother you anymore."

Jeremiah wiped his face and took the short walk back to his car. In his blasphemous rant, he hadn't noticed another car had pulled up. Even in the dark, he was able to recognize the figure waiting for him.

"Pastor, I don't feel like being all Christiany right now," he said rudely. He would apologize later but he was in no mood to hear about God's faithfulness.

"You don't have to be any kind of way, Jeremiah. Let's go someplace and talk," Pastor Gregory responded, ignoring his curtness.

"Elise told you?" Jeremiah asked, realizing in the confusion and chaos of his thoughts, that his pastor didn't just happen to show up at a cemetery in the middle of the night.

"Yes, she did," Pastor Gregory confirmed. "And she knew you would be here."

"You know, I thought God was finally going to let up on us. I thought it couldn't get worse. I thought he was turning it all back around. And now this? And I'm supposed to trust Him?" Jeremiah asked seriously.

"Yes," Pastor Gregory replied emphatically. "Now is the time to trust him like never before. Now is the time to lean into the love of Jesus Christ like you never have in your life!"

"Pastor, what the hell you think I been doing?" Jeremiah shouted angrily. "I knew you was gon come talkin' all that bullshhhh…," Jeremiah stopped himself. "Pastor, please. You've been like another father to me. I don't want to disrespect you. But I don't have it in me right now to pretend that everything is okay."

"I don't want you to pretend, son. Just let me be here for you. Let me pray with you," he said gently.

"I don't feel like praying, Pastor."

Pastor Gregory took a step toward him. "You don't have to pray. We can just talk."

"I don't feel like talking," Jeremiah argued.

"You don't have to talk. We can just look at each other," Pastor Gregory countered.

"I'm not gonna make it back from this, Pastor," Jeremiah said as his whole body began to shake.

"Yes, you will," Pastor Gregory said, putting a hand firmly on his shoulder. "I don't know what to do," Jeremiah said as he started to weep uncontrollably.

Pastor Gregory put his other hand on Jeremiah's shoulder and pulled him close. "That's okay, son. He does."

CHAPTER 88

Mama Said

DAY 541

Jeremiah had been in the same hotel room for three days. He refused to go back home to Elise and had turned down Pastor Gregory's offer to stay with Faye and him. He felt alone and wanted to be alone. Elise had called and texted countless times, but he wouldn't pick up or acknowledge her efforts. He didn't even sleep in the bed. He barely slept at all. He couldn't. He just sat in the corner of the room with the curtains closed shut, blocking out all the light. His only contact with the outside world was with Pastor Gregory, who had agreed to leave him in peace, provided he check-in with him every morning and every evening.

"Hey Pastor, just checking in," Jeremiah said.

"Hello, my son," Pastor Gregory responded. "You know I've been waiting on this call. It's good to hear your voice."

"Yours too. Thank you, Pastor," he replied politely.

"Jeremiah, I hate to burden you, but Elise has been worried sick."

"Pastor, please do not talk to me about Elise. I just can't right now," Jeremiah pleaded.

"Okay," Pastor Gregory acquiesced. "But can we bring you a plate? Or better yet, we can take you out or you can come by. You can't just hide in that room, son."

"I don't know what else to do," Jeremiah said dejectedly.

"I think you do, son. You can run. You can hide. But even now, you know where your help comes from. I wish I could tell you exactly what's going to happen, but I can't. But I know this. He is still on the throne and that throne is still one of grace. Go to the throne, Jeremiah. If your dad was healthy, that's what he would say. If your mother were here, she would say the same thing. You know Faye and I are praying for you. But what's happening here is very personal and unique, and you need to get up close and personal with the Lord yourself. Say what you need to say but make sure you listen too. I love you, son."

"Thank you, Pastor. I love you too," Jeremiah said, disconnecting the call.

Jeremiah sat there for a few moments. He loved Pastor Gregory dearly, but he truly could not relate. "You wouldn't think it was so simple if it were Faye," he said out loud. Still, something he said resonated. "If your mother were here, she would say the same thing."

But even though she wasn't there with him, Jeremiah knew his mother had already told him what to do. Now was the time to do what he refused to do three nights ago. He slid out of the chair and dropped to his knees. His mother told him that even when all was lost, he should open his mouth and give God the praise. So, that's exactly what he did. He was no singer, but he opened his mouth and sang praises to the Lord anyway. He sang praises to the One that he previously accused of ignoring him. He was never one to put too much emphasis on feelings and emotions, but even as he sought to draw near, he felt absolutely nothing. There was something in the way that needed to be moved.

"Father," he said reverently, "I have spoken against you. I have accused you of being unfaithful, untrustworthy, and uncaring. And even though I know you gave up Your Son for my sins, I accused you of being unloving. Whether or not you allowed all this or caused it, doesn't matter. It's too much for me to figure out. But even though I can't understand you, I know you are right."

"And Father, even against my own feelings, and even against everything I see, I want to tell you that I believe what your word says about you is true. You are good, Father."

"You chose me, Lord. And even with all that is against me, my failure, my rejection, my betrayal, my anger, my confusion, my sin…," Jeremiah stopped as he began to weep, "…even my own wife, right now, by your grace, I choose you and thank you that you are still for me."

"So, for every accusation I spat at you out of my angry and hurting heart, I confess, and I repent. You owe me nothing, Lord. But in Christ you have given me everything. I owe you everything and have given you nothing. I know you said I am more than a conqueror but I'm not feeling that right now. I am tired and I am weak, and I don't have anything left. But if you will forgive me, and if you will cleanse me, and if you will help me, then you can still have my praise."

Jeremiah continued to weep as he returned to his prayers and songs of praise. Were someone to hear, they likely would not be able to discern what he was saying, as he sang and blessed the Lord in anguish. He had confessed and repented. He felt no less betrayed, but he kept praising. His mind told him he still served a faithful God, but his pain said he should give up. Elise had betrayed him and the God he had just repented to moments ago, let it happen. The word he was trusting in told him the Lord was near, but in that dark hotel room, he was more alone than ever, and in that moment, despite his repentance, despite his praise, despite a fleeting hope that God would still come through, he no longer wanted to live.

"I can't do this anymore, Lord," he cried in frustration. "If this is it. If this is all you have left for me then I don't want to be here anymore."

Even through his tears, the words of his own lament pierced his soul. They reminded him of what Elise told him. She said she didn't want to be here anymore. "Is that what you would have preferred?" she had asked him. "A dead wife over a cheating one?"

"What were you going through?" he asked out loud. As disappointed, angry, and humiliated as he was, the thought of his wife being so lost that she wanted to die, further crushed his already broken heart. He was no less angry. No less hurt. But in his hurt and anger, he was thankful. If those were his only choices, a dead Elise or a cheating one, then he was thankful she was still there. He resumed his praise even as he struggled with the thought of his marriage being over. His life would never be the same, but he continued to praise until his tears slowed and his spirit calmed. In his calmness, he picked up the phone and dialed, remembering there was one more thing his mother told him to do.

"Hi Miah…I'm sorry…I mean, hi Jeremiah," Elise answered. "Hi Elise," he responded.

"Are you okay?" she asked.

Jeremiah paused as he tried to think of the right thing to say. "Yeah, I'm good.

I just know you've tried to call. I'm sorry but I wasn't ready to talk."

"I understand. Jeremiah, I'm so sorry. Please just come home. If you want me to, I'll leave."

"You don't have to leave, Elise."

"Well, then will you come home?" she asked.

"I'd better go. I was just letting you know I got your calls and texts," he said. "I saw Daddy today," she said, trying to keep him on the phone. "He's walking so much better. He's still struggling with his speech, but I think his mind is actually as sharp as ever. He's just having trouble expressing everything. I told him you had some business to take care of and would be by soon."

"I have to go, Elise," he said, stifling his tears.

"Okay, can I bring you anything? Do you need some clothes? Or your iPad?" she asked, desperately hoping he would soften and let her love him in some way.

"I don't need anything."

"Jeremiah, I know I deserve all this but it's killing me not to see you. I just want to tell you I'm sorry. Please, baby. Just come home!" she pleaded.

"I believe you. I know you're sorry. But I'm not ready to see you, Elise. Not yet. But if you give me a few days, maybe we can meet up at the church or over at Pastor's house."

"You mean for counseling?" she asked hopefully. "Does that mean you want to try?"

"Elise, I don't know what it means. I'm not even sure why I called," he told her, knowing that it was a lie. He called to tell her she was forgiven. That maybe things could never be the same but that he didn't want her to be in pain anymore. But he couldn't form the words. There was still a dark part of him that wanted her to feel what he was feeling.

"Jeremiah, are you there?" she asked.

"Yeah," he said suddenly. "Maybe for counseling...maybe for closure. I don't know."

"I guess that's fair," she said, crushed by his words. "I'll make an appointment for us."

"Okay, I'd better go," he said. "Thank you for calling, Jeremiah."

"You're welcome, Elise. I'll talk to you later." "I love you," she said.

"Goodbye, Elise," he said, disconnecting the call.

CHAPTER 89

Jeremiah and Elise

DAY 578

Elise put the finishing touches on dinner and waited for Jeremiah to come to the table. They had been in counseling for over a month now but hadn't made much progress. They slept in separate rooms and rarely spoke to each other besides polite hellos and goodbyes. First Lady suggested that Elise be more intentional in her efforts, so Elise prepared Jeremiah's favorite meal hoping they could enjoy an evening together without fighting or ignoring each other.

"Hey, how was your day?" Jeremiah asked politely as he joined her. "It was okay. Very busy. How was yours?"

"Same…that smells good, Elise."

"I hope you like it. I made it like Mama Etta used to. Do you want to say grace?" Elise asked him.

"Sure…Heavenly Father, we thank you for this food and we thank you for the hands that prepared it. Most of all, we thank you for Jesus. It's in His name that we pray, Amen."

"Amen. Somebody's hungry. That was a world record. If I would have known you were going to pray that quick, I would have skipped my premeal snack," Elise quipped.

"Oh, you got jokes," Jeremiah said, allowing himself to smile just a little.

Elise appreciated the response. They hadn't shared a smile or a laugh since the truth about her affair had been revealed. They both dug into their plates but neither said anything.

Elise turned on some music to cover their awkward silence as they ate.

"So, how's Chad's aunt's house coming along?" she asked, attempting to break the tension.

"Not too bad. We're painting it this week and replacing all the floors next week. His aunt should be able to move in before long. I hope she likes it."

"I'm sure she'll love it. I'd love to see it once it's done…if that's okay." "Yeah…that's okay. How's work with you?" he asked.

"It's good. I've got a few commercial properties lined up. If just one of them goes, we'll be looking at a sixty-thousand-dollar commission check."

Jeremiah's eyebrows raised at the figure. "Sixty thousand dollars? For one deal?" he asked.

"Yeah, commercial deals are harder to come by but when they do, the paychecks are nice. But my heart will always be in residential real estate, though. It makes me happy."

"Yeah, I know the feeling. I've been working on this house and it's hard…but it's a different kind of hard. I'm enjoying myself," he said.

"I'm glad. You deserve to enjoy what you're doing. I'm proud of you, Jeremiah. I know that doesn't mean as much as it used to, but I am."

"No, Elise. It means a lot. Thank you. This is good, by the way… but it's not Mama's recipe."

"What do you mean?" Elise asked, although she knew what he was referring to.

"Mama always put bell peppers in it. And I would always spend half the time

picking them out. So, thanks for remembering." "You're welcome. Hey…."

Elise's attempt to carry on the conversation was cut short by the next song on her phone. It was "Kiss," by Prince. Their song. There was a time when the song couldn't come on without Jeremiah serenading her or at least the both of them bobbing their heads to the funky beat and smiling. Now, it was just a painful reminder of what they no longer had. They both tried to ignore it until Jeremiah couldn't take it anymore.

"You mind turning that down? I'm not really in the mood for music right now," he said crossly.

"Yeah, I'm sorry," she said as she fumbled for her phone to cut it off.

Jeremiah ate a few more bites for the sake of being polite, then looked for his exit. "Hey, I just remembered…I've got some things to take care of. You can leave the dishes. I'll take care of them later. Thank you, Elise."

"Jeremiah, please. The song is off. You agreed we would have dinner together.

I'm trying."

"I know you are. This was nice. We sat down. We talked. We ate. And we didn't fight. Take the win."

"Fine, but I need to say something before you go lock yourself in your room and I need you to listen."

"Elise, I don't know if I can do this with you right now."

"Jeremiah, please just listen. I need you to be honest with me. We've been marking time for over a month but we're not going anywhere. I can't take much more of this. I've learned I don't do well with loneliness."

"So, is that another warning about what will happen if I don't do what you say?"

Elise ignored his accusatory tone. It was certainly understandable. "No. That's not what I mean at all. I just mean it's one thing to be alone, but it's another to be lonely when the one you want is right there. I just need to know if you're going to give me a chance, Jeremiah. Are you ever going to at least try to get past what I did? I was the one who cheated, and I can't take that back. But I can't do this by myself. If you don't want me or you can't forgive me, then just say that. There's no shame in it."

"Elise, I don't know what you want me to do."

"I just want you to try. I want you to want to make this work. I want us to eat together and go places together. I want us to work it out. I can't stand us being in this house and barely talking and not sleeping together. I know what I did to you and I will regret it for the rest of my life, but I need you to tell me if you are never going to be able to let it go. Just tell me the truth."

"I've told you the truth, Elise. I've told you in counseling and right here in this house. It's going to take a minute for me to get over this. And if we're keeping it a buck...you know what...never mind."

"Jeremiah, stop trying to be nice and say what's on your mind!"

"Fine," Jeremiah said as he leaned forward. "You don't get to rush me after what you did. You just get to sit back and be patient. I know you're sorry, but it doesn't change anything. You feel bad. I feel bad. So, I guess we're even."

"Is that what this is about, Jeremiah? Are you trying to get even with me?" "You sure you want to go there?" he asked, challenging her to back off. "You said keep it a buck, so yeah. Let's go there," she answered, not shrinking back.

"For me to get even with you, Elise, I would have to go find a woman and do with her what you did with Joshua. That would square us up."

"Is that what you want?" she asked, wondering how she would react if he did. "No. That's not what I want," he said honestly. "But you don't get to talk to me about us being even. I may not be smiling in your face all the time, but I'm not mistreating you. So quit acting like the victim. Like you said, you were the one who cheated. Look me in the eye and tell me you can imagine a situation where I would have done that to you."

"I can't. I know you wouldn't have ever done that," she admitted. "But I need to keep it a buck too. So, you look me in the eye and tell me you think that I would have done what I did if you would have stayed with me when I asked you to. I just needed you here. I just needed to know I was still important to you. Yes, I should have done better. Yes, I'm the whore who cheated on the best husband in the world. But I asked you for help and you ignored me when I needed you the most. And now I'm just asking you to do 90/10 with me. Miah, I will do the 90…can you please just give me 10? What we had is worth getting back. You can't tell me you don't believe that. It wasn't that long ago. Don't you remember? Don't you want that again?"

"I do…I'm just so tired, Elise. I have dreams about how we used to be, but then I wake up to this nightmare. And I'm like…this is real. You really cheated on me. And I don't know what to do because normally when I feel some kind of way about things…." Jeremiah paused as he held back his tears.

"You come and talk to me?" Elise said.

"Yeah, that part," he said as he turned his head and wiped his eyes. "I still want to be here for you, Miah."

"Then I have to be able to trust you," he said.

"That's fair. I know I have to earn that back. I want to be your Lise again and not ole girl you've had to live with lately."

"Yeah," Jeremiah agreed. "My Lise was amazing."

Elise smiled. "Your Lise was amazing because she knew you loved her. Does that make sense?"

"Yeah…it makes sense," he nodded.

"I need to say something else since we're on a roll," Elise said. "Okay," he agreed.

"Miah, I've owned my sin. And I've confessed and I've repented. I cheated on you but that's not the worst thing I did. The worst thing I did was turn away from the Lord."

"You've shared that," Jeremiah said sympathetically. "It was a bad time." "Yes, but you don't know everything. When J.J. died, I asked the doctors to bring him to me."

"You wanted to hold him?" Jeremiah asked.

"It was more than that. I don't know if you remember, but right before the accident you were assuring me that we were going to be okay. And in my mind, I think I felt like this might just be a test. So, I held our baby in my arms, and I lifted him up to the Lord for a resurrection. I believed with everything in me that my Daddy was going to come through for me, for you, for our baby. But he said no. And as I sat there, I felt the Holy Spirit reaching out to me that day. The Lord was calling J.J. home, and he was calling me to his peace and comfort right there in the middle of all my pain and confusion. He wanted to comfort me and reassure me that he was going to bring me through this, that he had a plan and I just needed to understand that it wasn't for me to understand but that I still had to trust him. And Jeremiah, I rejected him. If I was going to believe in a God of miracles who could bring the dead back to life and he wasn't going to give my baby back to me, then I had nothing else for him. I was going to get back at him for taking my baby by denying him myself. I was going to deny him his praise and I was going to deny him my prayers. I was like 'I am not asking you for anything else ever. How you like them apples, Lord?' After that, I cut myself off from the Lord. I refused to pray or give him thanks. That's the real reason I quit the praise team. No way was I going to stand in front of the church talking about how good God is. I know

I was wrong, but at the time, I just didn't believe it was true anymore. I know that's disappointing and hard for you to understand or relate to."

"No, Elise. I get it. I really do. After I found out about you and Joshua, I had… a moment. I said some things to the Lord that I've had to repent from. I was so angry. I blamed God for everything, and I wanted to walk away too. So, I know what it means to have your faith shaken and to want to give up on God."

"Yeah, but I actually did it. But there's more," Elise revealed. "I hate to rehash this, but I need you to have context. The day you told me you were taking the Denver job when I walked out on you after we had that fight, that was the day that things really started with Josh and me. It wasn't planned. I just wanted to get away from you for a minute. I just wanted to be mad. But I was out of fellowship with the Lord, and I was more vulnerable than I realized. I ran into Joshua. We saw a movie together and after that we got to talking."

Jeremiah still cringed every time Elise mentioned Joshua's name. "Elise, you've told me this. I don't need to hear it again."

"I know…it's hard to hear, but if we are going to ever move forward you have to know everything."

"What don't I know?" he asked, afraid of what she would say.

"You don't know that what I just told you…about J.J.…I told Joshua that night. I told him my pain, my betrayal, and my sins. That should have been something I shared with you, but I gave that to him. So long before I betrayed you in his bedroom, I betrayed you by giving him a trust that should only have been yours. I told him the worst thing I ever did in my life…intentionally turn my back on the Lord. Peter denied the Lord, but he was afraid. I did it because I was mad. I will always wonder what would have happened if I would have just taken the Lord's hand that day."

"Elise, I'm not sure what to say."

"It's okay. I just wanted you to know everything. How about you? Is there anything else you want to say?" she asked.

"Yeah…I'm still pissed that you called him that night," he said bluntly. "But you understand why I did, don't you?" she asked.

"Yeah…you had an affair with Mike Tyson's little brother, and you didn't want him to kill me. But you have to understand that, to me, you still had contact with him. And you had so much influence over him that he refused to fight me because of you."

"Jeremiah, I don't think that's all it was. I think he truly felt bad and ashamed.

I told you…he's not a bad person. He just did a bad thing."

"And there it is again! You don't know how it makes me feel to hear you defending him. Sometimes I wish it was just sex. But you actually like him."

"I don't know what to say," Elise said, throwing her hands up in frustration. "It's a catch-22, so all I can do is be honest. I was in sin, and I was in rebellion. You and I were apart, and I let myself get caught up. I'm not trying to defend him, but he wasn't some predator or evil guy. I saw in him a lot of the things that made me fall in love with you. But Miah…he was never you. All I can tell you is if you let me, I will do my best to earn your trust and your love back."

"You don't have to earn my love back, Elise. I've never stopped loving you. There are times where I wish that weren't true, but it is. And I'm sorry. I'm sorry that when you felt like you couldn't turn to the Lord, I wasn't there to guide you back. And I'm sorry I didn't call you that night. I mean the night you said you had those pills in your hand. I should have been there for you. But I wasn't. I still don't think it makes it right…but I can see how I left you out in the cold and you needed somebody."

"Thank you for saying that. That's actually very sweet. And I'm sorry about the song. I wasn't playing games. It came on randomly. I wouldn't do that."

"I know…it was just hard to hear, and I wasn't ready for it. But there is something else that's bothering me. I don't like it when you call yourself names. Please stop doing that."

"Oh, you mean like 'whore' or 'garden tool' or 'thot' or…."

"Yes, Elise!" he laughed. "All of that. Please stop…I still get mad sometimes, but I don't think of you that way. And I never will."

Elise smiled. She appreciated his kindness. "That's how I feel sometimes… but I appreciate you saying that. How you think of me will always be important to me. No matter what happens between us."

"Yeah…same here," he said. "Wow. Look at us. This is a conversation." "Pastor G. would be so proud," Elise said. "We should reenact this for him during the next counseling session."

"I know, right?" Jeremiah responded. "So…hug it out?"

"Yes," Elise smiled. "I would like to hug it out."

CHAPTER 90

Almost Miah and Lise

DAY 600

Although they were far from being reconciled, Jeremiah and Elise were making progress. Elise wanted to keep their positive energy going and invited Jeremiah to share pizza and have a movie night. They sat silently and awkwardly on the couch until a rather unbelievable only in Hollywood scene came on.

"OMG!" Elise exclaimed. "Girl, if you don't get yo tail up and run. That man ain't got time to come and get you. They shootin' bullets."

"Oh, so you wouldn't want me to come back for you?" Jeremiah asked. "Well, of course I would want you to, but you wouldn't have to. I would keep up. If anything, I would have to come back and get you."

Jeremiah paused the movie. "Elise Janelle Traylor, in what world would you have to come back for me? I would be just like ole boy there. I would grab your hand and I would lead you out of danger. And you know this…man!"

Elise laughed at his reference to one of their favorite movies. "Jeremiah, we tryna work on a marriage. Don't make me do this."

"Do what?" he asked.

"Destroy you in another argument," she giggled as she gently touched his thigh.

"Well, if you feelin' froggy…jump…shorty," he said as he motioned her to him with his hands.

"Okay, Lord…you heard him. He came for me, and I did not send for him." Elise scrunched her lips and cocked her head to the side. "Jeremiah, you wouldn't have to come back for me because I am a better athlete than you and you know I can outrun you."

"Whoa! Don't be lying just to win an argument!" he objected.

"I'm not lying, Jeremiah! Remember when you were in college when you were tryna holla and we would go running? I would legit have to slow down so I wouldn't make you look bad."

"Elise, no you did not! I remember you would be all like 'Whew, ya girl is tired.'"

"Tired of waiting on you is more like it. Jeremiah, I was in the military. I was in shape. I ran mini marathons."

"So why did I always beat you, huh, Elise?" Jeremiah said as he leaned forward and put his hand to his ear.

"I was faking it," she said simply.

"Really? You were just faking it? I don't believe that."

"Jeremiah, I hate to tell you this, but women fake it for men on much more ego-shattering things than this."

"You are one cold piece of work. I am so glad my mama is with the Lord, and she can't hear this foolishness."

"Boy, Mama Etta sittin' next to Jesus right now talkin' 'bout 'Lord, send yo Holy Spirit to comfort my baby. My daughter can outrun him and it's a hard pill to swallow.'"

"So, my mama would take your side?" he questioned. Elise gave him the hardest side-eye she could.

"Okay, you right," Jeremiah backed off. "But back to the race. Even if I believed you believe that, which you know you don't, and even if it were true that you could outrun me, which it's not. It's only because of distance. I don't do distance. Never have. I'm a sprinter. A swift and sleek cheetah blazing through the Serengeti."

"Okay, Chester Cheetah, then why were you running with me?" Elise asked him.

"Because I was in love with you, Lise!" he said, his words surprising him.

Elise blushed and smiled. "Well, first, you just called me Lise. I know I should just let that go, but we both know I'm way too petty for that. Second, that's why I slowed down…I was in love with you too."

Jeremiah nodded his head and wondered what he should say next. He hadn't anticipated this kind of conversation, but he was enjoying their playful banter.

Going back and forth over nothing was always their thing. He hadn't realized how much he had missed it. And he had forgotten how happy it made him feel to make her smile.

Elise was content with the small victory and let him off the hook. "You don't have to say anything else. Let's finish watching this silly-tail damsel in distress, but I will say this. If you did have to come back for me and you got shot? Ooooh, Miah, yo mama would come back and haunt me. That's when she would take your side. I could hear her now. 'Elise, why you let my baby get shot? You know he sweet. He ain't a thug like you.'"

"Wait," Jeremiah objected. "So now I'm soft?" I can't get gangsta with it.?

You think I'm soft? And you sayin' my mama thought I was soft?"

"Miah, really, sir? Round two? You just beat the standing eight count. You don't want this thug smoke. Please, baby. Let's just watch the movie."

"I don't believe this! You really do think I'm soft!" he said, feigning offense. "Aww, him so cute when him mad," Elise teased.

"I am not cute!" Jeremiah protested.

Elise laughed. "You're right, baby. I'm sorry. What I meant to say is that in comparison to me, you're not a thug. Me? I got a Batman vibe. You? Not so much?"

"So, what? I'm Robin?" Jeremiah asked.

"No, I didn't say that. You're not Robin. You're Superman. You're strong, pure, and wholesome…but ain't nobody scared of you," she laughed. "Me? I strike fear into the hearts of the scum and villainy of this world while you're more like 'Come on, guys. Really? Now would Jesus do that? Let's give the little old lady her purse back before this thing gets ugly.'"

"And what would you do…Batman?" he asked, anticipating whatever humorous response she would come back with.

"I'd be like 'Ma'am, here is your purse back. Sorry about the blood on it. But they won't be bothering you anymore.'"

Jeremiah didn't even try to hold back his laughter. He was truly enjoying her. Elise was thankful she could still make him laugh. His laughter and his smile were genuine. He wasn't just there because he had to be. He wanted to be there and though he might not admit it, he wanted to be with her.

They finished the movie, told each other goodnight, and returned to their rooms. Elise didn't want the evening to end, but her fear of rejection kept her from saying so. Still, she wondered if he was feeling the same way. She wanted to let him know the door was open. She ran to the bathroom, brushed her teeth, splashed some water in all the appropriate spots, put on a fresh layer of his favorite body lotion, and applied some lip gloss.

Should I knock? she asked herself. *Should I just call his name? Maybe I should strip and just walk in? No, strip and go back to the shower and scream, "Jeremiah, I fell! Come save me!" No,* she thought. *Don't play games. Just knock on the door and talk to your husband.*

"Okay, Daddy," she whispered. "It's your baby girl. I'm tryna get back what the devil stole. Yeah, I know I gave it away, but I still need your help. I trust you, Daddy. In Jesus' name, Amen."

Once they were in their rooms they usually didn't communicate until the next day, but she knocked on his door anyway. She heard him scramble from the bed and make his way to the door.

"You okay?" He seemed concerned as he opened the door. "Yes, I'm fine," Elise smiled. "I just wanted to say thank you." "Thank you for what?"

"For everything you did tonight. For chilling with me and laughing with me.

For taking another 'L' in one of our debates." "Oh, so I took an 'L'?" Jeremiah asked.

"You took two, baby, your wife can outrun you and out thug you, but I digress," she giggled. "I really want to thank you for trying and most of all for calling me Lise. That was nice to hear again." She placed her hands on his shoulders and kissed him on the cheek.

"You're welcome. I had a good time." He seemed happy to see her but didn't attempt to capitalize on her affectionate gesture.

"I'm glad," she said as she took a step back and gave a military-style salute. "Goodnight, sir."

"Goodnight, Lise."

Elise returned to her room. She was disappointed but tonight was definitely a win. Slow progress was better than no progress. She sat on the edge of her bed and was pleasantly surprised by a knock at her door.

"Thank you, Jesus!" she whispered as she fist-pumped the air. "Just one second, Miah," she said through the closed door. *Okay, Elise, it's just like riding a bike. Let's do this!* she encouraged herself. *Besides, that man ain't had none in a while. You just basically have to be here.*

She waited just a few more seconds before opening the door. "Hey," she said cooly. "I must have dozed off. Did you forget something?" she asked in her sexiest voice.

Jeremiah smiled at her. She was still the most adorable woman in the world to him…and the most hilarious. "You dozed off in the ninety seconds from when I last saw you?" he questioned.

"Yes, I did. It was a long night. But why are you counting the seconds, sir?" "I was hoping we could talk. I have some things I need to say. Can I come in?"

"Sure," she responded.

His serious tone concerned her. It was not one of an amorous husband who had not been with his wife in months. She wasn't sure what was on his mind, but she knew what wasn't.

They sat down on the bed.

"Can I hold your hand?" he asked.

"Yes," she said, hoping she had misread him.

"Lise, I feel like I need to be completely transparent with you."

"Okay…about what?" she asked.

"I've been thinking about it too." "It?" she asked.

"Yeah…it. The big it. The real reason you knocked on my door tonight. I know you didn't want our night to end. I didn't want it to either."

"Well…if you know how I feel, and you feel the same…why aren't we doing something about it?"

"Lise, I've fasted and prayed but every time I think about me and you being together, I…." He paused.

Elise finished his sentence for him. "You think about me and Joshua?" "Yeah, I do," he admitted.

"Miah, that's completely understandable. I broke trust with you and I don't expect to earn it back overnight. I know it will take time. But I'm here for it. You're right. I was hoping for something a little different when I knocked on your door, and I was definitely hoping for something different when you knocked on mine."

They both laughed together.

"I understand that an affair isn't easily forgiven," she continued, "and I'm willing to wait until you can welcome me back and accept me. I meant what I said, Miah. Tonight meant the world to me. It wasn't sexual but we connected. That's really all I wanted, so thank you for coming to talk to me. It means everything just to know that you care enough to come and share. You don't have to be here, but you are and I appreciate it. I love you, Miah. I just have to believe that forgiveness, healing, and reconciliation will come in time. And I'm willing to wait until you're ready."

She gently placed her other hand on his leg. He responded by taking her by both of her hands. But he held his head down, not making eye contact.

"Was there something else?" she asked. "I'm sorry. You know I can outtalk you. You know me and my mouth."

Jeremiah chuckled softly but when he raised his head, she saw the tears in his eyes.

"What's wrong?" she asked.

"Lise, I love you, too. And I need you to know you are forgiven and I will always want the best for you. But you told me that I should tell you the truth. The truth is I want to just move forward with our lives and for us to be Miah and Lise like we used to be. I want to let it go, forget what happened, and be your husband again."

"But you can't, can you?" Elise asked him.

Jeremiah shook his head. "I don't think I can. His face is engrained in my mind. And every time I think of you, I think of you being with him. I try to push it out of my mind, but I can't. I try to focus at work and it's there. I go to the gym and it's there. I pray but it's always there and I think it always will be. I don't see a way back to us."

Elise took her hands back. "So, are you saying you want a divorce?" Jeremiah said nothing but his silence spoke volumes.

"Miah, I know you want to spare my feelings, but you have to say it. Do you want a divorce?"

"Lise, I honestly don't. But I don't know how to be your husband anymore. If there were a pill I could take to fix this, I would. I don't want it to be this way, but I feel trapped. There's no good answer. I can't imagine how I would live without you, but I can't imagine things would ever be the same with us either."

"Miah, as much as I have prayed, I think I knew this was coming. God prepared my heart for it. I know you and the Lord have forgiven me, but there are consequences, and these are mine. I will always love you, but my sin has taken you away from me. It's like a thorn in my side that God won't ever take away. He won't let me stop loving you, but he won't bring you back to me either. I will just have to live with the fact that when my husband needed me the most, and when I had an opportunity to honor God, I completely and utterly failed. I will always know that if I would have just held on, the Lord would have brought you back to me, but I didn't."

"I'm sorry, Lise."

"Baby, you don't have to be sorry. You didn't break our marriage vows. I did." "But I should have been there for you. I should have listened."

"We both have regrets, Miah. But we have to let each other off the hook, even if it's over. Is that what we're saying? That it's over?"

Jeremiah still couldn't form the words.

Elise kissed him on his cheek and laid her head on his shoulder. "Miah, it's okay. I knew this was a bridge too far. If it were the other way around, I would have lost my mind. You see, I did the fool just with a little neglect from you, and there was some neglect mind you, but I know I didn't have to do this. Uggh! This would be so much easier if you weren't such an amazing husband."

"It would be so much easier if you weren't such an amazing wife!" Jeremiah agreed. "I don't want it to be like this. I want things to be like they used to be. I just don't see how they can be. So, I guess you're my thorn too."

"So, we're here? We're getting a divorce?" Elise asked.

"I'm not saying that. I'm just saying I don't know how things can be the same or how I could be your husband."

"Miah, I'm sorry, but if you can't be my husband, then you kinda want a divorce."

"No, I don't," he protested.

"Yes, Miah, you do. You just don't want to say it, so let this thug help you out. I cheated on you. You don't have to accept that. I know you don't want to hurt me, and I know you don't have it in you to go file for a divorce. So, I will handle it. You deserve to be free."

"Lise, stop. I didn't say all that."

"Then what are you saying? You don't want me, but you don't want me to go? I can't do that. I am willing to release you so you can be at peace, but you have to do the same for me. I understand that you can't see a way back to us, but I can't live like that. I can't have just part of you. I can't live with you across the hall anymore. I could do it when I thought there was still hope and it was just a matter of me being patient, but that's not why you came over here. You came over here to do the right thing. You came over here to tell me not to bother humiliating myself by knocking on your door because you can't stand the thought of making love to me. I get it and I can't say I would do much better. But if you do love me, you won't make me stay here. Not like this. Every time you don't touch me, I will know why. I can't do it, Miah. God will get me through this, but you have to let me go."

"Lise, you don't have to go. We can work something out."

"Miah, what did you think was going to happen? That we were going to be roommates? Buddies? We just keep on like we have been these last two months with more laughs and conversation?"

Jeremiah shrugged his shoulder and looked down.

"Oh, baby, you did, didn't you? So, what, you're just going to let your adulterous wife hang out? I'm sorry, but that's a hard no. I know pride comes before a fall, but I have too much pride for that. No, Miah, please don't do that to me. If you can't be my husband I get it, but you have to let me go."

"What are you going to do?" Jeremiah asked.

"I don't know. Probably get an apartment or something."

"Okay…that's not what I meant. I guess it's none of my business, but are you going back to Joshua?"

"It's okay for you to ask that and no, I am not going back to Joshua. I love you, and not him. I just can't stay here like this."

"Are you gonna be okay?" Jeremiah asked her.

"Your girl is a real estate shark. I will be fine. I'm more worried about you. Are you gonna need alimony? I need you to be gentle now," she said humorously, hoping to make him smile.

"No, this new deal you helped me get will hold me for a second. I'm gonna finish this job for Chad and then figure out my next step."

"Your next step is Jeremiah Traylor Investments. And if you let me, I will still help you."

"I love you, Lise."

"I know you do. But thank you for saying it. I love you, too." "So, what do we do now?" he asked.

"I think I will need some space to process and come to grips with the fact that there won't be a you-and-me anymore. Miah, I know you. You will try and see about me, but I don't need sympathy or false hope. For a little while, let's keep it business and only talk if we have to."

"You mean about the divorce?"

"That and about Daddy too. He's doing better, but if he needs anything I will be there."

"I know you will. Thanks. This really sucks," he said.

"Ha. Yes, it does but the failure is mine and I have to own it. I'm not going to do it by myself this time. I'm going to trust God and stay accountable and let him heal me. It's strange but I'm already praising him. I'm thankful that we can still be good to each other. You've been my best friend since I've known you. It will change but I don't want it to stop. I just need some space to readjust."

"So, you think we can just be friends?" Jeremiah asked.

"No, not just friends," Elise said. "It will be something different. It will take a while, I think, for both of us, but we just have to see what it looks like once God heals us. But rest assured, Superman. Let somebody mess with you and Batman will swoop in from out of the darkness and smite them with my wrathful vengeance. And when I do, don't be looking at my booty in my tights. No, Superman, the cookie shop is closed. You had your chance."

Jeremiah faked a smile. Elise could see his pain and wanted to comfort him. "Miah, it's going to be okay…for both of us. I just hit rock bottom and I can tell you, when Jesus is the rock at the bottom, you don't get crushed, you get caught. It doesn't get so bad that he won't heal. We just have to trust him."

Jeremiah eased closer to her and put his arm around her. "Okay. But you have to promise to let me know if you need anything."

Elise melted into his embrace for what she feared might be the last time. "I actually need something right now," she said. "Do you think you can hold your friend while she cries about her marriage breaking up?"

Jeremiah pulled Elise close to him as the tears formed in both their eyes. He whispered into her ear. "I can do that. I think I will even cry with her."

CHAPTER 91

Miah Against the World

DAY 617

"Jeremiah, this is amazing!" Chad said as he looked at his aunt's newly remodeled house.

"Yes, young man," Chad's Aunt Clarice agreed. "I can't believe you've taken it from what it was, to this! You really have a gift. Everything looks so nice."

"And you did it ahead of schedule and within budget," Chad added.

"I'm glad you're pleased, ma'am," Jeremiah said humbly. "I've been blessed to find good people to work with. I hope you can see the craftsmanship."

"I do," Clarice confirmed. "And your selections are amazing. I'm terrible at things like that but I can't imagine making better choices for the fixtures, floors, and colors. Did you work with an interior designer?"

"No ma'am. I...I...," Jeremiah stuttered as he thought about his muse, "I have a friend who has great taste. I just tried to imagine what she would like, and I put it in your house."

"Well, we appreciate you and your friend," Clarice said.

"For sure," Chad agreed as he handed Jeremiah an envelope. "And here's your final payment. I sorta figured you were going to go above and beyond, so I tried to do the same. This will hold you over until you start your new position as our National Operations Director," Chad winked.

Jeremiah smiled. "Nice try, Chad. And I appreciate it. But I think

I've found my passion. I'm gonna be launching Jeremiah Traylor Investments soon. I already have my eye on a few properties. I'm gonna do this full time and see what happens."

"I understand and I know you'll do well. My doors are always open Jeremiah.

For work or just to talk. It's been a pleasure, sir."

"Same here, Chad," Jeremiah said as he shook hands with him.

"I can't blame you for turning it down," Chad said. "I know you'd rather spend time with your wife than traveling three or four days a week."

"Yeah, you're right about that," Jeremiah said. "Take care, Chad."

Jeremiah left Chad and his aunt. The job was a complete success and Chad had given him a very generous bonus on top of their agreed payment. He should have been on top of the world, but Elise's absence took all the joy from his success. She had wanted to see the house once it was done but that was before she moved out. Now she needed space and other than some awkward moments at church, they had not spoken or even texted since she left. She had been gone for two weeks now. He had respected her request to keep a healthy distance so they could heal. But he missed her terribly.

Missing her wasn't particularly surprising to him. The fact that she had not reached out was. Every thought in his mind was of her. He wondered if she felt the same. They had parted on amicable terms, but they had still parted. This project had consumed his time and provided a much-needed distraction from his faltering marriage.

Now that the project was over, he would need to focus full time on getting things going for his own company. Just a few short weeks ago, he and Elise were going to do it together. Now, he was going to have to do it alone and the prospect was not nearly as appealing. It wasn't that he didn't think he could do it. He simply just didn't want to do it without her.

CHAPTER 92

Okay, You're Who?

DAY 670

Elise's mind wandered as she stood in line with her overflowing shopping cart. Semi-single life was bearable but not preferable. She missed Jeremiah terribly. Her desire to call him grew stronger every day. He was right when he said, "This really sucks." She agreed but they both needed space to heal and prepare for lives spent apart.

Her new apartment was fine, but it had no personality. She had spent the day shopping for various items to make her new place a home. As she waited for the cashier, an older lady with a toddler got in line behind her. She noticed she only had a few items and was struggling to control the squirming baby and manage the shopping cart.

"Ma'am. Please go ahead of me. You and little cute chunks there got places to go and things to do," she smiled.

"Oh, thank you, young lady. Are you sure? We can wait," the older lady replied. She seemed like she might be around the same age Mama Etta would have been.

"No, ma'am. Please go ahead," Elise said as she stepped aside. The baby grinned at Elise as the older lady rolled her cart past her. "He is soooo cute," Elise said. "What's his name?"

"This is Isaiah," she answered as Elise reached out and played with the baby's foot.

She realized just how little interaction she had had with small children since the death of her child. She was pleasantly surprised and thankful not to be overwhelmed with emotion. Elise was satisfied with the baby's smile and the foot play, but young Isaiah had more in mind and reached his chubby arms out to her. "Ooh, wee. He never does that," the older lady said. "I think I have him

spoiled. I can barely keep him off my hip, but he sure does like you." "May I?" Elise asked.

"Chile, please. Yes, take him," the older lady laughed.

Elise reached her arms to the little boy, who giggled as she took him. He played with her earrings as Elise spoke to her.

"How old is he?" Elise asked.

"He's almost fourteen months," the woman replied.

Elise beamed at her new little friend. "I bet you are into everything, aren't you?" Elise asked, again, surprised that she wasn't more emotional about snuggling with a little boy that was the same age her son would have been.

"Baby, you don't even know," the woman chuckled. "Granny can't turn her back on you for a second, can I?" she said to the little boy, who was totally enthralled with Elise.

"That will be $42.85, ma'am," the cashier informed her, causing the woman to grimace.

"I'm sorry, baby. I only have $35 today. I'm going to have to put some of this back."

Elise looked at the few items she was purchasing. She had the typical essential items for someone with a baby. But Elise noticed that she wasn't buying anything in bulk. This would only last her a few days at best.

"I will come back for these wipes," she said. She looked over at Isaiah. "Granny just gon wipe that little butt with some tissue and soap you down after."

"Ma'am," Elise chimed in. "Please, let me get it."

"No, sweetie," the older lady objected. "We will be all right. Baby wipes are a luxury."

"No, ma'am. Let me get it all. Please. I really want to do this. I insist. And you can pay me back by letting me play with little cute chunks here while you load my junk on the conveyer."

"Well, I guess I can't beat that deal. Are you sure?"

"Yes, ma'am. I'm totally sure. I should be paying you for this," Elise said as she snuggled her nose against his ear. "Ain't that right, little cute chunks? Tell Granny you worth more than $42.85."

They gathered their items and Elise paid the cashier. She was happy to be a small blessing but felt led to do more.

"Ma'am, are you sure this is all you need? I know it's not my place, but this isn't going to last him very long."

"Oh, I know, baby. This will hold him until I get my check and then I can stock up," the woman explained.

Elise scrunched her lips humorously at the older lady. "Well, my little cute chunks said he don't wanna wait that long. He said he ready now."

"You are so sweet, young lady, but you don't have to do anything else." "Yes, ma'am. I really do. Seriously, this is the Lord. Please let me be a blessing to you."

"Well, if you gon bring the Lord into it, then I'm not gon argue. I'm Patricia, by the way."

"Patricia, I'm Elise. It's a pleasure. Let's get these things to the car, and then me and my little cute chunks here are going to show you how to shop. You ain't ready," Elise teased.

They returned to the store after taking their items to the car. Elise still had not let Isaiah go, and Patricia was relieved for the help.

"Okay, Ms. Patricia," Elise directed. "First, we need to get you one of those strap-on carriers. You know, like a papoose. And we can get you a stroller too. Little cute chunks is too big to be carrying around like this."

"Well, yes, ma'am," Patricia agreed.

"And I want you to get fully loaded. Let the Lord bless you," Elise encouraged her.

"Well, we appreciate the Lord and you too, sweetheart. But we don't need that much."

Elise shook her head and looked at Isaiah, who had forgotten his fascination with her earrings and focused on her cheeks. "Little cute chunks, I see right now we gon have to school ya granny. But it's okay. We'll teach her."

Patricia tried to stay conservative, but Elise wanted Isaiah to have the very best and to have more than enough. She tried to only get the essential items, but Elise would double everything and then suggest others. By the time they were finished, they had two overflowing shopping carts. Elise was thankful as they walked to the cashier for the second time. She was thankful to be in a position to bless this woman but even more thankful that the Lord's healing allowed her to be a blessing without her heart being wrenched with the thoughts of her own child.

Elise helped Patricia to her car. Her heart was heavy as she placed Isaiah in his seat. Isaiah made it clear that he too was not eager to part with his new friend. "Isaiah, she can't hold you forever, baby," Patricia said. "Quit fussing so she can help Granny."

They got everything loaded into the car as Isaiah continued to voice his tearful objection to his abandonment.

"I'm sorry, little cute chunks. It was nice to meet you," Elise said as she kissed him on the top of his head.

"Elise, I can't repay you but if you have time, I've been called a pretty good cook. I have plenty at the house. I know we've taken up a lot of your time, but I'd love to have you over for lunch. It's not far."

"Ms. Patricia, that is so sweet. If it's not too much trouble, then I'd love to have lunch with you."

"Uh-huh. You ain't slick, girl. You just tryna get to yo little cute chunks," she laughed.

"Maybe," Elise laughed.

Elise followed Patricia to her home. It was in a modest older neighborhood not unlike Daddy and Mama Etta's. The house wasn't immaculate, but this older woman plus a little baby were probably never going to equal an immaculate house. Still, it had a very homey feel to it. There were pictures of what Elise assumed were various family members, but photos of Isaiah and another young man dominated the landscape. Elise was curious as to how this older lady had gotten the responsibility of caring for this little boy. She wondered exactly what Patricia's role in Isaiah's life was and where his mother and father were.

Elise sat at the kitchen table and gave Isaiah his sippy cup as Patricia prepared their lunch.

"So, little lady, where's your husband?" Patricia asked boldly.

"Ms. Patricia, you make me feel like the woman at the well. Why did you ask me that?" Elise asked.

"You're a beautiful young woman with a nice diamond wedding ring on your finger, and you are choosing to spend your time and your money with an old lady and her grandbaby. So, I have to wonder, where's your husband and what is he going to say when he sees this bill?"

"It doesn't matter. I'm pretty sure he's not going to be my husband much longer. It's hard to talk about it but it's me, not him. I really hurt him, and I don't think our marriage is going to recover," Elise confided.

"Baby, it's usually not just one person's fault, and you don't have to tell me what you did either. We've all sinned and fallen short," Patricia comforted.

"I know that, and I appreciate the grace. But some things can't be undone. We've been through a lot, but I really let him down. It's sad because we still love each other, but some things can't be overcome. It's just too much."

"I said the same thing recently," Patricia said. "I was looking at my bills and I was looking at my money and I said, 'Lord, it's just too much.' And then on the way back from Isaiah's doctor appointment, I felt the Lord telling me to go pick him up some things. I said, 'Lord, you know I don't have enough money to get him all he needs.' But I obeyed and I met you."

"Aww, that's sweet, Ms. Patricia. But I don't think it's the same thing."

"I know it's not the same thing, but it is the same God. He can handle things when they get to be too much. That's all I'm saying. Don't give up too soon. You don't sound like somebody who wants a divorce. Like me…your blessing may be just around the corner. And I'm not just saying this because you bought me and Isaiah a year's supply of groceries, but I don't care what you did. That man would be a fool to let you go."

"I appreciate that, Ms. Patricia, but since you all up in my bizness… are you married?"

"No, sweetheart. I was. But I raised Isaiah's daddy by myself. We were married for a short time, and I thought that things were okay. I got pregnant and it was a happy time until I found out another lady was having his baby too," Patricia chuckled.

"I'm sorry you had to go through that, Ms. Patricia."

"It's okay, baby. It was a long time ago, but I never found anybody that wanted me and Corey, that was my son's name. So, I just poured everything into him. I tried to be a good mother and raise him right. I wanted him to be a good, strong, loving, and kind man."

It seemed to Elise that Patricia wanted to say more but held back.

"I hope you don't mind me asking, but where is Corey and Isaiah's mother?"

Patricia set Elise's plate in front of her. "You sure you want to know? It's not a happy story."

"Ms. Patricia, I bet I could give you a run for your money on sad stories, but you go first. Oh, my," she paused as she looked at the plate. "This does look good. Thank you so much."

"You want me to take him while you eat?" Patricia offered.

"Uhh, my little cute chunk is fine," Elise objected. "Don't be tryna steal him.

Tell your story."

"Well, his mama came here when Isaiah was about two months old. She said she had to go out of town and needed me to watch him. That wasn't too unusual, so I didn't think anything of it. But that was the last time I ever saw her. I went to her apartment and the landlord said he hadn't been paid in two months and hadn't heard from her. I even filed a report, but the police couldn't find her either. So about three months ago, one of her relatives called me to tell me that she had killed herself."

"Ms. Patricia, that is awful. I'm so sorry," Elise said sympathetically.

"I told you it was sad. She left me a note saying that she was sorry, but she just couldn't do it anymore. She didn't know how to be a mother and she didn't know how to live without Corey."

"Did she and Corey break up?" Elise asked. "No, baby, Corey died over a year ago."

Elise's heart sank. "Ms. Patricia, I am so sorry. That's so much to deal with." "It's okay, sweetheart. You didn't do anything wrong. But you're right, it has been a challenge. I tried to work hard and make a good life, but I've had a few bouts with cancer and between the bills and just trying to live I don't have a whole lot in reserve. Plus, Corey… well, he was a good man, but he had some issues that drained me. I even had to get a loan against my house just to bury him. And your little chubby buddy there is expensive. But the Lord keeps providing. It's funny how he gives and takes away. I think it would have broke me to lose Corey if Isaiah hadn't been around. The Lord used him to give me the will to keep wanting to live and to keep trusting and believing. Now I just need about twenty-two more good years of strength. I will be ninety-five years old when this baby graduates high school."

"And it's just you? You don't have any family to help you?" Elise asked. "It's just me and Jesus, sweetheart. But he's enough," Patricia answered confidently.

"Well, we are just going to pray the Lord give you long life and strength so you can see little man grow up. I'm going to put you on a workout-and-nutrition plan. You can't be eatin' like this, Ms. Patricia. This is too good to be healthy," Elise laughed.

"Okay, coach, whatever you say," Patricia agreed. "It will be fine. Isaiah is my second chance."

"What do you mean your second chance?" Elise asked.

"I've had some failures, Elise. I hate to make excuses, but it's hard for a woman to turn a boy into a man. Children need both parents. I tried to raise Corey right. He was a sweet boy and a sweet man. But I guess what they say about generational curses has some truth to it. His daddy never spent much time with him, but he was a drinker. If

I would have known then what I know now, I would have told Corey to never take a drink. But when he got older, he started. It didn't seem like it was a big deal. It started with just a little beer here and there. But before I knew it that drinking had consumed him. He spent most of his life battling that alcohol. He would lose jobs because of it. He got in trouble with the law because of it. And every time I would come running to the rescue and he would promise, 'Mama, I'm gon stop.' And 'Mama, I promise this time I'm gon beat it.' But he never could. I prayed and I fussed but I just couldn't get him to stop, Elise!" she said as she struck her fist on the table, causing Isaiah to jump.

"Ms. Patricia, sometimes you can do everything right and still can't stop people from doing wrong," Elise comforted as she rocked the startled Isaiah.

"Sweetheart, a lot of people told me that. 'Make him be a man,' they told me. 'He won't learn if you keep savin' him,' they would say. Sometimes I wish I hadn't listened to them. Maybe Corey would still be alive."

"What do you mean, Ms. Patricia?" Elise asked sympathetically.

"Corey called me the night he died. I had just finished chemo and it took so much out of me. He already had a DWI, and we agreed that he would always call me if he was drunk. He said Isaiah's mama was in labor, and he wanted me to come and get him and take him to the hospital. I told him I couldn't drive. I didn't even drive myself home. I took an Uber. I told him that's what he should do. But he drove anyway and ended up getting himself killed."

Patricia tried to control her emotions as she relived the night, but Elise could see the pain on her face. Elise took her free hand and placed it on top of Patricia's. "It's okay, Ms. Patricia. You were sick."

"I think about it every day, Elise. It's an awful thing to know that your child would still be here if you would have just gotten out of the bed," Patricia sighed. "But anyway, that's why I say Isaiah is my second chance. If the Lord will give me strength, I'm determined to get it right with this one," she said as she pointed to Isaiah.

"Well, as much as I know it hurts, little man here is something to be thankful for," Elise said.

"Amen!" Patricia agreed. "And let me tell you something else. I am so thankful that the people in the other car didn't get killed."

"Oh, he hit someone else?" Elise asked.

"Baby, yes. They said he T-boned another car going around 80-90 mph. But they were fine," Patricia told her."

Elise's heart stopped as she considered what Patricia had just said. She looked at Isaiah as he was drifting off to sleep. If he was fourteen months old, then he was the same age as J.J. would have been. His father was a drunk driver who had died in an accident on the way to his birth. An accident where he T-boned another car. "Please Daddy, no," she prayed. "I'm not ready for another test."

"And he hit the other car?" Elise asked again.

"Yes, Corey died at the scene of the accident but the people in the other car survived," Patricia confirmed.

"And this happened the night Corey was born?" Elise asked as she looked at the little boy who was now sleeping in her arms.

"Yes. My son died the same night my grandson was being born," Patricia said. Elise allowed the tears to stream from her eyes. She had become very accustomed to crying. This was different though. Those feelings of anger, abandonment, and disillusionment with God that caused her to turn her back on him, rushed back like a flood. Patricia saw Elise's tears but completely misunderstood her distress. "Baby, you are too sweet but don't take my problems on you. I told you; the Lord is taking care of us. You dry those tears."

"Ma'am, when was Isaiah born?" Elise asked.

"He was born last year on November 13," Patricia said.

There it was. Isaiah was born on the same day of the crash. The same day J.J. was born. The same day J.J. died. But there was only one way to be sure. She had always known the name of the driver that was responsible for the worst day of her life. There was never any reason to pursue a course of justice since he died at the scene. But Elise always knew his name. Corey Caldwell.

"Ms. Patricia," Elise said, "Did I hear you say your last name was Caldwell?" "Well...yes, Baby," Patricia confirmed, trying to remember if she had actually told Elise her last name or not.

"And your son…he was Corey Caldwell?" Elise asked, her lips quivering. "Yes, baby. My son was Corey Caldwell."

"And he died the day Isaiah was born? In a car accident on November 13?

After he crashed into another car?" Elise questioned.

"Yes, baby. I said that. Now, you calm down, sweetheart. You're trembling. You're one of those people who feel other people's pain deeply, aren't you?" Patricia asked.

Elise's tears continued to flow. She had confessed and repented from her sins. The Lord had brought her back from her hog pen experience and even though she had to pay for the cost of her rebellion with her marriage, she was healed. She had accepted that it was not for her to understand why her baby had to die and she once again put her trust in the God who was always right, always good, and always for her. But would a good God keep playing these games with her? She had taken an opportunity she thought was provided by the Lord to be good to someone else, and the Lord's reply was to bring her face to face with the mother and child of her son's killer. She remembered the dark path she had chosen before and the consequences they had borne. If this was a test to see if she would offer the same forgiveness she had been given, then she was about to fail. This woman needed to know what her son had done to her. And she was going to tell her.

"Other people's pain?" Elise asked angrily. No, woman! I don't give a damn about other people's pain. What about my pain? I want you to know that the people your sorry-ass son hit weren't fine. They were far from it. How do I know? Because he hit me and my husband. We were on the way to the hospital too when your alcoholic son plowed into us. And you sit up here talking about a second chance. I had a son too and he was my last chance. I never even got to play with him or change him or breastfeed him. But you get a second chance because you don't know how to raise a child? Your son took everything from me! I lost my child. I lost my husband. I lost myself. I lost my faith. Why didn't you call him an Uber yourself? You know your child is a ticking time bomb and you just let him roam free on the street. How many times did you coddle him and give him another chance just so he could go out and kill somebody? You're just as responsible as him and you don't deserve to be rewarded with this baby!"

"Elise, here, sweetheart. Take a sip of this and breathe," Patricia said as she held the glass up to her lips. "You look like you're a million miles away. Are you okay?"

Patricia's voice calmed Elise and brought her back from the vengeance-fill rant she had just rehearsed in her mind. "No, Ms. Patricia. I'm not okay. I need to tell you something," Elise said.

Patricia gently rubbed Elise's hand. "Take your time, baby. I'm listening." "I want you to know…." Elise paused, as she looked down at the peacefully resting Isaiah, "…that whatever you and Isaiah need, I want to help. You will never have to do this by yourself. Life is not always what we call fair, but someone very special used to tell me that God is always right, always good, and always for us. I forgot that not too long ago and it cost me everything. But now I want you to trust that for yourself. I don't believe in coincidences with God. I don't know why but he put us together today and he has a plan. So, from this day forward, you can consider me your own personal ride-or-die. And please give yourself grace about your son. You did the best you could and trust me, the Lord forgives you. And if you could talk to the people in that car, I truly feel like they would forgive you and your son."

"Baby, I hope so. I am just so glad no one was killed or seriously hurt. I couldn't live with that."

Elise could only surmise that perhaps the full truth had been kept from her.

And if that was the case, she would not be the one to tell her any differently.

"But sweetheart, you don't owe me anything," Patricia continued. "You've done so much already."

"And whatever the Lord will allow, I'm going to do more. May I pray with you, Ms. Patricia?" Elise requested.

"Of course you can, sweetheart," Patricia said softly.

"Daddy, I come to you in the name of your Son, and my Savior, Jesus. I thank you for your strength and your grace in this moment. Your ways are higher than mine and your thoughts are different but even in the spaces where I don't understand, you still somehow, someway work all things together for my good, and I trust that is what you are doing right now."

Isaiah stirred gently in Elise's arms, and she recalled how she had prayed for

J.J. to do the same but the Lord chose not to respond. Still, she pressed on in prayer. "So, Daddy, since Ms. Patricia loves you, we are expecting you to work all things out for good in her life as well. I trust you, Lord, that you will make her

latter days better than her former days and that your joy would be her strength."

Elise recalled her wailing in the church floor when they closed J.J.'s little casket. Patricia's son had taken her son from her, but she knew the pain of that loss and she pressed on in prayer.

"Please be faithful to your promise to never leave her or forsake her. We give you praise, Precious Lord, because you never forget or fail. Please give her beauty for her ashes. Please make the dry bones live again. And please be close to Ms. Patricia where her heart is broken and please save her where her spirit is crushed. Lord Jesus, you know my failures and my sin, but I know your finished work on the cross is enough and your blood has purified me from my sin. So, I ask that you would use me, someone who is totally unlike you, to be a blessing to this sweet woman and this precious baby."

Isaiah smiled in his sleep. She never saw her son smile, but she remembered all the prayers Jeremiah and she prayed for him when she was pregnant. J.J. would never experience the fruit of those prayers but perhaps Isaiah could. So, she pressed on in prayer.

"Daddy, I want to thank you for my little friend," she prayed as she kissed him on his forehead. "Please protect my lil' cute chunks. May he know you all the days of his life as Lord, as Father, and as his very best friend. May he be a friend to you as you grow him in your grace and never let the enemy get a hold of his heart and mind. I pray for days of grace and wisdom for him. I pray for his future days to come and that he would personally know you as a provider and protector. Jesus, I pray you make him strong in you and your mighty power. I pray you show him how to love you with all his heart, mind, soul, and strength, and I pray you would use him to give your love to others. I declare your promises over Isaiah's life, Lord. He is a masterpiece who will do all the good works you prepared in advance for him to do. When the enemy attacks, may he know in the deepest part of himself that you are for him and that he is more than a conqueror. And since you are for him, I trust that along with Christ you will graciously give him all things. May he know the length, the width, the height, and the depth of your love as you make yourself at home in his heart by faith."

Elise recalled her failure in her hospital bed as the Lord offered his hand of grace as well as her failure with Joshua. But she felt in her spirit that if she asked the Lord would answer, so she pressed on in prayer.

"Lord Jesus, when you, in your sovereignty, allow the enemy to sift him as wheat, I trust that as you ever live to make intercession for him, you will not let his faith fail. Please don't let him stray from his intimacy with you and his trust in you. But Precious Jesus, if he does, I know you to be the good shepherd, and I know you will leave the ninety-nine and go and get him back so he doesn't stay away too long."

Elise looked at his adorable baby face. She had always imagined J.J. would look like Jeremiah, but he never grew to manhood. Somehow she knew this little boy would. And she pressed on in prayer.

"Precious Jesus, as you grow him into manhood, please make him ever mindful of the cross and your shed blood. May he offer himself to you daily as a living sacrifice, always being holy and pleasing to you. Please show him how to worship you with his life and give him strength so he is not like this hard cruel world, but please totally change him for you and your glory as he daily renews his mind. I ask that you make it so his days are lived out in your good, pleasing, and perfect will, as he becomes one with you as you are one with the Father. Daddy, I trust you for these things and believe that you will do even more than what I ask, imagine, or think for my son…I mean…my little friend, Isaiah. Thank you for the victory, peace, and love that only you can give. We pray and receive it together in Jesus' name, Amen."

"Lord," Patricia continued in prayer, "you know I can't pray like that, but I know when someone is weighed down with disappointment and pain. I thank you for this precious young child of yours, and I ask that you give her strength, joy, and peace. Whatever she feels like she has done wrong, Lord, I ask you to help her to experience your forgiveness. And Lord, as you have used her to perform a miracle in my life today, I ask that you perform some miracles in her life as well. Show her you are not done yet. Turn it around for her, Lord. I pray this in Jesus' name, Amen."

The two new friends sat in silence for a moment. Patricia's heart overflowed with gratitude. Elise's generosity would take care of her and Isaiah's basic needs for two months, but Patricia was more thankful for her presence. Her kindness and her humor seemed to lighten the load of her life and as much as she loved Isaiah, her assistance with the active toddler was right on time. She didn't want to burden Elise with her problems, but the same cancer she had been battling for years had returned. It was unlikely she would see Isaiah's next birthday much less his high school graduation.

Elise's emotions vacillated between light and dark. If there were a picture of love at first sight, Elise and the resting baby in her arms would be it. But this wasn't her baby. He belonged to the man who took her baby from her. She was thankful for the guard the Lord had put over her mouth but for now, it would be best that she exit stage left.

"Ms. Patricia, as much as I hate to, I had better go," Elise announced.

"Oh, sweetheart, I hate to see you leave but I understand. Don't you worry about me now. Me and Isaiah are going to be just fine," Patricia assured her.

"Yes, ma'am, but just the same, can I call you sometimes? Or maybe come by for a visit?" Elise requested.

"Of course you can,". Patricia agreed. "I'm sure Isaiah would love to see you again."

"I want you to take my number, Ms. Patricia. Please, if you need anything, let me know."

Reluctantly, Elise handed Isaiah back to Patricia. They embraced and she returned to her car. She couldn't tell Patricia what had really happened without revealing things that would hurt her, but she needed to talk to someone. She still had the scars from trying to process her emotions on her own.

She knew there was someone she could call who would listen to her and comfort her, but it wouldn't be fair to call him. After all, she was the one who had ended things and insisted they shouldn't talk to each other. But every time she had reached out to him before, he was there. And whether it was inappropriate or not, she needed him now. She dialed the number and thankfully, he picked up.

"Hi. I'm sorry to bother you,". Elise said. "I know I said we aren't supposed to see each other, and I really appreciate you respecting that and not reaching out. But there's a lot happening, and I need someone to talk to…just talk. Can I come over?"

"Okay. Come on over. I'm home," he said warmly. "Thanks. I'm on the way."

CHAPTER 93

A Safe Place to Land

DAY 670

"This is crazy," he said as he tried to process her close-to-unbelievable story. "If it wasn't you telling me, I wouldn't believe it."

"I can barely believe it!" Elise exclaimed. "And I was there."

"Are you okay? That's a lot to process and you've been through so much. I can't tell you what to do, but maybe you ought to give them some space. I really do feel bad for this old lady and the baby, but I don't want you getting overwhelmed. This shouldn't be your burden to carry."

It had been some time since they spoke, but it was nice to see he still wore his feelings for her on his sleeve.

"I'm still processing but the reality is I just realized just how much the Lord had healed me. I'm not saying it's not something I need to be careful about, but I really do feel whole. It was just the shock of realizing where I was. I looked around the house and saw his pictures and he didn't look like the devil. And O…M…G… that baby was so adorable. You should have seen him with his little ole cute chunky self. That's what I call him…my little cute chunks."

"Your little cute chunks?" he asked.

"I know what you're trying to say. I know that's not my baby," Elise said, trying to sound unemotional.

"Babies have a way of stealing hearts. Especially in a case like yours. You have to be careful. I'm glad you called. I really am. But I don't want you to get hurt and I don't want you to get taken advantage of," he said.

"She doesn't have that spirit. She didn't ask for anything. But I hear you and I will try to be careful."

"You get major points for not telling her," he said.

"I wanted to," Elise admitted. "My flesh had a speech written that was going to rival Martin's 'I Have a Dream' speech, but when I opened up my mouth nothing but blessing came out."

"Well, that had to be God," he responded. "Nobody but Jesus kept that mouth of yours in check," he laughed.

"Uhh…no, sir. Don't do me," she said. "Too soon?" he grinned.

"Just a little," she smiled.

"Well, I'm proud of you and I think the Lord would be very pleased. I don't know how you did it, but I think you did the right thing. It's crazy but it's not like it was her fault. Still, I can't get over it. For you to meet her after all this time? And she doesn't know about the baby and all the other stuff that happened that day?" he inquired.

"I couldn't tell her. It would have crushed her. Maybe it's not the same, but I know what it feels like to lose a son. And apparently, he was a tortured soul. I didn't want to give her another bad memory of him," Elise said sympathetically. "She called her grandson her second chance. I know how good it feels to get a second chance. I just want her to be at peace. And even if it's not the wisest move, I want to help her if I can."

"And your little cute chunks?" he grinned.

"Yes! My little cute chunks," she beamed. "You should have seen him looking at me with those adoring brown eyes. It was love at first sight."

"Well, I can tell you from personal experience you can have that effect on a brother," he said.

Elise smiled brightly at his words. He hadn't seen that smile in a while, but it still overwhelmed him with joy.

"Well, sir…we aren't supposed to be talking, but thanks for letting me come over. I knew you would understand."

"I think no matter what happens, I will always be here if you need me," he said, almost as if he was just coming to the realization himself.

"Even when another woman comes along?" she asked mischievously. "You're a tough act to follow. She'll just have to understand," he responded.

"That's sweet but I really just want you to be happy. Especially with all I've put you through."

"I know you do. And I appreciate it," he said.

They looked at each other and smiled. They both wanted to say more. They both wanted the other to take the short trip across the room and pull them into their arms. They both wanted to abandon wisdom. To forget the past and the future. To forget the risks and the consequences. But they were both afraid. There was a reason they were apart, and too much had happened to ignore those reasons.

"I'd better go," Elise said regretfully. "I know I shouldn't say this but if you need me, you call me."

"Are you sure your husband won't mind?" he asked with a sly smile. "Yes, Miah," she smiled. "I am sure my husband won't mind."

CHAPTER 94

Instant Family

DAY 730

"Excuse me. My name is Elise Traylor. I'm here to see Patricia Caldwell," Elise said, trying to remain calm.

She and Patricia had become fast friends, so she wasn't at all surprised to get a phone call from her. She was surprised when the other voice on the call didn't belong to Patricia. A nurse from the hospital had called her and said Patricia had to be brought in to the hospital and that someone needed to come and get Isaiah.

"Yes, ma'am," the nurse responded politely. "She's going to be in the first room on your left."

"And the baby?" Elise asked.

"Well, little man is in there cuttin' up, so if you can calm him down it would be much appreciated," the nurse told her.

"Oh, my goodness. I hear him! I'm sorry. He doesn't like strangers or doctors, so I can only imagine what y'all have been going through," Elise explained as she imagined Isaiah's behavior.

"Just follow the uncontrollable wailing," the nurse teased. "He's a mess."

Elise could joke with the best of them. She could give it and usually could take it. But she felt some kind of way about any implication that Isaiah was less than perfect.

"Saiah…stop it! You embarrassing us," she said as she entered the room. "Elise, is that you?" the woman holding Isaiah asked.

"Monique? Yes, it's me. What are you doing here?" she asked.

"Work," Monique said plainly as Isaiah squirmed and wailed. "Do you want him?"

"Yes, I'll take him," Elise said.

"Girl, here," Monique said, shaking her head. "I can't do anything to please him."

Elise took Isaiah, who was miraculously healed the moment he felt her embrace.

"Little boy, I know you didn't just do me like this," Monique complained. "Don't worry about him. He's just not a people person yet," Elise explained.

"Why are you here?"

Elise checked in with Monique quite often to see how Amari was doing. But seeing Isaiah in her arms brought back the memory of her taking her away.

"The doctor will be here in a moment. It's better for him to tell you," Monique explained.

"I'm here," a tall redheaded man said as he came into the room. "Ma'am…," the doctor said as he looked at Elise, "I'm Dr. Young. I'm Patricia's oncologist."

"I'm Elise. It's nice to meet you," Elise responded nervously. "So, what's happening?"

"Patricia, do you want to tell her?" the doctor asked. "You go ahead," Patricia said, looking rather annoyed.

"Elise, Patricia is a very sick woman. I've recommended she go into hospice care but she's resistant. Normally, I would say it's her life and let her do whatever she wants, but I'm bound by law and conscience to intervene when a baby is involved. Patricia is a wonderful woman, but she is no longer in any condition to care for this little boy."

"Elise, I told this man I'm fine. I can take care of Isaiah. People get sick sometimes. I just had a bad day," Patricia objected.

"No, Patricia. I'm sorry, but you're not fine. My heart goes out to you, but I told you months ago that you would need to consider other options for Isaiah. You were lucky today. Next time that might not be the case. What if you lose consciousness and no one knows? How do you think Isaiah would do if that happens?"

Patricia sighed and turned her head in frustration.

"Elise," Dr. Young continued, "Patricia doesn't have any family to take care of the baby, but she has you listed as an emergency contact. So, I had the nurse call you and Monique's office. My job is to take care of Patricia. You three can decide the best way to take care of this little guy. But if you want my two cents, it's pretty clear where he wants to be." He was thankful that the young boy's screams were no longer echoing through the hospital halls.

"Wait…," Elise said. "What's happening? Ms. Patricia has to go on hospice?" "That's my recommendation," Dr. Young confirmed. "We've done all we can for her."

"How long does she have?" Elise asked almost in a whisper.

Dr. Young looked over at Patricia for permission. Patricia simply nodded. "Three months at best," he said. "So, you can see, it's important that this little guy gets squared away."

"I'd like to talk to Elise alone if that's okay, Doctor," Monique requested. "Sure," Dr. Young agreed. "Patricia, I know you're upset with me. But I will be back in a little bit to check on you." "Whatever," Patricia said dryly.

"Ms. Patricia!" Elise scolded. "We will not speak to the nice doctor that way." "He need to mind his bizness," Patricia defended herself.

"I'm gon deal with you later," Elise said through gritted teeth. "Me and Saiah need to talk to Monique."

Elise stepped outside with Monique.

"Elise, I know this is sudden," Monique started. "Is this something you're prepared to do? You and Jeremiah have been through so much. If she only has three months to live, then that means you're going to have a two-year-old before long. That's a big commitment. I know your first instinct is to jump in, but you don't have to."

"And if I don't?" Elise asked, already knowing what her decision was.

"If you don't, we will have to monitor Patricia and Isaiah more closely to make sure he is taken care of. But based on what the doctor is saying and her having to call 911 today, it's clear he's probably right. She can't take care of this baby and she might not be around much longer regardless. Which means if they don't have family, we are going to have to find someone to take care of him."

As if on cue, Isaiah leaned in and kissed Elise on the cheek causing Monique to laugh out loud.

"He's a player," Monique teased.

"He think he slick," Elise said as she shook her head. "Listen, no offense, but I don't want him in the system. Can you just let me work this out with his grandmother? I promise you he will be taken care of."

"I understand. Talk to Patricia and let me know what you guys come up with. I am happy to stand aside as long as we can show that he's taken care of. I'll call you next week to see how things are going. Cool?"

"Yes. Next week is fine. I just have to figure some things out."

"So, what is Jeremiah going to think of all this? Or does little man have him charmed as well?" Monique asked, oblivious to Jeremiah and Elise's current situation.

"Jeremiah will support me in whatever I want to do," Elise said simply. There was no need for Monique to know all her personal business.

"Okay, well, I will talk to you next week," Monique said. "Bye, little angel," she said sarcastically.

"Say 'I am a little angel,'" Elise defended. "'You just can't see my wings yet.'" "Whatever...bye, Elise," Monique laughed.

"Bye, Monique...umm, hey...how's she doing?"

"I haven't seen her in a little while, Elise. She's with family so we don't check on them as much in a situation like hers. If I'm being honest...she's okay but she doesn't shine like she used to. It's a transition. You did all you could. She'll be fine. Amari's a tough little girl. And speaking of tough, you need to go and talk to that tough one in there."

"I will. Thank you, Monique."

Elise joined Patricia back in her room.

"Elise, I don't want to hear it. Don't come in here fussing. I only got one mama and she's in heaven," Patricia warned.

"Well, you got one Elise too and she don't play, so just hush and take this tongue-lashing like a woman. Why didn't you tell me you were sick? I said weeks ago you didn't seem like yourself."

"I didn't want to worry you about something you couldn't do anything about. And…." Patricia paused as she considered her words. "Never mind, it doesn't matter."

"It does matter, Ms. Patricia. And what?"

"I guess I just didn't want to talk about it, so I put my head in the sand and prayed that it would go away. Baby, you are such a blessing. And I'm not just talking about the way you watch out for us or the things you give us. Your presence is enough. I've been by myself so long and I started to enjoy you being around. I loved my Corey with everything in me, but it was tough raising him. It was even harder the last few years of his life. Then you came along. You got your little act together and you didn't want anything, you just wanted to give. I never had a daughter, so I guess I got to pretending that we were family. I was afraid that if you knew everything, you wouldn't want to go through all of that again, seein' as what happened with your husband's mother. And I know you love him, but I didn't want to guilt trip you into doing anything more for your little cute chunks. You got other things to do. I don't care what you say. You need to get your husband back, and you spending all your time with me and Isaiah ain't helping. That man wants you. He don't want you, an old lady, and another man's baby. I guess I just wanted to enjoy you while I could. It's not as heavy when you come around."

"What's not as heavy?" Elise asked her.

"Everything. Life. Death. Being sick. Not knowing how this thing will turn out…or worse, knowing how it will turn out and not knowing what will happen to my baby."

"But Ms. Patricia, it would have been so much better if you would have just told me what was happening. We could have already had this thing worked out. But we're talking now, so let me say a few things.

First of all, you don't have to pretend I'm family. Me, you, and Isaiah…
this is real." Elise smiled confidently. "And hey, I must admit I do have
that effect on people. Everybody want me to be their daughter but it's
okay. There's plenty of Elise to go around. And I want you to know I'm
not doing anything out of guilt. It's out of love. And not just for Isaiah.
It's for you too. You should know me well enough by now to know that
I don't say what I don't mean. I said I was going to be there for you two,
and I meant it. You don't have to do this alone. I know God is able, so
we can believe him for a healing, but no matter what happens I want
your days to be full of joy and peace. So, we need to make sure that
Isaiah is taken care of. As long as you are here then I am here to help you
with him, but if something happens to you I want him covered. And
please, stop worrying about my marriage. I destroyed that long before I
met you and Isaiah. You're not the downfall of my relationship, but you
are an example of the Lord being kind to me despite my foolishness.. I
closed one door, but his mercy opened another. You need to know that
whatever blessing you think I have been to you, you have been even
more to me. It's hard for me to not be wanted or needed. Or not to be
loved and appreciated. I don't do well when those things aren't in my
life. I'm more aware of it now, and there are some things that I won't
ever do again now that I know. Still, it's nice to have those things again.
That's what you and Isaiah do for me. So, if you want to treat me like a
daughter, I'm happy to treat you like a mother. But I have to warn you,
there will be some haters when you move in with me, but they will just
have to understand."

"Move in with you?" Patricia asked, shocked at her words.

"Oh, yes. This is happening. I insist. And it's not just for you. It's
for Isaiah and me too. It's too much on me to be going back and forth
to you, and now I know it's dangerous as well. I need to have closer
tabs on you in case you have an emergency, and my little man doesn't
like not seeing me every day. So, we just up in here killing all manner
of birds with one stone…I know…I'm a genius…you're welcome," she
beamed.

"Elise, no. That's too much. I'm not moving in with you," Patricia
objected. "And that's too much for you to do by yourself."

"I don't intend to. I'll hire someone who can help me look after you both." "That's gon cost money and I can't afford all that."

"Saiah, did we ask her for any money? No? I didn't think so." Isaiah looked at his grandmother and laughed.

"What else did you have to say, Saiah?" Elise continued. "Oh, okay, I will tell her. Ms. Patricia, your darling grandson wants to remind you his Auntie Elise is a mini real estate mogul and that her Daddy owns the cattle on a thousand hills. There's enough room in her apartment for both of you. The Lord has been good to her, so you need to chill. And he also says we need to get official legal papers drawn up, so she doesn't have any problems with taking care of you both."

"Is that what Isaiah said?" Patricia chuckled.

"Yes, and he also said you've never won an argument with us so don't try to win this one."

"You two think you runnin' thangs, don't you?" "We do," Elise giggled.

"Okay, but on one condition," Patricia said.

"Aww, Saiah. Her so cute. She think she has a choice. What you say? Go ahead and humor her? Okay, Ms. Patricia. Sure. What condition?"

"You need to talk to your husband and let him know what you're doing. This is a very independent-woman decision. If you don't get his input, it will make it look like you're moving on and don't care what he thinks. You need to talk to him."

"Ooh, Ms. Patricia, you be on one about this. I'm sorry, but I am kinda moving on."

"But you don't want to. And you need to be woman enough to tell him that.

Now once you've told him, if he don't have sense enough to step up, then I will leave it alone but you need to tell him. Then your little cute chunks and I will be happy to be your roommates."

Elise grunted. "You really grind my gears, old lady...and by the way, he also said he doesn't like being called little cute chunks anymore. He feels body shamed. I just call him Saiah now. But if you insist, I will have this awkward and unnecessary conversation with my soon-to-be ex-husband if you want. But then you gon have to sit yo little tail down somewhere. You ain't running nothing."

Patricia laughed at Elise's rant then reached for her hand.

"Thank you, Elise. I can take a lot, but I can't take the idea of him being in the system. I don't want him growing up and not being loved."

"That won't ever happen, Ms. Patricia. I promise you that."

CHAPTER 95

Partial Disclosure

DAY 733

"Shania, stop! I can't with you and Ms. Patricia. I'm a grown woman. I don't need Jeremiah's permission to do nuthin,'" Elise complained.

"That's exactly right. So, the fact that you're complying lets me know that this is something you want to do," Shania said.

"Don't analyze me. You are not a psychologist."

"No. But I am your sister. And I'm still pulling for you and Jeremiah," Shania encouraged.

"Shania…it's over," Elise said seriously. "People saying stuff like that only makes it harder."

"I'm sorry. So, what does your attorney say?" Shania asked. "I haven't gotten one yet."

"Oh…well, if it's over, you should get one. What is Jeremiah saying about the divorce papers he filed?" Shania dug.

"He hasn't filed yet. And I know what you're trying to imply, but that's not his style. He'll probably wait for me to file, and I've been too busy."

"Yeah, getting ready for a date with your husband," Shania teased. "This is not a date. It is a conversation over a meal," Elise clarified. "Okay. What are you wearing for this conversation?"

"I may have picked up a new dress," Elise said sheepishly. "And did you shave your legs all the way to the top?"

"As a matter of fact, I did not shave my legs at all."

"Oooo, you scandalous, slick, seducing vixen, you. You had them waxed, didn't you?"

Elise smacked her lips. "They had a special." "What else you wax?" Shania meddled.

"Shania, I am getting off the phone with you. He's here," Elise laughed. "Bye, girl. Tell my brother I said hi and let me know how it goes."

"I wanna laugh too," Jeremiah said as he approached the table. "What's up?" "Hey, Miah. How are you?"

"I'm good. What are you laughing about?"

"That was Shania. Need I say more?" Elise explained.

"Nope, I can only imagine," he said. "You look beautiful, Lise," he said as he leaned over and kissed her on the cheek.

She wasn't prepared for the gesture, and it flustered her a bit. "Oh…well.

Thank you. And you look nice in your little blue blazer and your dress jeans." "I didn't want to make you look bad. Is this place new?" he asked. "Yeah, Shania told me about it. She says the food is great."

"Cool. So, what's this important matter you needed to discuss?" he asked. "Sir…are you in a hurry? Let's just enjoy the ambience. Isn't this place beautiful?" she asked as she motioned with her hands.

"Yes, this place is beautiful," he said as he stared directly at her.

Elise felt herself blushing as she tried not to smile at his thinly veiled compliment. She couldn't tell if he was just being nice or if there was something more. She used to be able to read him like a book, but things were different now and she didn't want her heart to take her someplace that reality wouldn't allow.

"Oooo, Miah. On your left," she said, changing the subject. "Paw-Paw got it going on. Look at that PYT he's with!"

"I ain't sayin' she a gold digger," Jeremiah joked.

"Miah, stop it! I'm sure it's true love," Elise said, defending the May- December couple.

"Lise, you know good in heck well it's some sugar daddyness

coming all from that table."

"Well, I can't blame Paw-Paw. She is gorgeous," Elise exclaimed. "Can I have your jacket? I need to cover up my lil' blessings. Got me feeling all inadequate."

"She's not even in your league, Lise."

Now that was intentional, she thought. She found herself flustered again, but the waiter saved her when he came to take their order.

They enjoyed their food and one another's presence. It was nice to just talk without everything being so serious.

"Sooo…how's the business coming along?" Elise inquired.

"It's going well," he said happily. "I'm doing a property not too far from Mom and Dad's house. To be honest, I may have underestimated myself. I expected it to be a harder process than it's turning out to be. It's almost ready and I need to get it sold and get to another property."

"That's a perfect segue," Elise smiled. "Segue into what?" he asked.

"You know the lady and the baby I was telling you about?" "Yeah. How could I forget?"

"Well, we've got some challenges. I am thinking we need to sell her house. It would help us out financially. I was hoping we could be your second client."

"Lise, I'll help you out however I can, but you're saying 'we' and 'us' a lot.

What's going on?"

"I said 'we'? Oh, well…I meant her. Can I have some of your mushrooms?" "Elise Janelle Traylor, what did you do?"

"Don't call me by my government name," she giggled. "I ain't even do nuthin'…yet."

Jeremiah put his fork down. "Tell me." "Okay…what had happened was…." she laughed.

Jeremiah laughed with her and leaned back in his chair. After all they had been through, she could still easily disarm him. And he still loved it.

"Seriously," she continued. "Miah, she's sick. She's Mama Etta sick."

"I'm sorry to hear that. So, she found out you're a realtor and she asked you to help her sell her house?"

"Umm…not exactly."

"Well, what exactly? And why is it we?"

"The truth is, I've seen her and the baby almost every day since I told you about them. We've gotten very close. I'm her emergency contact. I help out when she can't quite make ends meet. I take the baby to the park and push him on the baby swings. And he just giggles. She wasn't feeling well a couple of weeks ago and I took him to the doctor. And Miah, he is so sweet but he is sooo clingy. I don't know what we're going to do when it's time to take him to preschool. Sometimes

I'm like 'Saiah! I can't take all the love in.' Then he looks at me with those bright eyes and it's like he knows he's in charge, and I just surrender."

Elised beamed as she spoke, but Jeremiah wasn't as excited. "What?" she asked as his expression brought her down to earth. "I'm just listening," he said.

"No, I know that look. That's the let me pee on Elise's emotional parade look.

So go ahead."

"Elise, we haven't fought in a while. I'm not doing this."

"Okay, okay, okay…I'm sorry. The truth is. I came here to…I don't know… at minimum get your opinion. Your feedback."

"Are you sure you want it?" Jeremiah asked hesitantly. "I'm sure."

"Elise, I see the healing and I see the joy. But…," he paused. "Go ahead, Jeremiah."

"I'm scared for you," he said. "You're in headfirst and I'm not sure if you know it. Lise, you call him 'Saiah.' To the casual observer, it means nothing, but I know what it means when you change people's names. For you to jump in with this woman and this baby, it is literally a repeat of all your past trauma. You have a sick woman who's terminally ill and you've gotten attached to her way too quick. And you have a baby you're getting attached to that's not yours. I don't want you to get hurt when you can't be in his life anymore."

"I'm not going to get hurt. This time there are no crazy relatives lurking. Patricia has full legal custody of him and if something happens, she will stipulate that I have guardianship."

"Guardianship?!" Jeremiah exclaimed.

"Yes, guardianship. More specifically, I'm planning to adopt him," she confessed.

"Elise, where is all this coming from? Help me understand."

"Listen, I know from the outside looking in it doesn't sound safe or healthy. I know what I've been through. But Miah, when I tell you I'm called to this, I mean it. Ms. Patricia is so special. I'm praying for a miracle but if I can be there for her in this last season of her life, I feel the Lord would be pleased. He's blessed me to be her blessing. Everything that she needs, he's given to me, and I can't withhold it from her. It's not his will that she die alone and separated from her grandson. It's not just me and my emotions. It's his Spirit. I know it. And I'm just going to be totally transparent even though you might not understand but Miah, I have fallen in love with this little boy. I loved J.J. from the second I knew he was growing inside of me, and I will never forget him, but Saiah and me…it was literally love at first sight. If the Lord would have let us keep J.J., I can't imagine loving him any more than I love this little boy. I know what you're thinking, but that's not what's happening."

"What am I thinking?" Jeremiah asked.

"You're thinking I'm afraid to be alone and I'm taking in these strays to fill the void in my life. Everything is changing and everyone is gone or going away and I'm trying to find a way to compensate."

"Is that what I think…or what you think?" Jeremiah asked plainly.

Elise kicked herself in her mind. She had given him too much ammunition with her words. "Well, maybe I am thinking that, but it doesn't change anything. You're right. I'm in headfirst. I can't leave them now."

Jeremiah's countenance softened as he tried to process her words.

"Lise, what do you need from me?" he asked sincerely. "And I'm not talking about the house. Why did you really ask me to meet you?"

She desperately wanted to lay her cards out on the table. She wanted to let him know that she wanted this new life and she still wanted him in it. Isaiah could be both of their second chances. He could be the baby he said they should adopt. He needed a mother and a father, and she would never find a better father for Isaiah than him. And she didn't want another husband. She had done the unforgivable, but she needed him to forgive and to forget. She wanted him to meet Isaiah the way he met Amari five years ago. If he did, he would see God was making all things new. She didn't just want his approval. She wanted his participation. But in this moment, she couldn't form the words. Her fear wasn't of rejection. Her fear was that he would say yes out of some sense of duty or obligation. She wanted him back, but she wanted it to be his idea.

"Miah, I guess I just want you to have my back. I want you to understand that I'm whole and not out of my mind. Being a caregiver and a single mom is scary even if I feel like I'm called to do it. I just need, no matter what happens with us, for you to keep those Jeremiah prayers going for me. I know it's not going to be the same, but I still need your support and your love. I know the love has to change shape, but I still want it. It was important for me to let you know what was going on, and I wanted to do it face to face. So that's why you're here."

"You'll always have my support, Lise. I will always be on your side. I'm scared for you but you're still the most amazing person I know. And if this is the next phase of your life, then I won't stand in your way or try to talk you out of it. But honestly…," he shook his head.

"What, Miah?"

"I don't know…I just feel like I could do more. Is that all you need? My prayers and support?"

The open door was there. All she had to do was walk through and tell him what was truly in her heart. But no. Jeremiah was just as much a grown man as she was a grown woman. If he wanted her and this new family, he would have to say so without coercion.

"Miah, whatever you want to give, I will take. But yes, all I can ask of you is your prayers and support."

"You will always have that, Lise."

"But I don't want them like this. Why are you looking so sad? I'm not going to war," she comforted him.

"I kinda feel like you are," he said.

Elise smiled and reached across the table to hold his hand. "Well, I'm not," she reassured him. "I'm going to my purpose. I'm walking in my forgiveness and my restoration. It doesn't look exactly like what I would have thought, but it's good because God is in it. And if you're going to support me, then you can start by just being happy for me. Because I am so happy for you. You've come out of all this mess, and by the Lord's grace you got the devil in the corner scratchin' his head. There's nothing lacking in your life and that's how it should be. And whether you need or want it, you will always have my prayers and support as well. You know that, right?"

"Yeah, I know that. Thank you, Lise."

"I know a way to turn that frown upside down," she said as she leaned forward.

"How?"

"I'm going to let you pick up the bill…oh, and buy me this chocolate cake," she grinned.

"And that's going to make me happy?" he said, smiling. "Oh, yes. You're going to be ecstatic," she laughed.

Jeremiah walked her to her car. There was so much she didn't know. She didn't know how naked his arm felt as they walked and how he wanted her to take it like she used to. She didn't know how empty his soul felt the last few months without her. She didn't know how excited he was for her to reach out. She didn't know how he looked forward to seeing her at church just for an opportunity to say hello and perhaps get a casual hug. Most of all, she didn't know that he was praying that someday, somehow, someway he could forget her failure with Joshua and they could be together again. She didn't know that even though he had never met Isaiah, that if she loved him, that was enough for him, and that he wanted to love him as well. She didn't know he didn't want her to have to do all this alone and that if she gave him more time, he would show up for her, for this baby, and even for this woman he had never met. She didn't know that he wanted a second chance as well. But she didn't ask him for that. She was at peace, and he didn't want to disturb it with his insecurities.

"So, you good?" he asked as they arrived at her car.

"I am…but you're not. Come here. And don't worry. I'm not gonna try to have my way with you in the parking lot. I'm a lady," she laughed as she pulled him close and laid her head in his chest.

"Daddy," she prayed, "I thank you for this amazing son of yours, and I thank you for all you have done for me through him. I surrender myself to you. As long as you will let me and as much as he will allow, I make myself available to love, to encourage, and to support him. I pray he would have total healing and victory so he can be everything you have called him to be. He has always worried more about me than himself, so please remove the heaviness from his heart and replace it with your assurance that you have me. And Daddy, if we can't love each other as husband and wife anymore, then please show us how to love each other in this new space. I trust you that even now you are working all things together for his good because he loves you and is called to your purpose. I praise you for this moment, Daddy. I know he will always be your son. He will always be a masterpiece. He will always be more than a conqueror. And no matter what, I thank you that he will always be my Miah. So, thank you for being there for him, Daddy, and thank you for showing him your glory. In Jesus' name, Amen."

Elise paused so she could collect herself. It felt good to have her head in his chest again. She felt like she had never left, but she also felt like this would be the last time. "Thank you for letting me do that," she said as she attempted to pull away.

But Jeremiah's arms remained snuggly around her. He didn't pray or say anything, but he wouldn't let her go either. She wasn't sure what it meant. Perhaps, like her, he thought it would be the last time they were with each other in this way, and he didn't want the moment to end. She leaned her head back into his chest and closed her eyes. If this was what he needed, then this was what he would have.

CHAPTER 96

Daddy's Girl

DAY 743

"No Jurmi today?" John asked.

"I thought I was always enough to make your day, Daddy," Elise pouted, hoping her expression would make John change the subject.

"Ahways, baby," John smiled.

"Daddy, you are talking so much better," Elise encouraged. He still struggled but his speech was much clearer and easier to understand.

"What jou wont...ta teh me?" he asked.

"Huh?" Elise played dumb. She understood exactly what he was saying, and there was much she wanted to tell him. She wanted him to know how little Isaiah had stolen her heart. She wanted to testify about God's restoring work in her life. She wanted him to join her in prayer for Ms. Patricia's healing. But telling him all those things would lead to him asking questions that she wasn't ready to answer. It was one thing to come clean to Pastor G. and even to the Lord, but Daddy? He never made her feel anything less than perfect, and she didn't know if she would ever be ready to let him know how she had betrayed his son. The thought of him looking at her with disapproval or, worse, contempt frightened her.

"Guh, jou her me! I shaid, what jou wont to teh me?" he asked again with more authority.

"I don't know, Daddy," Elise fidgeted. "What you want me to tell you? The Dallas Cowboys gon win the Super Bowl?"

"Jou...gah jokes," he said as he shook his head. "Fine...I go firs." "Yeah, Daddy. You go first. What's up with you?"

"Gowin' home," he said as he smiled proudly.

"You're going home?" she asked. John nodded as he continued to smile.

"Daddy, are you sure?" Elise asked. He was making progress. But he was still dependent on a walker and that was shaky at best.

"Sure," he insisted. "Few days be on j'all nerve."

"Daddy, you won't be on our nerves. We just have to get ready." Elise was happy he had gone from being written off, to never walking or talking again, to going home. But now that he was going home, he would expect Elise to be there with his son. Whether it was for his father's good or out of mercy toward her, Jeremiah hadn't told his dad everything that had happened. But if he was coming home, he would have to know.

"Jo turn. What jou got ta teh me?" he asked directly. "I'm so happy for you," Elise stalled.

John stared at her waiting for an answer.

"Daddy, this year has been hard. You got sick and we almost lost you. We lost the house. We lost Mama Etta. We lost Amari. And somewhere in all that loss, I lost my mind...and my faith. Daddy, I've done some horrible and unforgivable things. Things I never thought I would do. Lifechanging things."

"What hapund, babeh?" he asked sympathetically. "Tell Daddeh."

"Daddy, I can't. Please don't make me. Just know that I'm sorry," Elise pleaded.

"Come here," he said clearly.

Elise scooted her chair closer to his.

"Jou Daddeh's guh," he smiled as he interlaced his fingers with hers.

Elise giggled. She appreciated him sparing her the pain of describing what had happened. "Are you telling me I'm Daddy's Girl or asking me?"

"Tellin' jou."

"Thank you, Daddy. But things are going to be different now."

John shook his head. "No. No difwent. Jou go ahways be Daddeh's Guh."

CHAPTER 97

The Patriarch Returns

DAY 743

"Hey, Miah. Are you on your way to see Daddy?" Elise asked.

"Yeah, I'm about two minutes away. You still there?" he asked casually, hoping she would say yes.

"No, I left an hour ago. I have to go see Saiah and check on Ms. Patricia. But I need to tell you something. Miah, Daddy knows what happened."

"He knows what?" Jeremiah asked.

"The big 'know'…about me. I didn't tell him the details but stroke or no, he's a very smart man. I'm sure he can put the pieces together."

"I thought we agreed not to tell him. There's no reason for him to know. I didn't want you or him going through that," Jeremiah reminded her.

"And I've appreciated you covering me, Miah, but I had to tell him. He gets more and more suspicious every time we don't show up together. But that's not why I told him. I told him because he's about to go home. They're releasing him."

"What?!" Jeremiah exclaimed.

"You heard me right. And I confirmed it with his nurse before I left. The doctors say he doesn't need round-the-clock care anymore. We can work out a schedule and between the two of us and some in home nursing care, he'll be good. But Miah…they are expecting a full recovery. Won't he do it?" she asked joyfully. "Won't he will?" Jeremiah agreed. "But listen, you have the baby and Ms.

Patricia, I can't keep asking you to look after Pop too."

"Are you saying you don't want me to come around?" she asked.

"No, Lise. I'm not saying that at all. He wants you around…and so do I. I just don't want you burning yourself out."

"Miah, you know I will always do what I have to do for family. I'll be fine.

I'm more worried about you."

"Why are you worried about me?" he asked.

"He let me off the hook, but he's gonna press you harder for answers. I just want you to be prepared. Just so you know, I may have shed a tear or two before I left…you know…for dramatic effect."

"Elise, what you up in there cryin' for?" he asked, shaking his head.

"Miah, he said I would always be 'Daddy's Girl.' You know that man turns me to jelly."

"Great, so in other words be ready for my father to ask me what I did to you?" Jeremiah asked sarcastically.

"It beez that way sometimes," she giggled. "Your father loves me. What you want me to do?"

"Just keep being you, Lise," he said before he could stop himself.

He couldn't see her but even in her silence he knew his words brought her joy. The thought of her smiling on the other end of the line made him smile as well.

"Sooo…you there yet?" she asked, breaking their silence. "Yeah, getting out of the car now to go to the principal's office." "Let me know how it goes."

"Okay, I lo…," Jeremiah caught himself. "I'll see you later." "Bye, Miah. I lo…umm…I'll see you later too," she laughed. "You just couldn't let that go, could you?" he asked.

"Nope, but you go get 'em, champ!" she encouraged.

As he suspected, his father was waiting anxiously for him. "Shi down, son," John said.

It was all fun and games when he was talking to Elise, but now Jeremiah really did feel like he was in trouble.

"Whut wong…wif Elish?" John struggled to articulate.

"What's wrong with Elise? Pop, I just spoke to her. Nothing's wrong. She's fine. She says you're getting ready to be released? Wow, look at you."

John ignored his son's pitiful attempt to change the subject. "Whut hapund?

Teh me tha twoof."

"Okay, Pop. I'll tell you the truth. The truth is, I will always love Elise. But a lot has happened. We wanted to keep it from you because you were recovering, and the last thing we wanted was to stress you out. The reality is, we're really not together anymore. Elise is moving on and she has my support. I need you to trust me…and to trust us. We both love you and we want what is best for you. Let's not get into the details right now."

"Shun… jo daddeh is stwong. Can't tawk…but stwong. Teh me," he said.

It was ironic how well Elise knew their family dynamic. She was right. Pop was going to press him harder than he pressed her. Jeremiah hadn't thought much about this conversation. He knew eventually his dad would need to know. But he didn't expect to discuss it with him so soon.

"Pop," he started, "I'm not putting it all on her. Both Elise and I have been through a lot. I should have paid more attention. I should have listened to her. I should have been there for her to love her through everything. But Dad, she could have done things a lot differently too. I've made my mistakes…but I didn't do what she did."

John put his hand on his son's thigh. "Anutha man?" John asked, not nearly as shocked as Jeremiah thought he would be.

Jeremiah lowered his head and nodded. "Yeah, Pop. Another man."

Hearing about Amari being ripped away from them and being told he would never hold his grandson was devastating. But this latest revelation was unimaginable. Still, even with the little information he had, he knew in his spirit that Jeremiah still loved Elise and that Elise still loved Jeremiah.

"Whut jou gon do?" he asked his son.

Jeremiah shook his head. He had hoped he was finished crying about Elise but rehashing her infidelity with his dad re-surfaced his pain.

"I don't know, Pop," he answered. "She says she wants us to get a divorce and move forward but we haven't really talked about it.

"Do jou want a divorsh?" John asked his son.

Jeremiah shook his head and wiped his tears. "No, sir. I want my Lise back." "Well jou go get huh!" John said firmly, even if rather inarticulately.

"Pop, she cheated on me!" Jeremiah reminded him. "You don't know how that feels."

"No." John agreed. "Lot I don't know. But I know thish. Jou love Elish. And Elish love jou. Jou need huh. And she need jou. Sheez jour wife, shun. Not his wife…jours! Jou luv huh. Give jo sef up fa huh. Jou warsh huh with the word. Elish is jour wife. Jou can fix thish."

"Pop, I know all that. I know she's my wife. I love her. I need her. I've always tried to give myself up for her. I still pray for her and wash her with the word every day. I can't help it. I want her back more than you or she could ever know. I want to hold her and forget what she did, but I can't. Our marriage is broken, and she broke it! Not me."

John reached over and took his son's hand and spoke clearly for the first time since his stroke. "Jeremiah…real men can fix what they didn't break. You can do this, son."

CHAPTER 98

This Is How We Do It

DAY 750

"I'm sorry…I'm hosting a what?" Jeremiah asked.

Elise laughed out loud. It tickled her soul to have another opportunity to spar with him.

"Boy, you heard me! You're hosting a block party for Daddy," she said. "It'll be fun. You want to welcome him home right, don't you? I mean the poor man's already traumatized that I'm not going to be there. This will ease the blow."

"Lise, how are we not together and you still manage to pull me into these shenanigans?"

"Haaa!" she screamed. "That's shenanigans, hijinks, and tomfoolery sir. But anyway, when I was at the house last time, well, you could tell I hadn't been there. Don't get me wrong. It wasn't raw sewage, rats, and roach's nasty. But Daddy is used to the way Mama Etta used to keep it and I don't want him coming home to…well, you know, how you got it now. So, I told him, I would come over and put my touches on it before he came home."

"And how did that graduate to me throwing a block party?"

"He said it would be nice to have Pastor and First Lady over when he arrived. We got to talking and the next thing you know, the best son in the whole wide world is throwing his daddy a welcome home block party. Everybody on the block is going to prepare food. There's gonna be a DJ. Ooh, Miah, maybe you should set a band up in the cul-de-sac? You got some work to do. You need to get after it, son!" she teased.

"Elise, I'm not getting a band and a DJ."

"Jeremiah, I ain't gon let you poop on Daddy's party!" she said with authority. "I don't even know why you're arguing. You know you're gonna do it. Send me some pictures."

"You're not going to be there?" he asked, disappointed.

"I wasn't planning on it. That's why I think the party would be nice. He said he was looking forward to living with us. So, I was just trying to cheer him up. Breakups don't just affect the couple. We have to think about him too."

"So, if you're trying to cheer him up, don't you think you should come?" Jeremiah asked.

"Miah, I don't know. I wanted you to have that space with you and your dad. I didn't want to intrude. Plus, I have plus two if I ever go anywhere. Three if Saiah's nanny comes."

"You have a nanny for Isaiah?" he asked.

"Actually, she's a caregiver for Ms. Patricia and a nanny for him. I still have to work, and I don't want his spoiled butt in daycare. Ms. Patricia is doing okay but she needs someone there just in case."

"You're really doing this, aren't you?" Jeremiah asked seriously. "I told you I was. They're my family now too."

"Well, if Pop wants this, I'll do it. But only if you come. And you can bring the whole crew."

"Jeremiah, you don't have to do that."

"It's already done. We both know Pop wants you there, and I'm not sitting around with him for however many hours with him asking, 'Where's Elise?'"

"Well, as long as you're okay with it," Elise agreed. "I am, but I need one more thing," he said.

"You want me to organize the party, don't you?" she asked "You already know," he laughed.

Elise laughed sweetly. "I got you. I've already started putting things together. I just wanted to make you drop that little Jeremiah pride and ask. If I would've left it up to you, y'all would have been in the front yard listening to music on your I-phone and waiting for pizza to come. Don't worry...it will be nice. And yes, there will be a DJ...and a band."

"Thank you, Lise. I'm looking forward to meeting everyone." "I'm looking forward to you meeting them too, Miah."

CHAPTER 99

Time to Make a Change

DAY 750

"Daddy, I don't understand," Robin said to Joshua. "Baby, what's so confusing?" Joshua asked.

"What's in Atlanta that's not here? And why are you trying to ditch me?" she pouted.

"Baby girl, you know I'm not trying to ditch you but you're in college now. There's no limit for you. I want you to be able to go wherever God calls you and do whatever he tells you. But I need you to let your dad do the same."

"So, you're just going to pick up and move?" Robin questioned.

"Yes, I am. It's a great opportunity. It's a new start, in a new environment, with a new challenge. And that's what I need in this season of my life, and most importantly…this is what I feel God is calling me to."

"Daddy," Robin said seriously, "you know I know you, don't you?" Joshua laughed. "Yeah, girl, I know you know me. What's your point?"

"The point is, I don't think you're telling me everything. You were scared to death when I went to UCLA. You legit said you didn't want your baby going to Sodom, California. And now you're going to Atlanta? The Sodom of the South? So, why don't you tell me the real reason you're leaving?"

"If the warranty on you wasn't expired, I would take you back to the hospital I got you from," Joshua said jokingly.

"I'm waiting," she said, stone faced.

Joshua paused and sighed. Robin had stuck with him through the divorce. Even after she left for college, she would call, she would text, she even made him share his location. He would occasionally feign annoyance, but in reality, her love had kept him through a painful and confusing season. She was his baby, but she wasn't a baby anymore and she deserved the truth.

"Baby, there are a lot of bad memories for Daddy here. An ex-wife who doesn't want me. A son who doesn't wanna talk to me. And if we're gonna keep it real, there are some other failures too."

"Say more," Robin said authoritatively but sweetly.

"Baby, I've tried to teach you to live right. I tried to teach you to live for God and to trust him and to obey him. And I've tried the model what I've taught you. As hard as it is for me to admit, I haven't done a good job of the modeling part lately. I messed up…bad."

Robin scooted across the couch and got closer to her dad. She linked arms with him, took his hand, and laid her head on his shoulder. "What happened, Daddy?"

"I got involved with somebody and your dad fell hard. She was funny. She was sweet. And even if she didn't realize it, she loved the Lord. And yeah, I'm just gonna say it…she was fine."

"So, what was the problem with this funny, sweet, fine Christian woman?" she asked.

"She was also married."

"She didn't tell you she was married?" Robin asked.

"No…I knew," Joshua admitted. "I'm ashamed of it…but I knew."

Robin lifted her head and looked at her dad. "And I assume, young man," she said flippantly, trying to ease the tension, "that when you say you got involved with her, you're not just talking about Bible studies?"

"You would assume right," Joshua confessed.

"Ooh, Daddy, this is scandalous. Especially for you. But are you sure you're not running away? Why not just stay? You wouldn't let me leave school or move, just because of a breakup or a mistake."

"You're right, I wouldn't. But that's not the only reason I'm leaving. Robin, I really feel called to this place. It's a Christian school and they need leadership. All I will have to do is focus on those kids and that staff. I think it'll be a good place for me to refocus on God, get healed, and start my second act."

"What do you mean by second act?" Robin questioned.

"I mean the second half or back end of my life. I know I don't deserve it, but I'm praying God would make my latter days better than my former days. I'm praying for better relationships, better worship, better service, and a better life. I know God is not finished with me yet, but he's also shown me some things about myself that I didn't know were there. And I've got to deal with that stuff so I can be the man he wants me to be."

"Are you sure you're running to something and not away from something?" Robin asked.

"To be honest with you…it's both," he confided. "I need to get away from here and start fresh. But I'm running to where God has called me."

"So, who is this brazen hussy that seduced my daddy?"

Joshua laughed again and kissed her on her forehead. "No, baby girl, we not doing that. I know based on what I've said, it's hard to believe, but she's actually a great person. We were both hurt and lonely and we both made some bad decisions. But the reality is… I have this soul tie. I know it's not healthy and I know it's not from God. So, I have to make some changes."

"Okay, so when are we leaving?" Robin asked. "We?" Joshua questioned.

"Oh, yes. I'm coming with you to help you move. Your little mannish self obviously needs adult supervision. Plus, your next house will not… I repeat…will not… look like a frat house."

"I would really like that, baby girl. I was hoping to go down there a few weeks before they needed me to get settled in. So, if you want to drive down with me, I could fly you back," Joshua said happily.

"That would be nice, Daddy. And thank you for sharing. I know it took a lot for you to admit that to your favorite child. I won't say it's okay, because I know you don't think it's okay, but I will say I don't love you or respect you any less." "Thank you, baby girl. As much as I know I'm supposed to go, I wasn't looking forward to taking the trip by myself. Having you as my road dog would

be nice. And thank you for making it easy to talk to you about this."

"You're welcome, Daddy. I also plan on making it easy for you to add to my wardrobe this summer as well."

"Girl, get out!"

CHAPTER 100

Lil' Homey and Big Homey

DAY 757

"Amari, I'm gettin' ready to go. Ask Eric to get you something to eat!" Cherese shouted.

She was hoping for a relaxing Saturday but decided to check a few emails before she left. There were several from Amari's school. As was always the case with this little girl, there was more drama. The emails stated that Amari was constantly falling asleep in class, getting into fights, and on the verge of failing.

The reports didn't sound incredibly different from her own childhood experiences with school but failing at her age was ridiculous and embarrassing. Amari's teacher insisted that she come up to the school for a conference and noted that she had called her several times. Cherese's blood began to boil. Now Amari was making her look bad. She didn't need her caseworker or her school pestering her about this child.

"Amari!" she screamed again. "Get out here now."

Amari recognized the tone and knew she in trouble for something. It didn't matter for what. She knew she was about to be screamed at or hit on, no matter what she said. And a small part of her was ready for it. She was tired of being blamed for everything. She was little but maybe it was time to stand up for herself.

She intentionally took her time to finish dressing and walked casually out of her room to face her aunt. She walked up near Cherese but didn't say anything.

Cherese looked her up and down. "What you supposed to say when I call you?"

Amari took a deep breath and spoke. "Yes, ma'am."

"Girl, what you up at that school doin'? From what I can tell, all you doin' is going to sleep and fightin'. You obviously not doing your work. How the hell you on the verge of failing? Ain't all you do is ABCs and 123s? Sound like you worse at school than you are here at the house…and that's sayin' something."

"I got tired of the kids picking on me, so I fought them back. I told you they were bullying me, and you said to quit being a punk," Amari reminded her.

"All right. I see you," Cherese said, impressed with the comment. "Whoop they asses. I don't care. But why you fallin' asleep?"

"I don't know. I just get sleepy," Amari replied simply.

"Well, go yo azz to sleep at night. I keep telling you you ain't grown," Cherese scolded.

"You don't come home sometimes until late and it's never anything here to eat, so unless Eric brings me something I always have to wait until you get back to eat," Amari explained.

"Girl, quit lying. It be food here. Make a sandwich or eat some cereal and go to bed. You ain't a baby. And you sholé ain't my baby. You don't need me around here all the time. I got stuff to do. And if you stayin' up so late, at least have sense enough to do your homework. With these grades it will do you some good to stay up all night. Sorry self just bringing all sorts of shame to the family name," Cherese insulted.

Amari knew she would regret her words, but she was tired of Cherese and was going to let her know it. "I used to make good grades when I was with T Lise and Uncle J. I made the best grades in the whole class."

"Little girl…Don't. Test. Me," Cherese warned as she got up out of her chair. Amari knew what was coming but right now, she didn't care. She couldn't stop her, but she wanted Cherese to know she wasn't afraid. T Lise taught her that she never had to be afraid. If she were here, Cherese wouldn't act like this.

Eric was asleep but heard the commotion. The way Cherese treated this little girl made him sick. Technically, it wasn't his business, but he wanted to watch out for his Lil' Homey as much as he could. He came out of the bedroom and stood between Amari and Cherese.

"Hey, my ladies. Let's chill," he said calmly. "It's too early in the mornin' for y'all to be fightin' like this." He put his arms around Cherese. "Baby, don't get so mad. She's just a little kid. She ain't mean it."

He held Cherese close to him and turned his head toward Amari. "Amari, tell your aunt you're sorry," he said as he winked at her. Amari loved Eric. He was her only friend. But she didn't want his help.

"I did mean it!" the little girl insisted. "I used to be smart. My T Lise used to help me, and I did good in school. And I had friends who were nice to me. I played the piano at church and my whole family came to my recitals. And I played basketball and soccer, and I was the best player on the team because my Uncle J coached me. But you don't ever help me. You don't even talk to me except to yell." "Eric, let me go. This little heffa done lost her mind!" Cherese said as she jerked away from Eric. "Let me ask you something, Ms. 'I used to be smart.' Ms. 'I ain't got no job and don't bring nothin' to the table.' Ms. 'I don't appreciate nothin' or nobody.'" Cherese grabbed Amari by both her arms and pulled her to within an inch of her face. "Since you checkin' folks, let me check you. Yo mama didn't even want you. My mama begged me to take you, and you see how often she come around. We ain't heard from either one of them. Why you think you was in the system in the first place? Yo mama and yo grandmama didn't want you. And don't get me started on yo daddy cuz baby, we don't even know who he is. Yo own mama don't know. And if yo precious T Lise and Uncle J love you so much, where they at, Amari?"

Cherese paused and looked around the apartment dramatically.

"You talk about the house y'all had and yo big bedroom and how they loved you and how they mama and daddy loved you too. And let you tell it, they was rich. So, they loved you and they got all that money and couldn't keep you? Naw, boo-boo. Here's the real truth. They could have kept you if they wanted you. But. They. Didn't. Want. You. They told me to come and get you, babay. Ha, ha, ha," Cherese mocked.

"That's right. And you ain't heard from them since. They could call if they wanted to. Hell, they can come get you now for all I care. But I done told you I am all you got, and you gon stop talking to me like you crazy." Cherese let her go but emphasized her point by shoving Amari's forehead with her index finger.

"You're a liar!" Amari shouted, refusing to back down. "They do love me. They promised me they would always love me, but you took me from them. I know you did. And when I grow up, I am going to leave here and go to the Army like T Lise did and take care of myself. She didn't have anyone to love her either but now everyone loves her. And I am going to sell houses and sing. And I am going to be like her. I don't ever want to be like you. You say they don't love me, but you're a liar. When I grow up, I'm going to marry someone that loves me like Uncle J loves T Lise. You're just mad because nobody loves you. Eric doesn't even love you. And I don't love you either. I hate you."

The child's words made Cherese see red. Before Eric could stop her, she pounced on the little girl and began slapping and hitting her in her face and on her arms and legs. Eric pulled Cherese off her as Amari lay on the floor, weeping and defeated. Cherese wasn't finished but Eric wouldn't let her go.

"Get off of me, Eric!" she screamed.

"I'm not gon let you hit her again, Cherese," Eric defended.

"Get yo damn hands off me or my next phone call will be to your parole officer!" Cherese threatened.

Eric released her and Cherese stooped down over the still-crying Amari. "So, we keepin' it real, little girl? Fine. I. Hate. You. Too. Talkin' 'bout you smart and the dumbest thang up there. Talkin' 'bout what you used to do. You think I give a damn about what yo sorry ugly little ass used to do? You know so much? Then you know you just here so I can get a little extra cash. And you bet not say a word. You think I'm bad? Oh, baby, they told me everything. You always talking about T Lise and Uncle J, but what about the woman you stayed with before them?"

Even as she wept, Cherese's words got Amari's attention.

"Uh-huh," Cherese said wickedly. "That got yo attention, didn't it?

You remember her, don't you?"

"Yes, ma'am," Amari said through her tears. Her newfound boldness was gone.

"I bet you do. You remember this too, don't you?" Cherese said as she pulled up her skirt and pointed to a burn mark on Amari's leg.

Cherese was awful, but she didn't compare to the woman Amari stayed with before the Traylors. She was cruel and abusive. Amari tried her best not to think about her. One day Amari was playing with her curling irons. The woman had told her to leave them alone, but Amari was curious as to how they worked. Amari touched the end, and the heat surprised her. She dropped it on the floor and broke it. The woman was furious, and, in her anger, she picked up the curling iron and held it to Amari's thigh. She was very young, but she remembered it like it was yesterday. But it wasn't the pain she remembered the most, it was the look in the woman's eyes. They looked exactly like Cherese's eyes did now.

"So let me tell you something," Cherese said slowly and deliberately. "I'm the best thing you got going. Nobody is coming to get you. Nobody cares about your little piano recitals, your soccer games, your little grades you used to make. I'm all you got. So, get used to it. And guess what? When you get big, you can go join the Army and be like yo precious T Lise. I will drive you there but until then it's me and you. Now I got stuff to do. So go sit yo little self down somewhere and I might bring you back something to eat. But let me be clear. Next time you open yo mouth up to me like that again…I'm gon beat the literal living hell out of you… again. I am not the one. Go on now. I'm tired of looking at you."

Amari ran to her room and Cherese turned around to face Eric. He said nothing but the disgusted look on his face told her exactly what he thought. Cherese looked him in the eye as she picked up the phone and dialed. Eric's heart raced. Any accusation, true or not, could jeopardize his parole.

"Hey girl, yeah, I'm on the way. Okay, 'preciate ya," Cherese said.

Eric relaxed inwardly. Cherese hadn't called his parole officer. She had just called her hairdresser to confirm her appointment.

She hung up the phone and laughed. "What's wrong, baby?" she asked sarcastically. "You ain't gon take up for your little homey? Up here lookin' like a scared little—"

"Cherese! Not now," Eric interrupted.

"Whatever, Eric. I'm leaving," Cherese said as she grabbed her keys.

Eric went to Amari's room and opened the door. He didn't see her. He listened closely and heard her sobbing from inside her closet. He opened the closet door and saw his little friend crying into her pillow. He cleared a space on the floor near her and sat down. He searched his heart for something he could say to make her feel better, but Amari lowered her pillow and spoke before he did.

"You're leaving, aren't you?" she asked through her tears.

"I have to, Lil' Homey," he replied sadly. "Cherese is too much."

"Eric, please take me with you. Please don't leave me with her," Amari pleaded.

Amari couldn't imagine just how much he wanted to. She shouldn't have to endure Cherese. But he barely had anything for himself and even if he did, no one would entrust him with a child.

"Amari, I promise you I would if I could. But I can't. It wouldn't work. I don't know how to take care of a little girl."

"You don't have to take care of me. She doesn't take care of me. Just let me stay with you. I won't get in your way. I promise."

"Amari, you're just upset because she put a little whoopin' on you, but it's gon be all right, baby girl. That's just part of being a kid. I was bad as hell when I was little, and my mama used to tear my butt up."

"But I didn't do anything wrong, Eric," Amari objected. "She's just always mad at me no matter what I do."

"You're right. You didn't do anything wrong. I'm sorry."

"I hate her," Amari said coldly. "I hope she gets hit by a truck."

"Don't let her do that to you, Lil' Homey. Don't let her change you. I never told you this," Eric said as he put his arm around her, "but I got in trouble not too long ago. Not like you, where I didn't really do anything. No, I did some stuff I shouldn't have done and got caught.

Just being stupid. And when you do stupid stuff, you end up having to be around stupid people. So, I had to go to jail for a little while."

"What did you do?" Amari asked innocently. "That's not important."

"It is to me," she said.

"Okay. Well, somebody who I thought was my friend asked me to do a favor for them. They asked me to take some stuff to another friend and they said they would pay me for it."

"If they were your friend, why did you make them pay you?" Amari asked. "Well, they said they would pay me so I thought it would be cool. I could help

them out and I could get some money."

"And what was wrong with helping them?"

"There was some bad stuff my friend wanted me to take to the other friend," he explained, purposely leaving out the specifics.

"Eric, I told you before, I wasn't born yesterday. Sounds like you were selling crack or something."

"Well, fine. Anyway, I got caught and I had to pay for it," Eric confessed. "Did you know you were selling crack? Crack kills, Eric," Amari chastised. "First, can you quit sayin' crack? And, to tell the truth, I didn't ask. But yeah,

I knew. I just figured if I didn't ask or say anything, somebody might actually believe me if I did get caught. But it doesn't work like that. Now do you have any other questions? Because none of that is the point."

"Oh, I'm sorry. Go ahead," Amari said as she leaned her head on his shoulder. "So, while I'm locked up with these real drug dealers, gangbangers, and murderers. They decide they gon try me one day. They get to messin' with me and tryna punk me. Now, I don't want you to ever find this out, but you can't let that happen in prison. So, I had to fight."

"Did you win?" Amari asked excitedly.

"No, they beat the hell out yo boy," he admitted. "But they knew they were in a fight."

"So next time Cherese hits me, I should hit her back?"

"No. No. Uh-uh. I didn't say that. That would be a bad idea, Eric warned. "You not ready for that heat yet. Let me finish my story. So, I'm in the yard the next day and I'm all messed up. My eye is swole shut. My face is all cut up. And this old dude named Pops walks up on me. He said, 'Hey, Youngblood. Can I tell you a story?'"

"Like you just did with me?" she asked, excited.

"Yeah. But I wasn't as nice to him as you are to me. I said, 'What the hell you want, old man?' And you know what Pops told me?"

"What?" Amari asked, intrigued by his story.

Eric did his best to duplicate the old man's gravelly voice. "He said, 'Young brutha, I don't know you. And I don't necessarily want to know you. But let me tell you something about yourself.' He said, 'I've seen a lot of dumb knuckleheads come through here. You look like them. You talk like them. You even did what they did. But God told me to tell you that you ain't them. So don't let them turn you into something you ain't supposed to be. If you do, if you let them change you, then you will always be here. That's what they want to do. They want to make you like them. But if you remember you not like them. If you stay true to who you were meant to be, you can get out. They will still be here. But you will be gone, and you can live. God has something special for you, little brother. But it's up to you if you wanna get it.' I never forgot that. I held on to that and I only had to do a little bit of the time I was supposed to. And that's what I want you to know. Don't let your aunt change you. You're not like her. There's something special about you. What she is, she will always be. But you? Lil' Homey, you're different. Don't let her take that away from you no matter what she says."

"Did those guys leave you alone?" Amari asked.

"No, they didn't. I had to keep fighting them. Sometimes I lost and sometimes I won. But inside my heart and inside my mind, I started winning. I didn't really know what to say, but I just started asking God to help me be different so I could get whatever special thing Pops said he had for me. And I asked him to help me not become like what I was having to fight. And I guess that's what I want to tell you. You in a bad place but don't let nobody change you. Not those kids at school. Not those teachers. And not yo crazy-azz auntie either. One day, everybody is gon see what I see. They gon see you play yo piano and score yo goals and sing and all the other things you said. And when you make it big, I'm gon be right there saying, 'That's my friend Amari. They tried but can't nobody hold my Lil' Homey down.' Uh-oh. Is that a little smile I see on that face? Girl, smiling like that you gon make yo Big Homey take you to get some pancakes from McDonald's. How's that sound?"

"Good," Amari smiled.

"Cool. Let's go. Don't nobody want no ole funky cereal." "Eric, can I ask you a question now?"

"Yeah, what's up?"

"Did you ask Jesus to save you?"

"Huh?" Eric asked, confused by the question.

"You said Pops said God has something special for you and you asked God to help you. But did you ask Jesus to save you? The Bible says that Jesus is the way through the life. We only have God if we have Jesus. Do you believe in Jesus?"

"Umm, I guess so?" Eric asked hesitantly.

"You have to believe in Jesus, Eric. He died on the cross for our sins and God raised him from the dead. Do you believe that?" she asked seriously.

"I think I do," he answered rather unconfidently.

"No, Eric. This is important. You have to know. You have to believe Jesus loves you. Didn't you go to Sunday school? John 3:16 says, 'For God so loved the world so much that he be gotten his son to us to believe so we won't perish and have everlasting life.'"

Eric gave her the side-eye. "Baby girl, I don't really read the Bible that much, but I don't think that's how that go."

"Whatever, Eric I'm a little kid. You gotta do some of this. I'm just saying I want God to answer your prayers and I don't want you to go to hell. You don't want to go to hell, do you?"

"Well, when you put it like that, no, I don't want to go to hell," Eric said. This was not the conversation he had planned but she seemed to be feeling better, so he decided to just roll with it.

Amari continued her plea. "My Uncle J would know what to say, but I know he would tell you about Jesus. It's always about Jesus. I think you just have to ask Jesus to forgive you of your sins and to be your Savior. I remember that for sure. And I know you have to believe that Jesus is God's son. Here, let me show you." Amari got on her knees in front of Eric as he sat. He didn't know why, but Eric noticed his heart was beating faster than normal and his hands were shaking. "Oh...and this is important," Amari continued. "You have to believe that God raised him from the dead. Do you believe that? Do you believe Jesus died on the cross for your sins and God raised him from the dead?"

Eric thought about her words, still wondering how their conversation had taken such a dramatic turn. "Yeah, Amari. I guess I do."

"Whew. Okay. Good. Otherwise, I couldn't help you. Now give me your hands," Amari said. "Repeat after me. Lord Jesus."

Eric just sat there.

"Eric, say it. Jesus is listening! Don't make him mad. Are you ready?" "Yeah, okay, I'm ready," Eric said.

Amari recalled when she was younger and how Uncle J sat her in his lap and talked to her about Jesus. "Lord Jesus, help me remember what to say," she said.

"Lord Jesus, help me remember what to say," Eric repeated.

"No, no, no. I'm sorry," Amari said. "That's not your part. That was just for me. Okay. This time for real. Say 'Lord Jesus, I thank you for dying on the cross and rising from the dead for me. I ask that you forgive me of all my sins. I give my life to you and ask you to save me so I can go to heaven. In Jesus' name, Amen.'"

Eric repeated her words and they both sat in silence for a moment. "So, what now?" he asked.

"Do you feel different?" Amari asked him.

"I don't think so," Eric said, slightly disappointed.

"That's okay, Eric," Amari comforted him. "Uncle J says you don't always feel different at first. I probably didn't tell you the right words either, but all that matters is that you believe. You believe, right?"

"Yeah, I do," he said confidently. "Eric?" Amari asked.

"Yeah?" he responded.

"Are you sure you don't feel different? Because you're crying," Amari said. "I'm not...crying." Eric touched his face and realized tears were indeed coming from his eyes. "Oh, I guess I am. Is that good?"

"Yeah, I think that's good. Eric, I think it worked." "Maybe," Eric said.

"Stop saying maybe!" Amari corrected. "Try this. Say 'Thank you, Jesus!'" "Okay," Eric agreed reluctantly. "Thank you, Jesus," he said. It felt more natural than he expected.

"Try again and lift up your hands like this. Say 'Thank you for saving me, Jesus.'"

Eric lifted his hands and repeated her words, this time more confidently. "How do you feel now?" she asked him.

"I feel good," Eric said as he wiped his tears.

"Yay!" Amari clapped and smiled, then wrapped her arms around Eric's neck. "Thank you, Jesus. You saved my best friend! We love you."

Eric returned her sweet embrace. "Yeah, thank you, Jesus. We love you." Eric's tears returned and suddenly he no longer needed Amari to tell him what to say. "Jesus, I'm so sorry, Lord, for all I've done. I do want to be saved. I've gotten a lot of things wrong, and now I need another chance. I want to thank you for loving me and forgiving me. I know I let you down, Lord, but if you will help me, I want to be different. I want to be who you want me to be. So please help me, Jesus. I don't want this anymore. Please show me what you want for me."

"Eric?"

"Yes, Amari?"

"Are you finished praying?" she asked. "Uh-huh," he confirmed.

"Then you're supposed to say, 'In Jesus' name, Amen,'" Amari instructed. "Okay. I'm sorry. I'm new at this. In Jesus' name, Amen."

"Eric?"

"Yes, Amari?"

"Will you take me with you now?" she requested with a half angelic and half devilish grin.

Eric smiled. "I want to. But I can't. But I will take you to get some pancakes if you'll let me."

"Okay," Amari agreed reluctantly.

They got to their feet and started to the door. "Eric?"

Eric sighed, wondering what she was going to ask now. "Yes, Amari?"

"I don't know all the rules, but I'm pretty sure you're going to have to stop cursing now."

"That might take some time. But I'll try," Eric agreed. "Eric?"

"Amari, what now?"

"I just want to say I understand why you can't take me with you. But Pops was right. You are special. Thank you for being my friend. I mean my Big Homey."

"No, Amari. Thank you for being my Lil' Homey."

CHAPTER 101

Dream Drive

DAY 757

Eric enjoyed watching Amari have her pancakes. But he had made up his mind that he didn't want to see Cherese again. He needed to get Amari back before she came home.

"Amari, I'm sorry but after you're done, I have to take you back," he said sadly, hoping she would understand.

The glow that had been enveloping Amari's face disappeared before his eyes. He could normally tell when she was playing him. This didn't seem like one of those times. She looked truly sad.

"Do you have to?" she asked. "I do, lil' bit. I'm sorry."

"You're not going to come see me anymore?" she asked. "I want to, but I don't think I can."

"What if you got me a burner phone? I could call you and tell you when she's not there and you can come and see me then," Amari beamed.

"I don't know about that. Maybe," Eric said. "But for now, we gotta go. But I tell you what...we'll take the long way home. Okay?"

"Okay. Thank you, Eric," Amari smiled halfheartedly.

As promised, Eric took a longer route home. Amari still seemed down, and he wanted to cheer her up if he could.

"Hey," he said, smiling. "I got another story. You wanna hear it?"

"Uh-huh," she said as her eyes brightened. "Is it about a drug deal gone bad?" "No, Amari."

"Is it another prison story?" she asked.

"Amari! No, girl. You ack like I'm Al Capone or somebody. Now you want to hear it or not?"

"No. I do. What happened?"

"When I was little, maybe a little younger than you are now, we were poor. My mama had to use all of her money to pay bills and buy food. So, when Christmas came, she didn't have any money to get me anything. And I was real sad after she told me."

"I'm sorry, Big Homey," Amari said. "I used to never get Christmas presents before I started living with Uncle J and T Lise."

"Well, then you know how I felt. But my mama comes in my bedroom on Christmas Eve, and she says, 'Hey, Booty Butt.'"

"Booty Butt?" Amari laughed.

"Yeah, Booty Butt. That's what my mama called me. And?" Eric said, daring her to say something about it.

"And I bet you didn't tell them that in prison," Amari obliged.

Eric shook his head and laughed. "No. I didn't. Anyways, she tells me we don't have any money for Christmas, and she gets to crying and I start crying and said, 'Mama, one day I'm gonna get you everything you want for Christmas and forever. I promise.' And she goes, 'We don't have any money, but there is one thing we can do.'"

"What was it?" Amari asked.

"I'm glad you asked. She put me in the car, like me and you are right now, and we went out and looked at Christmas lights," Eric explained.

"Oh. That's nice. But Eric, it's not Christmas," Amari said, wondering what his point was.

"I know it's not Christmas, but remember I told you we were poor. Didn't hardly anybody in our neighborhood have Christmas lights. So, she took me to the rich white folks' part of town, and we looked at the lights over there. And she said, 'Booty Butt, one day I want you to live someplace like this. Someplace safe. Someplace clean. Someplace nice. I might not see it, but this is where I want you to live. So, you know sometimes when I get sad, I go to one of those places and I just kinda of dream that I can live there. I know it sounds stupid. But it makes me feel better. I call them my dream drives. I drive through a real nice part of town and just pretend I live there. I pretend I'm somebody different. I always have to go back home but it helps."

"Do the police bother you?" Amari asked him. "You look kinda sketchy, Eric." "Whatever, you wanna roast yo Big Homey or do you wanna go on a dream drive before I take you back?" Eric asked.

"I wanna go on a dream drive and I know exactly where we can go," Amari said confidently.

"Girl, what you know about some nice cribs?"

"Eric, you hear Cherese talk about it all the time. My uncle and aunt have a very nice house. You want me to show it to you?"

Eric's suspicions rose as he realized his well-intentioned plan was about to epically backfire. "Amari, are you trying to get me to take you back to your old foster family? Because that's not a good idea. You don't want me to get in trouble, do you?"

"Eric, you won't get in trouble. I just want to see them. I want to see my little brother. And Papa John. Eric, I know they want me back. I know they do. They wouldn't just leave me. They promised they would come and get me. Something must have happened."

"Amari. I told you I got in trouble once. If I get in trouble again, they might not let me out of jail. I can't do it. I have to take you home."

"My Uncle J won't let you go to jail. He is sooo smart. He can do anything. He can fix it. And my T Lise is smart too. Plus, she's got a little gangsta in her. They will figure it out."

"Amari, I can't just walk up to strangers and say, 'Hey, you want this kid?'" "Okay. Just drive in front of the house and if they come out, they will see me.

If they don't come out, then we can leave, and I won't ask you again. Please, Eric. If you can't take me with you, then take me to them. I have never asked you to do anything. I just want to see them. Pretty pleeeze," she said as she clasped her hands together and poked out her bottom lip.

Eric knew he was getting played. And he knew he needed to be careful. He didn't need smoke from Cherese or from the law. All his common sense said he needed to ignore this child's ludicrous and dangerous request. But something in him wanted to help her.

"Okay. Listen. We'll do a drive-by. I will let you see the house but Amari, that's it. We not getting out. I can't catch another charge for you."

"You won't. I promise."

"Amari, we're just going to drive by? We're not getting out, right?"
"Right. I promise. We won't get out," Amari smiled.

CHAPTER 102

Making Friends Along the Way

DAY 757

"Lord, I done got saved and I'm goin' back to jail on the same day!" Eric complained as Amari and he walked up to the front door of the luxurious house. "No, I'm going up under the jail. I don't believe you got me doing this! Do black people even live in this neighborhood?"

"Eric, come on. Quit acting scared," Amari said. "I ain't actin'!" he snapped.

"It's gonna be okay," Amari comforted, confident that her Uncle J and T Lise would know exactly what to do.

Amari ran to the front door of Jeremiah and Elise's house and began both knocking on the door and ringing the doorbell rather aggressively. She prayed her T Lise was working from home today. Maybe she was taking care of J.J.? She couldn't wait to see him.

Eric stood behind her and prayed. "Please, Jesus, I'm tryna do right. Please don't send me back to jail. You know I'm not tryna kidnap this girl."

He wondered how he had let her talk him into this but before he could imagine all the ways his current course could go wrong, the door opened. A rather disturbed- looking white woman answered the door.

"May I help you?" she asked, in a lyrical east Texas accent.

Amari was surprised. This was not who she expected to see. Who was this woman and why was she in Uncle J and T Lise's house?

"Are my auntie and uncle here?" she asked nervously.

The woman looked at the little girl noticing her cheeks were swollen and that the young man behind her was very nervous.

The woman's voice softened. "Sweetie, I don't think you have the right address. Nobody lives here but my husband and me. Are you okay?" she said as she looked past Amari at Eric.

It was just as he feared. He imagined hearing sirens in the distance and explaining to the police, with their guns drawn, that he was just trying to help.

"Yes, ma'am. She's okay. It's just a misunderstanding. We're sorry. We thought this was her aunt and uncle's house. We'll leave you alone. Come on, Amari. We have to go… now."

"Amari? Is that your name, sweetie?" the woman asked.

"Yes, ma'am," Amari answered, still processing that her T Lise and Uncle J were gone. Maybe Cherese was telling the truth. Maybe they didn't want her.

"You used to live here, didn't you, Amari?" the woman asked. "Yes, ma'am. With my aunt and uncle."

"Well, if you used to live here, can you tell me what it said on your bedroom wall?"

"It said 'Amari's Room - No haters or monsters allowed.'"

The woman smiled. "Yes. That's it. Sweetheart. I am not sure what's going on, but your aunt and uncle don't live here anymore. I'm sorry."

"Amari. We have to go," Eric said, hoping this seemingly kind woman wasn't about to call 911. "We tried but they're not here."

"Young man. Is there anything I can do to help?" the woman asked, still concerned about Amari's face, and still trying to determine if Eric was friend or foe.

"Ma'am, like you said, she used to live here. She convinced me to bring her so she could see her family. But I guess they've moved," Eric explained.

"Okay. Then since you're on my doorstep, I'm going to ask. What happened to her face?" the woman asked point blank.

"He didn't do it!" Amari said, coming to her ally's defense. "It was my aunt. He's just trying to help. Please. He's my friend. I promised him he wouldn't get in trouble if he helped me."

The woman looked at Amari as she clung to Eric's leg. Perhaps something wasn't right, but it was clear the little girl wasn't afraid of him.

"So where are you taking her now?" she asked.

"I guess I have to take her back to her aunt," Eric answered.

"The aunt who hit her little face? the woman questioned. "I'm sorry, young man, but that doesn't sound like help to me."

"I know," Eric admitted. "But I don't know what else to do. We don't know where her aunt and uncle are."

"Ooh, Eric. I know where we can go," Amari said as her face brightened. "Papa John's house. He's always home. We can go there. Thank you, ma'am. Let's go, Eric."

"Young man," the woman called to Eric. "Are you two going to be all right?" "Yes, ma'am. I promise you nothing will happen to her," Eric said.

"And you're sure you don't have anything to do with those marks on her face?"

"Yes, ma'am. I wouldn't do that."

"I guess it's none of my business, but I wouldn't take her back to this aunt," the woman cautioned. "My name is Mildreta Patrick. If you need anything, you come back here, and I will do whatever I can to help you."

"Thank you, ma'am. We appreciate that," Eric told her.

"You're welcome young man," Mildreta said, "Amari, I hope you find your Uncle J and T Lise. But if you don't, this other aunt's not going to hurt you again. I promise."

"Thank you, ma'am," Amari said as she grabbed Eric's hand and pulled him back to the car. "I think I can remember how to get to Papa John's house from here. Eric, this is so cool. I told you not to worry!"

Eric shook his head. "Amari, just get in the car."

CHAPTER 103

Party Time

DAY 757

"And she's been stickin' with us ever since," Patricia said to Pastor G. and First Lady Faye.

"So, our daughter just adopted you two in a Target?" Pastor G. asked. "Yes, she did. She's been such a blessing," Patricia said.

"I just want to know why this cute little fella won't let me hold him," Faye complained. "He is so precious. With those chubby cheeks."

"It takes him a few days before he warms up to people, but after that you'll have a friend for life. Ain't that right, Isaiah?" Patricia said.

"And look at him just following Elise's every move," Faye said, observing how Isaiah kept his eye on Elise. "Sweetie, she's just trying to get the party set up. She's not going to leave you. Elise, do you feel this child's eyes burning a hole in you?"

"First Lady, that little boy swear he my man. Saiah, stay with Granny. I'm almost finished," Elise said.

"The house looks wonderful, daughter. John will be very pleased," Pastor Gregory said.

"I hope so, Pastor. There was a time when we didn't think he would ever come home," Elise said.

"We said the same thing about you," Pastor Gregory teased her.

"Hursh, Pastor!" Elise laughed. "Ms. Patricia thinks I'm an angel and I'd just as soon keep it that way. Hold on…this is Jeremiah calling now."

"Hey, Miah, you almost here? Okay. Yes, we're ready. See y'all in a bit. Bye."

"Okay, everyone. Miah and Daddy are just a few minutes away. So, it's that time," Elise instructed.

The DJ turned up the music and all of John's neighbors, some of whom had known his wife and him for decades, lined up in their front yards waiting for their friend to make his triumphant return home. Their front yards were decorated with various welcome home signs. There were tables with various dishes lined up on the lawns. Some homes had bounce houses for the children. And of course, Elise had a band lined up on a stage at the end of the cul-de-sac for live music. Her Daddy was going to be welcomed home right!

"Elise, you shole is lookin' cute for your father-in-law's homecoming," Patricia teased.

"You noticed that too, Ms. Patricia?" Shania asked. "Mr. Traylor is certainly going to love that dress," she said sarcastically.

"Yeah, but which Mr. Traylor?" Faye asked. "Pastor G., they're bothering me," Elise tattled.

"Don't worry, daughter, when my friend gets here, we'll make them mean girls stop messin' with you," Pastor Gregory defended.

"Thank you, Pastor G.," Elise smiled at him before she stuck out her tongue at the ladies.

A few moments later Jeremiah called again, indicating they were turning the corner.

"Okay, everybody!" Elise announced. "They're coming."

CHAPTER 104

Blocked Shot

DAY 757

John's welcome home party was all the way live. There was dancing, laughter, and good conversation throughout the entire block. The aroma from the barbeque grills levitated people from one house to another to sample each grillmaster's selections. John should have been worn out but even from a seated position, he was a gracious host as he thanked all his guests for their well wishes. Most of the guests knew each other quite well, but there were some who hadn't met yet.

"Sooo…you gonna introduce me?" Jeremiah asked Elise.

"Jeremiah, she's right over there…sittin' right next to Daddy, Pastor G., and First Lady. Just go talk to her. You scared?" Elise teased him.

"I'm not scared!" he insisted. "I…you know…just never had to meet your parents, so this is new."

"Aww. Him nervous. Come on, Miah. I will take you to the mean old lady," Elise said as she instinctively grabbed his hand.

It felt natural at first. Then she realized it was no longer appropriate and released it.

"Sorry…old habit," she whispered to him. "Ms. Patricia, this is Jeremiah.

Jeremiah, this is Ms. Patricia."

"Well, hello, Jeremiah," Patricia said. "I was beginning to think you weren't real. The way Elise goes on and on about you, I thought I would meet a unicorn or a leprechaun before I met the legendary

Jeremiah Traylor."

"Is this what we doin', Ms. Patricia?" Elise asked.

"Hi ma'am," Jeremiah said, stepping in to save Elise. "It's nice to finally meet you as well. I've been praying for you," he said as he leaned over and gave her a hug.

"I feel like I already know you, Jeremiah," Patricia continued. "Your family has been telling me some stories about the both of you. They shared some stories about your mother as well. I'm sorry for your loss. It sounds like she was a wonderful woman."

"Thank you for saying that. Mama was the best," Jeremiah said reflectively. "Where's little man? I was hoping to meet him."

"His Auntie Shania took him inside to change him. They'll be out soon," Patricia explained.

"Can I get you anything?" Jeremiah asked Patricia.

"Yes, you can take Ms. Thang here out in the street and dance with her so we old folks can keep talking about y'all undisturbed," Patricia said as she shooed them away.

"Amen, Sister," Faye said. "Let the grown folks talk." "I'm so done with y'all," Elise said, shaking her head.

"Come on, Lise. We not winnin' this one," Jeremiah said, taking her hand and holding it tightly until they got to a part of the street where people were dancing.

"Old folks thank they can say anything!" Elise laughed. "Ha. That's cuz they can," Jeremiah confirmed.

They danced in the middle of the street. Elise did her best to ignore the smiling eyes of their tight circle of friends in the yard. She knew all of them were hoping that tonight would be more than just a homecoming for Daddy but that it would also be a reconciliation for Jeremiah and her. But this was their new normal. They would have to enjoy each other in this new way. And like Daddy, their friends and family would have to understand that their love was transitioning into something different. She wanted the same thing they did, but she was trying to accept that it wasn't going to happen.

Still, it was nice being out with him. To the uninitiated, they looked like a happy couple. What would be the harm of just enjoying him right now? They danced as one song melted into another. It reminded her of when they first met, and they would dance the night away. But they were no longer two young kids falling in love, and she no longer belonged to Jeremiah alone.

"I was trying to let you two have some grown folks' time but this little person is doing the most," Shania said as she put Isaiah in Elise's arms. "Here, little boy… go to your auntie, mama, big sister, sugar mama…whatever she is, but I am not going to let you clown me all day. Sorry, Jeremiah…didn't mean to block."

"It's okay, sis," Jeremiah smiled. "Hi Saiah, it's nice to meet you," Jeremiah said sweetly as Elise bounced him on her hip.

Hearing Jeremiah call him Saiah warmed her heart, but she didn't want to read too much into it.

"You wanna come to me, little man?" Jeremiah asked, extending his hands to the toddler. "Over there almost taller than Lise."

"Really, Miah?" Elise laughed. "I do all your work setting up this party for Daddy, and you still got short jokes? Besides, he's not going to let you hold him. He doesn't do strangers."

"I bet he will," Jeremiah disagreed confidently. He played with Isaiah's hand for a moment, then slowly reached under his arm and gently took him from her as they continued to dance.

"I don't believe it!" Elise exclaimed. "I hope he's not getting sick. You okay, Saiah? Do you have a fever?"

"Don't hate. Why he gotta have a fever just cuz he like me?" Jeremiah asked proudly.

"I'm not hating," Elise smiled as she resumed dancing. "I'm just not used to him being so cool with somebody he doesn't know."

"Well, you talk about me all the time, so he probably feels like he already knows me," Jeremiah said smugly.

"Jeremiah John Traylor. Don't make me hurt you in front of the baby. Ain't nobody talkin' bout you all the time," Elise argued.

"Well, that what Ms. Patricia say. She say you go on and on and on and on and on and on about your amazing husband Jeremiah Traylor.

Didn't she say that, Isaiah?" Jeremiah teased.

Elise stopped dancing. "Jeremiah, please don't do that," she said seriously. "Do what?" he asked.

"You know what," she answered. "Don't be insensitive. I'm trying to make this work. I'm trying to be around you and be there for you in a way that makes sense and is appropriate. But don't play in my face. I wouldn't do you like that."

"Do you?" he asked.

"Do I what?" Elise asked.

"Do you talk about me all the time?" Jeremiah smiled.

"That's what I mean," Elise said. "That's not funny. I don't wanna be ridiculed for my feelings. Patricia doesn't know any better, but you do. I know what I did, and I know I'm the cause of my own pain, but I've tried to do right by you ever since. And I…you know what? I have to go. Let me have him please."

"Lise, I'm sorry. I didn't mean it like that," he said as he gently placed Isaiah back in her arms.

"It's okay. But I'd better go," she said, walking back to where Ms. Patricia was seated.

Elise put Isaiah back in Shania's arms. "Hey, Daddy. It's getting late. We're gonna get little man home. I'll call you tomorrow. Ms. Patricia, I'm going to bring the car around. Pastor G., would you mind helping her to the car?"

"Whut's wong, babeh?" John asked.

"Daddy, it's nothing wrong," Elise said, trying to reassure him. "I just have to go. But I'll see you soon."

Patricia wasn't sure what was going on, but she could tell Elise was upset and that now wasn't the time to talk about it.

"Jou okay, shun?" John asked Jeremiah as he joined him, and Elise walked away.

"No, Pop. I'm not," Jeremiah answered honestly. "So jou jus gon let her go?" John asked.

Jeremiah turned to answer his dad and met Pastor Gregory, Faye,

Patricia, Shania, and even little Isaiah's gaze.

"No, Pop…and everybody. I'm not."

"Well, you better go, baby," Patricia chimed in. "Some of us don't have that much time."

"Elise…wait up!" Jeremiah said, trying to catch up to her. "Jeremiah, I'm fine," Elise said, not slowing down.

"No, you're not. Talk to me," he said as he ran in front of her. "I don't have anything to say," she said simply.

"Then just listen…please. I wasn't playing in your face. At least not to be insensitive or to ridicule you. I really just…I don't know…wow, I thought this would be easier."

"Jeremiah, it's just your emotions and feelings getting stirred up. Trust me, I get it. I thought we could be around each other but maybe…Mari?

"Maybe Mari? What are you talking about?" Jeremiah asked.

"Mari, is that you baby?" she asked, squinting off in the distance past Jeremiah.

"Why are you asking about Mari?" Jeremiah asked.

Elise didn't answer. She just ran past Jeremiah and screamed, "Mari!"

CHAPTER 105

Almost Home

DAY 757

Eric checked his phone. There were no phone calls from Cherese. So that likely meant she hadn't returned home. Eric didn't know much about parenting, but he knew enough to know that had he left, Amari would have been cooped up in Cherese's apartment all day with no supervision, nothing to do, and only junk food to eat. "Jesus," he prayed silently as he drove, "I haven't known you long and I know I haven't got much to offer you. But if you will just help me help this little kid…I don't know. Will you just help me? Please, God…if what I think you've done for me is real, then this is easy for you. Please help her.

"Amari, do I keep straight or turn?" Eric asked Amari, who had suddenly become a little quieter than usual.

"Turn here," she said.

She felt more nervous approaching Papa John's house than when they went to Jeremiah and Elise's home. What if no one was there either? What if they had to go back and Cherese found out? Or what if Eric really did get in trouble for trying to help her? Worst of all, what if they simply didn't want her back? Her confidence from a short while ago was giving way to fear. She began to see old familiar sights that should have brought her comfort, but instead she found herself shaking.

Eric turned onto the street expecting to find your average middle-class neighborhood. Instead, he found a full-blown party.

"They turnt up, ain't they, Lil' Homey? They have most of the street blocked off. Let's park down here and walk. Is it always like this?" Eric asked her as they got out of the car.

"No. I don't think so," Amari responded, curious as to what may have been happening.

"Their house is at the end, right?" "Yeah," she said as she grabbed his hand.

They approached the end of the cul-de-sac and Amari saw them! Her Uncle J held J.J. as he and T Lise danced in the middle of the street with some of the other partygoers. They looked so happy. T Lise smiled from ear to ear, and Uncle J looked like he always did when he was with her. She was glad they were happy. Even J.J. looked happy. Uncle J used to hold her like that, but he would probably think she was too big or too old to do that anymore. And even if she wasn't…now he had J.J.

"That's them," Amari said to Eric. "My Uncle J and T Lise…there, in the middle of the street dancing with the baby. That's J.J. That's their baby. He's so big."

"Well, come on then!" Eric said happily. "Let's go."

"Eric, I don't want to," Amari said in a panicked voice. "Let's just go. I know you can't take care of me. It's not your fault. You can take me back to Cherese or to that woman or wherever. They're fine without me."

"I thought you wanted to see your family?" Eric asked.

"I do. But they don't want to see me. Cherese is right. They would have come to get me if they wanted me. They're leaving anyway," Amari said, noticing them leaving the street.

Eric kneeled down in front of her. "Amari, listen. I know you're scared. And I thought this was kinda crazy at first too. But you know what, Lil' Homey? My money is on you."

"What does that mean?" Amari asked.

"I mean you convinced me to run these streets with you, out here defying the law and errthang. That's cuz you're special. And if I think you're special, I. Bet. They. Do. To," Eric said, gently tapping his finger against her little nose with each syllable. "I don't know a whole lot,

After the Crash

but I know what happened to me this morning was real, and I didn't deserve it. I don't deserve you either. So, if I can help you, if I can get you home, then I'm gon do it. I don't really have any friends. But you're my friend, Lil' Homey. Buzz and Woody for life! We started this day out trying to get some pancakes and take a ride. I think God had something else in mind, so let's finish this. I know my Lil' Homey ain't no punk," Eric said, punching her lightly in the chest.

"No…your Lil' Homey is a punk," Amari disagreed tearfully. "Eric. I'm scared. I'm scared they don't want me back and that I'm ugly like Cherese says and that nobody but her wants me. And I don't know what I'm going to say when I see them."

"Cherese is a liar, Amari! Don't worry about what she says. And don't worry about what you're going to say. If they're the same people you have been talking about, then they will know what to do. And don't forget…yo Big Homey just got saved. It's still much thug in me. So, if they get to trippin'…let's just say I got a little somethin' for 'em."

"Thank you…Booty Butt," Amari smiled. "I love you."

Eric laughed. "Yeah, I'm gon regret telling you that, ain't it?" But I love you too, Lil' Homey and no matter what, I'm goin' with you all the way to the end. So, we doin' this or what?" Eric smiled.

Amari wondered what she should say. Should she just run back to the car, or take Eric's hand and see what would happen? She opened her mouth to answer him, but before she could speak, she heard her name being called in the distance.

CHAPTER 106

Family Reunion

DAY 757

"Mari, baby, is it really you?" Elise said, flooding her face with kisses. "I missed you so much. You're so big."

"Yes, ma'am," Amari said, as her T Lise kissed all her fears away. "Miah, it's her!" Elise exclaimed, as Jeremiah approached.

Jeremiah was frustrated, confused, and overjoyed all at once. He had finally gotten the courage to shoot his shot with Elise, but instead of listening to him, she left him in the middle of the street screaming about Amari. But it really was Amari. A little older. A little bigger. But it was her. He wondered how she had gotten there and who the young man with her was. But most of all, he wondered if she resented him for not coming to get her. Amari quickly addressed his concerns as she ran to him and put her arms around him.

"Hey, beautiful. How did you get here?" he asked as he picked her up in his arms.

"We made a prison break," she said gleefully. "This is my best friend, Eric. I asked him to help me, and he did. He just became a Christian, but before that he was a thug and went to prison. He's not a bad thug, though. He used to lose most of his prison fights. He's really nice. His mama used to call him 'Booty Butt.' He's my Big Homey."

Eric smiled and waved as he observed this family reunion.

Jeremiah gave this stranger the onceover, still not sure what all was happening. "Mari, what happened to your face, baby?" Elise asked. "Did someone hit her?" she asked, looking back at Eric.

"It wasn't him, T Lise. I promise," Amari intervened.

"Eric, can you tell us what's happening, brother?" Jeremiah asked, gently stroking Amari's bruised face.

"It's like she told you," Eric responded nervously. "I was just tryna help. I don't want no problems. I got in trouble not too long ago but I'm tryna put all that behind me."

"Eric, baby, that's wonderful. But we can talk about your rehabilitation later. Right now, we wanna know who hit her!" Elise asked as she clapped out the last three words.

"Yes, ma'am," he responded, recognizing some of the attitude Amari had shared with him about his aunt. "Lil' bit and her aunt... they don't get along too well. Cherese got a temper, and it got out of hand this mornin.'"

"Out of hand?" Elise asked. "You call this out of hand?"

"Ma'am, I don't want any trouble. I'm just trying to help," Eric explained. "We understand, Eric," Jeremiah said, adjusting Amari on his hip and placing a calming hand on Elise's shoulder. "But how did you end up here? We're not coming for you. We just need to know what's happening."

"That's right," Elise agreed. "If Amari says you're her best friend, then you're our friend too. But if that...," Elise looked over her shoulder at Jeremiah and changed her words midway through her sentence, "... thang touched my child. Baby, Imma need you to give me an address."

"Nope! We don't need an address," Jeremiah intervened, knowing how catastrophic it could be if Elise came face to face with this infamous aunt who it now appeared was worse than they had ever imagined. "Amari, did she do this to your face, baby?" he asked.

"Yes, sir," Amari affirmed.

"It wasn't the first time either," Eric added. "And I'm not just talking about a normal whoopin' that kids get sometime. But today...it was bad. It was like she was possessed."

"So, you've seen it?" Jeremiah asked. "Yeah, I've seen it," Eric acknowledged. "Will you tell the police that?"

Eric drew back. Cherese meant what she said about calling his parole officer. He would never hurt Amari or any child, but his life still wouldn't hold up to close scrutiny.

"Sir, I'm on parole. I'd rather avoid the police if I can. I'm already out there further than I planned to be," Eric said.

"Yeah, when he tried to help me today, she threatened to call his parole officer," Amari confirmed.

"Eric, we don't want to get you in trouble. And we can't make any promises. But if Amari is your best friend, it might help if you can corroborate what she's saying," Jeremiah said.

"If I can what?" Eric asked.

"Baby, we need you to say you saw that thang hit my baby!" Elise translated. "Or you can just give me an address. Ever which way you feel the Spirit leading is fine with me."

Eric looked at Amari. For a few months, he had been her only source of happiness. And she had been his. But now she was with people who would not only love her, they could support her as well. Whatever the cost. Whatever Cherese's wrath would be. He needed to help his Lil' Homey.

"Tell me what you need," he said.

CHAPTER 107

Finally Home

DAY 757

Monique sat in the Traylors living room as the party that had morphed into a family reunion and now a possible police investigation continued on. Amari sat on the floor at John's feet playing with Isaiah. She wondered why they had decided to name him Isaiah instead of after Uncle J but regardless, she wanted to enjoy the moment. She looked over at Monique and even if it wasn't her fault, nothing good ever happened when she was around. She tried to focus on the attention she was getting as Papa John doted on her and Isaiah played with her. She was having trouble understanding everything Papa John was saying, but she didn't want to hurt his feelings. Besides, even if she couldn't understand everything he was saying, she could still look into his eyes and know everything she needed to know. And J.J.…Isaiah, rather, was wonderful. She recalled the dream she had before he was even born. As adorable as he was, this baby didn't look like the baby in her dream. But after all, it was only a dream. She was just glad he was okay even if he was a little chunkier than she imagined.

"So, how'd it go, Monique?" Jeremiah asked. "And what can we do to make sure she doesn't have to go back?"

"It went…okay," Monique answered with a slight chuckle. "I called Cherese and told her it was urgent I meet her and Amari, today. She resisted but when I told her it was not optional, she agreed. I met her at her apartment. I, of course, know Amari wasn't there. If it weren't so sad, it would have been very humorous, watching her search that two-bedroom apartment and yelling for Amari. She made up all sorts of stories. First, it was 'Amari likes to play hide-and-seek.' Then it was

'Oh, she's at my neighbor's.' She ran out of the house, and I assume Eric, that's when she called you.'

"Yes, ma'am. Must have been," Eric confirmed. "But I didn't answer, just like you said."

"Right," Monique continued. "So, she comes back and as disgusted as I am with her, I let her off the hook and laid it all on the line. I told her that Amari would not be coming back. And that further investigation into how she's been treated was pending."

"And what did she say to that?" Eric asked, wondering what Cherese's next step would be.

"Ah. Yes, Eric. Jeremiah and Elise told me there may be some concerns. All I can say is that people in glass houses shouldn't throw stones. Cherese put her hands on a child. She has other things to worry about. And just between us, if she wasn't there, if she didn't see it, she can't really testify to it. I would just suggest you get yourself together, so you don't have to worry about your parole officer. But I know some people. Just in case, give me your parole officer's name, and I will put in a good word for you. It was a big risk you took today, and you did it for a child. That means a lot in my book."

"Yeah…well, anything for my Lil' Homey," Eric said as he looked at Amari playing with the baby. "So, do you need anything from me?"

"Not right now," Monique replied. "I have your number. I will let you know if we need anything, but I think your part is done. Thank you, Eric."

"Yes. Thank you, Eric," Elise said as she stood up and gave him a hug. "You're welcome. I'm glad I could help. It feels good," he said as he walked

closer to where Amari was playing with Isaiah and got on the floor with them. "Lil' bit, I'd better go."

Amari had been so focused on getting back to her family that she hadn't thought about what Eric would do if she did.

"You don't have to go, Eric," she said, not really knowing what to say. She only knew she didn't want to trade her new family for her old one. That didn't seem right.

"It's okay, Lil' Homey. I don't belong here. But you do. I'll miss you, though." "I don't want you to go," Amari said as she stood up and wrapped her arms around his neck.

"I don't want to go either. But like you told me…you're a little kid. I'm not." "Uncle J, tell him he can stay," Amari pleaded.

"Amari, it's okay," Eric consoled her. "But I want to thank you. This is the best day of my life. I don't understand everything that happened or why, but I know there's a God who loves me and I don't think I knew that before. And I want to thank you for what you said when you introduced me to your aunt and uncle. You said I was your best friend…." Eric coughed in an effort to choke back his tears. "Nobody has ever called me that before. It means a lot."

"Will you come and see me again? Like you used to?" Amari asked him.

"I don't think it's gon be the same anymore, Lil' Homey. But I'll always be thinking about you."

"Eric," Jeremiah said, "I'm sure we can work out something for you to come visit Amari. Like Elise said, if you're a friend of hers, you're a friend of ours."

"Yes, sir. I appreciate that."

"He needs a job, Uncle J," Amari said. "What can you do?" Jeremiah asked. "Not much," Eric answered honestly.

"Do you want to learn how to do something?" "Yes, sir. I do," Eric said sincerely.

"Then let's meet up on Monday. We'll see what we can do for you. Deal?" "Deal," Eric agreed. "You feel better now, Lil' Homey?"

"Yes!" Amari said as she threw her arms around Eric. "Folks, I'm gon get out of your way," Eric said.

"Eric, there's plenty of food and plenty of time," Elise said. "This is a family reunion and in case you haven't picked up on it yet…you're family. Why don't you stay? It's been a long day."

"Yeah, I'm sorry, Eric. Where are my manners? Please stay. We'd love to have you," Jeremiah said. "We have to work out some things with Monique anyway."

"Actually, I don't think there's much to do, Jeremiah," Monique said. "You and Elise were Amari's foster parents before, so it's not like we have to do an extensive background check. And I'm assuming the way both of you have pestered me over the last few months, she can stay with you. Can I use your old address in Colonial Park?"

Jeremiah and Elise both stared at each other. They had been so concerned with Amari's safety, they had forgotten they no longer lived together.

"Actually, we don't live there anymore," Elise said.

"Oh, that's fine. Just let me know what address to use," Monique advised. "Funny story...," Jeremiah said, stalling for time. "We kind of have…some things hanging in the air right now as far as addresses. Like Elise said, we don't live at our old place right now. We were staying here and there…."

"Yeah, right. Here and there," Elise agreed clumsily. "Now Daddy is home… and it's going to be crowded."

"Yeah, real crowded. So, we…do some moving around," Jeremiah said. "Yes, they have places all over town," Shania added, trying not to laugh as they squirmed.

"But she can stay with you…right?" Monique asked, puzzled by their reaction. "Yes!" they said in unison.

"Okay, so I just need an address and I need to see it so I can have it on record.

You can let me know if anything changes."

"Well…you can use our address here," Jeremiah said. "Amari actually has a room here anyway."

"You don't think we should use the address at…our apartment?" Elise asked, cutting her eyes at Jeremiah.

"Yes, Jeremiah," Shania meddled, grinning from ear to ear. "What about your apartment?"

Jeremiah returned an annoyed gaze at them both. "Well, Elise…

Shania…she already has a room here that she's used to sleeping in. Her bed is in there and everything. So, it would make sense for her to stay here."

"Jeremiah…," Elise began to protest before Jeremiah cut her off.

"Monique, we need a second to work out some logistics," Jeremiah said as he grabbed Elise by the hand and led her to the front door.

"Is something wrong?" Monique asked.

"No, nothing's wrong," Jeremiah said. "I just need to talk to my wife."

CHAPTER 108

Beauty from Ashes

DAY 757

The party was over, but there was still a little activity on the block. A few neighbors were still congregating while others tidied up and put things away. Some of the more inquisitive neighbors couldn't help but turn their attention to the block's favorite couple. None of them really knew the story. They only knew they didn't see Elise quite as much as they used to. It was only natural for them to wonder what they had come outside to talk about. Jeremiah and Elise were as oblivious to the neighbor's curiosity as they were to the curiosity of their family and friends they had just left inside.

"Shania, girl…I know you not tryna lift up that window and eavesdrop!", Pastor Gregory chastised.

"Pastor, how can I hear if I don't open the window?" Shania questioned as she slowly tried to lift the window without Jeremiah and Elise noticing.

"You know you wanna know, Wayne," Faye said as she sat next to Patricia, snuggling Isaiah, who she had finally coaxed into letting her hold him.

"Faye, you just play with that baby. Don't be joining in with this foolery. John, this is yo house. Take over."

John leaned over toward his old friend. "I kinna wanna know myself," he chuckled.

"What's happening?" Amari asked.

"That's what I wanna know," Monique agreed.

"Gawd doin' sumthin,' John told them. "Jus watch." "Shush…and listen!" Shania added.

"Jeremiah," Elise whispered as they stood in the front yard, "what are we going to tell Monique?"

"Let's just tell her the truth," Jeremiah said simply.

"Boy, I ain't taught you nuthin'. That ain't gon work. We just got her back. I don't want her going to a group home or another family because we can't get our story straight."

"Lise, we have our story straight. She's not going to a group home. She can stay with us," Jeremiah said confidently.

"Jeremiah, there is no us. We're separated. I need you to get it together and think!" Elise barked.

"Ok…first of all…tone," Jeremiah chastised as he tried to make her laugh while he gathered his thoughts.

"Miah, you play too much. We need to focus," Elise insisted. "If Monique finds out we lied to her she might not let her stay, and she might take her anyway if she finds out what's really going on."

"What do you think is going on?" Jeremiah asked.

"Miah, do you smell burnt toast? Because I think you're having a stroke." Jeremiah shook his head and smiled. "I'm not having a stroke, Lise."

"Do you have a fever?" Elise asked as she put the back of her hand on his forehead.

"No," he chuckled. "I don't have a fever either."

"Well, then, why are you asking me what I think is going on when it's perfectly clear? Why are we out here? We need to clear this up."

"But what are we going to say?"

"Miah, what's wrong?" Elise asked seriously, realizing he had something important on his mind.

Jeremiah took a deep breath. "Lise… this isn't working."

"That's what I'm saying," Elise agreed. "But I'm not letting her go again. We just need to go in there and come clean. I'll ask Monique to list me as her sole foster parent and I will adopt her. I know you love her, we'll work that out, but Mari has to come first."

"No…that's not what I meant," Jeremiah said. "I meant my life isn't working…without you."

"Miah, hold on. I think I know where you're going, and I'm not going to let you do this. This is exactly why I was trying to leave in the first place. It's just some of those old feelings coming back up."

"They're not coming back up," Jeremiah insisted. "They never left. I've never stopped loving you or wanting you, Lise. I've loved you from the moment I saw you. I've loved you through all we've been through. And I love you now."

"Miah, I know you do. And I love you, too. But it doesn't change why we separated in the first place. I broke your trust; I broke my promise…and I broke our marriage. You are such an amazing man, but this is not on you to fix, baby."

"Pop says real men can fix what they didn't break," Jeremiah said.

Elise smiled and glanced back at the house. She thought she saw the blinds shake but ignored it. "I love that man," she said warmly. "But you're just in your feelings now. Mari's home. Daddy's home. And you want things to be like they were before. And as much as I do too, I'm afraid once that euphoria goes away, you're going to calm down and remember what I did to our marriage."

"You know what I remember, Lise? I remember when I first saw you and how you rocked a military police uniform but still managed to be the most beautiful woman in the world. I remember how you shot me down when I asked for your number and still managed to build me up at the same time. I remember crying when you went on deployment, and promising myself…and God, that if he brought you back to me, I would marry you, and love you, and take care of you, for the rest of our lives. I remember making good on that promise. It's still the happiest day of my life. And on that day, I promised to love you in sickness and health, for better or worse, until death do us part. And Lise…," he said, gently taking her hands, "we're both still alive."

"But Miah…," Elise tried to interject..

"Wait, babe. Please," he continued. "I remember the best twenty years in the history of mankind with the best wife in the world, who only a fool would let go. And I remember that wife pleading with me to just listen to her and to love her. I remember her telling me she needed me, and I just couldn't get it because my pride had to show this wonderful woman what a great man I could be. But I forgot that my only greatness came from Christ. And I forgot the grace he showed me when he gave me you. And I remember," Jeremiah paused and laughed softly, "an angel stopping us in a parking lot and telling me that no man could take away what the Lord had given me. I remember him promising us that God would heal our marriage and our life. And I remember Mama telling me that if you rob a bank, I should drive the getaway car."

Elise smiled, imagining Mama Etta saying those words as Jeremiah continued. "I remember her telling me that when everything falls apart to open my mouth and give God praise and when I did, God was going to turn it around. And when I found out about you and Joshua, I knew that then, everything had fallen apart. But I couldn't do it...or at least I wouldn't. But God joined me in that hotel room, and he softened me. And I praised him. I cried but I praised him. I still felt let down, but I praised him. I still didn't understand but I praised him. I don't know if I meant it or if the praise was sincere and from my heart, but I did it. But even as I was crying and slingin' snot and complaining and giving up, something happened when I told him that I didn't want to be here anymore. I remembered that you felt the same way. And that you didn't want to be here anymore. And in that space, hurt, angry, confused, betrayed, and alone as I felt, my praise became real. I knew God was still there and I gave him thanks that you were too. So, I just kept praising him. I got down on my knees and I opened my mouth and praised God like I never have before. And then I called you. I was too afraid and too mad to tell you everything and even after I hung up, I was still mad. I was still in my feelings. But every day, I've tried to praise him. And now, the more I praise Him, the more he reminds me that he's still right, he's still good, and he's still for me. He's for us, Babe. Miah and Lise against the world. Mama said I would have to forgive you, and at the time, I was like, 'For what?' And now here I am saying the same thing. For what? When I think about the way you have honored me, and loved me, and supported me, and prayed for me…I'm like forgive you for what?"

"Yeah, you're definitely having a stroke," Elise quipped, trying to mask her emotions.

"No, babe. I'm not," he said seriously. "I know what happened. But that's not who you are. The real Elise…my Lise…is the one who held this family together when everything fell apart. Now I'm asking you to let me be the real Jeremiah… your Miah, again. I'm asking for another chance to love you and to make it right."

"What about Isaiah?" she asked.

"We can adopt Isaiah and Amari…together." "What about Ms. Patricia?" Elise asked. "We can adopt her too," Jeremiah smiled.

"Miah and Lise against the world?" Elise asked, returning his smile.

"Yes. Miah and Lise against the world!" Jeremiah said as he got down on one knee and extended his pinky finger to her. "So, Elise Janelle Traylor, will you stay married to me?"

Elise paused…probably not for very long. But long enough to unnerve the audience she and Jeremiah didn't even know they had.

"Baby, say yes!" Ms. Patricia yelled through the window. "He wanna adopt me too!"

Elise and Jeremiah turned and laughed as they saw their family peering through the blinds of the living room.

"Yeah, say yes, T Lise!" Amari agreed, though she wasn't really sure what was going on or why all of this was necessary.

"Say yes, Lise," Jeremiah smiled, looking up at her. Elise sighed. "No," she said, smiling.

Jeremiah's face morphed from his confident smile to one of confusion. "No?" he asked, surprised.

"You know what I want," Elise said, grinning from ear to ear. "You sure?" he smiled.

"Yes, sir! And you need to make me believe it!" she grinned.

Jeremiah cleared his throat and serenaded her with their song. "You don't have to be rich, to be my girl, you don't have to be cool, to rule my world."

Their family, figuring their cover was blown, decided Jeremiah needed backup singers and joined him.

"Ain't no particular sign, I'm more compatible with, I just want your extra time and your…"

"Nananananananana," Amari scatted the guitar part.

"Kiss!" Elise said as she dropped down to her knees and kissed him.

Their family and friends cheered and applauded from the house which wasn't too much of a surprise. The surprise was the additional approval from the remaining neighbors on the block who added their own applause and cheers to the celebration. They didn't really know what they were celebrating, but it looked wonderful.

"So, can I go spend some time with my son?" Jeremiah asked. "Yes, baby. You can go spend some time with your son."

CHAPTER 109

Some Catching Up to Do

DAY 757

"Mari, I know it's a lot to take in, baby. But does it make sense?" Elise asked, attempting to help Amari process. Their special day was over but the recently reunited family still had a lot of catching up to do.

"So…this isn't J.J.?" Amari asked, kissing him as he slept in her arms. "I mean, I know his name isn't J.J., but you mean you didn't just change his name? You mean he's not your baby?"

"No, sweetheart. J.J. is in heaven," Jeremiah said, pulling her close to comfort her. "Isaiah is actually Ms. Patricia's grandson and she's a good friend of T Lise's."

"What happened to J.J.?" Amari asked.

"Baby, after they took you away from us, we had a very bad car crash. Your little brother didn't live," Elise explained.

"Are y'all okay?", Amari asked, concerned. "Do you miss him?"

"It's been hard," Jeremiah said. "We miss him every day. Just like we missed you. But we're making it."

"Cherese said that y'all didn't want me and that you asked her to come and get me," Amari said.

"That's not true at all," Jermiah said.

"Mari, we always wanted you. A lot has happened but that will never change," Elise said.

"Did you try to come and get me?" Amari asked.

"Baby, we wanted to," Jeremiah explained. "But we didn't know what Cherese was doing. Like T Lise said, a lot has happened. You know Papa John was sick when you left, and we lost your little brother, and I got hurt in the crash. It was pretty bad. Here let me show you."

Jeremiah lowered his head, parted his hair with his fingers, and showed Amari the scar on his scalp.

"I'm sorry we didn't come get you baby girl," Jeremiah said. "I know I let you down. T Lise tried and tried and maybe if I would have been stronger, we could have figured out a way to get you back."

"It's not your Uncle J's fault sweetheart," Elise said. "He has scars like that on his arm and leg too, sweetie. He had four surgeries. He even had to learn how to walk again. But we never forgot about you."

"I missed you too. I prayed every day that you would come and get me. I thought you forgot about me. But Eric would check on me and he made sure I was okay. He was my only friend."

"He seems like he's very sweet," Elise said.

"He is really sweet," Amari agreed. "He looked out for me. He would check on me, keep me company, and bring me stuff to eat. I don't think he has a family. I think I'm his only friend, too."

"We'll do whatever we can to help him, baby girl," Jeremiah reassured her. "We sure will," Elise confirmed. "But Ms. Patricia is my friend too. It's a lot to explain right now. But she doesn't know about J.J. So, don't say anything to her about him. Okay?"

"Okay," Amari agreed, not sure what the big deal was.

"And we're going to make up for all this lost time, too," Elise said. "I know one way you can make up for it," Amari said.

"Little Girl, you can get anything you want. You name it. Right, Uncle J?" Elise said.

"Anything," Jeremiah agreed.

"Can we all sleep together tonight?" Amari asked, smiling from one ear to the other.

"Yes, we can," Jeremiah said. "But it's getting late. You have to lay down and go to sleep."

"TT are you going to sleep in that?" Amari said, noticing Elise was still in her dress.

"No, I'm sure Uncle J has something I can sleep in," Elise answered.

"Why don't you have any sleep clothes?" Amari asked.

"Little girl…this is one of those things TT will tell you when you're older," Elise said. "All that matters is that we're together. Right Uncle J?"

"Right, babe. That's all that matters."

CHAPTER 110

Mildreta and Jasper

DAY 760

"Elise Traylor Real Estate. This is Elise. How may I help you?" Elise answered.

"Hi, this is Elise?" a male caller asked.

"Yes, sir. This is Elise. How can I help you?" Elise smiled patiently.

"Your husband is Jeremiah Traylor?" he asked in a thick east Texas accent. "Yes sir. I'm Elise and my husband is Jeremiah. Are you searching for real estate assistance?"

"Well…Elise, yeah I guess I kinda am. Did you folks used to live at 6422 Wilena Court over here in Colonial Park?"

"Sir, what is this about?" Elise asked, starting to get annoyed. Were this not her business phone this gentleman likely would not have gotten the same level of patience.

"Well, Elise, it's like this, and you might think I'm crazy but it's really not me, it's my wife," he said.

"Sir, how can I help you?" Elise said, one second from disconnecting the call. "Jasper, dang it! Try and let you handle business and ya just messin' every thang up," a woman interrupted. "Ms. Traylor," she said, her accent rivaling her husband's drawl. "Please don't be offended. But I just have to believe you are a

woman of God. Otherwise, the Lord wouldn't have told me to do this." "Do what ma'am?" Elise said, softening at her mention of the Lord.

"Well first, I do want to make sure that you and your husband are the former owners of our home. We own the property my husband mentioned. Over here on Wilena Court. I'm asking because a young man and a little girl were here a few days ago. She was just the cutest little thang. Poor baby had the awfulest bruise on her little face. He was a handsome little guy too. I thought he was a little suspicious at first…and mind you…it wasn't because he was black now. We feel like the good Lord made everybody the way he made them on purpose. It was just that he looked a little nervous though, but I could just discern in my spirit that little ole boy loved that little girl and wasn't gonna harm a hair on her sweet head. That's what I told my Jasper. That's my husband you were talkin' too. Sweetie, ain't men somethin' else? Can't get 'em to take care of nuthin'. Anyway…"

"Mildreta, would you get to the point! The poor girl gon be old as you by the time you finish," Jasper growled.

"I'm gon tell her! Hush now. Elise honey, well, you did used to live here… right? I just need to make sure I'm talking to the right family. That little girl… Amari…that was your niece?"

"Ma'am, yes that little girl is my niece…basically," Elise laughed, giving herself to the conversation. "Now, can you slow down and tell me how I can help you?"

"Elise, darlin'…I have barely slept a wink since that little girl and that young fella left here. At first, I thought I was just worried about her. She looked so sad when she came here and couldn't find you. But I kept on prayin' and the Lord just kept on a badgerin' me in my spirit, and I said, "Lord, I didn't even do nuthin' bad. Why are you displeased? And then it hit me. You know what I realized, darlin?"

"No, ma'am, what?" Elise asked as dramatically as she could. She wasn't going to make money on this call, but this laughter was good for her soul.

"Darlin, I realized this house ain't ours! The Lord said you find out who that little girls auntie and uncle are, and you work out something to give them their house back."

"Ma'am, did you say you want to give us our house back?" Elise asked, her laughter stopping.

"No, Darlin. I said the Lord told me to give you your house back. Now, we need you to be fair. But me and Jasper are fine. And we ain't tryna win the lottery off you folks. But we're hoping since you're a realtor already, we can work out somethin' that's fair."

"Ma'am…Ms. Mildreta…yes, we can work something out. I need to check with my husband, but you don't know how much of a blessing this would be."

"I'm so glad, sweetheart. And guess what? We've barely lived here. We had two grandbabies last year. One in California and the other in Florida. And we just been a spoilin' 'em. Shoot, I bet we ain't spent two months in this house since we bought it. But we can work with you and get it ready, and you guys can move in once we get all the paper work done."

"Ma'am, that would be indescribably wonderful. Thank God for you," Elise said, amazed at this sudden news.

"Oh, sweetheart, we're just bein' obedient. Now can I ask about that precious Amari? Is she okay?"

"Yes ma'am," Elise answered. "She's doing very well. It's almost like she was never away."

"Well, praise the Lord!" Mildreta exclaimed. "Darlin', I would love to chat with ya but I think me and Jasper had better go find some place to live. We're thinking about finding a place and fixin' it up."

Elise smiled. "Ms. Mildreta, I know just the right person to help you with that."

CHAPTER 111

Going Away Party

DAY 800

As much as Jeremiah and Elise were happy to be back in each other's lives, and their own home, there were still real-life issues to be overcome. There were now four adults and two children living under one roof. With their renewed commitment to marital counseling, Amari's schedule, and their own workload, their schedules left little alone time for them as a couple. When they did see each other, they were usually surrounded by attention-starved children, John's physical therapists, or Patricia's hospice nurses. Sadly, they knew that soon there would be more room in the house. Patricia's time on this earth was coming to an end, and Jeremiah wanted to make her last days special.

"Miah, this is so sweet. We should have done it for Mama Etta," Elise said. "We did…we just didn't realize it was happening. I think she did, though,"

Jeremiah said.

Elise leaned backwards into Jeremiah's arms, turned her head, and kissed him. "Thank you for thinking of this. If I can ever get you alone…and we're both awake at the same time…I'm going to thank you for real. I mean for real for real," she said as seductively as she could.

"Uh-huh," Jeremiah said skeptically. "You were supposed to thank me for real for real the other night…but you fell asleep…in the shower! Who does that? The tub? Okay. But in the shower? Standing up?"

"I'm sorry, baby," Elise laughed. "All I remember was saying to myself, 'I am just gon lean in this corner and close my eyes for a couple of minutes and after that…I'm gon rock my man's world.' Are you sure that didn't happen? I feel like that happened."

"It. Did. Not," Jeremiah insisted. "I came in there and you were propped up against the wall…knocked out. I dried you off and put you in the bed. And you never said a word. Just laid up there snoring while you gettin' tucked in. The only one in this family with those privileges should be Saiah."

Elise wanted to argue, but she noticed John staring at them. "Can we help you, Daddy?" she asked with an adoring smile.

"I'm just enjoying looking at you two. Looking at what God did," he said joyfully. "But when y'all are finished snuggling over there, you can join us."

"I was about to say get a room, but they might do it," Faye teased. "She can't get enough of a brutha," Jeremiah said.

Elise responded with another kiss on the cheek, followed by a gentle elbow to his gut as they joined the rest of the family in the crowded living room.

John, Pastor Gregory, and First Lady Faye sat around the hospital bed they had brought in for Faye while Eric played on the floor with Amari and Isaiah.

"How's our girl doing, Pop?" Jeremiah asked. "She's a little tired, son," John responded. "You okay, Daddy?" Elise asked.

"I'm fine, Daddy's Girl," he said, knowing she was concerned. He and Patricia had become good friends and now he was going to have to tell her goodbye. It naturally brought memories back of him having to say goodbye to his wife. "Today is all about Patricia. With her sleepin' self."

"I'm not 'sleep!" Patricia insisted. "I'm just restin' my eyes. I hear all this sweet ruckus."

"Well, it's about to get sweeter, so open up those pretty eyes so we can talk to you," Elise said sweetly.

"You really think you be runnin' stuff, don't you?" Patricia asked her.

"I really do," Elise agreed. "But this is Jeremiah's idea, so we will let him start."

"We want to thank you all for coming. The Lord put it on our hearts to make sure that this sweet lady got her flowers while she could smell them."

Jeremiah paused as Elise gently rubbed his arm to comfort him. He wanted the occasion to be joyful and sweet, but he couldn't help but think of his own mother. "It seems like just yesterday, we were at Pop's house, talking and laughing, rejoicing and reminiscing with Mama. We didn't realize it at the moment, but that was the last time we would do that. This family always holds out hope for God's miracles. And we've seen them too. They're in this room right now. We've seen a marriage healed, children returned and multiplied, and a man who wasn't even supposed to survive learn to walk and talk again. We've seen much of what the enemy stole be recovered. And the emptiness of things and people that haven't been recovered has been filled with God's all sufficient grace. So today we're celebrating the miracle of our good friend Patricia who, one day when she was down, obeyed the prompting of the Holy Spirit and went to Target, where she bumped into someone who it is impossible to meet without being changed. And that someone was my wife. Ms. Patricia, I want to thank you for taking care of her while I could not, and for sharing this amazing little boy with us. Today we want to celebrate you and a life well lived. I know it wasn't easy and I know it wasn't perfect. But I also know you're depending on the perfection that is only found in Jesus Christ, and I know you're trusting his all-sufficient grace for everything else. I said this family holds out hope for miracles, and I want to make it clear that you're a part of this family and we haven't given up hope for your miracle. But we also trust in the sovereignty of God and if He chooses to bring you home, then I am promising you that Isaiah is in good hands. I promise you that he will never forget you…or your son. You know how much you mean to Elise, but I also want you to know that I love you as well."

"Ms. Patricia…we are not going to cry…right?" Elise started. "But we've been praying and fasting and believing God for your healing. And now, as much as I don't want you to go, I can't deny the peace and joy I feel as I look at you now. Over the last few months, I have heard you say thank you more times than I can count. I don't think I've expressed enough how thankful I am to you. You let me be me. You let me love you. You let me love Isaiah."

"And I let you boss me," Patricia interjected as everyone laughed.

"You don't let me do nuthin'," Elise replied with a smirk. "I just do it… anyhoo…I just want you to know you have been a joy. I pray the Lord has allowed me to give you some joy. The Lord has given me more mothers as an adult than I ever had as a child, but he was just flexin' when he gave me you. You matter Ms. Patrica…and I love you so much. I gave up on God once and I refused to listen to his voice. I'm so glad you didn't."

One by one, their guests spoke words of encouragement to Ms. Patricia. They shared how she had impacted their life in their short time together and how her absence would be felt.

"I am not as good at words as you all," Patricia said. "All I can say as I look around this room is thank you, Jesus! I'm not a Bible scholar, but I know somewhere in there it talks about your latter days being better than your former days. Elise, that's what you did for me. I have more peace, joy, and love in this season than I have in my whole life. I know God did it. But he used you to do it. Thank you, baby."

"Ms. Patricia, why you making me cry?" Elise asked, letting her tears go. "They should be happy tears, baby. You've been a blessing. I was about to give up too. Then I met you. So go ahead and cry, but you make sure they are tears of joy."

"They are, Ms. Patricia," Elise sniffled.

"Tell that little boy to come over here," Patricia said. "Mari, can you bring Saiah here?" Elise asked. "No," Patricia corrected. "The big one. Bring him." "You mean Eric?" Elise asked.

"Yes. I want to talk to him," Patricia confirmed.

"Me?" Eric asked, confused as to what this woman he barely knew had to say. He only came because he knew Amari wanted to see him and as a courtesy to his new boss.

"Yes, ma'am?" he said respectfully as he stood up and went to

Patricia's bedside.

"Give me your hand, little boy," Ms. Patricia said, her voice beginning to lose its strength. "I know you don't know me. But whether you know it or not, I know you. You remind me of my son. Like you, he was sweet, strong, handsome and had all sorts of potential. But also like you, he was hardheaded. He never believed the stove was hot until he got burned. He had to learn everything the hard way. But you have something my son didn't have. You have good strong Christian men around you to show you the right way. You pay attention and you trust God. Your battles aren't over, but now you have God to fight your battles. You can't see it right now, but everything you've been through was for your good. Don't worry about what's behind you, because I'm living proof that God will turn it around before long."

Patricia paused. Then she smiled.

"I'll be there in a little bit, baby," she said, looking into the corner of the room. "Are you talking to me, ma'am?" Eric asked.

"No, son," Pastor Gregory said. "She's not talking to you."

CHAPTER 112

Beautiful Ending

DAY 800

"Uncle J, is Ms. Patricia going to heaven tonight?" Amari asked.

Their guests were gone, and Elise wanted to spend some time alone with Patricia. "She might, sweetie. Are you scared?" Jeremiah asked.

"A little. I didn't know what was happening when Mama Etta died, so I didn't have time to think about it. Is T Lise okay?"

"T Lise will be fine, baby. T Lise did what God wanted her to do for Ms. Patricia. She knows God is pleased. And plus, she has us." "Will Chunky remember her?" Amari asked.

"No, he won't remember her the way we do. But we will make sure that he knows he had a grandmother who loved him and gave everything for him."

"Isn't Papa John older than Ms. Patricia?" Amari kept up her inquiries. "Yes, he is," Jeremiah confirmed.

"Is he going to die soon, too?"

"I don't think so, baby. Pop is strong and he's doing fine. Don't worry about him." "Well, when you and T Lise get old, I'm going to take care of you both. And

if something happens to you, I'm going to take care of Chunky. Eric will help me." "That's sweet, baby. I know you will. But for now, we're going to take care of you.

"Can I go talk to Ms. Patricia?" Amari asked. "Let's go see."

"Lise, Amari wants to see Ms. Patricia," Jeremiah announced as

Amari, Isaiah, and he joined Elise in Patricia's room. Isaiah could barely stay awake.

"Okay, come on, baby," Elise said.

Amari came around the corner and stood next to Patricia's bed. The room was only lit by candlelight and soft music played in the background.

"Hi Ms. Patricia," Amari said.

"Hi little one," Ms. Patricia whispered weakly. "Are you going to heaven tonight?" Amari asked. "What do you think, sweetheart?"

"I think you are, but I still want to pray for you," Amari said as she climbed in the bed with her.

"Lord Jesus, I want to thank you for Ms. Patricia. Thank you for her giving me a little brother and for giving my T Lise and my Uncle J a son. Please make her happy and let her not be sad. Please don't let her hurt anymore and please don't let her be afraid. I promise to be good and help with Chunky…I mean Isaiah, so Ms. Patricia never has to worry about him. In Jesus' name I pray, Amen."

"Amen. Thank you, Amari. I wish I could have spent more time with you," Patricia said, closing her eyes.

"Can I stay, T.T.?" Amari asked. "I'll be quiet."

"If you're not afraid…it's okay, baby," Elise answered.

They sat quietly for the next few hours but sometimes Patricia would speak.

Some of her comments would make sense. "I love you," she would say. "Thank you for being here."

"I feel so full."

But as the night matured, some of her comments became very odd.

"Corey, I've never seen you look so handsome. Mama is so proud of you, baby," she said, her eyes still closed.

Elise turned around and looked at Jeremiah, who simply took his free hand and put it on her shoulder.

"Who?" Patricia continued. "Well, yes, I would. That would be wonderful." She sat silently for a few moments, then she spoke again, her eyes still closed.

"Elise, he looks just like Jeremiah."

"Who looks like Jeremiah?" Elise asked. "He has your eyes, though," Patricia said.

"Who has my eyes, Ms. Patricia?" Elise asked anxiously.

She took her by the hand to rouse her, but Isaiah was now awake and let out a joyful squeal that interrupted the calm of the room. Ms. Patricia opened her eyes and looked intensely to the corner of the room and smiled. Jeremiah, Elise, and Amari all followed her gaze to the seemingly empty corner. Isaiah looked into the corner as well. He giggled the same way he did when Jeremiah and Elise played with him, yet no one was doing anything to instigate his exuberant laughter. He wriggled around in Jeremiah's arms and reached out in the direction of Ms. Patricia's stare. It reminded Elise of when she had first met him and how he reached out to her. But no one was there to take him into their arms.

Ms. Patricia spoke again. Her voice was barely above a whisper, but her words were clear. "Yes. I'm ready. I want to see him."

In an instant, her eyes grew wide and a warm smile took over her tired face. She looked as if she had just gotten the sweetest and most wonderful surprise of her life. Her face transitioned from a warm smile to one of total awe. Tears came down her cheeks as she shook her head in amazement. Her mouth was wide open and, like Isaiah, her hands reached into the distance. She moved her lips, but no words came out. All that escaped her mouth was a huge gasp of air as her hands slowly lowered and her face transitioned from the awestruck expression back into a warm smile as she closed her eyes.

Isaiah settled down as his grandmother closed her eyes. He laid his head back on Jeremiah's shoulder and was back asleep as suddenly as he had awakened.

"Is she in heaven?" Amari asked.

Elise, still holding her hand, placed her fingers on her wrist. "Yes, she is, baby." "Miah," Elise said.

"Yeah, babe," he answered.

"I knew J.J. would look like you."

CHAPTER 113

Second Act

DAY 800

Joshua and Robin were having a wonderful road trip. They talked. They joked. They encouraged each other. And they had already made plans for the next time they would meet. But now, they were halfway to Atlanta, and his baby girl was knocked out as she reclined in the passenger seat of his truck.

He looked at her rest and, in the silence, he was reminded of what he was about to do. He still hadn't shared everything with Robin. The school he was taking over wasn't exactly thriving. There were challenges on every front, and he would be the third principal in as many years. It was a private school and enrollment was down. Not only were there no long-term guarantees of job security, he would actually be taking a pay cut to move. *Maybe I am running away,* he thought to himself. But he was past the point of no return, literally and figuratively. He had signed his contract, signed a lease on a new apartment, and was on the second half of their road trip to his new life. All he could do now to ease his anxiousness was pray.

"Father...Lord...," he said barely above a whisper so as to not disturb Robin. "I really thought I was doing this at your call. Now? That I'm on my way? I don't know. I've been so out of sync with you lately and I'm afraid. I'm sorry, but I am. I still have so many questions and even though I know you have the answers, it just doesn't seem like you want to share them with me. I know I messed up, Lord. I messed up with my family. I messed up with my son. I messed up with Elise. But Father God, I have confessed and I have repented, and now

I need you to have mercy on me, according to your unfailing love and according to your great compassion. Please don't treat me like my sins deserve. Father, I ask that by your Holy Spirit you guide me into all truth so I can help these kids, this staff, these parents, and even their communities. Please bless me with what I need so I can be a blessing to them and please give me grace to succeed, if only for the sake of not making you look bad. Father, even as there is more distance between me and Robert, I pray you make a way for him and I to drop our pride and our differences and to love each other again. Please show me how to be a father to him whether he wants me to or not. Lord, I'm praying for my second act. Please don't leave me where I am. Please take me to where you want for me to be and please stay with me. I need you, Lord. I can't make it without you, and I don't want to. But I may as well be real with you because you already know. I still miss Elise and I'm still so lonely. So please heal me. Please help me. And please give me your strength and give me joy for this journey. I love you, Lord. You said if I truly loved you then I would obey you. So, in faith, I give you a blank check that says, 'Yes, Lord.' I trust you to fill it out according to your purpose and calling on my life. Just please let it result in a life that is worthy of you and a life that would please you in every way. In Jesus' name, Amen."

His prayer left him somewhat comforted, but his anxiousness still lingered. He thought about some of the challenges he would have in his new endeavor as he realized the very present challenge of his empty gas tank. He pulled into a gas station and stirred Robin from her rest. Or at least he tried to.

"Robby, wake up. You need to go to the bathroom?" he asked. "Uh-uh," Robin said, hardly waking up.

Joshua stepped out to fill up and noticed a handsome young man approaching him. "That's a nice truck," the young man said to him.

"Thank you, man," Joshua replied. "Making a big move, I see."

Joshua looked at the bed of his truck filled with all his belongings. It was a fair assumption. "Yeah," he agreed.

"Atlanta's going to be good for you. You're needed there," the young man stated. Joshua turned and faced him. How did he know he was going to Atlanta?

The young man spoke again. "Even where the enemy wants to steal, kill, and destroy, the abundant life of Jesus Christ is yours. The Lord knows your eyes are on him and your feet are released from every trap. The Lord has turned to you with His grace even in your loneliness and affliction. The troubles of your heart are relieved, and He has taken away all your sin. There are tests before you, but the Lord will give you an amazing second act."

"Second act?" Joshua said out loud. "Man, how did you…?"

But the young man interrupted Joshua and continued speaking. "What the locusts have eaten will be restored and you will recover all the enemy has stolen. Your sins are forgiven, and he will make your latter days better than your former days. Your territory is going to be enlarged beyond what you could ever ask, imagine, or think. God sees you and he is for you."

Joshua shook his head. He didn't know who this brother was, but he was saying exactly what he needed to hear. "Thank you, man," Joshua said. "I receive that."

"May the Lord Jesus bless you continually, Joshua," the young man said. "How do you know my name?" Joshua said as the click of the gas pump

caused him to turn away. When he turned back around…the young man was gone. Joshua's heart raced, yet somehow, he was as calm as he had ever been. He finished pumping his gas and got back into his truck with the now wide-awake Robin.

"Daddy…why are you crying?" she asked. "I'm not crying, Robby," Joshua argued.

"Well, then your eyes are sweating. What's wrong?" she pressed. "Robby, give me a minute. I'll try to explain it to you later."

"Okay, but when you explain it to me, can you also remember to tell me why you're outside talking to yourself?"

"I wasn't talking to myself. I was talking to that guy." "What guy?" Robin asked seriously.

"The young brutha that looked like Bruno Mars," Joshua explained. "Daddy…the only person I saw was you…talking to no one. Trust me, if anybody who looked like Bruno Mars would have been in the vicinity, I would have noticed." "Robby, that dude was five feet away from me. You didn't see him? Looks

like he works out? Perfect teeth?"

"No, I didn't," Robin asserted as she scanned the parking lot for the invisible stranger her father had just described. "Umm, do you still see him?" she asked.

Joshua looked around but saw no signs of the young man. But the words the Lord has spoken through him were settled in his spirit.

"Daddy, are you going to be okay?" Robin asked. "Yes, Robby. Your daddy is going to be okay."

CHAPTER 114

The Traylors 2.0

DAY 1095

"You ready, babe?" Jeremiah asked Elise as they rode the elevator. "Baby, yes!" Elise answered.

"How about you, pretty girl? You ready?" he asked Amari.

"Good to go Daddy-O!" Amari said, giving him a military style salute. "But I still don't understand why Eric can't be included."

"Baby, we will always look out for Eric," Jeremiah reassured her.

"It's cool, Lil' Homey," Eric told her. "I know you think I'm yo little playmate but it's not the same with me. I'm a whole grown man."

"Well, the way Mommy spoils you, you would think you're Chunky's age," Amari said.

"My Big Baby is not spoiled," Elise defended as her family all turned and gave her the side eye.

"It's okay, Mama Lise. They don't understand," Eric grinned as he leaned over and kissed her on the cheek.

"Well, if I do be spoilin' folks, I learned from the best. Ain't that right, Daddy?"

"You did," John nodded proudly.

"No cap, Mama Lise be lookin' out for her boys though. Ain't that right, Chunky," Eric said as he switched Isaiah to his other hip.

"I have told y'all to quit body shaming my child," Elise scolded. "You started it!" they all exclaimed in unison.

After the Crash

"I can't stand y'all," she said with false anger.

"Yes, you can," they laughed as they exited the elevator and made their way to the assigned room.

Elise smiled as they entered. It warmed her heart that so many wanted to be there with them on this special day. The room was packed with their church family and friends.

"Well, well, well," the judge addressed them, "I didn't know we were going to have celebrities in my courtroom today."

"No, Your Honor," Jeremiah answered. "We're not celebrities. Our church family just wanted to celebrate with us."

"Well, I think that's wonderful. So, are we ready to make a family?"
"Yes, Your Honor," Jeremiah and Elise said in unison.

"So, where's Amari?" the judge asked. "Right here, Mr. Your Honor," Amari smiled.

"Well, aren't you the prettiest young lady I have ever seen. I don't think I'm going to let Mommy and Daddy adopt you. I think I might take you home to my wife. Would that be okay with you, Amari?"

"I think you would bring me back, Mr. Your Honor," Amari said without missing a beat.

"Oh, well," the judge said, feigning disappointment. "And who all do you have with you today, Amari?"

Jeremiah gave the judge a concerned look. He didn't know what he was in for by engaging Amari in conversation.

"Welll," Amari started. "This is Daddy, but I just started calling him that. I used to call him Uncle J because his name is Jeremiah. This is my mommy. I used to call her T Lise. That's short for Auntie Elise. That was way too many syllables, and she always shortens people's names anyway. That's why they call me Mari." "And who's that handsome little guy that nice young man is holding? That couldn't be Isaiah. Why, Isaiah is only supposed to be two years old. That fella there looks like he's in high school."

"No, Mr. Your Honor. That's Isaiah. He's still a baby. Mommy used to call him Lil' Cute Chunks because he's cute and chunky. But I just call him Chunky now. Everybody else calls him Saiah."

"Mari, wrap it up," Jeremiah whispered.

"But Daddy he wants to know," Amari explained.

Jeremiah looked at the judge, who not only seemed to be totally unbothered but overjoyed with Amari's introduction.

"I sure do, Mari," the judge affirmed.

"And this is Eric," Amari continued. "He's my best friend and my big brother too. He's too old to get adopted, but he's part of the family now too, and he works for Mommy and Daddy. He rescued me when I was living with my aunt. I got into a fight with her one day, but I sorta lost. Afterwards, Jesus saved him and he took me out for pancakes to make me feel better and I asked him to take me home and he did. He's my Big Homey and I'm his Lil' Homey. And my Papa John is here. He got sick the day Ms. Monique took me away…oh, but I'm not mad at her," Amari looked back at Monique and smiled. "She was just doing her job. I'm not supposed to be mad at my aunt either, but I still am sometimes. Daddy says I have to forgive her, but Mommy says, 'It's on sight!' That means…."

The judge laughed. "Mari, I think I know what 'It's on sight' means, and I bet your mommy would prefer we not discuss this in a room full of witnesses."

Elise nodded her agreement as Jeremiah gave her the side-eye. "So, who's Papa John?" the judge continued his questions.

"He's going to be my grandfather. My grandmother was going to be Mama Etta. Papa John called her Weenie. She's in heaven now with J.J."

"I'm sorry to hear that, sweetheart. Who is J.J.?"

"J.J. is my other little brother. But he died on the day he was born, so I never got to meet him. But I know he's happy."

"I know he is too, Mari. Are all these other nice folks who have filled up my courtroom with you too?"

"Yes, Mr. Your Honor. That's my T Shania and Pastor G. and First Lady. And that's our church family. They came to be with us today."

"That's wonderful, Mari. So, are you ready to get a new mommy and daddy?" "Yes, Mr. Your Honor!" Amari exclaimed. "I can't wait."

The judge looked at Jeremiah and Elise. "Mr. and Mrs. Traylor, it sounds like you two had a rough road getting here."

"Yes, Your Honor," Jeremiah responded. "But God has been faithful." "Always remember that, young man," the judge exhorted. "Raising a family isn't easy but when, as the young folks say, 'life gets to lifing,' I want you two to remember this day, and how you came into this court smiling from ear to ear, looking good, and surrounded by your friends and family. And even though I am probably not supposed to say this, surrounded by the Love of Jesus Christ."

"We got the right judge!" a random church member shouted from the back, followed by a chorus of "amens" from the others.

"Normally I would say 'Order in the court!' but I think I'll just let that one go," the judge laughed. "And before a revival breaks out or before Amari wants to talk again, let's get this show on the road. I think another 'Amen' would be okay right there," the judge said as he surveyed his packed courtroom.

"Amen!" the excited congregation responded.

The judge continued, this time sounding a bit more formal and authoritative. "With regard to case number GEN18-25-PS34-8-ROM8-31concerning the legal adoption of Amari Dawn Echols and Isaiah Jamal Caldwell by Jeremiah and Elise Traylor, I've reviewed the documents and find them to be in order. I'm going to ask our court clerk to bring them to the parents for signing."

The court clerk brought the adoption papers to Jeremiah and Elise and showed them where to sign. Jeremiah and Elise signed as Amari beamed And Isaiah squirmed in Eric's arms. The floor seemed to be so appealing, but for some reason his big brother wouldn't let him get down and play.

The clerk returned the newly signed documents to the judge, who quickly reviewed them to confirm that all was in order.

"I have reviewed the documents," the judge said. "They have been signed in my presence and confirm that everything is in order. I'm going to ask the family to approach the bench."

"Here you go, Unc," Eric said, handing Isaiah back to Jeremiah.

"You can keep him. You're coming with us," Jeremiah said, guiding him up to the judge's bench.

They stood in front of the judge who, for the first time today, looked less than pleased.

"Mari, can you help me get your mommy and daddy in order?" the judge asked. "Bring them up here with me."

"Yes, Mr. Your Honor," Amari smiled.

The judge turned his chair to face them and smiled warmly at the soon to be family. "Are you okay, Eric?" the judge asked.

"Yes sir. I mean, yes, Your Honor," Eric stammered. Everyone had been saying he was family. But he hadn't expected to be included in this special occasion at this level.

"Mr. and Mrs. Traylor," the judge said, "I know you are anxious to start your family but if you will humor this old judge, I would appreciate it if you would allow me to share a few words with you."

"Yes, Your Honor. We would appreciate that," Jeremiah said.

"Sometimes, life…no…that's not what I want to say," the judge said as he reconsidered his words. "Sometimes, the Lord places us on paths we would never choose for ourselves. These paths seem unfair, harsh, or even cruel. But when we trust him and stay on the path, we find once we get to the other side that it was the times he seemed the furthest away that he was actually the closest. We find that He stayed with us on those hard paths and as heartbreaking as they may have been, He had purpose behind them." The judge's gaze turned to Elise. "And I've learned that when I don't stay on His path that He doesn't give up on me. He just comes and gets me. I think you know what I'm talking about, don't you, Mrs. Traylor?"

Elise nodded. "Yes, I do, Your Honor."

"And I've also learned," the judge continued, "that it's not always the situation he wants to change. Sometimes, he just wants to change us. But every now and then, we see that when the hurt and tears are over, He comes in and makes things new for us. He rights the ship. He redeems the time. He shows us how he can bring joy out of the most intense pain. And he shows us how He's always doing more than one thing. I think that might be what I'm seeing here today."

Jeremiah and Elise smiled at each other and then at the judge.

The judge returned their smile and continued. "So now, before Almighty God, this Court, this great cloud of witnesses, friends, and family, I ask you, Jeremiah John Traylor and Elise Janelle Traylor, do you promise this day to love, protect, teach, and nurture Amari Dawn Traylor as your lawful daughter and Isaiah Jamal Traylor as your lawful son from this day forward?"

"We do," Jeremiah and Elise said together.

"Well, I would like to finish this thing up so you nice folks can go on your way, but I am getting a little old. Mari, can you help me?"

"Yes, Mr. Your Honor. What do you need?" Amari asked enthusiastically.

The judge rubbed his wrist and shoulder in a rather exaggerated fashion. "Well, sweetie, this gavel of mine is getting pretty heavy. Can you help me lift it?"

"Yes!" Amari said.

The judge moved his chair back and allowed Amari to stand in front of him. "Here we go," he said, placing his hand around Amari's as she picked up the gavel, but before he could speak Isaiah made it clear he did not like his sister

participating in an activity without him.

"Well, I see someone's a little spoiled, isn't he?" The judge's eyes found Elise's. "I wonder whose fault that is?" he winked.

Elise looked the judge squarely in the eye. "Your Honor, on the advice of counsel, I would like to plead the Fifth Amendment on the grounds that my answer may incriminate me," she said as the courtroom erupted in laughter.

The judge laughed and continued. "Well, Isaiah, if Eric will let you go, you can help too. I think I have enough lap for you, little buddy."

"Go sit next to Amari, little man. We're right here," Jeremiah encouraged as he gently placed his son into the judge's lap.

The judge beamed. "By the power vested in me, I now pronounce you parents and children. Come on, Amari. Hit it right there."

Amari raised the gavel and struck it.

"You wanna try it, little buddy?" the judge asked Isaiah as he handed him the gavel.

Isaiah needed no further instructions as he exercised no chill in banging the judge's desk as the courtroom filled with applause.

"Mr. and Mrs. Traylor, you may take your children home."

CHAPTER 115

Room for One More

DAY 1098

"Hey, Unc," Eric said to Jeremiah as he joined them for the family dinner. "I hope it's okay, but I cancelled the painters at 3000 Sheridan. It looks like rain."

"That's cool, Neph. Good job," Jeremiah replied.

"We're so proud of you, Big Baby," Elise said, pinching his cheek. "Thank you, Mama Lise," Eric smiled.

"Eric, me and Mama Lise have been talking," Jeremiah continued. "And after 3000 Sheridan is finished, we need to make some changes. You've been doing a great job, but we want you to have more options for your future. Have you ever thought about going to college?"

"Not really," Eric said. "I never thought I was smart enough to go to college." "Boy, don't make me whoop you!" Elise threatened. "You're smart enough to do whatever you want."

"Eric, you've been working with us for almost a year now. I know you're picking up the business on the project side, and Elise says you got some nice sales skills too. You're plenty smart, bruh."

"Even if I was, I can't afford to go to no college," Eric protested. "We'll take care of it, Neph," Jeremiah reassured him.

"You mean you gon pay for it?" Eric asked. "That's what I mean," Jeremiah confirmed.

"Unc...thank you but I don't want to let y'all down."

"You won't, Neph. You haven't so far," Jeremiah encouraged.

"Jerelise Properties is growing, and we need someone we trust to help us. But like I said, we want you to have options. One day you might want to do something different, and we want you to be able to pursue those opportunities. No matter what you do, we want to invest in you."

"Unc, I appreciate it, but I don't feel like I deserve it. All y'all have done is help me and now you tryin' to send me to college. Why y'all doing this?"

"Neph, man to man, I could say a lot of things. I could say we're doing this because when we couldn't take care of Amari …you did. Or I could say that we're trying to be good Christians and bless you. Or even that God told us to do it. Those things would be true. But the real reason is that we love you, son. Mama Lise loves you and I love you, too," Jeremiah said as he embraced him.

It was the first time Jeremiah had called him son. It was the first time he told him he loved him. It was also the first time any man had done either.

Eric cleared his throat and tried to control his emotions. "Thank you, Unc… I love you, too," he said returning the embrace.

"Aww, Mari, look at our big, stwong men tearing up and being mushy," Elise teased.

"I think Papa John is crying too, Mommy," Amari said.

"I ain't crying, little girl!" John said as he wiped his face with one hand and adjusted Isaiah on his hip.

"That's all right, John," Faye said. "I think your brother Wayne over here gettin' all misty-eyed too."

"It's my allergies," Pastor Gregory defended himself. "Do you gentlemen need some Benadryl?" Shania asked sarcastically.

"Mama, Brudda and Daddy baby cry?" Isaiah asked as he got down from his grandfather's lap to see what the problem was.

"That's right, mama little man," Elise answered. "Brudda & Daddy baby cry."

CHAPTER 116

After the Crash

DAY 1100

"This is fancy, baby. You sure know how to impress a girl," Elise said, teasing her husband.

"Ha, ha, ha. Very funny," Jeremiah responded dryly. "Don't worry. I have a nice little date night planned for us. I just feel like we need to be here."

"It's okay, baby. I'm just playing. I used to come here almost every week," Elise revealed. "Sometimes more."

"Really?" Jeremiah asked.

"Yeah, it would make me feel better. It's strange but I just wanted to make sure he knew I hadn't forgotten him. I haven't been here in a while, though," Elise explained as they strolled to their destination.

"Yeah, I haven't been here in a minute either. You used to bring him toys, didn't you?" he smiled.

"Did," she said, smacking her lips and rolling her neck. "I would also talk to him. Do you think that's weird?" she asked seriously.

"No, babe. Whatever you needed to do, or still have to do, is fine. As long as you know where he is. And as long as he doesn't talk back or start playing with the toys," he laughed.

Elise laughed with him. "Nope. It ain't that deep. I'd leave skid marks on this nice lawn if that happened."

"What would you say to him?" Jeremiah asked. "If you don't mind me asking." "Baby, of course I don't mind you asking," Elise said, reassuring him. "When I

first started coming, I wouldn't say anything. I would just cry. But later, I would mostly just tell him that I loved him and that I missed him. I know it may sound strange, but

I would also apologize a lot. Even though I knew he was perfect in Heaven, I felt like I wasn't setting a good example for him. You know what I'm saying?"

"Yeah, I get it," Jeremiah nodded.

"What would you do when you came?" she asked.

"I would mostly pray. I remember I would just keep telling the Lord how I didn't understand everything that was going on, but I trusted Him. I would repeat it over and over. 'I don't understand, Lord, but I trust you.' Sometimes, I don't think I was really talking to God. I think I was trying to convince myself of what I was saying. Because in the back of my mind…babe…I was like 'This is it. God has taken you as far as he's going to take you, and you may as well figure out the rest on your own.'"

"Miah, why do you think we've never come here together?" Elise asked as they reached their destination.

"Lise, you just said it, babe. We weren't together. And I didn't reach for you like I should have."

Elise nodded her head. "I wanted you to reach for me. I needed you to."

"I guess if I had, a lot of things wouldn't have happened," Jeremiah said somberly. "I'm sorry I put you through that, baby," Elise apologized.

"It's not just on you, babe," Jeremiah comforted. "I thought I was trusting in God, but I tried to do it on my own. I think that's why I wanted to bring you here. This is where it happened."

"Where what happened?" Elise asked.

"You remember your moment in the hospital? Where you…you know…" "You can say it. Where I slapped the Lord's hand away from me," Elise said bluntly. "Well, this is where I did the same thing. After I found out about you and

Joshua, I came here and told the Lord I would figure the rest of this stuff out on my own. I was done with this Jesus thing, babe. And I was as serious about walking away from the Lord here as you were in that hospital bed. But you knew where I would be, and you sent Pastor Gregory for me. You stayed out in the cold for a long time because I didn't come and get you. But even with all the things I said to you, you didn't let me go. I still wonder what would have happened if you hadn't sent Pastor Gregory for me that night. Even when you couldn't be here for me like you wanted to, you still figured out a way to make sure I was good. So, babe, I wanted to come here to say that that Miah and Elise against the world thing isn't just a catchy slogan. It's real. And whatever happens with us going forward… whatever God allows… we're going to trust Him…together. You won't ever have to figure it out on your own again, babe."

"I believe you, baby," Elise said. "But thank you for saying it."

"Come here. You know how we do it," Jeremiah said as he pulled her close. "Father, we come to you in the name of Jesus, and we come to you by His blood to give you thanks and to give you praise. You are so worthy of our praise, Lord. We haven't gotten it all right, but we still praise you. We don't understand, but we still want to praise you. Your sovereignty let the weapons be formed but your mercy, grace, and love didn't let them prosper. You let our hearts be broken but you stayed close. You let our spirits be crushed but you still saved us. We praise you for being faithful to your promise: You never leave and you never forsake. We give you praise for giving us beauty for our ashes. We give you praise for letting us recover what the enemy stole. We give you praise for joining us in the fire and not letting it destroy us. We praise you that when our faithfulness stopped, your faithfulness took over."

"You are faithful, Lord," Elise agreed, resting her head in his chest.

"Father, as we stand in this place where we had to bury our son, we still have so many unanswered questions. But we praise you for not having to ask you where our boy is. We know he is safe with you. We give you praise that we don't have to ask if we will ever see him again. We know one day we will see him again…and when we see him, he will be alive in you Lord. And our Precious Jesus, we don't have to ask if he is loved. We give you praise that he lives forever in your perfect love. We will always love him, Lord, and now that you've given us two children…"

"Three, baby," Elise whispered.

Jeremiah smiled and pulled Elise just a little closer. "Now that you've given us three children, we ask that you increase our love so they may receive it as from you. We praise you for being our light when it was darkest, and we praise you for being our salvation when we were defeated. You are always right. You are always good. And you are always for us. So, for all these things, and because of who you are, we give you praise. In Jesus' name we pray, Amen."

"Amen," Elise said. "And Daddy, I come with my husband in the name of your son and our Savior Jesus. Thanking you with him and praising you with him. You came and found me when I was lost, and you chased me down, with your grace, mercy, and love, even when I ran away. You've done so many things for us. You've healed our hearts and our souls and our lives. You've made all things new. But Daddy, before you did all those things, you gave us Jesus. I thank you that when I forgot that, you still didn't forget me. I ask for grace to never again forget you as my first love. I don't want to hurt or suffer, Lord, but if you will give me grace to suffer for your glory and if you will stay with me, then whatever you allow, I will choose you, Jesus."

"We will choose you, Jesus!" Jeremiah added as Elise continued.

"The devil did all he could to break us, but we praise your name, Jesus! You did not break your promise to work it together for our good. So, we just want to say that with all of our hearts, all of our minds, all of our souls, and all of our strength, we love you as our first love. We love you, Jesus, because you first loved us. You love us more than we love ourselves and you give better than what we could ask for ourselves. You forgave us when we were unforgivable. You loved us when we were unlovable. You remained faithful when we fell away. You answered before we even called. And when the devil had our life and our destiny lined up in his sights…Jesus, you protected us and kept us by the power of your great name, and by your grace… the devil missed."

"He missed! Thank you, Jesus," Jeremiah agreed.

"So, we thank you, Jesus. We praise you, Jesus. We worship you,

Jesus. And with all we have, by your grace, we love you, Jesus. It's in your name that we pray, Amen."

"Amen," Jeremiah whispered. "I love you, Miah."

"I love you, Lise," Jeremiah said, kissing her on her forehead.

Elise opened her eyes and looked to the sky as the sun set on the horizon.

What she saw reminded her of the words of an old friend.

"And when this time of testing is done, you will see his beauty in the sunset and his faithful promise in the sky and know like never before that the love of Jesus Christ did not, has not, and will not ever fail," she said confidently.

Jeremiah's eyes raised at the words they both heard three years ago. The words of a man Elise described as an angel. "Why'd you say that?" he asked.

"Look at the sky, baby," she said, pointing to the horizon.

Jeremiah looked up and saw the setting sun as its radiant light gently illuminated a glorious sea of clouds. The sky was decorated with a magnificent color palette of sapphire, gold, and auburn. Piercing the sky, was a brilliant rainbow, set in place by the Master Artist.

Jeremiah continued to hold his wife as he remembered his mother's words: *"But hear me, baby…after the crash, when all is lost and you are in your lowest valley, I want you to open your mouth and praise the name of Jesus. And soon after he will turn it around. The trial won't last forever. I won't be here when it happens but when God shows up, I'm gon climb up on Jesus' shoulders and I'm gon look down from Heaven, and I'm gon tell the devil, 'You shot yo best shot at my baby. But my Jesus is still on the throne and my baby boy is still standing.' And when that day comes, when God gives you your victory, you will look up in the sky and know that your mama is smiling down on you and the Lord will get his glory."*

Jeremiah smiled as he marveled at the sunset with Elise. "Go ahead and ride around on Jesus' shoulders, Mama."

"What are you talking about?" Elise laughed.

"I'll tell you in the car, babe. Let's go. We have a date."

"Nooo, Miah, not yet. I want to stay here in your arms until the sun goes down." "That's exactly what I wanted to hear, Lise. We can stay as long as you want."